THE
MIDWEST

THE
MIDWEST

A COLLECTION FROM
HARPER'S MAGAZINE

GALLERY BOOKS
An Imprint of W. H. Smith Publishers Inc.
112 Madison Avenue
New York City 10016

This volume first published in 1991 by
Reed International Books Limited
Michelin House, 81 Fulham Road, London SW3 6RB

This edition published in 1991 by Gallery Books
an imprint of W. H. Smith Publishers Inc.
112 Madison Avenue, New York 10016

ISBN 0 - 8317 - 4258 - 5

Printed in Great Britain by The Bath Press, Avon.

CONTENTS

THE MIDDLE WEST

ONE afternoon last summer three or four people from New York, two from Boston, and a young man from the Middle West were lunching at one of the country clubs on the south shore of Long Island, and there came about a mild discussion of the American universities.

One of the women from New York nodded pleasantly to the Westerner.

"I am sure, Mr. McWhirter, that you are too broad-minded to resent what I am about to say," she remarked,—a preface which of course braced the young man to receive with a winning smile any insult to his *alma mater* or to his section of the country. "It is only that I have decided that my sons must go to Harvard," she continued, turning to the Bostonians, "because at Princeton or Yale" (Mr. McWhirter's *alma mater* was Princeton) "they might be thrown in contact with Westerners."

She went on to declare that her feeling in the matter was not induced by ignorance; she knew the West well enough, she said, gayly, and did not judge it by its Congressmen alone, having spent some months in Indianapolis twenty years ago, and after that she had lived in Buffalo for a long, long time. Buffalo was sufficiently raw; but Indianapolis she described as a place where the women of a household spent their time sewing in an apartment called "the sitting-room," preserving for the occasional visitor a stiff, hard-swept stuffed chamber, "the parlor," never opened except to receive formal calls.

Another woman of the party at once

offered as a soothing draught the old, deadly formula, always an immediate restorative of good feeling, " But then, you know, Mr. McWhirter, we never think of *you* as a Westerner!" Variations of this formula are common enough on the lips of New-Yorkers and Bostonians; although no Philadelphian of really good feeling ever reminds the Westerner of his origin, because of a polite fear that the stranger may be sensitive about not being a Philadelphian.

However, this interesting provincialism is confined to no particular quarter along the Atlantic seaboard, neither to East Bridgewater nor to Elizabeth, New Jersey. It was an Albany clergyman who said to the writer, with the most genial approbation of the Central States: " Yes, indeed, the people from your part of the country are improving steadily. Members of the younger generation have come East to our schools and colleges; they visit our young people; they study our manners and ways of life,—and thus, returning home, bring the West more and more toward the standard." Nothing could have reminded one more vividly of the one-time popular song:

Of course you can never be like us,
But be as like us as it's possible to be.

Certainly " society " in a middle-sized town of the Central States is in a few respects unlike that to be found in Philadelphia, Boston, New York, or, indeed, anywhere else in the world, and possesses some characteristics of its own. There are no " professional society people "; and " social relaxation " for the young generation of men means a holiday; to the older generation it usually means the necessity for a tired man to go out and get more tired.

Towns, of course, differ in character quite as widely as individuals differ, and they do not greet with enthusiasm observations concerning their similarities any more than people do. Detroit does not enjoy hearing from the stranger that Detroit reminds him of Indianapolis; nor does Indianapolis too persistently urge any claim that it is like Detroit. Columbus is far from pressing upon the visitor its points of similarity to Detroit, Indianapolis, Springfield (Illinois), Omaha, or St. Paul, yet it is not bitterly resentful

of remarks to the effect that it reminds one of New York; though Louisville, which has more civic pride than any other place in the world, somewhat tolerantly allows you to say that New York reminds you of Louisville.

Nevertheless the polite visitor discovers an inward something in almost all the large towns of the Central States that he feels is typical; a resemblance in social spirit that is elusively prevalent, which, evading definition, though often showing itself quite tangibly, is almost as difficult to confine within the bounds of uncontradictory adjectives as that which we mean when we speak of the typically American. Nor can we wholly solve the difficulty by a study of the society of any particular city of this region, for there is none that we dare call an " average city " of the Central States. However, we may come near it by considering one of the large towns in its lighter aspects, forgetting ninety-nine and nine-tenths per cent. of its population and the graver potentialities which lie in the mass of its people.

An Easterner at a dance, a dinner, a club, or at a theatre in this city would observe very few differences between the people he would meet and those he might encounter in a place of like population (between 150,000 and 250,000) east of the Alleghenies; indeed, the difference that does strike the traveller at first glance is that the former are somewhat more cosmopolitan in point of view; they have " been about " more; they are more tolerant; and they have a greater breadth of thought, geographically.

They are pleasant people to know; easy-going, yet not happy-go-lucky; possessing energy without rush, and gayety without extravagance. They have a way of being hospitable without exertion, which they inherit from half their ancestry, which was Southern, and a way of competently entertaining each other and their visitors without lavishness,—a trait they inherit from the other half, which came from New England. Then, too, pioneer conditions are not so remote that the training of grandfathers and great-grandfathers has been lost. These forebears had a struggle with the earth and the wilderness severe enough to leave a mark upon the fourth generation; therefore the third and fourth generations feel

THE MEMBERS OF THIS SOCIETY LIVE ON TERMS OF SINGULAR INTIMACY it as a moral necessity that there should be caution in the husbanding of resources. And while nearly all are comfortable and well-to-do, none are "barons"; only a few are rich, and these few live like their neighbors, not displaying their advantage.

It is a society almost wholly without snobbishness. Now and then there becomes apparent a struggle to enter it on the part of some one outside of it; but, because access is so simple, the fact that a struggle is necessary nearly always creates in itself a perpetual disqualification. It is a society exceedingly friendly to the new-comer; very ready to receive him on his own merits; it has no feeling of its own insecurity to make it snub him because it does not know who he was before he came. And while the visitor will be asked many questions about his acquaintances in other cities, he will not be asked if he has met "the Rockmores of Germantown," in order to discover if he "knows the right people." The questions are put in a hopeful way, with the hospitable wish to find mutual friends of whom to talk, and to bring the visitor and native into closer touch.

There is a natural drawing together and interdependence, of course, among the people who form the nucleus of this society; whose fathers and grandfathers have been friends, watching the town grow from a village in the forties to a city of importance in the twentieth century; and although there is a small complacence among the families that were here "from the first," it amounts mainly to greater familiarity with each other, as among relatives. Conditions are all the happier for the absence of the pond-turtle who condescends to the new-comer because his relatives have been a long time in the same pond. Here and there there may be an individual who takes to himself some credit that his family have achieved distinction or continued in respectability through several generations; but he does not push the claim, because he lives among people who would laugh less at "the arrogant strut of new wealth" than at a claim of privilege for "high birth"; because (the people would

W. A. Rogers.

AT THE MEN'S CLUBS HE SOMETIMES HEARS THE VOICES OF WOMEN

TO SEE YOU OFF AND WAVE GOOD-BY

feel) to be tainted with the former means at least that you are proud of something you yourself have accomplished; to possess the latter means that you are in the ludicrous attitude of being proud of yourself because of something that somebody else did.

The members of this society live on terms of singular intimacy with one another, almost as in a village, meeting often, and rarely passing each other on the street without pausing for more than a greeting. When the warm weather begins one has only to stroll or drive about certain pleasant portions of the city during the early evening to see nearly all his friends, who will be lounging each on his lawn, or comfortably taking the air on the broad porches; and the older inhabitant easily remembers the day when he was acquainted with every person of respectable appearance in town. Such in-

timacy, of course, entails an amusingly large quantity of amazingly small gossip. The details of the arrangements for a wedding, a reception, or a dance receive eager attention in many quarters, nor is the watchful eye at the neighbor's window altogether unknown. Grotesquely impossible stories are passed about, as they are everywhere, and here they have a glamourous relish because every one knows every one else so very well. This latter fact usually precludes the scandal from entire credibility, but not from repetition, for that is "just plain human nature." And yet, in spite of the crossroads gossipiness, it is a society extraordinarily free from real scandal. Life is exceedingly dull at times, and there is a proper (or improper, if you like) proportion of divorce cases on the docket; but when the young couples separate, it is almost always "because they couldn't

ON THE RIVER-BANK BELOW . . . THE YOUTH OF THE CITY USUALLY PROPOSE get along together," and the married flirt who carries flirtation beyond a cheering interest is quite unknown. As the literary club essay might remark, "a highly moral tone prevails."

One of the things that surprise a male visitor at the men's clubs is that he sometimes hears the voices of women. Certain portions of the club-houses are accessible to women; they come there for lunch, attended and unattended by members; they give teas and dinners, and even children's parties, at the clubs; and daring indeed would be the bachelor (none but a bachelor can be conceived as thus foolhardy) who offered to amend the rules permitting them to do so.

Only a half-dozen or so families have houses in the country within driving distance of the city; many take cottages or gypsy it expensively in hotels during the summer; but the larger number spend the warm months contentedly at home; for the town is like gardens in a big grove. A bird's-eye view shows only a jutting roof-corner here and there among the thick foliage; and the country club is within easy reach. The country club gives the gayest and happiest and laziest part of town's life, from the first of May until November. It is on a high bluff among tall forest trees, where there is always a breeze and always some coolness. Here there are to be found, nearly always, out-of-town men who serve as an excuse for a dinner, and out-of-town girls for whom dances are arranged; and here, on the terrace or on the river-bank below, or in quiet corners of the long veranda when the music of the Saturday evening hop is going inside, the youth of the city usually propose. This has almost the sanctity of custom.

The vehicles which drive up to the porte-cochère are not such as you would see at Ardsley, for instance. Now and then will come one which might pass muster in that class, but rarely; most of them are of another character. The horses get over the ground rapidly, but without a suggestion of the park; and most of them are of trim, fast, Western breeds; about one in a hundred is docked —and that one wishing, in fly-time, that he were an automobile. Many automobiles come, of course, but runabouts and phaetons prevail, the harness being

as neat as it is plain. Sometimes a jovial party will arrive in several big park brakes, but these, alas! are rented, and the drivers slouch on the seats in the rustiest of mixed liveries.

It is an old cry of the Englishman, the objection to the voice and accent of the American woman. The Easterner passes on the complaint, alleging that it is the women of the West and of the Central States who are loud-voiced, nasal, r - burring, and twangy. Mr. Kipling vouchsafed expression of his opinion, once on a time, to this effect: "How pleasant in every way is a nice American whose tongue is cleansed of 'right here,' 'all the time,' 'noos,' 'revoo,' 'raound,' and the Falling Cadence."

Of course the question of rising or falling inflections is only an affair of personal preference with each individual; and the American has a perfect right to object to the rising inflection, what he has chosen to call the "English singsong"; and, as a matter by-the-way, Mr. Kipling's ear betrayed him when he thought he heard "revoo" for "review," no adult American (without physical impediment of speech) ever having pronounced "review" "revoo," though he does, in most parts of the country, say "constitootional," and has good authority therefor.

There are some peculiarities of the pronunciation in the Central States, common to educated people of such cities as Cincinnati, Omaha, Indianapolis, Columbus, Minneapolis, or Chicago—peculiarities which are not necessarily faults; but the voices of the women of these places have suffered less from the climate than from the old slander; and on the porches of the country club of the city at which we are glancing you will hear a twang no oftener than you will anywhere else. Every society in the world contains individual members who are precisians in speech, and individuals who have voices unpleasing in quality; and of course, as it is everywhere else, so it is here. Europe has long judged Americans by the loud and impertinent American tourist; that is natural, because the loud and impertinent attract attention, while the gentle and well-mannered travellers (largely in the majority) are not noticed. Thus the East has elected to sniff now

AND HELLO-BELLS EVEN TINKLING MILES AWAY

ly gives it breadth. The common fault of the whole country is elision; and the West elides no more than does the East. We are all so accustomed to elision that it needs a careful ear to detect it. East, South, and West, you will hear, not only on the street, but sometimes in "the best society," "Gimme," "Lemme," "Don'-chuh," etc., and no writer of fiction may write the American language precisely as it is spoken in any section of the country, because the transcription would be rough, possibly unintelligible, and would often be puzzling to the very reader whose actual manner of speech had been transcribed.

But to return to our own particular semi-typical city. While the hospitality of this place is neither lavish nor given to display, it has a way of being thorough and untiring and glad. You come to visit a friend for a time, which always expands, only to find yourself staying for many days afterward as guest of your friend's friends, who were previously entirely unknown to you. They do not weary you, and yet they have something for you to do all the time; and the weeks go by cheerily until a goodly number of your new acquaintances (who, somehow, already appear to be old friends) come down to the railway station with flowers to see you off and wave good-by.

and then at the West. The Bostonian or New-Yorker, observing a noisy young woman from somewhere in the upper Mississippi or Ohio valley disporting herself conspicuously by the sea or elsewhere, immediately sets her down as a "typical Westerner," whereas she is nothing of the kind, and the chances are does not "belong to the best" in her own home.

The Central West burrs the "r" in about the same proportion that the East snubs it, and shortens the "a" to the same extent that New England incorrect-

It is not only that the people are neighborly with each other, but the city is neighborly as well. It keeps in close touch with all the large towns within a radius of a hundred miles or more. In summer the golf clubs visit each other in squadrons, parties of women accompanying the men; and these friendly communities have developed a disposition to treat one another as suburbs. The pretty girls and the dancing men of each are well known to those of the others; there is a great deal of interurban dinner-giving, courting, and marrying; the coat-rooms of the clubs of each city know few seasons when they are not often littered with the bags and traps of visiting youth come from a distance to usher it, bestman it, to dance, ride, and dine.

One of the kindliest adjuncts of cheerfulness in this region has been the increase and growth of university clubs. They are the most homelike of all the clubs, especially to the wandering university man from anywhere, be his *alma mater* Oxford or Stanford; and when he enters the portals of any one of them he is on familiar ground again, even after a cold day's business with strange people in a strange city. A graduate of any of the larger universities, entering here, will be unlucky if he fails to run across classmates and old friends to his heart's content. As a New York Harvardian of the eighties said the other day: " In St. Louis, after a hard afternoon's work, somebody took me into the University Club, and there were only four or five men in the place that I didn't know or hadn't heard

of in one way or another; and the next morning there must have been a dozen of 'em dropped in at the hotel to meet my wife and take breakfast. And every one of them had plans for us — dinners, dances, polo, and what not—that would have kept us there for weeks if we could have stayed!"

The long-distance telephone is kept ringing across these Central States, ringing up people by their first names, from country club to country club and from one university club to another, old classmates continually arranging reunions, men who played opposite each other on Yale, Princeton, Harvard, and Cornell teams planning various festivities; the hello-bells even tinkling miles away for no more than a Cincinnati man to ask a Louisville girl if he can run over (seven or eight hours to go and come) and call in the evening. After all, though the horizon sometimes seems to bend in rather closely about the towns of this part of the country, there are apertures through which the atmosphere percolates with a very cheerful breeziness.

OHIO'S FIRST CAPITAL

TWO hours' railroad ride southward takes the traveller from the present capital of Ohio, the local seat of government for over three millions of people, to the quaint, conservative old town which was the birth-place and cradle of the State—its capital at the beginning of the century, when it contained only a few thousand scattered settlers.

Chillicothe presents at this

OLD STATE-HOUSE.

day an appearance which is suggestive of its age and early importance. Modern architecture has done but little to brighten the sombre aspect of the dignified, substantial old residences which line the quiet, deeply shaded streets, or to modify the antiquated and somewhat grimy appearance of the long lines of business blocks which many years ago formed the busy mart of "the ancient metropolis." One of the earliest settlements within the present boundaries of Ohio, Chillicothe, from a combination of natural advantages, as well as from the energy and ability of its leading men, came suddenly into prominence, and for many years occupied a position which made it the envy of all the other embryo cities of the West. It did not fulfill, however, the golden promise of its youth, and was eclipsed in a few decades by towns which had no existence until a score of years after the date of its own origin. It

was the adopted home of a class of men who were as judicious and as enterprising as any who came into the territory northwest of the Ohio, and as the residence of quite a coterie of eminent men and the capital of the infant commonwealth of the West, it was widely and favorably known throughout the Eastern States. Located in the heart of as rich a region as could be found from ocean to ocean, and favorably established at the start, there was a prospect that the prosperity of its early days would only be the forerunner of a long career of constantly increasing strength; but there was disappointment in store for those who had high expectations, even if they were founded upon the best of reasons. The great Ohio canal, of which De Witt Clinton was projector, gave the busy little town a powerful impetus of growth, and for many years its life was fed by this active artery of commerce. As the usefulness of this really vast internal improvement was superseded, however, by other means of transit, the stream of traffic upon the canal became rather venous than arterial in its flow, and Chillicothe lost its richest source of nourishment. Losing at an early day its political prestige as the State capital, it still continued to thrive in business; but losing the canal commerce, and being slow to secure the benefit of railroad stimulus, the old town which had proudly led all of its rivals, and passed through a period of phenomenal progression, arrived at almost a stand-still condition.

Chillicothe is classic ground. It was here that the first State northwest of the Ohio was ushered into organic being; and upon the heights of Cemetery Hill repose the mortal remains of four famous men who have been its Chief Executives. Two historic houses, rich in associations which recall the bravest of pioneers, men who were among the founders of the State, stand stately and sentinel-like upon a high plateau overlooking the old town. The academy, which was the *alma mater* of

NATHANIEL MASSIE.

the seat of empire, for nowhere else do memorial mounds exist in such numbers as upon its bottoms and uplands; nowhere else do so many defensive works appear, or such a number and variety of sacred inclosures. The Indians, too, regarded this as a favored land, and it was undoubtedly for centuries the abode of either the Delaware or Shawanese nation. The river was the war-way down which the braves of these tribes floated silently and stealthily to strike their implacable enemy the Creeks, and in later years the isolated stations of the whites in Kentucky. Logan, the Mingo, whose pathetic eloquence and sad story have stirred the hearts of so many modern sympathizers with his woe, delivered the impassioned speech upon which his fame rests, before Lord Dunmore's interpreter, only a few miles north of the site of Chillicothe, and his name has been honored, not by the rearing of any memorial, but by its application to the grandest of nature's monuments upon the Scioto—Mount Logan. The country is rich in legend of the dusky race, and history has preserved the annals of many a battle and skirmish in which the Indian sought to preserve a favorite hunting ground from the encroachments of his pale-faced brother.

Virginia, it is a notable fact, was the second one of the original colonies to cede to the United States its claim upon the ter-

a generation of men who have grown gray since they passed over its threshold, is still a place of learning for the youth of the town. Famous Ohio statesmen, men who have made their mark in high places, have been school-boys here. Not far away, in a quiet street, is a plain old house which is pointed out as the birth-place of the wife of an Ohio President, and scattered through the town are several humble places which have been the homes of men whose names were widely known in literature, politics, and law.

Chillicothe is charmingly environed. The broad valley through which the Scioto flows southward to the Ohio is bordered by high bluff banks upon the west, and by a chain of mountain-like hills upon the east, the highest of which lifts its timbered crest six hundred feet above the river which washes its base. The lover of the beautiful can here find elements of the rugged, wild, and picturesque in precipitous heights and rocky formations; or if he more admire the gentler aspects of nature, his eye may be guided along the far-sweeping slopes of green pasture-land, or from the crest of the valley wall he may let his vision wander from one fair feature of the landscape to another, through an infinite variety of form and wealth of color, to the dim blue hills miles away, or the valley fading to the horizon. This valley was the centre of densest population of the prehistoric race, and perhaps

EDWARD TIFFIN.

ritory northwest of the Ohio, doing so in 1784, preceded only by New York, while Connecticut was the latest, consummating a similar measure in 1786, "the last tardy and reluctant sacrifice of State pretensions to the common good." Virginia's act of cession contained a clause, reserving upon certain conditions a tract of land lying north of the Ohio, and between the Scioto and Little Miami rivers, for the payment of the bounty awards due her Revolutionary soldiers of the Continental line. This reservation, known as the Virginia Military District, was almost entirely settled by families from the Old Dominion, and thus a Virginia was formed in the Northwestern Territory. Chillicothe soon after it was founded became the place of location for the land-office of this district, and situated near the centre, north and south, of the enormous territorial county of Ross, which included nearly the whole of the reservation, it became its seat. It thus occupied a position which entitled it to the name (if it did not receive it) of the capital of New Virginia. As Marietta (more properly than Conneaut) may be called the Plymouth of the West, so can Chillicothe be termed the Jamestown of this New Virginia; and as the daughter of the Mother of Presidents, Chillicothe nobly maintained the family prominence and honor by becoming the Mother of Governors.

Of the five men elected Governors of Ohio whose homes were in Chillicothe, one, Nathaniel Massie, never served. Three others, Edward Tiffin, Thomas Worthington, and Duncan McArthur, were pioneer statesmen, and have long since passed away. The fifth, William Allen, only recently died, and his long life linked the past with the present, politically and socially.

The very earliest history of Central Southern Ohio brings before the reader Nathaniel Massie, the foremost pioneer of this region. Massie was a native of Virginia, and was a boy soldier in the Revolutionary war. When only twenty years of age, in 1783, he went out alone to seek his fortune in Kentucky. Employed by the Surveyor-General of the Virginia Military Reservations in that State and the Northwestern Territory, he soon became expert in the then useful and lucrative though dangerous calling of a surveyor, and as early as 1790 was the leader of an adventurous party locating land-warrants

north of the Ohio. Previous to Wayne's treaty in 1795, every survey in the Virginia Military District was made by stealth. In 1791, Massie formed the first settlement in the reservation, and from that time on-

THOMAS WORTHINGTON.

ward was almost constantly engaged in locating and surveying the best land along the streams northward, each year pushing further into the wilderness. In the midst of the most appalling dangers, suffering in the winter from the severe cold, sometimes almost starving, always subject to the sudden fierce attack of a wily, watchful, jealous foe, and sometimes having a sharp battle with the Indians, Massie and his men toiled on, the valiant van-guard of an army of peace.

Duncan McArthur, also destined to take a prominent part in the affairs of the State which was to develop from the wilderness, was with Massie in most of his expeditions, and was the hero of several daring adventures and hair-breadth escapes.

By the year 1794, such an enthusiasm had been created in Kentucky by the glowing descriptions of the beauty of the scenery and the fertility of the soil in the Scioto country, which were circulated by Massie's followers, that portions of two Presbyterian congregations in Bourbon County determined to emigrate thither in a body. Their dislike of slavery was also an inducement to them to make a change; and being both impelled and attracted, they were eager to emigrate as early as possible. Accordingly in the spring of 1795 we find a company of about sixty men met by appointment to penetrate the romantic wilds north of the Ohio. They reached a point near the site of Chillicothe, and there their progress was checked by a party of hostile Indians. As it was impossible to retreat with safety, they gave them battle, and the Indians, on being attacked, fled, leaving two of their number dead, and several wounded. Only one man of the Kentucky company was killed, and a white man who had long been a prisoner among the Indians made his escape to his own people. After gathering up all of the peltries left by the Indians, and plundering their camp, the whites retreated toward the Ohio, and, as they apprehended, were attacked the next morning by the pursuing and reenforced party of Shawanese. In the spring of 1796, Massie rendezvoused the same or essentially the same company of men, and dividing them into two equal parties, again sought the favored locality in which he hoped to see a great town grow up. One division of the colony went by land, and the other up the Scioto in pirogues, carrying implements of husbandry, and those few articles which were indispensable to the pioneer. They landed at the mouth of Paint Creek (Olomon Sepung), below the site of Chillicothe, at what has since been known as "the Station Prairie," and soon thirty ploughs had turned up three hundred acres of the fertile bottom-land, and it was planted in corn. Massie proceeded to lay out the town which a few years later became the scene of so many events important to the scattered settlers of the West. He was the owner of the tract on which the town was laid out, and he gave to each of the first settlers a lot within the plot, and a hundred acres of land near by. The town was laid out after the plan of Philadelphia, and in fact the situation also resembles much that of the city which it was sought to imitate, the Scioto River and Paint Creek representing the Delaware and Schuylkill rivers. The name, Chillicothe, chosen by Massie, was the generic name among the Shawanese for town, and although they had no village upon the site chosen, there was one not many miles distant—one of the several old Chillicothes celebrated in Indian narratives. The settlement thus established, the one furthest advanced toward the interior, increased very rapidly in population, and the surrounding country soon received large numbers of settlers. The influx of immigrants was something wonderful for those days of slow travel and slow growth. Men of great ability, energy, and foresight were attracted to Massie's settlement by the fame of his exploits and the *éclat* with which the pioneer village sprang into existence, as well as by the flattering prospect which the richness of the region warranted. In 1798, there came among the immigrants from Virginia three men who were

THE MASSIE MONUMENT, IN THE CHILLICOTHE CEMETERY.

to be notable in State history — Worthington, his brother-in-law Tiffin, and Robert Lucas—all three afterward Governors. The last-named located a few miles southward, but still in the valley, and the others in Chillicothe. But with the reputable element came also a rabble of rakes, gamblers, adventurers, and outlaws, worthless to the community in every sense—a heterogeneous herd, ready to defy decency and trample order and law under foot. Virginia vices were imported as well as Virginia virtues. A pioneer says: "When the settlers first came, whiskey was $4 50 per gallon, but in the spring of 1797, when the keel-boats began to run, and the Monongahela whiskey-makers having found a good market for their fire-water, rushed it in in such quantities that the cabins were crowded with it, it soon fell to fifty cents; men, women, and children, with some exceptions, drank it freely, and many who had been respectable became inebriates. Many of Wayne's soldiers and camp-women settled in the town, so that for a time it became a town of drunkards and a sink of corruption. There was a little leaven, which in a few months began to develop itself." In 1800, Congress, recognizing the growing importance of Massie's settlement, and doubtless, too, influenced by its central location as to population, made it the capital of the Northwestern Territory. Worthington and Tiffin had met with the first session of the Territorial Legislature at Cincinnati, and they retained their places, meeting with the second at Chillicothe, and also with the third, in 1801. Here then came Arthur St. Clair, Governor of the Territory, clothed in the august robes of state, and already disliked because of his haughty bearing, his arbitrary rulings, and more than all else because there still clung to him the odium of his unfortunate military defeat. During the session of 1801, "the Governor and several of the legislators having been insulted at Chillicothe," a law was passed removing the capital to Cincinnati again. But the Territorial Legislature was not to meet again anywhere.

ADENA, RESIDENCE OF GOVERNOR WORTHINGTON.

The unpopularity of St. Clair was causing many to long for a State government. The Federal Governor, to defeat the consummation of a plan which he foresaw would leave him without an occupation or an office, advanced a scheme for changing the ordinance of 1787 in such manner as to effect a division of the Territory, making the Scioto river the boundary line. This measure, had it been carried, would have long postponed the organization, as neither of the divisions of territory would have had for many years a sufficient population to have entitled it to a change in the administration of its civil affairs. Massie, Worthington, and Tiffin labored zealously against the change which was urged by St. Clair, and Worthington left late in the fall to lay before Congress a statement of the evils that must arise from a re-ar-

FRUIT HILL, THE RESIDENCE OF DUNCAN McARTHUR.

rangement of the boundaries of the prospective Northwestern States, and if possible to procure permission to call a convention for the formation of a State from the eastern portion of the Territory, having the boundaries originally provided by the ordinance, and to effect that organization " which, terminating the influence of tyranny, should meliorate the circumstances of thousands by freeing them from the domination of a despotic chief." In April, 1802, Congress passed an act to enable the people within the present boundaries of Ohio to form a Constitution, organize a State government, and to obtain admission into the Union on an equal footing with the original States. The people, eager to avail themselves of their new privileges, ordered and held an election, and chose delegates to represent them in a Constitutional Convention. This Convention assembled in Chillicothe on the first of November, 1802, and held its session in the "old stone State-house," in which the Territorial Legislature had assembled in 1801. The building was commenced in 1800, and finished in the following year. It was generally devoted to State purposes, and also served as the place for holding the local courts. Many years after the removal of the capital to Columbus, this first State-house of Ohio remained as a reminder of Chillicothe's proud early days; but about fifty years from the time it was built it was found that the plain, simple little struc-

ture, which was once thought amply commodious for the use of the State, was too small to serve the needs of the county, and it was destroyed to make room for a finer structure.

The Constitutional Convention brought to Chillicothe an assemblage of the ablest men in the Territory—such men as Charles Willing Byrd, William Goforth, and Jeremiah Morrow, of Cincinnati, Rufus Putnam and Judge Ephraim Cutler, from Marietta, and Samuel Huntington, from the Connecticut Reserve; but no locality had a stronger or more brilliant representation than Chillicothe. Among her delegates were Massie, Worthington, Tiffin, and Michael Baldwin, an erratic genius, who, previous to that time enjoying a local celebrity as the ablest and most brilliant member of the bar in the infant settlement, then first came before the people in a broader capacity. The Convention closed its labors after a session so short as to be worthy of the emulation of modern legislators, and it gave to the people a Constitution "which bore in every provision the marks of democratic feeling, of full faith in the people." And it may be added that the Constitution was never submitted to the people in whom it professed such full faith. Thomas Worthington is known to have been the member by whom was introduced the clause which secured to Ohio the mouth of the Maumee, the site of Toledo, and a valuable strip of territory, and he also was the originator of one or two other provisions; but Michael Baldwin, there is reason to believe, was the author of the greater part of the Constitution. No other man in the Convention possessed at the same time so large a legal knowledge and so great literary ability as he. He was one of that vast number of men to whom the world, or some part of it, has been indebted for most valuable services; but his great strength was handicapped by elements of weakness and venal faults—follies which impaired his usefulness, but did not destroy it. His ability, eccentricity, and prominence among the pioneer public men of the West entitle him to more than passing notice. He was both famous and notorious at an early day, and though his career in Chillicothe was short, and he left no monument or relic of his residence there, he was one of the marked characters of the town and State. He had located in the village as early as the last year of the last century, for the records show that he was in that year admitted to practice in the courts. Although he emigrated to the West from Connecticut, he was in all probability an Irishman, as his name would imply, and his character too, for that matter, for it was made up of all the incongruities, contrarieties, and contradictions that are popularly supposed to belong to the typical Irishman. He was strong mentally and physically, able to cope successfully with the best minds he met with, and equally well provided with that physical prowess which was necessary to the winning of respect from the roughs, and which brought victory in personal encounter. Well read in law, and familiar with general literature, he was, when he had a mind to be, as winning and graceful in private conversation as he was fluent and forcible in public oratory. These qualities won

for him many admirers, but other qualities which he possessed repelled the better element of the community; and thus losing the universal respect which he might have commanded, poor Baldwin suffered many falls in public favor, was only for brief periods successful, and led a sorry career, full of vicissitudes. He was kind-hearted and generous when he had means to be generous with, as he seldom did. Full of rollicking humor, and fond of wild fun, he developed a strong love for liquor, which was very naturally indulged in the unsettled town, until the once brilliant man sank from a high position into obscurity. Unrest or unhappy recollections of past life probably made him an easy prey to demoralizing influences, or at least such was the indication afforded by his actions. He became, very soon after his settlement in the West, recklessly dissipated, abandoning himself to the wildest orgies and protracted sprees, from which he would emerge into a condition of clear-headedness and temporary respectability to perform the most arduous legal labor, or to take a leading part in some political movement. The tavern of one William Keys was his favorite resort, and it is traditionally asserted that it was at this pioneer of pot-houses that he wrote the larger part of the Consti-

HALLWAY AT ADENA.

tution of Ohio, using a whiskey barrel for a table and a wine keg for a seat. It is a matter of record that the landlord sued Baldwin for the sum of £25 13s. 10d., which amount, with the exception of three items, was aggregated from a long list of charges for "toddy," "rum," "plain spirits," "brandy sling," and "drinks for the club." The exceptional items were three suppers at 6d. each, but with every one of these charges there was one of "3s. for 1½ pints of brandy," which was certainly quite a Falstaffian proportion of meat to drink. Baldwin was the captain of the "Blood-hounds," an organization of the roughs and fighting men of the town, who did his electioneering for him, championed him in his quarrels, and occasionally liberated him from jail. The "Bloodhounds" un-doubtedly constituted the club for which Baldwin ordered treats. Their captain was in the custom of drilling the "Blood-hounds" in mock military manner. Draw-ing the motley crowd up in line, Baldwin with great dignity would command, "At-tention—Bloodhounds!" And then after the orders to "uncase gourds" and to "case gourds" had been complied with, the company was put through the manu-al of arms—and legs—Baldwin giving with ringing voice the orders, "From the right shoulder—*strike!*" "From the left shoulder—*strike!*" "With the right foot—*kick!*" etc., greatly to the amuse-ment of the throng of spectators always present on the Bloodhounds' muster days.

Baldwin did not always need the serv-ice of his rough constituency. On one occasion, when imprisoned in the jail for debt, or perhaps for some wild freak when in one of his whirlwinds of dissipation, he awoke to the consciousness that his fellow-prisoners were not of the kind with which he could enjoy companionship. Being locked up with a lot of thieves and low marauders was more than his dignity and pride, which chanced then to prevail, could stand; and so he kicked the door down, and the jail-birds out, saying, "I'm a gentleman, and I can not share my apartments with such as you."

With the organization of the State gov-ernment there came into office several al-ready prominent Chillicotheans, Edward Tiffin being elected Governor, Nathaniel Massie Speaker of the Senate, Michael Baldwin Speaker of the House, and Will-iam Creighton, Jun., Secretary of State. The first General Assembly met in the old stone State-house at Chillicothe in March, 1803, and not long after the first great seal of the State was devised, exhibiting a sheaf of wheat and a bundle of arrows in

THE GOVERNOR'S ROOM, FRUIT HILL.

the foreground, with rugged hills beyond, supposed to represent in idealized or conventionalized forms Mount Logan and the other elevations which form a sort of mountain chain east of the old capital. Years afterward, when the great internal improvement was effected of which De Witt Clinton was the father, a canal-boat was added as emblematical of commerce.

Governor Tiffin made an excellent helmsman for the new ship of state, and in 1805 was unanimously re-elected. The most notable official act of his gubernatorial career was the arrest of the Burr-Blennerhasset expedition. There are a few old citizens who can remember Ohio's first Governor—the mild-mannered, pure, and scholarly man, who, after serving as the Chief Executive of the State, was United States Senator, and then refused other important offices because he could not wean himself from his Ohio home.

Michael Baldwin, the irrepressible and incorrigible, was no more dignified, abstemious, or moral in his position as Speaker of the first Ohio House of Representatives than he had been in former years or lesser stations. He presided over the Chamber in 1803, 1804, and 1805. It is a matter of tradition that for his own pecuniary benefit, and for the entertainment of those among the legislators who had a penchant for gaming, he established in his rooms the game of "vingt-et-un," himself acting as banker and dealer, and as a matter of course winning more frequently than any of the other players. On one occasion, after much drinking and a late sitting at the gambling table, Baldwin found himself in possession not only of all the money of his companions, but of many of their watches. In the morning the House of Representatives was found to be without a quorum; but Baldwin, accustomed to heavy drinking and late hours, was in his place back of the Speaker's desk. Rapping savagely with his gavel, he demanded the roll-call of the House, and then sent the sergeant-at-arms out with orders to bring in the delinquent members. After an hour or so that functionary returned, followed by about a dozen members of the Ohio Legislature, whose blood-shot eyes, suffused faces, unsteady, shambling steps, and general air of shamefacedness indicated the late hours they had kept and their heavy indulgences. With much austerity of manner, Baldwin reprimanded the tardy members, reminded them of the cost to which the infant State was subjected by payment of their *per diems*, and was proceeding to further elaborate his censure

WILLIAM ALLEN.

on their late arrival and the consequent delay of legislation, when one of the delinquents, exasperated beyond control, cried out: "Hold on there, Mr. Speaker, hold on! How could we tell what time it was when the Speaker of the House had all of our watches?"

Before and during the time when the State government was being organized, many local improvements were being made, which rendered the town more worthy of the honor which had been conferred upon it. Gradually the institutions of civilization were springing up in the new settlement. In 1800, Nathaniel Willis, grandfather of the poet, established in Chillicothe one of the earliest newspapers west of the Alleghanies, the *Scioto Gazette*, which has been published continuously ever since, and is now the oldest newspaper in Ohio. Churches were organized, and houses of worship built, schools provided, business projects entered upon, and an era of prosperity inaugurated which was unrivalled in any of the Western settlements. A little later than this period the Madeira House was built—a hostelry which in early times was known to all Western travellers, and famed for many years as the best tavern between Baltimore and Cincinnati. And here in this new town, then containing only a few hundred people, singular to state, in the year 1814, was issued the first number of the pioneer religious journal of America, the *Weekly Recorder*, founded and for several years successfully edited by John Andrews, a Presbyterian preacher.

Thomas Worthington, as has been stated, came from Virginia in 1798. Before leaving, he and his brother-in-law, Edward Tiffin, liberated a large number of slaves, some of whom, however, chose to remain with their masters, and accompanied them to Chillicothe, where a few of their descendants remain to this day. Worthington at first located in the village which Massie had laid out two years before, but he soon removed to a log-cabin on the plateau two miles northwest of Chillicothe, where he afterward built the large stone house known as "Adena."

The visitor finds this historic and picturesque house in almost exactly its original condition, and is received hospitably by a son of the old Governor, himself almost fourscore years of age. The house, we are told, was fully completed in 1806, the work having been begun in 1798, and progressing very slowly on account of the hugeness of the undertaking in a pioneer settlement, and the difficulty of obtaining many of the materials.

Thomas Worthington, on coming to Ohio, was possessed of considerably more of this world's goods than most of the pioneers enjoyed, and coming from a home of old-style luxury, he naturally desired to form one in the West which should supply some of the elegancies as well as the necessities of life, and one in which he could comfortably entertain his friends. Accordingly he took great pains to select a picturesque location upon the great tract of land which he bought, and employed that famous architect, the elder Latrobe, of Washington, to design his dwelling-place. The work was done strictly in accordance with the plans he furnished, and mostly by workmen who were sent West by him. The edifice rose slowly, and the utmost care was taken to secure thoroughness and insure durability. The heavy stones, quarried in the vicinity, were carefully laid by experienced masons in walls two feet thick, and all of the wood-work was made massive and strong, but simple. The nails and the iron and brass work were brought from Philadelphia, and the glass from Pittsburgh, at great cost. The marble for mantels was packed on horses across the

mountains from the Quaker City at an expense of seven dollars for every hundredweight. The cost of the house was, for the time, enormous, twice what it would have been a score of years later; but when completed, it was a marvel of beauty and luxury to the backwoodsmen—a palace in the wilderness. People flocked to Adena from all parts of the country round about, even from Kentucky, to gaze upon the massive walls of this many-chambered two-story stone mansion. The novelties of papered walls, the large panes of glass, curtains, and marble mantel-pieces, we are told, seemed especially to attract attention, and excite amazement and admiration. The house was seldom without visitors. During the earlier years of their occupancy the Worthingtons entertained hosts of people, among them some of the most eminent men of the time, who came to consult with their host upon grave public questions, as well as to enjoy the hospitality of the finest house in the West. Aaron Burr was at Adena not long before the dark close of his brilliant, audacious schemes. John Polk, James Monroe, Henry Clay, Lewis Cass, William Henry Harrison, Daniel Webster, and Thomas Corwin were among those whose footsteps have echoed in the old-fashioned hall, or upon the stone-floored veranda. And to this list may be added Paul Cuffey, the celebrated preacher; Judge Bibb, of the Supreme Court; Poletica, the Russian diplomate; General Macomb, commander of the army under Monroe; De Witt Clinton and Thomas A. King, Governors of New York; Thomas Ewing, Samuel F. Vinton, James Brown, member of Congress, and afterward ambassador to Paris; and a host of lesser lights among the statesmen of a past generation. Early in the history of the State, when the line of Indian battle had scarcely swept westward beyond the Miamis and the Whitewater, and when the settlements along the Scioto were still occasionally startled by rumors of danger, there was a great gathering of the braves of different tribes at Greenville, under Tecumseh, and his brother the Prophet. The Governor dispatched Thomas Worthington and Duncan McArthur to ascertain the object of such an assemblage. The commissioners were entirely convinced of the sincerity of Tecumseh in his protestations of pacific intentions toward the United States; but as there was a deep-seated and wide-spread feeling among the whites that the Indians had gathered for the purpose of attacking the scattered settlements, and making a general massacre, Tecumseh, Blue Jacket, Tahre (the Crane), and a chief called the Panther, were induced by Worthington and McArthur to accompany them to Chillicothe, to more effectually allay the feverish excitement and apprehension of the people. Tecumseh made a speech which gave the settlers perfect assurance of safety, and won for him many warm friends and admirers. He was the guest

TECUMSEH'S TOMAHAWK, AT ADENA.

for a fortnight of Mr. Worthington, and on departing left his tomahawk as a souvenir. It is still treasured among the articles of historic bric-à-brac at Adena.

Governor Worthington was not destined to enjoy an old age of retirement and rest in the happy home which he created. Active in the service of the State and the nation from the time he settled in Ohio until his untimely death (in 1827, at the age of fifty-four years), he had but little time to pursue the pleasures of study or the amenities of social life, and was only at Adena during the rare and brief intervals of absence from public duty. The great influence he brought to bear in securing the organization of the State government won for him the respect and gratitude of its people, and they evinced their appreciation of his character and work by electing him Senator from the new State—a position in which he became the participant in most of the important measures of the administrations of Jefferson and Madison. At the close of his career in the Senate he was elected Governor of the State, in which capacity he was the promoter of all those wise and beneficent measures which were the foundation of Ohio's prosperity. He founded, in 1815, the State Library, selecting in Philadelphia, with the aid of his son, the present occupant of the old homestead, the first installment of books which were placed in the Capitol at Columbus, the

nucleus of a vast library. He was elected Governor a second term, and on his retirement from the office was given important appointments which still kept him in the service of the State. For over thirty years in public life, no man in Ohio did more to form the character and advance the interests of the State.

Half a mile from Adena, and upon the same plateau, is Fruit Hill, the residence of two Governors—originally the homestead of Duncan McArthur, and latterly of William Allen.

Stern, rugged Duncan McArthur, whose name was a household word throughout the West—scout, surveyor, soldier, famous both as General and as civil leader—lived here in a log-cabin, and before the erection of the Worthington mansion built a large stone house on the site of the present structure. The original residence was, however, almost entirely destroyed by fire, and only a small portion remains, incorporated with the newer but still ancient pile of substantial masonry. McArthur's career was a curious one, and yet one which has had many parallels in the history of the Northwest. He was born in Dutchess County, New York, in 1772, and when eight years of age removed with his father to the Pennsylvania frontier. His parents were natives of the Highlands of Scotland, and his mother belonged to the Campbell clan, so celebrated in Scottish history. Young McArthur had a generous strain of the sturdy blood of the Highlands in his veins, and probably inherited something of the Scotch love of action and adventure, for at the age of only eighteen years we find him a soldier under General Harmer in his campaign against the Indians. In 1792 he acted with so much intrepidity at one of the most fiercely fought battles of the time that he immediately became a hero in the eyes of the hardy frontiersmen.

From that time on until after the settlement of Chillicothe he was constantly braving the dangers of the wilderness, either as a spy among the Indians or as a surveyor with Massie. He assisted Massie in laying out the "ancient metropolis," and in the course of his business became a rich landholder, and settled on one of his large tracts, now known as the Fruit Hill estate. He was a member of one of the early Legislatures, and being a high officer in the militia, on the breaking out of the war of 1812 went to Detroit, and was there, with the regiment he commanded, included in Hull's surrender. After his return as a prisoner of war on parole the Democratic party elected him by an immense majority to Congress, a position which he resigned to go into the field and to the front of action as Major-General. Under the "general call" he led to the Sandusky plains an army of nearly eight thousand men, mostly from the Scioto Valley, which, history says, "was almost wholly stripped of its male population." This general turn-out of the militia bore evidence that Massie, McArthur, and the few pioneers who followed them into the valley of the Scioto and made its first settlement had infused something of their own daring into the mass of the community. After the resignation of General Harrison, the command of the Northwestern army devolved upon McArthur, and from that time until the declaration of peace he conducted a most energetic and effectual campaign. Returning to his home, he again held many civil offices within the gift of a grateful State, and ten years after the close of the war in which he had won such high military honors was elected to Congress, in which body he became a strong supporter of what was then called the American system, and exerted a large influence in its favor, for although an uneducated man he had practical business habits, energy, perseverance, and the soundest of judgment. His enormous private business needing all his attention, he declined re-election for a third term, but a few years later he was brought forth from his retirement by the anti-Jackson party, which elected him to the Gubernatorial chair. Upon the expiration of his term of office he was a candidate for Congress, being put into the field to heal dissensions in the party. Upon McArthur's nomination the other candidates withdrew, and his friends everywhere were very confident that the ex-Governor, an old politician, and popular man of affairs, could sweep the district against a young and comparatively unknown man, a mere stripling — William Allen. Between McArthur and Allen there was a hot fight, or rather between Allen and the ex-Governor's friends, for McArthur himself made but little effort in the canvass, probably thinking it unnecessary. Some of his enemies used as a campaign document against him a small handbill headed with rude wood-cuts of coffins, and detailing in horrible colors the shooting of four deserters at the Chillicothe camp during the war of 1812 by McArthur's orders. This act, which was probably nothing more than one of the stern necessities of war, and perfectly justifiable under the circumstances, was denounced as the act of a blood-thirsty monster, and perhaps with some effect. It was the old campaign cry against McArthur, and had been used every time he was a candidate for office. Allen entered the contest with vigor, made speeches in almost every school-house through the country, and was elected by a majority of one in a total of ten thousand votes. This was the close of McArthur's political career and the opening of Allen's. By an accident McArthur met with in Columbus, while Governor, he was terribly maimed, and remained until his death a prisoner at his home.

The young man who won the victory over the ex-Governor of Ohio, and who was destined to hold the highest position within the gift of the State, came to Chillicothe as a poor boy one winter early in the twenties. He was a native of North Carolina, and born in 1806. His life, however, from early childhood until his eighteenth year, when he came to Ohio, was passed in Virginia. Making the entire journey from Lynchburg to Chillicothe on foot, and a large portion of it alone, he was warmly welcomed on his arrival by his half-sister and her husband, the mother and father of Allen G. Thurman, with whom he made his home. He attended for a time the "old academy," and then began the study of law. Young Allen was tall and large of his age, and he exhibited a mental precociousness which was in keeping with his physical advancement. He was soon admitted to practice at the bar, and almost immediately thereafter developed very unusual oratorical ability. After his first political success he rose rapidly in the favor of the public, and in 1836 was elected United States Senator. When he took his seat the year following he was the youngest man who ever had a place in that body, being in his thirty-first year. It is a fact not generally known that William Allen was offered the Democratic nomination for the Presidency in the Washington Convention of 1848. The friends of Cass and Van Buren being unable to agree, and the dissension having developed to such a degree that it was feared neither in the event of nomination could conciliate the partisans of his opponent, Allen was strongly urged to allow his name to go before the Convention as a compromise candidate. He declined on the ground that such action would be treachery to Cass, whose friend and adviser he was. After a second term in the Senate, Mr. Allen went into the retirement of private life. Marrying a daughter of Governor McArthur, and taking up his residence at Fruit Hill, he made no effort to emerge from his seclusion until 1873, when he accepted the Democratic nomination for the Governorship. Thus came before the people, in a personal canvass, a man who almost forty years before had entered the United States Senate, but who, from his long retirement, was almost unknown to the younger generation of politicians. On the expiration of his term of office, Governor Allen sought no further political preferment. He remained at Fruit Hill enjoying his books, and almost to the very last superintending the great farm which surrounded his home. His tall, erect form was a familiar sight upon the streets of Chillicothe, and as he was easily accessible, hosts of visitors from the town and from abroad, the distinguished and the obscure, sought "the sage of Fruit Hill," to converse with him and to receive his counsel. Even in the last few weeks of his life his physical and mental vigor seemed scarcely impaired. His voice was strong and clear, and as he warmed with the growing interest of conversation upon some broad topic, his manner became strangely impressive, and his words as eloquent as when he was a score of years younger. There was no indication of the near approaching close of life's earth chapter in the early summer of 1879, and yet, after a few days' illness, Death laid his hand upon the silvered, venerable head, and the clear blue eyes were closed forever.

The Governor's room in the old stone house, from which we have wandered to recount the lives of its two famous occupants, is still undisturbed. The vine which shades the window looking out upon the lawn and hill-slope, and upon Chillicothe beyond, has been bared by winter winds, and grown green again, but the fragrance of its blossoms floats through the open casement into a lonely chamber. By the reading table, with its homely device for holding books, there is a vacant, well-worn easy-chair, and all of the simple articles of furniture throughout the room remain in the position in which they were arranged by its departed occupant. Over thirty years of the Governor's life were passed at this historic house, and his powerful personality seems still to pervade the place.

A great concourse of people attended the funeral of the widely known and well-loved old man, and a long procession wound down the half-mile hill, and through the hushed streets of the town, and up to the summit of another high hill, following the remains of the last of Chillicothe's Governors to their final resting-place. No more beautiful cemetery can be found in the West than Chillicothe's city of the dead, overlooking the peaceful, sunny valley of the Scioto and its rambling, village-like city of the living. Poor mortality could have no resting-place hallowed by more harmonious beauty of nature, and glorious immortality no more suggestive earthly symbol or assuring mystic promise, than is here afforded.

Here sleep a goodly company of the distinguished dead—Massie, Tiffin, Worthington, McArthur, Allen, and many more, younger men—who by civil means fostered and with arms defended the State which their predecessors founded.

THE RELIGION OF THE SIOUX

TO the Sioux of the past, religion was truly a mystery. From the simple growth of the blade of grass to the complex phenomena of the thunder-storm, all life, power, and strength were interpreted as the physical acts of unknown gods. The Great Spirit is a name given us by the interpreter, for the Sioux had no conception of a single spirit, however great, capable of ruling the universe. Lightning was the anger of a thunder god, an awful bird, whose structure varied from wings containing only six quills to wings with four joints each, according to the imagination of the medicine-man. The moving god, he whose aid it was most difficult to invoke, was too subtle to be likened to any known form, but he controlled the intellect, passions, and mental faculties, abstractions for which the Sioux has not even a name. The Hayoka was the contrary god, who sat naked, and fanned himself in the coldness of a Dakota blizzard, and huddled shivering over a fire in the heat of summer, who cried for joy and laughed in his sorrow. Rocks and bowlders were the hardest and strongest things; hence they belonged to the oldest gods—smaller rocks were fetiches. On the barren buttes of the Dakotas may be seen many a crumbling pile of stones

erected in by-gone days to propitiate an unknown god. Many a forgotten chief has gone to the highest hill when his son was sick, and amidst fastings and incantations reared a mound of little stones in the hope that his loved one's life might be spared. And still another relic of the savage belief of the old Sioux is found on the bodies of the warriors themselves. Take almost any man who is thirty years old or more, and he can show you long scars on his back or breast, and dozens of smaller scars on his arms, all inflicted by himself in fulfilling his vows to the sun. The sun-dance was one of the great religious and political events of the Sioux life. Whole villages assembled and feasted, while the worshippers fasted and exhausted the strength they were to need so badly in the coming test of endurance. On the appointed day none but virgins were allowed to cut down and trim the tree that was to be used, while only chiefs and warriors of exceptional bravery were allowed to carry it to its place in the centre of the village. Here, with mysterious pipe-smokings and unintelligible incantations, the pole is planted, ropes of buffalo-hide having been fastened to its top, one rope for each worshipper. The men, already half dead from exhaustion, are then brought out and laid on the ground around the pole, always ready knives thrust through the muscles of their chests or backs, and in the holes thus made wooden skewers thrust, to which are fastened the loose ends of the ropes. Then round and round dance the worshippers, their eyes fixed on the blazing sun, while the jerk, jerk, jerk of the bleeding flesh beats a sickening time to the hi-yas of a Dakota song. Friends and relatives, men, women, and children, gash their arms and breasts to stimulate the dancers and keep up their courage. When the flesh is torn apart the dancer is released, his vow fulfilled, his bravery, his manhood, unquestioned..... These and a thousand other monstrous customs were what the early missionary had to combat.

The Sioux hereafter was a particularly happy idea, in the main in keeping with the advanced views of some of their white brothers of the present day. There were happy hunting-grounds, but there were no unhappy ones. When a Methodist minister, attending one of the Indian commissions in the 70's, painted a hell with colors of fire and brimstone, the only necessity for such a future abode was, as an old chief expressed it, for all the whites. Some Indians might lie, steal, or commit murder, but these were tangible offences receiving prompt punishment, and as such were violations of a social rather than a religious code. And, in fact, to kill a Crow Indian, steal his ponies, or lie to him and get him into trouble, were things that made the plenteous game, the clear waters, and the rich grass all the more abundant for the Sioux in the happy hunting-grounds. The medicine-man was not a priest; for their religion had no conception of such. He was self-appointed. Who could displace him or doubt his power? By some shrewdness he predicted a coming event, or by luck he performed an unheard-of act, and then his greatness was assured. Sitting-Bull, medicine-man rather than chief, once predicted rain in a season of drought. With mysterious pipe-smokings and vague incantations he prayed for rain, and sure enough it came. When the crops again needed water he was applied to, but he cautiously answered: "Too much rain will drown you. I can easily make it rain, but no one can make it stop." .... This utter lack of appreciation of moral right and wrong, combined with an ex-

ceptional craftiness, was a towering obstacle for the missionary to surmount.

This much has the missionary done. From the sorcery and jugglery of a weazened medicine-man he has brought the Sioux to confide in the simple teachings of the Bible. From the barbarous self-immolation of the sun-dance he has led him to the few rites of Christianity. From the gross sensuality and selfishness of the awful mystery, the Takoo Wakan, manifested and worshipped under the form of gods innumerable, he has built up a faith in one Supreme Being.

To-day Episcopalians, Roman Catholics, Presbyterians, and Congregationalists are all well represented in the Dakotas, and have rendered great assistance to the government in efforts toward civilization. The younger men wear their Y. M. C. A. badges, and the Roman Catholics their crosses, just as their forefathers wore the dirty medicine charms. The leading men are no longer those who have killed the most Crows or stolen the greatest number of ponies. War-songs are replaced by Christian hymns, and "Jesus Itancan" now bursts forth from the dusky throats that formerly knew nothing but the murderous "kte."

It would be an error, of course, to suppose that all the Sioux have embraced Christianity. Every one knows that there are still those malcontents who wear the hair long, who withdraw as far as possible from their agencies, and who still yearn for the extermination of the whites and the return of the buffalo. The late Messiah craze is still fresh in the public mind. The standing rock from which the principal Sioux agency takes its name is a large stone. One story makes it a runaway girl turned into stone with her baby on her back when pursued by her father and brothers. Another story makes it originally an Arickaree object of worship that became sacred to the Sioux when a warrior, defiling the idol, was killed shortly afterward by its worshippers. Whatever its origin, it was held in great reverence. Three years ago last summer an old Sioux suddenly felt himself possessed of divine power, and, as a proof, offered to make the stone remove itself from its masonry to a distant point. His bragging attracted considerable attention, but his hope of gaining followers was cut short when the Indian agent gave him twenty-four hours in which to remove the stone, or else remove himself to the guard-house. At the end of the time it was the Indian who moved.

It is probable that there are still messiahs who at times will give bullet-proof ghost-shirts to their followers and lead them against the law and order of government. The Indian who promised that

white lad after a vigorous perusal of the dime novel.

Smarting under wrongs, both real and imaginary, it was not natural for these Indians to receive the first missionaries with friendliness. Always suspicious, always keen to expect bad intentions, they regarded the early missionary in the general class of whites, and therefore

HAIRY-CHIN.

thirty feet of finely sodded and forest-planted soil should cover all the earth, smothering the greater part of the whites, but allowing a few to escape as fishes, will have successors whose fortune-telling, no matter how absurd, will gain them followers. For, stripped of power, it is but natural that the older chiefs should long for its return, and there is an analogy between the excitement produced on the ignorant and uncultivated brain of an Indian by dreams of old-time warfare and that aroused in the immature

unworthy of confidence. The chiefs dreaded a further loss of their following; the medicine-men feared that their enchantments would fall before the white man's god. Even the mass of the people, although afraid to forcibly interfere, nevertheless sought all other means to prevent the establishment of missions. Unlimited in hospitality among themselves, yet in many cases they forbade the missionary to use the water that flowed in the creeks. A missionary's horse had no right to eat a blade of the thousands of tons of grass that annually went to waste on the reservation. Armed with simple remedies, the missionary sought to win favor by healing the sick. If a cure were effected, no thanks were received; but if the patient died, the family of the deceased laid the death at the missionary's door and demanded payment for the loss. When the missionary sought to better their physical condition by giving to one a warm coat, the entire village demanded that they be likewise treated. If an Indian woman were given a dollar for doing a small washing, another woman would be angry unless she, for a like consideration, be allowed to carry the water; while a third woman would insist that she, for another dollar, be allowed to hang the clothes upon the line. When one considers that the good-will of these savages was the first requisite for mission-work, then the tact and untiring perseverance of the missionary will be appreciated. There was no Hiawathan romance about it.

Early converts were principally among the women. "Only a woman—it makes no difference," the warriors said. The woman was only the household drudge, and so long as she chopped the wood, carried the water, and took care of the ponies her religious beliefs were of small moment. But the man's life was a succession of paganish rites. Wild orgies celebrated all his actions from the time when, as a boy, he killed his first bird to when, as a stealthy old man, he stole his last pony from a Crow. To embrace Christianity was to give up everything that had been his pride. But, as admitted by the most experienced Indian agents, to allow his pagan belief to continue was to so shape his life in the wrong direction as to retard civilization many generations. An instance of the benefits of this change of belief is the report of the Presbyterian Church that of eleven hundred communicants only one was known to have joined in the ghost-dances of 1891.

While government officials could not directly promote Christianity among the Sioux, they have fully recognized its civilizing power. In 1876, with a view to allow the different sects to work harmoniously and to the best good of the Indian, the different Sioux reservations were assigned as fields for missionary work among the Episcopalians, the Roman Catholics, the Presbyterians, and the Congregationalists. This allotment in no way limited the work of the Churches to the fields assigned; it merely gave to each its starting-point, and the control of the contract-schools in that territory.

That the missionary's work has been well done may be judged from the following tables taken

STANDING ROCK, SACRED TO THE SIOUX.

from a late report of Mr. Daniel Dorchester, superintendent of Indian schools. I have made such changes in these tables as have come within my personal knowledge, and as the work of christianizing the Sioux has not been stationary, any errors that may still exist will be on the short side.

"The Roman Catholic Church has the following missions in the Dakotas:

Devil's Lake agency—3 priests, 2 boarding and 1 day school, 15 employés.
Standing Rock agency—3 priests, 2 boarding-schools, 25 employés.
Pine Ridge agency—2 priests, 1 boarding-school, 20 employés.
Rosebud agency—3 priests, 1 boarding-school, 20 employés.
Crow Creek agency—3 priests, 1 boarding-school, 15 employés.
Totals.—5 missions, 14 priests, 7 schools, 95 employés, 12 churches; Roman Catholic population, 4740; adult baptisms (for the year), 743; child baptisms, 1350.

"The Presbyterian Church has the following exhibit, furnished by one of its oldest ministers. Its missions are in the Yankton, Crow Creek, and Lower Brulé, Sisseton, and Devil's Lake agencies, and at Flandreau.

Native communicants..................... 1104
Native members of Sunday-school 736
Native churches organized 15
Native pastors installed over churches .. 8
Stated supplies in charge................. 7
Admitted on profession of faith last year. 120

"Congregational (A. M. A.) missions are as follows:

Cheyenne River agency — 9 stations, 25 laborers, 1 school.
Standing Rock agency—5 stations, 13 laborers.
Rosebud agency—3 stations, 6 laborers.

Totals.—3 missions, 6 ministers (4 at Cheyenne River agency, and 1 at each of the other places). 17 stations. 44 laborers, 1 school. Number of communicants not known.

"The Protestant Episcopal Church has the following:

Missions.	Churches.	Chapels.	Stations.	Clergy.	Deacons.	Catechists.
Cheyenne River agency	1	6	1	1	1	6
Crow Creek and Lower Brulé.	1	1	7	1	..	7
Pine Ridge agency............	1	6	3	1	1	9
Rosebud agency...............	1	6	3	1	3	4
Sisseton agency	1	2	..	1	..	3
Standing Rock agency	1	..	1	1	1	1
Yankton agency...............	1	2	..	1	1	2
Yanktonais.....................	1	2	2	1	1	3
Flandreau	1	..	..	1	..	2

Total.—9 missions, 9 churches, 25 chapels. 17 stations, 9 clergy. 8 deacons, 37 catechists; communicants, 1712; Indian contributions, $2575; average church attendance, 2609; church sittings, 4672; church property, $61,246. Total population Episcopal Indians, 6200.

"It is not a wild estimate to say that probably there are from 10,500 to 11,000 Indian adherents of the Protestant Episcopal, Presbyterian, and Congregational churches in the Dakotas."

The last two years have witnessed church convocations of the christianized Sioux, events of great importance to the Indians. The different agencies compete with one another for the honor of holding them, the voters good-naturedly swinging from one agency to another, as inducements of watermelons or tales of vicious snakes are held up to them. In 1892 the Episcopalians met at St. Elizabeth, the Roman Catholics at the Cheyenne agency, while the Presbyterians and Congregationalists combined, and held their Paya Owodake (united talk) at the Standing Rock agency.

This latter conference was held in a square booth built of young trees, with the branches strewn over the top for shade. Above the enclosure proudly floated the stars and stripes, borrowed for the occasion from the quartermaster at Fort Yates. One side of the booth was for the men, the other for women. All meetings, whether of a business or a purely religious character, were conducted in the prescribed form. Prayers were offered, hymns sung, and sermons preached—all in the Sioux language—sometimes by missionaries, more often by Indians. There is a terrible force in the prayer of an Indian—a wild, eloquent vehemence in all his petitions. When on Sunday, the last day of the conference, the sacrament was administered, there was an earnestness on every face that said dumbly, "We believe, and we are trying to do the best we can."

The Lord's Prayer may give some idea of the sound of the language of these people, together with the peculiar construction and the arrangement of the different parts of speech.

*Itaŋcaŋ tawoćekiye kiŋ.**
Lord   his-prayer   the

Ateuŋyaŋpi mahpiya ekta naŋke ciŋ;
Father-we-have   heaven   in   thou-art   the

Nićaźe kiŋ wakaŋdapi kte; Nitokićoŋze
Thy-name   the   holy-regarded   shall   Thy-kingdom

kiŋ u kte. Mahpiya ekta token
the   come   shall   Heaven   in   how

nitawaćiŋ ećoŋpi kiŋ, maka akan
thy-will   is-done   the   earth   upon

hićen ećoŋpi nuŋwe. Aŋpetu kiŋ de
so   done   may-it-be   Day   the   this

taku yutapi uŋku-po; ka waŋyhtanipi
food   us-give   and   our-trespasses

kiŋ uŋkićićaźuźu-po, uŋkiś iyećen
the   erase-for-us   us   like-as

tona ećiŋsniyaŋ uŋkokićihaŋyaŋpi
as-many-as   wrongly   have-done-to-us

* The character ŋ is n with a nasal sound, and is so represented in Sioux literature.

hena   iyećen   wicuŋkićićazuzipi   kiŋ.
those   even-as   them-we-forgive   the

Wawiwiyutaŋye   kiŋ   he   en   iyaya
Temptation   the   that   into   to-go

uŋyaŋpi śni-po, ka taku śića etaŋhaŋ
us-come   not   and what   bad   from

euŋhdaku-po. Wokićoŋze kiŋ, wowaśake
us-deliver   Kingdom   the   strength

kiŋ, wowitaŋ kiŋ, henakiya owihaŋke
the   glory   the   all-these   end

wàninca nitawa nuŋwe.   Aṃen.
none   thine   may-be   Amen

Cultivated by their mode of life, all Sioux have remarkable memories for sounds. Their singing is an agreeable surprise, the men, in their deep, rather rough, tones, chanting a thundering bass to the shrill treble of the women. Many of their hymns are merely Sioux words arranged to standard music; others are those that have been composed by educated Indians; while a few, the most popular, are native airs, queer tunes that have a distinctively Indian sound, and that run continually into minors. One of these, called Lacquiparle, runs as follows:

Sometimes at one of the conferences an old custom will crop out, when, on holding one of their society meetings in the open air, the women, with no apparent thought, arrange themselves in a great circle so nearly perfect that the eye glancing over it can suggest no change to make it more perfect. From this position the delegates rise and make their reports. In case of a contribution, one woman after another goes to the centre of the circle and deposits her offering, whether it be money, a strip of calico, or a fancifully worked bead bag. It is the desire of the missionary, as well as the government, to break up even the semblance of these old-time customs, but when one sees the readiness with which three hundred women will adapt themselves to this kind of a meeting there is some excuse for its preservation.

The christianized Sioux vote and elect officers of their religious societies much after the fashion of their white brothers. Their electioneering arguments, however, are distinctly Indian. In a recent election for secretary of one of their associations, a comely-looking woman nominated Miss Collins, a white missionary, who has been among the Sioux for seventeen years. Before the voting was begun, the same woman arose and declared that Miss Collins should not be elected. "For," said she, "I gave her a quilt, and asked her to hang it up at this meeting, but she wouldn't do it."

"Oh," said Miss Collins, "I was afraid it would rain; then the quilt would have been ruined, and that would have made me cry."

The explanation was satisfactory, and when the voting was begun, "Winona" after "Winona" was recorded for Miss Collins — Winona, signifying the first-born girl, being the name the Indians have given her.

Despite the awakening of Christian enthusiasm among the Sioux, the names frequently given their children show a desire to have them known as great warriors. At one of this year's conferences there was present a poor weakly little chap, with scrofula written all over him, but who bore the great-sounding name of "He-who-shoots-to-kill-past-beyond." In all his sickly existence the poor child has probably never killed anything as large as a field-mouse, yet should he live to be an old man, in some way or other the story will creep out that in his youth he stood in a circle of enemies and killed, killed, until there were none left to battle against him.

Sitting-Bull was a crafty old pagan,

but his two widows have stood up in church and said, "We want Christ." A deaf-and-dumb son of this same old fox was told by One-Bull, Sitting-Bull's successor, that he could not be received into the church on account of his infirmities. On hearing this the missionary, who was about to go on a journey, told One-Bull to tell the lad that on her return she would take him as a church member if he were still so inclined. When the little lady had travelled about ten miles on her journey she saw some one coming after her, riding fast over the prairie. It was the deaf-and-dumb boy, bearing a note from One-Bull that said, "We cannot make him understand." The boy dismounted and made signs, touching his eyes, straightening his form, and outlining his figure stretched upon the ground. That was his dead body. Then opening his eyes, he pointed to heaven, and afterward made on the ground the square enclosure of the church. . . . . He is now a constant attendant at all church meetings.

In connection with the fatality of revolution which seems to have followed the death of Sitting-Bull is the fact that in the hands of one of the christianized Indian policemen who killed Sitting-Bull was an old carbine which, as a hostile, the same policeman had picked up in the Custer affair.

The Churches and missionary societies were quick to grasp the idea that moral and mental training should go hand in hand. Government officials have stated that religion should be wholly ignored in government schools, but the same officials have never disputed the benefits of the moral teachings of any of the Christian Churches. In 1876, when the assignment of the reservations to the different Churches was made, many of the Churches were given control of the contract-schools in their fields. These are schools built by the government and controlled by a Church, the latter supplying teachers and receiving so much per scholar—about fifty dollars a year—for the average attendance. In addition to this amount the government allows such schools to draw the usual rations and clothing for the attendant pupils. These schools and the mission schools, the latter built and supported, except as to rations and clothing, by the various Churches, are the best schools on the reservation when properly con-

"MALCONTENTS WHO WEAR THE HAIR LONG."

ducted. With the exception of a few day scholars, the children are admitted on the first day of September, and educated morally, mentally, and industrially until the last of June, their training during this period receiving no set-back from contact with Indian village life. The government makes school attendance compulsory for all children between the ages of five and eighteen, and if the ringing of the bell on the first day of September does not bring them in, Indian policemen scattering over the reservation soon round them up. Washed from head to foot, and clothed according to civilized ideas, the scholars are then ready to learn to

ATTENDANTS AT THE PRESBYTERIAN AND CONGREGATIONAL CONFERENCE.

speak, read, and write English, to get some knowledge of arithmetic and the history and geography of their own country, while a few receive musical instruction. Industrially, the boys work in the school gardens, in the blacksmith, carpenter, and tin shops, and are taught the care of horses, cattle, and poultry. The girls receive instruction in domestic work, cooking, sewing, darning, and laundering. Aprons, blouses, cloaks, pillow-cases, towels — in fact, everything in needlework that is required for the school and scholars is made by the Indian girls. Morally, in addition to the beliefs of the different churches, the children are taught honesty and truthfulness, taught that girls and women are not household drudges, taught that dance rites and medicine charms are relics of the barbarism from which they have emerged.

As auxiliaries to their churches and chapels the Domestic and Foreign Missionary Society of the Episcopal Church has established five boarding-schools for the Sioux—St. Elizabeth's, on the Grand River, South Dakota, near the camps of Gaul and John Grass, two noted leaders of the hostiles who fought against Custer; St. Paul's, the oldest, at the Yankton agency; St. Mary's, at the Rosebud agen-

cy; St. John's, at the Cheyenne agency; and Hope School, at Springfield, South Dakota. In all, 228 children are under the control of principals and assistants. Godliness, usefulness, cleanliness, politeness, and learning are the points strived for. When I gave the customary " How, cola," to a little mite at the St. Elizabeth mission, the mite replied, " Good-morning, sir," in a way that made me feel decidedly at a disadvantage.

The churches and religious societies have certainly quenched the fire of barbarism in the Indian children. The Bible, translated into their native language, has been put before them, so that the younger element does not grow up with a belief in that convenient form of prayer—merely pointing the pipe—which expressed so little, but implied all manner of requests for ponies and meat and comfortable old age. Marriage according to Christian rites has succeeded the annual virgin-feast, where a slandered maiden stood face to face with her accuser by the sacred fire and swore a high-sounding oath to her purity. The disappearance of blanket and breech-cloth, long hair and highly painted faces, is a sign that the Sioux has succumbed to a stronger civilization, and with his old customs have fallen his old gods.

WHERE TIME HAS SLUMBERED

"MEBBY Mrs. Cap'n will have one," or, "You'd better go and see Mrs. Cap'n," or, "If there's any sich thing around, mebbe Mrs. Cap'n 'll have it." These things were so often said to the hunter from New York, who was down in West Virginia partly for deer, and largely for relics of a by-gone era, that he determined to see "Mrs. Cap'n," and to know more about her. There seemed to be little to know, and that was told readily in answer to his questions, for it was evident that she was the most conspicuous woman on the mountain on which she lived. All the mountain folk knew her or knew about her, but at the same time it became clear to the stranger from New York that there was some little mystery—something kept back. It was said of her that she was "more forehanded" than most women, that she was very industrious, that she was proud, and "kep' her head well up," and that she had been a widow through the best part of her life —a widow so stricken by her bereavement that no man had since been able to make any impression upon her affections, though the best men in that section had tried. That in itself was peculiar enough to make her conspicuous.

Freely as this was told, it was often accompanied by a manner that led the stranger to fancy there was more to learn. His failure to break through this reserve whetted his curiosity, and one day he went straight to the woman herself in her cabin. The cabin, externally, was very like all the rest—a little log house with a stone chimney projecting from one end, with a roof made of those large shingles that they call "clapboards" down there, with a row of three small window-panes set in the end opposite the chimney for an extra window, in addition to the real window that was beside the doorway, and that was also like a window in the daytime, and was usually left open to serve as such. Over and in front of the door was a rude, ramshackle porch. It was made of a few boards held up at the outer ends by a beam laid across two posts. It was apparently maintained to protect a flooring of rough logs sunk in the ground, but it could shelter them only from such rare rains as fell straight down from overhead, so that

perhaps its best service was to accommodate several bunches of dried or drying "yarbs." They hung at just the right height beneath the porch to hit a visitor's hat, and cause him to glance quickly around for the assailant who had made a target of his head-gear. The house or cabin stood in a little clearing of much trampled and furrowed dirt, with its chimney end toward the road, and its door and porch facing the rest of "Mrs. Cap'n's" buildings—a corn and tobacco house, a stable, and a pigsty—properties not altogether uncommon in those mountains, and yet not so common but that they reflected proudly upon the family as one that was pretty well-to-do as things go in that country. The corn-house and pigsty were commonplace, but the stable was one to arrest a stranger's attention. It was built on the plan of a canary-cage, with its sides almost as open as if you were expected to hand in hay by the half-bale to the horse through the space between the boards, or to pass him in a pail of water whenever he was thirsty, without bothering with the door. And even that kind of stable is commonplace in West Virginia, for that is the kind they build there, either because the climate is never severe, or possibly because a great storm would blow right through the building without carrying it away, as the winds pass through a net-work banner in the streets. But that is a mere ignorant conjecture, such as a stranger might make, since West Virginia is one of the few of our commonwealths that are free from really big American weather, with all that the term implies.

"Can I come in?" said the hunter from New York, pausing in the open doorway.

"Yaas; come in and hev a warm," said a man who sat before some blazing logs in the deep tall recess in the Dutch chimney. "Draw up a cheer by the fire and hev a warm."

"Is this Mrs. Captain's?"

"Yaas," said the man; "Mrs. Cap'n is my sister. She's up above. That's her a-shakin' things with her loom—makin' a little rag kyarpet fer Killis Kyar's folks. Sence Killis Kyar's moved into his new house on the valley road his gals is mighty ticky. And yit" (thoughtfully) "they ain't nothin' like's ticky as some. When I see the young folks that's so awful nice about hevin' kyarpets on the floor an' curtings on the winders and that-all, I often say to 'em, 'Ef you-all could see how yer fathers lived without none of them things, you-all wouldn't be so ticky.'"

"But you've got a carpet here—and curtains," said the stranger.

"Oh, we hev," said the man. "That's Mrs. Cap'n—she's different."

It was evident that she and much besides were different, as the old man said. We shall see that most mountain cabins are bare (floor, ceiling, walls, and all), but here was a floor-covering of rag carpet, and the window had a small section of a yellow lace curtain drawn across it, and the ceiling was clean, instead of being grimy with smoke like most others. And there were several tintypes grouped together not inartistically on one wall, and some gay lithographs, such as one gets at a country grocery, on the opposite wall. Two long mountain rifles, made pretty by brass-work inlaid in the stocks, ornamented two rafters, and some powder-horns and pouches and a dog-horn—the very sort of curios the hunter was seeking—hung upon other rafters. But the marvel of marvels in the cabin was one of the beds. It was a century-old "four-poster," standing so high above the floor that no man could reach the tops of the solid fluted posts, and no man would care to meet with such a mishap as to fall from the bedding to the floor. As the stranger looked about him the old man followed his eyes, and commented upon whatever they took in.

"Yaas," said he; "Mrs. Cap'n is different, you know. That's hern, that big bed. Me and young Cap'n, when he's to home, sleeps on that low bed thar" (nodding at an ordinary bed made up in a sort of low open box that sat on the floor without legs beneath it). "Them guns and things she takes fer the kyarpets and jeans she weaves, and sells 'em to strangers like you-all fer ten times what they're wuth. Them picters is hern too."

"Everybody speaks highly of her; she must be a remarkable woman," said the stranger.

"Waal, 'tain't that, so much," said the old man, pausing, and puffing at his pipe, and reflecting rather dreamily as he began to talk. "I reckon it's the hard times she's had, an' the way she's bore up

through it. Her husband bein' killed so quick, an' her mournin' for him so stiddy. I reckon that's it."

"How was he killed?"

"The Cap'n? He was shot takin' some deserters into camp; ambushed not more'n a mile away from here. I reckon that's why folks is so set towards her. He on'y was here a short time, but he stuck to her 'bout all the time he could spare. Our house was his quarters till the General give orders to forward the hull of the army on further west. I was away, 'listed on the Confed'rit side; but I'm Union now—because the Cap'n was Union. Anyhow, 'most nine in ten 'round here was always Union. My sister was Union soon as she seen the Cap'n, tho' she hadn't been before. That's near thirty year ago, and she's been mournin' and takin' on ever since. They were jist surely cut out for one another, and were agreed to be married, an' everything was arranged—and then he was ambushed by some friends of the men he was arrestin'."

"What was his name?"

"Thar, now," said the old man, "she kin tell you that. I never could just rightly remember it. Her bein' called 'Mrs. Cap'n' by they-all just drove his name outer my head. He was from Ohier—I know that—and had a name you couldn't take hold of easy, endin' in 'berger,' or—no, maybe it wasn't just 'berger' neither."

At this point a cessation of the regular thud-thud of the loom overhead gave notice that Mrs. Cap'n was resting. A moment later her voice sounded down through the square hole at the top of the ladder that served for the stairs to the second story.

"Pole!" the voice said; "what does he want, Pole?"

"Well, I declare; that's so," said the old man; "what did you want—anything 'sides a warm? I reckon maybe you'd like a cold slice."

"No," said the stranger; "I came to see if I could buy an old gun, like one of those I see you have there. I heard your sister had one or two."

"Reckon you'd better come down, Tish," said the old man. "He wants one o' your rifles, maybe."

With much deliberation and extraordinary disturbance of mind over her skirts, which were as contumacious as they might be expected to be when forced through a two-foot hole and down a ladder nailed against a wall, Mrs. Letitia Cap'n (for Tish is the diminutive of Letitia in those mountains) came down into the main room. Except that she was not as shy as most mountain women in the presence of a strange man, she was very like the rest—a spare angular woman of middle age, in a dress that was as simple as a woman's dress could be, and that consisted of a plain waist of pink calico, and a plain skirt of the same stuff that no more than reached to her shoe-tops. She differed from the other women whom the stranger had seen thereabouts in that she wore a white apron— a superfluity trifling in itself, and yet impressive in the effect of neatness and self-respect that it produced. Perhaps, too, she was more comely than her neighbors in the sight of the mountain men. They could make closer comparisons than a stranger might. To this stranger who now regarded her she had, in common with the rest, the colorless lips, the pinched features, and the lack-lustre eyes of all the typical, badly nourished, overworked, dyspeptic mountain folk. At the suggestion of an offer of his right hand by the stranger, she put both her long bony hands behind her back—not rudely, but from a blending of awkwardness and shyness. The bartering for the gun being over, the stranger remarked that he and her brother had been speaking of "the Captain." Something very like a spark of life lighted up the woman's eyes when the subject was introduced, and she stepped to the wall and took down two pictures —both tintypes.

"This is Cap'n's picture," said she, handling one tenderly, and offering it with a little enthusiasm, as something certain to be admired, though it was a wretchedly bad piece of workmanship. It was a photograph of a soldier in uniform.

"And hain't this one like him?" she asked, putting the other card in the stranger's hand. He saw no resemblance to one in the other, but understanding that even a bad picture may convey a perfect portraiture to the mind of one who knows the face that is hinted at, he avoided her question, and asked whose was the second portrait.

"It's young Cap'n's—my son's," said she, very proudly; "and I can see the Cap'n growing up in him all over again when I look at him. To me it's just like the Cap'n had come back, fer they're both

the same age. Young Cap'n is about twenty-nine, and so was his father when he was killed."

The stranger looked at the tintypes more closely. To him the face of the soldier appeared that of a vain and weak man. The low brow, the immense mustachios curled up at the ends, the small eyes, and the abnormal breadth of the face at the cheek-bones suggested something that quite startled him—the possibility that the Captain had been such a man as might, had he lived, have broken the heart of the woman who now held his memory so sacred.

"Young Cap'n's on the railroad— telegraph operatin'," said she. "When he comes home I see him and his father together. You hain't from Ohier, be yer? No? 'Cause there wuz a man from Ohier 'bout ten year ago—I just can't happen to think out his name—and he told 'round that the Cap'n was married a'ready when he 'listed fer the war. Pole here—my brother—might 'a' found out what the man knew, if he'd a-been more keerful. I was sorry fer what you done, Pole, and you know it—gittin' down your ole rifle and huntin' the man outen the country, the way you done."

"I'd like to 'a' raised my ole gyurl rifle on that critter till his head darkened the sight," said the old hunter. "That's all me and my old gyurl wanted that time, Tish. Reckon I was too keerful with Bird Jiney too, mebbe."

"I don't say you was, Pole," Mrs. Captain replied, "fer Bird Jiney was ornery."

She then explained to the stranger that a neighbor of the name of Jiney—a man so contemptible that even his folks were "mean" (a hard thing to say of any one) —had "dar'd" to speak slightingly of her and her widowhood, and that, after giving him fair warning to leave the country, her brother had met him on a mountain road, and jerking him from the back of his horse, had dropped him over the edge of a cliff. Mrs. Captain added that Jiney had not been killed, but, after his broken bones had healed, had gone away "to some of them cities in old Virginia" to start life over again. After an interval of several years he had sent her the bed on which she had slept ever since— the huge semi-royal four-poster close by— far and away the most impressive, pretentious, and costly article of household furniture in the county. Mrs. Captain had accepted the gift as a peace-offering, she being a very thrifty woman, and the bed being a thing that could not be sent back without great expense. After that she had expected Bird Jiney to limp back into the neighborhood among his friends and family, but he had never been heard from again.

It was evident that brother Pole's energy in protecting his sister was enough to account for the brake on the gossiping tendencies of the neighbors. He made it "unhealthy," as they say out West, to talk too much about Mrs. Cap'n, even though no one had anything but praise to speak of her.

"They-all round here says I'm proud, mebbe," Mrs. Captain continued; "but I'm only proud fer my husband. If he'd 'a' lived I'd 'a' been better off than any of they-all, and since he died I'm bound to work and save money, and live's near as I kin to the way he'd have had me. If I'm puttin' on, I'm on'y puttin' on fer Cap'n—hain't I, Pole? Mebbe he's where he kin see me and the kyarpet like he told me he had in Ohier, and the curting and—and the bed—and kin see me workin' and doing my best."

"She don't keer fer herself," said the old man; "she on'y thinks of him and young Cap'n. I never see anything like it."

"And I don't keer if you're f'om Ohier er not," she went on; "fer, tell the truth, your voice did naturally remind me of Ohier, somehow. I don't keer if Cap'n *was* married 'fore he 'listed in the war."

"Tish!" said the brother, warningly.

"No, Pole; mebbe it don't sound fittin'—and it ain't fittin'—fer any one to say that; and we know he *couldn't* 'a' been married; but yit if Cap'n had a wife in Ohier I pity her with all my heart. He might have had her, Pole, *but I just certainly had his love.*"

The stranger who told me of that adventure, as we sat before a log fire in a West Virginia tavern, told it to illustrate something of the peculiarity of the mountain people—not so much by the woman's history, for that was peculiar even there, but by the setting and accessories of the tale. After that I looked in many a cabin in the hope that I might see the great bed, which stood transfigured in my mind as a sort of altar, but I never saw it or the woman, who, without acknowledging or even realizing her fault, retrieved it so completely afterward.

The mountain districts of West Virginia are as strange in their primitive population as in their tossed and tumbled surface. The cities and larger towns and many of the cultivated valleys compare favorably with those of other States, and it is not of them that I am writing. But the greater part of the State is made up of mountains, and it is there that we see how unique are her people and their ways. New Mexico, with its glare of sands and its half-Mexican population, is more foreign, but it is not so picturesque nor nearly so peculiar as this abiding-place of a genuine and pure American population, whose civilization has stood still for more than a century. We go to Europe to seek what is less strange; indeed, it is a far journey to such another anachronism as West Virginia. Those reformers who fancy that legislation is a short-cut to virtue, and that nature can be altered by a change of statutes, might almost find their dreams realized in West Virginia; for when that State was cut off from old Virginia, leaving the old Mother of Presidents with her original boundaries on the West, the progress of two centuries and a half seemed also to have been cut off. And West Virginia began, thirty years ago, where old Virginia did, with a civilization that is to-day what might be expected of thirty years of settlement in a rough country.

It is not strange that travellers should find the scenery and flora of the Alleghanies so similar from Pennsylvania to Georgia that a blindfolded man taken to any part of them and uncovered could never tell in which State he stood. The mountain altitudes regulate the climate, and that makes all the rest nearly uniform. But it is strange to find the people so much alike from end to end of the great chain of mountains—to find them all so backward and simple, all so tall and spare and angular, all speaking so nearly the same dialect, all living in cabins of nearly one pattern, and copying one another even in such little details as lead them to use one sort of broad-strap harness that one sees put upon no other horses than theirs. To be sure, the valleys run parallel up and down the ranges, but there are passes from east to west, and through some of these are run latter-day railroads, with Pullman coaches, "diners," and the accompaniments of telephone and telegraph. And there are old railroads, too,

INTERIOR OF A MOUNTAIN CABIN.

which long ago broke through the fastnesses, and carried the nineteenth century in their wake. Yet the old life turned not aside. It still follows the trend of the valleys. And the new life hurries through as if it was conveyed "in bond," as we send goods through Canada to Chicago. At any point on the frontier or in the heart of West Virginia you step from your Pullman to the wagon that awaits you, and the length of a morning's "constitutional" finds you in the dominion of a belated century. The time is right by your watch, but your pocket-calendar is a hundred years too far ahead. It is true that the present era jars the past in places. The Chesapeake and Ohio Railroad, which bisects the State, is modern even to elegance, but thousands of the people near its steel threads have never ridden over a mile of it. That very modern statesman W. L. Wilson hails from there; but the life in the mountains is so ancient that George Washington, were he back on earth, would say, after a tour of the whole country, "At

last, here I find a part of the world as I left it."

I went into West Virginia over the Pennsylvania border last summer, and put up at a mountain-spring resort. There was a clashing of two centuries there. The arch city maiden in white flannel was there trimming her hat with butterflies, sticking a hat-pin into them at twenty places, "so as to find their hearts and kill them without hurting them too much," and at night she banged out Sousa's last two-step in a way that filled the old woods with the breath of a Michigan Avenue boarding-house. But in the early morning, when her flannel suit hung over a chair, and her "white sailor" sat the top of the bedroom pitcher with a rakish cant to one side, the squirrels and the locusts and katydids had the forests to themselves, and the early stirrers on the mountain roads were the old-time West-Virginians, as simple and genuine as fresh air.

Observing that the strangers at the Springs came from unthought-of dis-

THE MIDWEST

tances to drink the sulphur water that bubbled up in the meadow by the hotel, they too paid the tardy century the compliment of drinking its catholicon. But with never-failing shyness they always came at sunup, without noise or bustle, though in strong force, to fill their pails and cans and blickeys and carry the liquid away. They and the nineteenth-century boarders were impressed and cozened by the same fact: the water smelled so bad and tasted so nasty that it must certainly be good medicine. I never will forget how the mountaineers interested me. The women came sidewise, bobbing lightly up and down on the horses, with both feet side by side on the animal's ribs. The capes of their calico hoods waved prettily in the breeze. The teamsters knew better than to sit on the jolting wagons that pounded over the rocks in the roads, so each saddled the left-hand horse of his team and rode at ease, while the horses tugged up the hills with a force that had to be met and eased by means of the harness of broad straps which is the horse-gear of the entire Appalachian world. The little boys brought trousers that did not know their shoes, never having met them, and jackets that mimicked the trousers by being too short—in the sleeves as well as the body. The little girls were bare at both top and toe, as befitted creatures that did not have to go into the thorn and bramble thickets, as the boys had to do in order to be boys. But their tubular cotton drawers desired to see as much of life as possible, and therefore reached below their little dresses. All alike were simple, honest, unobtrusive, and shy. Nothing but a "bush-meeting" seemed powerful enough to bring them out in force, but at that they opened their shells like clams at high-water—for everywhere, from one end of the mountains to the other, they are deeply religious. They are "Baptis'" and "Methodys" wherever I saw them. Mr. Remington and I met one in the Potts Creek Valley, over near the old Virginia line, who had been out to Oregon, and was doing well there, but came back to Potts Creek "because they didn't respect the Sabbath out West."

There are church buildings in the villages, but the villages are few and far apart, and in this particular place the custom was for some preacher to spring as it were out of nowhere and to announce a bush-meeting by means of a written placard nailed to a tree by the spring. It was to be held at two o'clock in a certain patch of woods, so commonly and frequently the scene of such meetings that the rude benches made of planks nailed to tree stumps were always there, and kept in good order, apparently by a devout mountaineer who lived in the nearest cabin. The meeting lasted less than an hour, but the people made it the affair of a day. They came from as far as the news of the meeting had been carried by the equestrians and wagoners who had reined up at sight of the placard and halted "to see what's a-goin' on." Some, therefore, had been obliged to set out soon after breakfast—and that would not make a long journey where six miles of road may loop over the top of a tremendous mountain, up which the horses crawl, and the more humane men lead instead of riding them. Before noon the wagons began to come in. Bars were let down at various points near the camp-ground, and the teams were tethered to the trees in half a dozen scattered parts of the woods. The wagons were such as one sees all over the land, made in Racine, Wisconsin, or South Bend, Indiana, or Cortland, New York. Out of them came men and women, girls and boys, and even babies. By noon nearly all the worshippers were on hand—strolling from hitching-place to hitching-place to see who had come, and to gossip with friends and acquaintances. It is wonderful how far and wide men are known to one another in these mountains. The people are sociable in the extreme. We would call them "shiftless" as a race, for it is a fact that they have inherited the discouragement of their ancestors, who must have early given up the effort to wrest more than a bare living out of agriculture in a territory that is rich only where it is mined for coal and iron and stone.

Wherever nature refuses a living in return for fair effort, humanity becomes stagnant or demoralized, and in West Virginia, still the great game-preserve for the Middle and Atlantic States, the rod and gun were early found to be more profitable companions than the plough and shovel, so that a race of hunters developed there—hunters with the patience and philosophy that the Indian emphasizes, and that lead all such men, white, red, or black, to snub Dame Fortune if she comes with that heavy tax of care and responsibility which we call civilization, and which the woodsman sees through as if it were plate-glass, and regards as bringing very little at a very great cost.

Therefore these mountain folk take a great deal of time and pains to know one another, and having this wide acquaintance, they solder it to their lives with incessant gatherings like this bush-meeting.

go 'round 'mong the neighborhood women." Then there was "allers some of the neighborhood chillun and her chillun passin' to and fro; an' on'y night before last there was a corn-shuckin' and a dance here; on'y it wasn't so big but what the beds was left standin', 'stid of bein' sot out, same as when we hev a big dance; an' my man's got some corn to shuck yit."

THE OLD TAVERN IN THE VALLEY.

They hold "log-rollings" and "corn-shuckings" and dances and shooting-matches and "gander-pulls," and one thing or another, to make up a circle of gatherings that reaches around the whole year, and closes around every life in each district. I paid a visit one day at the tip-top of a mountain and at the end of a trail that hadn't one other cabin by its side. To me the cabin seemed a mere accentuation of a solitude I had scarcely believed possible. I remarked to the woman of the cabin that I should have thought she would be very lonely. Lonely? That showed my ignorance. Why, there never passed a day on which some of the "neighbors" did not drop in, and at least once or twice a week she would "git to

To return to the out-door church service, the interchange of visits was followed by a return of each party to its wagon for a picnic dinner upon whatever had been brought along — cold corn pone principally. When all the worshippers gathered at the bush-meeting it was seen not to be very different from a Northern camp-meeting, such as one sees in New Jersey particularly. The men wore soft felt hats and long beards, and seemed never to have combed their hair. The women had on broad-brimmed black straw hats, such as I was told a mountain woman is able to keep and use for "Sunday best" for a quarter of a century. The boys looked boldly at the girls, and the girls looked slyly at the boys out of the tails of their eyes. The sudden rattling of a wagon among the trees, followed by a loud "Whoa there!" occasionally sounded above the prayer and song. Some of the men who came without women stood away from the worshippers, smoking, and talking as countrymen converse, in broken sentences wide apart, with the fractures filled up by vigorous tobacco-chewing. The preacher was a woman—a "Mrs. Lawson of Kentucky, the celebrated evangelist." She brought a young man with her to "open with prayer," and to pass around his hat, and after his prayer she delivered an address, which, if it were right to pass judgment upon it, I should declare to be the most noisy and the least thoughtful sermon or talk that I ever heard. There was singing before and after her address, and it was noticeable that though the young man had to sing nearly the whole first verse entirely alone, the people afterwards sang the remaining verses, though there was not a book or printed copy of the hymn in the forest.

In the eastern part of the State, nearer to Virginia, I found that the circuit-rider still ministers to the religious welfare of the mountain folks. There are neat little white and green church buildings in the valleys, but they are opened only once a month. About as often as that, and in some cases regularly, the circuit-rider sends word of his coming to the elders or deacons, or puts the notice in the country paper if one is published near the meeting-house, and on the given day he appears on horseback, with a few extra belongings and his Bible and song-book rolled up behind him on his saddle. Wherever he preaches he has a large meeting, and he "boards 'round" with the religious families in the old time-honored way. But to end the glimpse I got of the State in the summer requires a mention of the mountaineer laundress at "the Springs." Her name was "Miss" Sony Bowyer—"Miss" meaning Mistress, and "Sony" being the abbreviation of the not uncommon name of Lasonia. She was down at the spring with her pitcher for the day's drinking water.

"I'd like to send up my washing to you this afternoon," said I.

"I'd ruther you wouldn't, not to-day," said "Miss" Bowyer. "It would just certainly muddle me. You see how it is: I'm ironin' the Adamses now, and I hate ter mix the families up. I'm so afraid

there'll be some mistake, so I wash and iron each family separate. To-day I'm ironin' the Adamses, and in the morning I'll wash the Browns. In the afternoon I'll iron the Browns, and by Wednesday I'll take up— What's your name? Ralph? Yes, by Wednesday I'll be able to wash the Ralphs."

Virginia, according to the historians, was settled in 1607; and West Virginia, the territory west of the mountains, was invaded by settlers nearly a century and a half later—in 1750. "Many a young man," as I read somewhere, "married the girl of his choice, and, with axe in belt and rifle on shoulder, accompanied by his bride, started out to locate on a purchase of land he had made in the wild but beautiful new country." Beautiful it is to-day, and very largely wild. The picturesque young pioneer felled trees, made logs, and put up a cabin, raising a chimney of rough stones at the end of the shanty against the arrival of the winter, if not to provide for immediate culinary needs. He hung his rifle and pouch and powder-horn on the rafters, and his wife got a spinning-wheel and loom somehow from old Virginia. As schools did not follow him into the woods he grew up with a mind as placid as a mill-pond, unruffled by any of those dreams and doubts which in other minds elsewhere became the fathers and mothers of progress. All that, says the historian, was in and after 1750, and yet it is very little different now in by far the greater part of West Virginia. The cabins are precisely the same as the first pioneer would have built when he let go his faithful bride's hand and began to swing his axe. The flintlock rifle, nearly seven feet long, that he first shouldered, he ordered cut down, and cut down again, in Richmond and Baltimore, as his carelessness allowed the saltpetre to corrode the pan; and at one time or another he allowed the gunsmith to tear off the flintlock and make his piece a "cushion" gun—that being what he calls a rifle that fires by means of a percussion-cap. Even the Winchester is creeping into the cabins now. The young bride, reproduced in her progeny, is slowly giving up the use of her spinning-wheel and loom, because there is no profit in the wondrous jean she makes, at less than a dollar a yard, and yet factory jean brings only a few cents. Nevertheless, there is still some

THE CIRCUIT-RIDER.

call for her art to-day. Plenty of mountain folk are wearing homespun stuff from their bodies outward, and I saw two spinning-wheels and two looms at work in one small valley, besides hearing of at least one other pair of these last-century machines in a cabin I did not visit.

The greatest difference between the present time and the long ago is seen in the presence of numerous free schools all over the mountains, and already they are awakening the people.

I made notes of the primitive out-door and in-door scenes in the parts of West Virginia where I wandered, and perhaps nothing that I could do would serve the purpose better than to smoothly transcribe them without their losing the freshness of the views they reflect. The scenery, I wrote, is the same from the middle of Pennsylvania to Georgia — the same rounded, wooded mountains; the same green, often fertile valleys, checkerboarded with farms; the same stone-strewn watercourses brawling down the hill-sides; the same frequent, almost general, forests; the same few roads and many trails; the same log cabins; the same clearings. Everywhere the same deep blue hangs overhead, and the mountains turn from near-by green to distant purple. The wood fires everywhere send up thin blue veils of smoke above the cabins, and the scenes in which humanity figures are played by characters that are everywhere very much alike. Perhaps in the North there are more covered bridges, but the rule, over the entire mountain system, is for the horses and wagons to cross the streams by means of fords over "branches" and creeks that are floored with great thicknesses of shaly, flat, smooth stones. The pedestrians get over the streams by means of foot-bridges, some of which are mere tree trunks resting on cross-bucks, and some of which are quite ornamental though simple suspension-bridges, with certainly one hand-rail, if not two, beside the planking.

a great population lives on the mountain-sides and mountain-tops, along bridle-paths that are mere trails, and these are not at all fit for wagoneering.

It has never occurred to any one to clear most of these trails. They run up and down the steepest inclines that a horse can climb, and they wind through forests and jungles of low growth so dense that I had to buy canvas "chaps" or leggings to ward off the thorns. Nevertheless, I met men, and even women, on these trails who were dressed just as they would be at home, and who got through without tatters—how, I don't know. Often the vegetation was so thick that if my companions or I halted for even less than a minute, those who kept on were totally lost to view. This wildness is on the steep hill-sides. Wherever there is a bench or a plateau one comes upon a clearing here and there, with fields sown in oats, potatoes, and buckwheat, and per-

A FOOT-BRIDGE, WEST VIRGINIA.

It's a horseback country. There are main roads and there are wagons to use upon them, but they are both "valley improvements," the products of the greater fertility of the lowlands, where the "quality" lived as planters before the war and worked large tracts with slaves, or where the small farms of the poor whites begat a prosperous middle class between the quality folk and the mountaineers. But

haps a little tobacco, to be rolled into twists for home consumption and for barter with the "neighborhood men."

It is on the wagon roads that one meets the greater number of people, but the roads are not exactly Parisian boulevards. Those roads that cross the mountains have a queer way of going into partnership with the streams. Sometimes they run up the streams, so that at high-water a

MOUNTAIN WOMEN.

farmer fording his way looks like a human Neptune floating in his wagon, while his horses, up to their bellies in the crystal water, show neither legs nor flippers. Sometimes the stream abandons its bed and takes to the roadway for a piece, each such interchange by the one or the other being made to get a clear right of way through the tree-cluttered, bowlder-strewn region. Down in the valleys the roads are latticed in by the very tallest fences that are anywhere used by farmers. They are called snake-and-rider fences, and the snake part is made of from seven to eleven rails laid zigzag, one pile of bars set this way and the next pile set the other way, with at least one "rider," and sometimes two, perched on tall crossed poles above the snake-work. Thus does West Virginia pay generous tribute to the agility of her mountain-bred cattle, poor and thin to look at or get milk or beef from, yet able to bound about like self-propelling rubber balls.

Between these towering gridiron fences one meets the people. Ah! those generous, hospitable, manly, frank, and narrow-minded people! Now it is two women that one meets—a mother and daughter, both on one horse, the mother on the saddle and the daughter behind her on an old shawl. They sit as if the horse was a chair, with their four shoes in a row, and their big hoods bobbing in unison. Next comes a farmer astride his steed, with a sack of meal in front of him, the wind blowing the front of his soft hat up against the crown, and the horse's sides working his trouser-legs up so as to show his blue and white home-knit woollen stockings. All along the sides of the road are pigs—the Africans of the brute creation—grunting contentedly, and eating, and clinging to the places where the sun is hottest. Deerhounds skulk along wherever there are houses—the instruments of a short-sighted people for the ruin of the game which brings them not merely food, but the generous patronage of holiday huntsmen from all over the North and East. And here comes a wagon with its driver a-horseback, driving two of the four horses that are hitched by a net-work of broad black leather bands to a rumbling green box-wagon, loaded either with lumber, stone, or corn, you may be sure. The district doctor, certain to be the only "citified" man in a rude district, comes lolloping along on a better horse than his neighbors own, with his medicines in a leather roll on the back of his saddle, under his coat tails.

"What sort of cases make up your practice, doctor?"

"Dyspepsia and child-birth—that is about all," he says, speaking the good English he learned at home in old Virginia and in college.

"And gunshot wounds?"

"Only accidental ones, and those very rarely," he replies.

"What of the morals of the people back in the mountains, doctor?"

"They have their own code, sir; one that differs slightly from that of more polished folk, but it is honest. They do not regard it as criminal to make moonshine whiskey. They make it because that is the only way they can get it. Marriages which you would say might better have been hurried are not uncommon, but here they preserve good names unharmed. There is little or no laxness beyond that. There is very little vagabondage of any sort. We have no tramps, no thieves, except a few who filch corn and meat rather than beg for it. Ambushing has not been practised for a long time, and only one murder has been committed in many years in the very large district in which I practise. Dog-poisoning by private hunters is the worst crime that is rampant. By-the-way, here comes a private hunter now."

It was Daniel Boone come back, in woollen clothes instead of buckskin, and in a soft felt hat instead of a 'coonskin cap. His tall lithe figure came rapidly, for his strides were long and light—a natural man who thought nothing of striding like that from sunrise until long after dark. Over his shoulder he carried a long old-fashioned rifle, and slung from his neck by a strap and leather thong were his powder-horn, his shot-pouch (with its deer-horn "charger" for measuring the powder, and its bent-wire hook crowded with cotton "patches" to wrap around the bullets). He had moccasins on

THE UNITED STATES MAIL IN THE MOUNTAINS.

A PRIVATE HUNTER.

his feet, and his trousers were tied tight around the ankles with brown twine. He was called a "private hunter" because he hunted by and for himself, without the dogs that are unleashed for strangers by men who hunt for pay. Pretty nearly every mountain man is a "private hunter."

"You private hunters hate the dogs, and drop poisoned meat about to kill them." I so spoke.

"Ya-a-s," said the private hunter. "Reckon some of 'em does."

"Why?"

"'Cause the dogs is driving the game away. Every season we has to go further and further away, and the deer gits sca'cer and sca'cer."

"I'll tell you what you do," said I. "Poison all the dogs you can. I am sorry to give you that advice, because the dogs are better than the men who use them—in fact, a good dog is better than any man. But keep on poisoning them."

The private hunter went off marveling, for he knew that the jolly doctor by my side had the best dogs in the country. So did I.

OLD MOUNTAIN TYPE.

"Strange advice to give," said the doctor, looking after the hunter, "for we've been saying that the dog-poisoner is the meanest varmint in the woods. I hunt with dogs myself, but I reckon you're right."

"Why do you do it? You surely know better."

"Oh, merely because everybody else does. It's got so that we cannot get deer without the dogs; and even then we have to go ten miles further from the railroad."

"'Eve tempted me and I ate,'" said I. "Well, soon you will go without eating —venison, at any rate."

We rode on, and presently the doctor met a patient. The meeting was peculiar, since it took place when both men were in the middle of a rushing stream, whose waters brawled over their stony course, and sent up little tongues that licked the knees of the horses. The patient wore a big soft hat and overcoat, and carried a pail in what should have been his free hand.

"Doctor," said he, "I've got a misery. They-all say you kin cure me. Kin you cure me, doctor?"

"Well, what's the matter with you?"

"I've got a smotherin' feelin', doctor," said the man, making up a face expressive of great distress. "'Pears like water washing 'round in my stummick." Here

he made a rotary movement covering his whole trunk, from his chin to his legs, to show what he appeared to regard as his stomach. "Old Charley Jones says you kin knock 'em out. Kin you do it, doc? They're smotherin' spells. I've been takin' pills. Dun'no' what they are, but they're right black; only they don't go for the misery. Kin you cure me, doc?"

"Oh, I think so," said the doctor.

"Well, if you kin git to go up to my place and bring some better pills, I'll be right glad, doctor."

To describe the in-door life of the people we will begin with their picturesque little cabins. They are nearly all log cabins, often of one room, occasionally of two, and never of three. Each has a heavy chimney on one end, built of the stones picked off the ground near by. The chimneys are all alike, broad at the base to allow for the fireplace, and either daubed with mud inside and out, or left in the rough on the outside. The fireplace is made of slabs of stone, and usually two large stones project into the room to keep the fire from the flooring. The thrifty folk maintain little door-yards, in which a few simple old-fashioned flowers grow without order or arrangement. Each place, whether it be a mere clearing or a tidy yard, maintains the man's dogs, a starving, snarling, barking breed of mongrel hounds, made up of ribs, spine, and an open mouth. Show me the dogs, and I can give you the commercial rating of a people. I have never yet seen dogs so mean and so numerous as those of the Swampy Cree Indians of Canada, therefore I know that those people are poorer than even the negro farmers along the Mississippi.

But let us step into a few West Virginia cabins. The door is the principal source of daylight, but some have daylight streaming in through many uncared-for cracks or chinks between the log walls. The draughts are such that one would think the bedclothes had to be nailed down to keep them on the beds in such cabins. Some cabins have regular windows, and others revel in a few panes of glass let into one wall. The lofts over the main room of each cabin are reached in different ways, but I did not see one that had a pair of stairs. There is not room for stairs, or talent enough to build a pair. Sometimes a ladder outside the house serves the purpose, and often as I reined up before a cottage I saw the women and girls—all as shy as deer—scamper out and up the ladder. If their curiosity was strong they came down again by-and-by, in their best but very cheap gowns, and it was delightful to see in them the same femineity that is observable on Madison Avenue, displayed in the way they smoothed down their dresses, disciplined their hair with their fingers, and tiptoed to glance into a cracked bit of mirror over one another's shoulders.

The rule is to reach the loft by a ladder inside, at the foot of the bed, but there are cabins so primitive that when the woman takes you up to show you her loom she calls to her eldest girl child, "Nance, git the pegs and set 'em in fer we-all to go up." Then the girl finds a number of rough-whittled wooden pins twice the size of clothes-pins, and fits them into the line of holes in the logs under the loft-hole. Such cabins are seldom found except in the true wilderness parts of West Virginia, the parts farthest from the railroads. In those parts we see truly preserved the mode of life of the picturesque pioneer of 1750, whom the historian describes as stalking into West Virginia with his gun, his axe, and his bride. In such cabins one finds beds made in the hollow trunks of trees, which have pegs set in the corners for legs to raise them up. It is said that the under-bedding is often nothing more than a mass of autumn leaves. The women in these most primitive homes make the corn-pone bread in dug-out troughs skilfully bitten out of a cucumber or poplar log with the husband's axe, and I have been told that travellers have frequently seen the youngest baby seated in one end of such a trough while the mother kneaded the dough in the other end.

To return to the average typical house, the routine of life is pursued in the one room. In one corner is the dining-table, in another is the closet or bureau, and in the others are the beds. The dreadful absence of privacy, or, to put it better, the incessant publicity, which shocks us so when we read of tenement-house life in New York, obtains in all the mountaineer homes, where land is abundant to a greater degree than it is scarce and hard to acquire in the metropolis. In these cottages other phases of life are as peculiar. A pail, a wash-bowl, and a dipper set out-of-doors serve for the requirements of the toilet. I am told that the people never

wash their bodies, and I judge that the men rarely comb their hair. The women "slick" theirs over with water and a comb. The children simply "grow up" in a long juvenile fight against heavy odds of dirt and tangles.

Over the yawning fireplace in each cabin one sees the beginning of the high colonial mantel which we so eagerly borrow for our houses—a tall narrow shelf bearing a line of bottles and cans. There or on a closet or bureau one is certain to see a cheap Connecticut clock, and under the tall old-fashioned principal bed is apt to be seen the most important article in a mountain household—the cradle. Never

A NATIVE SPORTSMAN.

thought of till the last minute, and there being no money to buy a thing that can be made at home, the cradle is usually a heavy pine box on a pair of eccentric rockers, so that it is apt to rock as a snake travels—one end at a time. In very tidy cabins the walls are covered with newspaper to keep out the draught; the wife has a little cupboard for her cups and dishes, her pepper, sugar, and salt, and a bureau for her clothing. Several times I saw some fresh flowers in a broken cup on the bureau, and a few noisy-looking chromos, usually presenting scenes of courtship, or pictures of women in gorgeous attire, stuck about on the walls. A lamp is a rare thing in a mountain cabin. Living there is simpler than the rule of three. When daylight fails, the people go to bed. If they sit up, they do so in the light of the logs in the fireplace. If they need to find anything which that light does not disclose, they pick out a blazing pine knot from the fire and carry it about as we would carry a lantern or a lamp. The pine knots smoke so prodigiously that the ceilings of these cabins are as black as ebony: not a bad effect from an artistic point of view, for the dead black is soft and rich, and shows off everything against and beneath it, particularly the brass-trimmed gun that is certain to hang on a rafter just in front of the door.

The mountain folk are often "squatters" on the land. A man plants two or three acres—rarely as much as ten acres —in corn, and if he has two apple-trees that bear fruit he is very lucky. He has the corn ground into meal by paying a tithe of it to the miller, and takes it home sitting on it on his horse. His wife makes it into big rocklike "dodgers" or pone-cakes with salt and water and "no rising." It gives out towards February, as a rule, and then come the annual hard times. Then the woman collects "sang" and herbs, and packs up bark for those who ship it to the distant tanners. "Sang" is a staple source of income in the mountains. It is so called as a nickname for ginseng, a root that is becoming more and more rare, and fetches $2 50 a pound now, whereas it used to fetch only fifty cents. It looks a little like ginger, and the authorities disagree as to whether it is the real ginseng of China, or, indeed, whether it is at all related to it. If it is not, it is used in China as a cheap substitute for that mysterious, most expensive drug, which the Chinese believe to be able to prolong life, and even to restore virility to the aged.

These should be the most ruggedly healthy of all us Americans. Their mountain air, sweetened by the breath of the pine forests, is only excelled in purity by the water they drink. They live sim-

ply and without haste or worry, as we know it would be better for us all to do. They are not an immoral or dissipated people. And yet they never know a day of health or bodily content. Dyspepsia is a raging lion among them all. This is because of the bad, the monstrously bad, cooking their food gets. That demon combination of the darky and the frying-pan which rules the entire South produces a mild and delectable form of cookery compared to the kind that gnaws the vitals of the West-Virginians. Smoking-hot, half-cooked corn-dodger is their main reliance, and it is always helped down with a great deal of still hotter and very bad coffee. Those who get meat at all get salt meat.

Let us drop in upon a mountaineer's home—one of the tidy sort, where they have apple-trees, and the woman has made a few pots of dark and lumpy apple-butter. The logs are blazing on the simple black andirons, and the kettle is sputtering as it swings on the pot-hook over the flames. As a preliminary to the meal the man takes down the bottle of "bitters" from the mantel-piece and helps himself to a goodly draught. He makes the bitters himself of new proof moonshine whiskey, tinctured with cucumber fruit, burdock or sarsaparilla root.

"I wuz down to the Springs," says the man, "an' I heard one o' them loud-talkin' city women fussin' a great deal 'bout the evils of drink. I wouldn't 'a' minded her ef she'd a - leaved me 'lone, but she kep' talkin' at me. After a bit I just let her have what was bilin' in me. 'I allers 'low,' says I, 'that whiskey is a good thing. A little whiskey and sarsaparil' of a mornin' fer me and the ole woman,' says I, 'an' a little whiskey an' burdock every mornin' fer the chillen—why, it's a pervision of natur' fer turnin' chillen inter men an' women, and then keepin' 'em men an' women after you've turned 'em that way.' Gosh! she didn't like me—that woman didn't."

The wife, as a first step, takes a tin can and goes out to milk the cow. A tomato-can serves for the milking of the average mountain cow, and the women hold the can with one hand and milk with the other. The appearance of the cow and the size of the can suggest the idea that it might be better to milk the wild deer, if one could catch them. Milking over, the woman comes in to cook the meal. Any

A MOUNTAINEER'S CABIN.

one can tell what meal she is preparing by the time of day. There is no other way, as all three meals of the day are precisely alike. She puts a handful of coffee-beans into a skillet, and holds them over the fire until they are coaled on the outside like charcoal. She empties the skillet into a coffee-grinder on the wall, and holds the coffee-pot under the grinder while she grinds the beans. She puts some corn meal into a box-trough or a dug-out trough, throws in a little water and salt, and works the dough with her fingers until it feels of the right consistency, when she takes it out in handfuls patted into cakes that are ornamented with her finger-marks. These she puts into a little iron oven shoved up close to the fire. She pours cold water into the coffee-pot, and presses that into the embers and close to the burning logs. Then she slices some bacon, and puts it into a long-handled frying-pan, where it is soon burned without being cooked. As soon as the coffee boils the work is done, and she says, "Your bite is ready; sit by." Earthen-ware plates, steel knives, two-pronged forks, cups and saucers, and a

dish of apple-butter are already on the table, with the milk-can, and another can which holds the sugar. A storekeeper in that region once tried to introduce forks with three prongs, but the people were not ready for such a revolution. "We want a fork that 'll straddle a bone," they said.

I wish there was room for descriptions of their dances, their old-fashioned shooting-matches and log-rollings, and of that queerest of all sports, the gander-pull, the fun of which consists in hanging a gander by the legs or in a bag from a tree limb or a gallows, and then greasing his neck, and offering him as a prize to whoever can grip his head and pull it off while riding beneath him at full speed. The old houses of the "quality folk" and their formal lives and warm hospitality shine like gems in this rough setting. The stealthy activity of the "moonshiners," who have the moral as well as the financial support of the people, would form a good part of still another chapter. But these subjects are not so new as the broader view of the simple habits and surroundings of these backward people who live as did the founders of our republic.

THE STATE OF WISCONSIN

NO region can be more appropriately designated the heart of North America, speaking geographically, than that which lies within the embrace of the upper Mississippi, Lake Superior, and Lake Michigan. The great natural arteries of the habitable continent issue from its borders, and grant to it, although inland a thousand miles, easy commerce with the ocean on the east, and the Gulf of Mexico on the south. In the ports of both lakes ships from Europe are to be seen which have passed, by the St. Lawrence gate, through the wall of mountains that from Labrador to Georgia defends the interior. The principal water channels of the wide plains between the Rocky and Alleghany ranges are gathered by the Mississippi into a tributary system of natural intercommunication available for its practical use.

Of this territory the State of Wisconsin embraces the greater part. In the plan of the nation's forefathers it was designed that a single State should comprehend substantially all of it; and it would, in some respects, have been convenient and beneficial to its inhabitants had the plan been more nearly adhered to in the adjustment of State lines. This was all parcel of the Northwest Territory, and was delivered from European dominion by the success of the Revolution, confirmed by the Treaty of Paris, by which instrument Great Britain surrendered the country to the Mississippi, the limit of her claim westward; and the northwestern corner on the Canadian boundary was fixed in the Lake of the Woods. Virginia, however, claimed the entire expanse beyond the Ohio, at least as far as the Illinois; Massachusetts asserted title, under her royal charter, to a belt of eighty miles in width, below the parallel of 43° 43' 12", extending to the river; and Connecticut to still another adjoining belt; but all relinquished their claims in the interest of common fellowship and good-will, and ceded full title and jurisdiction to the federal government. Thereupon, in consideration of their grants, the Congress of the old confederation passed the famous ordinance of 1787, and by one of its six special "articles of compact between the original States and the people and States in the said territory," which were to "forever remain

unalterable, unless by common consent," it was agreed and ordained that " not less than three nor more than five States" should be formed in the territory; of which, if but three, the third should be composed of the district of country lying west of a direct line drawn due north from the Wabash and Post Vincents to the Canadian boundary, and the division of this district to form two States, Congress was authorized to make *only* upon "an east and west line drawn through the southerly bend or extreme of Lake Michigan."

Had this "compact" been kept, the State of Wisconsin would have possessed northern Illinois, with the city of Chicago; northeastern Minnesota, with the cities of St. Paul and Duluth; and the richest portion of the upper peninsula of Michigan. But the insecurity of public engagements received signal illustration in the performance of this covenant in the first great instrument of national obligation after the establishment of our independence. Not one of the five States formed in the Northwest Territory is bounded according to the requirement of the celebrated ordinance, nor did any departure from it receive the common consent, which was the only contingency to modify the guarantee of perpetual observance. Ohio first, then Indiana, were permitted to crowd their northern lines upon Michigan; and Illinois to take 8400 square miles, in a strip of sixty-one miles width, from southern Wisconsin; in each instance the protesting Territory proving wholly defenceless in Congress, with no buckler but the nation's compact, "forever unalterable," against the arguments and influence of a new-coming State, immediately to possess votes in that body and the Electoral College. After long resistance, the people of Michigan were forced reluctantly into their lucky bargain, by which her territorial losses were far more than compensated in the gain of the entire upper peninsula; and Wisconsin was left with the usual portion, according to old customs, of the youngest in the family. Nor in the end was she permitted to keep what the others left. The great size of the remainder appeared to some of the older States dangerously disproportionate; the settlers in the northwestern portion were ambitious to secure a separate State, and exerted themselves diligently to influence Congress; and many in Wisconsin favored the division. It resulted in the excision by Congress of the northwestern corner of the old Territory, and Wisconsin entered the Union in 1848, with limits much less than were originally set apart for this State, yet substantially equal in area to Michigan and Illinois, and greatly beyond Ohio and Indiana, and with a country unexcelled, rarely equalled, in variety, extent, and quality of natural resources. The south boundary of the State lies on the parallel of 42° 30′ north latitude; the lakes, joined by the line of the Menomonee River flowing to Green Bay, and the Montreal in opposite course into Superior, are her eastern and northern confines; the northwestern limit proceeds from the end of Lake Superior up the St. Louis River to the first rapids, thence due south by a land line of about forty miles to the St. Croix River, and by its course to the Mississippi, which forms the western border. Its superficial measurement is 53,924 square miles. Its average length is approximately 260 miles, its average breadth, 215; but its shape is not regular, and the distance between its northernmost point and south line exceeds 312 miles, while its extreme breadth is nearly or quite three hundred. The little archipelago known as the Apostle Islands, in Lake Superior, lies within its northern boundary.

Protracted controversy attended all the adjustments of State lines which have been mentioned, much bitter feeling was aroused in the breasts of the pioneers and early statesmen of Michigan and Wisconsin, and for some time efforts were pressed to undo the dispositions which Congress had made. The northern counties of Illinois unwillingly parted at the time from the expected association with their neighbors above. The inhabitants of the western part of the upper peninsula of Michigan sustained more inconvenience, because their interests and intercourse naturally unite them to Wisconsin, and their readiest communication with their capital has long been by rail through this State and around Lake Michigan by the south. Yet, except in their case, it may be doubted whether much loss of material welfare has been sustained by the people chiefly affected by the deviations from

the lines originally fixed by the ordinance of 1787; and although States of vastly greater area have been since received, the opinions which prevailed when the limits of Wisconsin were finally settled might not improbably have operated to deny it extension to the shores of Lake Superior, and possession of much of its rich northern territory, if the southern boundary had been preserved on the line drawn through the "extreme of Lake Michigan."

The history of Wisconsin in all memorable particulars is not obscure. It opens under French auspices, and is separable by five divisions. The eras of French rule, of British authority, of pre-Territorial transition, of separate Territorial and State existence, are landmarked by events.

The elucidation of the circumstances of its discovery, from neglected and forgotten testimonies, has been in recent years accomplished to general acceptation by Professor Consul W. Butterfield, an industrious and intelligent student of the antiquities and annals of the State. He has not only brought out from long obscurity the true discoverer, but has set back by many years the date of the event. The little colony of the Pilgrims on the Massachusetts coast was only in its fourteenth year when first the white adventurer saw Wisconsin. He was Jean Nicollet, an early specimen of that unique and hardy race, the *coureurs des bois*, a graft of Indian savage life upon French character, who were for two centuries the curious common carriers of the wilderness. He had come to New France in 1618, a youth of twenty, for many years was immersed alone among the Hurons, in the wilds about Lake Nipissing and the upper waters of the Ottawa, and typically embodied the adventurous spirit, fortitude, cheerfulness, and zeal which always characterized his class. It seems to have been the old geographical fantasy, so oft pursued to bitter disappointments—belief of an easy way to Cathay and the realms of the East—that spurred him to his bold journey. Rumor passed among the Indians of eastern Lake Huron, then the terminal of exploration, of a tribe that dwelt some hundreds of leagues to the westward, called Ouinipigous, meaning "men of the sea." Significant name! Fancy-colored hope readily saw in the misty stories of their large wooden canoes, shaved heads, and beardless faces a people who knew the Western ocean, had mingled with, were even kindred to, the Chinese or Tartars of the East. It would seem that even Champlain, chivalrous old knight of the forest, lent his ear to the tale, and blew the flame of expectation. And Nicollet, in company with the good Father Brebeuf, then just setting forth on his dismal and fatal mission to the Hurons, again toiled up the St. Lawrence and Ottawa rivers to Allumette Island, and then on alone to the Georgian Bay, whence embarking with but seven Indian companions, he first of white men traversed the mist-covered waters of upper Lake Huron, paddled up the Strait of Mackinac, ascended the western coast of Lake Michigan, crossed the threshold of "Death's Door" into the sombre Green Bay, found at its head the mouth of the Fox, and at length, in the autumn-summer of 1634, set foot on the country of his venturesome search, of the "men of the sea." He despatched a messenger, to whom they hospitably responded, and, escorted by a company of their young men, he proceeded to their village. He knew the value of first impressions, and long before had studied the effects of this momentous meeting. Through all his tedious journeying he had borne with anxious care the garments suited to the tastes of this people he was then to see. The hour was now at hand, and, brilliantly apparelled in Chinese damask embroidered with many-colored birds and flowers, exploding pistols from both hands, he theatrically presented himself, the ambassador of New France. His illusion quickly vanished. No gorgeous mandarin welcomed him with Oriental grace; no road to Cathay opened there. They were simple savages like his own companions, who marvelled at the strange whiteness of his skin, and in a great assemblage feasted him magnificently on beaver; but he found a country marked by Nature's love, and her waterway to the Mississippi.

Notwithstanding his theory of raiment miscarried, the hands that clasped the thunder were objects of reverential awe, and Nicollet readily made friends of these Winnebagoes, and later of other tribes, and tarried for months among them. He continued his journey farther up the Fox River, to where but a short portage to the Wisconsin gives access to the waters that descend to the Gulf, and not improbably learned the general course of that river.

At that point, however, he turned southward by land, traversed the prairies into Illinois, and in the autumn of 1635 returned to Quebec. But the high-mettled Champlain lay sinking to his end, and there was none then to carry the flag of France to the new-found country of the prairies, and Nicollet's adventures and discoveries lapsed into story, fruitless, except of unacknowledged guidance to later explorers.

Twenty years afterward, two bold traders in quest of peltries penetrated the Northern forests, and probably visited Green Bay; but the beginnings of settlement were due to the Society of Jesus. In 1665 Father Claude Allouez pushed along the southern coast of Lake Tracy, as they called Superior then, to the Bay of Chegoimegon, and there established the Mission of the Holy Ghost. Near the head of the bay he built a house, sided and thatched with bark, the first dwelling of a white man in Wisconsin. Six years later this mission was abandoned from terror of the Sioux, and for above a century and a half was not resumed. The name of La Pointe de Saint Esprit, abridged to La Pointe in common speech, remained to the neighborhood, and afterward attached to the place on Madeline Island where an important post of Mr. Astor's famous company was located, in the prosperity of the fur trade. There Baraga, afterward bishop, re-established the mission in 1835, and for years wrought to construct in the wild Chippewa speech the gentle messages of Christianity.

He was born in Austria, near the close of the last century, studied law in Vienna, and theology in Laibach, where he was ordained. He came to America in 1830, burning with an ardor to bring the gospel to the hearts of the Indian people, which remained unquenched through all his long life. He began his Indian studies at Cincinnati, was first installed as pastor at Arbor Croche, afterward taught at a village near the site of Grand Rapids, in Michigan, and thence repaired to La Pointe. He became distinguished for his knowledge of the Chippewa tongue, wrote and published an Otchipwe dictionary and grammar, translations from the Bible, catechism, prayer and hymn books, besides works in the German and Slavonic languages. He was consecrated Bishop of Sault Ste. Marie in 1853, but subsequently transferred his episcopal residence to Marquette, and there he died in 1868, beloved and reverenced by all within a wide region upon which he had left the impress of his saintly purity, untiring zeal, and love for men. The humility and patience with which he labored and suffered, often in the extremest poverty and wretchedness of life, the constancy of his love for the benighted people to whom he was sent, the severity of his self-imposed tasks, his wonderful devotion and great accomplishments, have given him renown among missionaries hardly below those of earlier times who received the crown of martyrdom.

In 1669, the same missionary, Allouez, associated with Father Dablon, commenced at the head of Green Bay the enduring mission of St. François Xavier, and two years after built a chapel five or six miles above the mouth of the Fox, whence the present town of Depere derives its name, as the place *des pères*. Fort La Baye, an insignificant affair, was built where the city of Fort Howard now is, on the bank near the river's mouth. The point was one of activity in the Indian trade, but no settlement of the kind that indicates approaching civilization and development was begun there or elsewhere in Wisconsin until long after it was delivered from foreign hands. In 1761, a British officer, with less than a score of men, entered unopposed, and took possession of the post at Green Bay. Afterward, by the Treaty of Paris, negotiated in 1762, France entirely gave up the continent, yielding her northern possessions to England, and the territory of Louisiana to Spain. In the Green Bay neighborhood, the little fort, disused and decayed, the chapel and the mission house, a few families, a few *arpents* of cultivated ground, a few titles under French law, the disputed tradition of a "fort," or trading house, at Prairie du Chien, perhaps a factory at the foot of Lake Pepin, some inoculation of the French language on Indian dialects — these and nothing more were left to preserve the savor of New France in Wisconsin.

In June, 1763, on the breaking out of Pontiac's war, the Chippewas surprised and captured Michilimackinac, which necessitated immediate withdrawal of the garrison at Green Bay, and the British sway was thenceforth wholly nominal, neither settler nor soldier of England appearing afterward during its continu-

ance. Although that government surlily held the Northern posts until 1796, independence legally dates here, as in the original States, with the Declaration of 1776; and the twenty years between were free, in fact, of the manifestations of British authority.

The most interesting event of the French era was the famous voyage of Father Marquette and Sieur Joliet to the Mississippi in 1673, too often and too well described to admit repetition. It was not absolute discovery, for the great river had been De Soto's grave above a hundred and thirty years, and Indian report had also made known its existence and course toward the South. Yet the merit of discovery is theirs, because the story of De Soto's wanderings carried little geographical information, and none of the origin of the river; and it was their finding which made the world acquainted with it, even as the same that held his body.

The transitionary period before organization of the Territory of Wisconsin lasted sixty years. Until 1800 the Northwest Territory remained intact. The first division was made on the Fourth of July in that year, under an act passed in the preceding May, with a view to the erection of the State of Ohio, and all west of that proposed State was constituted the Territory of Indiana. The next step was taken in 1805, by setting out the Territory of Michigan within the lines designed for the fourth State by the ordinance of 1787; but this did not embrace any country west of the lake. In 1809 Congress created the Territory of Illinois, and, still pursuing essentially the lines of the ordinance, gave to it all west of the lower Wabash and the Vincennes meridian, thus comprising Wisconsin and northeastern Minnesota. Across this expanse the enabling act of Illinois drew the limit of that State, as already mentioned, in 1818, and annexed the northern remainder to Michigan Territory. This political association, to which was added in 1834 all the region west of the Mississippi which lies north of the State of Missouri and east of the Missouri and White Earth rivers, continued until the Fourth of July, 1836. On that day, by the act of April 20th, the Territory of Wisconsin came into being, with the area of Michigan Territory diminished by the excision of that State; Iowa, Minnesota, and the eastern half of the two Dakotas being thus included.

The first considerable immigration was due to the discovery of the lead mines. This mineral exists in great abundance in northwestern Illinois and southwestern Wisconsin, and when the fact became known, it was followed by a multitudinous rush to that region, then novel in character, though since witnessed in many other localities. Galena was the first seat of operations, and long the emporium of the trade. Its occupation began in 1822, and in three years the incoming tide was at flood. In the year 1828 the production of these mines amounted to nearly 13,000,000 pounds of the coveted metal.

The mineral district lay partly within the country claimed by the Winnebagoes, then numbering nearly 5000. They themselves had dug and reduced the ores, and looked upon the invasion with a jealousy which rose to bitter resentment. This brought about what is known as the Winnebago war, a war of no actual conflict of forces and but little bloodshed, owing to efficient measures of suppression promptly taken. General alarm, however, existed for a time, and doubtless the danger of a serious outbreak was imminent.

After a few years of peace came the Black Hawk war, the last desperate struggle of the red man east of the Mississippi. The honor of latest resistance belongs worthily to that brave tribe which in earlier days had waged so many wars in maintenance of their country—the Sacs and Foxes. The hostilities lasted from May to August, mainly in the Territory; several engagements befell, and many bloody deeds were done. The Indians were gradually driven from the mining districts, and finally, in swift retreat northerly through the Four Lake country to the Wisconsin River, on the banks of which, nearly opposite Sauk City, they were overtaken and defeated in a general engagement, on the 21st of July, 1832, with heavy loss. Their retreat and pursuit followed toward the west, and on the 2d of August the whole band—men, women, and children—were hemmed in on the banks of the Mississippi, near the mouth of the Bad Axe River. An armed steamer aided to prevent their escape, and the greater portion of the tribe was slain, little quarter being shown. The attack by the national troops was led by Colonel Zachary Taylor, afterward President. Black

HENRY DODGE.
From the painting by J. C. Marine, in possession of the Wisconsin Historical Society.

Hawk escaped at the time, but was in a few days captured and delivered up by Winnebagoes. He was detained in prison at Jefferson Barracks and Fortress Monroe until the succeeding June; then, being liberated, he was shown the principal cities of the country, to impress him with its power, and retired to Iowa, where he lived quietly till his death in 1838.

No one gained greater fame in this war than General Henry Dodge. He is sometimes called the hero of the war; and, so far as it afforded scope for the lofty title, was worthy of it. Black Hawk many times declared that but for the chief, Hairy Face—as his tribe had named him —he should have whipped the whites, and ranged the mining country at will. In his intrepidity, sagacity, skill, and conduct, General Dodge unquestionably manifested qualities which would have won him high renown on a wider field of arms. He commanded the mounted riflemen of the Territory, and by incessant vigilance and activity preserved the settlements from many scenes of horror, besides participating in nearly every engagement. It was his hot pursuit for over a hundred miles that secured the opportunity for battle on the Wisconsin River, and made the Indians' final escape impossible. But the little battle of the Pecatonica, some time earlier, remarkable for desperate fighting and result, gained him most repute for personal prowess. He had pursued a party of thirteen Indians, who had done recent murders, to a bend in that river covered by a deep swamp, where in the timber behind a high bank they found a natural breastwork. Dismounting, he charged upon them with eighteen men, and, notwithstanding that until the bank was surmounted the Indians were covered, within five minutes every savage was slain, Dodge losing three killed and one wounded.

General Dodge was a frontier boy, born at Vincennes, October 12, 1782, and removed in early manhood to a part of the new-bought Territory of Louisiana, within the present State of Missouri. In the war of 1812 he became a lieutenant-colonel in the Louisiana militia, and performed service up the Missouri, in watch of the Indians. The lead mines attracted him in 1827, where he had but lately arrived when called into service against the Winnebagoes. He pursued lead mining for some years, and built the first smelting furnace in the Territory. After the Black Hawk war, though already past fifty, he accepted the colonelcy of the newly authorized First Regiment of the United States Dragoons, and in 1835 marched to the Rocky Mountains. President Jackson appointed him first Governor of the Territory and Superintendent of Indian Affairs. Mr. Tyler removed him in 1841, and appointed James D. Doty, then the Territorial Delegate, in his stead. Thereupon the people elected the general as Delegate in place of Doty, and he served in the House of Representatives until 1845, when Mr. Polk restored him to the office of Governor, which he held until the admission of the State. He was then elected to the United States Senate, and re-elected in 1851. He enjoyed the singular parental felicity of the companionship in the Senate of his son, Augustus C. Dodge, a Senator from Iowa, highly distinguished for abilities and character, both having also previously sat together in the House as Delegates. At the end of his term he retired, in his seventy-fifth year, from public service, and in honored quietude enjoyed still ten years more of life, passing away at the home of his son in Burlington, Iowa, June 19, 1867. No man has ever possessed a greater, perhaps none so great a measure of affection and regard from the people of Wisconsin.

Its distance from Detroit by any practicable route of travel isolated the country west of the lake from the Territorial government, and begot early agitation for independent political life. The inhabitants on the eastern side also actively sought the erection of their State. But Congress, from embarrassment by the boundary disputes or other influences, delayed the necessary action. A bill to establish the new Territory was reported to the House in 1830; another passed that body in 1831; yet from year to year every measure halted incomplete. At last a novel remedy was applied, and proved successful. The Legislative Council of the Territory itself passed an act in 1835 to enable the people to form a State government without further waiting upon Congress. Provision was made for the assembling of a constitutional convention of delegates from the limits of the proposed State, while the people in the residue of the Territory were empowered to choose their Delegate to Congress and separate Legislative Council. Upon the constitution so formed, Michigan was admitted. In the west, George W. Jones was elected Delegate, and admitted to a seat in the House of Representatives in December following without a question. He rendered efficient service by procuring the act to establish the Territory of Wisconsin, and was re-elected, or chosen first Delegate of the new Territory, in the ensuing year, and served the full term. General Jones subsequently fixed his residence in Dubuque, where he had large business interests, and thenceforward his career, illustrated by eminent public services as a Senator and diplomatic representative, accrued to the benefit and honor of Iowa.

The member who introduced to the Council the bill which secured the accomplishment of the long-deferred wishes of the people was James Duane Doty, of Green Bay, one of the most eminent of Wisconsin's early settlers. Born in Salem, New York, in 1799, he had removed in 1819 to Detroit, and at once gained unusual favor and confidence; and though but twenty-four, President Monroe had appointed him to the independent judgeship provided for the region west of the Sault and Lake Michigan in the year

1823, in which capacity he had organized the courts and conducted the judicial business of the country for nine years. He had been chosen to the Council in 1834, and was at this time sitting in his second year. He became afterward Delegate to Congress for nearly three years, succeeding General Jones; Governor of the Territory from 1841 to 1844; and upon the admission of Wisconsin, for two terms a member of Congress; and rendered other useful services to the public. He settled at Green Bay in 1824, and resided there thirty years. Upon his retirement from Congress he changed his home to the pretty islet which divides the waters of the Fox as they issue from Lake Winnebago, still called Doty's Island. Earliest among the prominent pioneers of Wisconsin, he looked upon her as a father on his child, and was tireless in her service. He was strong and stubborn in his opinions, and sometimes whimsical. While Governor he denied the right of the Legislature chosen in 1843 to sit in December of that year, and after its assembling forced an adjournment to a date that obviated his objection; which led to acrimony of feeling, and an effort, though a fruitless one, for his removal. A humorous illustration of this characteristic was his persistence in spelling the name of the Territory Wis*k*onsan, which finally produced a joint resolution in the two Houses against the orthographic eccentricity. In 1861, the pioneer instinct still prevailing, he accepted appointment as Superintendent of Indian Affairs in Utah, and was subsequently made Governor of that Territory, in which office he died June 13, 1865. Strong-willed and honest men in public life usually make enemies, but deserve the highest respect. Judge Doty earned and received a large measure from the people of Wisconsin. Especially among old settlers are coupled the names, although their political views antagonized, of Dodge and Doty, as the two pillars of the Territory.

Extinguishment of the Indian title to the southern half of the State and opening of the lands to purchase took place about the time of the Territorial establishment, and progress was soon rapid. The history of the Territory mainly presents the usual features of a new country in

JAMES D. DOTY.
From a daguerreotype in possession of the Wisconsin Historical Society.

active growth, with its people laying the foundations of local government and the institutions of the future State.

The first session of the Legislature convened at Belmont, and was chiefly agitated upon the location of the seat of government. Early separation of the trans-Mississippi country being obvious, the convenience of Wisconsin ruled action; and the choice, largely influenced by the sagacious discernment of Judge Doty, fell upon the site of Madison, midway between the river and Lake Michigan, and, though yet untouched by settlement, already known for its extraordinary natural beauty. The fortunate selection has made their capital city always an object of pride to the citizens of the State.

The country west of the Mississippi was, in fact, set off as the Territory of Iowa in 1838. The enabling act for Wisconsin passed in 1846, but it required a second constitutional convention to achieve a satisfactory organic law, and it was not until the 29th of May, 1848, that the thirtieth State was received to the Union. The constitution then adopted still remains, unchanged but by a few amendments.

NELSON DEWEY.
From a photograph by Curtiss, Madison, Wisconsin.

Another prominent Territorial character was Charles Dunn, Chief Justice of the Supreme Court during the entire period. Born in Kentucky in 1799, he removed at twenty to Illinois, where he completed his legal studies and pursued his profession until 1836, when, upon his appointment to the bench, he fixed his residence at Belmont, and there he died in 1872. Strong but gentle in character and manner, assiduously faithful to duty, of perfect integrity and purity, he was an able and just judge, universally and affectionately esteemed by the bar and the people.

The first Governor of the State was Nelson Dewey, one of the earliest settlers, who had made his way unaided, by sheer force of character and ability. He was peculiarly adapted to the task of organizing the State government, and moulded the form and conduct of its affairs with great wisdom and care for the interests of the people. Of strong but not showy personality, well-trained business habits, firm in principles, and laboriously faithful to duty, Governor Dewey has not been surpassed in the executive office. He was re-elected, and remained in service until

January, 1852. He afterward rendered public service of valuable but inconspicuous character, and died in the past year at Cassville, his residence for more than fifty years.

The rapid influx of population to Wisconsin in the earlier days is shown in remarkable figures. In August, 1836, after the Territorial organization, the total number was 11,683; four years later, 31,000; in 1850, over 300,000; and 776,000 in 1860. After that year the tide of immigration was checked, and the ratio of gain became less than in the adjoining prairie States of Illinois and Iowa. Natural and adventitious causes conspired to this retardation. Southward from Lake Superior, for 150 miles, dense forests covered the State, and the lower third only, roughly speaking, was readily accessible to settlement. The southern counties filled quickly to the point of saturation for agricultural purposes, and outside of the cities have gained in numbers but little since 1860. This part of the State was peculiarly attractive, being mostly prairies, interspersed with oak openings, handsome as well-kept parks, and occasional tracts of fine forest trees, while its climate is unexcelled, and upon the whole may well be claimed the best for salubrity and comfort the temperate zone affords. Counting only the area substantially occupied during the early years, this country, perhaps the world, can show no instance of more rapid, healthy, and peaceful settlement. The subjugation of the northern forests, a slow task at the best, was further checked by the civil war, and the financial depression succeeding the business misfortunes of 1873. It resulted that for twenty years after 1860 the gain in population was less by over 200,000 than during the twenty years before, being little, if any, beyond natural increase, emigration and war losses counterbalancing immigration. Within recent years, however, the transformation of the northern region has been rapid, and the eleventh census raises the State from sixteenth to fourteenth on the scale of population, the enumeration, as last reported, reaching 1,687,000.

No State has been sought by a greater variety of immigrants—it may be doubted if any possesses representatives of so many races—and her mosaic citizenship comprises enterprising spirits from nearly all civilized countries of the globe. Next after our own land, most is due to Germany, which has given us a greater proportion than to any other State of the Union, one-sixth of our people having been born in the communities comprehended by that empire, besides probably as many more of German parentage but native birth. It need not be added that liberty, good order, and industrial prosperity will mark the State in which such blood is potential. The Scandinavian countries hold next place among the sources of our strength, having directly furnished above one-seventeenth of our population, a proportion to be reckoned a tenth, or ninth, by counting also those of the race born here. No foreigners more readily assimilate the customs and speech of America, surpassing in easy pronunciation of English with freedom from foreign accent. About two and one-third per cent. of our people were born in Ireland, and nearly as many more in Great Britain. British America has supplied one and a half per cent., Bohemia one, and other nations less. The Poles of foreign birth number near 10,000, the Dutch 7000 or 8000, the French approach 4000. In the town of New Glarus, a compact Swiss colony of nearly 1700 has reproduced upon the prairie many of the usages and faithfully maintained the virtues of their native mountains. Other nations have also their representatives, and to the resident of a quiet New England valley, the roster of our public officers or the signs on business houses might present a strange and unpronounceable aspect. But our prodigality of invitation has been on the whole well justified by those who have accepted it, and still keeping warm the memory of father-lands, their superior allegiance and duty to the State they have made their children's fatherland are faithfully maintained. Distinctive peculiarities gradually wear away and almost disappear in children grown; political and business intercourse leads to commingling of blood and social interfusion; our free people support the institutions of freedom with gaining, not failing power; and in the happy brotherhood of so various parentage, the great fact is apparent which Paul spake, that God "hath made of one blood all nations of men."

Illustration of fitness for their liberties was given by the nature of the State's participation in the civil war. The call to arms not only evoked a prompt response of five times the required number, but the continuing duty of maintenance was unfalteringly fulfilled. Every national demand was met, and the State's aggregate quota for the war was exceeded by 1260. Including 5784 veteran re-enlist-

ALEXANDER W. RANDALL.
From the painting by William Cogswell, Executive Chamber, Madison.

ments, she had credit for 91,379 men. The significance of these figures is better seen by the fact that they stand for one-fifth of the male population of the time, old and young, and exceeded one-half of the voters of the State at the Presidential election of 1864, including those who voted in the field. These soldiers won honorable fame in every quarter to which our arms were carried. Their command was prized by the fighting generals, and their service was, in consequence, so widely distributed that every revolting State witnessed their valor and was honored by their blood. It would be a pleasing office to recount the special services and gallant exploits of many who earned pre-eminent glory among our heroes. It is a story yet to be told with full justice, a story not less due the State than them. But the present is not the opportunity, and a partial tale or invidious mention would be a sin. Age fast masters the diminishing survivors of the war; a few years, and they will live in memory alone; but Wisconsin will ever have honor by the part she bore through the deeds of her soldiers in the struggle which preserved for men the government of liberty.

At the outbreak of the war the office of Governor was held by Alexander W. Randall. Quick of apprehension and ready in opinion and action, he was admirably suited to the hour. He declared at once, with eloquent patriotism, the devotion of Wisconsin to the Union, and the purpose of her people to fight for its integrity, in a tone and manner which drew national attention, and his prompt and efficient measures, well seconded by all, augmented the useful service of the State, and gave her character and standing.

Governor Randall was sent in 1862 as Minister to Rome; but after a year's residence abroad, accepted the post of First Assistant to Postmaster-General Denison. Upon Mr. Johnson's accession to the Presidency and Mr. Denison's resignation, he was appointed Postmaster-General, and served in the office to the end of that administration. He died in 1872 at Elmira, New York, before he finished his fifty-third year.

James R. Doolittle and Timothy O. Howe sat for Wisconsin in the United States Senate during the war period. There are interesting points of incidence in their careers. Judge Doolittle was the elder by a year, born January 3, 1815, in the State of New York, whence he came in 1851 to Wisconsin, with vigorous native powers ripened by liberal culture and years of practice at the bar. He was soon chosen to the Circuit Court bench, but resigned in 1856, after three years' service. Up to midsummer of that year he had been a Democrat, but he then announced his change, ably supported Mr. Fremont for President, and at once became prominent among Republicans.

Judge Howe was born in Maine, February 24, 1816, received there an academical and professional education, and served in the Legislature. In 1845 he removed to Green Bay. He also served as Circuit Judge, and resigned in 1855. In youth a Whig, he had been a Republican from the party's birth, and his fine abilities as a lawyer and speaker had easily given him first place, so that when the Legislature of 1857 assembled, it was hardly doubted he would be elected Senator. But his judgment refused the doctrine then ruling in his party that the State might set at naught an enactment of Congress—that is to say, the Fugitive Slave Law—and defy federal authority; and this was vociferously asserted against him by Mr. Booth, a prominent editor then recently convicted for aiding the flight of a slave, but yet was not generally credited. It led the party caucus, although in it his friends were a strong plurality, to adopt resolutions expressive of the extreme view, and to require the response of candidates. He alone among them refused assent, nobly disdaining the coveted office at the cost of subserviency. The point was not one of difficulty to Judge Doolittle, and, though so recent a convert, his conspicuous abilities commanded his choice. After four years more, the South's practical application of their doctrine of State resistance operated a change of sentiment in the party, and in 1861 Judge Howe was elected Senator, to the keen gratification of many citizens, who, though they contested his political views, profoundly admired and honored the rectitude of the man. He was twice re-elected, serving the full eighteen years. He declined, in his last term, the proffered appointment of Chief Justice of the Supreme Court, so it is said, from a sense of party duty, the opposition being then able to elect his successor. He went to Paris in 1881, as one of the government's Commissioners to the International Monetary Conference. In January, 1882, President Arthur called him to his cabinet as Postmaster-General; and while still in that duty he sickened, and died on the 25th of March, 1883, at Kenosha. Uprightly fixed in all his views, Judge Howe knew his friends and his enemies—having no enemies but in politics. From his opponents he exacted honor for his honesty, patriotism, and courage; by those he admitted to friendship he was loved and reverenced; and the people of the State hold him in honored memory.

To Judge Doolittle the trial of integrity came in turn, not as to his colleague to deny the Senatorial office in prospect, but in even the harder way, to cut it off in the flush of enjoyment. During his second term he found his convictions in radical disagreement with the dominant opinion of his party, and, its majority in the State being overwhelming, he sacrificed by his unflinching obedience to his sense of duty a career of official distinction which otherwise his strong hold upon the esteem of the State must have secured to him for an indefinite period. He still resides at his old home in Racine; but mainly his professional service has been given to Chicago as the head of an eminent legal firm in that city. Such worthy marks of honor and confidence as were possible to the party in minority have been repeatedly proffered him, and the people have freely manifested their unabated respect for his character and powers. He still retains, at the venerable age of seventy-six, the vigor and faculties of mid-manhood, and the genial kindness of heart and manner, always characteristic of his intercourse, returns in universal tenderness from all who know him.

A fair survey of her natural resources and the occupations of her people would exhibit the State with justice and to the best advantage, but the necessary limits of this article allow but the merest glimpse. Husbandry engages, according to the census of 1880, between fourteen and fifteen per cent. (then nearly 200,000 persons) of the whole population. The proportion is less than the average of the United States, which exceeds fifteen per cent., and it will doubtless be found still diminished by the census of last year, owing to increase of other pursuits. Depression is severe in this avocation, in common with the country at large. Yet it is difficult to find reason for it in the farms, which appear as productive as ever. The trouble would be more serious but for the wise changes from the earlier methods of our agriculture and the greater range and variety of production. The cultivation of wheat, formerly the chief end of our farming, has been subordinated to better objects, and it now employs hardly three-fourths the acreage of corn, and not half that of oats. The wheat yield is still ten to twelve million bushels annually, but the corn exceeds twenty-two, and oats thirty-two millions. Nearly as much

barley is grown as wheat, and the usual other grains and grasses in abundance. These facts suggest the greater attention given to domestic animals, in which farmers have shown wisdom. The economy

JAMES R. DOOLITTLE.
From a photograph by Mosher, Chicago.

of raising the best at whatever necessary cost no longer requires argument. Dairying has attained to much importance, the annual product of butter and cheese exceeding 60,000,000 pounds. The improvement of horses has been such in all classes that it is obvious to the ordinary observer. It may be shortly said, indeed, that, so much has animal culture been stimulated, there is hardly a species or breed of esteemed and valuable domestic animals, including bees and fowls, of which there are not now enterprising special breeders and importers in the State enjoying profitable success. Cranberries are indigenous to certain of the marshy lands and their cultivation, which requires peculiar conditions and care, has yielded excellent results. Tobacco culture, more especially in the counties of Dane, Rock, and Green, is extensive, and, though subject to vexatious uncertainty

TIMOTHY OTIS HOWE.
From a photograph by Bell, Washington.

of price, has upon the whole proven remunerative and helpful. In certain localities the grape has responded generously to intelligent care, and the smaller
fruits usually do well. Apples and pears
are grown in the southern portion, but
require more care and are less hardy than
in the Eastern States of the same latitude.

It was for a time supposed that the for-
est-covered region was generally unsuited
to agriculture. A better acquaintance
and the actual experiment, many farms
being now in cultivation, have demonstrated that the greater portion is available for excellent husbandry. The woodsman who harvests nature's great crop is
making way for the planting of man, and
the cleared fields will be occupied, with
adaptation to the circumstances, perhaps
as usefully as the prairies.

The timber which has until recent
years been the main source of profit in
the great forests is pine. No other wood
so well subserves the various demands of
new settlements for building, fencing,
and other immediate needs. Its lightness
makes its transportation easy, and its location in vast quantities upon the numerous rivers which rise near Lake Superior

and thence descend to the prairies is
significant of great design. That no
reproduction of the valuable pine
takes place, a worthless species only
springing up in its stead, seems a
pregnant testimony that the purpose
of this great provision was for temporary uses, more durable mineral
material being substituted in after-
developed prosperity. The active
business of the timber country turns
on logging and manufacturing this
wood, and in the number of men
engaged, the extent of operations and
value of product, it stands next to
agriculture. Immense as is the annual consumption, many years will
be required to exhaust the generous
supply of nature.

The pine is but one of the useful
trees of the forest. Other evergreens,
the cedar and balsam, spruce, fir, and
hemlock, are there in plenty; and the
hard-wood timber—and much of the
finest pine grows in the midst of the
hard-woods—is, perhaps, of greater
value than the pine. Manufacturing
of the other woods is now well established, and its increasing importance
promises generations to come a vast
source of wealth and profitable industry.
The oak, maple, ash, cherry, walnut, but-
ternut, hickory, birch, and many others
which grow in abundance, yield material
adaptable to more varied uses than the
pine, and will long survive it as manufacturing stock.

With the exception of such as relate to
lead and zinc, the mineral industries of
Wisconsin may fairly be said to be yet
mostly in their infancy. Discoveries of
rich promise have been many, particularly of iron, and mining enough has been
done to demonstrate that the mineral ores
are so abundant that industrial avocations
of great consequence will spring from
their possession. In the counties of
Dodge and Sauk, in the southern portion
of the State, valuable but not generally
extensive mines of iron have been worked
for a long time. But only seven or eight
years have passed since the mining district of the Gogebic range was inaccessible and almost unknown. Within that
time many rich mines of Bessemer ores
have been opened, and two railroads built
to carry out their product, while exploration continues eager, and fresh discoveries from time to time occur. The deduc-

tions of geology have had such proof in results secured that demonstration of its still richer anticipations seems only to require continuance of the energy of pursuit. The city of Ashland, not far from Allouez's first mission across the Chequamegon Bay, was, at the taking of the tenth census, a hamlet of a few hundred people almost isolated from the world. Its population now is estimated at 20,000; four railroads enter it, and numerous lumber mills fill the air with the quaver of machinery; it possesses in active operation a charcoal blast-furnace said to be the largest in the world; three great ore docks handled and shipped to the East in the last year over 2,000,000 tons of ore, and the spires that tell of busy commerce rise beside the long piers thrust from its coast. With the forest wall still surrounding the view on the landward side, the stump stubble of nature's fields fringing the town and crowding its vacant spaces, and, as one may fancy, the primeval spirits of the air yet hovering there, the spectacle of handsome modern buildings, gas and electric lighting, excellent water-works, horse-cars in the streets, moves the contemplative observer to interesting reflection. And this may be taken for a type and expression of the mighty stir of enterprise and industry which within a decade has penetrated with universal agitation the vast woods that have maintained their silent, majestic dignity for ages beyond reach of the retrospect of man.

No valuable deposits of other ores than iron have yet been brought to light in northern Wisconsin. Geologists affirm, however, that the course of the copper-bearing rocks in which lie the rich mines upon Keweenaw Point in Michigan runs in well-marked ranges southwestwardly from Lake Superior through Wisconsin, and the possibility of future copper-mining is scientifically shown—a possibility only, but perhaps as well justifying exploration as before discovery was presented by that part of the series in which copious wealth has been found. But the science stands opposed to any likelihood that the precious metals lie beneath our soil, and the expectation sometimes so highly excited cannot but be thought chimerical.

Even so rapid a glance at our subterranean resources must take observation of the non-metallic minerals. The clay from which are baked the fine cream-colored bricks known as Milwaukee brick, because first made there, exists in many localities, and a now long experience has proven them as useful and durable as they are pleasing to the eye. That clay which carries trace enough of iron to give the red color also abounds, and the manufacture of both sorts is extensive. No mineral of the State for the uses of architecture equals in beauty and excellence, however, the brownstone of Lake Superior. Its hue is usually of a reddish-brown, not sombre, but light of aspect, and it harmonizes or contrasts well with other material, and presents alone a fine appearance. Numerous quarries are open, shipments go to remote cities of the country, and this trade enlarges every year. Excellent stone of many other kinds is quarried in different parts, among which is a granite much esteemed, and marble, rated of inferior quality. Altogether, the stores of building material are as various and ample as the tastes and necessities of an old and wealthy civilization

JEROME I. CASE.
From a photograph by Thomas, Racine.

may be thought to hereafter reasonably require.

Kaolin, suitable with proper treatment for fire-brick and porcelain-ware, exists in sufficient plenty for extensive manufacture, but as yet awaits the attention of enterprise and skill for its profitable use. Cement-producing rock, limestone, and

ALEXANDER MITCHELL.

glass sand are embraced in the list of nature's useful gifts to the State, and cement and lime are made of good quality.

Such a store of natural material, above and below the surface predetermined the importance of manufacturing among Wisconsin industries. Transportation is so great a factor in production that competition requires the difference in freight of raw material and finished product to be saved, when possible, by planting the factory at the source of supply. The spirit of enterprise is contagious, and various advantages attach to the convenient contiguity of manufacturing establishments, although different in character. Many cities in the State are now the seats of active transforming industries, and the objects of production are numerous. The

hard-wood of the forest goes chiefly to furniture, wagon and carriage stock, agricultural implements, interior building material, and cooperage purposes. The construction of vehicles of every sort required by the affairs, convenience, or pleasure of men has attained great proportions, and large establishments in different towns maintain a trade extending to the limits of the country.

The manufacture of the tools and implements of husbandry comprehends nearly every species and form of the wonderful machinery which has so nearly transformed the farm to a factory, and delivered to ancient memories and poetic uses much of the toilsome drudgery by which our patient forefathers sorely won their scanty recompense from nature. It is carried on in above eighty establishments in different quarters of the State, but most prominently in the city of Racine. Long ago for Wisconsin, while the flail still flogged the too plenteous sheaves, an ingenious young mechanic built a threshing-machine for neighborhood use. It was a boon of mercy to farmers, and happily the resulting demand was addressed to a man of enterprise as well as ingenuity. From small beginnings, with courage and thrift, he raised the great establishment which has spread these useful machines, and the name of Jerome I. Case, to almost every quarter of the grain-growing world, and, still maintaining their superior excellence by constant improvement, finds a demand for many thousands every year. This proved a nucleus for other industries, and the energetic and skilful men who have gathered there have made Racine a city of manufacturing mechanics, approaching 25,000 in population, possessing numerous factories for a wide variety of objects, and manifesting the unmistakable aspect of high intelligence and prosperity. Mr. Case still lives there in enjoyment of his deserved fortune, and has amused his later years by rearing fine horses, one of them being the famous little trotter Jay Eye See.

Large tanneries are in operation at several places in the State, and the production of leather is considerable. The accessibility of the bark supply and the facilities for obtaining hides render the location advantageous for this business, which, though requiring large capital, commonly returns large gains.

Many mills for the manufacture of woollen goods are in active operation, and at least one prosperous concern has engaged in cotton manufacture. At Bay View, a suburb of Milwaukee, are extensive rolling-mills and furnaces for production of iron, and many establishments of iron-workers, though of less extent, are maintained in different localities.

The region of Lake Winnebago and the lower Fox is especially attractive to manufacturing. Fond du Lac, at the head of the lake, and Oshkosh, midway on its western side, at the mouth of the Wolf River, have from an early period been prominent in the lumber trade and kindred industries. The Fox flows from the northern extremity of the lake, with a strong current and in copious volume, the uniformity of which is so guaranteed by the large reservoir from which it issues that only a succession of dry seasons can materially affect its force. The river thence descends until near Green Bay upon such an inclination that its power for driving machinery is continuously enormous, and the succession of suitable sites for dams and mills renders nearly its entire course available to use. The general government made a grant of lands at an early day to aid its improvement for navigation, and in the prosecution of this object the company to which it was intrusted constructed many dams convenient for delivery of the force of the stream to the driving-wheels of the mills. Rapid development has taken place, and the valley is fast filling to its limits with mills and factories. The river-banks are generally high and bluffy, broken here and there by descending ravines, in places covered with trees, elsewhere with grassy verdure, and affording picturesque vistas, to which the numerous constructions by which the flood is put to work add effectively, the whole scene being of great beauty and interest. The objects of the industries are various, but the chief is paper, the aggregate daily production of which exceeds considerably, so it is said, any other paper-making locality in the United States. The aspect of this river when its harness shall become complete—not a distant day—will

C. C. WASHBURN.
From a photograph by Curtiss, Madison.

be among the most pleasing spectacles the country affords.

Other rivers furnish water-power of great value, as yet but slightly used. Particularly the Wisconsin is to be mentioned as one whose valley will some day teem with productive industries.

Ours would perhaps be commonly spoken of as an agricultural rather than a manufacturing State. The converse is probably now the fact, if all be reckoned who are fairly to be regarded as engaged in manufacture, or the value of products be compared. So many points naturally invite this form of industry that the manufacturing interests are diffused among numerous places of the State—a beneficial thing, but diminishing their apparent consequence until their large aggregate be summed. However it presently be, the promise of the future is favorable to the superiority of the manufacturing interests.

The railroads now afford the State so ample transportation service that comparatively little extension remains desirable. Their aggregate length is about 5425 miles, and but three counties are untouched by the rails—one in the forest and upon the course of lines projected, the other two being on the isolated peninsula which separates Green Bay and Lake Michigan. Four lines between Chicago and St. Paul traverse the State, eight cross it from east to west, four descend through it from Lake Superior, and shorter roads bring nearly all parts into convenient use of the general system. It may be doubted, indeed, whether the in-

MATTHEW H. CARPENTER.
From a photograph by Bell, Washington.

terests of rival companies have not increased the total mileage by needless construction to the disadvantage of the public in the added burden of their maintenance. One can hardly study the railroad map without thinking it might have been better for all interests if routes had been wisely prescribed with more reference to the common good, instead of having been left to the operation of the motives which have at times governed construction. The two dominant companies are known to Wall Street as the Granger roads—the Chicago, Milwaukee, and St. Paul, and the Chicago and Northwestern. The former

possesses above 1330 miles in Wisconsin, the latter nearly 950. Both own lines extending through many other States, the aggregate of each system, with its dependencies, approximating 6000 miles. These are the great trunk lines of the Northwest, binding the expanse between Lake Michigan and the Missouri, and gathering the trade and produce of a vast region beyond. The St. Paul was, by reason of two men, more particularly a Wisconsin road, and has been a large contributor to Wisconsin interests. These were S. S. Merrill, its general manager, and Alexander Mitchell, its president. Mr. Merrill was a strong example of a strong man, who rose from the lowest ranks of the service to the management of this road, and ruled it till his death. Mr. Mitchell presided over its growth and fortune, almost from its beginning, until his lamented decease in 1887. They fixed and kept its head-quarters in Milwaukee, and ever made it auxiliary to the interests of that city.

The foregoing is but a mere side look across the field of Wisconsin labor, rather than a bird's-eye view that, though swiftly, might observe the whole aspect. So much necessarily fails to appear that, without consideration and allowance, but short measure can be taken of the character and extent of material prosperity the State has attained and holds in prospect. A single additional object of view, even better illustrative, can be given a brief attention. Sharing the benefit of the wise federal policy that sought to promote education by grants of the public domain, the State upon its admission received the sixteenth section of every township for the use of common schools, and seventy-two sections, or two whole townships, for endowment of a State university. Had these gifts been husbanded with fidelity to the interests to which they were pledged, generous funds might have been realized. The eagerness for immigration characteristic of new communities, aided by some self-seeking, caused the sale of most of these lands at government price, realizing not more than one-third of what should have been their product. But the fault of the early days gave opportunity to the more enlightened spirit which now animates an intelligent and prosperous people, and the injury has been nobly repaired by laws which levy a permanent annual tax of a mill in the dollar on the entire assessment of the State, yielding nearly $600,000, for increase of the income of the common-school fund, and another of one-eighth of a mill for addition to the yearly revenues of the university, besides other aids, and a cordial warmth of interest not less nourishing than money. The common-school fund is now three millions, and gains something yearly from the proceeds of fines, forfeitures, and escheats. The income of it, augmented by the tax, is approximately $800,000, and its distribution proportionably to school-children is made to no district which has not raised by tax in the year the equivalent at least of its distributive share. Few districts fail to raise much more; so that the total expenditure for public schools, including the cities, now amounts to three and one-half millions each year.

To provide the instruction of teachers, the State set apart one-half the swamp and overflowed lands granted by the general government in aid of drainage, as a fund for support of normal schools. This was a wiser use than that purposed by Congress, and, though a departure from the trust, has met with merited acquiescence by the federal authorities. Upon this foundation five excellent institutions, under government of a common board of regents, are actively at work, and the university also gives instruction in didactics. A most useful system of institutes, holden throughout the State, assists in self-culture the teachers in service. These provisions mark increasing recognition of the important truth that teaching is a high profession to which persons of talent should be engaged, not for temporary relief, but as a life avocation, and that in the proper uplifting of that profession in ambition, scope, and rewards wisdom must largely rest hope for the thorough diffusion of knowledge which will elevate the race. Teachers are now admitted to service only after satisfactory examination, which, especially for the higher grades, is exacting; a worthy *esprit de corps* gains increasing power; and year by year useful progress yields encouragement for the gigantic task that confronts this profession.

A system of free high-schools has been

established, stimulated by State bounty, with good effects. Many are well equipped and fully graded, bear the fair rank of academies, and qualify their graduates directly for the university. Question is still occasionally raised of the right of the State to provide more than a common-school education for her children; but public opinion is steadfast that the knowledge which is the safe stay of liberty and civilization cannot be too thorough and abundant, and in hope for the day when the best shall be common, the State should proffer the best she can to all who will accept it now, and the rule of free tuition wisely governs the university not less than the district schools. In above six thousand school-houses distributed throughout the State is fixed the base of the educational system; the high-schools already number one hundred and fifty, shaping the upward course, with convenient gradation, to the university as the head.

This institution is located at Madison, upon a site of great natural beauty, with ample grounds of nearly two hundred and fifty acres in area, stretching over undulating hills along the coast of Lake Mendota. No seat of learning anywhere is more "beautiful for situation," and the wise providence of the State rapidly promotes its emulation of the best in all essentials of excellence. The national provision for an agricultural college was added to its endowment, and the university then undertook instruction in agriculture and the mechanical arts. The combination has proven fortunate, and, while the humanities suffer no lack of attention or consequence, its usefulness has been greatly augmented by fostering helpful scientific understanding of practical pursuits not long ago regarded beyond the pale of collegiate learning. Not failing to press upward the standard of all education, the university now holds down a helping hand to all the youth of the State, and its relation to the educational system is no longer distant, but close, cordial, and beneficent. No other similar institution in the country enjoys so large a proportional attendance from the State which maintains it—a clear proof of its benefits, as well as of popular appreciation. Co-education of the sexes, so absolutely free that entrance, class service, and graduation are common to both upon precisely the same terms, has now been the rule for a quarter of a century, and with such advantage that question is no longer raised of its value or propriety. It has been our good fortune to have largely escaped the distraction and enervation which have sometimes elsewhere befallen public agencies for higher education from independent establishments under exclusive control of different religious sects— although several usefully exist—or the futile efforts of wealthy men to cheaply gain remembrance by half endowing some weakling college; and in every particular of usefulness and strength the superiority of the public system stands here indisputable and dominant. The greater security of the public foundation over a memorial benefaction is shown by all history, and the utility of educational gifts is vastly enhanced when made auxiliary instead of rival and hostile to the general scheme of the State. Tribute is due, in this connection, to the memory of Cadwallader C. Washburn, who will be remembered as the giver to the university of a great instrumentality for the advancement of science, the Washburn Astronomical Observatory, long after the ephemeral glory of public station and personal consequence during a brief day and generation, so commonly the fatuous aim of ambitious effort, has faded to oblivion. Governor Washburn also rendered eminent service to the State and nation. For five terms, at different periods, he sat in the House of Representatives— one of the famous three brothers sitting together there from three several States, followed later by a fourth—was a Major-General of Volunteers in the civil war, and afterward Governor of the State. And better still than his excellent service was his example of unsullied public integrity and fidelity to public trust—a character beyond reach of the mean envy that so often barks at eminence in virtue and achievement.

Care for the blind and the deaf and dumb has provided two distinct establishments for their education, of sufficient capacity to embrace within their compass all instructible persons of either affliction within the State, and both aim to employ the most helpful methods of human kindness and skill. For the cure and comfort of the insane the State maintains two hospitals, and, with State contribution, Milwaukee County one, the three sufficient for 1400 patients. Besides these, twenty county asylums have been constructed for the care more especially of the incurable insane, under a law for encouragement of this system, which is peculiar to Wisconsin, by means of which the public compassion may now adequately reach out to every "mind diseased."

Separate reform schools for the criminal or vagabond youth of both sexes seek to save as much as to punish, while prisons are used for the elder offenders; and in all, humanity, not vengeance, inspires discipline, a spirit marked on our statute-book by freedom from the denunciation of death to any offender.

Government of the institutions maintained by the State is vested in a State Board of Supervision, under fair salaries, while the State Board of Charities and Reform exercises general censorship over all the eleemosynary, correctional, and penal establishments within our borders. In these measures of education and charity the thoughtful person will be apt to find the best evidence of true prosperity amidst the people.

To the roll of honored names in Wisconsin, the judiciary and the bar have furnished their customary share. The constitution committed the choice of judges to the people, and for limited terms. Their election is made in the spring, however, when partisan influences have less force, and generally with fortunate results. The wise rule that a good judge shall be re-elected, irrespective of political considerations, so long as he will serve, has become so fixed in common sentiment and custom that party whips cannot drive good citizens to its violation, and the attempt, even, is now an ancient story. The separate Supreme Court was organized in 1853, and since the expiration of the first terms of the Associate Justices, more than thirty years ago, although at times special interests have been stirred by necessary decisions to violent effort, no justice has been defeated at the polls, or left the bench but by voluntary resignation or the call of death. Four Chief Justices have presided in the Court with general approbation— Edward V. Whiton, Luther S. Dixon, Edward G. Ryan, and Orsamus Cole.

No man has gained the State a greater illustration beyond her borders than Matt. H. Carpenter. For many years he was a conspicuous figure in the nation, a leading counsel in celebrated causes before the highest tribunals, a Senator of acknowledged eminence among his fellows, and for a time acting Vice-President. In every relation the riches of his intellect, the bold spirit of his conduct, the graces of his manner, commanding respectful attention to his opinions, and charming all to admiration of his brilliant personality. Great as were his natural gifts, his capacity for labor, itself an unusual endowment, was unsparingly pressed to increase their usefulness, so that he appeared to advantage in the performance of every duty. No man had more attached friends, and though he encountered opposition in political life, it was little mixed with rancor, which could not withstand the genial warmth of his presence and kindliness. Mr. Carpenter began his professional practice at Beloit in 1848, but removed to Milwaukee eight years after, and there his grave is tenderly kept. He was chosen Senator in 1869, to succeed Judge Doolittle, was nominated in party caucus for reelection in 1875, but failed because of a combination between the opposition and some recalcitrants on his own side, which resulted in the choice of Mr. Cameron. On the happening of the next vacancy, in 1879, he was again elected, and his death befell him during the term, on February 24, 1881.

Philetus Sawyer and John C. Spooner now sit for Wisconsin in the Senate of the United States.* Mr. Sawyer was born in Vermont in 1816, but passed his youth in New York. In his thirty-first year he settled in Oshkosh, where his business career has been prosperous, mainly in lumbering, and he has amassed great riches. He served his city as Mayor and member of the State Legislature, for ten years was a Representative in Congress, and is now in his second term as Senator, having been first chosen in 1881.

Colonel Spooner, though born in Indiana, received his education in the State university, from which he was graduated in 1864, at the age of twenty-one, and enjoys the noble distinction of being first of her foster-children to bring her the honors of the Senate.

Our praise to Nature for her bountiful favor would be mean indeed if her gifts of material wealth alone inspired it. By salubrity of climate, abundance of wholesome water in streams and lakes and springs, and the most pleasing landscapes, she has marked her purpose to make the State a delectable home for man.

* This article goes to press before the session of the Wisconsin Legislature.

In general configuration the surface has been likened to a hipped roof. A water-shed of no great height stretches east and west, about thirty miles south from Lake Superior; and from that, at right angles, the line of highest ground passes southwardly through the middle of the State, descending as it goes, until it fades out of notice in the prairies of the southern border. The apex or junction of these lines of water-shed stands near the Montreal River, and rises only 1200 feet above the level of the lakes; but the descent to Superior is sharp enough to give rapid current to the frequent streams upon the northern slope, thus often broken into beautiful cascades. To the southeast and to the southwest alike the surface inclines with gentle declivity, not perceptible to the eye except in the flow of the rivers that wander in their long courses to the borders of the State on the lake and the Mississippi. No mountains add either sublimity to our scenery or isolation and severity to the lives of our people. But the superficial aspect is varied and relieved in outline by occasional hills, numerous streams, and especially by small lakes, which, to the number of thousands, dot the landscape like gems upon a handsome robe. For the most part these are of pleasing beauty, their waters supplied from springs fresh and wholesome, and filled with fine fish. The forests still contain game, but after it shall disappear the sportsman will find plentiful gratifications for rod and line in the lakes and streams; and year after year multiplies the number of tourists and summer residents who seek the delights of repose among scenes so blessed by nature.

Resulting, perhaps, from the surface shape, the privilege of artesian wells, from which streams of excellent water flow with force, is enjoyed in many places on either side of the State. At Racine and Kenosha, on Lake Michigan, such wells supply the public systems of water-works, by their own unaided force and volume carrying an abundant stream through all the ramification of pipes to the very tops of buildings. At Prairie du Chien, on the Mississippi, a flood sufficient almost to drive machinery pours vehemently from such a well; and many others, though of lesser power, exist elsewhere. The healing springs of the State are already famous. They issue from the earth in several places, but those of Waukesha have highest celebrity, and the bottled waters of Bethesda are drank on both continents.

The State is on three sides bordered with the beautiful scenery of the Great Lakes and a majestic river, in a charming succession of water landscapes that only artists of the pen and pencil can suitably tell the merit of, while its interior is as richly endowed to please the senses and gratify the tastes as to minister to the comforts of men. Summarizing with these all the other evidences which have been, though but unsatisfactorily, mentioned, can more be wanting to manifest the design of Heaven, to which from long aforetime the forces of nature have labored, that here shall be for a duration beyond all prescience of man an intelligent, prosperous, happy State?

THE CITY OF CLEVELAND

VIEW FROM THE VIADUCT.

THE CITY OF CLEVELAND.

BY EDMUND KIRKE.

TRAVELLING in 1796 was not what it is to-day. A journey which now is accomplished in a few hours, then occupied as many days, and in thinly settled portions of the country was often attended with hardships and dangers that led the stoutest-hearted to prefer a seat by their own firesides. This was, at least, the experience of a young New Hampshire farmer, who in the year I have mentioned set out to find for himself a home a thousand miles or more nearer to the setting sun. He was named James Kingsbury, and though born in Connecticut, had been reared among the granite hills, where the annual crop of stones is so large that the sheep's noses are said to be sharpened to enable them to nibble the thin grass that grows between them. He had heard of a country around the Great Lakes where the climate, being tempered by vast bodies of water, was mild and genial, and the soil so fertile that it only needed to be "tickled with a hoe to laugh into a harvest," and he determined to cast his lot in that delightful region.

The Revolution had left the country in poverty, and Kingsbury was no better off than the most of his neighbors, but though not yet thirty years of age, he had already attained to the rank of Colonel in the militia—a position which in those days implied character and a certain degree of social consideration. But he had a young family growing up around him, and it was probably more on their account than his own that he left the security of a settled district for the unknown hazards of a new country. Whatever may have been his motive, it is certain that in the early spring of 1796 he set out from Alstead, New Hampshire, with his wife and three children—the oldest not four years old—to find a home in what was then the far distant West.

He travelled by "private conveyance," taking with him a young brother of his wife to aid him on the journey. His outfit was a stout farm wagon drawn by a yoke of oxen, and laden with household goods and provisions; a horse to carry his wife and two younger children; a cow to supply milk during the journey; and for defense a rusty Queen's-arm musket, with which an older brother had in 1777 done effective service at Bennington. His first destination was Oswego, and after leaving Albany his route lay through a wild forest, where the road was merely a bridlepath blazed through the woods—the trail used from time immemorial by the Indians. Here no inn or friendly farm-house invited the traveller to lodge overnight, and the little company was forced to camp out among the trees, the woman and children sleeping in the wagon, while the man and the boy took turns in watching the fire, which had to be kept in a constant blaze to frighten away the wolves and panthers with which the forest was infested. Thirty days they journeyed in this manner, travelling perhaps ten miles in a day, before they came in sight of the little collection of log huts which then composed what is now the important port of Oswego.

Here Kingsbury found a scanty array of shipping, from among which he sought to find a craft suitable to navigate a lake subject at this season to violent storms, and at all times unsafe for any but skillful seamen. Nothing better presented itself than an open flat-bottomed boat, rigged with a single sail, and capable of carrying his family and household goods, but sure to have its gravity upset if freighted with animals ignorant of the science of equilibration. In this, however, Kingsbury embarked, closely hugging the land, and never venturing out in threatening weather,

the young lad meanwhile mounted upon his horse, and making his way through the woods along the shore with the cow and the oxen. At night the boat would be drawn up on the beach, and the camping-out experiences would be repeated. In this slow and toilsome way he journeyed another thirty days, when he arrived at Fort Niagara, which was the end of his route on Lake Ontario. Here the order of proceeding was reversed. The boat which had carried the wagon was now to be carried by that vehicle over the thirty miles of portage to Lake Erie. Here the little craft was again launched—trundled from the wagon into the lake—and here, at the future Buffalo, Kingsbury fell in with a gentleman who was to decide not only his destination, but his worldly destiny.

This was General Moses Cleveland— the Moses that was to lead a considerable part of Connecticut into the Ohio wilderness, and to come down to us as the founder of one of the most beautiful cities in the Union—Cleveland, Ohio. He was agent and director of the Connecticut Land Company, which had recently bought of that State the Western Reserve—a tract of about 3,500,000 acres, extending westward from Pennsylvania along the shore of Lake Erie, and "reserved" to Connecticut by the United States as its portion of the public domain. Cleveland was travelling in the wake of a surveying party of fifty, who had but recently gone forward to survey and lay out into townships and cities this immense tract, in readiness for the tide of emigration which was expected to follow. He had never seen his wide possessions, and they had never been explored; hence he could have given Kingsbury no reliable description of the country; but it is certain that he induced him to locate upon the reservation. In doing so, Kingsbury became the first white settler in northern Ohio.

Cleveland's first destination was Conneaut, a future village, near the junction of the lake and the line of Pennsylvania. Here Kingsbury selected a piece of ground on which the surveyors had already erected a cabin, and then broke up the soil and planted a few acres to serve his family for another season. During the winter that was approaching he expected to subsist on the provisions he had brought with him, eked out by what could be spared from the stores of the surveyors, whom he found at Conneaut, but who were soon to leave for a larger and more important town which was to be laid out at the westward.   To the site of this town, which had been fixed upon by the company in Connecticut as the capital of the reservation, Cleveland made an ex-

a shore everywhere overhung by a dense green forest, which was beautifully mirrored in the waters below, and before many hours came upon a narrow opening between two low banks of sand.   Pushing their canoes into this opening, they found a narrow channel, widening gradually to

MOSES CLEVELAND.

cursion with a small party soon after his arrival at Conneaut. The location had been determined on without any knowledge of the topography of the country, and merely because it was at the mouth of the Cuyahoga River.

The little party coasted closely along

the south, and bordered on the east by wooded bluffs, and on the west by broad flat marshes overgrown with reeds and coarse grass.   Near the entrance the beach was a miry sponge, and they had to proceed some distance up the muddy stream before they could find a patch of solid ground large enough to sustain a landing. While they were doing this, the squarely built, swarthy man who held the tiller of the leading boat had time to reflect upon the folly of locating a town without knowing something of the topography of the country. As the bow of his boat touched the land he sprang on shore, and clambering up the wooded slope at the east, looked off upon a broad level expanse rising gently from the lake, and stretching away as far as his eye could reach to southward. At a glance he saw that this was the true site for his future city, and the low ground along the river merely the water gateway that should admit to it the vast commerce of the future. Of this future he had great expectations, but he did not live to see them realized. Dying within ten years, and while Cleveland was still a mere hamlet of log houses, he beheld its future greatness only from the Pisgah of a somewhat active imagination.

Leaving a few men to erect a storehouse and cabin for the coming surveyors, Cleveland returned to Conneaut; and in the course of a short two months the city which is to bear his name to a late posterity came into existence—on paper. The map which was then made on the ground, by pasting together several sheets and parts of sheets of foolscap, was found a few years ago among the papers of ex-Governor Holley, of Connecticut, a son of one of the Cleveland surveyors. It is dated October 1, 1796; but the streets indicated upon it bear the same names and have the same locations as those now in existence.

Soon after the surveyors left Conneaut, Kingsbury was called by important business to return to his former home in New Hampshire. It must have been necessity which took him away, for he had to leave his wife and little ones, with only a lad of thirteen, exposed to the hazards of a wide forest frequented by roving bands of savages. Going on horseback by the shortest route—overland from Buffalo to Albany—he expected to return by the 1st of December; but the time came without him, or any tidings of him, for no mails as yet travelled west of Fort Stanwix, near Utica. The winter set in early with great severity. Snow fell deep late in November, and well-nigh blockaded the lonely cabin, and soon the little family ran short of provisions, and the cattle of fodder. Till the snow came, the In-

dians had brought the family game; but with the first very cold weather they had fled, with the birds, southward, and now the lone woman and her children seemed left to perish there in the heart of the wilderness. To add to her trials, another child was then born into the household. But even then, thus sick and alone and shut out from all human succor, this heroic woman did not lose hope or courage, for she trusted in a Providence who hears even the cry of the ravens. She knew that, if alive, her husband would soon come to her rescue; but day after day she watched and waited for him, measuring carefully her scanty store of food, and listening with anxious ear to every sound that broke the stillness of the forest; but the days lengthened into weeks, and still he did not come.

She ministered to herself as well as she could, and at the end of a fortnight managed to drag herself about the cabin; and during this time another furious storm broke over the little cabin, lasting, without intermission, twenty-one days, and piling still higher the heavy drifts that everywhere covered the forest. Could her husband survive, exposed to such a frozen tempest? or if he did, was there hope he could reach her, buried as she was under drifts as high as the roof of her dwelling? Terrible and desolate was the outlook to the lonely woman; but her faith and trust and courage did not even then forsake her, and at last her patient waiting was rewarded. It was Christmas Eve when the storm cleared away, and a gleam of sunshine broke at last through the long overhanging clouds. She went to the window to watch the welcome light, and then she caught sight of her husband, struggling painfully through the heavy drifts on his way to the cabin. He was on foot, and only an Indian guide was with him. Slowly he came on, but at last he reached the house, and, scarcely able to speak, fell exhausted in the opened doorway.

The reason of his long delay was soon made known to the overjoyed woman. He had no sooner arrived at his old home than he was stricken down with a fever, the seeds of which he had carried from the malarial swamps of Conneaut. As soon as able to mount his horse he had set out to return; but the heavy snows in western New York had so impeded his progress that he did not reach Buffalo till the 3d of December. There, though scarce-

TRAVELLING IN THE OLDEN TIME.

ly able to sit his horse, he had halted only long enough to secure an Indian guide—for the snow had obliterated the trail, and none but a native could find the way through the forest in such weather. They had set out together on the following day; and thus he had been exposed, day and night, for three long weeks, to the storm that she had heard howl so furiously around the little cabin. The drifts in many places had been higher than his horse's head; in one of them the animal had perished, and he would have shared its fate but for the fidelity of the faithful Indian.

The rest of this "winter's tale" may be briefly related. The revulsion of feeling consequent on the return of her husband prostrated Mrs. Kingsbury. She was herself now attacked with the fever, and unable to give her child its natural nourishment. The life of the infant then hung upon that of the half-starved cow, whose sole subsistence was the small twigs of the linn, elm, and beech, which had been gathered for the winter's fodder. It was a fortnight before Kingsbury was enough recovered to move about, and then he had to face another journey. The stock of provisions had now become all but exhausted, and no supply could be obtained nearer than Erie, twenty-five miles distant. The intense cold which had succeeded the storm had thickly incrusted the snow, and over it, on foot and alone, he dragged a hand-sled laden with the precious eatables. Flour could not be procured, and only a bushel of wheat; but on this, cracked and boiled, they managed to keep their souls and bodies together.

But a great calamity soon befell the lonely household. Among the browse for the cattle, the young lad had gathered some twigs of the oak, not knowing that they were poison to dumb creatures. Of these the cow had eaten, and died; and thus the little child was doomed to starvation. Day after day, and night after night, the little thing wailed its life away, and that father and mother, powerless to help, were forced to listen. At last its wailing ceased; and then the man and the boy made for it a rude coffin from a pine box which had been left by the surveyors, and scooped for it a narrow bed amid the snow. Lifting it upon his shoulder, the father bore the little body from the house, and the mother lifted herself up in her bed to catch a last glimpse

of it as he laid it away in a little mound not far from the dwelling. She watched him as he lowered it into the ground, and then she heard falling upon it the frozen sods that were to hide it from her eyes forever. With that sound she fell back unconscious, only to awake a fortnight later ignorant of all that had happened. Now the strange thing that we call life was in her only a flickering flame, which, if not quickly fed, would soon burn out in its socket. This the husband saw, and loading the old Queen's-arm, which is still a sacred relic in the family, he gathered up his little remaining strength and went out to secure some of the animal food that was necessary to the saving of his wife's life.

The severe weather had relaxed, and now, instead of cold blasts from the frozen lake, had come milder breezes from the south, bringing with them a few lonely birds into the forest. But the birds were shy, and Kingsbury would be fortunate to get within shooting distance. He trudged wearily on into the woods, but he saw no game, and at last, almost despondent, he sat down upon a fallen tree in the midst of a snow-bank. Soon a solitary pigeon came and perched itself upon the topmost branch of a tall tree at the utmost range of his musket. It seemed a hopeless chance; but he lifted his weapon and fired, and the bird fell, and he went home with it rejoicing. When he gave the broth to his wife she revived, and opening her eyes, asked, in a feeble tone, "James, where did you get this?" They were the first words she had spoken for a fortnight.

Such was the first winter of the first white settler in northern Ohio. It is not strange that, when the surveyors, coming to complete their work in the spring, told him that some of them intended to locate at the new city they had laid out at the westward, he should have decided to leave that desolate wilderness and build his cabin where he could occasionally see a human face of his own complexion. He did this, and thus became, in June, 1797, the first permanent settler in Cleveland, Ohio.

But he did not again make the mistake of locating near a marsh-bordered stream where the air was laden with malarial palsy. He moved back a mile and more from the Cuyahoga to a deserted cabin left by some Indian traders, who are supposed to have been there in 1786. This he occupied till he could build a cabin of his own, which he soon did, on a spot directly east of the public square, and not far from the present site of the Post-office. On the ground near by—now occupied by the City Hall and Catholic Cathedral—he planted a crop of corn, and thus provided against a repetition of the experiences of the previous winter.

Kingsbury's first neighbor, and the second settler at Cleveland, was one Lorenzo Carter, who soon afterward built a cabin at the mouth of the river, near the hut and store-house of the surveyors. These two families, in all nine persons, comprised the total population of Cleveland in 1797. In the following year four families were added to the settlement; but after that date the town increased very slowly, numbering in 1810 only fifty-seven persons, and as late as 1820 not more than one hundred and fifty. This snail-paced progress, due to a sterile soil and a malarial atmosphere, was, however, not shared by the adjacent country. More healthy and productive, this grew with amazing rapidity; and the consequence was that Cleveland, though small in itself, soon came to be of some importance as the mart and port of entry of a thriving farming region. This fact may justify a brief reference to the character, habits, and manner of life of its early settlers.

In 1800, Governor St. Clair appointed Kingsbury Judge of the Court of Common Pleas and Quarter Session of the county; and in the following year there came to reside in the place Samuel Huntington, a nephew of Governor Huntington, of Connecticut, and himself soon afterward Governor of Ohio. He was a man of cultivation, well descended, and eminent at the bar, and Kingsbury was a man highly esteemed; but in local influence they were both overshadowed by Lorenzo Carter, who had built his rough log cabin at the mouth of the river. This man was a genuine type of the pioneer. Though rude and uncultured, he was generous, kind-hearted, and neighborly.

LORENZO CARTER.

He had a shrewd, active intellect, great physical strength, and a keen though crude sense of justice; and these qualities, combined with a somewhat aggressive and domineering temper, gave him great ascendency over the simple-minded settlers and rude aborigines. As early as 1798 a whiskey distillery had been put up by a man named Bryant near the mouth of the river, and the Indians flocked to it in crowds for supplies of fire-water. Carter's house was near by, the Indians met him, and he soon acquired an influence over them greater than that of their own chieftains. His word became law among them, and so it soon was with the white settlers. Where there is no regular administration of justice it is natural that the strongest should rule; but what was known as "Carter's law" had control in Cleveland long after a regularly organized court existed in the county. But the court sat at Warren, fifty miles away, and was not at first attended with such a degree of state as was calculated to impress very much awe upon the community. The first session is said to have been held in the open air, between two corn-cribs, Judge Kingsbury occupying a rude bench beneath a tree, the jurors sitting around on the grass, and the prisoners looking on from between the slats of the corn-cribs. On other occasions court was held in a barn, as being the most commodious building in the town.

Carter's law was administered with quite as little state, but it had the advantage of being more accessible and of much speedier execution. One or two instances will serve as illustrations. In 1807 a farm hand who had been working for a neighbor suddenly decamped, and his disappearance was reported to Carter as a strange thing, for he had stolen nothing, and had left behind some unpaid wages. "No man can leave this town in that manner," said Carter, at once mounting his horse and going after the runaway. Overtaking him, he bade the man return to the settlement; but he declined, protesting that he owed no one anything, and had a right to go and come as he pleased. Upon this, Carter poised his rifle, and gave the runaway his choice between returning peaceably, or being shot and left in the road, a prey to the turkey-buzzards. The man knew that Carter had a way of suiting his actions to his words, and he sensibly returned, received his wages, and continued a good citizen.

But Carter's law produced its most salutary effects among the Indians. On one occasion a large band of Ottawas and Chippewas had gathered on the west shore of the river, while a smaller gang of Senecas were encamped on the eastern bank, and in their mingling together a Seneca had killed an Ottawa. The deed was done at night-fall, and early on the following morning the combined Ottawas and Chippewas were seen arrayed in war-paint, and about to descend in vengeance upon the little band of Senecas. This being reported to Carter, he went among them, and by the promise of a gallon of whiskey, succeeded in compromising for the offense of the Seneca. Unfortunately the distillery was not in operation at the time, and the whiskey could not be delivered before the day following. But the Indians were impatient, and not disposed to wait the slow movements of the distiller. Again they put on their war-paint, and now they threatened extermination to both the whites and the Senecas. For a time it seemed as if nothing could appease their wrath, and that Cleveland was about to be sacrificed for the lack of a single gallon

of corn whiskey. But, at the risk of his life, Carter went again among the infuriated savages, and again they took his word —this time, however, insisting upon two gallons of fire-water. Carter took good care that the distiller was not again tardy, and so the town, which had been kept awake by fear for a couple of nights, went again to peaceful slumbers.

Whiskey in the hands of Carter was a powerful persuader with the red man, as was shown on still another occasion. Cleveland had been made a county-seat in 1809, and this brought courts and justice nearer than fifty miles, and would be naturally expected to abolish Carter's law altogether. It did do this in a measure, but the sturdy pioneer had still so much influence as to be called upon in every sudden emergency. In 1812, an Indian was tried and condemned to death by the regular tribunal. Before being led to execution he boasted to Carter and others that he would show the white people how an Indian could die. He seemed to enjoy the ceremony of being drawn through the streets, to the sound of music, amid a crowd of people; but when he had ascended the scaffold, and the black cap was being drawn over his head, his fortitude forsook him, and he refused to be executed upon any consideration. In vain the sheriff appealed to his sense of manhood, and reminded him of his boast that he would die like a brave Indian. "Me will not die," was the only answer. Before resorting to unseemly force, the sheriff turned to Carter, who now ascended the scaffold, and said a few words to the Indian in his native language. Instantly the fellow wilted, and promised to die like a gentleman if Carter would give him just one-half pint of whiskey. The whiskey was sent for, but having imbibed it the Indian again refused to be executed. The sheriff was about to resort to force, but Carter suggested another glass of whiskey. The Indian accepted it, and then leaped fearlessly into eternity.

Whatever may be thought of his mode of conciliating the Indians, there is no question that Carter's popularity among them was a principal means of securing to the early settlers of Cleveland a freedom from savage molestation that was not enjoyed by other frontier settlements. There were among the early settlers men of greater cultivation and far higher character than Carter; but when he died, in

GOVERNOR HUNTINGTON ATTACKED BY WOLVES.

1814, he was universally regretted. Every one felt the community "could have better spared a better man."

More dreaded than the savages were the numerous wolves, bears, and panthers with which in those early days the woods were infested. They prowled about the highways, and often invaded the farm-yard of the settler. No one thought of going out at night unarmed, and though the dwelling-house was always unfastened—there being no fear of human intruders—a loaded musket hung constantly over the door as a defense from wild animals. As late as 1813 a large part of the town was covered with trees, and a forest of huge chestnuts skirted Superior Street, so dense as to completely shut the lake from the view of passers-by on the road. Near the corner of Euclid and Willson avenues was an extensive swamp, which was a favorite resort of wolves, and here, on one occasion, Governor Huntington was attacked by a pack of these hungry animals. He was mounted on a swift horse, and was returning from a circuit after dark, with no weapon but an umbrella, when in the midst of this swamp he was set upon by a score of these ferocious beasts. He laid about him right and left with his umbrella, and thus succeeded, not in beating off the attack, but in so frightening his horse that the latter outstripped the wolves and bore his rider off in safety.

But the panther was more dreaded than the wolf. He lurked everywhere about the wooded paths to spring upon the unwary traveller. Stretched along the overhanging branch of some tree, or concealed in the bushes by the way-side, he sought to take his prey unawares, and woe to the wayfarer who, after dark, had not both his eyes and his ears about him. In 1805, one of these creatures was killed in Euclid Avenue which measured nine feet from his nose to the tip of his tail. The bear, however, though less ferocious, was more troublesome than the panther. In broad daylight he entered dwellings and lapped up the housewife's cream, and at night he invaded barn-yards and pigsties, and made a feast of the calves and young porkers. If detected and pursued on such occasions, he would quietly walk off with a juvenile swine in his mouth, every now and then turning back and eying his pursuers with a cool impudence that defied everything but a well-loaded rifle. The passer to-day along Euclid Avenue, who witnesses everywhere about him the evidences of culture, refinement, and the highest civilization, finds it hard to realize that within three-fourths of a century it has been a lair of wild beasts, when a steady arm and a trusty rifle were the settlers' only safeguards.

But we shall mistake if we suppose that in such a condition of things the settler's life was not one of comfort and enjoyment. When danger has grown familiar to us, it has lost half its terrors. Men are known to walk unconcerned into a powder mill with a lighted candle. The settler carried into the Western wilds the same free, elastic spirit he had known in his old home in New England. In fact, his life was the same, modified only by his primitive surroundings. But it was not the life of the rural New England of this generation. He wore no broadcloth, and she was not clad in silks, satins, and laces. His coat and trousers were of homespun gray, and she was arrayed in a cottonade gown, somewhat scant in the skirts, but hermetically sealed across the bosom, and adorned with an unaffected modesty that enchanted the beholder.

And this was their best apparel, in which they went to balls, attended meeting, and now and then listened to a Fourth of July oration, wherein the eagle expanded his wings and screamed in the most approved fashion. Balls were frequent, and to them the lads and lasses gathered from all the country round, mingling in the "mazy dance," and cutting the "pigeon-wing" to the tune of "Hi! Betty Martin," played by the old-fashioned fiddle, till the stars faded away in the morning. "Billing and cooing," it is said, filled up the intervals of the dance; but there being of that no positive testimony, it can not be stated as a historical fact. That interesting exercise is more likely to have occurred in some more secluded quarter—under green boughs, with an overhanging moon, or in the chimney-corner, while the old folks were snoring soundly in the adjoining apartment. That it did actually occur may, however, be safely affirmed, not only on good circumstantial evidence, but from the positive testimony of a white-haired veteran who not long ago related his own experience of those old days, at a gathering of the early settlers of this part of Ohio. The old gentleman gave so good a picture of those primitive times, which will never again be repeated in any section of this country, that I am tempted to transcribe a portion of his experiences.

Said the old gentleman: "The boys and girls who were predisposed to matrimony used to sit up together on Sunday nights, dressed in their Sunday clothes. They occupied usually a corner of the only family room of the cabin, while the bed of the old folks occupied the opposite corner, with blankets suspended around it for curtains. About eight o'clock the younger children climbed the ladder in the corner, and went to bed in their bunks under the garret roof; and about an hour later father and mother retired behind the blanket-curtains, leaving the 'sparkers' sitting, at a respectful distance apart, before a capacious wood-fire-place, and looking thoughtfully into the cheerful flame, or perhaps into the future. The sparkers, however, soon broke the silence by stirring up the fire with a wooden shovel or poker, first one and then the other, and every time they resumed their seats, somehow the chairs manifested unusual attraction for closer contiguity. If chilly, the sparkers would sit close together to keep warm; if dark, to keep the bears off. Then came some whispering, with a hearty 'smack,' which broke the cabin stillness and disturbed the gentle breathing behind the suspended blankets, so as to produce a slight parental hacking cough. All this accords, in a great degree, with my own experience."

Then the ancient patriarch related his own courtship, told how he courted a girl of the "true Plymouth Rock stamp," who lived twenty miles away. As the course of true love never did run smooth, her mother objected to the match, and though he pleaded with her most pathetically, she refused to melt "worth a cent." Then he went about for a time "sighing like a furnace," and then he sent his father to the court of the old lady to contract an alliance, offensive and defensive, but with no better success. He, however, kept on courting the girl till he loved everything on her father's farm, and at last his perseverance was rewarded, and the wedding day was fixed. The ague and fever was on him, and now, as the "day of days" approached, he often detected himself feeling his pulse, in fear that the disease might increase, and add to the fever already consuming him. But he was married without accident, and election soon coming off, he offered his vote at the polls. It was rejected because of his youthful appearance, and this his wife took much to heart. On the morning of the next election day she presented him with a small counterpart of himself. The news had

ROLLING-MILL.

preceded him at the polls, and his vote was not again questioned, though he was not yet of the legal age.

They were a stalwart race of men, and a glorious race of women. All of New England blood, they had the Yankee's adaptedness to circumstances, and his universal genius. The men could repair a plough, build a house, or drive a sharp bargain, and at the same time chop logic, discuss theology, or deliver a Fourth of July oration; while the women could brew and bake, turn a spinning-wheel, and make their children's clothes; or entertain guests, execute embroidery, or sing Watts's hymns in a way to set the birds a-listening. And all these things they did with equal ease, as if born to the vocation. What would be thought nowadays of a young maiden who, single-handed, should worst a bear in a deadly encounter, or who, in her father's absence, should shingle the roof and nail the clapboards upon his unfinished dwelling, and all the while be as much of a lady as any countess? But such were the Ohio girls of 1800 to 1820, and they were the mothers of the men who built the city of Cleveland—for the town was built by men, and not made by nature. Other places on the south shore of Lake Erie have as great natural advantages; but no other has had its men, and hence Cleveland has outstripped them all in commerce, wealth, and population.

In 1817 New York began the construction of the Erie Canal, and soon afterward Ohio conceived the idea of a similar work to connect Lake Erie with the Ohio River. Cleveland was then an insignificant village of about one hundred and fifty people; but its leading men had the foresight to see the advantage of making it the northern terminus of the great waterway, and they planned and worked to that end until it was accomplished. In 1827 the canal was completed as far as Akron, and this opened to Cleveland a rich farming section, already thickly settled and overflowing with surplus products. This surplus was brought to Cleveland, and merchandise was wanted in exchange; and thus sprang up a business which in a little more than one decade amounted to the annual sum of twenty million dollars. The lake commerce of Cleveland, which began in 1808 with Lorenzo Carter's sloop *Zephyr*, of thirty tons, now aggregates an annual tonnage of one and a half millions. In the second year after the opening of the canal it brought to the city 500,000 bushels of wheat, 100,000 barrels of flour, 1,000,000 pounds of butter, and of other produce a like proportion ; and in the second year following (1830), the United States census found in the town 1075 people.

Among the earliest receipts by the canal was a boat-load of coal, for which an enterprising mine owner hoped to find a market in Cleveland. A wagon-load of it was hawked about the town, and attention called to its superior quality and great

ON THE RIVER.

THE RIVER FROM THE VIADUCT.

value as fuel. But the towns-people eyed
it with disfavor. It was filthy, inconvenient to handle, emitted an offensive smoke,
and not a few questioned if "stone" could
be made to burn at all. With wood growing at their very doorways, what sense
would there be in going a long distance
for a fuel neither so clean nor so pleasant
as the old-fashioned oak or hickory? All
day long the wagon went the rounds without a single buyer; but after a time a
good-natured innkeeper did consent to
try a small quantity at two dollars per
ton. This was the beginning of the coal
trade of Cleveland, which now exceeds
one million tons annually.

In 1832 the canal was finished to the
Ohio River, and about the same time the
advance-guard of that New England exodus which set in with the opening of the
Erie Canal began to reach Cleveland and
the outlying country. Its commerce grew
with amazing rapidity. It numbered, in
1846, 10,135 people, and in 1852, 25,670;
and this rapid growth was altogether due
to the foresight of the man who conceived
the idea of making it the northern terminus of the Ohio Canal. His name, I think,

was Alfred Kelley, the first president of
Cleveland village.

But about 1852 the commerce of Cleveland received a check, and its lake supremacy was threatened. The opening
of through lines of railway had now begun to carry past its doors the produce on
which its leading men had expected it to
grow into a great commercial city. But
these men were equal to the emergency.
It occurred to them that the town was
located about midway between the iron
mines of Lake Superior and the coal fields
of Ohio and Pennsylvania. They would
bring the two together, and convert Cleveland into a great manufacturing city.
This project resolved upon, they went
about it with surprising energy. They
erected foundries and factories, and set
on foot a railroad down the Mahoning
Valley, which should connect their furnaces with the immense coal fields of that
region. This road was completed in 1857,
and ever since the position of Cleveland
has been assured as the great iron centre
of the West. There is not here space to
note the successive steps by which the
place has since risen from a small town

to a great city, but its progress is clearly indicated in the following figures from the United States census tables. In 1860 it had a population of 43,838; in 1870, 92,829; in 1880, 160,146; and by the best estimates it numbers at the present date upward of 200,000.

iron foundries and factories, oil and chemical works, brick-yards, and other manufactories impossible to enumerate. Here ten thousand machines move night and day in ceaseless hum, sending away, upon the numerous rail tracks which everywhere interlace the district, iron in its va-

CHARLES F. BROWNE ("ARTEMUS WARD").

If we stand on the precise spot where General Cleveland landed on that summer day in 1796, and look about us for a moment, we shall be able to form some idea of the great wealth and immense activity of this teeming hive of human industry. At our feet is an irregular valley, from a half to three-fourths of a mile wide, and following the windings of the river, which here doubles on itself several times, thus affording a long line of dock front within the city limits. The outer edges of this valley are flanked by high bluffs, on which are built the main portions of the town; but here, along the bed of the river, is the industrial heart of Cleveland. Looking up the valley, we see hundreds of acres, stretching from the lake shore to the southern boundary of the city, which are covered by ship and lumber yards, planing and flouring mills,

rious forms to the value of $70,000,000, and other products amounting to $30,000,000; that is to say, a total value of $100,000,000 yearly—an amount equal to the whole taxable property of the city. Six great lines of railway dip into this valley, bringing to it uncounted tons of raw material, and bearing from it, in thousands of cars, its immense manufactured product, ready for use and consumption. The spectacle is confusing. The frequent scream of the steam-whistle, the ceaseless whir of the heavy machinery, the constant coming and going of the loaded trains, with the harsh grating of their iron wheels, all this gets into one's head, till it turns around, and if he is a quiet man, and somewhat given to day-dreaming, he longs to be wafted back some three-fourths of a century to a seat at the hospitable board of Major Carter in the old log cabin that stood just yonder. If the old pioneer comes down here now, and has eyes to see what is going on about his old home, what must be his sensations!

Branching from this valley to the right is another valley skirting a narrow stream, which for a mile and a half is crowded with woollen factories, slaughter and packing houses, and similar establishments; and farther up the Cuyahoga, along the margin of another brook, is still another valley which pours a ceaseless tide of manufactured products into the immense commerce of Cleveland. This last stream is called Kingsbury Run, and it is the only memorial that I know of which has been dedicated to the worthy first settler.

Here, at the mouth of Kingsbury Run, are the works of the Standard Oil Company, covering several acres, and turning out, when in full operation, 10,000 barrels of oil daily. This concern is a marvel of commercial enterprise. Starting about the time that petroleum was discovered in Pennsylvania, as a private firm, with a capital of only $20,000, it has grown into a mammoth corporation having branches in half a dozen States, employing thousands of men, and handling nine-tenths of the oil product that goes to Europe. It is said to have bought out and frozen out a hundred rival establishments, to have made its own terms with railroads and yet enriched them by its traffic; and to now control the crude oil market of Pennsylvania, and the refined oil market of the world. Its blue barrels are to be seen all over Europe. It is stated that the profits of the company up to 1883 had been $77,105,322. Some of its business methods have been criticised; but however unscrupulous they may have been, the company is a wonderful exhibition of what business energy and sagacity may accomplish in this country.

Another gigantic business that has its home in this valley is that of the Cleveland Rolling-Mill, which owes its origin and wonderful success to the almost unaided efforts of the late Henry Chisholm, who came to America from Scotland, at the age of twenty, with scarcely a dollar

in his pocket. By industry and energy he had, at the age of thirty-five, accumulated about twenty-five thousand dollars, and with this in 1857 he laid the foundation of this establishment, which is now one of the largest of its kind in the world, owning mines and mills in several of the States, and having, all told, a working force of 8000 men, 5000 of whom are employed in this valley. The rolling-mill has a capacity of 100,000 tons of steel rails per year, with four furnaces for the production of Bessemer metal. The aggregate business of the establishment amounts to $25,000,000 per annum.

Spanning this busy valley, and connecting the eastern and western halves of Cleveland, is a gigantic work, which has no parallel in any Western city. It is a stone causeway sixty-four feet wide, three-

LEONARD CASE.

fifths of a mile long, and carried over the Cuyahoga at a height of sixty-eight feet above the water. Its cost has exceeded two million dollars—an expenditure, in proportion to population, larger than that upon the Brooklyn Bridge.

If now we retrace our steps to the heart of the city, we shall see where the men live and transact their business who give life and movement to this busy hive of industry. Superior Street, the principal business thoroughfare, was laid out when land here was a drug in the market at one dollar an acre, and hence it is not surprising that the original surveyors made it a hundred and thirty-two feet wide. It is lined with stores, banks, and warehouses, some of which are business palaces; but midway up the street we will pause for a moment before one of the least pretentious of these buildings.

"I don't read anybody else," he answered, with a smile on his care-worn face; "he is inimitable." In the plain building before which we are standing the inimitable showman first set up his "wax figgers"; and if we enter here we may encounter the assistant editor of the *Plaindealer*, who was the associate and intimate friend of "A. Ward" when the latter was the city editor of this journal. He has many anecdotes to tell of the genial showman. He describes his appearance, when he first came

EUCLID AVENUE.

Calling upon Mr. Lincoln on one of the darkest days in the late war, I was surprised to see upon his mantel-piece a couple of volumes—one a small Bible, the other, *Artemus Ward, his Book*. "Do you read Artemus Ward?" I asked him.

to the office, as decidedly rustic. He was, he says, long and lank, with flowing hair, and loosely fitting coat, and trousers too short in the legs and bagging at the knees. His humor was irrepressible, and always bubbling over, and he kept all about him in a constant state of merriment. He was a wag—nothing but a wag—but in that line a genius. He could see only the ludicrous side of a subject. Going away once on a short vacation, he engaged this

San Francisco to deliver a course in California. The season being close at hand, the manager asked him by telegraph: "What will you take for forty nights in California? Answer immediately." Ward answered immediately, by tele-

JOHN HAY.

gentleman to perform his work during his absence. He carefully instructed him as to his duties, and in doing so drew from his pocket a tow string about a foot and a half long, and told him he must furnish that amount of copy per day, leaving on his desk the measure as a reminder of the quantity. About this time he was called upon to respond to a toast to the Press at a Ben Franklin festival held in Cleveland. He rose to his feet, hung his head for a few moments in silence, and then sat down, having said nothing. In his account of the festival in the next day's *Plaindealer* his speech was reported by a blank space of about half a column of eloquent silence.

This gentleman remembers that soon after "A. Ward" entered the lecture field he was invited by a theatrical manager in

graph, "Brandy and water." The joke was noised throughout the State, and the result was, when Artemus went there to lecture on his own account, he was met everywhere with overflowing houses. While engaged in lecturing in the West, he wrote this gentleman the following epistle:

"MY DEAR GEORGE,—I want you to do me a favor. I relied on one of my men to save me the press notices. He didn't. Will you collect them for me at once, and send them to me at the Bates House? Now this is taxing your good-nature, but you'll do it for me—won't you, George? Do you know that you remind me more and more of the noble Romans? I don't know who they were, but you remind me of them; you do, indeed. And could I have appealed to one of those noble Romans to cut out some press notices for me in vain? I guess not. Go on, young man, go on. Deal kindly with the aged. Remember that we are here for only a little while, and that riches take unto themselves wings and fly away. Intoxicate the shunning bowl. Support your county paper. Love the Lord, and send me those notices. Write likewise. And now, kind sir, farewell. Farewell.

    "'When other lips and other hearts—'
      "Your'n, my pretty gazelle,
          "A. WARD."

Passing along Superior Street, we soon come to the public square laid out by the original surveyors. It is now called Monumental Park, from the fact that in one corner of it, on a high pedestal, stands a statue of Commodore Perry, in the attitude he is supposed to have occupied when about to charge upon the British squadron. The battle took place at Put-in-Bay, some miles to the westward, but it is said that the day before it was fought the fleet lay to off Cleveland, and was boarded by Judge Kingsbury, who had been engaged to furnish it supplies. Having told him that he was in hourly expectation of encountering the enemy, Perry added, "What would you do, judge, if he should heave in sight before you leave the ship?" "Do, sir?" answered the judge, already venerable for his gray hairs—"I would fight. I can do it as well as the best of you." The enemy did not heave in sight, and so the judge missed being one of the heroes of Lake Erie, and died peacefully in his bed at the great age of eighty.

It is said that the monument stands on the precise spot where Major Carter administered his last glass of whiskey to the refractory Indian, and where, too, in 1808, occurred the first sham fight and general training ever witnessed in Cleveland. The company numbered about fifty rank and file, and the men were arrayed in all sorts of costumes, and armed with all kinds of weapons, from a peeled club to a rusty musket. The captain wore a gaudy uniform, and a cocked hat surmounted by a rooster's tail. He gave his commands in a stentorian voice, and with a pompous stride in pace with the martial music. After putting his men through all sorts of evolutions, he bade them to charge upon the enemy. They did so. It was a whiskey barrel. And when the encounter was over, not one of them was able to tell whether he was dead or wounded.

The Park as originally laid out was a square plot of ten acres, but by the extension through it of two streets it has been divided into four smaller parks, one of which is occupied by the monument, another by a stone oratorium for Fourth of July and other orators, and the two others are ornamented with fountains and small lakes, tastefully fringed with flowers and flowering shrubs. It is in the heart of the business portion of the city, and near it are the Post-office and other buildings.

Before the present Post-office was erect-

A PICTURESQUE RESIDENCE.

ed, its site was occupied by a low wooden
building, which was the meeting-place of
perhaps the most unique club existing in
this country. All may remember the story of "The First and Last Dinner," in
which it is related how twelve friends of
about the same age agreed one day, when
met together at the Star and Garter Inn
in Richmond, to institute an annual dinner among themselves, which each one
should yearly attend until he was removed
by death. The club should never admit
any but the original members, and when
one should die, his plate should be laid
and his vacant chair be set at the table as
if he were still with the remaining eleven.
And this should go on, as one after another dropped out of his place, till the last
one, the sole survivor of the twelve, should
take his solitary seat in the silent room,
and with the eleven empty plates and vacant chairs around him, should quaff his
lonely glass of wine to the memory of his
departed associates. This weird fancy of
a fictitious story-teller has been rendered
into actual fact in the intensely practical
and prosaic city of Cleveland. Thirteen
of the prominent citizens of the town met
in 1836—nearly fifty years ago—in that old
building, and formed a club, to include
none but themselves, and to go out of existence with the life of the last member.
There, in a quaint, old-fashioned room, furnished with a dozen or more chairs and a
large round table, and ornamented with a
few pictures, an old-fashioned fender and
andirons, and a huge mantel, on which
stood a couple of second-hand bottles doing duty as candlesticks, they came together week after week and year after year
to play whist and chess, discuss important
subjects, and talk over the news of the day.
In 1858 all of them were living. The old
building was christened "The Ark," and
this name was transferred to the club, its
members being called "Arkites." When
the old house was demolished to make
room for the Post-office, Mr. Leonard Case,
one of the members, deeded rooms in Case
Hall for the free use of the club till its last
survivor should be no more. One of the
members, an infirm, white-haired man of
seventy-five, not long ago said to me, with
a tremulous shake of the head, "We are
all old men now; Mr. Case and five of
the rest have gone, and very soon the last
one of us will sit here alone."

From Monumental Park the leading
streets ramify, not with the regularity of

RUINED TOWER IN WADE PARK.

the Detroit avenues, but in somewhat the
same manner—branching off from a central hub like the spokes of a gigantic half-
wheel, and spreading over the whole eastern part of the city. The most attractive
of these streets is Euclid Avenue, which
starts diagonally from the southwest corner of the square, runs to the city limits,
and for many miles beyond through a
most beautiful country. The portion
nearer the Park is occupied generally for
business purposes, and here are the Academy of Music, in which Clara Morris made
her first appearance before the foot-lights,
and other noticeable buildings. Beyond

the business quarter the avenue is lined with private residences of such elegance as to well entitle it to its reputation of being the most beautiful street in the country. For a distance of fully three miles it is finely paved, level as a floor, and bordered by lawns of velvety softness. Each house stands at a distance from the street, and all have grounds more or less spacious, which are ornamented with shrubs and beds of flowers, and every here and there dotted with stately trees which stood there when the bear and the panther crouched amid their branches. No sameness wearies the eye,

surface, and is being developed with so much taste and judgment that it will eventually be the equal of any cemetery in the country.

Abreast of the business portion of the town, and on the shore of the lake, the city has recently converted a strip of waste ground into a most attractive park, which is also called Lake View. It was an unsightly bluff, seamed with gullies, and covered with wretched shanties; but the city took it in hand, planted trees, piled up rock-work, converted springs into fountains, and ragged gullies into beautiful ponds, and now it is one of the most at-

LAKE IN THE CEMETERY.

for there is everywhere variety both in the architecture and the treatment of the landscape.

Beyond these republican palaces is an exquisite private park, on which large sums of money and great skill in landscape gardening have been expended. It occupies a deep ravine and the adjoining uplands, and is threaded by walks and drives under wide-spreading trees, or amid a dense shrubbery whose fragrance perfumes all the air. The public-spirited projector of this park, Mr. J. H. Wade, the well-known electrician, is to convey it to the city as soon as a few preliminary conditions are fulfilled by the municipality.

Opposite this park, and overlooking the lake, is Lake View Cemetery, where Garfield's body is laid, and where the monument is to be erected to his memory. It occupies a tract of rather more than three hundred acres of beautifully diversified

tractive spots of the kind to be found anywhere. Every pleasant evening it is crowded with people who come here to inhale the cool breeze from the lake, and to watch the white sails and smoking steamers as they come and go on the blue water.

Of the western portion of the city, on the opposite side of the Cuyahoga, I can speak but briefly. The part nearest the river was originally the farm of Lorenzo Carter, and by his son was in 1830 sold to a company of speculators, who laid it out in streets, and here built what was called Ohio City. In 1854 it was annexed to Cleveland, and it now contains 60,000 inhabitants. Here is located a new city park, and the distributing reservoir of the Water Department. This is fed by a tunnel five feet in vertical diameter, which, sunk ninety feet below the surface, runs a mile and a quarter into the

LAKE VIEW PARK.

lake to obtain water free from the impurities which are brought down by the river. The capacity of the reservoir is six million gallons, and the total length of pipe laid, one hundred miles. The entire cost of works and pipe, from the crib in, has been nearly two million dollars.

As was to be expected of pilgrims from Connecticut, the first thought of the first settlers was for churches and schools for themselves and their children. Accordingly we find that as early as 1800 they invited here from their native State the Rev. Joseph Badger, a Congregational missionary, who went about among them, and preached in the open air or in the settlers' houses; and that two years later, Anna Spofford, the daughter of one of the first comers, gathered the little ones of the township into the "parlor" of Major Carter's log cabin, and taught their young ideas how to shoot in the right direction. This open-air church has grown into one hundred and fifty sacred edifices, some of them of the highest architectural beauty; and that one improvised school, into scores of educational palaces, where gather 50,000 children. And not content with providing the best system of instruction for the children, the people of Cleveland have organized an "Educational Bureau," managed by the first citizens, with the purpose to afford instruction and entertainment to the adult working classes by concerts, lectures, and gratuitous distribution of small books on useful subjects. Ten public entertainments have been given each season for three winters, the average attendance at which has been four thousand. The total distribution of books and pamphlets during the three years has been 167,200, and the average cost to each member, of each concert, lecture, and pamphlet, has been only three cents. The system is a most admira-

THE GARFIELD MONUMENT.

SCHOOL OF APPLIED SCIENCE.

ble one, and it deserves to be copied in other cities. The School of Applied Science is another of Cleveland's educational features.

Growing naturally out of the many churches of Cleveland are a host of benevolent institutions—hospitals, orphan asylums, retreats for the aged, children's homes, and Friendly Inns, in which latter the poor may find free reading-rooms, with the best of papers, magazines, and books; and also good meals and comfortable lodgings at a cost of merely enough to pay the expenses of the establishment.

Cleveland can not be called a literary centre, its men being of the class not of writers, but of workers; and yet it has been the home of several authors who have achieved distinction. Beside Artemus Ward, of whom I have spoken,

it was at one time the residence of William Dean Howells, the most popular among living American novelists. Constance Fenimore Woolson, the author of "Anne" and "East Angels," was born in New Hampshire, but Cleveland has been the home of her girlhood and early womanhood. Here too resides John Hay, the widely known author of "Little Breeches" and "Castilian Days."

As every man is different in form, feature, and character from every other man, so in all these respects every town is different from every other town. In the youth of towns this individuality is more marked and observable than when, in their older years, foreign elements have blended with the native, and they have become more cosmopolitan. But even then, down at the root, in the inner spirit, the native

THE CRIB.

element controls, and gives its peculiar characteristics to the engrafted branches. So it is with Cleveland. A large foreign element has blended with the native, and somewhat modified its surface character, but the prominent features are still Yankee, and Connecticut Yankee at that. As Connecticut was sown with culled grain from Massachusetts, so northern Ohio was sown with culled grain from Connecticut, and this seed has produced a crop the like of which can be found nowhere else in this country. None of the first settlers are now living, but hundreds still linger on the Western Reserve whose memories go back to the time when Cleveland was an inconsiderable hamlet of not more than twenty houses. Some of these old worthies I have met, and one needs to meet them to realize what kind of men sprang from the loins of the New England of the year 1800.

Such a race accounts fully for the present generation which has builded Cleveland. If one were asked what is the prominent characteristic of these men of to-day, I think he would have to say, A large-minded and large-hearted liberality that does not stop to count any expenditure which may result in public good or benefit Cleveland. Scores of living men might be mentioned who would justify this remark. I may not speak of them; they are too many; but I may refer to two or three who are not living. One of these was Leonard Case, whose benefactions were simply princely; another was the late Henry Chisholm, whose benevolence flowed in a constant but unobtrusive stream, and who cared for the interests and studied the improvement of his army of 8000 workmen as if they had all been his own children; another was Joseph Perkins, who has recently died, mourned by the whole community; and still another was Amasa Stone, who while living gave half a million to Western Reserve College, and in dying left immense sums to educational and charitable institutions. And such men are still left in Cleveland. Now and then they are to be found in other cities, but here they are numerous enough to give character and tone to the whole community. With such men, and with its population increasing, its manufactures growing, and its trade expanding year by year in an almost unprecedented manner, it is not hazardous to predict that Cleveland will number five hundred thousand people by the close of this century.

Building the Grass House of the Wichitas.

QUIVIRA AND THE WITCHITAS

LATE in 1540 the general Francisco Vasquez de Coronado, with three hundred Spanish cavaliers and the usual Indian following, come up from Mexico in quest of golden kingdoms in the north, and made winter quarters in the Indian pueblo of Tiguex, on the Rio Grande, about the present Bernalillo in New Mexico. After the good old fashion of the *conquistadores*, they at once proceeded to help themselves to what they wanted, without taking the trouble to ask leave of the owners, until their exactions led to an open revolt, culminating in the storming of the pueblo and the butchery of the defenders. So the Spaniards proved very bad neighbors, and the Indians were heartily wishing to be rid of them.

While visiting the neighboring pueblo of Cicuye—identified by Bandelier as the old Pecos ruin near the head of Pecos River—the soldiers met an Indian whom they called the Turk, a captive from a far-eastern tribe. They hired him to guide them on a buffalo-hunt, but on the way he had such stories to tell of the wealth of gold in his country of Quivira that, as the chronicler says, they did not care about looking for buffalo, but returned with the news to their general. And no great wonder, for he told of a river two leagues wide, with fishes as large as horses, and boats with sails and golden prows. The lord of the country prayed before a golden cross, or took his ease under a great tree, and was lulled to sleep by the tinkling of innumerable little golden bells in the branches. Even the bowls and dishes of the common people were of gold, which he knew well, and called *acochis* in his language.

A fair story, and it found ready listeners, for everything was possible in this New World. Cortez had taken a golden

Mexico and Pizarro a golden Peru, and why should not Coronado find a golden Quivira? Notwithstanding that the Pecos people called the Turk a liar, while one of the soldiers solemnly swore that he had seen him talking with the devil in a pitcher of water, Coronado made preparations to start for Quivira as soon as the spring opened. The Pecos chief gave him as additional guides two other Quivira captives, one of whom discounted the golden story very considerably, while the other, Ysopete, constantly insisted that the Turk was lying; but for a long time the Spaniards gave no heed to the warning.

Toward the end of April, 1541, the army left Pecos to cross the buffalo plains to Quivira. At the very outset we encounter difficulties and discrepancies in tracing the line of march. Of several contemporary narratives, no two agree in details, and some differ widely on important points. The only agreement is in the general statement that Quivira was beyond the plains eastward from Pecos, and that, after wandering about aimlessly for more than a month, Coronado finally reached it by taking a north course from the country of the Teyas. We shall therefore interpret the narrative in the light of some years of acquaintance with the tribes and territories under discussion.

Crossing the Pecos River below the pueblo, the army struck out toward the great Staked Plain. On account of the scarcity of water the regular Indian trails usually avoided the plateau by circling around its southern border, and it is probable that Coronado did the same. The chroniclers are full of wonder at the immense numbers of the buffalo, and at the terrible monotony of the grassy plains; as Coronado himself says, "with no more landmarks than if we had been swallowed up in the sea, because there was not a

stone, nor a bit of rising ground, nor a tree, nor a shrub, nor anything to go by."

Ten days after leaving the river they began to meet the roving Mescaleros, called in the narrative Querechos—the name still applied to them by the old people of Pecos, according to the researches of Bandelier and Hodge. They were then, as they were always, until confined upon their present small reservation in south-

A WICHITA MOTHER AND CHILD.

ern New Mexico, typical nomads, shifting constantly from place to place, and depending entirely upon the buffalo.

Proceeding still toward the east, they came next to the Comanches, or Teyas, as they were called by the people of Pecos, who knew them as alternately doubtful friends or open enemies, according as it suited the purpose of these wild raiders.

A WICHITA VILLAGE ON THE NORTH FORK OF THE RED RIVER IN 1834.
From the painting by Catlin, now in the National Museum.

Some of these Comanches, while roving somewhat farther south, had met Cabeza de Vaca and his companions, survivors of the ill-fated Narvaez expedition of 1528, whose story forms another of the romances of the old heroic period of Spanish discovery.

The account given of these two tribes is a perfect description of the plains Indians from Canada to Mexico, as known to us later, excepting that they had as yet no horses: "Two kinds of people travel around these plains with the cows [i. e., buffaloes]. One is called Querechos, and the others Teyas. They are very well built, and painted, and are enemies of each other. They have no other settlement or location than comes from travelling around with the cows. They kill all of these they wish, and tan the hides, with which they clothe themselves and make their tents, and they eat the flesh. The tents they make are like field-tents, and they set them up over some poles they have made for this purpose, which come together and are tied at the top; and when they go from one place to another they carry them on some dogs, of which they have many; and they load them with the tents and poles and other things, for the country is so level that they can use them, because they carry the poles dragging along on the ground. They trade robes with the people of the river for corn." They had neither corn nor pottery of their own.

The army had now been on the march thirty-seven days, but moving very slowly, and in such devious course that the return by a more direct route occupied but twenty-five days, even with several stops made to hunt buffalo. They learned afterward that they had made a great détour toward Florida—that is, toward the southeast, instead of going northeast, the direction in which Quivira lay. Ysopete had repeatedly declared that the Turk was deceiving them, and now the Comanches, on being questioned, said that his story was false—that Quivira was toward the north instead of the east, and that instead of the great stone structures and golden magnificence which he had described, it had only houses of dried grass occupied by other Indians who cultivated corn. A council was held, and Coronado decided to send the army back to Tiguex, while he pushed on to Quivira with thirty horsemen, under the direction of Ysopete and some guides furnished by the Comanches. He took the Turk along in chains. They were now apparently in the cañon country about the head-waters of the Colorado and the Brazos, described in the chronicle as abounding in mesquite beans—a favorite food of the Comanches—wild plums and grapes, turkeys, and pecans.

With the return of the army to Tiguex we need not concern ourselves, beyond noting the remarkable fact that, through a captive Indian woman, who made her escape only to be retaken soon after by other white men, the Spaniards learned long afterward that they had been within a few days' march of De Soto's men, advancing at the same time from the opposite direction of Florida. How differently might history have read had they met!

Under the direction of Ysopete and the Comanche guides, Coronado and his small party turned squarely to the north, probably about the line of the one-hundredth meridian, and after a month or more—for the accounts do not agree — reached a great river, which his Indians said was the river of Quivira. All the evidence indicates that this was the Arkansas River, in western Kansas. Crossing to the farther side, probably about where the Santa Fe trail crossed it three centuries later, they followed it for some distance northeast, and at last came upon a hunting party of Quivira Indians, who were about to flee until Ysopete hailed them in their own language, when they approached, and soon agreed to escort the strangers to their villages, some distance beyond.

Coronado now called the Turk to account, and he confessed, "like one who had given up hope," that he had deliberately misled the Spaniards by order of the Pecos people, in order that they might

lose their way and perish upon the plains, or be so weakened by exposure and hardship that they would fall easy victims to Pueblo vengeance upon their return. For himself, he had hoped to escape to his own people. He was at once strangled, and the Spaniards went on with their new friends to Quivira—the villages of the Wichitas—then about the middle course of the Arkansas, below the Great Bend, and no great distance from the present city of Wichita, Kansas.

And now, to his bitter disappointment,

A WICHITA GIRL OF FORMER DAYS.

Coronado found only houses of grass occupied by very ordinary savages, instead of the magnificent storied structures and golden civilization which the Turk had promised. He says: "Not only are they not of stone, but of straw, and the people in them are as barbarous as all those whom I have seen and passed before, but have the advantage in the houses they build and in planting corn." An officer who accompanied him says: "The houses were of straw, and most of them round, and the straw reached down to the ground like a wall. They have something like a sentry-box outside, where the Indians sit or recline." The Franciscan chronicler describes the people as barbarous and without decency, living in straw houses, and planting corn, beans, and melons. It being now the middle of summer, the men wore only the G-string.

Coronado spent nearly a month exploring the vicinity, visiting other grass-built villages, and receiving the submission of the inhabitants, who, it is to be hoped, understood what it all meant. Then, after setting up a cross of discovery, he started to rejoin the army at Tiguex, where he arrived in October, 1541, having made the return journey by a more direct route in forty days. From his letter to the King it is evident that he felt keen regret at

AN OLD-FASHIONED WICHITA HAIR-CUT.

the small result of the expedition, and he soon after resigned his offices and retired to private life.

Among those who had accompanied the army was a heroic Franciscan priest, Father Juan de Padilla, who had resolved to remain in the Indian country to devote his life to the salvation of souls. With a single white companion and some Indian guides and helpers, and some sheep and mules, with which he hoped to introduce stock-culture among the wild tribes, he recrossed the plains from Tiguex the next year, but was murdered soon after his arrival by those whom he had come to befriend. Other missionaries and other commanders kept up the tradition of Quivira, until with more exact knowledge of the country and people the newer names gradually superseded the old.

We come now to the modern period. While there may be doubt as to the exact location of the so-called province of Quivira in 1541, there can be no doubt as to the identity of the people, the Wichita Indians. No other tribe of the southern plains lived in grass houses and practised a native agriculture before the coming of the whites. The rolling *r*, so prominent in the names mentioned as those of villages or allied tribes of Quivira, is the most characteristic sound of the Wichita language, and the name *acochis*, given by the Turk as his people's name for gold, is simply the Wichita word *akwichish* (metal), according to the linguistic researches of Gatschet.

The name Quivira, like the modern name Wichita, is probably of foreign origin, perhaps having been learned by the Spaniards from the Pecos Indians. The Wichitas call themselves *Tawéhash* and *Kitikitish*. From a former custom, not yet entirely obsolete, of tattooing the eyelids, chin, and breast, they were called by the French traders *Panis Piqués*, or "Tattooed Pawnees," the Pawnees being their first cousins, and speaking nearly the same language. They had several subtribes, the best known being the Wacos and Tawaconis, who have given their names to a city and stream of Texas. They are closely related to the Pawnees of the Platte and to the Rees of the upper Missouri, and there is traditional evidence that at an early period the three tribes were neighbors in the country of the lower Arkansas, from which they were driven by the pressure of invading tribes from the east.

Although sedentary, as compared with

ON THE WICHITA RESERVATION.

the roving plains tribes, the Wichitas seem to have kept up a constant slow migration toward the southwest, until the hostile pressure was removed by the interference of the United States government, when they began to return along their track. In 1541 Coronado found them on the middle Arkansas, the whole course of which stream, from the Santa Fe crossing near Fort Dodge down to the Kansas line, was always a favorite gathering-place of tribes for the winter camp or the summer dances. In 1719 La Harpe found them lower down, about the junction of the Cimarron. Later on, their tradition says, they lived on the North Canadian; and about the opening of the present century they had their village on Red River, at the mouth of the Big Wichita. In 1834 we find their main settlement on the North Fork of Red River, at the west end of the Wichita Mountains, and twenty years later they had removed to the present site of Fort Sill, to the eastward of the same mountains. In 1859 they were gathered upon the reservation north of the Wichita, where they have resided ever since, excepting during the troublous period of the civil war, when for some time they were refugees in Kansas, near their old homes on the Arkansas, where the town bearing their name now stands. They have been reduced by wars and disease, until they number to-day but 320 souls.

In color the Wichitas are rather darker than their neighbors. As has been already stated, they practised tattooing. The men wore the scalp-lock, with the hair shaved from one side of the head and flowing loosely on the other. Parents still sometimes cut their children's hair after the old style, as shown in the portrait. They wore but little clothing, the women having only a short skirt in addition to the leggins. Their peculiar

DANCE LEADERS.

grass houses, with the grass-roofed arbors and drying-frames — the "sentry-boxes" of the old chronicle — are still in use, probably more than half the tribe being housed in this fashion. They raised large quantities of corn, which they ground upon stone *metates* or in wooden mortars. Their women were expert pottery-makers, and the art yet survives among them.

Their present chief is Tawaconi Jim, as he is known among the whites, a man of commanding presence, who rules with absolute control over his people, and defends their rights with equal force and eloquence, either in his native language or in English, which he acquired in

years of faithful service as a government scout.

A characteristic incident will illustrate his quickness of repartee. At a council held some years ago at the agency to negotiate the purchase of the reservation, Jim was present as spokesman for his tribe. The commissioners had exhausted every effort to induce the Indians to sell out for fifty cents an acre, but the latter preferred to keep their lands, and stood firm. At last one of the commissioners undertook to persuade the Indians that after they had selected their allotments the rest would be only worthless sand, for which the purchase-price would be clear gain. Quick as a flash the chief retorted, "Then why do you want it?" With a magnificent gesture, he girded his blanket about his waist, and stooping, took up a double handful of dust and scattered it to the winds, saying, "You white men have that many ways to cheat Indians!"

Having spent some years in ethnologic investigations among the Wichitas and other tribes of that section, the writer was requested by the Department of Justice, some five years ago, to visit a location on the upper Red River and examine some ancient remains which had an important bearing upon a pending controversy between the government and the State of Texas, the latter having claimed them as those of an old Spanish mining settlement, with a view to proving that the region was within the original Texas jurisdiction. On visiting the spot, we found, as I had suspected, that the remains were no other than those of an old Wichita village, the identical one visited by Colonel Dodge in 1834 in connection with the first expedition sent out by the government to initiate friendly relations with the southern plains tribes. The artist Catlin, painter of the noted Catlin Indian Gallery now in the National Museum, accompanied the expedition, and has left a detailed diary of its march and the subsequent negotiations at the village,

A WICHITA DANCE FEAST.

of which he has given us a painting, which, however, is considerably idealized, as will be seen by comparing his drawings with the photographs of actual houses. The village was upon a narrow strip of level bottom on the north bank of the North Fork of Red River, at the extreme western end of the Wichita Mountains, and within the present limits of the Kiowa reservation. We found the grass-grown circular foundations of the lodges as distinct as they might have been sixty years ago, and picked up arrow-heads, stone hammers, and *metates*. Largely upon the result of this examination, the question was decided in favor of the government.

On being detailed for the ethnologic work at the Omaha Exposition last year, I resolved to give the American people an opportunity to see one of the grass houses of Quivira, described by the old Spanish conqueror so long before. As

TAWACONI JIM, CHIEF OF THE WICHITAS.

Coronado was the first explorer of the Western plains, such an exhibit should have a special interest at a trans-Mississippi exposition. Accordingly, in making up my delegation from the southern tribes, I included a party of forty Wichitas, and contracted with them for one of the large grass houses then in actual occupancy on the reservation, which they agreed to take to pieces and set up again at Omaha.

The house having been taken down and the materials transported to the railroad in Indian wagons, a special train was made up to accommodate the delegation, consisting of nearly one hundred and fifty Indians from five tribes, with their ponies, tepees, and baggage, and the grass and poles of the house. The Wichitas had brought their drum, and as the train sped on they started up the music of the old dance songs, in which the other tribes joined, until the chorus went up from a hundred Indian throats.

As we sighted the Arkansas, which the Wichitas still recognize as the great river of their old home country, Tawaconi Jim clapped his hand to his mouth and gave a series of yells, which were echoed by every man in the car, while the drummers pounded away with all the strength of their arms, and we pulled into Wichita with a burst of noise that must have made the citizens believe for a moment that the Indians had broken out again in good earnest. The performance was repeated on the return trip, and also on coming in sight of the Platte, which the Wichitas know as the river of their kinsmen the Pawnees.

On arriving at the exposition grounds the grass house was unloaded, and set up as the central piece of the Indian camp. The supporting timbers were upright logs, forming the sides of a square, with forks at the tops, across which other timbers were laid. Long flexible poles, planted in a circle outside of this square, were then pulled over against the cross-pieces, when their tops were brought together to

A WICHITA HORN-DANCE.

form a dome, and firmly bound with elm bark. Lighter rods were fastened horizontally around the circumference, and finally the bundles of long grass were laid on, round after round, in shingle fashion, beginning at the ground, in such a way that each round was overlapped by the next above. All the tying was done with elm bark, so neatly that it needed a sharp eye to detect it. Two doorways were made on opposite sides of the house, so as to allow the breeze free play, and a small smoke-hole was left near the top. Inside were high platforms, which served both as seats and as beds. Fifteen persons were comfortably accommodated in the house, which, from the outside, looked very much like a well-built hay-stack. The building required the labor of several women for about a week, every detail being supervised by the chief himself. The rest of the party were housed in canvas tepees.

Adjoining the house they put up one of the grass-roofed arbors, under which they love to sit in the hot summer days; and the old men constructed for their own use one of the little rounded sweat-lodges of willow rods which belong to every Indian camp. With the strings of corn hanging from the rafters, the mortar and *metate* near the door, the drum in its place, the men and women at work, and the children at their play, it was all very homelike.

The Wichita camp formed one of the main attractions on the Indian grounds while the exposition lasted, and almost every night a dance or a hand game, to which all the other tribes were invited, made the place resound with shout and song. When the great show was at an end, the grass house and its belongings were bought for the National Museum. The structures were taken down, and the materials again packed and shipped, this time to Washington, where I hope at some favorable opportunity to set up in the beautiful park on Rock Creek one of the last remaining specimens of the straw houses of Quivira.

NOTE.—The account of Coronado's march is based chiefly upon Winship's translation in the Fourteenth Annual Report of the Bureau of Ethnology, supplemented by Bandelier and others. The identification is my own.—J. M.

THE SECOND MISSOURI COMPROMISE

I.

THE Legislature had sat up all night,
much absorbed, having taken off its
coat because of the stove. This was the
fortieth and final day of its first session under an order of things not new only, but
novel. It sat with the retrospect of forty
days' duty done, and the prospect of forty
days' consequent pay to come. Sleepy it
was not, but wide and wider awake over a
progressing crisis. Hungry it had been
until after a breakfast fetched to it from
the Overland at seven, three hours ago.

It had taken no intermission to wash its
face, nor was there just now any apparatus for this, as the tin pitcher commonly
used stood not in the basin in the corner,
but on the floor by the Governor's chair;
so the eyes of the Legislature, though
earnest, were dilapidated. Last night the
pressure of public business had seemed
over, and no turning back the hands of
the clock likely to be necessary. Besides Governor Ballard, Secretary (and
Treasurer) Hewley was sitting up too,
small, iron-gray, in feature and bearing

every inch the capable, dignified official, but his necktie had slipped off during the night. The bearded Councillors had the best of it, seeming after their vigil less stale in the face than the member from Silver City, for instance, whose day-old black growth blurred his dingy chin, or the member from Big Camas, whose scantier red crop bristled on his cheeks in sparse wandering arrangements, like spikes on the barrel of a musical box. For comfort, most of the pistols were on the table with the Revised Statutes of the United States. Secretary and Treasurer Hewley's lay on his strong-box immediately behind him. The Governor's was a light one, and always hung in the armhole of his waistcoat. The graveyard of Boisé City this year had twenty-seven tenants, two brought there by meningitis, and twenty-five by difference of opinion. Many denizens of the Territory were miners, and the unsettling element of gold-dust hung in the air, breeding argument. Against the windows distant from the stove the early thin bright morning steadily mellowed, melting the panes clear until they ran, steamed faintly, and dried this fresh May day after the night's untimely cold; while still the Legislature sat in its shirt sleeves, and several statesmen had removed their boots. Even had appearances counted, the session was invisible from the street. Unlike a good number of houses in the town, the State-House (as they called it from old habit) was not all on the ground-floor for outsiders to stare into, but up a flight of wood steps to a wood gallery, from which, to be sure, the interior could be watched from several windows on both sides; but the journey up the steps was precisely enough to disincline the idle, and this was counted a sensible thing by the lawmakers. They took the ground that shaping any government for a raw wilderness community needed seclusion, and they set a high value upon unworried privacy.

The sun had set upon a concentrated Council, but it rose upon faces that looked momentous. Only the Governor's and Treasurer's were impassive, and they concealed something even graver than the matter in hand.

"I'll take a hun'red mo', Gove'nuh," said the member from Silver City, softly, his eyes on space. His name was Powhattan Wingo.

The Governor counted out the blue, white, and red chips to Wingo, pencilled some figures on a thickly ciphered and cancelled paper that bore in print the words "Territory of Idaho, Council Chamber," and then filled up his glass from the tin pitcher, adding a little sugar.

"And I'll trouble you fo' the toddy," Wingo added, always softly, and his eyes always on space. "Raise you ten, suh." This was to the Treasurer. Only the two were playing at present. The Governor was kindly acting as bank; the others were looking on.

"And ten," said the Treasurer.

"And ten," said Wingo.

"And twenty," said the Treasurer.

"And fifty," said Wingo, gently bestowing his chips in the middle of the table.

The Treasurer called.

The member from Silver City showed down five high hearts, and a light rustle went over the Legislature when the Treasurer displayed three twos and a pair of threes, and gathered in his harvest. He had drawn two cards, Wingo one; and losing to the lowest hand that could have beaten you is under such circumstances truly hard luck. Moreover, it was almost the only sort of luck that had attended Wingo since about half after three that morning. Seven hours of cards just a little lower than your neighbor's is searching to the nerves.

"Gove'nuh, I'll take a hun'red mo'," said Wingo; and once again the Legislature rustled lightly, and the new deal began.

Treasurer Hewley's winnings flanked his right, a pillared fortress on the table, built chiefly of Wingo's misfortunes. Hewley had not counted them, and his architecture was for neatness and not ostentation; yet the Legislature watched him arrange his gains with sullen eyes. It would have pleased him now to lose; it would have more than pleased him to be able to go to bed quite a long time ago. But winners cannot easily go to bed. The thoughtful Treasurer bet his money and deplored this luck that seemed likely to trap himself and the Governor in a predicament they had not foreseen, else they had never begun the game. All had taken a hand at first, and played so for several hours, until Fortune's wheel ran into a rut deeper than usual. Wingo slowly became the loser to several, then Hewley had forged ahead, winner from everybody. One by one they had dropped out, each meaning to go home, and all lingering to see the luck turn. It was an extraordinary run, a rare specimen, a breaker of records, something to refer to in the future as a standard of measure and an embellishment of reminiscence; quite enough to keep the Idaho Legislature up all night. And then, it was their friend who was losing. The only speaking in the room was the brief card talk of the two players.

"Five better," said Hewley, winner again four times in the last five.

"Ten," said Wingo.

"And twenty," said the Secretary and Treasurer.

"Call you."

"Three kings."

"They are good, suh. Gove'nuh, I'll take a hun'red mo'."

Upon this the wealthy and weary Treasurer made a try for liberty and bed. How would it do, he suggested, to have a round of jack-pots, say ten — or twenty, if the member from Silver City preferred—and then stop? It would do excellently, the member said, so softly that the Governor looked at him. But Wingo's large countenance remained inexpressive, his black eyes still impersonally fixed on space. He sat thus till his chips were counted to him, and then the eyes moved to watch the cards fall. The Governor hoped he might win now, under the jack-pot system. At noon he should have to disclose to Wingo and the Legislature something that would need the most cheerful and contented feelings to receive with any sort of calm. Wingo was behind the game to the tune of—the Governor gave up adding as he ran his eye over the figures of the bank's erased and tormented record, and he shook his head to himself. This was inadvertent.

"May I inquah who yo're shakin' yoh head at, suh?" said Wingo, wheeling upon the surprised Governor.

"Certainly," answered that official. "You." He was never surprised for very long. In 1867 it did not do to remain surprised in Idaho.

"And have I done anything which meets yoh disapprobation?" pursued the member from Silver City, enunciating with care.

"You have met my disapprobation."

Wingo's eye was on the Governor, and now his friends drew a little together, and as a unit sent a glance of suspicion at the lone bank.

"You will gratify me by being explicit, suh," said Wingo to the bank.

"Well, you've emptied the toddy."

"Ha-ha, Gove'nuh! I rose, suh, to yoh little fly. We'll awduh some mo'."

"Time enough when he comes for the breakfast things," said Governor Ballard, easily.

"As you say, suh. I'll open for five dolluhs." Wingo turned back to his game. He was winning, and as his luck continued, his voice ceased to be soft and became a shade truculent. The Governor's ears caught this change, and he also noted the lurking triumph in the faces of Wingo's fellow-statesmen. Cheerfulness and content were scarcely reigning yet in the Council Chamber of Idaho, as Ballard sat watching the friendly game. He was beginning to fear that he must leave the Treasurer alone and take some precautions outside. But he would have to be separated for some time from his ally, cut off from giving him any hints. Once the Treasurer looked at him, and he immediately winked reassuringly, but the Treasurer failed to respond. Hewley might be able to wink after everything was over, but he could not find it in his serious heart to do so now. He was wondering what would happen if this game should last till noon with the company in its present mood. Noon was the time fixed for paying the Legislative Assembly the compensation due for its services during this session; and the Governor and the Treasurer had put their heads together and arranged a surprise for the Legislative Assembly. They were not going to pay them.

A knock sounded at the door, and on seeing the waiter from the Overland enter, the Governor was seized with an idea. Perhaps precaution could be taken from the inside. "Take this pitcher," said he, "and have it refilled with the same. Joseph knows my mixture." But Joseph was night bar-tender, and now long in his happy bed, with a day successor in the saloon, and this one did not know the mixture. Ballard had foreseen this when he spoke, and that his writing a note of directions would seem quite natural.

"The receipt is as long as the drink,'

said a legislator, watching the Governor's pencil fly.

"He don't know where my private stock is located," explained Ballard. The waiter departed with the breakfast things and the note, and while the jack-pots continued, the Governor's mind went carefully over the situation:

Until lately, the Western citizen has known one every-day experience that no dweller in our thirteen original colonies has had for two hundred years. In Massachusetts they have not seen it since 1641; in Virginia not since 1628. It is that of belonging to a community of which every adult was born somewhere else. When you come to think of this a little, it is dislocating to many of your conventions. Let a citizen of Salem, for instance, or a well-established Philadelphia Quaker, try to imagine his Chief Justice fresh from Louisiana, his Mayor from Arkansas, his tax-collector from South Carolina, and himself recently arrived in a wagon from a thousand-mile drive. Such was the community that Ballard from one quarter of the horizon had travelled to in a wagon to govern, Wingo arriving on a mule from another quarter. People reached Boisé in three ways: by rail to a little west of the Missouri, after which it was wagon, saddle, or walk for the remaining fifteen hundred miles; from California it was shorter; and from Portland, Oregon, only about five hundred miles, and some of these more agreeable, by water up the Columbia. Thus it happened that salt often sold for its weight in gold-dust. A miner in the Bannock Basin would meet a freight teamster coming in with the staples of life, having journeyed perhaps sixty consecutive days through the desert, and valuing his salt highly. The two accordingly bartered in scales, white powder against yellow, and both parties content. Some in Boisé to-day can remember these bargains. After all, they were struck but thirty years ago. Governor Ballard and Treasurer Hewley did not come from the same place, but they constituted a minority of two in Territorial politics because they hailed from north of Mason and Dixon's line. Powhattan Wingo and the rest of the Council were from Pike County, Missouri. They had been Secessionists, some of them Knights of the Golden Circle; they had belonged to Price's Left Wing, and they flocked together. They were seven—two lying unwell at the Over-

land, five now present in the State-House with the Governor and Treasurer. Wingo, Gascon Claiborne, Gratiot des Pères, Pete Cawthon, and F. Jackson Gilet were their names. Besides this Council of seven were thirteen members of the Idaho House of Representatives, mostly of the same political feather with the Council, and they too would be present at noon to receive their pay. How Ballard and Hewley came to be a minority of two is a simple matter. Only twenty-five months had gone since Appomattox Court House. That surrender was presently followed by Johnston's to Sherman, at Durhams Station, and following this the various Confederate armies in Alabama, or across the Mississippi, or wherever they happened to be, had successively surrendered—but not Price's Left Wing. There was the wide open West under its nose, and no Grant or Sherman infesting that void. Why surrender? Wingos, Claibornes, and all, they melted away. Price's Left Wing sailed into the prairie and passed below the horizon. To know what it next did, you must, like Ballard or Hewley, pass below the horizon yourself, clean out of sight of the dome at Washington, and find in remote, snug Idaho (besides wild red men in quantities) a white colony of the ripest Southwestern persuasion, and a Legislature to fit. And if, like Ballard or Hewley, you were a Union man, and the President of the United States had appointed you Governor or Secretary of such a place, your days would be full of awkwardness, though your difference in creed might not hinder you from playing drawpoker with the unreconstructed. These Missourians were whole-souled, ample-natured males in many ways, but born with a habit of hasty shooting. The Governor, on setting foot in Idaho, had begun to study pistolship, but acquired thus in middle life it could never be with him that spontaneous art which it was with Price's Left Wing. Not that the weapons now lying loose about the State-House were brought for use there. Everybody always went armed in Boisé, as the gravestones impliedly testified. Still, the thought of what it might come to at noon, a bad quarter of an hour, did cross Ballard's mind, raising the image of a column in the morrow's paper: "An unfortunate occurrence has ended relations between esteemed gentlemen hitherto the warmest personal friends. . . . They will be laid to rest at 3 P.M. . . . As a last token of respect for our lamented Governor, the troops from Boisé Barracks. . . ." The Governor trusted that if his friends at the post were to do him any service it would not be a funeral one.

The new pitcher of toddy came from the Overland, the jack-pots continued, were nearing a finish, and Ballard began to wonder if anything had befallen a part of his note to the bar-tender, an enclosure addressed to another person.

"Ha, suh!" said Wingo to Hewley. "My pot again, I declah." The chips had been crossing the table his way, and he was now loser but six hundred dollars.

"Ye ain't goin' to whip Mizzooruh all night an' all day, ez a rule," observed Pete Cawthon, Councillor from Lost Leg.

"'Tis a long road that has no turnin', Gove'nuh," said F. Jackson Gilet, more urbanely. He had been in public life in Missouri, and was now President of the Council in Idaho. He, too, had arrived on a mule, but could at will summon a rhetoric dating from Cicero, and preserved by many luxuriant orators until after the middle of the present century.

"True," said the Governor, politely. "But here sits the long-suffering bank, whichever way the road turns. I'm sleepy."

"You sacrifice yo'self in the good cause," replied Gilet, pointing to the poker game. "Oneasy lies the head that wahs an office, suh." And Gilet bowed over his compliment.

The Governor thought so indeed. He looked at the Treasurer's strong-box, where lay the appropriation lately made by Congress to pay the Idaho Legislature for its services; and he looked at the Treasurer, in whose pocket lay the key of the strong-box. He was accountable to the Treasury at Washington for all money disbursed for Territorial expenses.

"Eleven twenty," said Wingo, "and only two hands mo' to play."

The Governor slid out his own watch.

"I'll scahsely recoup," said Wingo.

They dealt and played the hand, and the Governor strolled to the window.

"Three aces," Wingo announced, winning again handsomely. "I struck my luck too late," he commented to the onlookers. While losing he had been able to sustain a smooth reticence; now he gave his thoughts freely to the company,

and continually moved and fingered his increasing chips. The Governor was still looking out of the window, where he could see far up the street, when Wingo won the last hand, which was small. "That ends it, suh, I suppose?" he said to Hewley, letting the pack of cards linger in his grasp.

"I wouldn't let him off yet," said Ballard to Wingo from the window, with sudden joviality, and he came back to the players. "I'd make him throw five cold hands with me."

"Ah, Gove'nuh, that's yoh spo'tin' blood! Will you do it, Mistuh Hewley—a hun'red a hand?"

Mr. Hewley did it; and winning the first, he lost the second, third, and fourth in the space of an eager minute, while the Councillors drew their chairs close.

"Let me see," said Wingo, calculating, "if I lose this—why still—" He lost. "But I'll not have to ask you to accept my papuh, suh. Wingo liquidates. Fo'ty days at six dolluhs a day makes six times fo' is twenty-fo'—two hun'red an' fo'ty dolluhs spot cash in hand at noon, without computation of mileage to and from Silver City at fo' dolluhs every twenty miles, estimated according to the nearest usually travelled route." He was reciting part of the statute providing mileage for Idaho legislators. He had never served the public before, and he knew all the laws concerning compensation by heart. "You'll not have to wait fo' yoh money, suh," he concluded.

"Well, Mr. Wingo," said Governor Ballard, "it depends on yourself whether your pay comes to you or not." He spoke cheerily. "If you don't see things my way, our Treasurer will have to wait for his money." He had not expected to break the news just so, but it made as easy a beginning as any.

"See things yoh way, suh?"

"Yes. As it stands at present I cannot take the responsibility of paying you."

"The United States pays me, suh. My compensation is provided by act of Congress."

"I confess I am unable to discern your responsibility, Gove'nuh," said F. Jackson Gilet. "Mr. Wingo has faithfully attended the session, and is, like every gentleman present, legally entitled to his emoluments."

"You can all readily become entitled—"

"All? Am I — are my friends — included in this new depa'tyuh?"

"The difficulty applies generally, Mr. Gilet."

"Do I understand the Gove'nuh to insinuate—nay, gentlemen, do not rise! Be seated, I beg." For the Councillors had leaped to their feet.

"Whar's our money?" said Pete Cawthon. "Our money was put in thet yere box."

Ballard flushed angrily, but a knock at the door stopped him, and he merely said, "Come in."

A trooper, a corporal, stood at the entrance, and the disordered Council endeavored to look usual in a stranger's presence. They resumed their seats, but it was not easy to look usual on such short notice.

"Captain Paisley's compliments," said the soldier, mechanically, "and will Governor Ballard take supper with him this evening?"

"Thank Captain Paisley," said the Governor (his tone was quite usual), "and say that official business connected with the end of the session makes it imperative for me to be at the State-House. Imperative."

The trooper withdrew. He was a heavy-built, handsome fellow, with black mustache and black eyes that watched through two straight narrow slits beneath straight black brows. His expression in the Council Chamber had been of the regulation military indifference, and as he went down the steps he irrelevantly sang an old English tune:

"'Since first I saw your face I resolved
    To honor and re—'

I guess," he interrupted himself as he unhitched his horse, "parrot and monkey hev broke loose."

The Legislature, always in its shirt sleeves, the cards on the table, and the toddy on the floor, sat calm a moment, cooled by this brief pause from the first heat of its surprise, while the clatter of Corporal Jones's galloping shrank quickly into silence.

II.

Captain Paisley walked slowly from the adjutant's office at Boisé Barracks to his quarters, and his orderly walked behind him. The captain carried a letter in his hand, and the orderly, though distant a respectful ten paces, could hear him swearing plain as day. When he reached his front door Mrs. Paisley met him.

"Jim," cried she, "two more chickens froze in the night." And the delighted orderly heard the captain so plainly that he had to blow his nose or burst.

The lady, merely remarking "My goodness, Jim," retired immediately to the kitchen, where she had a soldier cook baking, and feared he was not quite sober enough to do it alone. The captain had paid eighty dollars for forty hens this year at Boisé, and twenty-nine had now passed away, victims to the climate. His wise wife perceived his extreme language not to have been all on account of hens, however; but he never allowed her to share in his professional worries, so she staid safe with the baking, and he sat in the front room with a cigar in his mouth.

Boisé was a two-company post without a major, and Paisley being senior captain was in command, an office to which he did not object. But his duties so far this month of May had not pleased him in the least. Theoretically, you can have at a two-company post the following responsible people: one major, two captains, four lieutenants, a doctor, and a chaplain. The major has been spoken of; it is almost needless to say that the chaplain was on leave, and had never been seen at Boisé by any of the present garrison; two of the lieutenants were also on leave, and two on surveying details—they had influence at Washington; the other captain was on a scout with General Crook somewhere near the Malheur Agency, and the doctor had only arrived this week. There had resulted a period when Captain Paisley was his own adjutant, quartermaster, and post surgeon, with not even an efficient sergeant to rely upon; and during this period his wife had staid a good deal in the kitchen. Happily the doctor's coming had given relief to the hospital steward and several patients, and to the captain not only an equal, but an old friend, with whom to pour out his disgust; and together every evening they freely expressed their opinion of the War Department and its treatment of the Western army.

There were steps at the door, and Paisley hurried out. "Only you!" he exclaimed, with such frank vexation that the doctor laughed loudly. "Come in, man, come in," Paisley continued, leading him strongly by the arm, sitting him down, and giving him a cigar. "Here's a pretty how de do!"

"More Indians?" inquired Dr. Tuck.

"Bother! they're nothing. It's Senators—Councillors—whatever the Territorial devils call themselves."

"Gone on the war-path?" the doctor said, quite ignorant how nearly he had touched the Council.

"Precisely, man. War-path. Here's the Governor writing me they'll be scalping him in the State-House at twelve o'clock. It's past 11.30. They'll be whetting knives about now." And the captain roared.

"I know you haven't gone crazy," said the doctor, "but who has?"

"The lot of them. Ballard's a good man, and—what's his name?—the little Secretary. The balance are just mad dogs—mad dogs. Look here: 'Dear Captain'—that's Ballard to me. I just got it—'I find myself unexpectedly hampered this morning. The South shows signs of being too solid. Unless I am supported, my plan for bringing our Legislature to terms will have to be postponed. Hewley and I are more likely to be brought to terms ourselves—a bad precedent to establish in Idaho. Noon is the hour for drawing salaries. Ask me to supper as quick as you can, and act on my reply.' I've asked him," continued Paisley, "but I haven't told Mrs. Paisley to cook anything extra yet." The captain paused to roar again, shaking Tuck's shoulder for sympathy. Then he explained the situation in Idaho to the justly bewildered doctor. Ballard had confided many of his difficulties lately to Paisley.

"He means you're to send troops?" Tuck inquired.

"What else should the poor man mean?"

"Are you sure it's constitutional?"

"Hang constitutional! What do I know about their legal quibbles at Washington?"

"But, Paisley—"

"They're unsurrendered rebels, I tell you. Never signed a parole."

"But the general amnesty—"

"Bother general amnesty! Ballard represents the Federal government in this Territory, and Uncle Sam's army is here to protect the Federal government. If Ballard calls on the army it's our business to obey, and if there's any mistake in judgment it's Ballard's, not mine." Which was sound soldier common-sense, and happened to be equally good law. This is not always the case.

"You haven't got any force to send," said Tuck.

This was true. General Crook had taken with him both Captain Sinclair's infantry and the troop (or company, as cavalry was also then called) of the First.

"A detail of five or six with a reliable non-commissioned officer will do to remind them it's the United States they're bucking against," said Paisley. "There's a deal in the moral of these things. Crook—" Paisley broke off and ran to the door. "Hold his horse!" he called out to the orderly; for he had heard the hoofs, and was out of the house before Corporal Jones had fairly arrived. So Jones sprang off and hurried up, saluting. He delivered his message.

"Um—umpra—what's that? Is it *imperative* you mean?" suggested Paisley.

"Yes, sir," said Jones, reforming his pronunciation of that unaccustomed word. "He said it twiced."

"What were they doing?"

"Blamed if I—beg the captain's pardon—they looked like they was waitin' fer me to git out."

"Go on—go on. How many were there?"

"Seven, sir. There was Governor Ballard and Mr. Hewley and—well, them's all the names I know. But," Jones hastened on with eagerness, "I've saw them five other fellows before at a—at—" The corporal's voice failed, and he stood looking at the captain.

"Well? Where?"

"At a cock-fight, sir," murmured Jones, casting his eyes down.

A slight sound came from the room where Tuck was seated, listening, and Paisley's round gray eyes rolled once, then steadied themselves fiercely upon Jones.

"Did you notice anything further unusual, corporal?"

"No, sir, except they was excited in there. Looked like they might be goin' to hev considerable rough house—a fuss. I mean, sir. Two was in their socks. I counted four guns on a table."

"Take five men and go at once to the State-House. If the Governor needs assistance you will give it, but do nothing hasty. Stop trouble, and make none. You've got twenty minutes."

"Captain — if anybody needs arrest-in'—"

"You must be judge of that." Paisley went into the house. There was no time for particulars.

"Snakes!" remarked Jones. He jumped on his horse, and dashed down the slope to the men's quarters.

"Crook may be here any day or any hour," said Paisley, returning to the doctor. "With two companies in the background, I think Price's Left Wing will subside this morning."

"Supposing they don't?"

"I'll go myself; and when it gets to Washington that the commanding officer at Boisé personally interfered with the Legislature of Idaho, it 'll shock 'em to that extent that the government will have to pay for a special commission of investigation and two tons of red tape. I've got to trust to that corporal's good sense. I haven't another man at the post."

Corporal Jones had three-quarters of a mile to go, and it was ten minutes before noon, so he started his five men at a run. His plan was to walk and look quiet as soon as he reached the town, and thus excite no curiosity. The citizens were accustomed to the sight of passing soldiers. Jones had thought out several things, and he was not going to order bayonets fixed until the final necessary moment. "Stop trouble and make none" was firm in his mind. He had not long been a corporal. It was still his first enlistment. His habits were by no means exemplary; and his frontier personality, strongly developed by six years of vagabonding before he enlisted, was scarcely yet disciplined into the military machine of the regulation pattern that it should and must become before he could be counted a model soldier. His captain had promoted him to steady him, if that could be, and to give his better qualities a chance. Since then he had never been drunk at the wrong time. Two years ago it would not have entered his free-lance heart to be reticent with any man, high or low, about any pleasure in which he saw fit to indulge ; to-day he had been shy over confessing to the commanding officer his leaning to cock-fights—a sign of his approach to the correct mental attitude of the enlisted man. Being corporal had wakened in him a new instinct,

and this State-house affair was the first chance he had had to show himself. He gave the order to proceed at a walk in such a tone that one of the troopers whispered to another, "Specimen ain't going to forget he's wearing a chevron."

III.

The brief silence among the Councillors that Jones and his invitation to supper had caused was first broken by F. Jackson Gilet.

"Gentlemen," he said, "as President of the Council I rejoice in an interruption that has given pause to our haste and saved us from ill-considered expressions of opinion. The Gove'nuh has, I confess, surprised me. Befo' examining the legal aspect of our case I will ask the Gove'nuh if he is familiar with the sundry statutes applicable."

"I think so," Ballard replied, pleasantly.

"I had supposed," continued the President of the Council—"nay, I had congratulated myself that our weightiuh tasks of law-making and so fo'th were consummated yesterday, our thirty-ninth day, and that our friendly game of last night would be, as it were, the finis that crowned with pleashuh the work of a session memorable for its harmony."

This was not wholly accurate, but near enough. The Governor had vetoed several bills, but Price's Left Wing had had much more than the required two-thirds vote of both Houses to make these bills laws over the Governor's head. This may be called harmony in a manner. Gilet now went on to say that any doubts which the Governor entertained concerning the legality of his paying any salaries could easily be settled without entering upon discussion. Discussion at such a juncture could not but tend towards informality. The President of the Council could well remember most unfortunate discussions in Missouri between the years 1856 and 1860, in some of which he had had the honor to take part—*minima pars*, gentlemen ! Here he digressed elegantly upon civil dissensions, and Ballard, listening to him and marking the slow, sure progress of the hour, told himself that never before had Gilet's oratory seemed more welcome or less lengthy. A plan had come to him, the orator next announced, a way out of the present dilemma, simple and regular in every aspect. Let some gentleman present now kindly draft a bill setting forth in its preamble the acts of Congress providing for the Legislature's compensation, and let this bill in conclusion provide that all members immediately receive the full amount due for their services. At noon both Houses would convene; they would push back the clock, and pass this bill.

"Then, Gove'nuh," said Gilet, "you can amply vindicate yo'self by a veto, which, together with our votes on reconsideration of yoh objections, will be reco'ded in the journal of our proceedings, and copies transmitted to Washington within thirty days as required by law. Thus, suh, will you become absolved from all responsibility."

The orator's face, while he explained this simple and regular way out of the dilemma, beamed with acumen and statesmanship. Here they would make a law, and the Governor must obey the law!

Nothing could have been more to Ballard's mind as he calculated the fleeting minutes than this peaceful pompous farce. "Draw your bill, gentlemen," he said. "I would not object if I could."

The Revised Statutes of the United States was procured from among the pistols and opened at the proper page. Gascon Claiborne, upon another sheet of paper headed "Territory of Idaho, Council Chamber," set about formulating some phrases which began "Whereas," and Gratiot des Pères read aloud to him from the statutes. Ballard conversed apart with Hewley; in fact, there was much conversing aside.

"'Third March, 1863, c. 117, s. 8, v. 12, p. 811,'" dictated Des Pères.

"Skip the chaptuhs and sections," said Claiborne. "We only require the date."

"'Third March, 1863. The sessions of the Legislative Assemblies of the several Territories of the United States shall be limited to forty days' duration.'"

"Wise provision that," whispered Ballard. "No telling how long a poker game might last."

But Hewley could not take anything in this spirit. "Genuine business was not got through till yesterday," he said.

"'The members of each branch of the Legislature,'" read Des Pères, "'shall receive a compensation of six dollars per day during the sessions herein provided for, and they shall receive such mileage as now provided by law: Provided, That

the President of the Council and the Speaker of the House of Representatives shall each receive a compensation of ten dollars a day.'"

At this the President of the Council waved a deprecatory hand to signify that it was principle, not profit, for which he battled. They had completed their whereases, incorporating the language of the several sections as to how the appropriation should be made, who disbursed such money, mileage, and, in short, all things pertinent to their bill, when Pete Cawthon made a suggestion.

"Ain't there anything 'bout how much the Gove'nuh gits?" he asked.

"And the Secretary?" added Wingo.

"Oh, you can leave us out," said Ballard.

"Pardon me, Gove'nuh," said Gilet. "You stated that yoh difficulty was not confined to Mr. Wingo or any individual gentleman, but was general. Does it not apply to yo'self, suh? Do you not need any bill?"

"Oh no," said Ballard, laughing. "I don't need any bill."

"And why not?" said Cawthon. "You've jist ez much earned yoh money ez us fellers."

"Quite as much," said Ballard. "But we're not alike—at present."

Gilet grew very stately. "Except certain differences in political opinions, suh, I am not awah of how we differ in merit as public servants of this Territory."

"The difference is of your own making, Mr. Gilet, and no bill you could frame would cure it or destroy my responsibility. You cannot make any law contrary to a law of the United States."

"Contrary to a law of the United States? And what, suh, has the United States to say about my pay I have earned in Idaho?"

"Mr. Gilet, there has been but one government in this country since April, 1865, and as friends you and I have often agreed to differ as to how many there were before then. That government has a law compelling people like you and me to go through a formality, which I have done, and you and your friends have refused to do each time it has been suggested to you. I have raised no point until now, having my reasons, which were mainly that it would make less trouble now for the Territory of which I have been appointed Governor. I am held ac-

"'DON'T NOBODY HURT ANYBODY,' SAID SPECIMEN JONES."

countable to the Secretary of the Treasury semiannually for the manner in which the appropriation has been expended. If you will kindly hand me that book—"

Gilet, more and more stately, handed Ballard the Revised Statutes, which he had taken from Des Pères. The others were watching Ballard with gathering sullenness, as they had watched Hewley while he was winning Wingo's money, only now the sullenness was of a more decided complexion.

Ballard turned the pages. "'Second July, 1862. Every person elected or appointed to any office of honor or profit, either in the civil, military, or naval service, . . . shall, before entering upon the duties of such office, and before being entitled to any salary or other emoluments thereof, take and subscribe the following oath: I—'"

"What does this mean, suh?" said Gilet.

"It means there is no difference in our positions as to what preliminaries the law requires of us, no matter how we may vary in convictions. I as Governor have taken the oath of allegiance to the United States, and you as Councillor must do the same before you can get your pay. Look at the book."

"I decline, suh. I repudiate yoh proposition. There is a wide difference in our positions."

"What do you understand it to be, Mr. Gilet?" Ballard's temper was rising.

"If you have chosen to take an oath that did not go against yoh convictions —"

"Oh, Mr. Gilet!" said Ballard, smiling. "Look at the book." He would not risk losing his temper through further discussion. He would stick to the law as it lay open before them.

But the Northern smile sent Missouri logic to the winds. "In what are you superior to me, suh, that I cannot choose? Who are you that I and these gentlemen must take oaths befo' you?"

"Not before me. Look at the book."

"I'll look at no book, suh. Do you mean to tell me you have seen me day aftuh day and meditated this treacherous attempt?"

"There is no attempt and no treachery, Mr. Gilet. You could have taken the oath long ago, like other officials. You can take it to day — or take the consequences."

"What? You threaten me, suh? Do I understand you to threaten me? Gentlemen of the Council, it seems Idaho will be less free than Missouri unless we look to it." The President of the Council had risen in his indignant oratorical might, and his more and more restless friends glared admiration at him. "When was the time that Price's Left Wing surrendered?" asked the orator. "Nevuh! Others have, be it said to their shame. We have not toiled these thousand miles fo' that! Others have crooked the pliant hinges of the knee that thrift might follow fawning. As fo' myself, two grandfathers who fought fo' our libuhties rest in the soil of Virginia, and two uncles who fought in the Revolution sleep in the land of the Dark and Bloody Ground. With such blood in my veins I will nevuh, nevuh, nevuh submit to Northern rule and dictation. I will risk all to be with the Southern people, and if defeated I can, with a patriot of old, exclaim,

'More true joy an exile feels
Than Caesuh with a Senate at his heels.'

Ay, gentlemen! And we will not be defeated! Our rights are here and are ours." He stretched his arm towards the Treasurer's strong-box, and his enthusiastic audience rose at the rhetoric. " Contain yo'selves, gentlemen," said the orator. "Twelve o'clock and our bill!"

"I've said my say," said Ballard, remaining seated.

"An' what 'll ye do?" inquired Pete Cawthon from the agitated group.

"I forbid you to touch that!" shouted Ballard. He saw Wingo moving towards the box.

"Gentlemen, do not resort—" began Gilet.

But small, iron-gray Hewley snatched his pistol from the box, and sat down astraddle of it, guarding his charge. At this hostile movement the others precipitated themselves towards the table where lay their weapons, and Governor Ballard, whipping his own from his armhole, said, as he covered the table: "Go easy, gentlemen! Don't hurt our Treasurer!"

"Don't nobody hurt anybody," said Specimen Jones, opening the door.

This prudent corporal had been looking in at a window, and hearing plainly for the past two minutes, and he had his men posted. Each member of the Council stopped as he stood, his pistol not quite yet attained; Ballard restored his own to its armhole and sat in his chair; little Hewley sat on his box; and F. Jackson Gilet towered haughtily, gazing at the intruding blue uniform of the United States.

"I'll hev to take you to the commanding officer," said Jones briefly to Hewley. "You and yer box."

"Oh my stars and stripes, but that's a keen move!" rejoiced Ballard to himself. "He's arresting *us*."

In Jones's judgment, after he had taken in the situation, this had seemed the only possible way to stop trouble without making any, and therefore, even now, bayonets were not fixed. Best not ruffle Price's Left Wing just now, if you could avoid it. For a new corporal it was well thought and done. But it was high noon, the clock not pushed back, and punctual Representatives strolling innocently towards their expected pay. There must be no time for a gathering and possible reaction. "I'll hev to clear this State-House out." Jones decided. "We're makin' an arrest," he said aloud, "and we want a little room." The outside by-standers stood back obediently, but the Councillors delayed. Their pistols were, with Ballard's and Hewley's, of course in custody. "Here," said Jones, restoring them. "Go home now. The commanding officer's waitin' fer the prisoner. Put yer boots on, sir, and leave," he added to Pete Cawthon, who still stood in his stockings. "I don't want to hev to disperse anybody more'n what I've done."

Disconcerted Price's Left Wing now saw file out between armed soldiers the Treasurer and his strong-box; and thus guarded they were brought to Boisé Barracks, whence they did not reappear. The Governor also went to the post.

After delivering Hewley and his treasure to the commanding officer, Jones with his five troopers went to the sutler's store and took a drink at Jones's expense. Then one of them asked the corporal to have another. But Jones refused. "If a man drinks much of that," said he (and the whiskey certainly was of a livid, unlikely flavor), "he's liable to go home and steal his own pants." He walked away to his quarters, and as he went they heard him thoughtfully humming his

most inveterate song, "Ye shepherds tell me have you seen my Flora pass this way."

But poisonous whiskey was not the inner reason for his moderation. He felt very much like a responsible corporal today, and the troopers knew it. "Jones has done himself a good turn in this fuss," they said. "He'll be changing his chevron."

That afternoon the Legislature sat in the State-House and read to itself in the Revised Statutes all about oaths. It is not believed that any of them sat up another night; sleeping on a problem is often much better. Next morning the commanding officer and Governor Ballard were called upon by F. Jackson Gilet and the Speaker of the House. Every one was civil and hearty as possible. Gilet pronounced the Captain's whiskey "equal to any at the Southern, Saint Louey," and conversed for some time about the cold season, General Crook's remarkable astuteness in dealing with Indians, and other topics of public interest. "And concernin' yoh difficulty yesterday, Gove'nuh," said he, "I've been consulting the laws, suh, and I perceive yoh construction is entahley correct."

And so the Legislature signed that form of oath prescribed for participants in the late Rebellion, and Hewley did not have to wait for his poker-money. He and Wingo played many subsequent games; for, as they all said, in referring to the matter, "A little thing like that should nevuh stand between friends."

Thus was accomplished by Ballard, Paisley—and Jones—the Second Missouri Compromise, at Boisé City, Idaho, 1867—an eccentric moment in the eccentric years of our development westward, and historic also. That it has gone unrecorded until now is because of Ballard's modesty, Paisley's preference for the sword, and Jones's hatred of the pen. He was never known to write except, later, in the pages of his company roster, and such unavoidable official places; for the troopers were prophetic. In not many months there was no longer a Corporal Jones, but a person widely known as Sergeant Jones of Company A; called also the "Singing Sergeant"; but still familiar to his intimate friends as "Specimen."

WHEATFIELDS OF THE NORTH WEST

IN the summer of 1879 a number of agricultural meetings were held in different parts of England to consider the influence of American competition on the price of wheat—a subject which the farmers and land-owners were then learning to regard as one destined to receive more anxious consideration from them than any other of a political nature. At one of these meetings Lord Beaconsfield, in the course of an address, is reported to have said that supremacy as a grain-growing country would soon be attained by Canada, and that with this expectation thousands of persons from the States were hastening to change their homes to the other side of the boundary line. This statement, brought into general notice on this side of the Atlantic at the time by the eminent position of the speaker, was held plainly to lack trustworthiness; and our press, having simply compared the quantities of wheat raised in the year preceding by the two countries assumed to be rivals, and having proved that the movement of immigration between Canada and the United States was in favor of the latter, deemed further refutation unnecessary. But the editors of our press, in common with other persons, do not at present appreciate that part of the United States which lies west of Lake Superior, and it may be doubted if it is generally known further than as a country the failure of which to sustain the Northern Pacific Railroad project was the harbinger of the unwelcome financial crisis of 1873, and now more lately as the location of several noted wheat farms conducted on a gigantic scale; whilst hardly so much could be told of the larger and more valuable portion of this land, distinguished throughout its extent by certain peculiarities of soil and climate, which lies north of the boundary line, and forms the new provinces of Canada. However, this country has the elements to support the most prosperous people on the continent, if it is not destined soon to put the established districts of our grain supply into the same position as they have put the farming lands of England.

The Red. River of the North rises near the head-waters of the Mississippi, but flowing in the opposite direction to the larger river, forms the boundary between Minnesota and Dakota, and entering the Canadian province of Manitoba, finally discharges itself into Lake Winnipeg. The prairie drained by this river and its tributaries contains, roughly, 40,000,000 acres, and, speaking from our stand-point, is the beginning of the vast section of fertile land which, stretching in a widening belt to the Rocky Mountains, is drained by the Saskatchewan rivers, and further north by the Athabasca and the Peace. This Canadian division contains certainly 150,000,000 acres of land, and may probably be found to include 250,000,000 acres when a thorough survey shall have been made by the Dominion government. The southern limit of this section of fertile land has a latitude as high as that of Montreal, and what may be called its northern limit lies distant one thousand miles. The climate, however, differs essentially from that found in Eastern British America at a corresponding distance from the equator. The isothermal lines, as they approach Hudson Bay from the Pacific Ocean, bend decidedly to the south. The mean temperature of the Peace River Valley varies but little from the mean temperature of the valley of the Red River. Throughout the country wheat may be planted in April, or fully as early as spring wheat is sown in the United States. But as the summer is not warm enough to ripen Indian corn, and the winter, while it lasts, permits no thaw to take place, the climate is a cold one, compared with that over the grain States of the Mississippi Valley; and to this fact, doubtless, the superior quality of the cereals raised here is due. In 1872, railway construction had extended far enough in the Northwest to afford an entrance to this new territory. But the disasters which speedily overtook the two pioneer lines stopped at once all immigration. Three years ago it was resumed. Since that time, it may be safely asserted, in no other part of the United States has it gone forward with so much vigor, and been attended with so much prosperity, as in the Red River Valley. The towns of Fargo and Grand Forks in Dakota, and Winnipeg across the border—the country around them presenting no resources except a prolific soil—exhibit a growth as rapid, and commercial transactions as heavy, as cities which have sprung up in the richest mining districts of the Rocky Mountains. Intense as the character of the immigration has been, it has not yet exercised any disturbing influence on the grain market. The part of the land reclaimed is comparatively trifling. At various points in the valley farms have been laid out, and fields of wheat, some of which are thousands of acres in extent, have been cultivated, but the greater part of the land is still an unbroken prairie, without a trace of settlement. The immigration into the valley of the Red River, and the smaller immigration into the valleys of the Saskatchewan, have been of most importance in proving that this country produces the cereals in a state of perfection which has not manifested itself farther south—a result possibly to have been anticipated from its latitude and soil. In a climate warmer than is needed to bring it to maturity, wheat shows an imperfect development of grain, with a deficiency in weight. It is always more subject to drought, the hot sun acting both to evaporate moisture from the ground and to burn the plant afterward. The same facts are observable in the growth of other cereals. Even grass shows a marked change in value made by latitude. Many of our stock-raisers in the Southwest do not sell their cattle in Texas or New Mexico, but drive them from the coarse and poor vegetation there to feed on the sweeter and more nutritious grasses of Montana, the increased price which the cattle bring in their improved condition paying for a drive of fifteen hundred miles.

The superior quality of the wheat raised in this new country will be best shown by a comparison made in figures. Duluth and Chicago are selected to furnish a comparison, as the former is the general point of shipment of the northern wheat, and the latter is the place of largest receipts in the grain States further south. To explain the use of the figures below, it may be noted that, for the convenience of trade, on arrival at one of the larger places of receipts, grain is inspected by experts who are public officers, and graded according to its soundness and weight. The difference in market value between the grades is considerable. Take for the purpose the crop of 1880. During the last three months of that year there were inspected at Duluth 1,778,764 bushels of wheat. Leaving out of consideration the fraction 86,000 bushels, which were of the soft variety, and, it is assumed, came to this port from southern counties of Minnesota, the wheat graded as follows, the amounts being expressed by per cent.:

AT DULUTH.

Grade No. 1, Hard................. 87 per cent.
Grade No. 2 .... 11 "
Grade No. 3 .... 1 "
Rejected .... 1 "

During the same months there were inspected at Chicago 1,571,262 bushels of winter wheat, and 7,988,816 bushels of spring wheat, which graded as below:

AT CHICAGO.

Winter Wheat.	Spring Wheat.
Grade No. 1.. 1 per cent.	Grade No. 1.. 1 per cent.
Grade No. 2..53 "	Grade No. 2..66 "
Grade No. 3..34 "	Grade No. 3..23 "
Rejected ....12 "	Rejected ....10 "

As to the respective market values: at the city of Buffalo, where the northern and southern grain, coming over the lakes from Duluth and Chicago, first meet in a general market, the following were the average prices per bushel during the months mentioned above:

No. 1, Hard Duluth............... 1.18
No. 2,   " 1.15¼

No. 1, Red Winter..1.14	No. 1, Spring 1.13½
No. 2, " ..1.11	No. 2, " 1.08
No. 3, " ..1.06	No. 3, " 0.95
Rejected " ..1.00	Rejected " 0.80

The southern grown wheat may have in the future, it is probable, a still lower relative value. It alone has been used for export to foreign countries, whose mills were not adapted for grinding with the best results the hard Manitoba wheat, even if the production of the latter were large enough to bring its merits into notice. Now, however, that the improved methods of milling employed at Minneapolis are being introduced into England, with an increased supply of hard wheat, there will doubtless come the same preference as exists in this country for a grain having its special properties. These improvements in milling have had a most important bearing on the value of all the varieties of hard wheat. The secret of the higher price which the Duluth wheat commands over the best grades from other localities is the fact that it makes a flour of greater strength. The northern wheat is flinty, and contains more gluten; the southern is soft, and contains more starch. Until lately, however, the farmer in Northern Minnesota found that his grain, although by an analysis of its parts most valuable, brought the lowest prices paid in market, because, with the method then used for separating bran from the middlings, it made a dark-colored flour. A few years ago the defects were remedied by the millers at Minneapolis, and so successfully that their method of treating wheat has been very generally adopted throughout the country. The result has been that the strong flour made of Red River wheat is quoted at a price of two dollars per barrel over other kinds—a difference which the baker is willing to pay, because from a given number of pounds it makes the greatest number of pounds of bread; and the private consumer is willing to pay, because it furnishes the most nutritive food. The hard Northern wheat, instead of being the lowest, has taken its rightful place as the highest priced on the list of grain.

The land is also more prolific. The experience of the wheat-raisers in Manitoba has now been of sufficient length to make understood some of the natural advantages extended to this country for returning large and certain crops. Situated in a high latitude, there is afforded to vegetation a greater number of hours of sun each day during the entire season of growth. The winter cold, continuous and with light falls of snow, freezes the ground to an extraordinary depth. Under the disintegrating power of frost, the lower soil is broken up each season for the sustenance of plants as thoroughly as if done by the best artificial means. This is not the only service performed by the frost; later, throughout the period of growth, it keeps within reach of the roots a moisture which renders drought impossible. But most noteworthy is the soil itself—an alluvial black loam, with an average depth of twenty inches, resting on a subsoil of clay. It is very heavy, when wet having a tar-like consistency, and rich in the elements which are believed to nourish vegetation. Dropped into this soil, with the other favoring circumstances, seed springs up and grows with an extraordinary vigor, and gives a sound and abundant crop. The average yield of wheat per acre in the Red River Valley, north of Fargo, where the soil becomes heavier and more characteristic, is twenty-three bushels. In Manitoba and the Saskatchewan region the average is greater, and amounts to twenty-eight bushels. These facts become more striking when compared with results in the district of the wheat supply at present. In Illinois the average for wheat to the acre is seventeen bushels; in Iowa, ten; in Wisconsin, less than ten; in Kansas, ten; while in Texas it is eight and one-half bushels. Nor does the land seem to deteriorate under a course of cropping, as does the lighter soil of States in the south. In the early part of the century, Lord Selkirk, fascinated by the resources which he beheld in the Lake Winnipeg region, formed the idea of developing them with colonists from his country. Shut off from any market for their grain, and located in a spot at that time practically inaccessible, the Highlanders who came over in accordance with the ill-considered plan of Lord Selkirk were subjected to a great deal of hardship. But many families staid. The town of Kildonan, near the mouth of the Red River, started by these colonists, has been occupied by them and their descendants ever since. By their farming the powers of the soil have been pretty thoroughly tested. In this settlement there are fields which have been sown to wheat every season for the last thirty-five years without the application of any fertilizers, and which in 1879 yielded an average of over thirty bushels to the acre. A soil which raises one grain in such perfection is, of course, suitable for other purposes. Stimulated by the presence of buyers for the mills making the high-priced flour, who offer immediate payment for all their crop, the farmers have so far devoted all their energy to increasing their acreage of wheat. But the other cereals—oats, rye, and barley—sown to supply local needs, show a like abundant yield, and when brought to outside markets these products of northern soil will be found entitled to the high estimation accorded to the present staple.

Of equal importance with the natural resources here is the means of getting the products to market. In the United States the importance of this question will be fully appreciated, and it becomes a matter deserving attention when directly at our doors a large body of land of unusual fertility is being invited to compete in markets which have been opened to us by an efficient system of transportation, and found very profitable. Apart from any question of loss or gain to the trade of the United States, the subject itself presents many features to excite an interest. The scheme of the roads for traffic at present is so little complicated as to be readily understood. The projects now under way are to cost vast sums of money. Their completion will present much that is novel in the systems of the continent. On the American side, the Northern Pacific Railway, at the end of 1880, had built west of the Rocky Mountains a section of 150 miles, beginning at a point 260 miles from the terminus on Puget Sound, and extending eastward. During the year they had pushed westward the main road from Duluth to the Yellowstone River in Montana. By the collapse in 1873 the company were left with a very poor credit, and to continue their work they have been obliged to rely mainly on the earnings of the completed part and the proceeds of the sale of the land grant. The progress made since that time toward completing the transcontinental line illustrates the rapid way in which this country has of late been developing. The construction last year was 360 miles of new road. Recently measures to secure money for continuing the work as fast as it may be required have been successfully taken, and it is believed that the line from Lake Superior to the Pacific Ocean will be finished in 1883. As a terminus, the port of Duluth has hitherto been sufficient during the season of navigation, which lasts, however, only six months. During the remainder of the year grain is left to go eastward by rail transportation around the southern end of Lake Michigan. This lake has been the means of shutting off the Northwestern States from any direct land communication with the East. North of Chicago there is not at present a single line of railway from the prairies. The States of Wisconsin, Iowa, Minnesota, and the adjoining portion of Dakota are covered with iron roads, but they are all tributary to the Eastern system at the head of Lake Michigan—a fact which sufficiently accounts for the steady and rapid growth of the city at that point. The presence of Lake Michigan and Lake Superior, and the character of the country north and south of the latter, which is hilly, and abounds in immense ledges of rock, render direct rail connection of the Red River territory with the East a difficult and expensive matter. But the development of resources which are so valuable and complete will doubtless in time create an extensive system of rail communication, which shall form the shortest possible routes to the sea-board, and be free of the charges at an intermediate point of distribution. The construction of two lines, one along the south shore of Lake Superior and the other on the north shore, has been definitely decided upon, and work on the first line has been begun. The Northern Pacific Railway is now engaged in building a road from Duluth eastward to the charter terminus at Montreal River. From this point a road, part of which is finished, is to be extended to Sault Ste. Marie. Here a combination of Canadian railways is to give communication with Montreal and New York. The distance from the Red River to New York by this route, when completed, will be at least two hundred miles shorter than by the expensive one through Chicago. Another railway, the St. Paul, Minneapolis, and Manitoba, located at right angles to the line of the Northern Pacific, extends from St. Paul, on both sides of the Red River to the international boundary, where it is met by a branch of the Canadian Pacific. This road carries a large part of the wheat raised in the Red River Valley to the mills at Minneapolis, and until the present time has furnished the only adequate means of entrance to the province of Manitoba. By the construction of 230 miles in 1880 this company now owns nearly one thousand miles of road, and its extensions westward bid fair to make it equally active with the Northern Pacific in developing this country.

On the Canadian side, Hudson Bay may eventually become of the first importance as an outlet for foreign shipments of grain. The bay is free of ice, and its southwestern harbors are open fully three months—a short season of navigation, but sufficient for a sailing vessel to clear with two cargoes for Liverpool, which ships carrying grain from California around Cape Horn can not accomplish, taking the entire year. But it may be doubted whether the hope of utilizing this short road to Europe will be realized for a considerable time. At York Factory, the Nelson, a river flowing from the lakes of Manitoba, empties into the bay. Surveys have lately been made

to locate a line for a railway down this river from the city of Winnipeg. The want of material to provide this road with local traffic, and the brief period during which the Atlantic port, its proposed terminus, is accessible, would probably deter private enterprise from undertaking its construction until the surplus of grain in Manitoba had become much larger than it is at present, and a sufficient number of vessels for the Hudson Bay trade could be assured to move accumulated freight at York Factory. The river Nelson itself is not now navigable. Improvements in its channel would give a depth of water sufficient for vessels of large draught to pass through to the lakes above, and other natural obstacles are not so great as to render its future navigation improbable. But until the completion of other schemes for promoting trade in their new territory, which are now being carried out at great expense, it is hardly to be thought that the Canadian government will attempt improvements in the Nelson, or the construction of the Hudson Bay railroad, more especially as the success of these would tend to weaken certain direct benefits to the old provinces which the present plans of internal improvement are expected to bring.

The old route for inland navigation through the great lakes is now being subjected to changes which promise to establish it as a way for ocean vessels to reach inland ports with certainty, and to change materially its status as a means of communication between the interior and Atlantic sea-board. When the plan of enlargement has been fully carried out, the Welland Canal will admit steamers of two thousand tons, and drawing thirteen and one-half feet of water. Work on the first enlargement has now advanced so far that it is expected the canal will be opened to navigation this season. Upon the completion of improvements corresponding to this in the St. Lawrence, vessels drawing eleven and one-half feet of water will be able to load at Chicago, and sail through this river to Montreal, or directly across the Atlantic. The outlay of $30,000,000 on the Welland Canal, however, has not had as its object chiefly the American trade of Lake Michigan, but it has been in accordance with the comprehensive policy of the Canadian government for the development of their Northwestern territory, and for keeping within national lines the right to handle its valuable products. The money expended by the Dominion on internal improvements is nearly ready to yield its return. On the north shore of Lake Superior, one hundred miles northeast of Duluth, the pioneer railway, now almost finished, to connect the Canadian prairies with the water route to the Atlantic, terminates at the lake. Its starting-point is the city of Winnipeg, on Red River.

The Canadian Pacific road, of which this is the Lake Superior section, is to form a transcontinental line in British America, and may in time become the most important of the railroads to the Pacific. Its construction was a measure taken by the government, by whom the existing parts have been built. At a session of Parliament the present year, however, it was decided to intrust the construction to a private company, who are obliged to preserve the full route adopted by the government. Great as will be the facilities offered at the eastern end of this road for transporting grain to the seaboard by way of Lake Superior, the Dominion government has taken care to secure the construction of one overland route from the new provinces. The road from Winnipeg to the lake terminus at Fort William is to be extended on the north shore to the town of Callander, near Montreal, and to a union with the railway system of the old provinces. The extension was to be begun the present summer. From Winnipeg westward the road is to traverse the full length of the Saskatchewan prairie, and cross the Rocky Mountains to an ocean port near the United States border. The section through the prairie to the foot of the Rocky Mountains it is expected to have ready for traffic within three years. This briefly is the main line of the Canadian Pacific Railway. When completed, the distance from the Pacific Ocean overland to Montreal will be 2960 miles, or about 500 miles less than the distance by the Union Pacific road to New York.

The larger yield to the acre, the better quality, and higher grade of crop shown in this Northern country, are matters lifted by the vast extent of the land above a question of individual profit to the persons now cultivating the soil. If one-half the ground of that comparatively small portion which is drained by the Red River and its affluents were sown to

wheat, the product at an average yield would be 500,000,000 bushels, or more than the entire amount raised in the United States in 1880. The attention of the United States within a few years will certainly be drawn sharply to the supply of grain coming from this new quarter, if the reclamation of land goes on with its present movement. With the advent of a system of inland navigation greatly improved, and made the most perfect in the world, indeed, there is every reason to believe that the development of the interior will continue at its present rate, and even go forward with a rapidity never witnessed before. An immense amount of money is ready for employment. By the Canadian government and railway companies the news of these unsettled fields will be spread among the populous countries of Europe. A populous country lies directly adjoining. The land itself, level and rolling prairie, will allow railways to be built with the utmost rapidity and cheapness, and furnish no obstacle to cultivation. Scattered plentifully throughout Dakota and the valleys of the Saskatchewan are beds of the soft coal which has supplied the fuel of our Western States. That necessity, iron, is not lacking. The extensive region north of Lake Superior is known to be rich in this ore. In 1880, from the mines on the south, at present the more accessible shore of this lake, were taken 1,900,000 tons of easily worked ore, which had a value of $13,000,000.

Within ten years it is certainly possible that there will be ready for shipment at the edge of Lake Superior an amount of wheat which shall equal the total quantity now received yearly at all the Atlantic ports, at a price of seventy cents per bushel. Low as this price would be, compared with prices heretofore prevailing at the lakes, southern-grown wheat of the average quality would be worth ten cents a bushel less. Wheat can be raised in the Red River Valley and delivered to the railroad at a cost of less than forty cents to the bushel. Fifteen cents more, the rate for transportation to the lake from Fargo, which will probably be the rate also from Winnipeg over the Canadian Pacific, deducted from the price above, leaves remaining a high profit to the grower. This is in the Red River Valley, and with a yield of twenty-three bushels to the acre. With a yield of twenty-eight bushels, the increase would pay cost of transportation from far within the territory of the Saskatchewan.

What will be the effect on agriculture in the United States of this tremendous addition to the wheat land, and on present routes of traffic of a division in a valuable trade, it is impossible to foretell, and without the scope of this article to consider. That it will exercise some influence on our agriculture can not be doubted. Wheat could not now be raised in the Mississippi Valley at the price supposed above. The land of the United States has no longer the richness of unbroken ground; at least, very generally throughout its extent the best parts have been tilled. There is a wide margin for profit left in higher and more laborious cultivation of the soil. This, however, is not the method to which we have been trained. Hitherto our crops have been increased by cultivating new land. A course of giving more attention to the plants, notably Indian corn, for whose cultivation we have special advantages, it may be found expedient to follow. On the other hand, a decided fall in the price of the other cereals would probably affect maize also.

However uncertain may be effects on the United States, we may expect that the centre of activity in wheat, never very stable, will soon pass to the Red River Valley; to go later, possibly, still further northward. Most valued by the farmers in Minnesota for seed is the grain coming from the Red River Valley, and especially that from Manitoba. Taken southward, if not renewed frequently from the original source, it tends to degenerate, and become soft. Harder and better still is the wheat coming from the region of the Upper Saskatchewan and the Peace River. This perfect grain has the greatest weight of all, and by cultivation even in the Red River Valley shows a loss of its original quality.

THE GRAY CHIEFTAIN

ON the westernmost verge of the Cedar Butte stood Haykinskah and his mate. They looked steadily toward the setting sun, over a landscape which up to that time had scarcely been viewed by man—the inner circle of the Bad Lands.

Cedar Butte guards the southeastern entrance of that wonderland, standing fully a thousand feet above the surrounding country, and nearly half a mile long by a quarter of a mile wide. The summit is a level, grassy plain, its edges heavily fringed with venerable cedars. To attempt the ascent of this butte is like trying to scale the walls of Babylon, for its sides are high and all but inaccessible. Near the top there are hanging lands or terraces and innumerable precipitous points, with here and there deep chimneys or abysses in the solid rock. There are many hidden recesses, and more than one secret entrance to this ancient castle of the Gray Chieftain and his ancestors, but to assail it successfully required more than common skill and spirit.

Many a coyote had gone up as high as the second leaping bridge, and there abandoned the attempt. Old Grizzly had once or twice begun the ascent with doubt and misgiving, but soon discovered his mistake, and made clumsy haste to descend before he should tumble into an abyss from which no one ever returns. Only Igmutanka, the mountain-lion, had achieved the summit, and at every ascent he had been well repaid; yet even he seldom chose to risk such a climb, when there were many fine hunting-grounds in safer neighborhoods.

So it was that Cedar Butte had been the peaceful home of the Big Spoonhorns for untold ages. To be sure, some of the younger and more adventurous members of the clan would depart from time to time to found new families, but the wiser and more conservative were content to remain in their stronghold. There stood the two patriarchs, looking down complacently upon the herds of buffalo, antelope, and elks that peopled the lower plains. While the red sun hovered over the western hills, a coyote upon a near-by eminence gave his accustomed call to his mate. This served as a signal to all the wild hunters of the plains to set up their inharmonious evening serenade, to which the herbivorous kindred paid but little attention. The phlegmatic Spoonhorn pair listened to it all with a fine air of indifference, like that of one who sits upon his own balcony, superior to the passing noises of the street.

It was a charming moonlight night upon the cedar-fringed plain, and there the old chief presently joined the others in feast and play. His mate sought out a secret resting-place. She followed the next gulch, which was a perfect labyrinth of caves and pockets, and after leaping two chasms she reached her favorite spot. Here the gulch made a square turn, affording a fine view of the country through a windowlike opening. Above and below this were perpendicular walls, and at the bottom a small cavity—the washout made by a root of a pine which had long since fallen. To this led a narrow terrace—so narrow that man or beast would stop and hesitate long before making the venture. The place was her own by right of daring and discovery, and the mother's instinct had brought her here to-night.

In a little while relief came, and the ewe stood over a new-born lamb, licking tenderly the damp, silky coat of hair, and trimming the little hoofs of their cartilaginous points. The world was quiet now, and those whose business it was to hunt or feed at night must do so

SHE TENDERLY CARESSED THE LAMB

in silence, for such is the law of the plains. The wearied mother slept in peace.

The sun was well above the butte when she awoke, although it was cool and shadowy still in her concealed abode. She gave suck to the lamb, and caressed it for some time before she reluctantly prepared its cradle according to the custom of her people. She made a little pocket in the floor of the cave and gently put the baby in. Then she covered him all up, save the nose and eyes, with dry soil. She put her nose to his little sensitive ear and breathed into it warm love and caution, and he felt and understood that he must keep his eyes closed and breathe gently, lest bear or wolf or man should catch his big eyes or hear his breathing if they should find her trail. Again she put her warm, loving nose to his eyes, she patted a little more earth on his body and smoothed it off. The tachinchana closed his eyes in obedience, and she left him for the plain above, in search of food and sunlight.

At a little before dawn two wild hunters left their camp and set out for the Cedar Butte. Their movements were marked by unusual care and secrecy. Presently they hid their ponies in a deep ravine and groped their way up through the difficult Bad Lands, now and then pausing to listen. The two were close friends and rival hunters of their tribe.

"I think, friend, you have mistaken the haunts of the Spoonhorn," remarked Grayfoot, as the pair came out upon one of the lower terraces. He said this rather to test his friend, for it was their habit thus to criticise and question one another's judgment, in order to extract from each other fresh observations. What the one did not know about the habits of the animals they hunted in common, the other could usually supply.

"This is his home. I know it," replied Wahye. "And in this thing the animals are much like ourselves. They will not leave an old haunt unless forced to do so, either by lack of food or overwhelming danger."

They had already passed on to the next terrace and leaped a deep chasm to gain the opposite side of the butte, when Grayfoot suddenly whispered, "Inajin!" (Stop!). Both men listened attentively. "Tap, tap, tap," an almost metallic sound came to them from around the perpendicular wall of rock.

"He is chipping his horns," exclaimed the hunter, overjoyed to surprise the chieftain at this his secret occupation. "Poor beast! they are now too long for him, so that he cannot reach the short grass to feed. Some of them die starving, when they have not the strength to do the hard bucking against the rock to shorten their horns. He chooses this time, when he thinks no one will hear him, and he even leaves his own clan when it is necessary for him to do this. Come, let us crawl upon him unawares!"

They proceeded cautiously and with catlike steps around the next projection, and stood upon a narrow strip of slanting terrace. At short intervals the pounding noise continued, but, strain their eyes as they might, they could see nothing. Yet they knew that a few paces from them, in the darkness, the old chief was painfully driving his massive horns against the solid rock. So they lay flat upon the ground under a dead cedar, whose trunk and the color of the scanty soil resembled their clothing, and on their heads they had stuck some bunches of sage-bush, to conceal them from the eyes of the Spoonhorn.

With the first gray of the approaching dawn the two hunters looked eagerly about them. There, in all his majesty, heightened by the wild grandeur of his surroundings, stood the Gray Chieftain of the Cedar Butte! He had no thought of being observed at that hour. Entirely unsuspicious of danger, he stood alone upon a pedestal-like terrace, from which vantage-point it was his wont to survey the surrounding country every morning. If the secret must be told, he had done so for years, ever since he became the head chief of the Cedar Butte clan.

It is the custom of their tribe that when a ram attains the age of five years he is entitled to a clan of his own. He must thereafter defend his right and supremacy against all comers. His experience and knowledge are the guide of

his clan. In view of all this, the Gray Chieftain had been very thorough in his observations. There was not an object anywhere near the shape of bear, wolf, or man for miles around his kingdom upon Hanta Pahah that was not noted, as well as the relative positions of rocks and conspicuous trees.

The best time for Haykinskah to make his daily observations is at sunrise and sunset, when the air is usually clear and objects appear distinct. Between these times the clan feed and settle down to chew their cud and sleep; yet some are always on the alert to catch a passing stranger within their field of observation. But the old chief Spoonhorn pays very little attention. He may be nestled in a gulch just big enough to hold him, either sound asleep or leisurely chewing his cud. The younger members of the clan take their position upon the upper terraces of the great and almost inaccessible butte, under the shade of its projecting rocks, after a whole night's feasting and play upon the plain.

As Spoonhorn stood motionless, looking away off toward the distant hills, the plain below appeared from this elevated point very smooth and sheetlike, and every moving object a mere speck. His form and color were not very different from the dirty gray rocks and clay of the butte.

Wahye broke the silence: "I know of no animal that stands so long without movement, unless it is the turtle. I think he is the largest ram I have ever seen."

"I am sure he did not chip where he stands now," remarked Grayfoot. "This chipping-place is a monastery to the priests of the Spoonhorn tribe. It is their medicine-man's lodge. I have more than once approached the spot, but could never find the secret entrance."

"Shall I shoot him now?" whispered his partner in the chase.

"No, do not do it. He is a real chief. He looks mysterious and noble. Let us learn to know him better. Besides, if we kill him we will never see him again. Look: he will fall to that deep gulch ten trees' length below, where no one can get at him."

As Grayfoot spoke, the animal shifted his position, facing them squarely. The two men closed their eyes and wrinkled their motionless faces into the semblance of two lifeless mummies. The old sage of the mountains was apparently deceived; but after a few moments he got down from his lofty position and disappeared around a point of rock.

"I never care to shoot an animal while he is giving me a chance to know his ways," explained Grayfoot. "We have plenty of buffalo meat. We are not hungry. All we want is spoons. We can get one or two sheep by and by, if we have more wit than they."

To this speech Wahye agreed, for his curiosity was now fully aroused by Grayfoot's view, although he had never before thought of it in that way. It had always been the desire for meat that had chiefly moved him in the matter of the hunt.

Having readjusted their sage wigs, the hunters made the circuit of the abyss that divided them from the ram, and as they looked for his trail, they noticed the tracks of a large ewe leading down toward the inaccessible gulches.

"Ah! she has some secret down there. She never leaves her clan like this, unless it is to steal away for a personal affair of her own."

So saying, Grayfoot and his fellow tracked the ewe's footprint along the verge of a deep gulch with much trouble and patience. The hunter's curiosity and a strong desire to know her secret impelled the former to lead the way.

"What will be our profit if one slips and goes down into the gulch, never to be seen again?" remarked Wahye, as they approached a leaping-place. The chasm below was of a great depth and dark. "It is not wise for us to follow farther; this ewe has no horns that can be made into spoons."

"Come, friend, it is when one is doubting that mishaps are apt to occur," urged his companion.

"Koda, heyu yo!" exclaimed Wahye the next moment in distress.

"Hehehe, koda! hold fast!" cried the other.

Wahye's moccasined foot had slipped on the narrow trail, and in the twinkling of an eye he had almost gone down a precipice of a hundred feet; but by a desperate launch forward he caught the bough of an overhanging cedar and swung by his hands over the abyss.

Quickly Grayfoot pulled both their bows from the quivers. He first tied himself to the trunk of the cedar with his packing-strap, which always hung from his belt. Then he held both the bows toward his friend, who, not without difficulty, changed his hold from the cedar bough to the bows. After a short but determined effort the two men stood side by side once more upon the narrow foothold of the terrace. Without a word they followed the ewe's track to the cave.

Here she had lain last night! Both men began to search for other marks, but they found not so much as a sign of scratching anywhere. They examined the ground closely, but without success. All at once a faint " ba-a-a " came from almost under their feet. They saw a puff of smokelike dust as the little creature called for its mother. It had felt the footsteps of the hunters, and mistaken them for those of its own folk.

Wahye hastily dug into the place with his hands and found the soil loose. Soon he uncovered the little lamb. "Ba-a-a," it cried again, and quick as a flash the ewe appeared, stamping the ground in wrath.

Wahye seized an arrow and fitted it to the string, but his companion checked him. "No, no, my friend. It is not the skin or meat that we are looking for. We want horn for ladles and spoons. The mother is right. We must let her babe alone."

The wild hunters silently retreated, and the ewe ran swiftly to the spot and took her lamb away.

"So it is," said Grayfoot, after a long silence, "all the tribes of earth have some common feeling. I believe they are people as much as we are. The Great Mystery has made them what they are. Although they do not speak our tongue, we seem to understand their thought. It is not right to take the life of any of them unless necessity compels us to do so.

"You know," he continued, "the ewe conceals her lamb in this way until she has trained it to escape from its enemies by leaping up or down from terrace to terrace. I have seen her teaching the yearlings and two-year-olds to dive down the face of a cliff which was fully twice the height of a man. They strike on the head and the two forefeet. The ram falls largely upon his horns, which are curved in such a way as to protect them from injury. The body rebounds slightly, and they get upon their feet as easily as if they had struck a pillow. At first the yearlings hesitate and almost lose their balance, but the mother makes them repeat the performance until they have accomplished it to her satisfaction.

"They are then trained to leap chasms on all fours, and finally the upward jump, which is a more difficult feat. If the height is not great they can clear it neatly, but if it is too high for that, they will catch the rocky ledge with their forefeet and pull themselves up like a man.

"In assisting their young to gain upper terraces they show much ingenuity. I once saw them make a ladder of their bodies. The biggest ram stood braced against the steep wall as high as his body could reach, head placed between his forefeet, while the next biggest one rode his hind parts, and so on until the little ones could walk upon their broad backs to the top. We know that all animals make their young ones practise such feats as are necessary to their safety and advantage, and thus it is that these people are so well fitted to their peculiar mode of life.

"How often we are outwitted by the animals we hunt! The Great Mystery gives them this chance to save their lives by eluding the hunter, when they have no weapons of defence. The ewe has seen us, and she has doubtless warned all the clan of danger."

But there was one that she did not see! When the old chief left his clan to go to the secret place for chipping his horns,

the place where many a past monarch of the Bad Lands has performed that painful operation, he did not intend to rejoin them immediately. It was customary with him at that time to seek solitude and sleep.

The two hunters found and carefully examined the tracks of the fleeing clan. The old ram was not among them. As they followed the trail along the terrace they came to a leaping-place which did not appear to be generally used. Grayfoot stopped and kneeled down to scrutinize the ground below. "Ho!" he exclaimed, "the old chief has gone down this trail, but has not returned. He is lying down near his chipping-place, if there is no other outlet from there."

Both leaped to the next terrace below, and followed the secret pass into a rocky amphitheatre, opening out from the terrace upon which they had first seen the old ram. Here he lay asleep.

Wahye pulled an arrow from his quiver.

"Yes," said his friend, "shoot now! A warrior is always a warrior—and we are looking for horn for spoons!"

The old chief awoke to behold the most dreaded hunter—man—upon the very threshold of his sanctuary! Wildly he sprang upward to gain the top of the cliff. But Wahye was expert and quick in the use of his weapon. He had sent into his side a shaft that was deadly. The monarch's forehoofs caught the edge—he struggled bravely for a moment, then fell limply to the floor below.

"He is dead. My friend, the noblest of chiefs is dead!" exclaimed Grayfoot as he stood over him, in great admiration and respect for the Gray Chieftain.

OHIO

BY PRESIDENT CHARLES F. THWING, WESTERN RESERVE UNIVERSITY.

OHIO is a State of individualisms. The principle emerges in its settlement, and moves as a constant element in its history of one hundred years.

Previous to the Revolutionary war no less than four distinct claims, having at least some evidence of validity, were made to that territory a part of which is now called Ohio. New York, by a grant of 1664, claimed a part. Massachusetts also put forth claims, which were in conflict with the claim already mentioned. Virginia, by right of conquest and by act of her Legislature, annexed the territory as a county. It is also to be said that the Indians claimed the entire territory of the Northwest as their own. In addition to all these specific demands, France and England, at different times and with different degrees of force, proclaimed their ownership and exercised their control.

This diversity of claims to original proprietorship is still further accentuated by the variety of the early settlements. In the score of years that divide the close of the Revolution from the admission of the State to the Union no less than six bodies of people established themselves in the territory. Men of Virginia, of Massachusetts, of Connecticut, of Pennsylvania, of New Jersey, and of France hither came, and here made homes. It is significant that few of these six colonies came from the States which had laid a claim to the territory in the early period. The Virginia company largely consisted of soldiers, who found in the land granted to them compensation for their services in the war. The Massachusetts men, led by Rufus Putnam, made, in 1788, a settlement on the Ohio, at the place now known as Marietta—a name which these chivalric Americans composed by uniting the first syllable and the last of the name of Marie Antoinette. The Connecticut men, of the same type as the Massachusetts, settled in the northern part of the State, on the lake, in a section which was long known as New Connecticut, and which has taken its place in history as the Western Reserve. The Pennsylvania men were German and Scotch-Irish, who entered the middle belt. The New Jersey colony, inspired to emigration by the representations of a fellow-citizen touching the fertility of the soil and other conditions of an easy existence, came into the south. The Frenchmen, some five hundred souls, left France near the breaking out of the Revolution, moved by the persuasions of Joel Barlow to inhabit a land which was to them described as "the garden of the universe, the centre of wealth, a place destined to be the heart of a great empire." With the men of Massachusetts, and in a secondary degree with those of Connecticut, as well as with those of the Virginia colony, the motive of securing compensation for service rendered in the war had value. The Federal government owned land; it lacked money. It had at the close of the Revolution paid off its soldiers in certificates, which soon came to be greatly depreciated, a dollar having the value in certain instances of only twelve cents. The government was willing to accept its own notes in payment for land. With the Pennsylvania and the New Jersey colonists and with the Frenchmen commercial motives of a more ordinary type prevailed.

Few of the reasons which brought the Pilgrims from Leyden to Plymouth moved the Connecticut or other emigrants. The same motives urged people to come to Ohio a hundred years ago that were at that time moving people to go from Cape Cod to the District of Maine—a better living. There were few or none of those motives which Bradford, in his history, says moved the Pilgrims: the Pilgrims came to save their mother-tongue for their children, to worship God in freedom, and to establish a free commonwealth. But people came to Ohio not so much to lead a better life as to get a better living. Yet, outside of motives, there was much in common between these two emigrating bodies. The people who emigrated to Ohio came, most of them, poor in purse, like the Pilgrims; only a few of them came with a purse well filled, like many Puritans who came to Massachusetts Bay. They were the first of the great emigrations into the Northwest Territory. They had, moreover, the same experiences of want and plenty, of hope abounding and of hope disappointed, which the Pilgrims had, and which, indeed, is the usual lot of pioneers. They were, both of these sets of people, first farmers, and afterwards manufacturers. Some of them breathed the same ethical and Christian atmosphere and possessed the same educational purposes which the Puritans had. They were, like the Pilgrims, of the great body of the common people. Like both Pilgrims and Puritans, they gave the names of the towns of the old home, like Keene and New Lyme, to their new dwelling-places. They were orderly men. They believed in the constituted order of human society. They were neither cranks nor bigots. They had no unreasoning enthusiasms. They came to make homes, not to establish trading-posts.

The movement of five hundred Frenchmen in 1790 from their native land to the valley of the Ohio was a movement of greater daring and of stronger emotional enthusiasm than the emigration from any

New England State. It was a unique undertaking. The American spirit had touched France. French soldiers who served in the Revolution had, returning home, aroused the enthusiasm of their fellow-countrymen with pictures of the free life of the new land. It was a time of excitement in Paris and France. A sense of great events that had come or that were to come was moving among the people. "Nothing was talked of in every social circle," says Volney, with of course some degree of exaggeration, "but the paradise that was opened for Frenchmen in the western wilderness, the free and happy life to be led on the blissful banks of the Scioto." And they came, saw, suffered.

It was about the time that Barlow was persuading the Frenchmen to come to America that Jefferson wrote from Paris to Monroe urging him to come to Paris, for "it will make you adore your own country, its soil, its climate, its equality, liberty, laws, people, and manners." Jefferson also prophesied that though many Europeans might come to America, "no man now living will ever see an instance of an American removing to settle in Europe and continuing there." It is not unreasonable to infer that Jefferson, holding such sentiments, may have directly promoted the emigration of the Frenchmen. He returned to the United States a few months before the French colony reached the banks of the Ohio—*la belle rivière*.

The men of Paris, on reaching the banks of the Ohio, however, did not find that the representations of Barlow and Playfair were quite true. Rice, cotton, and indigo were not products of the Ohio Valley. Frost was not unknown, and the river did freeze. Among those who came were carvers, gilders, coach and peruke makers, accustomed to the conditions of life in the gayest metropolis. They did not find the work of felling trees and of grubbing up the soil fitted to their strength or to their tastes. A few of them may have returned home, a few of them remained, but the larger part of them scattered among the older States. And yet for all of them there must have been a certain sense of satisfaction filling their disappointed hearts. Some of them were Royalists. If they had remained in their own country, they might have suffered something more severe than fear of starvation and cold weather.

It was the same kind of satisfaction which
the Pilgrims of Plymouth must have felt
when tidings came to them in their free
life of Laud and Strafford. The presence
of this body of Frenchmen is still evidenced in Ohio by the names of Gallipolis and of Belpre. Welshmen are now
far more numerous in Gallipolis than
Frenchmen.*

In general it is to be said that the earlier settlers of Ohio possessed the best
blood of the parts from which they came.
In their vocations they represented all
the works and workers which go to make
up a well-ordered and civilized society.
In learning they were more of the type
of the Pilgrims who came to Plymouth
than of the Puritans who came to Massachusetts Bay. It is probable that in the
Bay Colony in the first twenty years after
its settlement were to be found as many
college men as could be found in any
population of a similar size anywhere, but
among the Pilgrims of Plymouth was not
a single man who had taken a collegiate
degree. Elder Brewster had received a
part of his training at the university, but
had failed to finish the course. But the
men who came to Ohio were, like both
Puritans and Pilgrims, possessed of high

* The following incident may be worth preserving among the annals of the little French settlement: "Louis Philippe went down the Ohio in 1798
and stopped at Gallipolis. Years afterwards, when
he occupied the throne of France, a distinguished
citizen of Ohio was presented at his court by the
American minister. The King received him very
graciously, and learning that he resided in southern
Ohio, led the conversation to Gallipolis and the
French settlers, and asked him if he knew a French
baker there named ——. The gentleman replied
that he knew the man very well, but confessed his
surprise at finding him among his Majesty's acquaintances. The King then spoke of his visit to
Gallipolis, and said he had improved the opportunity
of his stop there to have a supply of bread made
for his voyage. While the bread was baking, word
came that the ice was coming down the river, and
that it would be necessary for his boat to start at
once in order to keep ahead of it. What was to be
done? It was impossible to delay his departure,
and it seemed equally impossible to go without the
bread. In this dilemma the baker offered to go
along with him, with his ovens, down the river far
enough to finish the baking of the bread. He was
accordingly hurried on board the boat, ovens and all,
and they started ahead of the ice. When the bread
was done, the baker with his ovens was put on
shore, and returned to Gallipolis."—*Ohio: 1788.*
Translated from the French by John Henry James.
Columbus, 1888. This little tract was itself translated into French from the English for the use of
Barlow. This incident is taken from the notes of
the Introduction.

ideals of education, and were moved in
sympathy with the best learning of the
time. In point of social respectability
they were families out of the stock which
had peopled the Bay Colony and the colonies of Hartford and of New Haven. They
represented officers of the Revolutionary
war—men who had been accustomed to
command, who were without wealth, and
also free from extreme poverty.

After the disintegrations and attritions
of a hundred years, the conditions and
the influences which many of these bodies
brought are still quite intact and distinct.
It is not difficult to trace through the
northern part of the State the southern
line of the Western Reserve purchase.
The Western Reserve people are inclined
to pride themselves upon the fact that
evidences of thrift, economy, and energy are to be observed in their villages,
churches, school-houses, and homes not
found in certain parts of the territory
south. A friend of mine, whose business
calls him up and down and across the
State, tells me that a dull observer can
trace with ease the southern line of the
Western Reserve territory. In this territory he is in New England; out of this
territory he is out of New England. Marietta, too, and its neighborhood are still
distinct and integral. The other original
colonists have scattered more or less in
various parts of the State — a leaven
which has helped to leaven the whole
lump.

The noble character of the settlers gave
promise of a noble character in those who
might follow them. Like attracts like.
The presence of the best people con-
strained others also of the best people, who
were following the star of empire, to take
up their abode with the original inhabitants. At the close of the first decade of
the century not far from a quarter of a
million of people, and at the close of the
second decade somewhat over half a million people, had become citizens of Ohio.
A few centres of large influence had been
established. Among them were Cincinnati, Zanesville, and Chillicothe (the first
capital of the State). Throughout the
State also, in small towns as well as in the
larger, were people of genuine culture.
Though their homes might be quite unlike Blennerhasset's villa, yet in village
and even in the lone settler's cabin were
found men and women who had "light"
and whose lives were "sweetness." I of-

ten talk with the sons and daughters of the founders of the Western Reserve, and I constantly hear stories of the books that were read, which, though few in number, were rich in power. The memories of the noble and beautiful lives which were lived are yet green and fragrant. To Ohio also came not a few of the best people of the older States as visitors. Lafayette visited Ohio in 1825; and his secretary, Levasseur, says that Lafayette was simply astonished at this new creation of a commonwealth. The attentions shown him gave him delight. Ohio to him seemed "the eighth wonder of the world."

Although in the time of settlement colonies came from several parts, yet at the present time Ohio is less dependent upon other commonwealths for her people than any other of the north central States. Only thirteen per cent. of the native American population were born outside of her borders. The States which have contributed the more largely to the 441,000 Americans who have moved on to and are now living on her soil are—Pennsylvania, with 121,000; New York, with 57,000; Virginia, with 41,000; Kentucky, with 38,000; and Indiana, with 35,000. The Connecticut and Massachusetts immigration continues; for 9000 persons born in Massachusetts and 6000 born in Connecticut are among her present citizens. But above most States her American citizens are her own production.

The progress of a people in a new country is well measured by the simple element of roads and of other means of communication and transportation. In the beginning there is no road. The beginning of civilization and the beginning of a road are contemporaneous. Turkey has no roads; England has turnpikes. The explorer makes for himself a path. He or his successors blaze a line. A bridlepath is subsequently cut, along which the lone traveller, the circuit-rider, the solitary postman, stubs his way on horseback. The next step is the felling of trees, the laying of the fallen trees into corduroy roads in case the way is over a bog, or removing and burning these trees and the pulling out of stumps. Thus a way is made for "teams." Presently the road is improved. Population increases. The demands of life become more numerous and more urgent. The road becomes a turnpike; over it the coach, bearing the goods and folks of and for

the new State, goes twice or thrice a week. Presently the railroad surveyor emerges as silently as the sun rises, and within a few months after his appearance rails themselves are laid. Such is the history of Ohio. Governor St. Clair in 1795 wrote, "There is not a road in the country." In as many years after the beginning of the century as there elapsed between the remark of St. Clair and the close of the century roads had their beginning. They were few, and the few were bad. But among the earliest internal improvements made by the United States was a road called the Mail Route from Wheeling to the West. This road, built by Ebenezer Zane, of Wheeling, was known as "Zane's Trace." It was first a bridlepath cut through the woods. In a few years corduroy bridges were built over bogs and marshes. The road-wagon, with its four and six horses, presently supplanted the pack-horse. Along this road for forty years went the mails between Washington and Kentucky. In 1832 the first railroad was built.

But Ohio above most Western States was favored with means of communication other than of the land. On its southern and eastern boundary it had a great river; on its northern, a great lake. Long before the roads became moderately passable, on both river and lake was passing the commerce of vigorous and ever-increasing peoples. In October, 1811, the steamboat *Orleans* departed from Pittsburg for the South. It excited wonder among all those living on the banks between which it passed. Some supposed that a comet had fallen and come into the river. Some supposed that it was an English boat, for the war with England was already in the air. She did not reach her destination until more than two months after her departure, and it was not till the next year and the year following that two other steamers from Pittsburg followed her down the Ohio. But no one of these boats ever came up the river against its current. It was not till 1815 that a steamer which in December, 1814, had taken a cargo of ordnance stores from Pittsburg to General Jackson in fourteen days, succeeded in stemming the tide, although she was twenty-five days in making the distance from New Orleans to Louisville. But in this time, although steamers were not proving inefficient, sail-boats were doing a great business. It is said that Marietta alone sent to the sea before the war of 1812 no less than twenty-five sailing craft, seven of which were ships, eleven brigs, and six schooners. In this time, too, the flat-boat played a most important part. Every spring, at full water, flour, bacon, pork and other products of the country were taken to New Orleans and to the markets that lay this side of the Southern metropolis, and the boats returned with cargoes in which were many tropical and foreign goods. As the southern part of the State was the earlier settled, so also the commerce of the river preceded the commerce of the lake. At the time when the Ohio River was the scene of an active business, Lake Erie had but a few little schooners. Lake Erie sprang into prominence not through its commerce, but through Commodore Perry's victory of 1813.

But it was not alone the river and the lake to which the people looked for easy communication. The Ohio Canal, in association with the Erie Canal, played a most important part in the development of the State. This canal stretched from the river to the lake. The Miami Canal, that ran from the river to Dayton, begun in 1826, was, with the great canal, completed in 1833. In 1842, when the entire canal system was finished, there were found to be 796 miles of navigable water opened for commerce. The entire cost was between fourteen and fifteen millions of dollars. The effect of these improvements it is now hard to overestimate. The canals opened the markets of the world to the farmer of central Ohio. Wheat doubled in value; land greatly appreciated; the population rapidly grew; capital flowed into the State; villages became towns; towns became cities. Ohio began to take its large place among the great commonwealths.

In 1800 Ohio had 45,000 people, and ranked eighteenth among the States in point of population. In the next ten years its rate of increase was greater than that obtaining in any other State, being 408 per cent., and in 1810 it had 230,000 inhabitants, and came to be the thirteenth most populous commonwealth. In 1820 it sprung to the fifth place, having 581,-000 people; in 1830 it advanced to the fourth; in 1840 to the third place; and the third place it continued to hold till 1890, when it fell back to the fourth, Illi-

nois having come to have 150,000 more people than her own 3,672,316.

In Ohio, as in most of the Western States, agriculture was the first employment of the early settlers. The immigrant found the State well wooded, and he, unlike the colonists in such States as Wisconsin and Minnesota, cut down the walnut and the pine not to make lumber, but to get a patch for planting corn and potatoes and wheat. It is probable that the present value of the timber destroyed by the settlers in Ohio would be more than the present value of the cultivated land on which that timber stood. But necessary as the soil was to the settler, he did not know that beneath the sod lay a treasure far more valuable than the soil itself. The coal-mine and the oil-well have proved to be in not a few counties of far greater worth than the loam lying above them. Ohio has thus become, through the same condition which makes England a great manufacturing nation, a great manufacturing commonwealth. These manufactures are largely of iron and of allied products. The conditions of the problem are very simple. Iron ore is taken from the mines of Michigan and Minnesota. Soft coal is necessary to its manufacture. Manufactured iron is needed in every part of the country. Iron ore is not adequately produced in Ohio; soft coal is not adequately found in Michigan or Minnesota—"useless each without the other." The definite part of the problem is, where can iron ore and soft coal best meet? From what point can the results of the meeting of iron ore and soft coal be best transported to those points where they are needed? It is now known and confessed that the spot where iron ore and soft coal can best meet, and the spot whence can best be shipped the products of their union, is to be found on the shore of Lake Erie between Toledo and Buffalo. Upon this curve lies the meeting and the distributing point of iron products.

Since 1872 Ohio has been the second State in the making of iron and steel. Pennsylvania was then and is still ahead of her neighbor. The Lake Superior mines produce more than one-half of the iron ore of the United States, and these mines are very largely owned in Ohio, and mostly in Cleveland. The total value of the products of iron and steel in this country in 1890 was $478,687,519, and about one-seventh of this value is to be credited to

Ohio. In the making and distribution of iron, the ship plays a part second only to the furnace. The chief city of the State on its northern boundary has become one of the great ship-building points of the world. If the construction of war-ships be omitted, it has become the second greatest ship-building port in the world, being excelled alone by the Clyde. When war-ships are included, Cleveland is obliged to fall behind Philadelphia. The total foreign and coastwise commerce of New York is, of a year, somewhat more than 12,000,000 net tons; of Cleveland, about 10,000,000 net tons. Thus the State, which was primarily agricultural, has become, though still remaining agricultural, a State of iron and steel makers, of mine-owners, and of ship-builders.

The development of Ohio, like the development of Plymouth Colony and of the Massachusetts Bay Colony, has been a development led by great men. The names of the leaders of the two colonies that went to make up Massachusetts are the names of great men. Take away the Winthrops, the Mathers, the Adamses, the Bradfords, the Brewsters, the Everetts, and Massachusetts history would be a thing quite different from what it is. A great people creates and demands great leaders. Great leaders create and demand a great people. But the demand of a great people for great leaders is the more imperative. In Ohio great men have led. Its earlier history is woven with the names of Putnam, Manasseh Cutler, and Moses Cleveland, the founder of the great and beautiful city bearing his name; and in the early middle and present history are stitched in silver threads the names of Ewing, Corwin, Giddings, Stanton, Chase, Wade, Waite, Hayes, and Garfield. It is significant that the great men of Ohio have usually been men engaged in political life. There are of course certain exceptions, to which I shall allude, but on the whole the great men have been statesmen and generals. There are a few lawyers, Ohio born and bred, who can be seen from beyond the boundaries of the State, so tall are they. One of them is Chief-Justice Waite, respected in Ohio before his great elevation, as he was respected beyond Ohio after it. His associate, too, Stanley Matthews, is regarded in Ohio as not unworthy of his high office. Allen G. Thurman, also, was for almost half a century one of the great

lawyers of the State, a man, too, whose political service was greatly enriched by his legal knowledge and training. In northern Ohio was one lawyer who has received large recognition aside from his official position, and that is Judge Rufus P. Ranney, of whom Rhodes, in his history, says: "He was a profound jurist. . . . As a member of the Ohio Constitutional Convention he had a great share in making the organic law; as judge of the Ohio Supreme Court, he interpreted it in a series of decisions which for sound doctrine, and clearness of thought and expression, are probably not surpassed in the court records of any State."—(*History of the United States*, vol. ii., pp. 380–81.)

The annals of Ohio in medicine are quite vacant of the greatest names. The two names that occur first of the great religious leaders of the State were not of Ohio origin, and the work of one only was done in large degree in Ohio. Lyman Beecher came to Cincinnati, and helped to mould that part of the State to a liberal orthodoxy and to civic freedom. Finney came to the northern part of the State, to Oberlin, a radical, a man of strong brain, of unique personality, and helped to form an emotional but vigorous type of piety. The great editors in Ohio have been few, but one does not forget that Whitelaw Reid was here born and educated. The great educators have been few also, but certain names at once occur to one. The greatest by far of these is Horace Mann. Short and sad was his Ohio life. He dug his grave in Antioch College. Of him Theodore Parker said, writing to him in 1854: "I am glad that you are there,—sad enough for my own sake; sympathizing, too, for the heartache which I know often comes over the homesick man. But I think of the generations which will rise up and call you blessed. I think New England had no seed in her granary which the West needed so much as yourself. Now God has sown you in Ohio, I look for great harvests which mankind shall one day reap therefrom."—(*Life of Horace Mann*, pp. 458–9.) But, alas! it must be said that the prophecy of Theodore Parker has not come true. Before Mann's death, too, Antioch College had come almost to its grave. Horace Mann's life is a power in American life because of his work in the common schools of Massachusetts, not because of his work in a college of Ohio. Following Mann was another great educator, Thomas Hill, who went from Antioch to Harvard, but greater as an educator, scholar, thinker, than as an administrator. Probably the next greatest name in Ohio's educational history is that of Fairchild of Oberlin, who has occupied almost every position in that college, and taught almost all branches, from mathematics to dogmatic theology, and who has brought to every task a clear mind, a sympathetic heart, and a calm judgment.

When one thinks of the great authors one finds that they are men and women whose association with Ohio has been brief. Of all these the most famous probably is William D. Howells. But does not all the world know that Howells left Ohio almost as soon as he had left his teens? Here also Rhodes the historian was born, and worked many years, but when he wished to begin in earnest the writing of his volumes he went to Cambridge. Here also that noble man and charming, John Hay, has a home, but Washington is his more permanent dwelling-place. Constance Fenimore Woolson spent her girlhood in Cleveland, and her relations with that city were always intimate, but her residence in late years was abroad, and abroad she died. The Cary sisters began their popular and inspiring writings near Cincinnati, but they drifted soon, like many others, to the metropolis. No one forgets that Artemus Ward had a service on the Cleveland *Plaindealer* in the troublous times before 1860, but it was brief. His Cleveland life is still preserved in his name, which is given to a club of journalists. No journalist has been more prominent in Ohio than Murat Halstead, and though his residence is now outside the State, his name and work are here honored. Albert Shaw and Edith Thomas were born in Ohio—the one, at a place in the south having the name of Paddy's Run (a name which the postoffice authorities tried to change, but failed), where also was born Murat Halstead; the other, at Chatham, and was educated in a high-school and normal institute at Geneva.

It must be confessed that the great men of Ohio, and the men who have helped to make Ohio great in itself and great in reputation, have been men engaged in civil and political life. In his *Twenty*

Years in Congress, Mr. Blaine, writing of the time of the beginning of the war, says: "The Ohio delegation was especially strong. John A. Bingham, the oldest in service on the Republican side, was an effective debater, well informed, ready, and versatile. A man of high principle, of strong faith, of zeal, enthusiasm, and eloquence, he could always command the attention of the House. His colleague, Samuel Shellabarger, was distinguished for the logical and analytical character of his mind. Without the gift of oratory, paying little heed to the graces of speech, Mr. Shellabarger conquered by the intrinsic strength of his argument, which generally amounted to demonstration. His mind possessed many of the qualities which distinguished Mr. Lincoln. In fairness, lucidness, fulness of statement, the two had a striking resemblance. Valentine B. Horton was a valuable member on all questions of finance and business; and on the issues touching slavery James M. Ashley followed the radical example of Mr. Giddings. Among the Democrats, George H. Pendleton, Clement L. Vallandigham, and Samuel S. Cox were especially conspicuous. Mr. Pendleton was regarded as the leader of the Democratic side of the House by a large section of his party, and his assignment to the Committee of Ways and Means by the Speaker was intended as a recognition of that fact. Mr. Cox gave much attention to foreign affairs, to which his mind had been drawn by a brief but fruitful participation in the diplomatic service of the country. Mr. Vallandigham possessed ability, and a certain form of dogged courage, combined with a love of notoriety, which allured him to the assumption of extreme positions and the advocacy of unpopular measures. No other State was in the aggregate so ably represented as Ohio" (p. 328). But it must be said that probably the Ohio delegation was never again so strong as it was at this time. The names of Ewing, Corwin, and Giddings are now becoming rather a memory; but the stories of Corwin are still told by men who heard him tell them, and they still arouse many a laugh. The name of Wade, too, is not familiar to the younger generation, and, like the names of so many of his companions who were leaders in the times between 1856 and 1866, is swiftly passing from the recollection of the common people. The name of

Chase still lives, and possibly, of all the names, is the only one which is in common thought associated with the names of Hayes and Garfield—as great a man as either of these, and whom some hold to Garfield have given him a place which no one else will occupy in the present generation. Hayes was loved throughout the length and breadth of the State. He was, for a dozen years following his

SHIPPING IN THE OLD RIVER-BED, CLEVELAND.

have been greater than either. He holds a position in American as well as Ohio history absolutely unique. He was one of the men who had a part in shaping the movements which resulted in the war; he was one of the three or four great men whose conduct was most influential in carrying on the war; and thirdly, he was the one who, above any one else, aided in the settlement of the constitutional principles involved in the war. As an orator and candidate for office, as Secretary of the Treasury, and as Chief Justice, he took a mighty threefold share in the great issues. The names of Garfield and of Hayes are dear to every heart. The public career and the ending of the life of retirement from the great office, the first citizen, and he bore himself in ways worthy of the first citizen. He said to me at different times: "I wish to do useful things which no one else will do. I am president of the Prisoners' Aid Society, a worthy work, I think. Who cares for the poor prisoner? Possibly I can help him a bit." "My chief work," he said at another time, "is to advertise good things; my one wish is to be useful."

Ohio as the mother of great men becomes possibly more conspicuous in war than in peace. The number and character of the men who were leaders on the field between 1861 and 1865, whose birthplace was in Ohio or whose early training was there received. are pre-eminent. Among them were such commanders as McDowell, McPherson, Buell, Cox, Rosecrans, and also Sheridan, Sherman, and Grant. McClellan went to the war from Ohio, and was first appointed to the command of Ohio troops. It is only not to be forgotten that Hayes and Garfield won the title of "General" long before that of President. But these names are to me hardly so significant as the fact that one-eighth of all the Federal army of the great war came from Ohio.

The similarity between Ohio and Maine in having its great men political leaders is striking. The delegation of Maine in Congress, like the delegation of Ohio, has always been one of pre-eminent ability. George Evans and William Pitt Fessenden, Lot M. Morrill, Hannibal Hamlin, and James G. Blaine—not to mention men who are now in Congress—illustrate the character of the timber which the Pine-tree State has sent to Washington. An Ohio Governor was the rival of the great Maine man as a candidate for the Republican nomination for the Presidency in 1876, and four years later a like condition prevailed. The Ohio men won both in the conventions and at the polls.

But the contrast between the vocations and avocations of the great men of Ohio and the great men of Massachusetts is most striking. One who visited Boston twenty or forty years ago wanted to see literary men—Longfellow, Whittier, Emerson, Lowell, and Holmes. Sumner did not attract the public notice that Longfellow called out, nor Wilson that of Whittier, nor Winthrop that of Holmes. There are two exceptions. One, Daniel Webster. No man probably ever filled the public eye in any State as did Webster in Massachusetts. I have heard Colonel Higginson say that when Webster walked down State Street, State Street seemed to stop its business, look out of the windows of counting-rooms, cease its walk and turn round in order to look at the great man. Men and boys said, in bated breath, "There goes Webster!" The other exception is Wendell Phillips, great orator, who thought he was a statesman, but who helped to make the events which called into service the greatest of statesmen.

The origin of the remark, made half in jest, half in earnest, as to the ubiquity and power of the Ohio man, lies largely in his ubiquity and power as a statesman. The causes that have contributed to this civic greatness are of course general and particular. One cause to which I allude is the ubiquity of the Ohio college. Ohio is a State of colleges. And yet it must be acknowledged that many of the great political leaders were not college men. Giddings was not. Wade was not. Chase was a graduate of Dartmouth. Ewing was a graduate of Ohio University, at Athens, and received the first degree of A.B. ever given in Ohio. Hayes was a graduate of Kenyon. Garfield was educated in part at Hiram, in Ohio, but finished his education at Williams. But the rank and file of these men who have made Ohio history have been college-trained. The typical Ohio college of forty years ago was a very sorry institution, except in the nobility of its purposes and in the character of two or three men who sat in its professors' chairs. There were of course exceptions. The old Western Reserve College, at Hudson, was an exception, in which such teachers as Laurens P. Hickok, afterwards President of Union, Professor Loomis, of mathematical fame, Barrows, the great Hebrew scholar, President Bartlett, Clement Long, Henry N. Day, Professor Charles A. Young, and the elder Seymour were gathered. But any college, poor in money and resources, if it be true and honest, may do a great work for the student if he be honest and not too poor. And these Ohio boys went to college, and in the college they were trained to think. From the college they went to the lawyer's desk and the bar, from the bar to the State-house, the Governor's seat, and to places in the national Congress.

The principle of individuality which is manifest in the beginnings of Ohio receives illustration in its collegiate system. The first college founded in Ohio was not only the first college founded in the whole Northwest Territory, but also it was the first college founded in the United States having an endowment in land given by the national government. It bore the ambitious name of the American Western University, and the act establishing it passed the Territorial Legislature in January, 1802. The college preceded the State. In the century that has since elapsed more colleges have been founded in Ohio than in any other State.

JUDGE RUFUS P. RANNEY.

Although the present number of colleges may be somewhat less than is found in Illinois, yet the number is sufficiently great to illustrate the principle of individuality. Instead of having one university, as has been the method in most States of the West, Ohio has continued to have three. The oldest is still at Athens, where it was founded; a second is at Oxford — Miami; and the third, technically known as the Ohio State University, which has just celebrated its twenty-fifth anniversary, is at the capital of the State. Throughout this period, too, in all parts of the State colleges have sprung up. They have usually had their origin in religious or sectarian motives. Kenyon, the college of the Episcopalians, laid its corner-stone in June, 1827. Western Reserve was founded in 1826 by Congregationalists and Presbyterians, among whom the influence of Yale was pre-eminent. Oberlin followed in 1833 as a part of an evangelistic movement. Marietta was founded in the south in 1835, also as the agent of the Congregationalists. Ohio Wesleyan was founded in 1843 by the Methodist Episcopal Church. Antioch was founded in 1853 as the organ of a liberal Christianity. Denison was founded by the Baptist denomination, and in 1856 took its present name, although the institution had under other names been engaged in educational work for several years. These and other colleges, to the number of some thirty or more, at present represent the higher education in the State. They represent the obliged to solve her problems for herself, without the help of precedents made under similar conditions. Oberlin represented a movement in coeducation. Antioch stood for a free type of Christianity, as well as for the education of women and of men upon the same basis. Western Reserve stood for the highest and strongest intellectual education and for a liberal culture. The State University for many years represented the technical side of education.

At the present time the movement in the State is away from the tendency of

A CHARACTERISTIC OHIO HOMESTEAD.

policy of decentralization, a policy which is opposed to the policy that has prevailed in New England, for Ohio has twice as many colleges as all the New England States, and as many as New York, New Jersey, and Pennsylvania combined.

As one reads the history of the higher education in the State he is impressed with the method of experiment which has prevailed. It has been the State of educational reforms and of educational reformers. The first State formed out of the great Northwest Territory, she has been the century. The educators are sympathetic with the centralizing tendency of modern education. When this State was without roads, or had only poor ones, it was fitting to have many colleges. For the local influence of any college is great. Many boys and girls went to colleges scattered throughout the State who would not have gone to a university situated in one part of the State. It is significant that more than half the students of a national university like Harvard come from the State in which it is located. But when

THE CAPITOL AT COLUMBUS.

railroads penetrate every town the special reason for many colleges in a State
is removed. Therefore the only reason
for the present existence of many colleges
in Ohio is the reason that they have existed; it is the reason of prescription. The
value of many colleges in a State is also
lessened by the fact that many colleges
usually means colleges small in endowment, poor in equipment, and weak in
teaching force and illustrative apparatus.
For the modern college demands an equipment in libraries, museums, and laboratories which is extremely expensive. Colleges in Ohio, like colleges in New England such as Amherst and Williams and
Dartmouth, should have at least a million dollars of endowment. They cannot properly do their work without an income of fifty thousand dollars, aside from
fees of students. The colleges in Ohio
which have an income of fifty thousand
dollars can probably be counted on the
fingers of one hand.

In the making and maintaining of these
educational foundations the laws of the
State have been exceedingly and, some
would say, excessively liberal. For no
endowment of any amount worth speaking of is necessary for granting a charter
to an institution of the higher education.
New York and more recently Pennsylvania have set an example to the sister upon
their western boundary in having laws
requiring a large endowment for institutions conferring collegiate degrees. But
already in Ohio a movement is under
way which represents the thought of the
best educators and wisest citizens, declaring that henceforth no charter shall be
granted to any institution for the higher
education unless it is in the beginning
properly endowed.

But the Ohio people have not forgotten
that all colleges are not in Ohio. There
are 135 graduates of Harvard and 174
graduates of Yale living in Ohio now.
In Ohio, as in most Western States, Yale
is more popular than Harvard with the
people, but less popular with scholars.
One college in northern Ohio was for a
long time known as the Yale of the West;
the faculty was composed of Yale men.
As northern Ohio was called New Con-

necticut, it was natural, therefore, that boys going away to college from northern Ohio should go to the college of old Connecticut. But this condition has now passed away.

The public-school system of Ohio is better for a public-school system than the college system is for a college system. The system is good; the teachers as a body are well trained, as compared with teachers in other States, although in no State are they as well trained as they ought to be. The school-houses are excellent—far better than one finds in Maine or in the country districts of the other New England States. I have sometimes thought that the farther west one goes, the better one finds the school-houses in comparison with the churches. And the farther east one goes, the better he finds the churches in comparison with the school-houses. To foster education has been the policy of the West. The large proportion of the public domain that has been set apart in the Northwest for the purposes of higher education has resulted, and will result, in giving a magnificent system of education without large draughts upon the purses of the people.

In all these manifestations of its life Ohio is essentially a State of individualisms. The communistic system or method has not prevailed. Political parties have been more split than in most States. The large number of colleges represent, as I have said, the individualistic principle. Normal schools have been founded, but they have usually been private normal schools. The efficiency with which the Underground Railroad was run in Ohio illustrates the individualistic quite as much as the co-operative system and method. The laws in respect to corporations and commercial enterprises have been far more severe than New York laws of the same kind. Individual legal rights have been respected. The greatest corporation of modern times was organized in Cleveland, but it was found wise to transfer its headquarters to the city of New York. A Republican Legislature has been known to choose a Democrat as United States Senator. The Ohio man is an individual.

The individualisms of the State also receive illustration in its ecclesiastical history. I do not know how many of the different denominations are represented in Ohio, but I am sure that most of them are, and I am also sure that most of their churches are vigorous. Although the northern part of the State was peopled by those who were originally Congregationalists, and who, coming to Ohio, became Presbyterians—and it is always to be said

OHIO STATE UNIVERSITY AT COLUMBUS.

THOMAS EWING.

that Congregationalism stands for individualism, and Presbyterianism for cooperation—yet the Presbyterianism has been of a very independent and free-thinking sort. The Mormon faith had in a large degree its origin in Ohio, and here it has perpetuated itself in a narrow though lasting stream. Here also the Disciples have had from the first a very large following, and the personality of Alexander Campbell is still felt. Perfectionism also burned over Ohio. Perfectionism represents anarchy; it is individualism gone to seed.

But with these individualisms the people are usually conservative. Although there have been great discoveries made in Ohio in oil and coal and gas, it is not a State of booms. It has known less of the ups and downs of commercial crises than any State. No bank in Cleveland failed in the crises of 1873 and 1893. This conservative condition arises in part from the fact that the State has been essentially an agricultural State. Farmers are conservative. This condition is now passing away, and Ohio is becoming a great manufacturing State; and possibly the State is less conservative than it was forty years ago. Another cause of its conservatism may lie in the equanimity of its climate. More than any other State does it seem to be neither hot nor cold, neither wet nor dry. Possibly also its conservatism may have relation to what may be called its self-contentment and self-sufficiency. I believe Ohio raises everything which the American eats, excepting perhaps two or three tropical fruits. It is certainly true that the mental and emotional state of which Bryce writes, "the temper of the West," does not belong to Ohio.

The standard of wealth and of living greatly differs in different parts of the State. The standard of living in the country is somewhat better, I think, than can be found among the farmers of Vermont and Maine. Ohio farmers have more money and provide a better table. The life in the two great cities of Cleveland and Cincinnati is somewhat similar to the life in Boston and New York, though the similarity of life in Cleveland and Boston is greater than that which obtains between Cincinnati and New York. People in Cleveland spend money more freely than people in Boston, because they get it from a larger rate of interest and more profitable commercial ventures. The tax laws of the State, however, have driven a good many rich men to New York. The departure of millionaires from their native State and town in order to avoid swearing to the amount of their property is evidence of the uprightness of their consciences, but it does tend to make Ohio poor.

I have suggested that the Ohio man is ubiquitous. It is a constant surprise to me to find how many people have had some relation to Ohio. If Ohio shares with Massachusetts and Connecticut the privilege of being the mother of great men, it may be also said that with Illinois she shares the honor of being the mother of great States. A million of her children now have their homes in States west of her own boundaries. To her next-door neighbor Indiana she has contributed 164,000 people; and to her second-door neighbor Illinois, 126,000 — a number greater than has been contributed by any other State. To Iowa she has given 102,-000; to Kansas, 116,000; to Michigan, 80,-000; to Missouri, 70,000; to Nebraska, 59,000; to California, 28,000; to Colorado, 21,000; to Oregon and Washington, 24,-000; and to Texas, 10,000. Few of her people have turned against the movement of the star of empire, and fewer still have entered the South, though Kentucky has 31,000 of native Ohioans; West Virginia, 31,000 also; Pennsylvania, 34,000; but New York has only 15,000; New Jersey only 3000; and the New England States so small numbers that the Census Reports fail to specify them.

Thus in her emigrations in the last decades of her century, as well as in her immigrations during the first decades, Ohio is still a State of individualisms.

KANSAS

THE other continents are convex, with an interior dome or range, from whose declivities the waters descend to the circumference; but North America is concave, having mountain systems parallel with its eastern and western coasts, whose principal streams fall into the Atlantic and the Pacific.

Between the Appalachian and the Cordilleran regions, a vast central valley, more than two thousand miles wide from rim to rim, extends with uniform contour from the tropics to the pole. The crest of this colossal cavity nearly coincides with the boundary between the Dominion and the United States, its northern part drained by the Mackenzie and Red rivers into the Arctic Ocean, and its southern by the Mississippi and its six hundred tributaries into the Gulf of Mexico.

In a remote geological age this continental trough was the bed of an inland sea, whose billows broke upon the Alleghanies and the Rocky Mountains—archipelagoes with precipitous islands rising abruptly from the desolate main.

The subsiding ocean left enormous saline deposits, which at varying depths underlie much of its surface, and which later were succeeded by tropical forests and jungles, nurtured by heat and moisture, their carbon stratified in the coal measures of the interior, and beneath whose impervious shadows, after many centuries, wandered herds of gigantic monsters, their fossil remains yet found in the loess of the Solomon and the Smoky Hill. In a subsequent epoch, as the land became cooler by radiation and firmer by drainage, the saurians were succeeded by ruminants, like the buffalo and the antelope, which pastured in myriads upon the succulent herbage, and followed the seasons in their endless migrations.

Mysterious colonizations of strange races of men—the Aztecs, the moundbuilders, the cave-dwellers—whose genesis is unknown, appeared upon the fertile plains and perished, leaving no traces of their wars and their religions, save the rude weapons that the plough exhumes from their ruined fortifications, and the broken idols that irreverent science discovers in their sacrificial mounds.

Upon the western acclivity of the basin, where its synclinal axis is intersected by its greater diameter, lies the State of Kansas—"Smoky Waters"; so called from the blue and pensive haze which in autumn dims the recesses of the forests, the hollows of the hills, and broods above the placid streams like a covenant of peace. It is quadrangular—save for the excision of its northeastern corner by the meanderings of the Missouri—200 miles wide by 400 miles long, and contains the geographical centre of the territory of the United States. Its area of 52,000,000 acres gradually ascends from an elevation of 900 feet above tide-water to the altitude of 4000 feet at its western boundary. It has a mean annual temperature of 53°, with a rainfall of 37 + inches; an average of 30 thunder-storms, 198 days exempt from frost, and 136,839 miles of wind every year. This inclined plane is reticulated by innumerable arroyos, or dry runs, which collect the storm waters, whose accumulations scour deepening channels in the friable soil as they creep sinuously eastward, forming by their union the Kaw (or Kansas) and Arkansas rivers, two of the most considerable affluents of the Missouri.

The confines of the valleys are the "bluffs," no higher than the general level of the land, worn into ravines and gulches by frost and wind and rain, carving the limestone ledges into fantastic architecture, and depositing at their base an alluvion of inexhaustible fertility. Dense forests of elm, cottonwood, walnut, and sycamore, mantled with parasitic growths, clothe the cliffs and crags with verdure, and gradually encroach upon the "rolling prairies." The eye wanders with tranquil satisfaction and unalloyed delight over these fluctuating fields, treeless except along the margins of the indolent streams, gorgeous in summer with the fugitive splendor of grass and flowers, in autumn billows of bronze, and in winter desolate with the melancholy glory of undulating snows.

By imperceptible transition the rolling prairies merge into the "Great Plains," plateaus elevated above the humid currents of the atmosphere, rainless except for casual showers, presenting a sterile expanse, with vegetation repulsive and inedible, a level monotony broken at irregular intervals by detached knobs and isolated buttes. Above their vague and receding horizon forever broods a pathetic and mysterious solemnity, born of distance, silence, and solitude.

The dawn of modern history broke upon Kansas three and a half centuries ago, when Marcos de Naza, a Franciscan friar, returning from a missionary tour among the Pueblos, brought rumors of populous cities and mines richer than Golconda and Potosi in the undiscovered country beyond the Sierra Madre. In 1541, twenty years after the conquest of Mexico by Cortez, Francisco Vasquez de Coronado, under the orders of Mendoza, Viceroy of India, with a little army of 300 Spaniards and 800 Mexicans, marched northward from Culiacan, then the limit of Spanish dominion, on an errand of discovery and spoliation. Crossing the mountains at the head of the Gila River, he reached the sources of the Del Norte, and continued northeasterly into the Mississippi Valley, descending from the plains to the prairies, crossing the present area of Kansas diagonally nearly to the fortieth degree of north latitude.

At the farthest point reached in his explorations he erected a high cross of wood, with the inscription, "Francisco Vasquez de Coronado, commander of an expedition, reached this place." He left some priests to establish missions among the Indians, but they were soon slain. In his report to Mendoza, at Mexico, Coronado wrote: "The earth is the best possible for all kinds of productions of Spain. I found prunes, some of which were black, also excellent grapes and mulberries. I crossed mighty plains and sandy heaths, smooth and wearisome and bare of wood, and as full of crooked-back oxen as the mountain Serena in Spain is of sheep."

Coronado was followed sixty years later by Don Juan de Onate, the conqueror of New Mexico, and in 1662 by Penalosa, then its governor, who marched from Santa Fe, and was profoundly impressed by the agricultural resources of the country which he traversed.

The desultory efforts of the Spaniards to subdue the savages and acquire control of the territory continued for a century, when the French became their competitors, under the leadership of Marquette, Joliet, Hennepin, Iberville, and La Salle, by whom formal possession of the Missis-

sippi Valley was taken in 1682 for Louis XIV. By this monarch the whole province of Louisiana, including what is now called Kansas, with a monopoly of traffic with the Indian tribes, was granted in 1712 to Crozat, a wealthy merchant of Paris, who soon surrendered his patent, and its privileges were transferred to the Mississippi Company. Under their auspices the city of New Orleans was founded in 1718 by Bienville, who, in the following year, despatched an expedition under the command of Colonel du Tissonet, who visited the Osages at their former location in Kansas, and crossed the prairies 120 miles to the villages of the Pawnees at the mouth of the Republican River, where Fort Riley now stands. He continued his march westward 200 miles, to the land of the Padoucahs, where he also set up a cross, with the arms of the French king, September 27, 1719.

In 1724, De Bourgmont explored northern Kansas, starting from the "Grand Detour," where the city of Atchison now stands. In 1762, Kansas, with the rest of the Louisiana territory, was ceded by France to Spain. In 1801 it was retroceded by Spain to France. On the 30th of April, 1803, it was sold by Napoleon, then First Consul, to the United States. Thomas Jefferson, President. This was the largest real-estate transaction which occurred that year, being 756,961,280 acres, for $27,267,621, being at the rate of about 3½ cents per acre. The Anglo-Saxon was at last in the ascendant.

Attached in 1804 by act of Congress to the "Indian Territory," the following year to the "Territory of Louisiana," and in 1812 to the "Territory of Missouri," Kansas remained, after the admission of that State in 1820, detached, without local government or a name, until its permanent organization thirty-four years afterwards.

This mysterious region, so far, so fascinating, the object of so much interest and desire, inaccessible except by long voyages on mighty rivers whose sources were unknown, or by weary journeys in slow caravans disappearing beyond the frontier, had for some unknown reason long been marked on the maps of explorers and described in the text of geographers as "the Great American Desert."

Though for many centuries populous and martial Indian tribes, the aristocracy of the continent, making war their occu-

pation and the chase their
pastime, had without hus-
bandry sustained their
wild cavalry upon its harvests; though the Spanish
adventurers had reported
that "its earth was strong
and black, well watered by
brooks, streams, and riv-
ers"; though the French
trappers and voyageurs
had enriched the mer-
chants of St. Louis, New
Orleans, and Paris with its
furs and peltries; though
Lewis and Clarke had
penetrated its solitudes
and blazed a pathway to
the Pacific; though Pike
had discovered the frown-
ing peak indissolubly as-
sociated with his name;
and Pursley and the trad-
ers of Santa Fe had trav-
ersed the prairies of the
Arkansas and the mesas
of the Pecos—yet in pop-
ular belief half a century
ago the trans-Missouri
plains were classed with
the steppes of Tartary and
the arid wastes of Gobi.

CHARLES ROBINSON.

The flight of the Mormons to Salt Lake
in 1844, and the California exodus in 1849,
following the trail which was succeeded
by the pony express, the overland stage
line, and the Union Pacific Railroad, fa-
miliarized thousands of travellers from
all parts of the country with its enchanting landscape, its superb climate, and its
unrivalled though unsuspected capacities
for agriculture and civilization. To them
it was not a desert; it was an oasis, compared with which, in resources, fertility,
and possibilities of opulence, all the rest
of the earth was Sahara.

The surf of the advancing tide of population chafed restlessly against the barrier, realizing the truth of the majestic
and impressive sentence of Tocqueville,
written a quarter of a century before:
"This gradual and continuous progress
of the European race toward the Rocky
Mountains has the solemnity of a provi-
dential event; it is like a deluge of men
rising unabatedly, and daily driven onward by the hand of God."

The origin or genesis of states is
usually obscure and legendary, with pre-

historic periods from which they gradually emerge like coral islands from the
deep. Shadowy and crepuscular intervals precede the day, in whose uncertain
light men and events, distorted or exaggerated by tradition, become fabulous,
like the gods and goddesses, the wars and
heroes, of antiquity. But Kansas has no
mythology; its history has no twilight.
The foundation-stones of the State were
laid in the full blaze of the morning sun,
with the world as interested spectators.
Its architects were announced, their plans
disclosed, and the workmen have reared
its walls and crowned its dome without
concealment of their objects, and with no
attempt to disguise their satisfaction with
the results. Nothing has been done fur-
tively nor in a corner.

The first bill for the organization of
Kansas was presented by Senator Douglas in 1843, under the name of the Territory of Nebraska. The next, two years
later, named it the Territory of Platte, and
afterwards it was again twice called Nebraska.

January 23, 1854, Senator Douglas reported as a substitute for his former measure the bill for the organization of the Territories of Kansas and Nebraska, which, after fierce and acrimonious debate, passed both Houses of Congress, and was approved by President Pierce on the 30th of May. The eastern, northern, and southern boundaries of Kansas were the same as now. Its western limit extended 673 miles, to the summit of the Rocky Mountains, including more than half of the present area of Colorado, with its richest mines and its largest cities.

Intense political excitement preceded and followed the repeal of the Missouri Compromise, which gave the measure its chief political significance, and the conquest of Kansas was not the cause but the occasion of the conflict which ensued. The question of freedom or slavery in the Territory, and in the State to be, was important, it is true, but it was merely an incident in the tragedy, unsurpassed in the annals of our race, opening with the exchange of fourteen slaves for provisions by the Dutch man-of-war in the harbor of Jamestown in 1619, and whose prologue was pronounced by the guns that thundered their acclamations when the Confederate flag was lowered for the last time upon the field of Appomattox.

The incipient commonwealth lay in the westward path of empire—the zone within which the great commanders, orators, philosophers, and prophets of the world have been born; in which its Saviour was crucified; in which its decisive battles were fought, its victories over man and nature won, the triumphs of humanity and civilization achieved.

Had the formation of its domestic institutions alone been the stake, it would still have been compensative for the valor of heroes and the blood of martyrs. The diplomacy of great powers has often exhausted its devices upon more trivial pretexts, and nations have been desolated with wars waged under Cæsars and Napoleons for the subjugation of provinces of narrower bounds and inferior fertility.

But there was a profound conviction, a premonition, among thoughtful men that vastly more was involved; that further postponement of the duel between the antagonistic forces in our political system was impossible; that the existence of the Union, the perpetuity of free institutions, and the success of the experiment of self-government depended upon the issue.

The statesmen of the South, long accustomed to supremacy, had beheld with angry apprehension the menacing increase of the North in wealth and population; the irresistible tendency of emigration to the intermontane regions of the West and the Northwest, already dedicated to freedom. With prophetic vision they foresaw the admission of free States that would make the South a minority in the Senate, as it was already in the House, and hasten the destruction of the system of servile labor upon which they wrongly believed their prosperity to depend.

The conscience of the North apparently became dormant upon the subject of the immorality of slavery when, ceasing to be profitable, it disappeared, by the operation of natural laws, from the valleys of the Merrimac, the Connecticut, and the Hudson. It seemed to have been lulled into an eternal sleep by the anodyne of the Missouri Compromise; but it was roused into renewed activity when the repeal of that ordinance, supplemented by the Dred Scott decision, disclosed the intentions of the Southern leaders to maintain their ascendency by the extension of slavery over all the territories of the republic, a policy whose success threatened their political supremacy and their industrial independence.

Events have shown that the magnitude and significance of the Kansas episode were not exaggerated. It was the prelude to a martial symphony, the preface to a volume whose finis was not written until the downfall of slavery was recorded.

It would be a congenial task, but the present scope and purpose neither require nor permit a detailed narrative of the tumultuous interval from the organization of the Territory to the admission of the State. Its history has been written by its partisans. Its actors have been portrayed by their foes or their worshippers. The contests waged by Atchison and Stringfellow against the "abolitionists," and by Brown and Montgomery against the "border ruffians," the battles and murders and sudden deaths, the burning of houses and sacking of towns, the proclamations, bulletins, and platforms, the fraudulent elections and the dispersion of legislatures, form a unique chapter in our annals that waits the impartial chronicler. Neither side was blameless. Each was guilty of wrongs, begotten of the passions of the crisis, that culminated during the rebellion in border forays, encounters, reprisals, and retaliations, shocking to humanity, whose memory time cannot obliterate nor charity condone.

In the preliminary movement for the occupation of the new Territory, the slavery propagandists had the advantage of proximity. They swarmed across the Missouri border, establishing camps, taking possession of the polling-places, securing eligible sites for towns, and by obstructing the navigation of the river, compelled the emigrants from the North to make a long circuitous land journey through Iowa and Nebraska. They received re-enforcements and contributions of money, stores, and arms from many Southern States, and elected the first Territorial Delegate, J. W. Whitfield, who sat from September 20, 1854, till the adjournment of the Thirty-third Congress.

By the census taken in February, 1855, the number of legal voters in the Territory was 2905, but at the election of members of the first Legislature, four weeks later, 5427 votes were cast for the Southern candidates, and 791 for their opponents, the increment being largely due to the importation of electors from Missouri, who came into the Territory on the day of the election, and having voted, returned home at night.

By this guilty initiative they obtained on the threshold an immense advantage. They secured absolute control of the political agencies of the Territory. The Legislature which assembled at Pawnee in July adopted the slave code of Missouri *en bloc*, supplementing these statutes with original laws making many new offences against the slave system punishable with death, and compelling every official, candidate, and voter to take an oath to support the fugitive-slave law.

The idea of permanently colonizing Kansas with free labor from the North by systematic migration, and thus determining the question of the institutions of the new empire of the West, originated with Eli Thayer, of Massachusetts, who organized the Emigrant Aid Society in that State in 1854. The example was immediately followed in other parts of the North, and the pioneer colony reached the mouth of the Kansas River July 28th. Among the most prominent leaders of the colonists from New England were Samuel C. Pomeroy, afterwards for twelve years a

Senator of the United States, and Charles Robinson, an early settler in California, where he had fallen wounded in an armed struggle for what he believed to be the cause of popular rights against corporate injustice and tyranny. By one of those singular and pleasing coincidences which the judgment would reject as an unreal and extravagant climax in a romance or drama, he camped for the night on his overland journey in 1849 in the enchanting valley of the Wakarusa, to which five years later he returned to found the city of Lawrence, the intellectual capital of the State, of which he became the first Governor, and where, in the afternoon of an honorable, useful, and adventurous career, he still survives, his eye not dim nor his natural force abated, the object of affectionate regard and veneration.

The emigrants from the North were almost without exception from civil life, laborers, farmers, mechanics, and artisans, young men of the middle class, reared in toil and inured to poverty, unused to arms and unschooled in war. They were intelligent, devout, and patriotic. They came to plough and plant, to open farms, erect mills, to saw lumber and grind corn, to trade, teach school, build towns, and construct a free State. But one of them —James Henry Lane—had any military experience. He had been a colonel in the Mexican war, of an Indiana regiment, and was afterwards a Democratic Lieutenant-Governor and member of Congress from that State. He had an extraordinary assemblage of mental, moral, and physical traits, and with even a rudimentary perception of the value of personal character as an element of success in public affairs, would have been a great leader, with an enduring fame. But in arms he was a Captain Bobadil, and in politics a Rittmeiter Dugald Dalgetty. He proposed to "settle the vexed question and save Kansas from further outrage" by a battle between one hundred slave-holders, including Senator Atchison, and one hundred free-State men, including himself, to be fought in the presence of twelve United States Senators and twelve members of the House of Representatives as umpires!

He was the object of inexplicable idolatry and unspeakable execration. With his partisans the superlatives of adulation were feeble and meagre. With his foes the lexicon of infamy contained no epithets sufficiently lurid to express their grace ; but the multitudes to whom he perpetually appealed hung upon his hoarse and harsh harangues with the rapture of devotees upon the oracular rhapsodies of a prophet, and responded to his apostrophes with frenzied enthusiasm.

He gained the prize which he sought with such fevered ambition ; but after many stormy and tempestuous years, Nemesis, inevitable in such careers, demanded retribution. He presumed too far upon the toleration of a constituency which had honored him so long and forgiven him so much. He transcended the limitations which the greatest cannot pass. He apostatized once too often; and in his second term in the Senate, to avoid impending exposure, after a tragic interval of despair, he died by his own hand, surviving ten days after the bullet had passed through his brain.

The Northern press, alive to the importance of the struggle, united in an appeal to public opinion such as had never before been formulated, and despatched to the Territory a corps of correspondents of unsurpassed ability and passionate devotion to liberty. Foremost among these apostles were William A. Phillips, who, after long and distinguished service in the army and in Congress, lives in literary retirement upon a magnificent estate near the prosperous city of Salina, which he founded; Albert Dean Richardson, whose assassination in New York in 1869 prematurely closed a brilliant career; and James Redpath, subsequently editor of the *North American Review*. Their contributions reached eager readers in every State, and were reprinted beyond the seas, chronicling every incident, delineating every prominent man, arousing indignation by the recitation of the wrongs they denounced, and exciting the imagination with descriptions of the loveliness of the land, rivalling Milton's portraiture of the Garden of Eden. No time was ever so minutely and so indelibly photographed upon the public retina. The name of no State was ever on so many friendly and so many hostile tongues. It was pronounced in every political speech, and inserted in every party platform. No region was ever so advertised, and the impression then produced has never passed away.

The journalists were re-enforced by the poets, artists, novelists, and orators of an age distinguished for genius, learning, and

JAMES HENRY LANE.

abhorrence and detestation. They alleged that he never paid a debt nor told the truth, save by accident or on compulsion, and that to reach the goal of his ambition he had no convictions he would not sell, made no promise he would not break, and had no friend he would not betray.

A lean, haggard, and sinewy figure, with a mephistophelian leer upon his shaven visage, his movements were alert and restless, like one at bay and apprehensive of detection. Professing religion, he was never even accused of hypocrisy, for his followers knew that he partook of the sacrament as a political device to secure the support of the church; and that with the same nonchalant alacrity, had he been running for office in Hindostan, he would have thrown his offspring to the crocodiles of the Ganges or bowed among the Parsees at the shrine of the Sun. His energy was tireless and his activity indefatigable. No night was too dark, no storm too wild, no heat or cold too excessive, no distance too great, to delay his meteoric pilgrimages, with dilapidated garb and equipage, across the trackless prairies from convention to convention. His oratory was voluble and incessant, without logic, learning, rhetoric, or inspiration. Lincoln, Douglas, Seward, and Sumner delivered their most memorable speeches upon the theme. Phillips and Beecher, then at the meridian of their powers, appealed to the passions and the conscience of the nation by unrivalled eloquence and invective. Prizes were offered for lyrics, that were obtained, so profound was the impulse, by obscure and unknown competitors. Lowell, Bryant, Holmes, Longfellow, and Emerson lent the magic of their verse. Whittier was the laureate of the era. His "Burial of Barbour" and "Marais du Cygne" seemed like a prophet's cry for vengeance to the immigrants, who marched to the inspiring strains of "Suona la Tromba," or chanted, to the measure of "Auld Lang-Syne,"

"We cross the prairies as of old
Our fathers crossed the sea."

The contagion spread to foreign lands, and alien torches were lighted at the flame. Walter Savage Landor wrote an ode to free Kansas. Lady Byron collected money, which she sent to the author of *Uncle Tom's Cabin* for the relief of the sufferers in Kansas. Volunteers from Italy, France, and Germany, revolutionists and exiles, served in the desultory war, many of whom afterwards fought with distinction in the armies of the Union. It was the romance of history. The indescribable agitation which always attends the introduction of a great moral question into politics pervaded the souls of men, transforming the commonplace into the ideal, and inaugurating a heroic epoch. The raptures that swelled the hearts of the pioneers yet thrill and vibrate in the blood of their posterity, like the chords of a smitten harp when the player has departed.

The free-State settlers, being powerless to overcome or reverse the political action of their adversaries, adopted the policy of ignoring it altogether. They resolved to endeavor to change the Territory into a State without the formality of an enabling act of Congress. Their competence to do this was denied on the ground that it was in opposition to the regularly organized political authorities, but they chose delegates to a convention, which met at Topeka, and framed a Constitution that was adopted in December, 1855, by 1731 for to 46 against, its friends only participating in the election.

A Governor and other State officers

and a Delegate in Congress were chosen in January. The national House of Representatives, July 3, 1856, passed a bill for the admission of the State under this Constitution, but it was rejected in the Senate.

Acting, however, upon the theory that the State existed, the Legislature chosen under the Topeka Constitution assembled July 4, 1856, but was dispersed by United States troops commanded by Colonel Sumner, on the order of President Pierce, who denounced the movement as an insurrec-

MARCUS J. PARROTT.

tion requiring the forcible interposition of national authority. Further attempts to organize were thwarted by the arrest of the leaders for usurpation of office and misprision of treason.

Immigration from the North increased, and under the assurance of Governor Walker that the election should be honest and peaceable, the two parties had the first actual test of their relative strength, October, 1857, when the Free-State electors chose 33 out of 52 members of the Legislature. For Delegate in Congress 3799 votes were cast for Epaphroditus Ransom, who had been Governor of Michigan, 1848-9, and 7888 for Marcus J. Parrott, an ambitious and popular member of the Leavenworth bar.

Born in South Carolina, of Huguenot ancestry, Parrott was at an early age domiciled in Ohio, whither his family had removed to escape the contaminating influences of slavery. He was graduated at Yale, and trained to the law. He came to the Territory two years before, at the age of twenty-six, politically in sympathy with the party in power, and expecting to be the recipient of its favors. Imbued with a passion for liberty, he revolted at the methods pursued by its foes, and espoused the cause of freedom with the ardor of a generous and impulsive nature. Reared in affluence, and of easy fortune, he was familiar with the ways of the world, and united to the bearing of a

MARTIN F. CONWAY.

courtier a captivating suavity of address which propitiated all sorts and conditions of men. He was like a thread of gold shot through the rough woof of the frontier. Though not of heroic stature, his dark vivacious countenance, the rich melody of his voice, and his impressive elocution gave him great power as an orator. He possessed the fatal gift of fluency, but wanting depth and sincerity, seemed like an actor seeking ap-

plause rather than a leader striving to direct, or a statesman endeavoring to convince the understanding of his followers. His service in Congress demanded the indulgent judgment of his constituents, and failing of an election to the Senate when the State was admitted, he yielded to the allurements of appetite, squandered two fortunes in travel and pleasure, and the splendid light of his prophetic morning sank lower and lower until it was quenched in the outer darkness of gloom and desolation.

The leaders of the pro-slavery forces from this time practically abandoned their aggressive efforts, admitting that they had been overcome by the superior resources of the North; but the so-called "bogus Legislature," before its expiration, called another convention, which sat at Lecompton, and adopted the Constitution known in history by that name. It recognized the existence of slavery in the Territory, forbade the enactment of emancipation laws, and prohibited amendments before 1864. Knowing its fate if submitted to the people, it provided that only the clause relating to slavery should be voted upon, but that the instrument itself should be established by act of Congress admitting the State. The slavery clause was adopted by 6256 to 567, the Free State men refraining from voting; but as soon as the new Legislature met, an act was passed submitting the entire Constitution to the popular vote, January 4, 1858, when it was rejected by 10,256 to 162, the pro-slavery men not appearing at the polls.

The debate was then transferred to Congress, and the effort to admit the State under the Lecompton Constitution failed, although the President urged it, and its friends were in a majority in both Houses. The tempting bribe of the English bill, which was offered as a compromise, was rejected by the people in August by 11,088 to 1788, and thus the curtain fell on Lecompton.

The abortive series of Constitutions was enlarged by the formation of the fifth at Leavenworth, which was also ratified by the people, but rejected by Congress on the ground that the population was insufficient. The Territorial existence of Kansas closed with the adoption, October 4, 1859, by a vote of 10,421 to 5530, of the Wyandotte Constitution, under which, the Southern Senators having departed, Kansas was admitted into the Union January 29, 1861.

The long procession of Governors and acting Governors sent to rule over the Territory vanished away like the show of eight kings, the last having a glass in his hand, Banquo's ghost following, in the witches' cavern in *Macbeth*—Reeder, Shannon, Geary, Stanton, Walker, Denver, Medary, and Beebe—"come like shadows, so depart!"

It is a strange illustration of Anglo-Saxon pride of race, and of its haughty assumption of superiority, that in a State which apotheosized John Brown of Osawatomie, and gave a new definition to the rights of man, suffrage was confined to "white male citizens." But the people of Kansas were too brave and strong to be long unjust. The first colored man regularly enlisted as a soldier was sworn and mustered at Fort Leavenworth. The first colored regiment was raised in Kansas, and the first engagement in which negroes fought was under the command of a Kansas officer, October 26, 1862. The citizen longest in office in the State—for nearly thirty years—was colored, and born a slave.

The admission of the State and the outbreak of the rebellion were coincident, and, as might have been predicted from their martial gestation, the people devoted themselves with unabated zeal to the maintenance of the Union. Being outside the field of regular military operations, inaccessible by railroads, exposed to guerilla incursions from Missouri, and to Indian raids from the south and west, the campaign of defence was continuous, and for four years the entire population was under arms. Immigration ceased. By the census of June, 1860, the number of inhabitants was 143,463; at the close of the war it had declined to 140,179. Fields lay fallow, and the fire of the forges expired. Towns were deserted and homesteads abandoned. The State sent more soldiers to battle than it had voters when the war began. Under all calls, its quota was 12,931; it furnished 20,151, without bounty or conscription. Nineteen regiments, five companies, and three batteries participated in 127 engagements, of which seven were on her own soil. From Wilson Creek to the Gulf every great field in

the Southwest was illustrated by their valor and consecrated by their blood. Her proportion of mortality in the field was the largest among the States, exceeding 61 in each 1000 enlistments, Vermont following with 58, and Massachusetts with nearly 48. Provost-Marshal-General Fry, in his final roster of the Union armies, in which all are alike entitled to honor, be-

EDMUND G. ROSS.

cause all alike did their duty, wrote this certificate of precedence in glory: "Kansas shows the highest battle mortality of the table. The same singularly martial disposition which induced about one-half of the able-bodied men of the State to enter the army without bounty may be supposed to have increased their exposure to the casualties of battle after they were in the service."

With the close of the war the first decennium ended, and the disbanded veterans returned under the flag they had redeemed to the State they had made free. Attracted by homesteads upon the public domain, by just and liberal exemption laws, and by the companionship of the brave, those heroes were re-enforced by a vast host of their comrades, representing

PRESTON B. PLUMB.

commonwealth, which resembles primitive Massachusetts before its middle classes had disappeared and its society become stratified into the superfluously rich and the hopelessly poor.

Within these pastoral boundaries there are no millionaires nor any paupers, except such as have been deprived by age, disease, and calamity of the ability to labor. No great fortunes have been brought to the State, and none have been accumulated by commerce, manufactures, or speculation. No sumptuous mansions nor glittering equipages nor ostentatious display exasperate or allure. Legislation protects wages and cabins no less than bonds and palaces, and the free school, the jury, and impartial suffrage have resulted in the establishment of justice, liberty, fraternity, and equality as the foundations of the State.

Politically, as might have been predicted, the Republican party, whose birth is indissolubly associated with the efforts to dedicate Kansas to freedom, continued supreme for thirty years. During that period the State had but one Governor and one member of Congress of another faith, and there have been few Legislatures in which the membership of the opposition has risen as high as 20 per cent. This supremacy has not been favorable to national leadership, both parties having reserved their allegiance and their favors for more doubtful constituencies.

every arm of the military and naval service from all the States of the Union. Not less than 30 per cent. of its electors have fought in the Union armies, and the present commander of the Grand Army of the Republic, Timothy McCarthy, witnessed the defence of Sumter and the surrender at Appomattox.

Population increased from 8601 in 1855 to 140,179 in 1865, 528,349 in 1875, 1,268,562 in 1885, and 1,427,096 in 1890. In a community so rapidly assembled the homogeneity of its elements is extraordinary. Kansas is distinctly the American State. Less than 10 per cent. of its inhabitants are of foreign birth, principally English, Germans, and Scandinavians, and less than four per cent. of African descent. The State is often called the child of the Puritans, but, contrary to the popular impression, the immigration from New England was comparatively trivial in numbers, much the larger contributions having been derived from Iowa, Indiana, Illinois, Missouri, Pennsylvania, New York, and Kentucky. It is the ideas of the Pilgrims and not their descendants that have had dominion in the young

An equilibrium which compels the presentation of strong and unexceptionable candidates and the practice of honesty and economy in administration is better than a disproportionate majority which makes the contest end with a nomination. When one party has nothing to hope and the other nothing to fear, degradation and decay are inevitable. Intrigue supplants merit; the sense of responsibility disappears; manipulation of primaries, caucuses, and conventions displaces the conflict and collision of opinion and debate. Paltry ambitions become respectable. Little men aspire to great places, and distinguished careers are impossible.

In addition to those elsewhere mentioned, others who have been prominent in State and national affairs are Martin F. Conway, the first Representative in Congress, a native of Maryland, a diminutive, fair-haired, blue-eyed enthusiast, with the bulging brow and retiring chin of Swinburne, an erratic political dreamer whose reveries ended at St. Elizabeth; Generals James G. Blunt, Robert B. Mitchell, George W. Deitzler, Charles W. Blair, Albert L. Lee, and Powell Clayton, military leaders, and eminent also in civil life; Edmund G. Ross, the successor of Lane in the Senate, who forfeited the confidence of his constituents by voting against the impeachment of President Johnson, and was subsequently appointed by President Cleveland Governor of New Mexico; Thomas A. Osborn, who, after serving as Governor (1873-7), had a remarkably successful diplomatic career as United States Minister to Chile and Brazil; John P. St. John, twice Governor, prominently identified with the cause of prohibition, and the candidate of its advocates for the Presidency in 1884; John A. Martin, a distinguished soldier, editor of a leading journal, Governor 1884-8, in whose administration the municipal organization of the State was completed; Preston B. Plumb, Senator from 1877 until his untimely death, December 20, 1891; and Bishop W. Perkins, his successor by appointment, after several terms upon the bench, and eight years of distinguished service in the House of Representatives; Thomas Ryan, ten years member of Congress, and now representing the United States as Envoy Extraordinary and Minister Plenipotentiary to Mexico.

Philosophers and historians recognize the influence of early settlers upon the character and destinies of a community. Original impulses are long continued, like the characteristics and propensities which the mother bestows upon her unborn child. The constant vicissitudes of climate, of fortune, of history, together with the fluctuations of politics and business, have engendered in Kansas hitherto perpetual agitation, not always favorable to happiness, but which has stimulated activity, kept the popular pulse feverish, and begotten a mental condition exalted above the level monotonies of life. Every one is on the *qui vive*, alert, vigilant, like a sentinel at an outpost. Existence has the excitement of a game of chance, of a revolution, of a battle whose event is doubtful. The unprecedented environment has produced a temperament volatile and mercurial, marked by uncalculating ardor, enterprise, intrepidity, and insatiable hunger for innovation, out of which has grown a society that has been alternately the reproach and the marvel of mankind.

For a generation Kansas has been the testing-ground for every experiment in morals, politics, and social life. Doubt of all existing institutions has been respectable. Nothing has been venerable or revered merely because it exists or has endured. Prohibition, female suffrage, fiat money, free silver, every incoherent and fantastic dream of social improvement and reform, every economic delusion that has bewildered the foggy brains of fanatics, every political fallacy nurtured by misfortune, poverty, and failure, rejected elsewhere, has here found tolerance and advocacy. The enthusiasm of youth, the conservatism of age, have alike yielded to the contagion, making the history of the State a melodramatic series of cataclysms, in which tragedy and comedy have contended for the mastery, and the convulsions of nature have been emulated by the catastrophes of society. There has been neither peace, tranquillity, nor repose. The farmer can never foretell his harvest, nor the merchant his gains, nor the politician his supremacy. Something startling has always happened, or has been constantly anticipated. The idol of to-day is execrated to-morrow. Seasons of phenomenal drought, when the sky was brass and the earth iron, have been followed by periods of indescribable fecundity, in which the husbandman has been embarrassed by abundance, whose value has been diminished by its excess. Cyclones, blizzards, and grasshoppers have been so identified with the State in public estimation as to be described by its name, while some of the *bouleversements* of its politics have aroused the inextinguishable laughter, and others have excited the commiseration and condemnation, of mankind.

But as in spite of its anomalies and the obstacles of nature the growth of the State in wealth and numbers has been unprecedented, and its condition is one of stable and permanent prosperity, so, notwithstanding the vagaries and eccentricities into which by the appeals of reformers and the pressure of misfortune they have sometimes been betrayed, the great body of the people are patriotic, conservative, and intelligent to a degree not surpassed elsewhere, and seldom equalled among the children of men.

The social emancipation of woman is complete. The only limitation upon her political equality with man is in the right of suffrage, which is confined to municipal and school-district elections. Women are exempt from jury duty, from military service, and from work upon the highways; but, whether married or single, they can practise the professions, engage in mercantile business, follow any industry or occupation, and pursue any calling, upon the same conditions as men. The distinction of sex is recognized only in its natural sense and use. The property, real and personal, of a single woman remains her own after marriage, unless voluntarily alienated. She can sue and be sued in her own name, and her estate is not liable for her husband's debts, nor can the homestead be sold or encumbered without her consent. When the marriage is ended by death, the survivor is entitled to a moiety of the joint and several estate, with the remainder to the children. Agitation for full suffrage is active, and will undoubtedly ultimately prevail.

The first bonds voted in the State were for school-houses, and the first tax levied in every community, the largest tax, and the tax most cheerfully paid, is the school tax. For the education of her children Kansas has already spent the enormous total of forty million dollars, nearly one-half the entire cost of State and municipal government. Equal facilities are afforded to whites and blacks. More than twenty-one million dollars are invested in school-houses, State buildings, lands, and other property for educational purposes. The average school year is twenty-seven weeks, supported by State, district, and county taxation, amounting in 1890 to $5,696,659 69.

This magnificent educational system wears the triple crown of the State University, at Lawrence, with a faculty of thirty-six members and 474 students, the State Normal School, at Emporia, with a faculty of eighteen members and 1200 students, and the Agricultural College, at Manhattan, with an endowment from public lands of $501,426 33, $15,000 annu-

ally from the government as an experiment station, an annual income of $65,000, a faculty of eighteen members, and 575 students.

Public education is supplemented by private and denominational schools, with an average yearly attendance of 6500, and buildings and endowments valued at two and a quarter million dollars. Such efforts and sacrifices have already produced perceptible and gratifying results. The illiterate fraction in Kansas is the smallest save one in the nation. The general standard of intelligence is unusually high. The State publications and reports are models for imitation, notably the Biennial of the State Board of Agriculture, speaking whereof the London Times in 1880 said, "the resources the book describes fill the English mind with astonishment and envy."

The curse and bane of frontier life is drunkenness. The literature of the mining camp, the cross-roads, and the cattle ranch reeks with whiskey. In every new settlement the saloon precedes the school-house and the church, is the rendezvous of ruffians, the harbor of criminals, the recruiting station of the murderer, the gambler, the harlot, and the thief; a perpetual menace to social order, intelligence, and morality, above whose portal should be inscribed the legend engraved on the lintel of the infernal gates, "Lasciate ogni speranza voi ch' entrate."

Agitation against the evils of intemperance was contemporary with the political organization of the Territory. The founders of Topeka and Lawrence forbade the sale of intoxicating beverages within their corporate limits, and the debate continued until 1881, when a constitutional amendment was adopted forever prohibiting the manufacture and sale of intoxicating liquors, except for medicinal, mechanical, and scientific purposes. This was enforced by appropriate legislation, and the validity of the amendment and of the statutes was sustained by the Supreme Courts of the State and of the nation. After futile and costly resistance, the dram-shop traffic has disappeared from the State. Surreptitious sales continue, club drinking and "joints" are not unknown, but the saloon has vanished, and the law has been better enforced than similar legislation elsewhere. In the larger towns prohibition is not so strictly observed as in the rural districts, where public opinion is more rigid; but in all localities the beneficent results are apparent in the diminution of crime, poverty, and disorder. Banned by law, the occupation is stigmatized, and becomes disreputable. If the offender avoids punishment, he does not escape contempt. Drinking being in secret, temptation is diminished, the weak are protected from their infirmities, and the young from their appetites and passions.

Much of the prominence of Kansas is due to the novel and startling methods employed by its journalists to invite public attention to the opportunities found here for success and happiness. They have been the persistent and conspicuous advocates of immigration, railroads, schools, churches, manufactories, and improvements.

The first printing-press was brought by Jotham Meeker in 1833 to Shawnee Mission, a station of the Methodist Church, established in what is now Johnson County, in 1829. Upon its primitive platen were printed religious books, pamphlets, tracts, and a newspaper in the Indian tongue, in a region then more remote and inaccessible than Alaska now. This venerable relic, after nearly sixty years of service, is still on duty in one of the southern counties of the State. The first newspaper in the Territory was the Leavenworth *Herald*, printed in the open air under an elm-tree on the levee of the city of that name. It has been succeeded by a swarming multitude of original, ingenious, and brilliant ventures in journalism, magazines, reviews, periodicals, papers, daily and weekly, varying in excellence, but united in vociferous and persistent affirmation that Kansas is the best State in the most glorious country on the finest planet in the solar system; that its soil is the richest, its climate the most salubrious, its men the most enterprising, its women the most beautiful, its children the most docile, its horses the fastest, its cattle the largest, its sheep the woolliest, its hogs the fattest, its grasshoppers the most beneficent, its blizzards the warmest, its cyclones the mildest, its droughts the wettest, its hot winds the coldest, its past the most glorious, its present the most prophetic, its destiny the most sublime.

They remind the bewildered reader of the feat of the Hindoo necromancer who throws a ball of cord into the air, catches the depending end, and climbing hand over hand, disappears in the blue abyss of the sky. Their versatile and extravagant spirit appears in the extraordinary nomenclature which serves to attract the attention of the searcher after truth. Among them may be found *The Thomas* (County) *Cat, The Wano Rustler, The Paralyzer, The Cherokee Cyclone, The Cimarron Sod House, The Lake City Prairie Dog, The Bazoo, The Lucifer, The Prairie Owl, The Kincaid Knuckle, The Bundle of Sticks, The Cap-Sheaf, The Dodge City Cowboy.*

The newspapers have been the advance-agents of civilization, often the voice of one crying in the wilderness. They have reversed the ancient order, and instead of waiting for subscribers and advertisers, they have been the sappers and miners of the assault upon the solitudes of nature. The moral tone of the press is exceptionally pure, its intellectual plane unusually elevated; it is generous in the treatment of public men, just in the criticism of opponents, broad and liberal in views of State and national policy and administration.

The hunger and thirst for knowledge, which has created and in turn is stimulated by the press, has a wider scope, and the people are omnivorous readers of metropolitan journals and leading periodicals. With the church and the school have been established great numbers of public and private libraries, so that religion, learning, and literature have become the moving forces of every community. The State library and the collection of the State historical society at the capital, and the public libraries in other localities, are richer and larger than those of many of the older States.

The venerable jest that there is no Sunday west of the Mississippi is not entirely jocular. It has a suggestion of truth. The same influence which makes men indifferent to the past renders them careless also of the future. Ambition and cupidity are the ruling passions in new communities, and the chief end of man is not to glorify God and enjoy Him forever, but to make money and run for office. The concern for this world is much greater than for that which is to come. Religion is conservative. It stands upon authority, and demands obedience. The pioneer is radical, impatient of dogmas, and a "kicker" by instinct. He detests bigots, hypocrites, and fossils. His mind being inquisitive, its tendency is toward materialism and rationalism rather than faith. He is not disturbed by anathemas, and with composure hears himself described as an agnostic; but he is reverent, tolerant, and devout. He recognizes religion as one of the great beneficent forces of the universe, an indispensable premise in the syllogism of human destiny, without which society would be a sophism and the soul of man a fallacy. Kansas attests her convictions by 4000 church organizations, representing every denomination, with an aggregate membership of nearly 317,000, having 2339 houses of worship, and property valued at about $9,000,000.

The first railroad track was laid in Kansas March 20, 1860, on the Elwood and Marysville line, opposite the city of St. Joseph. On the 23d of April the Albany, a pioneer locomotive, a veteran which had been used from Boston to the Missouri as railroads advanced across the continent, was ferried over the river, and drew the first train on the first section of the Pacific Railroad. Construction ceased with the breaking out of the war, but was resumed with great vigor at its close. Stimulated by liberal donations from cities, towns, and counties, railroad building became a mania, with disastrous results. In addition to the great trunk lines through populous and productive regions, subsidiary branches, unnecessary auxiliaries, and superfluous feeders were built, without earning capacity, burdening communities with irretrievable self-imposed debts, absorbing the revenues of those which were remunerative, giving poor service, and rapidly deteriorating from neglect and poverty.

In August, 1863, the grading of the Kansas Pacific Railroad was begun at the State line between Kansas and Missouri, in the dense forest of cottonwoods that then shaded the site of what has since become a populous suburb of one of the great cities of the West. The contractor erected at the initial point a pillar, inscribing on the face towards the east "Slavery," and on the face towards the west "Freedom." This line was completed to Lawrence in November, 1864, but the first 40 miles were not accepted by the government until October, 1865.

There are now 109 railroad companies in the State, many of them consolidated, with more than 10,000 miles of track, assessed at $50,865,825 34. Of the 106 counties, all but five are traversed by railroads, and the traveller entering a Santa Fe train at Atchison can within a week, in a Pullman car, reach the city of Mexico over almost the identical route followed by Coronado in his expedition 350 years ago.

This great corporation, chartered in 1857 and permanently organized in 1864, was not operated until 1869, and then only as a local line from Topeka to the Osage coal fields, 30 miles southwest. Its land grant was considered of doubtful value, and capitalists looked askant upon the project of constructing a railroad along the unpeopled sands of the Arkansas Valley, which were still the grazing-ground of the buffalo and the hunting-ground of the savage. The site of Wichita, alliteratively described by M. M. Murdock, its prophet and herald, as "the peerless princess of the plains," with its palaces, temples, marts, electric lights, and railways, water-works, elevators, flouring-mills, and packing-houses, had not been traced among the whispering reeds and scattered cottonwoods of the meadows bordering on the American Nile. The subirrigation which makes the corn and wheat crops independent of the rainfall had not been discovered. The fertility of the loose and shifting soil was not suspected, and the vast region seemed doomed to perpetual solitude and sterility.

Some bolder spirits, gifted with the prescience essential to great designs, foresaw the future, and sent the surveyors and graders, the advance-guard of civilization, into the desert. Contemporaneously with construction, they advertised the lands and the State, sending agents to all parts of the Union and to every country in Europe, penetrating Russia to the Crimea; inviting immigration; selling farms at low rates on long time; extending payments and giving aid in time of distress; exhibiting the productions of orchards and farms; bringing harvest-home excursions from other States; distributing maps, pamphlets, and statistical tables as numerous and as chromatic-colored as autumnal leaves. Similar methods, though not as extensive nor as liberal, were employed by the managers of the Missouri Pacific, Fort Scott and Gulf, the Union Pacific, and other trunk lines, under the stimulus of which lands rapidly advanced in value, and much that was sold at from three to five dollars is now worth as high as one hundred dollars per acre.

The farms of Kansas were not made to order. They waited for the plough. There were no forests to fell, no stumps to extract, no rocks to remove, no malaria to combat. These undulating fields are the floors of ancient seas. These limestone ledges underlying the prairies, and cropping from the foreheads of the hills, are the cemeteries of the marine insect life of the primeval world. This inexhaustible humus is the mould of the decaying herbage of unnumbered centuries. It is only upon calcareous plains in temperate latitudes that agriculture is supreme, and the strong structure and the rich nourishment imparted essential to bulk, endurance, and speed in animals, to grace, beauty, and passion in women, and in man to stature, courage, health, and longevity.

Here are valleys in which a furrow can be ploughed a hundred miles long, where all the labor of breaking, planting, cultivating, mowing, reaping, and harvesting is performed by horses, engines, and machinery, so that farming has become a sedentary occupation. The lister has supplanted the hoe; the cradle, the scythe, and the sickle are as unknown to Western agriculture as the catapult and culverin to modern warfare. The well-sweep and windlass have been supplanted by the windmills, whose vivacious disks disturb the monotony of the sky. But for these labor-saving inventions the pioneers would still linger in the valleys of the Ohio and Sangamon, and the subjugation of the desert would have been indefinitely postponed.

The ozone of the air, its dryness, and the elevation of the land produce nervous exaltation, which creates enthusiasm, movement, energy, push, vigor, and "go"; by whose operation men are transformed into "rustlers" and "boomers," inventors of new methods to overcome the hostility of nature, and coiners of novel phrases to express their defiance of destiny. Platitudes are unknown, and all epithets are superlative. Imagination predominates; established formulas and maxims are disregarded. Upon the rainless and sterile uplands the strata of the earth are pierced for water; and marble, paint, cement, fire-clay, gypsum, coal, and salt are discovered in the descent. If chinch-bugs and noxious insects attack his crops, parasites and epidemics are imported for their destruction. Foiled and thwarted by the baffling clouds, the undaunted husbandman bombards the invisible moisture of the firmament with explosive balloons, and effusively welcomes the meteorological juggler who summons with his incantations aqueous spirits from the vasty deep. The faith which removes mountains into the sea animates every citizen, and rejects the impossible with calm disdain.

The present wealth of Kansas, real and personal, reaches the astounding aggregate of nearly seventeen hundred million dollars*—many times more than the valuation of all the States in the Union when the government was established, after one hundred and fifty years of colonial existence. This enormous accumulation nominally represents a period of forty years, but has actually been created in much less, for life in Kansas from 1854 to 1865 was a bivouac, and the real development of the State did not begin until peace was restored. Twenty years ago half its area was pastured by buffalo, and a considerable part was covered by the reservations of hostile Indians, whose depredations continued until 1880, resulting in more than two hundred deaths, or captivities less merciful than the grave, and the expenditure of millions for the defence of the frontier.

Even as late as 1875, agriculture beyond the Blue was regarded by many as an uncertain and by some as a desperate experiment. Nature appeared to resent the invasion of her solitudes. The horrors of internecine war were followed by a succession of droughts and hot winds, that, in turn, were re-enforced by swarms of locusts, which descended from the torrid mesas of New Mexico and the sterile Piedmont of Colorado and Wyoming, obscuring the pitiless sun by their desolating flights, leaving the earth they devastated defiled by their loathsome exuviæ, and poisoning the atmosphere with the fetor of their decay. It was like the incarnation of nature's secret and evil forces, as if the bacilli and microbes of "the pestilence that walketh in darkness and the destruction that wasteth at noonday" had become visible, endowed with wings, malignant intelligence, and insatiable voracity.

That the State survived the infliction of this series of disasters seems incredible. A people less sanguine, buoyant, and res-

* Extra Census Bulletin No. 14, October, 1891.

olute, more unschooled in the lessons of adversity, would have succumbed. They would have surrendered unconditionally, and abandoned their parched fields and farms to the coyote and the prairie-dog. But the malevolent energies of the desert, having been marshalled for this final onset, were repulsed by an indomitable persistence superior to their own, and sullenly withdrew. While envious rivals were jeering, and jealous competitors were flouting, pointing with scorn's slow, unmoving finger at the droughts, grasshoppers, hot winds, crop failures, and other calamities of Kansas, the world was suddenly startled and dazzled by her collective display of horticultural and agricultural products at the Centennial at Philadelphia, which received the highest awards. Since that time there has been no arena in Europe or America in which Kansas has declined competition, and at the New Orleans exposition, in 1885, she took sixty-five first and second premiums on wheat, corn, flour, sugar, fruit, and cattle, leading all the States in the Union.

This year (1891) the yield of wheat has been 58,550,653 bushels, nearly one-tenth of the entire crop of the country; of oats, 40,000,000 bushels; unfavorable conditions have reduced by one-third the average corn crop of 200,000,000 bushels. These, supplemented with roots, sorghum, broom-corn, millet, hay, rye, barley, garden vegetables, honey, and wine, have enriched the farmers of Kansas with wealth far exceeding the year's yield of the gold and silver mines of the United States. The total aggregate value of all farm products for the years 1889 and 1890 was $283,740,491, and that of the present biennial, judging by the previous rate of increase, will exceed $300,000,000.

The courage, sand, and grit of the people, their nervy faith in fortune, the confidence of capitalists in the staple value of Kansas lands and in the industry and integrity of their owners, have marvellous illustration in the fact that during the ten years between 1880 and 1890 a recorded real estate mortgage indebtedness was incurred of nearly five hundred million dollars, exclusive of loans upon chattels, State and railroad land contracts, personal liabilities, city, township, and county subsidies for railways and other public objects, aggregating probably two hundred millions more. This feverish period culminated in a delirium of public and private credit known in local history as "the boom of 1887," whose frenzy and disaster have not been exceeded since the bursting of the "Mississippi bubble," or the collapse of the "tulipomania" of the seventeenth century.

The building of superfluous towns, the construction of unnecessary railroads, the organization of counties and the location of county-seats, the entry of public lands for the sole purpose of mortgaging the inchoate title at excessive valuations, became established industries. The agents of Eastern companies eagerly competed for the privilege of placing loans upon quarter sections without a fence or furrow, often far beyond their market value. Professional "boomers," with a retinue of surveyors and cappers and strikers, invaded the State, bought and platted additions, which they sold at exorbitant prices to resident and foreign speculators, victims to the epidemic passion for sudden wealth, whose inexplicable contagion infected the reason of men with its undetected bacteria.

The reaction came like the "next morning" after a night of revelry and debauch. The plunderers disappeared with the ready money of the people, leaving, instead of anticipated wealth, an intolerable burden of maturing indebtedness upon deluded purchasers. Empty railroad trains ran across deserted prairies to vacant towns. Successive droughts and siroccos destroyed the crops in the western half of the State. The laborers, mechanics, and speculators, having erected costly business blocks that found no tenants, and residences that remained uninhabited, being without further occupation, sought employment elsewhere. The population declined. Pay-day came. The coupon matured. Taxes fell due. Creditors became clamorous. Merchants refused credit, and public and private treasuries were depleted.

These accumulated misfortunes were supplemented in 1890 by an irruption of false teachers, with the instruction that such disasters were the result of vicious legislation, and could be cured by statute; that banks should be destroyed, debts repudiated, property forcibly redistributed, and poverty abolished by act of Congress. It was an exhibition of what Burke described as the "insanity of nations." Conservative, thoughtful, and patriotic men yielded to an uncontrollable impulse of resentment against society. This outburst shocked the public credit, temporarily destroyed the ability of the debtor to borrow or to pay, diminished the value of property, and inflicted an irremediable wound upon the State's good name. But it vanished like one of the ominous and sudden catastrophes of the sky. With the return of prosperity came the restoration of reason. More than half the enormous indebtedness has already been liquidated, and the whole will be honestly and resolutely paid. A Kansas loan is as secure as a government bond.

The Arabs say that he who drinks of the Nile must always thirst; no other waters can quench or satisfy. So those who have done homage and taken the oath of fealty to Kansas can never be alienated or forsworn. The love of the people for their State is not so much a vague sentiment as an insatiable passion. The anniversary of its admission is observed by the schools as a festival and holiday, with commemorative exercises. Days are set apart in spring, by Executive proclamation, to decorate the hills and road-sides with trees, as a lover adorns his bride with jewels. The defects of climate and the disasters of husbandry are indulgently explained and excused as the foibles of a friend from whom better things may be anticipated hereafter. The wanderers, whom caprice or misfortune may temporarily banish, are recalled by an irresistible solicitation as they remember the bright aspect of its sky, which is like a smile, and the soft touch of its atmosphere, which is like a caress.

The cross which Coronado reared at the verge of his wanderings long since mouldered, and the ashes of the adventurer have slept for ages in their ancestral sepulchre in Spain. He found neither Quivera's phantom towers nor Cibola's gems and gold; but a fairer Capital than that he sought to despoil has risen like an exhalation from the solitude he trod, and richer treasure than he craved has rewarded the toilers of an alien race. Upon their effulgent shield shines a star emerging from stormy clouds to the constellation of the Union, and beneath they have written, "*Ad astra per aspera*," an emblem of the past by whose contemplation they are exalted, the prophecy of that nobler future to which they confidently aspire.

MINNESOTA

LEWIS and Clarke, sent out by Mr. Jefferson in 1804 to discover the Northwest by the route of the Missouri River, left the town of St. Charles early in the spring, sailed and poled and dragged their boats up the swift, turbulent, and treacherous stream all summer, wintered with the Mandan Indians, and reached the Great Falls of the Missouri in about a year and a quarter from the beginning of their voyage. Now, when we wish to rediscover this interesting country, which is still virgin land, we lay down a railway track in the spring and summer, and go over there in the autumn in a palace-car —a much more expeditious and comfortable mode of exploration.

In beginning a series of observations

and comments upon Western life it is proper to say that the reader is not to expect exhaustive statistical statements of growth or development, nor descriptions, except such as will illustrate the point of view taken of the making of the Great West. Materialism is the most obtrusive feature of a cursory observation, but it does not interest one so much as the forces that underlie it, the enterprise and the joyousness of conquest and achievement that it stands for, or the finer processes evolved in the marvellous building up of new societies. What is the spirit, what is the civilization of the West? I have not the presumption to expect to answer these large questions to any one's satisfaction—least of all to my own—but if I may be permitted to talk about them familiarly, in the manner that one speaks to his friends of what interested him most in a journey, and with flexibility in passing from one topic to another, I shall hope to contribute something to a better understanding between the territories of a vast empire. How vast this republic is, no one can at all appreciate who does not actually travel over its wide areas. To many of us the West is still the West of the geographies of thirty years ago; it is the simple truth to say that comparatively few Eastern people have any adequate conception of what lies west of Chicago and St. Louis: perhaps a hazy geographical notion of it, but not the faintest idea of its civilization and society. Now a good understanding of each other between the great sections of the republic is politically of the first importance. We shall hang together as a nation; blood, relationship, steel rails, navigable waters, trade, absence of natural boundaries, settle that. We shall pull and push and grumble, we shall vituperate each other, parties will continue to make capital out of sectional prejudice, and wantonly inflame it (what a pitiful sort of "politics" that is!), but we shall stick together like wax. Still, anything like smooth working of our political machine depends upon good understanding between sections. And the remark applies to East and West as well as to North and South. It is a common remark at the West that "Eastern people know nothing about us; they think us half civilized"; and there is mingled with slight irritability at this ignorance a waxing feeling of superiority over the East in force and power. One would

not say that repose as yet goes along with this sense of great capacity and great achievement; indeed, it is inevitable that in a condition of development and of quick growth unparalleled in the history of the world there should be abundant self-assertion and even monumental boastfulness.

When the Western man goes East he carries the consciousness of playing a great part in the making of an empire; his horizon is large; but he finds himself surrounded by an atmosphere of indifference or non-comprehension of the prodigiousness of his country, of incredulity as to the refinement and luxury of his civilization; and self-assertion is his natural defence. This longitudinal incredulity and swagger is a curious phenomenon. London thinks New York puts on airs, New York complains of Chicago's want of modesty, Chicago can see that Kansas City and Omaha are aggressively boastful, and these cities acknowledge the expansive self-appreciation of Denver and Helena.

Does going West work a radical difference in a man's character? Hardly. We are all cut out of the same piece of cloth. The Western man is the Eastern or the Southern man let loose, with his leading-strings cut. But the change of situation creates immense diversity in interests and in spirit. One has but to take up any of the great newspapers, say in St. Paul or Minneapolis, to be aware that he is in another world of ideas, of news, of interests. The topics that most interest the East he does not find there, nor much of its news. Persons of whom he reads daily in the East drop out of sight, and other persons, magnates in politics, packing, railways, loom up. It takes columns to tell the daily history of places which have heretofore only caught the attention of the Eastern reader for freaks of the thermometer, and he has an opportunity to read daily pages about Dakota, concerning which a weekly paragraph has formerly satisfied his curiosity. Before he can be absorbed in these lively and intelligent newspapers he must change the whole current of his thoughts, and take up other subjects, persons, and places than those that have occupied his mind. He is in a new world.

One of the most striking facts in the West is State pride, attachment to the State, the profound belief of every citizen that his State is the best. Engendered perhaps at first by a permanent investment and the spur of self-interest, it speedily becomes a passion, as strong in the newest State as it is in any one of the original thirteen. Rivalry between cities is sharp, and civic pride is excessive, but both are outdone by the larger devotion to the commonwealth. And this pride is developed in the inhabitants of a Territory as soon as it is organized. Montana has condensed the ordinary achievements of a century into twenty years, and loyalty to its present and expectation of its future are as strong in its citizens as is the attachment of men of Massachusetts to the State of nearly three centuries of growth. In Nebraska I was pleased with the talk of a clergyman who had just returned from three months' travel in Europe. He was full of his novel experiences; he had greatly enjoyed the trip; but he was glad to get back to Nebraska and its full, vigorous life. In England and on the Continent he had seen much to interest him; but he could not help comparing Europe with Nebraska; and as for him, this was the substance of it: give him Nebraska every time. What astonished him most, and wounded his feeling (and there was a note of pathos in his statement of it), was the general foreign ignorance abroad about Nebraska—the utter failure in the European mind to take it in. I felt guilty, for to me it had been little more than a geographical expression, and I presume the Continent did not know whether Nebraska was a new kind of patent medicine or a new sort of religion. To the clergyman this ignorance of the central, richest, about-to-be-the-most-important of States, was simply incredible.

This feeling is not only admirable in itself, but it has an incalculable political value, especially in the West, where there is a little haze as to the limitations of Federal power, and a notion that the Constitution was swaddling-clothes for an infant, which manly limbs may need to kick off. Healthy and even assertive State pride is the only possible counterbalance in our system against that centralization which tends to corruption in the centre and weakness and discontent in the individual members.

It should be added that the West, speaking of it generally, is defiantly "American." It wants a more vigorous and assertive foreign policy. Conscious of its power, the growing pains in the limbs of the young giant will not let it rest. That this is the most magnificent country, that we have the only government beyond criticism, that our civilization is far and away the best, does not admit of doubt. It is refreshing to see men who believe in something heartily and without reserve, even if it is only in themselves. There is a tonic in this challenge of all time and history. A certain attitude of American assertion toward other powers is desired. For want of this our late representatives to Great Britain are said to be un-American; "political dudes" is what the Governor of Nebraska calls them. It is his indictment against the present minister to St. James that "he is numerous in his visits to the castles of English noblemen, and profuse in his obsequiousness to British aristocrats." And perhaps the Governor speaks for a majority of Western voters and fighters when he says that "timidity has characterized our State Department for the last twenty years."

By chance I begin these Western studies with the Northwest. Passing by for the present the intelligent and progressive State of Wisconsin, we will consider Minnesota and the vast region at present more or less tributary to it. It is necessary to remember that the State was admitted to the Union in 1858, and that its extraordinary industrial development dates from the building of the first railway in its limits—ten miles from St. Paul to St. Anthony—in 1862. For this road the first stake was driven and the first shovelful of earth lifted by a citizen of St. Paul who has lived to see his State gridironed with railways, and whose firm constructed in 1887 over eleven hundred miles of railroad.

It is unnecessary to dwell upon the familiar facts that Minnesota is a great wheat State, and that it is intersected by railways that stimulate the enormous yield and market it with facility. The discovery that the State, especially the Red River Valley, and Dakota and the country beyond, were peculiarly adapted to the production of hard spring-wheat, which is the most desirable for flour, probably gave this vast region its first immense advantage. Minnesota, a prairie country, rolling, but with no important hills, well watered, well grassed, with a repellent reputation for severe winters, not well adapted to corn, nor friendly to most fruits, at-

tracted nevertheless hardy and adventurous people, and proved specially inviting
to the Scandinavians, who are tough and
industrious. It would grow wheat without end. And wheat is the easiest crop
to raise, and returns the greatest income
for the least labor. In good seasons and
with good prices it is a mine of wealth.
But Minnesota had to learn that one industry does not suffice to make a State,
and that wheat-raising alone is not only
unreliable, but exhaustive. The grass-
hopper scourge was no doubt a blessing
in disguise. It helped to turn the attention of farmers to cattle and sheep, and to
more varied agriculture. I shall have
more to say about this in connection with
certain most interesting movements in
Wisconsin.

The notion has prevailed that the
Northwest was being absorbed by owners
of immense tracts of land, great capitalists who by the aid of machinery were
monopolizing the production of wheat,
and crowding out small farmers. There
are still vast wheat farms under one control, but I am happy to believe that the
danger of this great land monopoly has
reached its height, and the tendency is
the other way. Small farms are on the
increase, practising a more varied agriculture. The reason is this. A plantation
of 5000 or 15,000 acres, with a good season, freedom from blight and insects, will
enrich the owner if prices are good; but
one poor crop, with low prices, will bankrupt him. Whereas the small farmer
can get a living under the most adverse
circumstances, and taking one year with
another, accumulate something, especially if he varies his products and feeds them
to stock, thus returning the richness of
his farm to itself. The skinning of the
land by sending away its substance in
hard wheat is an improvidence of natural
resources, which belongs, like cattle-ran-
ging, to a half-civilized era, and like cattle-
ranging has probably seen its best days.
One incident illustrates what can be done.
Mr. James J. Hill, the president of the
Manitoba railway system, an importer
and breeder of fine cattle on his Minnesota country place, recently gave and loaned a number of blooded bulls to farmers
over a wide area in Minnesota and Dakota. The result of this benefaction has
been surprising in adding to the wealth
of those regions and the prosperity of the
farmers. It is the beginning of a varied

farming and of cattle production, which
will be of incalculable benefit to the Northwest.

It is in the memory of men still in active life when the Territory of Minnesota
was supposed to be beyond the pale of desirable settlement. The State, except in
the northeast portion, is now well settled,
and well sprinkled with thriving villages
and cities. Of the latter, St. Paul and
Minneapolis are still a wonder to themselves, as they are to the world. I knew
that they were big cities, having each a
population nearly approaching 175,000,
but I was not prepared to find them so
handsome and substantial, and exhibiting
such vigor and activity of movement.
One of the most impressive things to an
Eastern man in both of them is their public spirit, and the harmony with which
business men work together for anything
which will build up and beautify the city.
I believe that the ruling force in Minneapolis is of New England stock, while St.
Paul has a larger proportion of New York
people, with a mixture of Southern; and
I have a fancy that there is a social shad-
ing that shows this distinction. It is
worth noting, however, that the South-
erner, transplanted to Minnesota or Montana, loses the *laisser faire* with which he
is credited at home, and becomes as active
and pushing as anybody. Both cities
have a very large Scandinavian population. The laborers and the domestic servants are mostly Swedes. In forecasting
what sort of a State Minnesota is to be,
the Scandinavian is a largely determining force. It is a virile element. The
traveller is impressed with the idea that
the women whom he sees at the stations
in the country and in the city streets are
sturdy, ruddy, and better able to endure
the protracted season of cold and the
highly stimulating atmosphere than the
American-born women, who tend to become nervous in these climatic conditions. The Swedes are thrifty, taking
eagerly to politics, and as ready to profit
by them as anybody; unreservedly American in intention, and, on the whole, good
citizens.

The physical difference of the two cities
is mainly one of situation. Minneapolis
spreads out on both sides of the Mississippi over a plain, from the gigantic flouring
mills and the canal and the Falls of St.
Anthony as a centre (the falls being, by-
the-way, planked over with a wooden

apron to prevent the total wearing away of the shaly rock) to rolling land and beautiful building sites on moderate elevations. Nature has surrounded the city with a lovely country, diversified by lakes and forests, and enterprise has developed it into one of the most inviting of summer regions. Twelve miles west of it, Lake Minnetonka, naturally surpassingly lovely, has become, by an immense expenditure of money, perhaps the most attractive summer resort in the Northwest. Each city has a hotel (the West in Minneapolis, the Ryan in St. Paul) which would be distinguished monuments of cost and elegance in any city in the world, and each city has blocks of business houses, shops, and offices of solidity and architectural beauty, and each has many private residences which are palaces in size, in solidity, and interior embellishment, but they are scattered over the city in Minneapolis, which can boast of no single street equal to Summit Avenue in St. Paul. The most conspicuous of the private houses is the stone mansion of Governor Washburn, pleasing in color, harmonious in design, but so gigantic that the visitor (who may have seen palaces abroad) expects to find a somewhat vacant interior. He is therefore surprised that the predominating note is homelikeness and comfort, and he does not see how a family of moderate size could well get along with less than the seventy rooms (most of them large) which they have at their disposal.

St. Paul has the advantage of picturesqueness of situation. The business part of the town lies on a spacious uneven elevation above the river, surrounded by a semicircle of bluffs averaging something like two hundred feet high. Up the sides of these the city climbs, beautifying every vantage-ground with handsome and stately residences. On the north the bluffs maintain their elevation in a splendid plateau, and over this dry and healthful plain the two cities advance to meet each other, and already meet in suburbs, colleges, and various public buildings. Summit Avenue curves along the line of the northern bluff, and then turns northward, two hundred feet broad, graded a distance of over two miles, and with a magnificent asphalt roadway for more than a mile. It is almost literally a street of palaces, for although wooden structures alternate with the varied and architecturally interesting mansions of stone and brick on both sides, each house is isolated, with a handsome lawn and ornamental trees, and the total effect is spacious and noble. This avenue commands an almost unequalled view of the sweep of bluffs round to the Indian Mounds, of the city, the winding river, and the town and heights of West St. Paul. It is not easy to recall a street and view anywhere finer than this, and this is only one of the streets on this plateau conspicuous for handsome houses. I see no reason why St. Paul should not become, within a few years, one of the notably most beautiful cities in the world. And it is now wonderfully well advanced in that direction. Of course the reader understands that both these rapidly growing cities are in the process of "making," and that means cutting and digging and slashing, torn-up streets, shabby structures alternating with gigantic and solid buildings, and the usual unsightliness of transition and growth.

Minneapolis has the State University, St. Paul the Capitol, an ordinary building of brick, which will not long, it is safe to say, suit the needs or the pride of the State. I do not set out to describe the city, the churches, big newspaper buildings, great wholesale and ware houses, handsome club-house (the Minnesota Club), stately City Hall, banks, Chamber of Commerce, and so on. I was impressed with the size of the buildings needed to house the great railway offices. Nothing can give one a livelier idea of the growth and grasp of Western business than one of these plain structures, five or six stories high, devoted to the several departments of one road or system of roads, crowded with busy officials and clerks, offices of the president, vice-president, assistant of the president, secretary, treasurer, engineer, general manager, general superintendent, general freight, general traffic, general passenger, perhaps a land officer, and so on—affairs as complicated and vast in organization and extensive in detail as those of a State government.

There are sixteen railways which run in Minnesota, having a total mileage of 5024 miles in the State. Those which have over two hundred miles of road in the State are the Chicago and Northwestern, Chicago, Milwaukee, and St. Paul, Chicago, St. Paul, Minneapolis, and Omaha, Minneapolis and St. Louis, Northern Pacific, St. Paul and Duluth, and the St.

Paul, Minneapolis, and Manitoba. The names of these roads give little indication of their location, as the reader knows, for many of them run all over the Northwest like spider-webs.

It goes without saying that the management of these great interests—imperial, almost continental in scope—requires brains, sobriety, integrity, and one is not surprised to find that the railways command and pay liberally for the highest talent and skill. It is not merely a matter of laying rails and running trains, but of developing the resources—one might almost say creating the industries—of vast territories. These are gigantic interests, concerning which there is such sharp rivalry and competition, and as a rule it is the generous, large-minded policy that wins. Somebody has said that the railway managers and magnates (I do not mean those who deal in railways for the sake of gambling) are the *élite* of Western life. I am not drawing distinctions of this sort, but I will say, and it might as well be said here and simply, that next to the impression I got of the powerful hand of the railways in the making of the West, was that of the high character, the moral stamina, the ability, the devotion to something outside themselves, of the railway men I met in the Northwest. Specialists many of them are, and absorbed in special work, but I doubt if any other profession or occupation can show a proportionally larger number of broad-minded, fair-minded men, of higher integrity and less pettiness, or more inclined to the liberalizing culture in art and social life. Either dealing with large concerns has lifted up the men, or the large opportunities have attracted men of high talent and character. And I sincerely believe that we should have no occasion for anxiety if the average community did not go below the standard of railway morality and honorable dealing.

What is the *raison d'être* of these two phenomenal cities? why do they grow? why are they likely to continue to grow? I confess that this was an enigma to me until I had looked beyond to see what country was tributary to them, what a territory they have to supply. Of course the railways, the flouring mills, the vast wholesale dry-goods and grocery houses, speak for themselves. But I had thought of these cities as on the confines of civilization. They are, however, the two posts

of the gateway to an empire. In order to comprehend their future I made some little trips northeast and northwest.

Duluth, though as yet with only about twenty-five to thirty thousand inhabitants, feels itself, by its position, a rival of the cities on the Mississippi. A few figures show the basis of this feeling. In 1880 the population was 3740; in 1886, 25,000. In 1880 the receipts of wheat were 1,347,679 bushels; in 1886, 22,425,730 bushels; in 1880 shipments of wheat 1,453,647 bushels; in 1886, 17,981,965 bushels. In 1880 the shipments of flour were 551,800 bushels; in 1886, 1,500,000 bushels. In 1886 there were grain elevators with a capacity of 18,000,000 bushels. The tax valuation had increased from $669,012 in 1880 to $11,773,729 in 1886. The following comparisons are made: The receipt of wheat in Chicago in 1885 was 19,266,000 bushels; in Duluth, 14,880,000 bushels. The receipt of wheat in 1886 was at Duluth 22,425,730 bushels; at Minneapolis, 33,394,450; at Chicago, 15,982,524; at Milwaukee, 7,930,-102. This shows that an increasing amount of the great volume of wheat raised in north Dakota and northwest Minnesota (that is, largely in the Red River Valley) is seeking market by way of Duluth and water transportation. In 1869 Minnesota raised about 18,000,000 bushels of wheat; in 1886, about 50,000,000. In 1869 Dakota grew no grain at all; in 1886 it produced about 50,000,000 bushels of wheat. To understand the amount of transportation the reader has only to look on the map and see the railway lines—the Northern Pacific, the Chicago, St. Paul, Minneapolis, and Omaha, the St. Paul, Minneapolis, and Manitoba, and other lines, running to Duluth, and sending out spurs, like the roots of an elm-tree, into the wheat lands of the Northwest.

Most of the route from St. Paul to Duluth is uninteresting; there is nothing picturesque except the Dalles of the St. Louis River, and a good deal of the country passed through seems agriculturally of no value. The approaches to Duluth, both from the Wisconsin and the Minnesota side, are rough and vexatious by reason of broken, low, hummocky, and swamp land. Duluth itself, with good harbor facilities, has only a strip of level ground for a street, and inadequate room for railway tracks and transfers. The town itself climbs up the hill, whence there is a good view of the lake and the Wisconsin shore, and a fair chance for both summer and winter breezes. The residence portion of the town, mainly small wooden houses, has many highly ornamental dwellings, and the long street below, following the shore, has many noble buildings of stone and brick, which would be a credit to any city. Grading and sewermaking render a large number of the streets impassable, and add to the signs of push, growth, and business excitement.

For the purposes of trade, Duluth, and the towns of Superior and West Superior, in Wisconsin, may be considered one port, and while Duluth may continue to be the money and business centre, the expansion for railway terminal facilities, elevators, and manufactures is likely to be in the Wisconsin towns on the south side of the harbor. From the Great Northern Elevator in West Superior the view of the other elevators, of the immense dock room, of the harbor and lake, of a network of miles and miles of terminal tracks of the various roads, gives one an idea of gigantic commerce; and the long freight trains laden with wheat, glutting all the roads and sidings approaching Duluth, speak of the bursting abundance of the tributary country. This Great Northern Elevator, belonging to the Manitoba system, is the largest in the world; its dimensions are 360 feet long, 95 in width, 115 in height, with a capacity of 1,800,000 bushels, and with facilities for handling 40 car-loads an hour, or 400 cars in a day of ten hours. As I am merely illustrating the amount of the present great staple of the Northwest, I say nothing here of the mineral, stone, and lumber business of this region. Duluth has a cool, salubrious summer and a snug winter climate. I ought to add that the enterprising inhabitants attend to education as well as the elevation of grain; the city has eight commodious school buildings.

To return to the Mississippi. To understand what feeds Minneapolis and St. Paul, and what country their great wholesale houses supply, one must take the rail and penetrate the vast Northwest. The famous Park or Lake district, between St. Cloud (75 miles northwest of St. Paul) and Fergus Falls, is too well known to need description. A rolling prairie, with hundreds of small lakes, tree fringed, it is a region of surpassing loveliness, and already dotted, as at Alexandria, with summer resorts. The whole region, up as far as Moorhead (240 miles from St. Paul), on the Red River, opposite Fargo, Dakota, is well settled, and full of prosperous towns. At Fargo, crossing the Northern Pacific, we ran parallel with the Red River, through a line of bursting elevators and wheat farms, down to Grand Forks, where we turned westward, and passed out of the Red River Valley, rising to the plateau at Larimore, some three hundred feet above it.

The Red River, a narrow but deep and navigable stream, has from its source to Lake Winnipeg a tortuous course of about 600 miles, while the valley itself is about 285 miles long, of which 180 miles is in the United States. This valley, which has astonished the world by its wheat production, is about 160 miles in breadth, and level as a floor, except that it has a northward slope of, I believe, about five feet to the mile. The river forms the boundary between Minnesota and Dakota; the width of valley on the Dakota side varies from 50 to 100 miles. The rich soil is from two to three feet deep, underlaid with clay. Fargo, the centre of this valley, is 940 feet above the sea. The climate is one of extremes between winter and summer, but of much constancy of cold or heat according to the season. Although it is undeniable that one does not feel the severe cold there as much as in more humid atmospheres, it cannot be doubted that the long continuance of extreme cold is trying to the system. And it may be said of all the Northwest, including Minnesota, that while it is more favorable to the lungs than many regions where the thermometer has less sinking power, it is not free from catarrh (the curse of New England), nor from rheumatism. The climate seems to me specially stimulating, and I should say there is less excuse here for the use of stimulants (on account of "lowness" or lassitude) than in almost any other portion of the United States with which I am acquainted.

But whatever attractions or drawbacks this territory has as a place of residence, its grain and stock growing capacity is inexhaustible, and having seen it, we begin to comprehend the vigorous activity and growth of the twin cities. And yet this is the beginning of resources; there lies Dakota, with its 149,100 square miles (96,596,480 acres of land), larger than all the New England States and New York

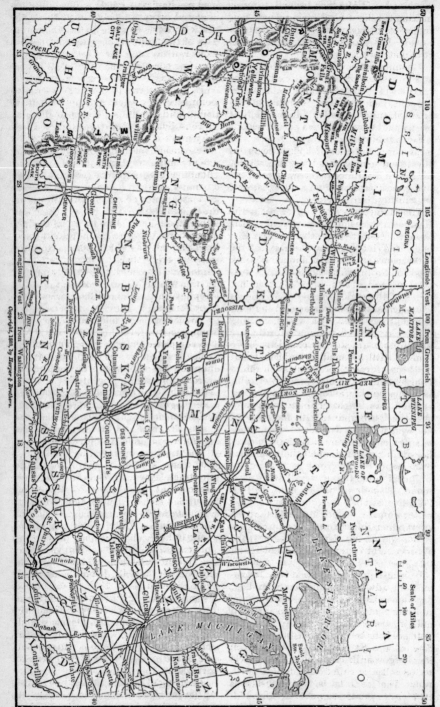

MAP OF THE NORTHWEST, SHOWING THE MANITOBA RAILROAD AND ITS CONNECTIONS.

Copyright, 1888, by Harper & Brothers.

combined, and Montana beyond, together making a belt of hard spring-wheat land sufficient, one would think, to feed the world. When one travels over 1200 miles of it, doubt ceases.

I cannot better illustrate the resources and enterprise of the Northwest than by speaking in some detail of the St. Paul, Minneapolis, and Manitoba Railway (known as the Manitoba system), and by telling briefly the story of one season's work, not because this system is bigger or more enterprising or of more importance in the West than some others I might name, but because it has lately pierced a comparatively unknown region, and opened to settlement a fertile empire.

The Manitoba system gridirons north Minnesota, runs to Duluth, puts two tracks down the Red River Valley (one on each side of the river) to the Canada line, sends out various spurs into Dakota, and operates a main line from Grand Forks westward through the whole of Dakota, and through Montana as far as the Great Falls of the Missouri, and thence through the cañon of the Missouri and the cañon of the Prickly-Pear to Helena—in all about 3000 miles of track. Its president is Mr. James J. Hill, a Canadian by birth, whose rapid career from that of a clerk on the St. Paul levee to his present position of influence, opportunity, and wealth is a romance in itself, and whose character, integrity, tastes and accomplishments, and domestic life, were it proper to speak of them, would satisfactorily answer many of the questions that are asked about the materialistic West.

The Manitoba line west had reached Minot, 530 miles from St. Paul, in 1886. I shall speak of its extension in 1887, which was intrusted to Mr. D. C. Shepard, a veteran engineer and railway builder of St. Paul, and his firm, Messrs. Shepard, Winston, and Co. Credit should be given by name to the men who conducted this Napoleonic enterprise; for it required not only the advance of millions of money, but the foresight, energy, vigilance, and capacity that insure success in a distant military campaign.

It needs to be noted that the continuation of the St. Paul, Minneapolis, and Manitoba road from Great Falls to Helena, 98 miles, is called the Montana Central. The work to be accomplished in 1887 was to grade 500 miles of railroad to reach Great Falls, to put in the bridging

and mechanical structures (by hauling all material brought up by rail ahead of the track by teams, so as not to delay the progress of the track) on 530 miles of continuous railway, and to lay and put in good running condition 643 miles of rails continuously and from one end only.

In the winter of 1886–7 the road was completed to a point five miles west of Minot, and work was done beyond which if consolidated would amount to about fifty miles of completed grading, and the mechanical structures were done for twenty miles west from Minot. On the Montana Central the grading and mechanical structures were made from Helena as a base, and completed before the track reached Great Falls. St. Paul, Minneapolis, and Duluth were the primary bases of operations, and generally speaking all materials, labor, fuel, and supplies originated at these three points; Minot was the secondary base, and here in the winter of 1886–7 large depots of supplies and materials for construction were formed.

Track-laying began April 2, 1887, but was greatly retarded by snow and ice in the completed cuts, and by the grading, which was heavy. The cuts were frozen more or less up to May 15th. The forwarding of grading forces to Minot began April 6th, but it was a labor of considerable magnitude to outfit them at Minot and get them forward to the work; so that it was as late as May 10th before the entire force was under employment.

The average force on the grading was 3300 teams and about 8000 men. Upon the track-laying, surfacing, piling, and timber-work there were 225 teams and about 650 men. The heaviest work was encountered on the eastern end, so that the track was close upon the grading up to the 10th of June. Some of the cuttings and embankments were heavy. After the 10th of June progress upon the grading was very rapid. From the mouth of Milk River to Great Falls (a distance of 200 miles) grading was done at an average rate of seven miles a day. Those who saw this army of men and teams stretching over the prairie and casting up this continental highway think they beheld one of the most striking achievements of civilization.

I may mention that the track is all cast up (even where the grading is easy) to such a height as to relieve it of drifting snow; and to give some idea of the character of the work, it is noted that in preparing it there were moved 9,700,000 cubic yards of earth, 15,000 cubic yards of loose rock, and 17,500 cubic yards of solid rock, and that there were hauled ahead of the track and put in the work to such distance as would not obstruct the track-laying (in some instances 30 miles), 9,000,000 feet (board measure) of timber and 390,000 lineal feet of piling.

On the 5th of August the grading of the entire line to Great Falls was either finished or properly manned for its completion the first day of September, and on the 10th of August it became necessary to remove outfits to the east as they completed their work, and about 2500 teams and their quota of men were withdrawn between the 10th and 20th of August, and placed upon work elsewhere.

The record of track laid is as follows: April 2d to 30th, 30 miles; May, 82 miles; June, 79.8 miles, July, 100.8 miles; August, 115.4 miles; September, 102.4 miles; up to October 15th to Great Falls, 34.6 miles—a total to Great Falls of 545 miles. October 16th being Sunday, no track was laid. The track started from Great Falls Monday, October 17th, and reached Helena on Friday, November 18th, a distance of 98 miles, making a grand total of 643 miles, and an average rate for every working day of three and one-quarter miles. It will thus be seen that laying a good road was a much more expeditious method of reaching the Great Falls of the Missouri than that adopted by Lewis and Clarke.

Some of the details of this construction and track-laying will interest railroad men. On the 16th of July 7 miles and 1040 feet of track were laid, and on the 8th of August 8 miles and 60 feet were laid, in each instance by daylight, and by the regular gang of track-layers, without any increase of their numbers whatever. The entire work was done by handling the iron on low iron cars, and depositing it on the track from the car at the front end. The method pursued was the same as when one mile of track is laid per day in the ordinary manner. The force of track-layers was maintained at the proper number for the ordinary daily work, and was never increased to obtain any special result. The result on the 11th of August was probably decreased by a quarter to a half mile by the breaking of an axle of

an iron car while going to the front with its load at about 4 P.M. From six to eight iron cars were employed in doing this day's work. The number ordinarily used was four to five.

Sidings were graded at intervals of seven to eight miles, and spur tracks, laid on the natural surface, put in at convenient points, sixteen miles apart, for storage of materials and supplies at or near the front. As the work went on, the spur tracks in the rear were taken up. The construction train contained box cars two and three stories high, in which workmen were boarded and lodged. Supplies, as a rule, were taken by wagon trains from the spur tracks near the front to their destination, an average distance of one hundred miles and an extreme one of two hundred miles. Steam-boats were employed to a limited extent on the Missouri River in supplying such remote points as Fort Benton and the Coal Banks, but not more than fifteen per cent. of the transportation was done by steamers. A single item illustrating the magnitude of the supply transportation is that there were shipped to Minot and forwarded and consumed on the work 590,000 bushels of oats.

It is believed that the work of grading 500 miles of railroad in five months, and the transportation into the country of everything consumed, grass and water excepted, and of every rail, tie, bit of timber, pile, tool, machine, man, or team employed, and laying 643 miles of track in seven and a half months, from one end, far exceeds in magnitude and rapidity of execution any similar undertaking in this or any other country. It reflects also the greatest credit on the managers of the railway transportation (it is not invidious to mention the names of Mr. A. Manvel, general manager, and Mr. J. M. Egan, general superintendent, upon whom the working details devolved) when it is stated that the delays for material or supplies on the entire work did not retard it in the aggregate one hour. And every hour counted in this masterly campaign.

The Western people apparently think no more of throwing down a railroad, if they want to go anywhere, than a conservative Easterner does of taking an unaccustomed walk across country, and the railway constructors and managers are a little amused at the Eastern slowness and want of facility in construction and management. One hears that the East is antiquated, and does not know anything about railroad building. Shovels, carts, and wheelbarrows are of a past age; the big wheel-scraper does the business. It is a common remark that a contractor accustomed to Eastern work is not desired on a Western job.

On Friday afternoon, November 18th, the news was flashed that the last rail was laid, and at 6 P.M. a special train was on the way from St. Paul with a double complement of engineers and train-men. For the first 500 miles there was more or less delay in avoiding the long and frequent freight trains, but after that not much except the necessary stops for cleaning the engine. Great Falls, about 1100 miles, was reached Sunday noon, in thirty-six hours, an average of over thirty miles an hour. A part of the time the speed was as much as fifty miles an hour. The track was solid, evenly graded, heavily tied, well aligned, and the cars ran over it with no more swing and bounce than on an old road. The only exception to this is the piece from Great Falls to Helena, which had not been surfaced all the way. It is excellent railway construction, and it is necessary to emphasize this when we consider the rapidity with which it was built.

The company has built this road without land grant or subsidy of any kind. The Montana extension, from Minot, Dakota, to Great Falls, runs mostly through Indian and military reservations, permission to pass through being given by special act of Congress, and the company buying 200 feet roadway. Little of it, therefore, is open to settlement.

These reservations, naming them in order westward, are as follows: The Fort Berthold Indian reservation, Dakota, the eastern boundary of which is 27 miles west of Minot, has an area of 4550 square miles (about as large as Connecticut), or 2,912,000 acres. The Fort Buford military reservation, lying in Dakota and Montana, has an area of 900 square miles, or 576,000 acres. The Blackfeet Indian reserve has an area of 34,000 square miles (the State of New York has 46,000), or 21,760,000 acres. The Fort Assiniboin military reserve has an area of 869.82 square miles, or 556,684 acres.

It is a liberal estimate that there are 6000 Indians on the Blackfeet and Fort Berthold reservations. As nearly as I could ascertain, there are not over 3500 Indians

(some of those I saw were Crees on a long visit from Canada) on the Blackfeet reservation of about 22,000,000 acres. Some judges put the number as low as 2500 to all this territory, and estimate that there was about one Indian to ten square miles, or one Indian family to fifty square miles. We rode through 300 miles of this territory along the Milk River, nearly every acre of it good soil, with thick, abundant grass, splendid wheat land.

I have no space to take up the Indian problem. But the present condition of affairs is neither fair to white settlers nor just or humane to the Indians. These big reservations are of no use to them, nor they to the reservations. The buffalo have disappeared; they do not live by hunting; they cultivate very little ground; they use little even to pasture their ponies. They are fed and clothed by the government, and they camp about the agencies in idleness, under conditions that pauperize them, destroy their manhood, degrade them into dependent, vicious lives. The reservations ought to be sold, and the proceeds devoted to educating the Indians and setting them up in a self-sustaining existence. They should be allotted an abundance of good land, in the region to which they are acclimated, in severalty, and under such restrictions that they cannot alienate it at least for a generation or two. As the Indian is now, he will neither work, nor keep clean, nor live decently. Close to, the Indian is not a romantic object, and certainly no better now morally than Lewis and Clarke depicted him in 1804. But he is a man; he has been barbarously treated; and it is certainly not beyond honest administration and Christian effort to better his condition. And his condition will not be improved simply by keeping from settlement and civilization the magnificent agricultural territory that is reserved to him.

Of this almost unknown country, pierced by the road west from Larimore, I can only make the briefest notes. I need not say that this open, unobstructed highway of arable land and habitable country, from the Red River to the Rocky Mountains, was an astonishment to me; but it is more to the purpose to say that the fertile region was a surprise to railway men who are perfectly familiar with the West.

We had passed some snow in the night, which had been very cold, but there was very little at Larimore, a considerable town; there was a high, raw wind during the day, and a temperature of about 10° above, which heavily frosted the car windows. At Devil's Lake (a body of brackish water twenty-eight miles long) is a settlement three years old, and from this and two insignificant stations beyond were shipped, in 1887, 1,500,000 bushels of wheat. The country beyond is slightly rolling, fine land, has much wheat, little houses scattered about, some stock, very promising altogether. Minot, where we crossed the Mouse River the second time, is a village of 700 people, with several brick houses and plenty of saloons. Thence we ran up to a plateau some three hundred feet higher than the Mouse River Valley, and found a land more broken, and interspersed with rocky land and bowlders—the only touch of "bad lands" I recall on the route. We crossed several small streams, White Earth, Sandy, Little Muddy, and Muddy, and before reaching Williston descended into the valley of the Missouri, reached Fort Buford, where the Yellowstone comes in, entered what is called Paradise Valley, and continued parallel with the Missouri as far as the mouth of Milk River. Before reaching this we crossed the Big Muddy and the Poplar rivers, both rising in Canada. At Poplar Station is a large Indian agency, and hundreds of Teton Sioux Indians (I was told 1800) camped there in their conical tepees. I climbed the plateau above the station where the Indians bury their dead, wrapping the bodies in blankets and buffalo-robes, and suspending them aloft on crossbars supported by stakes, to keep them from the wolves. Beyond Assiniboin I saw a platform in a cottonwood-tree on which reposed the remains of a chief and his family. This country is all good, so far as I could see and learn.

It gave me a sense of geographical deficiency in my education to travel three hundred miles on a river I had never heard of before. But it happened on the Milk River, a considerable but not navigable stream, although some six hundred miles long. The broad Milk River Valley is in itself an empire of excellent land, ready for the plough and the wheat-sower. Judging by the grass (which cures into the most nutritious feed as it stands), there had been no lack of rain during the summer; but if there is lack of water, all the land can be irrigated by the Milk River, and it may also be said of the country beyond to Great Falls that frequent streams make irrigation easy, if there is scant rainfall. I should say that this would be the only question about water.

Leaving the Milk River Valley, we began to curve southward, passing Fort Assiniboin on our right. In this region and beyond at Fort Benton great herds of cattle are grazed by government contractors, who supply the posts with beef. At the Big Sandy Station they were shipping cattle eastward. We crossed the Marias River (originally named Maria's River), a stream that had the respectful attention of Lewis and Clarke, and the Teton, a wilfully erratic watercourse in a narrow valley, which caused the railway constructors a good deal of trouble. We looked down, in passing, on Fort Benton, nestled in a bend of the Missouri; a smart town, with a daily newspaper, an old trading station. Shortly after leaving Assiniboin we saw on our left the Bear Paw Mountains and the noble Highwood Mountains, fine peaks, snow-dusted, about thirty miles from us, and adjoining them the Belt Mountains. Between them is a shapely little pyramid called the Wolf Butte. Far to our right were the Sweet Grass Hills, on the Canada line, where gold-miners are at work. I have noted of all this country that it is agriculturally fine. After Fort Benton we had glimpses of the Rockies, off to the right (we had seen before the Little Rockies in the south, toward Yellowstone Park); then the Bird-tail Divide came in sight, and the mathematically Square Butte, sometimes called Fort Montana.

At noon, November 20th, we reached Great Falls, where the Sun River, coming in from the west, joins the Missouri. The railway crosses the Sun River, and runs on up the left bank of the Missouri. Great Falls, which lies in a bend of the Missouri on the east side, was not then, but soon will be, connected with the line by a railway bridge. I wish I could convey to the reader some idea of the beauty of the view as we came out upon the Sun River Valley, or the feeling of exhilaration and elevation we experienced. I had come to no place before that did not seem remote, far from home, lonesome. Here the aspect was friendly, livable, almost homelike. We seemed to have come out, after a long journey, to a place where one might be content to stay for some time—to a far but fair country, on top of the world, as it were. Not that the elevation is great—only about 3000 feet above the sea—nor the horizon illimitable, as on the great plains; its spaciousness is brought within human sympathy by guardian hills and distant mountain ranges.

A more sweet, smiling picture than the Sun River Valley the traveller may go far to see. With an average breadth of not over two and a half to five miles, level, richly grassed, flanked by elevations that swell up to plateaus, through the valley the Sun River, clear, full to the grassy banks, comes down like a ribbon of silver, perhaps 800 feet broad before its junction. Across the far end of it, seventy-five miles distant, but seemingly not more than twenty, run the silver serrated peaks of the Rocky Mountains, snow-clad and sparkling in the sun. At distances of twelve and fifty miles up the valley have been for years prosperous settlements, with school-houses and churches, hitherto cut off from the world.

The whole rolling, arable, though treeless country in view is beautiful, and the far prospects are magnificent. I suppose that something of the homelikeness of the region is due to the presence of the great Missouri River (a connection with the world we know), which is here a rapid, clear stream, in permanent rock-laid banks. At the town a dam has been thrown across it, and the width above the dam, where we crossed it, is about 1800 feet. The day was fair and not cold, but a gale of wind from the southwest blew with such violence that the ferry-boat was unmanageable, and we went over in little skiffs, much tossed about by the white-capped waves.

In June, 1886, there was not a house within twelve miles of this place. The country is now taken up and dotted with claim shanties, and Great Falls is a town of over 1000 inhabitants, regularly laid out, with streets indeed extending far on to the prairie, a handsome and commodious hotel, several brick buildings, and new houses going up in all directions. Central lots, fifty feet by two hundred and fifty, are said to sell for $5000, and I was offered a corner lot on Tenth Street, away out on the prairie, for $1500, including the corner stake.

It is difficult to write of this country without seeming exaggeration, and the habitual frontier boastfulness makes the acquisition of bottom facts difficult. It is plain to be seen that it is a good grazing country, and the experimental fields of wheat near the town show that it is equally well adapted to wheat-raising. The vegetables grown there are enormous and solid, especially potatoes and turnips; I have the outline of a turnip which measured seventeen inches across, seven inches deep, and weighed twenty-four pounds. The region is underlaid by bituminous coal, good coking quality, and extensive mines are opening in the neighborhood. I have no doubt from what I saw and heard that iron of good quality (hematite) is abundant. It goes without saying that the Montana mountains are full of other minerals. The present advantage of Great Falls is in the possession of unlimited water-power in the Missouri River.

As to rainfall and climate? The grass shows no lack of rain, and the wheat was raised in 1887 without irrigation. But irrigation from the Missouri and Sun rivers is easy, if needed. The thermometer shows a more temperate and less rigorous climate than Minnesota and north Dakota. Unless everybody fibs, the winters are less severe, and stock ranges and fattens all winter. Less snow falls here than farther east and south, and that which falls does not usually remain long. The truth seems to be that the mercury occasionally goes very low, but that every few days a warm Pacific wind from the southwest, the "Chinook," blows a gale, which instantly raises the temperature, and sweeps off the snow in twenty-four hours. I was told that ice rarely gets more than ten inches thick, and that ploughing can be done as late as the 20th of December, and recommenced from the 1st to the 15th of March. I did not stay long enough to verify these statements. There had been a slight fall of snow in October, which speedily disappeared. November 20th was pleasant, with a strong Chinook wind. November 21st there was a driving snow-storm.

The region is attractive to the sightseer. I can speak of only two things, the Springs and the Falls. There is a series of rapids and falls for twelve miles below the town; and the river drops down rapidly into a cañon which is in some places nearly 200 feet deep. The first fall is twenty-six feet high. The most beautiful is the Rainbow Fall, six miles from town. This cataract, in a wild, deep gorge, has a width of 1400 feet, nearly as straight across as an artificial dam, with a perpendicular plunge of fifty feet. What makes it impressive is the immense volume of water. Dashed upon the rocks below, it sends up clouds of spray, which the sun tinges with prismatic colors the whole breadth of the magnificent fall. Standing half-way down the precipice, another considerable and regular fall is seen above, while below are rapids and falls again at the bend, and beyond, great reaches of tumultuous river in the cañon. It is altogether a wild and splendid spectacle. Six miles below, the river takes a continuous though not perpendicular plunge of ninety-six feet.

One of the most exquisitely beautiful natural objects I know is the Spring, a mile above Rainbow Fall. Out of a rocky ledge, sloping up some ten feet above the river, burst several springs of absolutely crystal water, powerfully bubbling up like small geysers, and together forming instantly a splendid stream, which falls into the Missouri. So perfectly transparent is the water that the springs seem to have a depth of only fifteen inches; they are fifteen feet deep. In them grow flat-leaved plants of vivid green, shades from lightest to deepest emerald, and when the sunlight strikes into their depths the effect is exquisitely beautiful. Mingled with the emerald are maroon colors that heighten the effect. The vigor of the outburst, the volume of water, the transparency, the play of sunlight on the lovely colors, give one a positively new sensation.

I have left no room to speak of the road of ninety-eight miles through the cañon of the Missouri and the cañon of the Prickly-Pear to Helena—about 1400 feet higher than Great Falls. It is a marvellously picturesque road, following the mighty river, winding through crags and precipices of trap-rock set on end in fantastic array, and wild mountain scenery. On the route are many pleasant places, openings of fine valleys, thriving ranches, considerable stock and oats, much land ploughed and cultivated. The valley broadens out before we reach Helena and enter Last Chance Gulch, now the main street of the city, out of which millions of gold have been taken.

At Helena we reach familiar ground. The 21st was a jubilee day for the city and the whole Territory. Cannon, bells, whistles, welcomed the train and the man, and fifteen thousand people hurrahed; the town was gayly decorated; there was a long procession, speeches and music in the Opera-house in the afternoon, and fireworks, illumination, and banquet in the evening. The reason of the boundless enthusiasm of Helena was in the fact that the day gave it a new competing line to the East, and opened up the coal, iron, and wheat fields of north Montana.

Further comments, economic and social, upon the Northwest, including Wisconsin, must be deferred to the April number.

THE EARLIEST SETTLEMENT IN OHIO

IN the whole West there is no other colony in which original and distinguishing characteristics are so distinctly preserved as in Marietta, Ohio, one of the fairest of the many towns which beautify the shores of *la belle rivière*. The Western Reserve, as a whole, is essentially a reproduction of Connecticut—a copy in which the colors of the prototype appear at once faded and freshened; but Marietta is a brilliant, faithfully exact miniature of New England—a picture in which not only the outward form of resemblance, but the very spirit of likeness, is presented. Possibly the peculiarly Eastern or New England aspect of the town is heightened by contrast with its near neighbors upon the Virginia side of the river, and with the composite population of southeastern Ohio surrounding it. At any rate, the traveller from Massachusetts or Connecticut, who feels a most uncomfortable stranger within the gates of almost any other town along the Ohio, finds himself at home in Marietta. If he sojourns there a few days, he discovers that the names of the people whom he meets are familiar ones in his native State. It requires no stretch of imagination to detect resemblances to New England facial types, to New England manners, and to New England speech. The substantial dwellings have a comfortable, thrifty appearance, a homely dignity of expression which recalls those of the older Eastern States; the stately elms which shade the streets and spacious door-yards offer a pleasant suggestion of the New England village; the surrounding landscape seems but to sustain the illusion; and even the little steamboats upon the Muskingum are like those which ply upon the Connecticut River, far up in Massachusetts. The visitor is surprised at nothing which meets his eye—except the whole. How came it here, this typical New England village, set in its amphitheatre of wooded hills upon the banks of the Ohio? As the earliest settlement in Ohio—in fact, the first organized permanent English settlement in the old Northwest Territory, from which were carved the States of Ohio, Indiana, Illinois, Michigan, and Wisconsin—Marietta possesses a peculiar historic interest.

The spirit of emigration was very naturally developed in the young, strong, expansive nation, born amid the throes of the Revolution, and yet the first movement westward was as much the result of a pressing necessity as of the growth of independence and enterprise among the people. During the closing years of the war the subject of Western colonization was strongly agitated among the officers of the colonial army. In 1776 the Congress of the confederation had taken steps toward making an appropriation of lands for these officers, and passed laws prescribing the number of acres each one, according to his rank, should receive. In 1783, seeing that the final reduction of the army must soon take place, the officers, to the number of two hundred and eighty-eight, anxious for definite action, petitioned Congress to locate the lands they were entitled to somewhere in the region now known as eastern Ohio, but even the great influence of Washington was not sufficient to bring about the object sought, and no legislation affecting the interests of the petitioners was enacted. Congress had not yet a perfect title to the territory northwest of the Ohio. It must be remembered that the officers and soldiers of the Revolutionary army did not receive money for their priceless services, but almost valueless certificates. In 1784 they were worth only about 3s. 6d. to 4s. to the pound, face value, and as late as 1788 they brought not more than 5s. or 6s.

Such was the situation when a new scheme, and one which finally proved effective—that of buying outright what the nation refused to bestow—began to form itself in the minds of a few earnest thinkers in Massachusetts.

Early in January, 1786, a conversation occurred between General Rufus Putnam and General Benjamin Tupper, which led to the organization of the New England Ohio Company, and the founding of Marietta. This conference took place at Putnam's home, in Rutland, Worcester County, Massachusetts. At the close of the war General Putnam retired to his farm and followed agriculture and surveying. He was not contented, however, with a quiet life; his energy sought grander channels of action. He was foremost among the men who sought by argument and appeal to induce Congress to grant the petition of the officers for the bestowal of their bounty lands. He carried on a long correspondence with

Washington upon the subject, in the course of which he proposed the admirable system of township division which was ultimately adopted in the West, and which was the natural precursor of the planting of the township organization called by Tocqueville the "miniature republic." General Putnam was not an educated man, but he possessed strong native ability, keen judgment, steadfastness of purpose, and an almost superhuman energy. Like most of his fellow-officers, he was in reduced circumstances.

To this man came General Benjamin Tupper, just returned from the West, whither he had gone in 1785 as one of a company of surveyors, appointed by Congress to lay out in ranges and townships the lands now comprised in southeastern Ohio. Like Putnam, Tupper was a native of Massachusetts, and he had fought bravely in two wars, his gallant services in the Revolution resulting in his being made a brigadier.

These men, formerly comrades in arms, seated before the great fire-place in Putnam's farm-house, upon a winter evening, conversed earnestly and long—so long that the massive logs before them burned to crumbling embers, and the gray light of dawn came to mingle with the fire-glow while they were still engaged. Their eventful past, their campaigns and victories, their troubled present, their poverty and disappointments, their hopeful future, their anticipation of adventure in a remote wilderness, which General Tupper probably painted in roseate hues, were probably all touched upon. Doubtless the conversation was desultory, but it bore definite results. The old soldiers so strengthened each other's faith in the future that they could no longer rest inactive. They joined in a brief address to the people, proposing a plan of organization. This first appeared in the newspapers of Boston upon the 25th of January, under

RUFUS PUTNAM.

the caption of "Information," signed by Rufus Putnam and Benjamin Tupper, and dated Rutland, January 10, 1786. The subscribers stated that they took "this method to inform all officers and soldiers who have served in the late war, and who are by a late ordinance of the honorable Congress to receive certain tracts of land in the Ohio country, and also all other good citizens who wish to become adventurers in that delightful region, that from personal inspection, together with other incontestable evidences, they are fully satisfied that the lands in that quarter are of a much better quality than any other known to the New England people; that the climate, seasons, products, etc., are, in fact, equal to the most flattering accounts that have ever been published of them; that being determined to become purchasers, and to prosecute a settlement in that country, and desirous of forming a general association with those who entertain the same ideas, they beg leave to propose the following plan, viz.: That an association by the name of the Ohio Company be formed of all such as wish to become purchasers, etc., in that country, who reside in the Commonwealth of Massachusetts only, or to extend to the inhabitants of other States, as shall be agreed on."

It was further proposed that in order to bring such a company into existence all persons who wished to promote the

POWDER-HORN OF ISRAEL PUTNAM.

scheme should meet in their respective counties, at places designated, on the 15th of February following, and choose delegates, who should assemble at the Bunch of Grapes Tavern, in Boston, on Wednesday, the 1st of March, 1786, and there determine upon a plan of association.

The plan proposed was duly executed, the delegates meeting at the time appointed, and three days later adopting articles of agreement, and electing officers. The delegates at this historic meeting, which, small as it was, may, from the nature of its object, have attracted some attention in colonial Boston, consisting of less than twenty thousand inhabitants, were Manasseh Cutler, of Essex County; Winthrop Sargent and John Mills, of Suffolk; John Brooks and Thomas Cushing, of Middlesex; Benjamin Tupper, of Hampshire; Crocker Sampson, of Plymouth; Rufus Putnam, of Worcester; Jelaliel Woodbridge and John Patterson, of Berkshire; and Abraham Williams, of Barnstable. It was decided to raise a fund of not less than one million dollars, in shares of one thousand dollars each. After the lapse of a little more than a year, upon March 8, 1787, the second meeting of the Ohio Company was held at Brackett's Tavern, Boston, and it was reported that although only two hundred and fifty shares had been subscribed for, there were many in Massachusetts, also in Connecticut, Rhode Island, and New Hampshire, who were inclined to become adventurers, and who were only restrained by the uncertainty of obtaining a sufficient tract of country, collectively, for a good settlement.

It was now decided to make direct and immediate application for the purchase of lands in the territory northwest of the Ohio River, and as an agent to negotiate with Congress the associates chose one of their own number, the Rev. Manasseh Cutler, pastor of a little Congregational church in the hamlet of Ipswich (now Hamilton), Massachusetts.

The company could have employed no better man than Dr. Cutler. In the prime of life, forty-five years of age, he was, perhaps, second in general genius and culture to no living American, except Franklin, and his name possessed a prestige in the literary and scientific circles of Boston, New York, and Philadelphia. Since his graduation from Yale, twenty-two years before, he had studied and taken degrees in the three learned professions,

divinity, law, and medicine. His education was one of unusual solidity, and the versatility of his genius was attested by the fact that in addition to his clerical duties he had written upon meteorology, astronomy, and botany. His strength was rendered readily effective by the possession of a keen insight into human nature and of a courtly grace of conversation. He was further qualified for the duty he was to undertake by his deep sympathy with the Revolutionary soldiers. He had been among them as chaplain through two campaigns.

Had Dr. Cutler gone forth as the ambassador of a powerful nation, his mission could not have been more vastly important than it was in his capacity as agent for this feeble, struggling colonization society, nor could it have demanded more consummate tact. He journeyed in humble style in his one-horse shay or gig, and there was nothing in the appearance of the quiet, comfortable, dignified New England parson, leisurely jogging along the country roads of Massachusetts and Connecticut, suggestive of the mighty influence he was to exert in moulding the future of the West and of the nation. He left his home in the latter part of June, preached in two towns (Lynn, Massachusetts, and Middletown, Connecticut), where he tarried for Sunday rest, and arrived in New York, where the Continental Congress was then in session, on July 5, "by the road," he chronicles, "that enters the Bowery." He put up his horse "at the sign of the 'Plow and the Harrow' in the Bowery barns."

The work which this man was to perform in Congress was twofold. He sought to purchase a large tract of public land at the most advantageous terms possible, and to procure such legislation for the territory as would be satisfactory to those intending immigration to it. The purchase would have been almost entirely valueless, in the minds of a majority of the Ohio Company associates, if they could not have it clothed with the laws to which they were accustomed. They were almost to a man fully in accord with the spirit which seven years before had prohibited slavery in Massachusetts. Thus it came about that the prospective purchase was used as a powerful lever to effect the formation and passage of the Ordinance of 1787, or, as it is commonly called, the Ordinance of Freedom. The details of the plan by which

Dr. Cutler accomplished his dual object would fill a volume. In brief, he used every argument, every element of personal persuasion, every art of diplomacy, which could have an effect in his favor. He pictured the needs of the brave men who sought to make the purchase and the debt of gratitude which the nation owed them. He urged as an important consideration the revenue which would accrue to the government from the sale, and from others which would probably quickly follow. There was at this time a strong feeling of disaffection in Kentucky, and imminent danger that that Territory would embrace the first opportunity to join her fortunes with Spain. The planting beyond the Ohio of a strong colony of men whose patriotism was unquestioned, Dr. Cutler argued, would be a measure well calculated to bind the West to the East and promote union. Virginia and the South generally were intensely patriotic, and it is probable that this consideration was of great importance in the opinion of their delegates in Congress, and led them not only to favor comparatively easy terms of sale to the Ohio Company, but to permit the enactment of such an ordinance as that body of men desired. Up to this time every ordinance for the government of the Northwest Territory containing an antislavery clause had been voted down, and even the inoperative ordinance of 1784, of which Thomas Jefferson was the author, had before its passage been shorn of its article prohibiting slavery after the year 1800. The ordinance before Congress when Dr. Cutler arrived in New York contained no restriction of slavery whatever. Still, it had come down to the 9th of July, and passed its second reading. Upon that day was appointed a new committee, which was authorized to prepare and submit a plan of government for the Federal territory, and four days later, upon the 13th of July, the result of their labors, the Ordinance of Freedom, passed. The committee had sent a draft of the ordinance to Dr. Cutler, " with leave to make remarks and propose amendments," and he found afterward that the amendments suggested by him were all made, except one (relating to taxation), which was better qualified. There is evidence extant, indisputable, that the measures introduced by his agency, and the passage of which was secured

through his sagacity, were those forever proscribing slavery and encouraging religion, morality, and education. A concession made to the South, which doubtless had some weight in influencing the vote

MANASSEH CUTLER.

approving the ordinance, was the insertion of a clause allowing owners to reclaim runaway slaves who escaped into the territory.

Dr. Cutler labored most zealously with the Southern members of Congress, and it was by their votes the law was passed. His jovial conversation and genial, hearty manner evidently won their friendship, as his culture commanded their admiration. In the divine, the bookworm, the scientist, they doubtless failed to see the skillful diplomatist with a shrewd knowledge of men—the pioneer and the prince of lobbyists. Dr. Cutler in his journal mentions one of them, who, he says, "calls me a frank, open, honest New England man, which he considers as an uncommon animal."

At the time the ordinance was passed, Dr. Cutler was in Philadelphia visiting Benjamin Franklin, but he returned to New York upon the 17th of July. Upon the 27th of that month Congress passed an act authorizing a sale of lands to the

GENERAL RUFUS PUTNAM'S LAND-OFFICE.

many difficulties. The public prints were used to disseminate knowledge concerning the Ohio country and the scheme for its settlement. Dr. Cutler published anonymously at Salem, Massachusetts, a small pamphlet, in which was presented the fullest information attainable in regard to the region beyond the Ohio, and especially that part about the Muskingum. It contained also some prophecies which were undoubtedly regarded as the wildest of improbabilities or impossibilities, born in the brain of a sanguine visionary. Among other things, the pamphlet set forth what was probably the first suggestion ever made in print of the mighty commerce that the future would witness upon the Western rivers, and of the employment of steam in its service. The author said that the "current down the Ohio and Mississippi" would be "more loaded than any streams on earth," and "in all probability steamboats will be found to do infinite service in all our river navigation." This was published just twenty years before Fulton's successful application of steam to navigation; but it is worthy of note that Miller in Scotland had that very year demonstrated the practicability of propelling boats by this power, and Dr. Cutler being a scientist, fully abreast with the times, and in communication with certain *savants* and scientific societies of Europe, in all probability had had early knowledge of the fact.

Ohio Company upon the precise terms offered by Dr. Cutler and his associate, Winthrop Sargent. The contract, far exceeding any ever before made in the United States, was closed in New York on the 27th of October following, being signed by Samuel Osgood and Arthur Lee of the Board of Treasury, and Cutler and Sargent for the Ohio Company. It covered 1,500,000 acres of land upon the Ohio, about the mouth of the Muskingum, for which the price to be paid was one dollar an acre, with an allowance for bad land not to exceed one-third of a dollar per acre. Dr. Cutler secured the grant of two townships of land for the support of a university, and incorporated in the contract clauses setting apart one mile square in each township for the maintenance of schools, and the same amount for religious institutions. Thus it came about that the declaration of the ordinance, "schools and the means of education shall forever be encouraged," did not stand upon the statute-books as an empty flourish of words.

Prior to the time the ordinance was passed and contract secured, Generals Putnam and Tupper, Dr. Cutler, General Samuel H. Parsons, Winthrop Sargent, and other prominent men were actively engaged in advancing the interests of the Ohio Company, and they now redoubled their efforts, and sought everywhere for responsible people who would become subscribers to their fund, and for men who were willing to go to the West as pioneers. The work of arousing a spirit of emigration among the masses was attended with

It was natural that a publication containing the predictions that many people then living would see the Western rivers navigated by steamboats, and that in fifty years the Northwest Territory would contain more people than all New England, should be very generally ridiculed, for the masses then more universally than now were wont to receive new ideas with skepticism and scoffing. The idea of Western emigration and its enthusiastic advocates were alike the subjects of wide-spread scorn and derision. The accounts of the Western country circulated by the leading men of the Ohio Company were very generally received with incredulity, and commented upon with sarcasm. The Ohio Valley was derisively dubbed "Putnam's Paradise" and "Cutler's Indian Heaven," and the wags of the day exercised their wit in the invention of extravagant and burlesqued recitals of the charms of the region to Ohio"—the Marietta which was to be—laid out on paper.

On the 1st of December, 1787, the advance detachment of the company's first band of pioneers departed for the West from Danvers, Massachusetts, under the

SITE OF MARIETTA IN 1788.

which a few of their fellow-citizens were endeavoring to turn the serious attention of the people. There was opposition, too, of a more dignified and possibly more dangerous order. There was really much to be feared from the hostility of the Indians, and many influential men in Massachusetts from various motives were seeking to direct the tide of emigration toward Maine. Nevertheless, the Ohio Company associates were enabled to carry out their long-cherished plans. In spite of all obstacles, they seem never to have wavered in their faith of ultimate success. At meetings of the directors held at intervals in Boston taverns (the Bunch of Grapes, Brackett's, and Cromwell's Head) the financial affairs of the organization had been arranged, multitudinous details decided upon, a plan for surveying the lands of the purchase formulated, and "a city at the confluence of the Muskingum and command of Major Haffield White, being sent ahead to build boats upon the Youghiogheny, a small affluent of the Monongahela, in western Pennsylvania. Another party, including the surveyors and a number of the Ohio Company proprietors, under Colonel Ebenezer Sproat, left Hartford, Connecticut, January 1, 1788. General Putnam, who was to have commanded the march, was detained by business in New York, and overtook the company in eastern Pennsylvania on the 24th of the month. Their progress from this time was slow and tedious, owing to the severity of the weather and a heavy fall of snow. When they arrived at the Alleghanies the situation was such as might have appalled men less brave and less inured to hardship. General Putnam in his journal says they "found nothing had crossed the mountains since the great snow, and in the old snow, twelve inches

FORT HARMAR, BUILT IN 1785.

deep, nothing but pack-horses." The trail, difficult of travel at any time, was now almost impassable. But the march of these hardy, resolute men toward their destination was not to be stayed by storm or danger. "Our only resource," continues the leader of the expedition in his simple narrative, "was to build sleds and harness our horses to them tandem, and in this way, with four sleds, and men marching in front, we set forward." Winding slowly and with infinite toil through the mountain passes, the men breaking a way in the trackless, drifted snow along which their jaded horses could more easily draw the cumbrous, heavily laden sledges, the little company, consisting of less than a score of souls, journeyed on. At night they slept around huge blazing fires, which, however, they often had difficulty in kindling. They were two weeks in the mountains, and suffered much from excessive cold and the arduousness of their labors. General Putnam, writing to Dr. Cutler, says, "It would give you pain, and me no pleasure, to detail our march over the mountains, or our delays afterward on account of bad weather and other misfortunes." On the 14th of February, a month and a half after leaving Hartford, they arrived at Sumrill's Ferry, on the Youghiogheny (in pioneer parlance the "Yoh"), where they met the men who had preceded them. The remainder of February and the whole of March was consumed in the building of boats, and on the 1st of April the united company, embarking upon a little flotilla consisting of three log canoes, a flat-boat, and a galley of fifty tons burden, called originally the *Adventure Galley*, but afterward the *Mayflower*, left Sumrill's Ferry, on the Youghiogheny, and floating down that stream to the Monongahela, was borne onward to the Ohio. Peacefully and uneventfully the great river swept them southward, the weather becoming daily more balmy and vegetation farther advanced as they proceeded. They arrived and disembarked at the site of Marietta upon April 7, 1788, and thus by forty-eight men was begun the settlement of the State of Ohio and of the Northwest Territory.

Tradition has it that the first two men who sprang ashore from the *Mayflower* began a good-natured but zealous rivalry to see who should chop down the first tree, one of them selecting a buckeye, and the other, in his undue haste, some species of hard timber, and it has been asserted that, from the very natural circumstance of the former being the first brought to the ground originated the application of the name to the people and the State which afterward came into existence. It seems more probable, however, that the *sobriquet* had its origin in another way.

The attention of the Delaware Indians who greeted the pioneers was quickly attracted by the tall, erect, soldierly figure of Colonel Ebenezer Sproat, whom they designated as Hetuck, or the big Buckeye—an appellation which might easily have grown into use as a generic one for the pioneers, as the majority of them possessed figures which would suggest to the Indians, always poetical and descriptive in their nomenclature, a comparison with the stately, symmetrical tree which grows by the Western water-courses.

sides measured one hundred and eighty feet, surrounded by a line of heavy palisades. It contained seventy-two rooms, each one eighteen feet square or more, and it was estimated that in case of necessity nearly nine hundred people could live within its walls. Tastefully as well as strongly constructed, Campus Martius doubtless merited the words of one of the pioneers who, in writing to relatives in Massachusetts, said, "It is the handsomest pile of buildings this side of the Alleghany Mountains."

CAMPUS MARTIUS, THE FIRST HOME OF THE PIONEERS.

Fort Harmar, the second fort erected by the English west of the Ohio, and at the time the colonists arrived the only one in existence, had been built in 1785 at the mouth of the Muskingum, opposite the site of Marietta. Very likely the Ohio Company, in selecting the locality for their city, had been influenced in some measure by the idea of securing its protection. General Putnam, however, with the prudence and good judgment which ever characterized him, took immediate measures for the building of another defense, exclusively for the people of the colony. This was Campus Martius, the first home of the pioneers, and destined to be for five long years the military camp which its name implied. It was a substantial structure of timber, a parallelogram or hollow square, of which the

The same somewhat pedantic predilection for classical nomenclature which led to the naming of Campus Martius accounts for the terms applied to portions of the extensive and wonderful system of ancient works which the colonists found covering the ground on which they proposed to build their city, as *Quadranaon*, *Capitolium*, and *Cecelia* (elevated squares of earth apparently constructed as the foundations of temples), and *Sacra Via* (a great graded way, leading from the walls of the Mound-builders' fortification down to the Muskingum). For the town such names were proposed as Castrapolis, Protepolis, Urania, Tempé, Adelphia, Genesis, and the like. The name adopted—Marietta—was taken from that of the then Queen of France, Marie Antoinette, and its bestowal was a graceful tribute from

RETURN JONATHAN MEIGS, JUN.

the Revolutionary soldiers to the sovereign of a people who had aided them, and whom they gratefully remembered.

The initial movement from New England to the West was watched with great interest by some of the leading characters of the country. While the first little company of pioneers were painfully making their way through Pennsylvania, George Washington, writing to Lafayette, said: "A spirit of emigration to the western country is very predominant. Congress have sold in the year past a pretty large quantity of lands on the Ohio for public securities, and thereby diminished the public debt considerably. Many of your military acquaintances, such as Generals Parsons, Varnum, and Putnam, Colonels Tupper, Sproat, and Sherman, with many more, propose settling there. From such beginnings much may be expected." Later in the same year, in a communication to an inquirer concerning Western lands, he wrote: "No colony in America was ever settled under such favorable auspices as that which has just commenced at the Muskingum. Information, property, strength, will be its characteristics. I know many of the settlers personally, and there never were men better calculated to promote the welfare of such a community. If I was a young man just preparing to begin the world, or if in advanced years and had a family to make a provision for, I know of no country where I should rather fix my habitation than in some part of the region for which the writer of the queries seems to have a predilection."

Among the pioneers who arrived at Marietta during the first year were many able, well-educated men, and some who were distinguished. The Territorial Governor, Arthur St. Clair, who had been President of Congress when he received his appointment, and Generals Samuel H. Parsons and James M. Varnum, Territorial Judges, became residents of the settlement, and so also did the Secretary, Major Winthrop Sargent, Return Jonathan Meigs, afterward Governor of Ohio, and Postmaster-General of the United States, General Benjamin Tupper, and Commodore Abraham Whipple, of Rhode Island, who was the reputed leader of the company who burned the schooner *Gaspé* in Narragansett Bay in 1772, and had the honor later of firing the first gun at the British on the sea.

Governor St. Clair formally inaugurated government in the Northwest Territory, with simple ceremonies but profoundly impressive effect, upon the 15th of July, and the first court in all that region was opened upon the 2d of September following. Dr. Manasseh Cutler, who had come out on a visit to the colony, riding a large portion of the way in his sulky, had the honor of opening with prayer the exercises upon the latter occasion, and perhaps that privilege was regarded by him as a sufficient recompense for all his labors on behalf of the pioneers and those who were to come after them. The good doctor also preached in Campus Martius the second sermon ever delivered in Ohio to other than an Indian congregation.

The prosperous condition of which it was hoped the success and happiness of the first year were the harbinger, and of which the superior character of the colonists was almost an earnest, was not to be speedily or easily attained; the sanguine predictions of Washington and others having the interests of the pioneers at heart, not to be immediately or fully realized. A combination of disastrous circumstances, which would have completely overwhelmed a less vigorous outpost of civilization, seriously retarded progression in the affairs of the Ohio Company pioneers, and defeating in a measure, still longer deferred the hopes of those brave men. In the East the idea of emigration A penny anti-moving-to-Ohio pamphlet bore upon its cover a rude wood-cut in which "a stout, ruddy, well-dressed man on a sleek fat horse," with the legend appended, "I am going to Ohio," was repre-

ARTHUR ST. CLAIR.

was still obstinately opposed by many influential men, and derided by newspapers and pamphleteers. Dr. Cutler's departure upon his journey to the settlement had been made the subject of doggerel verses in the public prints of Salem, and caricatured and exaggerated stories were widely circulated, relating the reputed wonders of the West. There were springs which flowed brandy, and there was flax that bore little pieces of cloth instead of leaves. The country was said to be fairly fertile, but to possess a very unwholesome climate. sented as meeting a pale and ghastly, skeleton-like figure, clad in tatters, astride an almost inanimate animal, underneath which was the label, "I've been to Ohio." Horrible stories of Indian massacres were told, and for these, unhappily, there was some foundation of truth, though slight compared with the superstructure of fiction which was built upon it. The five years of Indian war, but for the firmness of General Putnam and his sagacious management, would have resulted either in the withdrawal or annihilation of the colony.

THE MUSKINGUM ACADEMY.

exception of one to the State of Pennsylvania, the first issued by the United States.

When peace came, in 1795, it was too late for the Marietta region to rejoice in all of the benefits which at an earlier date would have been possible. The Miami settlements, which eventually developed Cincinnati, were already assuming importance, and thousands of pioneers passed down the river to them. A little later the Connecticut Western Reserve, in northeastern Ohio, was thrown open to settlers, and drew a strong current of immigration from the very fountain-head to which the Ohio Company had looked for its chief re-enforcement of population. Many, however, from Massachusetts and the other New England States became residents of the Muskingum country, and an era of fair prosperity was begun.

As it was, the pioneers were confined much of the time to their garrisons. Thirty persons were killed within a radius of twenty or thirty miles of Marietta, and more than once the inmates of Campus Martius, and of the block-houses at Belpre and Waterford, which settlements had been established as offshoots of Marietta, were threatened with the horrors of starvation. Added to these evils—the practical existence of a state of siege, enforced idleness, and the cessation of immigration—the financial affairs of the company became involved through the failure of its treasurer in the East. Many of the shareholders who had subscribed to the fund for purely speculative purposes, gaining no immediate benefit from their investment, desired to withdraw, and it thus became, through the operation of many causes, imperatively necessary for the association to seek a release from their original contract. Here Dr. Cutler and General Putnam became the saving, as they had been largely the creating, geniuses of the company and its settlement. The amount of lands which the Ohio Company finally received was less than two-thirds of that for which they originally contracted. The patents, bearing date of March 3, 1792, and signed by George Washington, President, and Thomas Jefferson, Secretary, were, with the

It was natural that in a New England colony, and the first planted under a law of which one of the provisions declared that "schools and the means of education shall forever be encouraged," an institution of learning should be brought quickly into existence. As early as the spring of 1797 a subscription list, headed by General Rufus Putnam, was circulated, and a fund raised for the building of a school-

GENERAL RUFUS PUTNAM'S HOUSE.

house. Primary schools had been held in Campus Martius, but in the house now provided there was opened, in the year 1800, the Muskingum Academy, the first advanced school in the State of Ohio, presided over by David Putnam, the grandson of General Israel Putnam, and a graduate of Yale College. In the same year Marietta delegates in the Territorial Legislature procured the passage of a law go down to the sea in ships," which may account for their making Marietta, nearly two thousand miles from the ocean by a water route, a port of clearance whence full-rigged barks and brigs laden with the produce of the country sailed for foreign ports. Down the devious channel of the Ohio and the Mississippi more than a score of ships made their way to the Gulf of Mexico between the years 1800 and 1808,

ABRAHAM WHIPPLE.

authorizing the leasing of the school lands and lands set apart for religious purposes in the Ohio Company's purchase, and creating a corporate body whose duty it should be to carry out that important and beneficent measure. This corporation impressed upon its indentures a seal bearing as its device an altar, and the legend "Support Religion and Learning." Then the spirit of the Ordinance of 1787 was a living influence in the land, and thus New England's favorite institutions were literally made to grow upon the soil of the West.

One of the curious industries in which the energy of Marietta pioneers found exercise was the building and sailing of ocean ships. Many of them had come from the sea-coast, and some of them had been familiar with the ways of men "who when the embargo act first put a stop to this commerce. The first full-rigged vessel built at Marietta, the *St. Clair*, commanded by Commodore Whipple, who was no stranger to the sea, left the Muskingum in May, 1800, went to Havana, and thence to Philadelphia. One of the Marietta sea-captains greatly astonished a Liverpool official when, after vainly endeavoring to make him understand what port he hailed from, he took a map, and sweeping his hand across the broad Atlantic and around Florida, he traced the Mississippi to the Ohio, and the latter stream to the Muskingum.

But it was not in material prosperity that Marietta was to attain its highest success or fulfill its highest destiny. Its first citizens came to Ohio, whether consciously or not, as the guardians of an

MARIETTA COLLEGE.

idea which was to be the most valuable heritage of the whole State and of the nation. Had slavery gained a foot-hold north of the Ohio River, it is probable that it would have gained such strength as to have resisted overthrow in the United States. Although Dr. Manasseh Cutler never became a resident of Marietta, his son Ephraim immigrated at an early day to the settlement, and was one of its most eminent citizens. It was his privilege to perpetuate in Ohio the work his father had begun in New England and in the Congress of the confederation. Few people of this day know how narrowly the State of Ohio escaped being made slave territory in the year 1802. When the Constitutional Convention was in session in Chillicothe, the committee appointed to draft a bill of rights, notwithstanding the terms of the Ordinance of 1787, sought to introduce a clause allowing limited slavery. It was believed by many that the exclusion of slavery would operate against immigration to Ohio from the Slave States, and that the insertion of a clause allowing

modified slavery would encourage such immigration. This consideration led a number of delegates, whose districts depended principally upon the South for population, to labor for the pro-slavery clause with great pertinacity. The influence of Jefferson was doubtless exerted to advance the cause. In the committee of the whole it was found that there was a majority of one in favor of the introduction of slavery. The defeat of the measure and the vindication of the Ordinance of Freedom in the formation of the first State government under its provisions rested upon and was accomplished chiefly through Judge Ephraim Cutler. Among his colleagues in the Convention from Marietta, or Washington County, were General Rufus Putnam and Benjamin Ives Gilman. They came to him in his room, to which he had been confined by sickness, and urged that he should immediately exert his influence against the obnoxious clause.

"We must prevent this," said Gilman. "I can not, will not, live in a community

where such injustice is sanctioned by
law."

"Cutler, get up, get well; be in your
place to-morrow," exclaimed Putnam.

He did get well, or at least forced himself into a condition in which he could
make a speech, and that speech brought
over the one vote necessary to defeat the
slavery clause.

Judge Cutler was also the author of
those sections of the Constitution which
related to education and religion. In 1819,
in the Ohio Legislature, he began the agitation which resulted in giving to the
State an excellent public-school system
and a just plan of taxation.

The quality which Marietta possessed in
1802, and which, as exemplified in one of
its citizens, served the State so well at its
founding, has never ceased to be a characteristic of the community. It has produced more than its full quota of men willing and able to defend the principles which
prevailed among the people who planted
the colony. Socially and intellectually
it is the peer of any of the smaller towns
of the West. Prominent in its population,
after the lapse of almost a century, are the
Putnams and Cutlers and a score more of
the families who were in the van-guard of
the army of civilization which has occupied
the West. As these old families are represented in the community, so are the old
New England ideas which were dominant

EPHRAIM CUTLER.

when the Ohio Company was formed. Particularly is this noticeable in the staid religious status and advanced condition of
education and culture which are characteristics of the town. In Marietta College,
which has already filled a half-century of
usefulness, and been "justly regarded as
the child of the pioneers," the seed of education planted and nurtured by the founders of the colony has flourished to a fru-
ition grander than they could possibly
have foreseen.

NOTE.—The celebration of the centennial of the settlement of Marietta and of Ohio, upon April 7, 1888,
for which judicious preparations are already making, will be an occasion interesting not only to the people
of Ohio and its sister States of the old Northwest Territory, but to many in New England whose ancestors
and kindred laid the corner-stone of civilization in the West. The year 1888 will close the first century
of Western development and round the most wonderful chapter in the history of the continent, and it is
proposed to make the 7th of April anniversary at Marietta not merely a pleasant holiday, but a memorial
observance worthy in dignity and meaning of the event which it will commemorate, and which led to the
vast accomplishment that a hundred years have witnessed.

THE OLD ICHABOD FRYE HOUSE.

THE GEOLOGY OF CHICAGO

IT is not the intention of this paper to confine itself to a bald statement of the geological facts of this vicinity; such a statement could be better found in the excellent reports of our government surveys. Rather it is proposed to apply these facts to a setting forth of some of the principles and methods of geological research, and also to try to make this little area of the earth's surface illustrate the close relation between geology and human destiny; for, after all, geology is interesting in proportion as it connects itself with man, while man becomes increasingly interesting in proportion as we associate him with the long geological preparation for his successful existence.

When we inquire into the remoter causes whereby a race, a nation, or even a city has reached a position of superiority, we are certain to come at last upon some peculiar physical advantages, some happy combination of climate and soil with river plain or many-harbored peninsula, or perhaps inland sea, by means of which nature has met man's needs halfway, as it were, thenceforward enabling him to surpass those less favored in kind. In short, history is what it is because physical geography is what it is.

Applying this principle directly to our subject, let us inquire why Chicago has become a great city. Many attribute her growth and prosperity to her harbor and her proximity to the southern end of Lake Michigan as the head of navigation. True; but there are other and better harbors along our coast than our river affords; while for sightliness any point between Evanston and Milwaukee would have been preferable. It is also claimed that this particular location was due to the erection of a fort in 1803, thus forming a nucleus around which population naturally collected. But what determined the location of the fort? It was needed, the historian says, to protect white and Indian traders, who had long met on this far frontier to exchange their commodities, and also because it was a point convenient for the distribution of government supplies to the Indians.

But how came this to be a convenient point for Indian supplies and commercial interchange? Because this strip of ground and this only on which we live forms so low a divide between the eastward and westward flowing waters of the great central plain of our continent that easy communication could at all times be maintained between the two.

For more than a century previous to the erection of Fort Dearborn, indeed ever since the days of La Salle and Marquette, white men came by lake from Mackinac to meet at this point the Indians of the great Northwest Territory; while these in turn could come all the way in canoes if they chose from the great river to the great lake with scarcely a portage to obstruct their transit.

It was then the brave and adventurous Jesuit fathers who located Chicago, because of its unique natural advantages for inland communication. So carefully did they explore this region, and so accurately did they describe its topography, that but for the dates one might imagine himself reading a recent argument in favor of the great ship-canal.

This now takes us back to 1673, so far have we ascended the stream of time in our search for causes. We have reached the physiographical explanation usually deemed most distant by the historian. Chicago has become a great city because it rests upon a low water-shed.

We have now to inquire what caused the low water-shed.

Our native rock lies deeply buried under a mass of miscellaneous materials. Occasionally it rises to the surface, as at the quarries of Stony Island, Bridgeport, and a few other places. Here it can be studied. It is of limestone throughout, with occasional patches saturated by petroleum products. While these are not present in quantity sufficient to warrant the cost of extraction, they impart to the stone a mottled antique appearance, which enhances its value for building purposes. This is especially agreeable to the residents of a city whose chief characteristic, whether a fault or a merit, lies in its youth or brand-newness. Much of this rock is arranged in horizontal layers, evidently deposited under water—sedimentary; but this layer structure frequently disappears or merges into a crystalline formation that refuses to split or cleave with any certainty of result. If used at all, it is simply crushed into irregular fragments for road-beds.

Again, this hard crystalline formation is everywhere penetrated by a porous, honey-combed structure, consisting of very symmetrical five-sided cells. Yet these three varieties—the sedimentary, the crystalline, and the pentagonal—are one in composition; they glide so insensibly into each other as to suggest a common origin.

We can explain how sedimentary rocks are deposited by what we see going on at the outlet of any running stream. We can also explain the crystalline formation by fusing processes that could be approximated in the laboratory. But we will not be able to explain the honey-combed cellular structure by any process, artificial or natural, in this part of the world. Florida or the Bahama Islands will furnish for this purpose the nearest point of observation. There among the coral reefs that form both foundation and border to these semi-tropical lands will we recognize the analogue of our five-sided cell-like limestone formations. There, among the living reefs, men have studied the habits of coral animals, have measured their rate of growth, and discovered the conditions necessary to their existence. Years of patient study not only there, but among the islands of the Caribbean Sea and those of the South Pacific, have furnished sufficient data whereby we can apply the conditions of coral life to the interpretation of our conditions when our rocks were being formed.

The coral demands, first of all, warm water: none exist in temperatures lower than 68° Fahr. These waters must also be salt and shallow: no corals can live below a hundred feet from the surface. As reefs often extend downward thousands of feet, their depth is explained by a slow sinkage of the sea-bottom, a subsidence that must bear a close relation in time to the upward growth of the reef-builders, else they would be destroyed. Another condition is great purity of water, hence they cannot live near the mouths of rivers, nor in the track of sediment-bearing ocean currents, nor in the vicinity of volcanic discharges. Let us make of these conditions the outlines of a picture to be filled in later.

We have now found through observation of similar building in tropical oceans that our rocks are composed of great coral reefs, built partly *in situ* and partly by the broken and comminuted pieces of coral lodged among them by the action of the waves.

We have next to find when, at what stage of the world's history, this reef-building was done.

The keys that unlock the doors of time to the geologist are fossils, and the combination or guide to their successful use is this: the simplest life forms came first—a great geological principle, involving the idea of a progressive development from lower to higher, from simpler to more complex. Without fossils and without this principle for their interpretation rock systems would fail to account for the earth's history. It becomes, then, of vital importance to acquaint ourselves with the nature of the fossils associated with our corals and embedded with them in our rocks.

Our rocks fairly swarm with the petrified remains of animals and plants. They are all marine. They have no living duplicates, yet all can be classified under some of the existing orders of life. They have modern representatives, but as varieties, as species, as genera, with perhaps one exception, they are extinct.

For us at present the most significant fact respecting them is this: among all their abundance and variety, not one fossil form belongs to the class of vertebrates. No animals with backbones are represented here. This fact alone places our rocks in the Silurian age of the world's natural history—that period of earliest life forms of which the rocks yield any certain record. It is also called the age of mollusks, because this type of animals then attained a superiority in size, numbers, and variety which made them the rulers of the ancient seas. One class, known as orthoceratites, whose remains are very abundant in our limestones, were ten and even twenty feet in length. They lived in straight shells, separated into compartments, only the front one of which the creature occupied, withdrawing himself from each chamber in turn as he secreted a new one in front. From this chamber protruded enormous arms or tentacles for feeling and grasping; he possessed a sharp beak for tearing, and lidless eyes, with which to sweep the surrounding waters for prey. A modern representative of this terrible mollusk is the chambered or pearly nautilus.

While a molluscan type of animal gave name to the age, there existed a higher type of organization, known as the trilobite. This animal, abundant in some Silurian formations, is not so here. The collector always counts the trilobite to be a rare find. It was a highly specialized form ; its nervous system was complex and delicate, its movements active. Although breathing by gills, it was an insect in structure—a water breather. It is a characteristic animal of the Cambrian and Silurian ages, passing away with the carboniferous. Among living animals its nearest relative is the king-crab.

Another form, whose remains, next to those of the corals, make up the mass of our limestones, is the crinoid, a creature often spoken of as a sea-lily. These crinoids attach themselves, as though rooted, to shallow sea-bottoms; thence they send up long stems ending in cup-shaped bud-like bodies, whose slowly moving arms are highly suggestive in their arrangement and coloring of the petals of a flower. This deceptive appearance is increased by the transparent gelatinous structure of the animal enclosing the stony skeleton. Both the softer and harder parts of the animal resemble so closely some forms of vegetable life that the older zoologists were greatly puzzled over their classification. The question was not in what family to place them, but in what kingdom. This issue was not confined to crinoids alone, but included other marine forms, especially the corals. In despair of agreement, they finally compromised by calling them zoophytes—animal plants. The skeletons of crinoids are composed of successive rings of limy material. One hundred and forty thousand rings have been counted on the stem of a single animal. These characteristic rings form of themselves a large constituent part of the substance of our rocks.

It would be tedious to spend further time in describing these fossilized life forms. Details are for the laboratory and class-room. Suffice it to say that the entire mass of limestone rocks in our vicinity is composed almost exclusively of the shells and skeletons of animals. They are technically known as the Niagara section of the Silurian formations. These rocks descend to a vertical depth of three hundred feet and more, the materials of every cubic inch of which were collected from the sea-water and manufactured by living processes. Limestone of similar origin forms not only the principal rock of the entire Mississippi Valley, but it is the most abundant surface rock in the world.

Limestone has been compared to coal. As coal represents so much carbon withdrawn by plants from the air, so limestone represents so much carbon withdrawn by animals from the water.

We are now ready, through data furnished by our rocks, to picture to ourselves Chicago in the Silurian age. In Silurian times Chicago lay at the bottom of a salt, warm, and shallow sea. To the north lay a land area of unknown extent, the oldest of our continent, if not in the world. We will call it Laurentia. To the east, bordering what is now our Atlantic coast, lay another strip of land we will call Appalachia; to the west, bordering the Pacific, lay still another we will name California. These lands furnish thus early by their position and arrangement the first rough sketch of North America. It is more than probable that along their shores stretched the primordial beaches, whereon the lowest, simplest, earliest forms of life appeared. But the lands themselves were without life. Rain and streams cut down their bald rocky surfaces, ocean waves ate into their coast lines, the air above conveyed clouds and transmitted sunlight; yet aside from these there was no sign of movement. But these lands were distant; they do not concern us most. Let us fix our thoughts on this particular spot.

The point is indicated by long white lines of surf, thrown into spray as it encounters the submerged reefs. There were teeming populations then as now, but they moved in water and not in air. There was consciousness, there was great activity, there must have been enjoyment, since without it life cannot be keenly active. There must have been also pain, for life was over-abundant. There was a struggle to elude, a struggle to capture. There were eyes for seeing, teeth for tearing, claws for grasping, tentacles for feeling, stinging, or paralyzing.

There was color, from the iridescent pearly lining of sea-shells to the gorgeous banks of coral flower beds. There were waving meadows of sea-plants, fairy groves of sponges, amid which each lived according to his kind. But in this exuberant existence there was no voice; all animate nature was mute. There was no sound save from the dashing surf; ears, such as they were, gave heed to vibrations only. Yet these were the possessors of the earth. For them at that time "all things were made that were made." Nor is this all. They possessed a form of life as unique as were their physical conditions. The world and its inhabitants were suited to each other.

Can we form any estimate, however rough, of the length of time these latter-day Silurians owned and ruled this part of the world? Our coralline limestone rocks are here about 300 feet in depth. We must remember they have been compacted through heat and pressure into less than half their former depths. There is evidence also of their being worn down more than a hundred feet at least by succeeding denuding forces. As they were built by corals mainly, it is proper to ask how fast coral reefs grow upward nowadays. Careful investigations in different parts of the world yield varied results. Professor Agassiz from his studies in Florida clearly established the fact that the living species of corals have been at work on that coast for more than 70,000 years. Captain E. B. Hunt, of the United States Corps of Engineers, stationed many years at Key West, expressed the opinion that the existing species of corals have been at work on the Florida coast not less than 5,400,000 years. This estimate, enormous as it may seem, is predicated upon well-demonstrated facts, derived from observations and measurements made upon the spot. (Worthen.) Professor Dana, a most cautious geologist, says, "Coral reef limestones are of slow formation, the rate of increase in thickness, where all is most favorable, not exceeding perhaps one-sixteenth of an inch a year, or five feet in a thousand years." Mr. Huxley is disposed to endorse Dana. According to this estimate our Niagara limestone was at least 200,000 years in building. When we remember that the Niagara period is only one of many divisions of the Silurian age, that elsewhere Silurian rocks are known to be many thousand feet in depth, we must conclude that for the entire period all our time estimates are relative only, the absolute time being inconceivable.

So ends our picture of Chicago in the molluscan age, as we have been able to restore it from the hieroglyphics engraven in our rocks. Of the long geologic periods following, few traces are here recorded.

The conclusion, then, is that before the close of this age Chicago and vicinity were elevated above sea-level, and remained there until a comparatively recent period. During this infinitely long interval our land, washed by rain and rivers, became the source of sediments accumulating to the south of us. As Laurentia had furnished the materials in which to entomb our fossils, so Siluria furnished in turn the sediments in which to record a later and in some respects a higher fauna and flora. Progressively southward the continent grew. Progressively from cooling the earth shrank, folding and wrinkling her level surfaces. Slowly Appalachia lifted into the upper air her masses of stratified rocks thousands of feet in depth. Then the western Cordilleras, youngest of our mountain systems, followed. With these physical changes came corresponding changes in the life forms. Mollusks gave place as leaders to fishes. They, in turn, to reptiles. Then interest in the dramatic procession is diverted for a time by the abundance of plant life. An enormous vegetation, luxuriating in marshy soils and a warm, moist atmosphere, stretches from polar to equatorial regions, a band of tropical growth. This life also was entombed in the rocks, furnishing now in our coal fields the basis of existing civilization. At last mammals emerged from their lowly and obscure beginnings. They moved as now along many diverging roads. While we recognize no familiar forms, they abound in prophecies of the present. But of all these rock and life systems elsewhere so abundantly recorded, Chicago seems to be oblivious.

We have not, however, exhausted all the sources of investigation touching our past history. So far nothing has been said of the soil overlying the native rock of our vicinity. It is of great depth, varying from ten to eighty, to two hundred, feet. It is composed of a miscellaneous mass of clay, sand, and gravel, with bowlders of all sizes scattered indiscriminately through the whole. Now since most soils are made by the disintegration of the surface rock, we should expect ours to be chiefly composed of limestone, more or less pulverized. We should expect the bowlders and larger masses to differ in hardness only from the rest, thus resisting for longer time the crumbling effects of our moist atmosphere. But our soil is unmistakably foreign. Its pebbles are made of agates, flints, jasper, quartz; they have no relation to limestone. These clays were never limestone before the pulverizing. These bowlders, large and small, are hard and crystalline, refusing to be shaped by tools — unutilizable — whereas our native rock is easily cut, cleaves readily into uniform layers, and so becomes a useful and inexpensive building material. Evidently our soil has been transported. But from where? By what agencies could such vast amounts have been removed?

It needs no expert to tell us that rivers are the great soil carriers, and deltas their great dumping-grounds. We know that "Egypt is the gift of the Nile"; Holland and Belgium, of the Rhine; Louisiana, of the Mississippi. Is the soil of Cook County also the gift of some river? The answer is not far to seek, for water has a wondrous sorting power that reveals at once its agency. Drop a handful of sand and gravel into still water, what results? The coarsest, being heaviest, reaches bottom first; the next lighter following; while only the finest silt covers the whole. Drop another, and now the coarsest falls upon the finest of the previous deposit; the rest arranges itself as before. These alternations of coarse and fine form true stratification. Had our soil been deposited on the margin of a lake by the action of a river, it would present more or less of this assorted appearance. As it shows no such regularity, we must look further for its explanation.

We know that rivers, long before reaching their outlets, deposit vast amounts of eroded materials upon their own margins and channels. We know that such alluvial accumulations have made rich the river bottoms of all continents, and for this reason they became the sites of man's earliest civilizations. Let us drop our handful of mixed material into swiftly running water, what results? Again the coarsest, because the heaviest, will be carried the shortest distance; the next lighter, further on; while the finest silt will be carried farthest away. So a river rising in highlands will, through its superior velocity, do there its most devastating work. There, too, for the same reason, will it transport in its mad progress the largest fragments of its own wreck-

age. Arriving at lower levels, each check to its flow will cause corresponding deposit of material, the heaviest fragments being the first burdens to be dropped, while down the stream, in the order of their respective weights, will gravity distribute with an unerring precision the freight of sediments, until in the lower course no gravel, or even sand, may be found. Little save the finest silt builds a delta. In other words, running water distributes horizontally that which quiet water distributes vertically. In both cases the order of distribution is the same.

But our mixed soil, save on the lake margins past and present, yields no evidence of an orderly deposit either in time or space. Pushing investigation further, it is noticed that many of these foreign stones of our soil possess smoothly polished surfaces, with innumerable small striations and scratches engraved upon them. These markings are usually parallel and firm, as though there were no variation in the pressure of the hand that made this etching. Moreover, our bedrock, when laid bare, is observed to possess similar markings upon a surface sometimes as smoothly polished as though sandpaper and pumice had completed the process. The surface besides is not level, but undulating, rolling, giving the effect of stony billows with furrows of irregular depth and width between. These, like the finer markings, trend in one general direction. In our locality they run from northeast to southwest. Nor are these phenomena confined to our particular region, but they range over New England and the Middle States, running as far south as the fortieth parallel, where they end in an irregular terminal line, extending from the Atlantic west of the Mississippi. Everywhere north of this line the native country rock lies deeply buried under this burden of foreign materials, some of which is crystalline, some granite-like in structure and composition, all metamorphic and unstratified. Travelling north, we shall not find the counterpart of these bowlders as native rock until we reach the old Laurentian Canadian formation, many hundred miles away. Lake Superior is contained in them. The city of Duluth is perched high upon their bare and rugged cliffs, while from the southern shore of that lake long spurs trend southward and westward into Minnesota and Wisconsin. We shall meet them at the Dalles of the St. Croix, and again, for the last time, as I remember them, forming the picturesque shores of Devil's Lake.

One more link in the chain of evidence revealing their origin must be furnished. These transported foreign stones are mainly without fossils. So is it also with the Canadian formations of which they seem to be a part. They may antedate the time when life existed on the earth, as they certainly indicate by their location the oldest portion of our continent.

I need not dwell longer on the mysterious origin of the drift, for that is the name given this unsorted mixture of sand, gravel, and bowlder clay. Almost every intelligent man or woman now knows it was brought here by the action of glaciers and icebergs during the great North American ice age. And while no fact in geological history is now more firmly established and more generally understood, yet it is worth while to note how short the time since it was regarded as "but a brilliant hypothesis, or the vagaries of a wild but harmless theorist" at the worst. In 1846 Louis Agassiz, then a young and unknown man, advanced, as an explanation of the drift, the theory of an ice sheet covering the entire northern part of Europe and America to the depth of many thousands of feet. This conclusion was based upon studies of glaciers in Switzerland.

Observing the unsorted mixed deposits of these torpid icy rivers; observing also the characteristic parallel striations, scorings, and polishing of the rocky surfaces both below and throughout the enormous masses of enveloping ice; observing the furrows made by these giant ploughshares in the country rock; above all, noting the great erratic bowlders stranded high upon hill and mountain sides, like great beasts come out to sun themselves — Agassiz and Forbes observing these things (in the living phenomena), declared the track of a glacier as constant and unmistakable as the track of a wolf or a horse. And since these tracks are found abundantly over large areas, reasonable minds at least are forced to admit the fact, however unexplainable the cause. This "sweeping generalization," so sceptically received at first, has through scores of subsequent investigators been verified. Agassiz's conclusion has "passed from the realm of hypothesis to the realm of fact." The ice

age has added another period to the myriads of centuries behind us.

But the glacial period brought great changes to our local physiography. To realize them more fully, let us picture to ourselves successively some of the more prominent events. Previous to the change of climate, this particular intersection of latitude and longitude was probably situated near a pre-glacial river of unknown length and width. This river drained the long valley now occupied by Lake Michigan, and was probably tributary to an inland system of drainage, although this fact is not perfectly established.

To us the surprising fact is the comparatively recent origin of our Great Lakes. There is reason to believe that their present basins up to the ice period were simply broad and shallow valleys of erosion, whose gentle slopes would if uncovered resemble ordinary prairie-land, with a meandering river occupying their lowest depressions. (Claypole.) Whether a vegetation covered these ancient slopes we cannot say, since glaciation has removed all its traces. From the abundant coal beds south of us, we may infer that here also plants were storing the sun's energy for future ages to liberate. We do know that the on-coming ice sheet enveloped not only every surface object in its path to a depth of hundreds of feet, but it carried them forward in its slow, resistless grasp toward the terminal moraines near the southern part of our State. Hills and mountains were no obstruction to its course, either it rode over them granite shod, rounding their ridges into domes, or it picked them up piecemeal and carried them along. Valleys were choked with its débris, and the pre-glacial system of drainage rearranged or obliterated. Yet all this advancement was probably so slowly made, as men count time, that a yearly observer of this region would have noted few changes; scarcely would the centuries have brought consecutively prominent or conspicuous contrasts in ice scenery.

Greenland is now covered with an ice sheet from eight to ten thousand feet in depth. As that inaccessible region is to-day, so was this part of the earth then. To the arctic man the Greenland ice seems fixed and unchangeable, yet we know it is constantly moving forward, thrusting vast icebergs into the surrounding ocean. Could we see the surface rock beneath this ever-moving mass, we would find it furrowed, scarred, and polished by this mightiest of levelling agencies. It would look as our own surface rock does to-day wherever any considerable area is exposed. If one questions the adequacy of glaciers alone to transport vast quantities of material, he has but to become acquainted with their action at present in polar and mountainous regions to allay his doubts. He will find it no "geologist's dream" that an ice sheet whose depth from the evidence on mountain and hill sides must have been not less than from six hundred to one thousand feet was capable of transporting the foreign deposits we know as drift. The mountains of New England show glaciation to their summits, except perhaps Mount Washington, whose top alone held itself above the crystalline pall. In our own locality, while there are no existing mountains to register the height of glaciation, we have evidence equally reliable in the sites of ancient hills or mountains now completely levelled by erosion and covered by accumulations of drift. The rocks of our quarries reveal by their tilted and distorted condition an ancient upheaval, probably hundreds of feet in height. They are believed to be the remnant of a mountain range extending from Lake Superior southward to this point, thence eastward through northern Indiana. This ancient range is known as the Wabash Arch. As its elevation occurred about the close of the Silurian age, it was possibly the means of raising our region above old sea-levels. (S. S. Gorby, Fifteenth Geological Report of Indiana.) Can we get any idea of how long a time Chicago was buried under this burden of congelation? On this subject Professor Claypole says: "Allowing what would be a rapid rate of advance, we cannot assign to the ice sheet a movement of more than a quarter of a mile in a year. At this rate the Canadian bowlders which exist in great numbers along the terminal moraine must have required at least sixteen hundred years to travel from their northern home in the Laurentine mountains to the south of Ohio." As the terminal moraine in Illinois extends still further south, this estimate of time cannot be exaggerated, at least for us.

How long a time "elapsed between the cessation of the advance and the commencement of the retreat" of the glacier can be estimated only from the "huge mounds or hills of drift which mark its southern line," quoting again the same author. "From combined testimony we are almost compelled to believe that the meridian of the glacial day existed for centuries, perhaps thousands of years." But these time estimates, extraordinary as they seem, shrink to small dimensions compared with the exceeding slowness of recession of the ice sheet. Some hint of this may be obtained from the location of ancient terraces far above present levels, when the melting resulted in lakes of great size, on whose margins rivers dropped their assorted deposits. These deposits formed successive terraces of great extent, indicating long periods of time at which the lakes remained at these levels.

It is with this lake and flood period that we as Chicagoans have a very personal interest, this time of "combat between sun and frost," due to the slow amelioration of climate. From the front of a glacier there runs always a milky white river, noisy and tumultuous in summer, frozen and silent in winter. So from the great ice front stretching from the Atlantic to the Rockies there leaped and flowed countless streams. So long as the ice margin lay on the southern side of slopes the water found easy access to the sea. But after it crossed the divides between northern and southern bound waters, these turbid milky streams collected in numerous lakes between the ice front and the water-sheds. These lakes, separated at first, filled the valleys, then overflowing their brims, or bursting their self-made ice dams, they coalesced with more or less of violence as their altitude or volume of waters varied. The basins now occupied by lakes Huron, Erie, and Ontario were thus united in a single lake, extending from the State of Michigan to the Highlands of New York. This enormous sheet of inland water, blocked by the ice to the north and east, found an outlet for an unknown length of time at Fort Wayne, Indiana, whence, through the Ohio, it reached the Mississippi. In a similar manner the valley now occupied by Lake Michigan was flooded. Mackinac, its present outlet in latitude 46°, must have been ice-locked long after this end of the basin was uncovered. Glaciers must have filled the entire depression of our lake and greatly deepened and extended its area. As these retreated, the waters therefrom must have collected in this end of the basin, blocked by the elevation south of us, not yet entirely removed. Slowly the waters deepened and spread, reaching at last a height of forty feet above the present level. Chicago is again submerged, while miniature icebergs detached from the northern glacier cliffs float on the surface above, dropping their enclosed rocky materials as they slowly melt in the chilly waters. At last these pent-up waters find an outlet into the valley of a free glacial stream, now known as the Des Plaines River. This outlet is well defined at a point called the Summit, about ten miles southwest of Chicago. Another outlet at a later stage of lower level is also defined at the meeting of the Calumet and Des Plaines rivers, at a point called the Sag, about four miles from Lemont and Athens (well-known quarries), and about seven miles southwest of the Summit. These two outlets form the point of a triangle whose base, thirty-seven miles in length, gives the width of the bay out of which the glacial waters escaped, a line extending from Winetka to the southern end of the lake. This bay covered twelve townships of Cook County, including many suburban towns, in particular those east of a line prolonged south from Winetka, through Grosse Point, Niles Centre, Norwood Park, Oak Park, Riverside, Willow Springs, to Lemont.

Out of these openings at the Summit and the Sag the waters poured, we can believe, with great velocity. Their erosive power, correspondingly great, was intensified by ice and the frozen rocky materials derived from the glacier. At Athens the "evidences of a powerful stream are numerous in the shape of water-worn surfaces, pot holes," etc. (Bannister, *Geology of Illinois*.) Thus the water-shed between Lake Michigan and the valleys of the Des Plaines and Illinois rivers was cut deeper and deeper, wearing finally a passage two hundred feet lower than found elsewhere on the rim of the lake. *And so, in that far-off time, was made the most important physical preparation that determined the location of Chicago of the nineteenth century.*

But we are not quite through the records as revealed by our soil. Judging from the terrace deposits before mentioned, the lake must have made long stands at various levels above the present. During all which time its waters drained into the Mississippi River. As the glacier slowly deserted these lands an arctic vegetation covered their baldness. This vegetation, driven southward by the advancing ice, had gradually replaced the destroyed or exiled tropical forms of the preceding period. The ground, rich with the varied deposits of the drift, supported a flora which soon acquired a hardy luxuriance. Pines, firs, cedars, and arbor-vitæ bordered the lake shores with a dark forest. Beneath this shelter northern plants and animals found a congenial home.

As in Alaska to-day we see the glacier and an Alpine flora side by side, so then the retreating land ice and flowering mosses overlapped each other. Occasionally we find a little remnant of this arctic flora lingering under a combination of favorable conditions even to the present. Such a little survival may be found at Miller's Station, on the Baltimore and Ohio Railroad, where clusters of hardy Northern pines overshadow a cool marshy ground, on which grows the rare little trailing vine *Linnæa borealis*—the one flower of all the flora he knew so well that Linnæus wished named after himself, not only for its delicate beauty and fragrance, but because it was a plant of the cold and the North, his native land. The trailing arbutus is another and a more conspicuous relic of this frigid interval.

But of greater interest to us is the fact that man, as a fisher and hunter, was present in this vicinity before the close of the glacial epoch. So persistently do his remains accompany the deposits of terminal moraines that he is known as the man of the drift, otherwise the man of the stone age. Human skulls have been unearthed on the banks of the Des Plaines River of types lower than any existing races, not excepting the lowest Australian. Foster, in his *Prehistoric Races of the United States*, says of one of these: "It is undoubtedly the most remarkable skull hitherto observed, affording the nearest approximation to the skulls of the anthropoid apes. It is difficult to bring it within the reasonable bounds of conjecture as to our ideas of what a human cranium in its widest deviation from a supposed type ought to be." Unfortunately these remains were destroyed in the fire of 1871.

These palæolithic men must have existed in large numbers, as their stone implements show. Their distribution seems to have been determined by the length of the ice front, close to which they lived. They must have been terrified witnesses of the sweeping floods that characterized this era. Floods on a smaller scale, but for similar reasons, have occurred in modern times in Switzerland, where, through breakage of ice dams, upper lakes have burst their torrents of destruction upon the valleys below. Remembering that the ice cap covered northern Europe as well as America, that drift men dwelt along its borders there as here, we realize that floods must have been equally destructive in both continents. Being probably helpless to forecast their coming, whole populations may have been swept away. A writer suggests that "in these catastrophes it is easy to see the far-off basis of a traditional universal deluge, a belief in which is said to be held in some form by most savage nations, especially those of the north temperate zones."

One more important episode in our past history is yet to be described.

At length the ice front retired beyond the Strait of Mackinac. Previous to this the compound lake to the eastward, covering an area of forty thousand miles, had maintained for ages a level two hundred feet above Lake Michigan, and seven hundred feet above the Atlantic. As the supply of water lessened, this body diminished in size. Lakes Huron, Erie, and Ontario became differentiated. Niagara began to cut its famous gorge between the last two named. Whether the whole system of inland waters will flow to the Atlantic or the Gulf will depend upon the relative length of time between the excavation of Niagara channel and the melting of Mackinac glaciers. It was a neck-and-neck race between erosion and evaporation. The water-shed west of us at its lowest point is but ten feet above Lake Michigan. The Niagara outlet near Buffalo is but twelve feet lower than this. Had the country near Buffalo been a few feet higher, or the water-shed at the summit west of us a few feet lower, the entire lake drainage would have gone over this region to the Mississippi. Niagara would never have been, neither would the modern St. Lawrence with its Thousand Isles Buffalo and Chicago would have exchanged places in commercial functions.

The whole development of this continent would have been changed. Upon such small geological differences do sometimes such great results depend. But the Mackinac glaciers lingered obstinately, Niagara took permanent advantage of the delay, and when the lakes became confluent, their waters sought the Atlantic.

With the establishment of an eastern drainage Chicago again emerged from the receding waters as a low flat, maintaining a precarious amphibious existence between the land and water.

A new factor now enters into its evolution. An oblique shore line to the northeast became the cause of sand deposits at the foot of the lake, whose pocket shape favored its lodgement. The sand collected in bars running parallel to our shore lines. Rising above the surface, another agent took part in the land construction. The winds picked up the finer materials, and lodged them, as water does, in the order of their respective weights. Thus the sand dunes were formed that figure so prominently in our Calumet region. Sand hills of great extent, hundreds of feet in height, covered with forest trees of centuries in growth, testify to the amount of work and length of time required to build our present lake frontage.

Between the low sand bars, which in turn became sand dunes, there lay long narrow strips of water more or less separated from the restless lake. In these sheltered, quiet lagoons another agent took up the work. A water vegetation, consisting of mosses, sedges, and rushes, came into luxurious growth, converting by their own accumulations the strips of water into swamps. These, through further filling in, became slowly drained and covered by coarse prairie grasses, as we now know them.

We have advanced with ridiculous speed in our description of Chicago since the glacial epoch. It remains to correct our time estimates since then by a few reflections. We left our county emerging from the lake and covered by an arctic vegetation. The moose, the reindeer, and the mammoth were disputing for supremacy with ancient man. Their bones were laid away together amid the drift. With the retreat of the glaciers went not only these Alpine plants and animals, but palæolithic man as well. Habits too deeply organized for eradication held them alike in bonds far stronger than the ice itself. To this day his descendants, the Esquimaux, still prefer to hunt and fish along the borders of that zero line above which the moisture never melts.

To the ice age we owe the countless beautiful lakes stretching from Maine to Minnesota. To the drift we owe that remarkable variety and fertility of soil which is the real source of the marvellous prosperity and rapid development of our Northern and Middle States.

Estimates of time since its close vary widely. Allowing for all possible mistakes, we are safe in considering it proven that no less a period than forty or fifty thousand years has elapsed since the retreat of the ice sheet from temperate latitudes. The ice age forms the nearest fixed date from which all modern geology reckons. To us it answers for "In the beginning."

My task is ended, though far from completed. In the desire to make prominent the more striking features of our past much has been omitted, much more awaits further investigation.

Matthew Arnold in one of his latest essays lamented the absence in the United States of ancient monuments of man's industry and devotion. He noted the vulgarity of our names at railway stations as he crossed the continent, that even of these such was our poverty we were obliged to use duplicates. He probably had in mind the long line of Celtic names trailing across Europe as memorials of stations in the progress of our Aryan ancestors. In short, he complained we had no historic past to inspire us to reverence and kindle the imagination, nothing to throw a mysterious haze over the crude strong realism of the present. That for lack of this we are not "interesting."

There may be truth in this, but Mr. Arnold offered us no remedy. There is one, however, close at hand. Our land has had a history, if our civil polity has not.

THE DAKOTAS

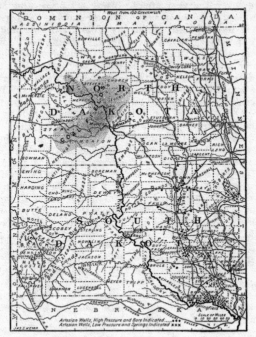

MAP OF NORTH AND SOUTH DAKOTA.

IN entering upon a study of the newly admitted States, and beginning with those of the Northwest, we are confronted by new scenes, new peoples, and new conditions, in which we shall find far fewer reminders of our Eastern life than greet us in some regions which we regard as quite foreign, as in old Canada, for instance. We are putting a new slide into the American magic-lantern. We are opening a new volume added to our own history, and we are to read of new characters moving amid surroundings quite as new; to them almost as new as to us.

Beginning with the Dakotas, we enter the vast plains country—monotonous, all but treeless, a blanket of brown grass almost as level as the mats of grass that the Pacific coast Indians plait. It is only a little wrinkled in the finishing—at the top edge and down in the southwest corner. On its surface the houses and the villages stand out in silhouette against a sky that bends down to touch the level sward. Here we find the western edge of the lands which the Scandinavians who have come among us prefer to their own countries. Here we come upon the yellow wheat-fields that turned their kernels into millions of golden dollars last year. Here, also, we see the more than half savage cattle whose every part and possession, except their breath, is converted into merchandise in Chicago. The hard-riding cowboys are here "turned loose," and the not less domesticated Indians in their blankets are cribbed in the national corrals. A great thirst would seem to overspread the Dakotas, for the lands are arid, while the people possess prohibitory liquor laws, and water that is poisoned with alkali.

In the Black Hills we prepare ourselves for Montana by a first glimpse of mining. In Montana, where the very first merchant's sign-board announced "pies, coffee, and pistols for sale," we now see the legend "licensed gambling saloon" staring at the tourists, who may walk into the hells more easily than they can into the stock exchanges of the East In Montana we feel an atmosphere of speculation. Every store clerk hoards some shares in undeveloped mines for his nest-egg. It is natural that this should be. The stories of quick and great fortunes that daze the mind are supported by the presence of the millionaire heroes of each tale. Moreover, the very air of Montana is a stimulant, like champagne. Perhaps it gathers its magic from the earth, where the precious metals are strewn over the mountains, where sapphires, rubies, and garnets are spaded out of the earth like goober nuts in the South, and where men hunt for the diamonds which scientists say must be there.

Montana is a land of ready cash and high wages. Lumbermen and miners get as high as seven dollars a day, and the very street-sweepers get twice as much as politicians pay to broom-handlers in New York to keep in favor with the poor. Here we find wealth, polish, and refinement, noble dwellings, palatial hotels, and numerous circles of charming, cultivated folk. Their mistake has been to despise agriculture. They know this, and with them, to see an error is to repair it.

The mining camps and California-colored characteristics of the mountainous half of Montana spread over into Idaho, a baby giant born with a golden spoon. The cattle ranges and cowboy capitals of Montana's grass-clad hills are repeated upon the gigantic but virgin savannas of Wyoming. In Washington all is different again. The forests of Maine and of the region of the Great Lakes are here exaggerated, the verdure of the East reappears, and passes into semi-tropic and incessant freshness and abundance. Here flowers bloom in the gardens at Christmas, small fruits threaten California's prestige, and the aborigines are bow-legged, boating Indians who work like 'longshoremen. Cities with dozen-storied buildings start up like sudden thoughts, and everywhere is note of promise to make us belittle our Eastern growths that startled the older world.

With surprise we find the New England leadership missing. Here is a great corner of America where the list of the *Mayflower's* passengers is not folded into the family Bibles! The capitals of the older Northwest are dominated by the offspring of Puritans, but we must journey all across the Dakotas and Montana, among a new race of pioneers, to have New England recalled to us again only in Spokane and Tacoma—and but faintly there. The new Northwest is peopled by men who followed the Missouri and its tributaries from Kentucky, Indiana, Iowa, Arkansas, and Missouri. Others who are among them speak of themselves as from California and Utah, but they are of the same stock. Broadly speaking, they founded these new countries between the outbreak of the rebellion and the end of the reconstruction period in the Southern States. They are not like the thrifty, argumentative, and earnest New-Englander, or the phlegmatic Dutch and hard-headed English of the Middle States. These new Americans are tall, big-boned, stalwart folks, very self-assertive, very nervous, very quick in action, and quicker still in forming resolutions. If it would be fair to treat of them in a sentence, it could be said that they act before they think, and when they think, it is mainly of themselves. Their European origin is so far behind them that they know nothing of it. Their grandfathers had forgotten it. They talk of Uter, Coloraydo, Illinoise, Missourer, Nevadder, Ioway, Arkansaw, and Wyóming. The last two names are by them pronounced more correctly than by us. In a word, they are distinctly, decidedly, pugnaciously, and absolutely American.

Because it is impossible to picture the novelty—to an Eastern reader—of life in the Northwest, and because it nevertheless must be suggested, let me tell only of four peculiar visitations that the new States experience—of four invasions which take place there every year. In May there come into the stock ranges of Montana shearers by the hundreds, in bands of ten or twenty, each led by a captain, who finds employment and makes contracts for the rest. These sheep-barbers are mainly Californians and New-Yorkers, and the California men are said to be the more skilful workers. To a layman, all seem marvellously dexterous, and at ten cents a head, many are able to earn $6 to $8 a day. They lose many days in travel, however, and may not average more than $5 on that account. Their season begins in California in February, and they work through Oregon, Washington, and Montana, to return to a second shearing on the Pacific coast in August. Some come mounted and some afoot, and some are shiftless and dissipated, but many are saving, and ambitious to earn herds of their own.

They come upon the Montanan hills ahead of another and far stranger procession—that of the cattle that are being driven across the country from Texas. This is a string of herds of Texas two-year-olds coming north at middle age to spend the remaining half of their lives fattening on the Montana bunch-grass, and then to end their careers in Chicago. The bands are called "trails," and follow one another about a day apart. With each trail ride the hardy and devil-may-care cowboys, led by a foreman, and followed by a horse-wrangler in charge of the relays of broncos. A cook, with a four-horse wagon-load of provisions, brings up each rear. Only a few miles are covered in a day, and the journey consumes many weeks. These are enlivened by storms, by panics among the cattle, by quarrels with settlers on guard at the streams and on their lands, by meals missed and nights spent amid mud and rain. That is as queer and picturesque a procession as one can easily imagine.

Then there is the early autumn hop-picking in the luxuriant fields of the Pacific coast in Washington. Down Puget Sound and along the rivers come the industrious canoe Indians of that region in their motley garb, and bent on making enough money in the hop-fields to see them through the rainy and idle winter. They are not like the Indians of story and of song, but are a squat-figured people, whose chests and arms are over-developed by exercise in the canoes, which take the place of the Indian ponies of the plains, as their rivers are substituted for the blazed or foot-worn trails of the East. To the hop-fields they come in their dugouts from as far north as British Columbia and Alaska. When all have made the journey, their canoes fret the strand, and the smoke of their camp fires touches the air with blue. Women and children accompany the men, all alike illuminating the green background of the hop-fields with their gay blankets and calicoes, themselves lending still other touches of color by means of their leather skins and jet hair. They leave a trail of silver behind them when they depart, but the hops they have picked represent still more of gold—a million last year; two millions the year before.

Again, a fourth set of invaders appears; this time in Dakota. These are not picturesque. They come not in boats or astride horses, but straggling or skulking along the highways, as the demoralized peasantry made their way to Paris during the French Revolution. These are the wheat-harvesters, who follow the golden grain all the way up from Texas, finding themselves in time for each more and more belated ripening in each more and more northerly State, until, in late autumn, they reach the Red River Valley, and at last end their strange pilgrimage in Manitoba. The hands and skill they bring to the dense wheat-fields of eastern North Dakota are most welcome there, and these harvest folk might easily occupy a high niche in sentimental and poetic literature, yet they don't. As a rule, they are not at all the sort of folk that the ladies of the wheat lands invite to their tea parties and sewing bees. On the contrary, far too many of them are vagabonds and fond of drink. In the Red River country the harvesters from the South are joined by lumbermen from Wisconsin and Minnesota, who find that great natural granary a fine field for turning honest pennies at lighter work than felling forests.

In area, the half-dozen new States in the Northwest are about the size of Alaska, and they are larger than France, Germany, Italy, and Holland combined. One of the States is greater than Great Britain and Ireland, and one county in that State is larger than New Hampshire, Massachusetts, and Connecticut. The population of those six States is about like that of little New Jersey, yet it is thought that at least half as many persons as are now in the entire country could maintain life in that corner of the nation. Three of the names the new States took are criticised. There are many persons in the Dakotas who now realize that a foolish mistake was made in the choice of the names North Dakota and South Dakota. Both fancied there was magic in the word Dakota, and wanted to possess it. By succeeding in that purpose they ridiculed the noble word, which means leagued or united.

To the traveller who crosses North Dakota in the thoroughly modern and luxurious easy-rolling trains of the Northern Pacific Railroad, the region east of the Missouri seems one dead-level reach of grass. It appears to be so level that one fancies if his eyesight were better he might stand anywhere in that greater part of the State and see Mexico in one direction and the north pole in the other. Everywhere the horizon and the grass meet in a monotonous repetition of unbroken circles. As a matter of fact, there is a slight slope upward from the Red River of the North at the eastern edge of the State, there is a decided valley south of Jamestown, and for fifty miles before the Missouri River is reached the land begins to slope slightly towards that stream. There are hills, too, called by the French the "Coteau du Missouri," and never yet rechristened, to mark the approach to the river. The country west of the Missouri is more attractive to the sight-seer, though far less so to the farmer. It looks like a sea arrested in a storm, with all its billows fixed immutably. It is partly a mass of softly rounded, grassy breasts; and beyond them, in the Bad Lands, the hills change to the form of waves that are ready to break upon a strand. Farther on, the change is into buttes, into peaked, columnar, detached hills. On the light snow that merely frosted this broken country last winter, when I crossed it twice, there seemed not a yard of the earth's surface that was not tracked with the foot-writing of wild animals and birds —that kitchen literature which the red men knew by heart—the signs of coyotes, jack-rabbits, prairie-chickens, deer, and I know not what else besides. It is a 350-mile journey to cross the State from east to west, a 210-mile trip to cross it from the north to the south.

It has been a one-crop State, and the figures that are given of its yield of that crop are not what they pretend to be, for four-fifths of the wheat is usually grown on the eastern edge, in the Red River Valley. In the rest of the State the crops have failed year after year, and even the grazing of stock, for which alone the critics of the State say it is fit, has been attended with some serious reverses. The most extravagant lying indulged in to boom the State has failed to alter nature—just as it failed in Canada, where it was followed by even greater hardship and disappointment. The lying on behalf of North Dakota took the form of applying the phenomenal figures of the rich Red River Valley to the whole State, quoting the earnings of Red River farms and the experiences of Red River settlers as applicable to all Dakota.

Having gone to Dakota because of the marvellous yield of wheat in the Red River Valley, the unfortunate settlers put all their holdings in wheat. It is customary in Dakota for people to say that these poor fellows bought their experience dearly, but they did not pay as much for it as the two Dakotas have paid for the carnival of lying that began the business. A succession of extraordinarily bad seasons followed, owing to lack of sufficient moisture to grow the grain. In one year there was not enough to sprout it. There were five years of dire misfortune, and they brought absolute ruin to all who had no means laid by. Many were ruined who had money, and thousands left the Territory, for it was a Territory when the wholesale lying was at its height.

The soil in the Red River Valley is a thick vegetable deposit, while that of the remaining nine-tenths of the State is of a mineral character, lime being a notable factor in the composition. It is very productive if water can be got to it. In that case the Red River country would be no better than all the rest. And there is the rub. With irrigation, North Dakota will become a rich farming State. Without it, the State has enjoyed one rich harvest in six years. The irrigation cannot be accomplished by means of any waters that are now on the surface of the State; it must be by means of wells, or by "bombs bursting in air," or by Australian alchemy. And yet it is not fair to the State to say that it can do nothing without irrigation. We shall see that the belief is that its worst misfortunes have come from its dependence upon a single crop, and that by diversified farming the wolves can be kept from the doors when the wheat crop fails.

Last year came a change of luck and a year such as North Dakota has not enjoyed in a long while. Between 50,-000,000 and 55,000,000 bushels of wheat were harvested; and if the Red River Valley's yield was 35,000,000, it is apparent that the rest of the State must be credited with from 15,000,000 to 20,000,000 of bushels. Of corn, 300,000 bushels were raised; of oats, 10,000,000 bushels; of cattle, a million dollars' worth; and of hay and potatoes, a very great deal. This was good work for a population of 200,000 souls. It is estimated that the money product of the entire harvest was sufficient to pay off the indebtedness of the farmers, and leave an average of $250 to each farming family. At the beginning of 1892 it was prophesied that the farmers would free themselves of only those debts upon which they had been paying a high rate of interest, so as to be in a position to borrow at lower rates and to improve their farm buildings. They have been paying all the way from 12 to 24 per cent. a year for loans. They have also been obliged to give bonuses to the loaning agents at renewal times, getting $180,say,when they were charged with $200. These agents are terrible sharks, and there are crowds of them in the State, calling themselves real-estate and loan agents, getting money from the East, paying the capitalists 6 and 8 per cent. for it, and then exacting as high as 24 per cent., and these stiff bonuses besides. They have made a fine living upon the misery and distress and upon the bare necessities of those around them. An organization of capitalists to loan money at reasonable rates would be a godsend there, and full security for their money could be obtained by them.

How the poor victims lived through these exactions is a mystery. Many did not. They abandoned their farms and the State. A great many came back last year on hearing of the likelihood of a good season. But the best news is that last year nearly all the farmers began to turn their attention to diversified farming and to stock-raising in conjunction with agriculture. North Dakota was always a good cattle State at least three years in five, and the manner in which the farmers are going into the business ought to make the industry successful every year. Those who can afford it are acquiring herds of from 50 to 300 head. In the winter,when the beeves need attention, the farmers will have nothing else to attend to. They calculate that they can raise a three-year-old beef at an expense of from $12 to $15, and market it at from $30 to $40. At the least, they figure on a profit of $5 a head each year. It would appear that cattle thus looked after, with hay in corrals for the winter, may some day be rated between stall-fed and range cattle. In the summer these farmers are advised to put into wheat only that acreage which they can handle without hired help, for help is hard to get in the western part of the State. The mysterious nomads of the wheat belt do not go there.

On the Missouri slope, where most of the corn was raised last year, that crop never was a failure. It has been culti-

vated there for twenty years. In fact in some Indian mounds above Bismarck corn-cobs are found along with the pottery and trinkets for which the mounds are constantly ravaged. Potatoes also grow well on the Missouri slope. Starch is being made from them at a factory started by a New England man at Hankinson, in Richland County. From eight to ten tons of starch is being made daily at that place.

The range land for cattle is in that district which may be roughly described as the last three rows of counties in the western end of the State. Dickinson, on the Northern Pacific Railroad, is the shipping-point for the stock. In order to exact a revenue from the cow-men, the people have agreed to reconstruct into five organized counties the whole country west of the Missouri and the extreme northwestern counties. By the time this is published, the change will, in all probability, have been accomplished. There are thirteen counties west of the Missouri on the present maps, and only four of these have county governments. The new arrangement will complete the political machinery for assessment and taxation in the grazing lands. The cattle-men are supposed to be taxed for their cattle as upon personal property, but they have heretofore evaded the impost. The cattle business in these counties is rapidly being revolutionized. All the stock-men agree that the most return is gotten from small holdings with winter corrals. There are five horse ranches west of the Missouri. At one point Boston capitalists are raising thoroughbreds from imported stallions. The rest of the stock is of the common order, herded loose on the ranges.

But there is some farming even west of the Missouri. Corn, wheat, and oats are successfully raised in Morton County. Mercer County produced a splendid quality of wheat at 25 bushels to the acre, and across the river, in McLean County, a farmer succeeded in getting 31 bushels to the acre. In these two counties we come upon that vast bed of coal which underlies parts of eleven counties in North Dakota. In Mercer County this coal crops out on the riverbank, and a company backed by Chicago capital has been organized to build barges and ship the coal to points down the river. It can be sold at wholesale in Bis-

marck at $2 40 a ton, and in Pierre, South
Dakota, for $3 50 a ton. In Bismarck
soft coal now sells for $8 and $8 50, and
anthracite for $11 a ton. The Dakota
coal is a lignite—an immature coal—but
it serves well for ordinary uses, making
a hot fire, a white ash, and no soot. Its
worst fault is that it crumbles when it is
exposed to the air. Dakota coal from Morton County is already marketed. There
seems to be an inexhaustible supply of it
in that county. The veins that are now
being worked are between eight feet and
fourteen feet in thickness, and they crop
up near the surface. It is in use in the
public buildings of the State, in the flouring-mills, and in many hotels and residences. It sells in Mandan for $2 50 a
ton. It is said that there are 150,000
acres of these coal beds east of the Missouri, and the coal area west of the river
is almost as great. The veins vary in
thickness from half a dozen to thirty
feet. Farmers find it on their lands close
under the surface, and with a pick and
shovel dig in one day sufficient to last
them all winter. It is a most extraordinary "find"—a bountiful provision of
nature. It greatly alters the former view
of the future of North Dakota—and of
South Dakota also, since there is enough
for both States. It adds to the comfort
of life there, it provides a coal at least
half as good as anthracite at one-quarter
the cost, and it would seem that it must
become the basis of manufacturing industries in the near future. A good terra-
cotta clay in great quantities is found
near the coal in many localities.

In showing that the future of the State
depends upon diversified industries, and
in calling attention to the newly exerted
efforts of the people to meet this condition,
I have omitted to mention the fact that
many capitalists who had loaned money
to farmers west of the Red River country
are now supplying sheep to their debt-
ors. Between 75,000 and 100,000 sheep
were put upon farms in the State in
that way last summer in herds of from
50 to 100 head. The plan generally adopted is for the farmer to take care of the
sheep for five years, taking the wool
for his pains, and at the end of that
term for the farmer and the capitalist to
divide the herd between them, increase
and all. I do not find it to be the general opinion that this will turn out well
in most cases. Sheep require constant at-

tention, and the raising of them is a business by itself, not to be taken up at hap-
hazard by men who are not experienced.
Moreover, the land east of the Missouri
is said not to be the best sort for that
use.

The proportion of unoccupied land in
the whole State is one-third. The western grazing counties form a third of the
State, but much of their land is taken up
by farmers—along the streams and the
railroads. In all probability one-quarter
of it that is not taken up is arable land,
but until railroads reach it there will be
no profit in tilling it. The land yet obtainable is part railroad and part government land. It fetches from $1 25 to $4
an acre. Two railroads cross the State
from east to west, and two new ones are
in process of construction across the State
from the southern border over to Canada.

North Dakota is a prohibition State;
that is to say, the making and selling of
alcoholic stimulants are forbidden there.
One effect of the operation of this law
was the driving of thirty-six saloons out
of Fargo across the Red River into More-
head, Minnesota. Another effect was the
transformation of a brewery in the Red
River Valley into a flouring-mill. Yet
another effect was the semi-prostration of
business in Bismarck, the capital of the
State, where the electric-light plant was
shut down, for one thing, because of the
loss of the saloon custom. The prohibitory clause was put into the new State Constitution and the whole measure was carried with a rush. The clause was asked
for more earnestly by the Scandinavian
element than by any others, and their
votes, especially in the Red River Valley,
greatly assisted in making it the law; but
intelligent men, who are in a position
to know whereof they speak, assert that
hundreds of votes were cast for the
clause by men who had no idea that it
would become a law—men who promised
to vote for it, or who voted for it because
they thought nothing would come of their
action. The Scandinavians are alcohol-
drinkers, and many who serve as spokes-
men for them frankly declare that their
countrymen need prohibitory laws because they are not mild and phlegmatic
beer-drinkers like the Teutonic people,
but are fond of high-wines, and are terribly affected by the use of them. If an
attempt be made to alter the law or repeal
it, the process will consume five years.

It is impossible to say what the temper of the majority of persons in the State now is, but the exodus that has taken place from the Dakotas, as it is recorded in the archives of Western general passenger agents, tells of one damaging effect of such a law; the disinclination of Europeans to take up land in prohibition States tells of another; and the failure of mankind to enforce the law in any State in which it has been included in the statutes would seem to make a mockery of the principle that underlies it.

The local geologists say that the Red River Valley is the bed of a former sea. Enormous rivers poured into it, and washed a great depth of alluvial deposit there, to make the extraordinarily rich soil that now supports the most prosperous farming population of the West. The valley forms the eastern face of North Dakota, half of its width being in that State and half in Minnesota. The outlines of the valley are traced over a region nearly 300 miles long, and between 50 and 100 miles wide. It extends from a point 100 miles above the Canadian border down to the southern edge of North Dakota. The western or Dakota half of it takes in the six easterly counties of the new State; but it is not all typical Red River soil, for the western edge is inclined to be sandy.

The soil is a rich black loam. In the old days the hieroglyphs of the buffalo, written in their trails, seemed to be lines of black ink upon the brown grass. This

black soil is 15 to 25 inches thick, and under that is a thick clay, which, when turned up by the spade or plough, is as productive as the soil itself. To the eye the valley appears to be level as a billiard table, but in reality it dips a little toward the unpretentious river that cleaves it in twain. It is not beautiful. No one-crop country can be either beautiful or

MAP OF NORTH AND SOUTH DAKOTA.

continuously active in life and trade, no matter how rich and productive it is. In summer this is a wilderness of grain; in winter, a waste of stubble. But we shall see further on that this cannot long be the case.

The certainty of the wheat crop is the best gift the good fairies gave it at its christening. Any farmer who attends to his business can make $6 to $8 an acre on wheat at its present price, and, considering that he buys his land at about $25 an acre, that is an uncommonly good business proposition, in view of the intellectual ability that is invested in it. I use these figures because the average crop of the valley is 19 or 20 bushels to the acre. That they told me on the ground, where they said, "There's no use lying when the truth is so good." There are higher yields. One large farm near Fargo returned above 30 bushels, and others have done better in the past year, but the average is as I have stated. And this brought a profit of $9 to the acre last year. One man with 6000 acres cleared $40,000; one with 3500 acres made a profit of $25,000. Many paid for their farms; scores could have done so, but wisely preferred to put some of their money in farm betterments.

There has never been a failure of crops in the valley. It sometimes happens that men put in their wheat too late, and it gets nipped by frost, but there is no excuse for that. Barley is what the prudent men put in when they are belated. They raise good barley, and a great deal of it, in the valley, the main products being wheat, oats, barley, some flax, and some corn, the latter being the New England flint corn. Such corn has been raised near Fargo seven years in succession without a failure. Irrigation is not needed or employed in the valley, but artesian wells are very numerous there, as well they may be, since the water is reached at a depth of 20 feet and a cost of $100.

To go to the valley is not to visit the border. It is a well-settled, well-ordered, tidy farming region, of a piece with our Eastern farm districts, with good roads, neat houses, schools, churches, bridges, and well-appearing wooden villages. The upper or northern end of the valley is the finer part, because there the land was taken up in small plots—quarter sections of 160 acres each, or at the most whole sections. Therefore that end is the most populous and prosperous, for it is the small farms that pay best. The southern end of the valley was railroad land, and as much of it was sold when the railroad needed money, an opportunity for big holdings was created and embraced. These so-called bonanza properties do not pay proportionately, and are being diminished by frequent sales. In one year

(1888) no less than twenty-four thousand acres on one of these farms were sown in wheat.

The present population of the Red River Valley is of Norwegians, Swedes, Irish, English, and Canadians, all being now Americanized by law. It is strange—to them it must be bewildering—to think that in that valley are women who were once harnessed with dogs to swill-wagons in Scandinavian cities, and yet are now the partners of very comfortable, prosperous farmers. The Scandinavians are spoken of in the valley as being good, steady, reliable, industrious folk, but eminently selfish and lacking in public spirit, and yet they and all the other residents of the valley have been in one respect both prodigal and profligate, for it has been a rule there never to cultivate or make anything that can be bought. In this respect the people are mending their ways. They are learning the lesson taught in the Southern States, where, to put the case in a sentence, the people were never prosperous until they raised their own bacon. So, latterly, these Red River people have been venturing upon the cultivation of mutton, pork, wool, horses, vegetables, and small fruits. But the first efforts at saving are as hard as learning to swim, and so as soon as these farmers learned that Europe was clamoring for wheat, they lost their heads. It is said that they abandoned fifty per cent. of the dairy farming that had grown to be a great source of income there, and in all the towns where the farmers' daughters were at work as domestic servants, the kitchen industries were crippled by a general homeward flight of the girls. "Our fathers are rich now, and we won't have to work any more," they said.

A leading railroad man in the Northwest, who is noted for his luminous and picturesque way of talking, is fond of calling the Red River farmers "the leisure class of the West." He says: "They only attend to their business for a few weeks in the spring and fall, and that they do sitting down, with splendid horses to drag the farming implements on which they ride around. When their grain is ripe, they hire laborers to cut and harvest it. and then they cash it in for money, fill the banks of the valley with money to the bursting-point, and settle down for a long loaf, or go to Europe or New York." Yet they must find a continuance of their strength and prosperity in diversified farming and in hard work, and this is being taught to the rest by the shrewder ones among them. Such men are making the breeding of fine draught-horses a side reliance, and very many farms now maintain from 1500 to 2000 Percheron, Norman, and Clydesdale horses, as well as pigs, sheep, and poultry. The country is too level for the profitable raising of sheep, however. They need uneven land and a variety of picking; moreover, the soil clogs in their hoofs, and subjects them to hoof rot, and other diseases prey upon them there.

There are nearly 9,000,000 acres in the valley, and one-sixth of it is under the plough. One hundred and fifty million bushels of wheat could be raised there if every acre was sown with seed, but there is no such demand for wheat as that would require to be profitable. As it is, less than a quarter of the valley is cultivated, and only three-quarters of that fraction are given up to wheat, so that last year's yield was about 30 to 37 millions of bushels. That would have brought $27,000,-000 had it been sold, but while this is being written (in the holidays of '91–2), a great many farmers are holding their grain in the firm belief that Russia's needs will determine a rise of 20 cents in the price. Those who sold got 80 cents; those who are holding back want a dollar a bushel.

The climate is, of course, perfect for farming. Some very lively tornadoes go with it, and in the winter it is sufficiently cold to freeze the fingers off a bronze statue. But these are trifles. The windstorms do their worst damage in the newspapers and the public imagination, and the cold of the winter is not as intense or disagreeable as the cold of more southerly States. It is a dry cold, and plenty of glorious sunshine goes with it. There are plentiful rains in the spring and the autumn, with intensely hot weather at midsummer. The moisture is held in the soil by the clay underneath, and in hot summer weather the surface cakes into a crust, still leaving the moisture in the earth.

I am so explicit about this great "breadbasket of America," as it is called, because it is by far the best part of North Dakota —so very much the best that in the valley the people are heard to say that they wish they were not tied to the rest of the

State. "What a marvellous State it would have made to have taken the eastern half of the valley from Minnesota, and put it all under one government!" they cry. And others say that the whole valley should have been given to Minnesota, and North Dakota should have forever remained a Territory. But even in view of the excellence of this Red River region there would be little use in exploiting it were it all farmed and populated. On the contrary, there is room for thousands there—for many thousands. The land now obtainable cannot be purchased for less than $25 an acre, but not more than $30 need be paid. Money down is not needed. The system called "paying with half crops" obtains there. The farmer pays half of what the land produces each year until the sum of the purchase price is met, with interest, of course. Under this system the land cannot be taken away from him unless he fails to farm it. He will need to house himself and buy horses and tools. However, one owner of 910 acres came to the valley with nothing but an Indian pony and a jack-knife. A great many others brought only their debts.

All that I have said about the productiveness of the valley applies particularly to the six valley counties of North Dakota. The Minnesota land is not so good.

Here, then, is a region that must feel the greatest increase in population that will come to any part of North Dakota. The river that curves and twists its way between the farms has been rightly nicknamed the Nile of America. In the twelve counties that border upon it in Minnesota and Dakota are 61 banks, with deposits amounting, in last December, to $6,428,000, or $65 for every man, woman, and child in the region. The farmers are the principal depositors, and they had this amount to their credit when a very large fraction of their grain crop had not been sold. The valley has two thrifty towns—Fargo, with 7000 population, and Grand Forks, with 6000.

I have spoken of the custom in the valley of relying upon a swarm of nomad harvesters to fall upon the wheat and garner it in the autumn. They make a picturesque army of invaders, led by the men from the Minnesota forests and Wisconsin pineries, in their peculiar coats of checked blanket stuff, but far too many of them form a hardened lot of vagabonds —"a tough outfit," in the language of the country. They have been in the habit of dictating how much help a farmer shall employ when they are in the fields, their idea being that the fewer the laborers the more work for those who are employed. They will abandon a farm on half a day's notice, and between the laziness and drunkenness of numbers of them there is little chance for either good or hard work. Prohibition gets more praise here than in other parts of the State, because, even with bottles hid in the fields, the harvesters only get a thimbleful where they once got a quart of rum. Another thing that eases the strain of prohibition is the plenteousness of rum just across the river in Minnesota. The system which relies on these harvesters is a bad one, and in time, with smaller holdings, the farmers will mainly harvest their crops with their own hands and neighborhood help.

North Dakota has many attractive towns, those that I have mentioned in the Red River country being the largest. Bismarck, the capital, on the Missouri River, has 2500 population. It has more than its share of brick buildings, and in its numerous pretty villas are families of a number and character to form an attractive social circle. By great enterprise it secured the position of capital of the Territory in '83, raising $100,000 for a capitol building, and adding a gift of 160 acres for a park around the edifice, as well as 160 acres elsewhere "wholly for good measure." Mandan is a flourishing railroad town across the river, with about 2000 population; Jamestown, near the eastern end of the State, is as big as Bismarck; and Devil's Lake, in the northern part of the State, is the same size. North Dakota has 1500 free schools, supported by a gift of 3,000,000 acres of public lands, set apart for the purpose when the State was admitted. As these lands cannot be sold for less than $10 an acre, the schools would appear to be certain eventually to have the support of a fund of $30,000,000.

South Dakota is 360 miles long and 225 miles wide. It contains 76,620 square miles, and is therefore larger than North Dakota by 2308 square miles. The population is estimated at 325,000, or more than half as much again as the other half of the old Territory. It is another blanket of grass like North Dakota, a little tattered and rocky in the northeast, and slight-

ly wooded there and in the southeasterly corner. Just as North Dakota has a vastly wealthy strip called the Red River Valley, and triumphing over all the rest of the State in its wealth, so South Dakota has its treasure land, the Black Hills mineral region, a mountainous tract in the southwestern corner of the State, 120 miles long and 35 or 40 miles wide. But North Dakota's bread-basket netted $27,000,000 last year, whereas South Dakota's precious metals are worth but $3,000,000 or $3,500,000 a year. Right through the middle of the State runs the Missouri River, with its attendant hills of gumbo clay and its slender groves of cottonwood to relieve the dreadful monotony of the plains, and to give a beauty that no other settlements in the State possess to such towns as lie along it.

Both States have the same story to tell. The people of South Dakota rushed into exclusive wheat-growing, leaving themselves nothing to carry them along if the crops failed; and fail they did in 1887, '88, '89, and '90. Then came a prohibitory liquor law, which is already set at naught in the cities, and settlers left the State by the thousands. But last year brought great crops, and good fortune was never, perhaps, better deserved. Estimates made before the threshing showed a wheat yield of 31,178,327 bushels, but the editor of the *Dakota Farmer* at Huron, a first-rate authority, told me he believed time would prove that 40,000,000 bushels had been reaped. The other yields were as follows: oats, 33,000,000 bushels; corn, 30,000,000 bushels; barley, 6,000,000 bushels; potatoes, nearly 5,000,000 bushels; flax, nearly 4,000,000 bushels; and rye, 750,000 bushels. This astonishing agricultural success in an arid State was achieved in 50 counties, nearly all east of the Missouri River. Some farming in the western or cattle-grazing half of the State was done in what may be loosely called the Black Hills region in the southwest, where there are railroads and local government and numerous settlements.

But little new sod had been broken to produce these crops. The wheat acreage had decreased by 70,000 acres. The acreage in flax also decreased, but in all the other cereals the acreage was more than in 1890. Notwithstanding the flight of so many farmers, there were only 400 acres less under the plough than during the preceding years. In the middle of the agricultural or eastern half of the State is a fertile, great, and well-watered valley. It is the valley of the James, but is seldom spoken of otherwise than as "the Jim River Valley." It passes through both Dakotas from Devil's Lake in northern North Dakota to the Nebraska border of southern South Dakota. It is watered by artesian wells, of which there is much to be said later on. There are many little streams in the rocky northeastern corner of the State, and here is the best sheep-raising district in South Dakota. Around Sioux Falls, in the southeastern corner, the farmers who had grown flax to rot the sod and to harvest the seed are now growing it for its fibre, and a company proposes to put up a linen-mill in that little metropolis. There is a notable industry in granite there, the stone being pink, red, and flesh-colored, and susceptible of as high a polish as Scotch granite. Hogs, too, are being raised down in that part of the State, and a packing concern is under way. Pierre also has a packing establishment.

Hundreds of thousands of sheep are being taken into central South Dakota. It is called a common thing to keep 95 per cent. of the lambs, because there are no cold rains there to kill them. There are few diseases, and foot rot is unknown. The farmers hope to be able to make from $2 to $3 50 a head in the sheep business. I have their figures, but I will spare those readers who know what a complex, delicate, and precarious business sheep-raising is, except where the conditions are exactly right as to climate, ground, and skilled ability on the part of the herders.

I have a friend, a lawyer, who, whenever he visits the farm on which he was born, vexes his father by asserting that there is a higher percentage of profit in farming than in mining or banking. He cites the enormous profit that attends the birth of a colt or a calf, or the sale of a bushel of corn gained from planting a few kernels. It is far easier to figure big profits in the sheep business. A lamb costs $2 50, yields wool worth 12 shillings a year, sells for $5, and creates several other sheep of equal value. Unfortunately there is another side to the story—but this is not the place for telling it. It is devoutly to be hoped, however, that sheep-raising may be a success in the Dakotas, as, indeed, it has already proved

with some extra intelligent and careful men there.

The Black Hills are cut off from the rest of the State. I could not find any one to tell me anything about them until I went to them. The Black Hills business is mining, while that of the rest of the State is all transacted on the surface. Between the Missouri and the Black Hills was, until lately, the great Sioux reservation of twenty-three millions of acres, or practically one-third of the State. That was cut in two a little more than a year ago, and eleven millions of acres were thrown open for settlement. But no railroad yet bisects the tract; no governments administer the affairs of the counties; there are no schools or post-offices there.

The newly opened land lies between the White and Big Cheyenne rivers. The land had offered such rich pasturage that the Interior Department found it next to impossible to keep the cattle-men out. Some white men actually were making use of it; but the greater number of men who had cows in there were squaw men, remnants of a band of French Canadians who came thither in the fur-trading era, married squaws, and grew to be more Indian than the Indians. One rich old squaw man in that region, who caches his wealth rather than risk it in a bank, lives close to Pierre, the capital, but has only once visited the town. To-day white men have 50,000 cattle there.

It is a superb range cattle country where it is watered, and the stock keeps seal fat all the time. Shipments from there have gone straight to Liverpool on the hoof. But, on the other hand, other parts are too dry for use; the springs that are there dry up in early summer. The bother of it is, so far as the cattle-men are concerned, that settlers are taking up the land by the streams, and eventually wells must be sunk in the arid country or the stock-men must retire from it. The farms there are fenced, as the law requires, while east of the Missouri there are no fences, and what cattle or sheep are there must be herded and guarded by day and corralled at night.

The government is selling this reclaimed reservation land at $1 25 an acre for first choice during the first three years, for 75 cents during the next two years, and for 50 cents for all lands not taken after five years. After that the government will pay the Indians for what remains. The money obtained by the sales goes to the Indian fund, and the plan is designed to help to make the Indians self-support- ing. What it means to the white men is that the people who have been the most distressed and unfortunate class in the Northwest are practically subjected to an especial and additional tax for the sup- port of Indians who are not their wards, but the wards of the nation. One small and poor county has already paid the red men $570,000.

What the Indians think of it and of the entire behavior of the white men is illus- trated by the best Indian story I have heard in a long while. An old grizzled Sioux dropped into a bank in Pierre, and upon being asked what he thought of the government purchase of half his reserva- tion, made an attempt to reply in broken English as follows:

"All same old story," said he. "White men come, build chu-chu [railroad] through reservation. White men yawpy- yawpy [talk]. Say: 'Good Indian, good Indian; we want land. We give muz-es- kow [money]; liliota muz-es-kow [plenty money].' Indian say, 'Yes.' What Ind- ian get? Wah-nee-che [nothing]. Some day white man want move Indian. White men yawpy-yawpy: 'Good Indian, good Indian; give good Indian liliota muz-es- kow.' What Indian get? Wah-nee-che. Some day white man want half big reservation. He come Indian. Yawpy- yawpy: 'Good Indian; we give Indian liliota muz-es-kow.' Indian heap fool. He say, 'Yes.' What Indian get? Wah- nee-che. All same old story. 'Good In- dian, good Indian.' Get nothing."

What the white men of South Dakota want now is to have the government of the United States spend a little of the muz-es-kow it is getting from the sale of these lands in driving wells in the newly opened lands for irrigation and the sup- port of stock. It is not positively known that there is an artesian basin under the land in question, but wells have been suc- cessful at both sides of it, in the east and the west, and many students and experts have declared that water will be found there. As the wells will cost $5000 each, no one is going to risk the experiment of driving them, unless it be the govern- ment. The only arguments that recon- cile those who dislike all approaches to Federal paternalism are that the govern-

ment is charging for what should be pub- lic land, and that since it seeks to sell the land, it will be a good business proposition to improve those parts of it which cannot otherwise be sold. It is believed that wells will work there, and it is certain that once the fact is proved, the whole great tract will be settled and made to blossom like a garden.

The story of the artesian basin under part of South Dakota seems fabulous. It is even more astonishing than the wealth of coal that underlies the farms of North Dakota. God does, indeed, move in mys- terious ways His wonders to perform when to the poor farmer, amid the cold blasts of the Northern winters, He distributes coal that is to be had for the taking of it, and when under the South Dakotan soil, that would be as rich as any in the world were it but moistened, He seems to have placed a great lake or, as some would have us believe, a vast sea.

On a foregoing page I have given the location and dimensions of that basin which the Dakotans affectionately speak of as the Jim River Valley. Under it all, in both States, there is said to lie a vast lake of crystal water. The fact is amply proven in South Dakota, where, between the northern and southern boundaries, there are already more than fifty high- pressure wells, or "gushers," as they call them there. A hundred, or perhaps more, low-pressure wells, reaching a flow closer to the surface, are at the foot of the same basin. In Sanborn, Miner, and McCook counties almost every farmer has his own low-pressure well. But the won- derful wells are the high-pressure, deep ones, wherein water is struck at from 600 to 1200 feet. The pressure in some of these wells is 200 pounds to the square inch. One at Woonsocket supplies 5000 gallons a minute. One at Huron serves for the town's water system and fire pro- tection. One at Springfield has force enough for more than the power used in a sixty-barrel flour-mill. One at Tyndall is expected to irrigate 800 acres. It is calculated that a two-inch well will water 160 acres; a three-inch well, 640 acres; and a four-inch well, 1280 acres or more. Eight miles above Huron a well is used on a farm that produced 53 bushels and 20 pounds in wheat to the acre, as against 15 bushels in the unirrigated land of the neighborhood. Some who profess to know say that the great basin is inexhaustible, and that the opening of one well near another does not affect the first one. Then, again, I read that this is not wholly true. But, at all events, no one doubts the presence of a vast body of water, and no well, even among those that are five years old, shows any sign of giving out. A law called the Melville Township Irrigation Law, approved on March 9, 1891, authorizes townships to sink wells for public use, and to issue bonds to defray the cost. This aims to make the mysterious basin the property of the people. For farming, the flow of water is not needed during half of each year. It is said that if the subsoil is wet, the crops will need no more water. The water should be turned on to the land after the harvest, and kept soaking into it for four or five months. The drilling of wells goes on apace. In one county where there were eight wells a year ago, there will be one hundred this summer.

The James River Basin is 400 miles long and 40 to 50 miles wide. Well-boring has been a failure to the eastward of it, but to the westward there are several splendid wells, some even as far away as Hughes County, near the Missouri. The boring is very costly, some wells having cost $5000, and even more. At first a soft shale rock of white sand is pierced, and then there is reached a sticky clay like gumbo. Minnows of brilliant colors and with bright and perfect eyes have been thrown out of these wells, as if to prove that the water comes from surface streams somewhere. The theory is that its course is from the west, and an official of the Department of Agriculture holds that several rivers to the westward lose all or part of their volumes of water at certain places where they meet the outcropping of this same sandstone which is found by boring. The Missouri, for instance, is said to lose two-thirds of its bulk after its flight over the cascades at Great Falls. The Yellowstone diminishes mysteriously in bulk. Three or four streams in the Black Hills run their courses and then disappear in the neighborhood of this outcropping of sandstone. When I was at Great Falls in Montana, I was not able to prove that the Missouri loses the greater part of its bulk below there, but it was said that engineers have investigated the subject, and are to report upon it to the government. I was told, however, that several streams which seem to be heading toward

the Missouri in that neighborhood suddenly disappear in the earth without effecting the junction.

With water thus apparently plenteous; with cattle-raising, flouring-mills, linen manufacture, wool, and diversified farming, all newly started; with the coal of North Dakota brought cheaply down the Missouri, and with better coal in the Black Hills, to be brought eastward when railroads are built across the State—the prospect is that South Dakota will stride onward to a degree of prosperity that her people cannot have expected, and yet richly deserve.

It is said that there is more mineral wealth in the Black Hills than in any other territory of the same scope in the world. Gold is the principal product, but silver, nickel, lead, tin, copper, mica, coal, and many other valuable sorts of deposits are there. The output of gold has been about $3,300,000 a year, and of silver from $100,000 to $500,000. The Black Hills are so called because the pine-trees which cover them look black from the plains. The numerous villages of the region are agricultural settlements or mining towns, and are connected by two trunk lines among the foot-hills and by three narrow-gauge roads in the hills. These smaller railways turn and curve through the valleys amid very beautiful and often grand scenery. It is wonderful to see the enormous machines at the greater mines, and to know that they, and nearly all the principal appointments of the buildings of every sort, were packed across the plains in ox carts; for the first railroad—the Fremont, Elkhorn, and Missouri Valley Railroad, of the Chicago and Northwestern system — reached the hills less than two years ago. It was in February of last year that the Burlington road came there.

The great gold-mining company, the Homestake, is said to have taken fifty millions of dollars' worth of gold out of the hills. The Homestake Company is the name of a group of five or six corporations, all under the same ownership. Messrs. J. B. Haggin, Lloyd Tevis, and the Hearst estate, all of California, are the principal owners. They have the largest gold-reduction works in the world. For labor alone they pay out $125,000 a month. Their mills contain 700 stamps. The last year was the first one of notable activity outside the Homestake plants, and one or two very much smaller ones, because the railroads have only just made it possible to get the ore to the smeltery, or to effect the construction of such works. The ores are all low grade, and will not pay the heavy tolls for wagon transportation. The profits in the free milling Homestake ores have been found in their quantity and the cheapness with which they have been reduced. Five smelteries have been put in within a year, others are projected, and others are being enlarged. It is said that within two or three years no ore will be sent out of the hills, but it will all be reduced there by fifteen or twenty smelteries that will then be operated. It is further predicted that when both reduction works and means of transportation encourage activity in all the districts, the yield of the hills will amount to twenty or twenty-five millions of dollars a year.

The tin in the Black Hills is almost as much a bone of contention there as it is in the columns of the political organs throughout the country. But in the hills all question of the existence of the metal is lifted from out of the controversy, and the only subjects of discussion are the quantity of tin and the reasons why the marketing of it has so long been delayed. There is no doubt that there are surface indications, to say the least, to mark a tin deposit along two great belts. More than 7000 locations have been made, and "development work" (required by law from those who would hold their claims) has been done to the extent of nine miles of drifts, shafts, cuts, and tunnels. The famous Harney Peak Company works as if it had great faith in its future, its work being in the construction of an extensive plant in readiness for the prospective mining. The railroads also, by a rivalry in building spurs to the mines, give signs of perfect faith in the new industry. The local criticism on the situation is best expressed in the pamphlet issued by the merchants of Rapid City: "The reason why tin has not been produced for market is that those who can produce it do not seem disposed to do anything except development work. The men who own ninety per cent. of the valuable claims are poor prospectors, who are unable to erect mills and reduction works. So far, it has been almost impossible to enlist capital in the purchase or development of Black Hills tin mines. With the exception of the Harney Peak and Glendale companies, no money has been invested in the mines of the Black Hills. Why it is that American capitalists refuse to invest in or to investigate the tin mines is a question that yet remains unanswered."

The Black Hills smelteries are closely connected with the coal of the hills, one mine at Newcastle (in Wyoming), being worked to the extent of 1500 tons a day. It is a soft coal, and makes a high-grade coke. It is coked at the mines. A great field of coal, estimated at 4000 acres in extent has been opened at Hay Creek, in the north. It is said to burn with only seven per cent. of ash. It awaits the railroads, whose lines are already surveyed to the fields. The financial and mining capital of the hills is Deadwood, a very picturesque, active, orderly, and modern city of 3500 souls, caught in a gulch, and obliged to climb steep mountain walls for elbow-room. It has a lively rival in Rapid City, in the foot-hills. Lead City is another place of importance, and Hot Springs is a resort of the character implied by its name. Pierre, the capital, on the Missouri River, is very enterprising and modern, and has a fine district of stores, and a still finer one of residences. Huron is a lesser place, and Sioux Falls is the industrial capital, a lively and promising town of more than 12,000 persons.

South Dakota is diversifying her farm industries, and insuring them by utilizing nature's great gift, artesian water. It is said that central South Dakota has the climatic conditions for the successful cultivation of the sugar-beet, for ripening it while it contains the greatest proportion of sugar. One sample grown in this region last year showed nineteen and a half per cent. of sugar. In 100 samples the sugar averaged above fifteen per cent.; in Germany the average is less.

But the best news about both the Dakotas is that the moisture in the soil last New Year's day was said to be such as to warrant firm faith in another splendid year like the last. With that to put the people and their industries upon their feet, and with all the new lines of development and maintenance that are being tried or established, the outlook for both States is very encouraging.

THE NEW GROWTH OF ST LOUIS

POPULATION and wealth are classified by the same standards. In both cases a million is the utmost figure that is popularly comprehended. A million of citizens or of dollars suggests the ripening of success in both fields. It is true that London has five millions of citizens and the Astors have thirty times as many dollars, but London is simply one of the world's capitals and the Astors are but millionaires in the general thought and speech. In America we are growing familiar with big figures, and now it seems logically likely that another town will soon increase our acquaintance with them. It startled the English-speaking world to learn that Chicago had reached the million mark, but to-day we foresee that in a few years—perhaps the next census will record it—St. Louis is to share the honor with her. No other Western city has such a start in the race. It is true, if the signs are to be trusted, that the Twin Cities—Minneapolis and St. Paul—may then have a joint population of a million, but St. Louis is the commercial rival of all three of her great Northern neighbors, and is drawing trade which they were seeking, while the Twins are separate cities. The only millionaire towns, so to speak, will be Chicago and St. Louis.

St. Louis is already the fifth in size among the cities of the land, and would be fourth if Brooklyn were rated what she is in fact—a bedchamber of New York. But it is the new growth of St. Louis, her re-start in life, that is most significant and interesting; it began so recently and is gathering momentum so fast. And we shall see that never was city's growth more firmly rooted or genuine. What is accomplished there is performed without trumpeting or bluster, by natural causes, and with the advantages of conservatism and great wealth. More remarkable yet, and still more admirable, the new growth of the city is superimposed upon an old foundation. It is an age, as this world goes, since this proud city could be called new and crude. The greater St. Louis of the near future will be a fine, dignified, solid city, with a firmly established and polished society, cultivated tastes, and the monuments, ornaments, and atmosphere of an old capital.

I have had occasion once or twice in the course of these articles upon the development of our West to speak of what may be called the "booming organizations" which father the commercial interests of the more ambitious cities, and in some instances of the newer States. These should have had more prominence, and should have been mentioned more frequently. Though they have nothing to do with the governments of the cities, they are, like the governments, the instruments of the united will of the people, working for the general good, and when they and the governments conflict, the will of "the boomers" often rises supreme above the local laws. For instance, it was announced in one city that the excise laws would be ignored, in order that the place might prove more attractive to a convention of politicians while they were the city's guests. There are good reasons for such supremacy of these powerful and active unions. Their leading spirits are always the most energetic and enterprising men in the cities, and their interest in their schemes for the general advantage is more enthusiastic than that which is felt in the government.

The phrase "booming organizations" is applied to these institutions for the benefit of Eastern and transatlantic readers. It is not altogether satisfactory to the persons to whom it is applied, because in parts of the West booming is a word that has come to be coupled with unwarranted and disastrous inflation, as when a new town is made the field of adventure for town-site and corner-lot gamblers. I use the phrase as we do who have succeeded in getting General Horace Porter to "boom" the completion of the Grant monument in Riverside Park. To "boom," then, is to put a plan generally and favorably before the people, to put a scheme in motion with *éclat*, to vaunt the merits of an undertaking. And that is what is done with and for the interests and merits of the Western cities by these organizations, which are there variously known as Boards of Trade, Chambers of Commerce, and Commer-

cial Clubs. They are in essence what
our Chambers of Commerce in Eastern
seaports are, but in some cities they
work apart from the Chambers of Commerce and on separate lines, while in
others they do some of the same work,
and a great deal else that is very different. They are in some cities what an
engine is to a machine-shop or a locomotive is to a railway train. Whoever
visits a city that is well equipped in this
respect feels the pulsations and is conscious of the power and influence of its
Board of Trade, as we note the presence
of the dynamo in a boat that is lighted
by electricity.

These unions consider the needs of
their cities, and set to work to supply
them. They raise the money for a fine
hotel, if one is lacking; and in at least
one city of which I know they turn what
trade they can over to the hotel after it
is built, even going to the extreme of
giving a grand annual banquet there,
and paying a purely fancy price per plate
to the lessee of the house, in order that
he may get a sort of *pourboire* out of it.
They raise the means to build street railroads; they organize companies for the
erection and maintenance of a first-class
theatre in such a city, for the holding of
an annual fair or carnival parade, for the
construction of a great hall, to which
they afterward invite conventions. These
ventures are not all expected to be profitable by any means, particularly in the
smaller cities; but they are "attractions,"
they swell the local pride, they promote
that civicism which is such a truly marvellous factor in the even more marvellous progress of our Western cities. But
these local unions go farther. They obtain the passage of laws exempting certain manufactures from license fees and
taxes on the buildings in which they are
carried on, and then they induce manufacturers to establish their workshops in
those cities, giving them bonuses in the
form of exemption from taxes, in the
form of a gift of land, or even of a gift
of a building designed and constructed
as the recipients desire to have it. To
give one illustration out of ten thousand,
the little town of Rapid City, South Dakota, gave a noble store-house of brick
and stone to a wholesale grocery firm
for coming there to do business. To
give another view of the subject, the editor of an influential newspaper in one

of the ambitious smaller cities of the
West resigned his membership in the local Board of Trade because he said it contained so many wealthy men, and they
so frequently subscribed large sums of
money for public improvements, that he
was uncomfortable at the meetings, and
preferred to do his share of the work outside "until he had made his pile" and
could "chip in with the rest."

These commercial circles send committees to Congress, to the heads of great societies, to the capitalists of the East and
of the Old World, to urge their needs
and merits, for especial ends. They
cause the building of railroads and railroad spurs; they print books, pamphlets,
and "folders," to scatter praise of their
cities wherever English is read. They
stop at nothing which will tend toward
the advancement of their local interests.
They are unions of business men, land-
owners, and capitalists; but, as in all
things, one man is the dominant spirit
and the most fertile in expedients. This
is usually the secretary, who is a salaried
officer. Men with an especial genius for
the work drift into such positions, and
when they prove especially and signally
capable officials, such as those are who are
in St. Paul, Spokane, and St. Louis, other
cities try to secure them.

St. Louis has one of the most progressive and influential bodies in the West in
its Merchants' Exchange. It is by no
means a mere exchange. It does very
much of the work toward the public and
general good of which I have spoken;
indeed, it may be said that the entire
Southwest, and the immense territory
drained by the Mississippi, find in it the
ablest and most active champion of their
needs. It is to the central West and the
Southwest what our Chamber of Commerce is to New York and the commercial interests of the Atlantic coast. But
with the sudden assumption of a new
youthfulness in old St. Louis there has
sprung up an auxiliary, or, at all events,
another organization for the exploitation
and advancement of local interests. It
is called "the Autumnal Festivities Association," and is one of the most remarkable of the mediums through which
Western enterprise works.

The story of its inception and organization, with the incidents I gathered
concerning the firelike rush of the movement among all classes of St. Louis citi-

zens, presents a peculiarly clear reflection of the character of the new life that now dominates that city, as well as of the forcefulness and ambition of the Western people generally.

When St. Louis failed to secure the World's Fair, instead of sinking back discouraged, its leading men concluded that one fault with the city must be that its merits were not as widely or as clearly understood as was necessary. Therefore, in the spring of 1891, a meeting was called at the Exposition Building to discuss the advisability of forming an organization which, for three years at least, should devote itself to celebrating the achievements and adding to the attractions of the city. From the stage the crude plan of the campaign was announced, and suggestions from the audience were asked for. As my informants put it, "the first 'suggestion' was a subscription of $10,000 from a dry-goods firm; the second was a similar gift from a rich tobacconist. Then came two subscriptions of $7500 each, and others of amounts between $5000 and $1000. Mr. John S. Moffitt, a leading merchant, as chairman of the Finance Committee, promised to undertake the raising of one million dollars within three years, and received promises of sums amounting to $100,000 on that first evening. The sense of the meeting was that this large amount should be expended in attracting visitors to the city, and in interesting and caring for them after they came.

A sum of money was set aside as a bonus for any persons who should build a one million dollar fire-proof hotel in the city on a site to be approved by the executive committee. It was resolved to appropriate as much as would be needed to illuminate the city with between 20,000 and 100,000 gas and electric lights on especial evenings during each year's autumnal festivities, and committees were appointed to look after illuminations, transportation, and whatever. It was also arranged that one-third of the full amount raised should be expended under the supervision of a branch of the organization to be called the Bureau of Information, and to be headed by Mr. Goodman King as chairman. Mr. James Cox, who had been the managing editor of one of the daily newspapers, became the secretary of this bureau. It has offices in St. Louis and it arranged to open others in London and other cities in pursuit of a systematic effort to advertise the commercial, social, and sanitary advantages which St. Louis possesses.

Without waiting for the raising of the prescribed amount of money, the association fell to work at once, and the illuminations and festivities of the autumn of 1891 attracted hundreds of thousands of persons to the city, and were characterized as the finest displays of their kind that had up to that time been made in the country. In the mean time the finance committee began its task of raising a million of dollars. It adopted a shrewdly devised plan. Every trade was appealed to with a request that a committee be appointed and a canvass be made within its own field. Within a week 200 such sub-committees were at work. Each vied with the other in an effort to secure the largest sum, and subscriptions, in sums that ranged between three dollars and $5000, poured in. Those who did not subscribe promised to do so at a later time. In answer to about 4000 applications by these committees, it is said that there were only five refusals to join the popular movement.

It had not occurred to the leaders, even in this general sifting of the population, to ask the police for any subscriptions, the feeling being that the money was to be expended for purposes that would greatly increase their work; but, after waiting for months to be asked to join the movement, the police force applied for a thousand subscription cards, appointed their own collectors, and sent the money to the association headquarters in silver dollars carried in sacks. The citizens who were not directly appealed to—the lawyers and doctors and all the rest — sent in their checks, and five months after the organization was effected the finance committee reported the receipt of two-thirds of the total amount that was to have been raised in three years, or $600,000. It is not to be supposed, at this writing, that there will be a failure to raise the remaining $400,000 within the period in which it will be needed.

It will be seen that this association was formed after the city failed to secure the World's Fair, and that its term of duration covers the period of preparation for and the holding of the exposition. It is not antagonistic to the fair, however, but is simply due to the determination of St. Louis not to be lost sight of, and not to hide its light under a bushel, while the country is filled with visitors to Chicago.

It may cause a smile to read that Chairman King and Secretary Cox report, in a circular now before me, what work the Bureau of Information has done "to correct any false impressions which have been created by the *too great modesty* of St. Louisans in the past." But they are right, for, as compared with its rivals, St. Louis possessed that defect, and the frank admission of such a hated fault shows how far removed and reformed from retarding bashfulness that city has since become. The bureau reports that it is causing the publication of half-page advertisements of St. Louis, precisely as if it were a business or a patent-medicine, in sixty-two papers, circulating more than a million copies; that it has obtained reading notices in all those dailies; that "articles on St. Louis as a manufacturing and commercial metropolis and as a carnival city" are sent out every day; that arrangements are making for a weekly mail letter to 500 Southern and Western journals; and that once or twice a week news items are sent to the principal dailies of the whole country. It was found that St. Louis was not fairly treated in the weekly trade reports published generally throughout the country, and this source of complaint has been removed. Invading the camp of the arch-enemy — Chicago — the bureau has caused a handsome "guide to Chicago" to add to its title the words "and St. Louis, the carnival city of America." It is also getting up a rich and notable book, to be called *St. Louis through a Camera*, for circulation among all English-speaking peoples. The local service for the press telegraphic agencies has been greatly improved, "and the efforts of the bureau to increase the number and extent of the notices of St. Louis in the daily papers throughout the United States have continued to prove successful," so that "instead of St. Louis being ignored or referred to in a very casual manner, it is now recognized as fully as any other large city in America."

I have described the operations of this association and its most active bureau at some length because they exhibit the farthest extreme yet reached in the development of the most extraordinary phase of Western enterprise. There we see a city managed by its people as a wide-awake modern merchant looks after his business. It is advertised and "written up" and pushed upon the attention of the world, with all its good features clearly and proudly set forth. There is boasting in the process, but it is always based upon actual merit, for St. Louis is an old and proud city; and there is no begging at all. The methods are distinctly legitimate, and the work accomplished is hard work, paid for by hard cash. It is considered a shrewd investment of energy and capital, and not a speculation. If we in the Eastern cities, who are said to be "fossilized," are not inclined to imitate such a remarkable example of enterprise, we cannot help admiring the concord and the hearty local pride from which it springs.

St. Louis is the one large Western city in which a man from our Eastern cities would feel at once at home. It seems to require no more explanation than Boston would to a New-Yorker, or Baltimore to a Bostonian. It speaks for itself in a familiar language of street scenes, architecture, and the faces and manners of the people. In saying this I make no comparison that is unfavorable to the other Western cities, for it is not unfriendly to say that their most striking characteristic is their newness, or that this is lacking in St. Louis. And yet to-day St. Louis is new-born, and her appearance of age and of similarity to the Eastern cities belies her. She is not in the least what she looks. Ten or a dozen years ago there began the operation of influences which were to rejuvenate her, to fill her old veins with new blood, to give her the momentum of the most vigorous Western enterprise. Six or seven years ago these began to bear fruit, and the new metropolitan spirit commenced to throb in the veins of the old city. The change is not like the awakening of Rip Van Winkle, for the city never slept; it is rather a repetition of the case of that boy god of mythology whose slender form grew sturdy when his brother was born. It was the new life around the old that spurred it to sudden growth.

There is much striving and straining to fix upon a reason for the growth of St. Louis, and in my conversations with a great number of citizens of all sorts between the City Hall and the Merchants'

Exchange, I heard it ascribed to the cheapness of coal, iron, and wood; to river improvement, reconstructed streets, manufactures, and even to politics. All these are parts of the reason, the whole of which carries us back to the late war. In the war-time the streets of St. Louis were green with grass because the tributary country was cut off. After the war, and until ten years ago, the tide of immigration was composed of the hardy races of northern Europe, who were seeking their own old climate in the New World. Chicago was the great gainer among the cities. That tide from northern Europe not only built up Chicago, but it poured into the now well-settled region around it, where are found such cities as St. Paul, Minneapolis, Duluth, Milwaukee, Omaha, and a hundred considerable places of lesser size. It was a consequence of climatic and, to a less extent, of political and social conditions, and it caused St. Louis to stand still. But for the past ten years the tide of immigration has been running into the Southwest, into Missouri, and the country south and southwest of it.

St. Louis is commonly spoken of as the capital of the Mississippi Valley, but her field is larger. It is true that there is no other large city between her and New Orleans — a distance of 800 miles — but there is no other on the way to Kansas City, 283 miles; or to Chicago, 280 miles; or for a long way east or southwest. Her tributary territory is every State and city south of her; east of her, to the distance of 150 miles; north, for a distance of 250 miles; and in the west and southwest as far as the Rocky Mountains.

Between 1880 and 1890 the State of Missouri gained more than half a million of inhabitants; Arkansas gained 326,000; Colorado, 300,000; Kansas, 430,000; Kentucky, 200,000; Nebraska, 600,000; Texas, 640,000; Utah, 64,000; New Mexico, Arizona, and Oklahoma, 114,000. Here, then, was a gain of 3,174,000 in population in St. Louis's tributary country, and this has not only been greatly added to in the last two and a half years, but it leaves out of account the growth in population of the States of Illinois, Iowa, Indiana, Mississippi, and Louisiana. St. Louis had 350,518 souls in 1880; now she calls herself a city of half a million inhabitants. Her most envious critics grant that she has 470,000 souls. In 1891 permits were granted for 4435 new buildings, to cost $13,259,370, only eleven hundred thousand dollars of the sum being for wooden houses.

The city now has 347½ miles of paved streets, and they are no longer the streets of crumbling limestone, which once almost rendered the place an abomination. They now are as fine thoroughfares as any city possesses, 272 miles being of macadam, 41 of granite blocks, and the rest being mainly of wooden blocks, asphaltum, and other modern materials. A system of boulevards, of great extent and beauty, is planned and begun. New waterworks are being constructed beyond the present ones at a cost of four millions of dollars, but with the result that a daily supply of one hundred millions of gallons will be insured. The principal districts of the city are now electrically lighted. A new million dollar hotel is promised.

The old city, with its stereotyped forms of dwellings and stores, is being rapidly rebuilt, and individual tastes, which search the world for types, are dominating the new growth. The new residence quarters, where the city is reaching far from the river in the vicinage of the great parks, are very pretty and open, and are embellished with a great number of splendid mansions. In the heart of the city are many high modern office buildings. They are not towering steeples, as in Chicago, nor are they massed together. They are scattered over the unusually extended business district, and in their company is an uncommon number of very large and substantial warehouses, which would scarcely attract the eye of a New-Yorker, because they form one of the striking resemblances St. Louis, both new and old, bears to the metropolis. The most conspicuous of the office buildings are distinguished for their massive walls and general strength. Beside some of the Chicago and Minneapolis buildings of the same sort they appear dark and crowded, and are rather more like our own office piles, where room is very high-priced. But they are little worlds, like their kind in all the enterprising towns, having fly-away elevators, laundry offices, drug shops, type-writers' headquarters, barber shops, gentlemen's furnishing shops, bootblacks' stands, and so on.

But in praising the new orders of architecture in St. Louis I do not mean to condemn all of the old. The public and

semi-public edifices of its former eras
should be, in my opinion, the pride of her
people. That cultivated taste which led
to the revival of the pure and the classic
in architecture, especially in the capitals
of the Southern States, found full expression in St. Louis, and it commands praise
from whoever sees such examples of it as
the Court-house, the old Cathedral, and
several other notable buildings. What
was ugly in old St. Louis was that cut-
and-dried uniformity in storehouses and
dwellings which once made New York
tiresome and Philadelphia hideous.

But to return to the size and growth of
the city. It reaches along the river-front
19 miles. It extends six and sixty-two
one-hundredth miles inland, and it contains 40,000 acres, or 61.37 square miles.
This immense territory is well served by
a great and thoroughly modern system
of surface street railways, having more
than 214 miles of tracks, and run almost
entirely by electric and cable power.
Some of the newer cars in use on the
electric roads are as large again as our
New York street cars, and almost half
as large as steam railway coaches.
Their rapid movements, their flashing
head-lights at night, and the cling-clang
of the cracked-sounding gongs in the
streets seem to epitomize the rush and
force of Western development. There is
an element of sorcery in both of them—
in modern progress and in the electric
cars. Was it not Dr. Holmes who likened
those cars to witches flying along with
their broomsticks sweeping the air?

If Chicago was not the first, it was at
least a very early railway centre in the
West, and her citizens are right in as-
cribing to that fact much of her prosperity. To-day St. Louis has become remarkable as a centring-place of railways.
The city is like a hub to these spokes of
steel that reach out in a circle, which, unlike that of most other towns of prominence, is nowhere broken by lake, sea, or
mountain chain. Nine very important
railroads and a dozen lesser ones meet
there. The mileage of the roads thus
centring at the city is 25,678, or nearly
11,000 more than in 1880, while the mileage of roads that are tributary to the city
has grown from 35,000 to more than
57,000. These railways span the continent from New York to San Francisco.
They reach from New Orleans to Chicago, and from the Northwestern States to

Florida. Through Pullman cars are now
run from St. Louis to San Francisco, to
the city of Mexico, and to St. Augustine
and Tampa in the season. New lines
that have the city as their objective
point are projected, old lines that have
not gone there are preparing to build
connecting branches, and several of the
largest systems that reach there are just
now greatly increasing their terminal facilities in the city with notable works and
at immense cost. The new railway bridge
across the river is yet a novelty, but it is
to be followed at once by a union depot,
which is promised to be the most commodious passenger station in the world.
It will embrace all the latest and most
admirable concomitants of a first-class
station. It will be substantial and costly, and will follow an architectural design which will render it a public ornament.

But St. Louis is something besides the
focal point of 57,000 miles of railways.
She is the chief port in 18,000 miles of
inland waterways. She is superior to the
nickname she often gets as the mere "capital of the Mississippi Valley," but her
leading men have never been blind to
the value of that mightiest of American
waterways as a medium for the transportation of non-perishable and coarse
freights, and as a guarantor of moderate
freight rates. The Merchants' Exchange
of St. Louis has for twenty years been
pressing the government to expend upon
the improvement of this highway such
sums as will render it navigable at a
profit at all times. The government has
greatly bettered the condition of the river, but it will require a large expenditure
and long-continued work to ensure a fair
depth all along the channel at low water.
What is wanted is a ten-foot channel.
Now it drops to five feet and a half, and
even less where there are obstructions
in the form of shoals and bars. It is argued that the improvement asked for
would so reduce the cost of freighting on
the river as to bring to the residents of
the valleys of the river and its tributaries a gain that would be greater than
the cost of the work. In the language
of a resolution offered in Congress by
Mr. Cruise, of Kansas, "it would reclaim
an area of lands equal to some of the
great States, and so improve the property
of the people and increase their trade relations with other sections of the United

States, and improve the condition of our foreign trade, as to benefit every interest and every part of the whole country."

This year the Exchange and the city government, with the leading industrial bodies of the city, sent a memorial to Congress which they called "a plea in favor of isolating the Mississippi River, and making it the subject of an annual appropriation of $8,000,000 until it shall be permanently improved for safe and useful navigation." They said that the removal of a snag or a rock anywhere between Cairo and New Orleans extends relief to Pittsburg, Little Rock, Nashville, and Kansas City. This is because the stream runs past and through ten States, and (with its tributaries) waters and drains, wholly or in part, more than one-half the States and Territories of the Union.

After proving that 28,000,000 persons inhabit the region directly interested in the improvement of the river, the memorialists proceed to show that the railroads in 1890 carried freight at .941 cents per ton per mile, and that this amounted to $11 29 for 1200 miles, the distance between Boston or New Orleans and St. Louis, whereas the river rate for that distance was $2 20 a ton. They show that whereas it cost 42½ cents to send a bushel of wheat by rail from Chicago to New York in 1868, the rate had decreased in 1891 to .941 of a cent. This saving to the people was not brought about solely by competition among the railroads; the competition of the water lines with the railroads also influenced the reduction. Upon the basis of an estimate that fifty millions of dollars must be spent upon the river, they offer other reasons for believing that the money will be well spent. They assert that before the jetties deepened the mouth of the river, only half a million bushels of wheat were annually exported to Europe from New Orleans. Now eighteen millions of bushels are shipped thus, and the amount is increasing. Had that wheat not gone by that route at the rate of 14⅓ cents a bushel from St. Louis to Liverpool, it must have been sent by rail to New York at 21¼ cents a bushel — a difference of seven cents a bushel in favor of the river route, or a saving of $1,260,000 on the annual shipment of wheat alone. The census figures of 1890 show that the amount of freight carried on the river and its tributaries in 1889 was 31,000,000 tons. It is impossible to here follow the arguments and pleas that are embodied in the memorial, but it is well to know that they are not the outcome of the interests and ambition of St. Louis alone, but of the entire region which makes use of the now erratic, destructive, and uncertain river. What St. Louis asks is what New Orleans wants, and this is what Memphis, Vicksburg, Cairo, and the masses of the people in several large and populous States believe should be granted for their relief and gain.

The bill that was prepared in this interest provides that the river, from the Falls of St. Anthony to the jetties, be permanently improved under the direction of the Secretary of War and the chief engineers of the army; that $8,000,000 be appropriated for said improvement, and that a similar sum be annually expended under the direction of the Secretary of War until the river is permanently improved for safe and useful navigation.

The coal supply, which has had so much to do with the development of the new St. Louis as a manufacturing centre, comes from Illinois, the bulk of it being obtained within from ten to twenty miles of the city. St. Louis is itself built over a coal bed, and the fuel was once mined in Forest Park, though not profitably. The Illinois soft coal is found to be the most economical for making steam. It is sold in the city for from $1 15 to $1 50 a ton. The Merchants' Exchange has it hauled to its furnaces in wagons for $1 56 a ton, but Mr. Morgan, the secretary—to whom I am greatly indebted for many facts respecting the commerce of the city—says that those manufacturers who buy the same coal by the car-load get it cheaper. All southern Illinois, across the Mississippi, is covered with coal. Fifty or sixty miles farther south in that State a higher grade of bituminous coal is found, and marketed in St. Louis for household use. It is cleaner and burns with less waste, but it costs between 25 and 30 per cent. more.

The Exposition and Music Hall Building was the subject of what was perhaps the first great expression of the renewed youth of the city. It is a monument to the St. Louis of to-day. It is said to be the largest structure used for "exposition" purposes in this country since the Centennial World's Fair at Philadelphia.

It is 506 feet long, 332 feet wide, and encloses 280,000 feet of space. The history of its construction is one of those stories of popular co-operation and swift execution of which St. Louis seems likely to offer the world a volume. A fund of three-quarters of a million was raised by popular subscription six or seven years ago, and the building was finished within twelve months of the birth of the project. It is built of brick, stone, and terra-cotta, has a main hall so large that a national political convention took up only one nave in it, contains the largest music hall in the country, with a seating capacity for 4000 persons, and a smaller entertainment hall to accommodate 1500 persons. The famous pageants and illuminations which mark the carnival in that city are coincident with the opening of the exhibitions. Six of these fairs have been held in this building, each continuing forty days, and showing the manufactured products of the whole country, but principally of the Mississippi Valley. The merchants and manufacturers of St. Louis naturally make a very important contribution to the display.

I say "naturally," because this busy capital of the centre of the country and of its main internal water system has an imposing position as one of the greatest workshops and trading-points of the nation. In the making of boots and shoes no Western city outstrips St. Louis, and her jobbing trade in these lines is enormous, and rapidly increasing. Boston, the shoe-distributing centre of the country, sent 310,500 cases of goods to St. Louis in 1891, as against 288,000 to Chicago and 284,000 to New York. The gain in the manufactured product of St. Louis was 17 per cent. last year, and in the jobbing trade it was more than 40 per cent. *The Shoe and Leather Gazette* of that city makes the confident prediction that, "at this rate of progress, in five years St. Louis will lead the world in the number of shoes manufactured and in the aggregate distribution of the same."

She has an enormous flour-milling interest, having sold in 1891 no less than 4,932,465 barrels of flour. Her 14 mills in the city have a capacity of 11,850 barrels a day, and her 16 mills close around the city, and run by St. Louis men and capital, grind 9850 barrels a day. The city turned out 1,748,190 barrels and the suburbs 1,542,416 barrels in 1891. In the neck-and-neck race in flour-milling between St. Louis and Milwaukee, St. Louis has recently suffered through the loss of a large mill by fire. The figures for the two cities are, St. Louis, 1,748,190 barrels; Milwaukee, 1,827,284 barrels. It is seen that our reciprocal treaties with the Central and South American countries and the islands off our coast will open up a large and lucrative trade in flour, as well as in many other commodities. While I was in St. Louis, in the early spring of 1892, a large shipment of flour had been made to Cuba, where the duty on that staple had been reduced from nearly five dollars to one dollar a barrel. The city exported 344,506 barrels to Europe, and sold more than two millions of barrels to supply the Southern States.

Cotton is received in St. Louis from Missouri, Oklahoma, Kansas, Arkansas, Texas, and Indian Territory. It seeks that way to the East, and as much passes on as is stopped in St. Louis. It is used to a slight extent in manufactures there. A wooden-ware company in the city sells fully one-half of all that ware that is marketed in the country, and manufactures, or controls the manufacture, in many places. The largest hardware company in the country which does not make, but carries on a jobbing trade in those goods is a St. Louis institution. The saddlery and harness makers do a business of three millions; the clothing-makers have a trade of six millions; the new and growing trade in the manufacture of electrical supplies reached a value of five millions last year; four millions in wagons and carriages was an item of the city's manufactures; the making of lumber, boxes, sashes, doors, and blinds amounted to five millions; of paints, to three millions, and of printing, publishing, and the periodical press, to eight and a quarter millions. The businesses of the manufacture of iron and iron supplies, brass goods, and drugs and chemicals are all very large.

NEW ERA IN THE MIDWEST

I.

INTO three periods may be divided the business history of the western Mississippi Valley — settlement, extravagance, and depression. Upon a fourth it is now entering, and to the millions who, seeking new homes, have there invested their all, as well as to the Eastern friends whose money they have borrowed, the outcome thereof is of deep interest. Over rich-soiled prairies, six hundred miles north and south, and reaching from the foothills of the Rocky Mountains to the Missouri River, the States of Nebraska and Kansas and the Territory of Oklahoma, because of the energy of the people and their remarkably rapid development, form a widely advertised and much-discussed section. The business thermometer, telling of advances and retrogressions in the new lands, has been closely watched, and those who have had faith during the time of depression are pleased to find the present readings encouraging.

The prairies were settled at high-pressure; life has been at high-pressure ever since. The throngs that rushed into the virgin lands in the early seventies, settling on the first claim that offered, making contracts for payment without thought of possible crop failure, and hoping and believing all things told them by voluble land agents, laid thereby the foundation for disappointment and setbacks. Those who followed during the next decade gave but little more consideration to the climatic conditions and the needs and resources of the soil. The claims along the Colorado border at an elevation of 3500 feet were as eagerly taken as those near the Missouri bottoms at 750, and it was believed that all would prove equally productive. The population of Kansas in 1870 was 364,399; in 1880, 996,096; in 1888, 1,518,552. Nebraska had, in 1870, 122,-923; in 1880, 452,402; in 1890, 1,058,910. This enormous influx, largely of people without means, and in a majority of instances without practical experience in the development of raw lands, was unprecedented. The most extravagant plans were laid, and everything was done on the largest possible scale. Even the State documents of the earlier times boasted of the wonderful riches and teeming population the commonwealths would have in 1890, "if the present rate of increase keeps up." Wheat raising was found to be successful. Fields were sown of such size that the overland trains on the just completed railroads were stopped between stations to enable the passengers to feast their eyes on the wondrous sight. Sheep thrived, and flocks were driven from New Mexico numbering tens of thousands, while wrinkled merinos were imported from New York and Ohio to be placed on farms whose value that of a dozen of the animals would have more than equalled.

From the farms the desire for speedy riches spread to the towns, and in the summer of 1885 began the "boom." Additions were laid out for miles around the county-seats; stakes for lots and alleys, and furrows bounding boulevards and avenues, disturbed the pasturing cattle and awakened the interest of the farmhand. People look back to those days now and wonder if a wave of insanity swept over the West. It seemed plausible then that every town would be a commercial metropolis or a great railway centre—or both; twenty villages in each State coveted the capital, and not a few believed that in time the greatness of the new West would necessitate the abandonment of Washington for a national headquarters on the plains. It was not joking, this wild inflation—never were men more in earnest. The evidence of their sincerity exists to-day in handsome brick and stone blocks unoccupied, in carved marble pillars and staircases ornamenting half-empty school-houses and office buildings, and in uneven road surfaces telling of the sometime presence of street-railway ties.

This it was that burdened the plains with debt. To adorn the farms, to build the blocks and school-houses, to equip the railway lines, the people issued their due-bills in the shape of mortgages, bonds, and corporation stock. It was the capital with which was constructed the fabric of their dreams. By this means the settlers had at their command the coffers and savings of the East, and even much from across the Atlantic. While it was welcome, it was not altogether the fault of the West that it came. Said the manager of a large investment and loan company, which failed some years ago with liabilities of over ten million dollars: "It is a fact that during many months of 1886 and 1887 we were unable to get enough mortgages for the people of the East who wished to invest in that kind of security. My desk was piled every morning with hundreds of letters, each enclosing a draft, and asking me to send a farm mortgage from Kansas or Nebraska." Is it any wonder that men were urged to borrow more than they needed, or that rascally agents were tempted to place a larger loan on a farm than its value warranted?

In the winter of 1887-8 the end came. Every one wanted to sell at once, and none could find a buyer. The story of what followed is an old one. The collapse of the boom was not confined to the West; the South suffered as well. The enormous depreciation of property was followed by a succession of short crops on the plains, and accentuated by political vagaries that attracted attention throughout the civilized world. Yet the story of the past decade is not less interesting than that of the years when frontier life was testing the courage and endurance of the hardy pioneers. It has been a time of struggle with debt, with bad credit, with decreasing values, and lessening population. Thousands of farmers deserted the much - mortgaged claim, loaded the family into a white-covered prairie-schooner, and, in current phrase, "went back to the wife's folks." From the western third of Kansas and Nebraska one hundred thousand people departed. In one season eighteen thousand prairie-schooners passed east over the Missouri River bridge at Omaha— never to return. Loan companies could not collect the interest on the mortgages they had negotiated, and failed. Out of about three hundred that were chartered in Kansas, six stood the test and pulled through. The Middle West was called on to meet its obligations, and could not find the resources therefor. It was practically impossible to sell real estate for money—land had no cash value. There was a trading value and a taxable value —that was all. The Western people did not tell the world how bad it was. The papers cheerfully prevaricated when they

reported large "sales" that were actually trades. Foreclosure notices and bank statements were hidden away on the inner pages of the paper, and failures were, by common consent, not published at all. In the assets of the suspended banks and loan companies were found lots in boom "additions." The receivers sold them under the hammer for from one to three per cent. of their cost, and were glad to get it.

The Eastern investors tried to realize on the securities they had bought, and could not. They foreclosed the farm and city mortgages and took the property. Mortgagee and mortgagor were alike displeased, and demagogues took advantage of the situation to trade on the feeling of antagonism. They said hard and abusive words concerning the "plutocrats," and found a means to ride into political power through the echo of their own bitter rantings. The men and women who had worked for years to make homes had no sympathy with this abuse of the East. "Back East" was for them, and is to-day, the land of halcyon memories. There they played beneath stately elms, studied in old-fashioned school-houses, and loved and married. But the frenzy of depression was contagious, and sentiments were uttered and printed which have since brought blushes to their authors.

In the East the effect was less marked, but not the less definite and positive. The investors felt that they had been defrauded, and resented it by refusing to place more funds beyond the Missouri— except in special instances.

The Middle West was experiencing such conditions when Oklahoma was opened. The two great rushes for homes in that splendid expanse of fertile acres took thousands out of the two States to the north. All who failed in their desires saw here a chance to retrieve their fortunes, and many abandoned their claims in order to begin over again in the new lands. When it is remembered that in the four and eight years that have elapsed since the openings the Territory has come to a population of 275,587, and an assessed valuation, on a basis of one-fourth to one - third the real value, of $35,034,752, the importance of the drain on the adjoining commonwealths can be understood. At the beginning there was not a white man inside the entire expanse of the Territory: now it is an empire in itself, outranking a dozen different States in population. But the people there had the same experiences as to crops and business conditions for several years as the rest of the prairie West, and the stories of want were not unlike the ones that reached the East in the old times of the grasshoppers on the plains.

The West was many years paying the debt incurred by its overweening ambition and its indiscreet speculations. The period of depression, beginning in 1888, covered eight years. In it were learned lessons of saving, of thrift, of endurance. They were lessons that the West needed to learn. Partly because it was very difficult to borrow, few new debts were incurred. Partly because creditors were pressing, old scores were reduced as much as possible. It was a time of severe business methods, of caustic criticisms from friends in the East, of sackcloth and ashes for those who could not meet the hastily assumed obligations.

II.

With 1897 the clouds lifted. It was in many respects a year of surprises to the business world of the plains. Few realize why its record stands out so brightly compared with the half-dozen seasons gone before. There have been published glowing reports of the wheat raised in Kansas, yet in two years in the past decade there have been larger yields. The corn is a boast, yet four years in the decade have done better. The live-stock products are pointed to with pride, yet three years have shown larger cash returns. The aggregate value of all products of farm and ranch has been exceeded twice in ten years. The same is true of Nebraska. Notwithstanding this, it is doubtful if in all the history of the prairies there has been a year when the workers had so much to show for their efforts—both in material values and in enhanced credit—as in the one just past. It was the first step forward that manifested itself prominently. The advance had been going on, but it had not come to the surface.

The crops were above the average, the prices were good, new sowing favorable. But above these things, and working with them, was the fact that the debts, public and private, were no longer nerve-wearing burdens—they had been reduced in

the years of economy to reasonable proportions. Herein lies the key to the new era that is opening for the prairie West; it has resources gained through its own toil, and its obligations occupy the place of servant, not of master.

The returns of the grain-fields were most clearly marked in the western third of the section named. For ten years the people there had been hoping for the good crops that once or twice before had been the cause of lifting their hopes, and making them believe that there was a possibility of making permanent homes through the ordinary methods of agriculture. Many of the original settlers had left, discouraged, but those who remained were rewarded by a wonderful return for their labor. On farms that were worth $500 to $800, wheat was taken that brought at the market $1200 to $2000. The high prices that came in midsummer, added to a generous yield and good quality, made the settlers happy. They had the best profit on their investment of any body of people in the nation, probably, and it made them take cheer again—and put in more wheat. In the middle section the year was an average one, except for the better prices for grain; in the eastern portion it was perhaps scarcely up to the usual standard.

But there was money to pay debts, because the savings of the past years had been sufficient to bring the interest charges down and make the burden light. Here is an example: A farmer came into my office one day last summer wearing ragged, faded clothes, and appearing very shabby. "Look pretty tough, don't I?" he remarked, laughing. "Well, it will be better next time. I am going to buy a new suit of clothes this afternoon. I have not had a new suit for five years—just couldn't afford it. My wife has been saving her egg-money, and I have kept up the taxes and interest. Now we are getting out of the woods, and I am to have a suit and she a dress from the egg-money." He said it without any bitterness or regret, as if it were a perfectly natural situation. He felt that he had done his duty, and the new clothes were doubtless worn with a pride and satisfaction unknown where less sacrifice was needed to procure fresh raiment.

The hens are said to have saved Nebraska. From the stations in the interior of the State were shipped thousands of dozens of eggs every week. The money received for them was about the only clear cash that came into the household, and kept the children fit for school and the wife in presentable clothes. In Kansas the humble cow was more in evidence. Scattered over the plains are the creameries, to which every morning wends a procession of farm-wagons, each containing a dozen or more high tin cans filled with milk from the farms. One county has for six years received from the creameries $250,000 annually in monthly payments. It has been the salvation of the settlers. Others have done nearly as well, and the annual value of the milk products has been from $4,500,000 to $5,000,000. This, added to the help of the hen and the returns of the swine-yard, has been the resource upon which many a family has depended to tide over the lean years. The creameries have also extended into Oklahoma, and, with the trade of Texas and the Gulf ports so close to its gates, the Territory has, relatively, realized more out of the business, perhaps, than its neighbor on the north. Here, too, the wheat was of much value last season. One could stand on the court-house tower at Newkirk in the early days of July and within a radius of six miles count 1960 wheat stacks and 186 stacks of straw. A Nebraska man bought a farm in Garfield County for $600 in March, and sold $900 worth of wheat from it in June. This was perhaps not so striking as the yield in six western Kansas counties, where it was over 235 bushels for every man, woman, and child living therein, but it was enough.

The disposition made of the generous returns of the fields can, of course, be determined only approximately. While court records show some of the business transactions, there is a vast amount that is known only to the people interested. Extended tables of statistics are often misleading, but there are some facts that cannot be controverted, and which are reliable evidence of the extent to which the Middle West has assumed an independent financial position. For instance, the State mortgage report for Nebraska, for the first six months of 1897, showed 6589 mortgages filed and 8004 released. The amount represented by those released exceeded that of those filed by $913,366. The farm mortgages released amounted to $7,210,240. This sort of reduction has

been going on more rapidly since that time, and it has been in course for years, though at a lesser rate. It is estimated by the bank commissioner of Kansas that that State has paid off $30,000,000 of indebtedness in the past year. There has been altogether a reduction of more than two-thirds of the $290,000,000 of mortgage debt with which the State was credited by the government census in 1890. It would be useless to deny that much of the release of mortgage debts has come through the process of foreclosure; especially is this true of the western portion. But probably not more than one-fourth has been so released. The remainder has come through the little savings of the men and women who have toiled faithfully to make homes for their children. The interest charges on the debt owed to foreign capitalists in Kansas and Nebraska is probably not one-tenth of the amount required five years ago. Local capital is taking up the mortgages and bonds, and the people of the West are showing their faith in their own communities by placing their savings there.

A most vital and important problem before the West is the management of the bonded indebtedness assumed in the boom days. Some of this is backed by such wealth that there is no doubt of its future. But in the boom there was little inquiry made as to the reliability of the enterprise for which bonds were sought. Railroads were wanted, and any proposition that would secure them was accepted. Court-houses were built with little regard for the needs of the counties. Out in western Kansas is a court-house costing $20,000. With scarcely a load of wood in the county, there is a handsome fireplace in every office. The total population of the county is but 1800, and the bonds of the county have not yet been reduced. Several court-houses, through the process of mechanics' liens and other legal processes, have come to be owned by individuals, who have been puzzled to know what to do with them. Some of the bonds were issued without the proper formalities, and the counties are taking advantage of this to refuse to pay. Many cases are in the courts, growing out of such issues. It is safe to say that few boom-time bonds that can be defeated will be paid. In many instances, in the newer counties of western Kansas and Nebraska, where there are such contests, the counties are unable to pay even if they wished. The falling off in valuation has been such that it is out of the question for the people who remain to pay the interest, to say nothing of the principal. Here there must be a scaling down, and mutual forbearance on the part of creditors and debtors, to refund the debts on a basis that can be borne. Many towns are in the same condition—mostly small cities that allowed their ambitions to outrun their income. They sought electric lights, water-works, and street improvements that were out of proportion to their ability and size. When the boom additions were turned back into farm-land by the Legislature, and were assessed by the acre instead of by the square foot, they found the tax-levying and tax-paying ability greatly reduced. It became necessary to reduce the municipal expenses, and sometimes even the most rigid economy on the part of the management has been ineffectual in producing a balance between the receipts and disbursements. Here, too, must there be a scaling down and concessions. Several cities have done this already, having frankly informed their creditors that something of the kind must take place or the town site would be vacated. The investors were shrewd enough to see that half a loaf with certain interest payments was better than their former holding.

It is not that the towns are dishonest; the sneer of "repudiation," flung so readily by those who do not understand the situation, is not applicable. It is a condition which the investor does not regret more than the people who have taken up their residence in the towns so situated. It is one that can best be arranged on a friendly basis, not by force. Debtor and creditor are coming together on these matters, and such concessions as have been indicated are taking place. It means much for the debtor—self-respect, hope, encouragement in making improvements, and the feeling that eventually there will be clean pages in the municipality's bond-book.

Another thing the West has learned. For years it has talked of manufacturing the articles that it uses, but so disastrous have been its attempts to start great manufactories off-hand that now there are few business men who favor bonuses or other extraneous aids to the establishment of such enterprises. Many a town is yet owing the heavy bonds issued to

secure a carriage-works or a sugar-mill, that went into bankruptcy a few years after starting—some in a few months. The remoteness from great population centres, the high cost of fuel, and the magnificent distances that are necessary factors of transportation make the task a severe one. The West can manufacture many articles; it has the raw material, and can, by proper development, save freight to the East and back. But it is not trying to achieve all this at a single bound. It is satisfied to have its manufacturing industries developed as are the business investments of the country. In this way they will be on a firm foundation and will stand. The West needs more men at work in mills and shops, but it does not need them if they are to be kept there by issuing bonds.

III.

Two elements that were neglected by the first comers to the plains have been brought to prominence in the past few years, and are now among the most important of the plains region's resources. They are the cattle industry and the raising of such crops as are suitable to the climate. Kaffir corn, the hardy food product that thrives when the drouth is the most severe, did not appear in the reports of the boards of agriculture until about 1892; yet last season nearly ten million dollars' worth was taken from the fields. It is planted in the place formerly occupied by less sturdy crops. Then there are the sorghums, the Jerusalem corn, the millet and maize—they mean the adoption of a system of agriculture that is permanent, that will furnish "roughness" for the stock and make bread for the family, no matter if the rainfall is below the average. It means that there will be no more free seed-wheat or appeals for aid for the West. The cattle industry is of another sort, yet related to this, as it is an adaptation of agricultural pursuits to the climate. Thousands of abandoned claims exist in western Kansas and Nebraska, and thereon graze the herds that have taken the place of the ploughs and harrows. In the western third of the Middle West is the stockman's elysium. There he can turn the herds out on the close-curled "buffalo-grass," and pasture them from Christmas to Christmas. There is no thought of shelter, and but little feed is provided outside the pastures. They are not needed. To be sure, cattle die. After one storm a few years ago fifty thousand hides were shipped from one station; but the percentage of loss is, on the whole, small. The owners of the cattle are the dictators of the land. They commence with their wire fences at the quarter section forming their home ranch, and forget to stop when they reach the corner. On and on they go, until thousands of acres are enclosed. The owner of the land, who has perhaps taken much of it under foreclosure, hears of it. He writes that the land must not remain under fence without rent. "Come and take it out of the pasture," replies the cattle-man, and the incident is closed. One may drive for sixty miles in western Kansas and Nebraska and western Oklahoma and never be out of cattle-pastures. Fence after fence crosses the road. Probably not more than twenty per cent. of the land is owned by the users, but it is all appropriated. This is a pursuit that will be permanent. It will make its followers well-to-do. It is a money-making, certain line of business.

For a time much was said and written about the promise of irrigation. It was believed that it would revolutionize the plains, and make of them gardens. But that day is past. Irrigation without water is a failure, and the plains have not enough water for the ditches that have been already dug. Vast reaches of upland cannot be reached by water except by pumping it out of the ground, and frequently it is nearly as far to water in that direction as it is overland. Windmill and pump can supply the vegetables, and make sure that there will be enough flour in the bin, but it cannot moisten the whole claim. This has been demonstrated. Along the river bottoms there is hope, and many flourishing irrigation plants exist. Numerous other ditch properties, however, are in the hands of receivers, and are losing money. The future usefulness of irrigation seems likely to be confined to small territories favorably situated, rather than to be applied to the plains generally.

The houses need paint; the yards need shrubbery and flowers. The "new" has worn off the buildings erected during the boom, and there has been little renovation. The picture of a plains village has been one heavy with unpainted or faded

houses of simple lines, of square-fronted store structures and offices. Here and there looms up a "block" of stone or brick, which does not pay one-half of one per cent. on the investment it represents. In the hard years property has been neglected, and there has been a feeling on the part of the occupants that somehow they would leave the place soon. They put off the improvements, and consequently the towns present a neglected appearance. This is passing away now. The painters are busy; there is a new roof here and there to tell of progress; the feeling of unrest has been succeeded by one that the West is a pretty good locality after all; that the East has forgotten its children after so long an absence, and that it is as well to prepare to reside in the present abiding-place.

The era of prosperity has done a great deal for the people in contentment. There is less talk of "back East," though it is as dear as ever. Little graves are in the Western cemeteries—those squares of hallowed sod fenced off from the far reaches of level land—and make a new tie for those to whom they are a shrine. The people are holding "old settlers' reunions," proud of their long residence on the plains. This is a good sign. It marks the beginning of a time when the land shall be to them a home, not merely a stopping-place. And then there are more people each year. The low-water mark came about 1896. Then the tide turned, and each census shows a growth over the preceding year. In the past few weeks reports have come of the arrival of special trains bringing immigrants from farther East. Every real-estate agent reports sales far in excess of the past half-dozen years. The farms are selling, and the land all over the plains region is increasing in price. City property is not yet gaining so much as farm-lands, but it is in better condition than in a long time. The additions are being ploughed up and planted to wheat. The surplus houses are moved to the country, and are making pleasant homes for farmers' families. The towns are thus being reduced to a size appropriate to the number of people who inhabit them. The banks have vastly increased their deposits. The latest statement shows that in the banks of Nebraska is deposited $33,914,406, an increase over last year of about $7,000,000. In Kansas is deposited $41,094,712, an increase of

$9,000,000. In both States the reserve in the banks' vaults is over fifty per cent. of the deposits. The fifty-four banks of Oklahoma have on deposit $1,982,385, of which fifty-one per cent. is in cash in the vaults. These figures tell more eloquently than can words the position of the people of the plains in saving their earnings.

Western Kansas and Nebraska have many problems to solve. They comprise the difficulty of handling the semi-arid section where the rainfall is deficient. It has been demonstrated that agriculture will not succeed. Empty sod cabins are plenty; school-houses have no occupants; cattle are stabled in what were once store-buildings; whole town sites are deserted; the people have begun over again. Business is yet a speculation, though it is passing out of that stage. The debts must be adjusted, the bonds arranged so that the payments can be met and the conditions simplified. It will never be a thickly settled country, but there will be prosperity and good returns on the investments made. In central and eastern Nebraska and Kansas the same solidity that exists in the East may be expected, and will be found. The crop failures are an exception; the agriculture is so diversified and the pursuits so varied that no general failure is possible. Big barns, that would do credit to Pennsylvania, are scattered over the well-fenced farms; the farmers ride in carriages, and the farmers' boys and girls have bicycles. It is becoming more Eastern every day, and one may well forget that it is in the West at all. Oklahoma is looking earnestly forward to Statehood, with all the Indian Territory added to its present extent. This will make a great commonwealth, rich in all the natural resources that fertile soil and mineral riches can give. With a climate that will raise corn or cotton, wheat or sugar-cane, it is located near to the rapidly advancing Gulf ports, and has thus an advantage over the country farther north. In a short time the claims will all have been "proved up," and the settlers will own them in fee-simple. Then they will have a start, such as no other body of settlers of the West ever enjoyed—out of debt, and with the improvements secured from the land itself. One county of Oklahoma is the most evenly settled of any territory in the world, probably—one family on every quarter section, and only one. The people are among the most energetic and progressive in the nation, and they have had the experience of other settlements by which to profit. If they cannot make a model commonwealth, it will be strange.

IV.

The period of settlement in the Middle West is gone, never to return. The time of extravagance will not be repeated, for its lessons were burned deep into the hearts of all. It left behind broken hopes, tormenting debts, ruined homes, blighted ambitions. The prophecies upon which it was based can again receive no credence from those who saw the wreckage of the receding financial wave. Without extravagance there is little danger of great depression. Short crops may, and doubtless will, come; prices may fluctuate and localities have their rise and fall; but with plans laid on conservative lines, and the motto "Pay as you go" made the underlying principle of the people's business dealings, widespread or long-continued backslidings will be impossible.

The period on which the West is entering gives promise of being one of permanent prosperity; it is based on those things which are not influenced seriously by climatic vagaries. The hot winds may come, but the Kaffir corn and cane will wave green banners. The rains may be far between, but the milk-cart will continue its journey to the creamery. Hail may fall, but the cattle on the level reaches will not be hurt. Diversified agriculture will provide for failure in a single crop by giving yields of others. Irrigation will lend its aid in opportune places to insure bountiful gardens. In short, the West is settling down to make the most of the resources which it possesses, and has ceased worrying about those it possesses not. In that lies the secret of its future, and so generally is this recognized that the prairies ought to be taken out of the "doubtful list" and placed with those portions of the nation of which certain results can be predicted, and where unvarying advances follow the seasons round. This is the ideal of the West; for this it is working, and over the threshold of such an experience its people believe it has passed.

DECORATIVE POTTERY OF CINCINNATI

VARIETY OF PLAQUES. —[SEE PAGE 840.]

DECORATIVE POTTERY OF CINCINNATI.

THE first occasion on which the decorated ware of Cincinnati was shown in a quantity to be specially remembered was in May, 1875, at the "International Entertainment" given by the "Women's Centennial Executive Committee of Cincinnati," in the old Elm Street Exposition Building, on the site of which the College of Music now stands. In the general aim of this committee to make a creditable addition to the work of women at the Centennial Exposition, the specialty of china-painting, then exciting some interest among the women here and in other parts of the country, was looked upon as promising a possible field of lucrative work for women. The exhibit, prepared by a few ladies of Cincinnati for this occasion, consisted of several dozen pieces—cups and saucers, pitchers and plates. The excellence of its execution excited attention, and many of the articles, together with subsequent work, were sent to the Centennial Exposition the next year.

The newspapers of that day (May 23, 1875) gave the following as the list of ladies who prepared this first exhibit of china-painting: Mrs. S. S. Fisher, Miss Clara Fletcher, Mrs. L. B. Harrison, Mrs. William Hinkle, Mrs. E. G. Leonard, Miss M. L. McLaughlin, Miss Lincoln, Mrs. A. B. Merriam, Mrs. Richard Mitchell, Miss Clara Newton, Mrs. Maria L. Nichols, Miss Rauchfuss, and Miss Schooley.

These ladies were invited to prepare the work by the Centennial Committee, who provided the china and the firing; the decorators gave their work. The articles were sold at auction during the entertainment, bringing good prices, the highest being twenty-five dollars for a cup and saucer; thirty-five cups and saucers were sold, aggregating three hundred and eighty-five dollars.

The origin of the movement can not be more precisely told, perhaps, than by saying that in the summer of 1874 Mr. Benn Pitman, of the Cincinnati School of Design, started a class of ladies (who had had some practice in water-color painting) in china-painting. The specialty of china-painting was not included in the curriculum of the School of Design, and could not, under the rules, be taught there. Mr. Pitman procured the necessary materials, invited the ladies to meet at his office for instruction, and engaged the late Miss Eggers as teacher. The ladies forming the class were Mesdames William Dodd, George Dominick, and E. G. Leonard, and Misses Charlotte Keenan, Florence Leonard, M. Louise McLaughlin, Clara Newton, and Georgie Woollard. At that time Miss Eggers and Mr. Hartwig were the only persons to be found in the city who practiced and taught china-painting. Although some of the class generously insisted on sharing the expense of this experiment, Mr. Pitman declined their assistance, and bore it entirely himself.

The work shown on the occasion referred to in 1875 was for the most part the outgrowth of this experiment, and although imperfect, when compared with later results, it was unquestionably the most extensive and satisfactory exhibit of amateur overglaze decoration made up to that time in the United States. The work was deeply interesting as so many careful experiments. Each one made her own trials, and gained knowledge and courage from her failures. Modes of firing were as imperfect as all other means and appliances; but the interested workers were undismayed by difficulties and mistakes, and eagerly pressed on to higher degrees of excellence.

Prominent among the ladies whose work gave character to this early exhibit in 1875 were Mrs. E. G. Leonard and Mrs. Andrew B. Merriam, whose interest has continued unabated, and whose delicate and finished overglaze work has caused their names to be well known among the best amateur artists of the country.

Among the efficient means of popularizing china decoration in Cincinnati at an early day were the establishment of a small oven, and the teaching of overglazed painting, by Mr. Edwin Griffith, in the spring of 1877. He visited the New Jersey potteries, learned something of the processes of using the oxides and of firing, and being skillful in the use of the brush, and pleasant in his ways, he became a successful teacher. The classes of Mr. Griffith were taught, and the process of firing was carried on, in the third story of the old building on the southwest corner of Fifth and Race streets, above the carving school of Messrs. Henry L. and William Fry. The house has since been removed. Mr. Pitman was instrumental in starting Mr. Griffith in this work.

From 1874 to 1877, the attention of the ladies was exclusively given to overglaze painting.

In 1877, Miss M. Louise McLaughlin, who had been among the foremost in her success in china-painting in 1875, published a hand-book on china-painting, for the use of amateurs in the decoration of hard porcelain, and also began to experiment in her search for the secrets of the Limoges faience.

The first results in this direction shown in Cincinnati were in the fall of 1877.

In the next year specimens of this work were sent to the Paris Exposition. At about the same time, or soon after, Miss McLaughlin painted the first successful piece of blue underglaze on white ware.

It is said that unsuccessful efforts have been made in different parts of Europe to imitate or reproduce the faience of Limoges. However this may be, there is no doubt that in the United States we are indebted to the intelligent interest and persistence of Miss McLaughlin for its accomplishment. Months of labor and considerable money were spent before success was achieved: the preparation of clays, the adaptation of colors, suitable firing for underglaze decoration, were all matters of vital importance in the accomplishment of the new decorative process. Down to this time there were no facilities for firing decorated wares beyond the very imperfect means used for firing the overglaze work of jars, and the ordinary kilns of the potters.

During the process of her experiments in 1877–78, the work of Miss McLaughlin was done at the pottery of P. L. Coultry and Co., where special pride was felt in the matter by members of the firm and employés, and where everything in their power was done to insure success.

In giving credit where credit is due, it may be added that Mr. Joseph Bailey, Sen., and his son Joseph, of Mr. Dallas's pottery, gave her many practical suggestions, derived from their long experience in the business. It required the union of the knowledge of the artist, the chemist, and the potter to conduct the experiments to a successful termination.

The glaze used was that of Messrs. Coultry and Co., and was found to be admirably adapted to the decorative process which Miss McLaughlin had discovered.

The clays, of which she used a variety, were brought from different parts of Ohio; the vases, jugs, etc., many of them her own designs, were at that time made by the firm of Coultry and Co.

In the latter part of 1879, two kilns for firing decorated wares were built at the pottery of Frederick Dallas, one for underglaze, the other for overglaze work, the latter said to be the largest of its kind in the United States. The cost of these kilns was advanced by two ladies, respectively Miss McLaughlin and Mrs. Maria Longworth Nichols. During the year 1879, the work of Miss McLaughlin was transferred to the Hamilton Road pottery of Frederick Dallas.

In her specialty, which may be called Cincinnati faience, Miss McLaughlin has been constantly at work, month by month increasing her knowledge of methods, etc., until the results show a high degree of excellence and beauty. Many of her pieces have found homes in New York and other

FIG. 1.—VASE DECORATED BY MRS. WILLIAM DODD.

cities, but some of her largest and most successful specimens have not been seen outside of Cincinnati. Her "Ali Baba" vase, forty-two inches high, was produced in the winter of 1879–80, and has been presented by Miss McLaughlin, with other pieces, to the Women's Art Museum Association of Cincinnati. In the rooms of the association, with other ceramic work, it forms the nucleus of a collection probably destined to have historic interest in future years. This "Ali Baba" vase, or jar, has a groundwork of sage green, blending the gradations of color from the full tone up to a fleecy, cloud-like greenish-white; the decoration is a Chinese hibiscus, the colors being held in subdued tones. The potting of this piece, said to be the largest made down to that time in the United States, is the work of Frederick Dallas.

The success of the Cincinnati faience by Miss McLaughlin led to numerous experiments by others toward the same end. A number of them were successful in the discovery of the principles involved in the

new process, and all were distinguished by individual characteristics of style. Notable among the discoverers and workers in this specialty are Mrs. William Dodd, Mrs. M. V. Keenan, Mrs. Dr. Meredith, and Mr. J. T. Wheatley.

In the spring of 1879, a "pottery club" of ladies was organized, with twelve active and three honorary members. Each one of the ladies is at work upon some specialty, or at least bringing to her work so marked an individuality as to characterize it with distinctive features. All have painted, and still paint, overglaze; each works in incised design, in relief decoration, and in underglaze color.

The Pottery Club has rented a room at the pottery of Frederick Dallas, where it is convenient to work in the various specialties in the "green" clay and "biscuit" ware. Their room is perhaps fifteen by twenty-four feet, having windows on the east, south, and west, in front of which, running round the three sides, is a shelf, or work-table, some two feet wide. A few plain chairs, modelling stools, a stove, and wash-stand comprise the fittings and furniture of the room. The building in which this pottery studio is found was the home of Mrs. Trollope during the time of her residence in Cincinnati. The access to the studio, which is on the second floor, is through the yard of the pottery, in which stand some of the kilns.

The members of the Pottery Club are as follows: Miss M. Louise McLaughlin, president, Miss Clara C. Newton, secretary, Miss Alice B. Holabird, treasurer, Mrs. E. G. Leonard, Mrs. Charles Kebler, Mrs. George Dominick, Mrs. Walter Field, Miss Florence Carlisle, Miss Agnes Pitman, Miss Fannie M. Banks, Mrs. Andrew B. Merriam, one vacancy; honorary members, Mrs. M. V. Keenan, Miss Laura Fry, Miss Elizabeth Nourse.

While it would be difficult to describe in this article the character and quality of the work of each member of the Pottery Club, any sketch of the decorative pottery-work of Cincinnati would be incomplete and unjust which failed of a due recognition of its excellence. Calling the roll of its membership brings into review much of the best of the enamelled faience, of the underglaze color, of the incised design, of the relief-work in clay, and of the exquisitely finished overglaze painting, which have given reputation to the work done in Cincinnati.

To a smaller room, perhaps ten by twelve feet in size, also in the second story of one of the buildings of the pottery, two ladies, not of the Pottery Club, daily take their way through the dusty floors, piled high with partially dried "biscuit" and glazed wares. For them the hours of daylight are too few and short. From this dim and unattractive little nook comes a succession of creations unique in character and beauty. The vase of "green" clay, brought up from the hands of the thrower below, is submitted to the artistic fingers of Mrs. William Dodd and

FIG. 2.—VASES DECORATED BY MRS. MARIA L. NICHOLS.

Mrs. Maria L. Nichols, who practice every style of work on "green" and "biscuit" ware, from incised design as delicate as the spider's web, to Cincinnati faience, and relief-work in clay so bold that one is tempted to reach forth her hand and take the bird from the bough.

A piece of Mrs. Dodd's (Fig. 1) is a vase thirty inches high, buff body (Rockingham and white pastes), with bough of apple blossoms in high relief and natural colors, in which is a nest of eggs, and perched on the bough two brown birds of life size. To this extent the color is underglaze. Subsequently Mrs. Dodd added an overglaze decoration, by which the surface is flecked with clouds of gold here and there, and the neck of the vase enriched with a twining wreath of apple blossoms, and the base with a fringe of grasses and marsh plants.

The work of Mrs. Nichols is shown in vases of all sizes, and in wonderful variety of style, for her talents enable her to throw off work with uncommon rapidity. Among her pieces, during the last year, has been a succession of vases, each some thirty inches high. The body is of Rockingham in some cases, in others a mixture of Rockingham and white pastes, giving a soft buff color in some pieces, in others a rich cream. A majority of the large pieces of Mrs. Nichols are Japanese grotesque in design, with the inevitable dragon coiled about the neck of the vase, or at its base, varied with gods, wise men, the sacred mount-

ain, storks, owls, monsters of the air and water, bamboo, etc., decorated in high relief, underglaze color, incised design, and an overglaze enrichment of gold. (See Fig. 2.) The large vases are thirty-two and thirty inches high.

Other pieces of Mrs. Nichols are in the fine-grained red clays of Ohio, decorated in incised and relief work, and an illumination of dead gold; surface finished with semi-glaze; also in a mixture of blue and yellow clays, producing charming tints of sage green, blue-gray, etc.

It is an interesting commentary upon the occupations of our women that the dusty quarters of the manufacture of iron-stone and Rockingham should be the point of attraction for so many of the refined and cultivated women of the city.

So much interest has been felt by the public in the practical work of the Pottery Club, that to avoid inconvenient interruption they decided to give an occasional reception, to which visitors would be admitted by cards of invitation. The first of the series was held in May, 1880. On this occasion not less than two hundred pieces were shown, which, from their variety of style and excellence of execution, formed a most interesting exhibit.

Early in 1878 the first effort in underglaze color in the Lambeth style, or, as it should be called, the "Bennett"* style, was made by Miss McLaughlin.

---

* Mr. Bennett's attitude toward Mr. Doulton is so respectful and deferential, and in regard to what he

FIG. 3.—WORK OF MRS. DOMINICK.

In 1879 the attention of a number of ladies was given to underglaze color work: during the year experiments in this direction became general. Success in using blue was not found difficult, and unremitting efforts have finally triumphed in the satisfactory use of a variety of colors.

FIG. 4.—WORK OF MISS HOLABIRD.

The work of Mrs. Dominick (Fig. 3), Miss Holabird (Fig. 4), Mrs. W. P. Hulbert (Fig. 5), Mrs. Kebler, and Miss Newton, in underglaze color, in the style of John Bennett, is full of interest and promise.

The relief-work in clays by Mrs. C. A. Plimpton is distinguished by features so marked as to make it unique and original among the various styles of work being done in Cincinnati. The decoration is generally on a body of Rockingham (Figs. 6 and 7), or one of the fine red clays of Ohio, on which the design is painted, so to speak, in varying relief, with clays of different colors and shades. A landscape, for example, upon a dark red or brown body, is artistically and delicately wrought, as if with the engraver's burin, in brown clays of different shades, with yellow and white pastes for high lights. Or on a close-grained, soft-toned red body of Scioto clay (Fig. 8), a branch of grape-vine in high relief encircles the rim of the vase, while delicate sprays spring from the base, the entire decoration being in clays of different colors. The largest diameter of this piece is sixteen inches. Her surface work is substantially that of pâte-sur-pâte, so beautifully shown by Solon, and it demonstrates in a most interesting manner

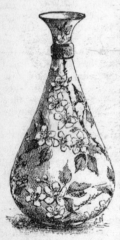

FIG. 5.—WORK OF MRS. W. P. HULBERT.

FIG. 6.—WORK OF MRS. C. A. PLIMITON.

has himself done is so modest, that his own statement in answer to an inquiry on this point is not without interest. It is as follows: "Your impression respecting Doulton Lambeth faience is right. I introduced it, and taught all the pupils, glazed and burned; but in justice to Mr. H. Doulton, the principal, I must say it is very doubtful whether I would have brought it to the success it attained had I not been engaged by him: his natural good taste and desire to improve in art pottery always had a stimulating effect upon me. You will gather from the above that I think the Lambeth faience ought to be called 'Doulton'; at the same time, I have felt slighted by no mention being made of my name in Mr. Sparkes's paper on Lambeth pottery."

At the time of Mr. Bennett's employment by Messrs. Doulton, the only artistic work done by them was in the gray stone-ware which they were producing in their establishment: they had no studios for *painting*, either over or under glaze, till Mr. Bennett went there.

the decorative uses to which our common clays may be put. No work yet done here has so much originality, and promises so much in the use of our common clays, as this work of Mrs. Plimpton.

Mrs. Leonard's work has been chiefly overglaze (Fig. 9), but her work in underglaze color has all the delicacy and artistic skill which characterize her china-painting. Fig. 10 shows a vase of stone-china, covered with blue slip, and decorated with Parian paste, in low relief, by Mrs. Leonard.

The use of Parian paste for light relief-work, or for modelling in high relief, has received special attention from a number of ladies. Misses Elizabeth and Adelaide Nourse have produced some effective work in pottery in bold relief. Fig. 11 shows a piece of carving in yellow clay, unglazed, by Miss Adelaide Nourse; Fig. 12, a vase of cream-colored clay, carved by Miss Fannie M. Banks.

An interesting specialty is seen in the work of Miss Agnes Pitman, a part of the design being incised on a common clay body, which is then covered with a colored slip; finally other designs in low relief are laid on in Parian paste, modelled, and wrought with delicacy and skill. Miss Pitman also shows work in incised and low-relief decoration covered with dark glazes. A vase by Miss Pitman (Fig. 13) is of yellow clay, with incised designs and low-relief work in brown and white clay, semi-glaze finish.

The point of interest in the work of these Cincinnati women (leaving out of the question the excellence of its execution) is in the decorative uses which have been made of the common clays, and the

FIG. 8.—WORK OF MRS. C. A. PLIMPTON.

variety and originality of the styles in which they are working. The various kinds of work mentioned in this article, except the few pieces of overglaze-work on European porcelain, are all done in Ohio clays from Cincinnati potteries, and, with few exceptions, are from the pottery of Mr. Frederick Dallas.

A piece by Mrs. William Dodd (Fig. 14), body of sage green (a combination of blue and yellow clays), shows a landscape in low relief, in red, brown, and white clays, with a garniture of woodbine in white clay; semi-glaze finish.

Fig. 15.—Stone-china tea-pot: blue glaze; decoration in gold and white enamel, low relief, by Mrs. Walter Field.

Fig. 16.—Cincinnati

FIG. 9.—WORK OF MRS. E. G. LEONARD.

FIG. 10.—WORK OF MRS. E. G. LEONARD.

FIG. 11.—WORK OF MISS A. NOURSE.

faience vase: soft green ground, with tiger-lilies, by Miss Laura Fry.

Mrs. Merriam's work is shown in group Fig. 17. The central piece is overglaze; a gold and silver decoration on a rich dark green glaze; stone-china body. The end pieces are underglaze on cream-colored body.

Group Fig. 18 shows the work of Miss McLaughlin. The vase decorated with branches in relief is of dark brown clay; branches in red-brown clay. The four other pieces are in the enamelled faience.

The illustration at the head of this paper shows a variety of work in plaques:

FIG. 12.—WORK OF MISS F. M. BANKS.

the central piece at top, by Mrs. Frank R. Ellis, is blue glaze on white body, decorated in gold and white enamel; the plaque to the right, by Mrs. M. V. Keenan,

is of Cincinnati faience; that to the left, by Miss Sarah Schooley, is in low relief, overglaze decoration, on soft buff clay body; below, an arabesque design in blue, underglaze, on white ware, with overglaze lines in gold, by Miss Clara Newton.

Fig. 19. — Mirror frame: designs in brown, on tiles, by Mrs. Charles Kebler.

The experiments of Mr. J. T. Wheatley in Cincinnati faience were begun in 1878. For a time his work was done at the pottery of P. L. Coultry and Co., but in the spring of 1880 he established himself in quarters of his own on Hunt Street, where he built a kiln for firing decorated wares (underglaze), and where all the processes of the preparation of clays, of moulding, glazing, and firing, are performed by him. It is understood that Mr. Wheatley has been unselfish in regard to his discoveries of modes and processes, freely communicating them to any who wish to learn, and

who are welcomed to work at his establishment. Mr. Wheatley is busily engaged in experiments with colored glazes, and in the preparation of new shapes and moulds, some of which rank with the largest yet made here.

During the spring of 1880, a class was taught in the practice of Cincinnati faience by Messrs. Retig and Valentine. These young gentlemen were pupils of the School of Design for a number of years. Mr. Retig had established some reputation as a designer of frescoes, and for artistic talent generally; in his quickness and accuracy of hand and appreciation of color Mr. Pitman saw the kind of skill to make a successful decorator of pottery, and at his suggestion

FIG. 14.—WORK OF MRS. W. DODD.

FIG. 13.—WORK OF MISS PITMAN.

Mr. Retig prepared himself for this work. Here again we recognize the unfailing interest of Mr. Pitman. His encouragement and aid in all practical ways have been intelligently bestowed, as many can testify who have felt the benefit of his knowledge and liberality of spirit. In reference to the growth of interest and advance in decorative pottery, as well as some other branches of industrial work, it can be said that no one in Cincinnati has done more toward making an industry into an industrial art than Mr. Pitman.

The class of Messrs. Retig and Valentine numbered sixty at the close of the spring term, and showed some encouraging work. The pieces decorated by Mr. Retig are said to be among those which have brought the highest prices in New York.

No porcelain clay has been found in Ohio, and we have the authority of Professor Orton, State Geologist, for saying that we are not likely to find it. Professor Orton says: "We have in Ohio the main elements of a successful manufacture of porcelain and pottery, the fine varieties of porcelain clay being excepted. The two main elements are coarse clay and fuel. It is always counted an object to locate the manufactories near these supplies. The finer material can be brought a long way, if need be, for the amount required is very small in proportion to the pottery clay used in baking the porcelain, and the fuel."

FIG. 15.—WORK OF MRS. WALTER FIELD.

FIG. 16.—WORK OF MISS LAURA FRY.

But if not within the State, we have at our very

door an abundant supply of fine china clay.

Of this Indiana clay Professor E. T. Cox, State Geologist of Indiana, says: "The Indiana porcelain clay is the very best quality known to the world for the manufacture of fine porcelain. It is not, properly speaking, a kaolin, since the latter is derived from the decomposition of feldspathic rocks, and the former is a precipitate from a water solution. It is a new mineral, and I have named it 'Indianaite,' from Indiana, and *ite*, a stone (Indiana stone). It is found in the greatest abundance three and a half miles north of Huron, Lawrence County, Indiana." In addition to this "Indiana stone," a fine china clay is now brought here over the Southern Railroad from near Chattanooga.

Professor Cox was appointed one of the judges on fictile products at the Centennial Exposition, where he had rare opportunities of comparing the raw material, as well as the manufactured products, of the United States with those exhibited by foreign countries.

In regard to the "Indianaite," he says: "I saw no porcelain clays at the Centennial from other portions of the world which were equal to it in color or purity. This fact must speak for the future success of porcelain manufacture in the West. . . . European potters were much astonished at the excellence of American wares. Only a few pieces of porcelain were exhibited by our potters, but this was enough to show our ability to produce fine grades of ware. The body and glaze of our iron-stone and granite ware was in every way equal, if not superior, to that made in England and France."

Professor Cox also says, February, 1878: "I have just received a sample of pure white silica, in powder, from Perry County, Missouri. It is found there in extensive beds, and may be had at much less cost than the white quartz of the New England States, which is found in lumps, and has to be burned and crushed. The Missouri silica will save all of this labor, and is naturally prepared for use."

It is obvious from these statements that Ohio is favorably situated for the manufacture of fine porcelain, and the economic value of her common clays is a compensation for the absence of a porcelain clay within her borders.

So great an advance has been made in the use of underglaze color within a few years in Europe, and especially in England, that soft pottery for certain decorative and domestic uses has become popular, and the distance between it and its more pretentious sister, porcelain, has been lessened. Its perfection of glaze, and the consequent pleasure of handling, and the richness, depth, and blended quality of its coloring, appeal so pleasantly to the senses as to give it a certain superiority above overglaze work, especially where it is to be handled. The Ohio clays are all that could be desired for this wide and interesting field of work, and their uses are being shown by the potteries of Cincinnati. Experiments with the clays long used, and with those less known, from various parts of the State, with the introduction of new colored glazes which are especially needed for delicate incised and relief work, the making of new and improved shapes for table-ware and decorative pieces, show an impulse at the same time interesting and encouraging. Doubtless pure porcelain will be made in Ohio; but she can well afford, if she chooses, to rest her chances of reputation as a centre for the production of pottery upon her own varied and beautiful clays.

The pleasing tints of buff and cream pastes, with the soft, charming blue slip made by Frederick Dallas, seem as great an improvement among us over the glaring iron-stone, as was the invention, one hundred and twenty-five years ago, by Josiah Wedgwood, of his cream-color (C.C.) body. May we not draw a parallel between our own country at this time and the condition of England, in respect of her pottery, when Wedgwood lifted the industry from the low state in which he found it? It is true that the English had begun to make porcelain at that time, but ordinary table-ware was so rude and imperfect that the C.C. body of Wedgwood was considered an important advance.

The interest in this part of the country is not confined to Cincinnati, but to some extent pervades the towns and cities of Ohio generally. Ladies from Dayton, Hillsborough, and more distant points come here for lessons, send to the potteries for clay and "biscuit" ware, and return their decorated work for firing and glazing. Decorated work is sent here to be fired from New York, Iowa, Kentucky, Michigan, Minnesota, and Indiana. The number of amateurs in the city alone whose work is fired at the pottery of F. Dallas

FIG. 17.—WORK OF MRS. MERRIAM.

is more than two hundred, and of this large number all but two are women.

It is curious to see the wide range of age and conditions of life embraced in the ranks of the decorators of pottery: young girls twelve to fifteen years of age find a few hours a week from their school engagements to devote to over or under glaze work, or the modelling of clay; and from this up, through all the less certain ages, till the grandmother stands confessed in cap and spectacles, no time of life is exempt from the fascinating contagion. Women who need to add to their income, and the representatives of the largest fortunes, are among the most industrious workers; and it is pleasant to know that numbers of these self-taught women receive a handsome sum annually from orders for work, from sales, and from lessons to pupils.

As a purely social and domestic entertainment, much is to be said in its favor as an educating and refining influence. Taking the broader view, we are led to the conclusion, from the signs everywhere pervading the country, that the times are ripe for the introduction of a new industry in the United States, in which the feeble instrumentality of women's hands is quietly doing the initial work.

Any appreciative or correct estimate of the work done by the women of Cincin-nati must be based on the fact that, like amateurs elsewhere in this country, they have had no instruction in the art of decorating pottery, for the reason that there was no practical teaching to be had. With the single exception of Mr. Lycett, who taught a few months here, we have had no help from any practically and artistically educated decorator. The realm of underglaze painting was an unknown land, the use of color on the "biscuit" an experiment, and success only to be achieved after repeated failures.

An effort was made in the fall of 1878 to secure the instruction of John Bennett, of New York, for a class in Cincinnati in underglaze painting; but Mr. Bennett replied that he had been at considerable expense to bring his family from Lambeth and to establish himself in New York, and that for the present the secrets of his processes must be confined to his own studio. He was willing to instruct in his fine, broad, free-hand style, overglaze, but not in underglaze work.

Looking back through six or seven years to the beginning, as it may be called, of the movement in china-painting, or the decoration of pottery, in the United States, we can not fail to be struck with its significance, taken in connection with the steady growth in the pottery trade, and the improvement in American wares.

FIG. 18.—WORK OF MISS McLAUGHLIN.

The little exhibit in 1875 was a suggestion of suitable work for women, and also of a future of commercial importance for Cincinnati as a centre of activity in pottery-work. Certainly the results have far exceeded the most rose-colored expectations of those days, in the growth of the interest, and in the quantity and quality of the work done. As might be expected, in the amount of work done by so many untrained hands, much of it is crude and inartistic; but a collection such as may at any time be brought together of the decorated work of Cincinnati, in the various specialties which have been enumerated, would excite attention and interest, in proportion to the intelligence of those who saw it, wherever it might be shown. It is not too much to say that in the history of the potter's art in Europe, so far as we have accounts of it, there has at no time been a beginning more full of promise than that which this sketch has attempted to describe.

The impossibility of procuring skilled teachers has developed the best efforts of the amateur decorators, and may in the end prove a fortunate circumstance; it certainly will, should it result in the development of a distinctive type, which may in time become a national style. It is too early to predict what the American style will be, but it is encouraging that the tendency is to broad and pronounced effects rather than to pettiness of detail.

The aim of this sketch has been to present a historical outline of the beginning and progress of the decorative pottery work of Cincinnati from 1874 down to the time of this writing, mentioning some of the different varieties which have succeeded each other in the short space of a few years. The attempt to convey a distinct impression by verbal description must be to a great extent unsatisfactory, since so much of the advance has been made in the successful use of color, and so much of the effect is dependent on it.

To name personally the numbers of women who have done good and promising work is beyond the possibilities of such an article, and the mention of names is limited to those whose work has rather led the way in distinctive directions.

Begun by a few thoughtful women of taste and social influence, who foresaw possible results of importance to their city, as well as pleasant occupation to women of leisure, and a solution, to some extent, of the problem of self-support and independence for women, the work has gone on, one successful experiment after another marking its advance.

If, in the earlier part of the movement, clays from distant parts of the State were wanted, a woman sent for them; if kilns for firing decorated wares were needed, the money was provided by women. A young woman, after patient experimenting, and the bestowal of time and money, discovered the process of making Limoges faience; an amateur, self-trained, she has published a little volume of instructions to amateurs on overglaze painting, now in its ninth edition; and a similar handbook from the same pen, "*Pottery Decoration Under the Glaze*, by Miss M. Louise McLaughlin," has recently been issued from the press of Robert Clarke and Co.

A woman's taste and interest were influential in the manufacture of the Capo-di-Monti porcelain of Naples, and for the faience of Oiron the world is indebted to a woman, these two specialties combining more of originality and beauty than anything Europe has produced in porcelain and faience.

In Cincinnati, the crowning result of the six years' work by women, and the earnest of the future, is also inspired and executed by a woman. During last autumn a new pottery for decorative work went into operation in the suburbs of the city. In addition to toilet sets, pitchers, etc., to which attention will be given, it is the intention to manufacture gray stone-ware, which is not now made in Cincinnati, and to put upon the market a class of articles for which there is a practical and constant demand, of shapes so help of the potters of the city, who have aided and fostered the interest by all the means at their command, and without whose practical sympathy and co-operation no such advance could have been made.

At the close of this sketch, it is interesting to turn for a moment to the advantages which the coming Art Museum (made possible by the generous gift of

FIG. 19.—MIRROR FRAME DESIGNED BY
MRS. CHARLES KEBLER.

good that the simplest article of household use shall combine the elements of beauty.

These are pleasant times and places, when women give their leisure and means to the founding of an artistic industry. Mrs. Maria Longworth Nichols, by this use of time and money, practically opens a path in which unlimited work for women may eventually be found.

This sketch of women's work would be incomplete without mention of the hearty Mr. Charles W. West and the liberality of many citizens) holds in store for these women who have already accomplished so much. They have long nourished hopes of help from its educational treasures and its training schools, and have gone on courageously, supported by their own constancy and faith, until public opinion sees in the not distant future an artistic industry added to the attractions and prosperity of the city, and respectfully gives the credit where it is due.

ST LOUIS

SOME years ago the journals of the country were laughing at a person whom they called "The Capital-Mover." This was one T. U. Reavis. Caricatures were made of Reavis in which he was represented as carrying the Capitol at Washington on his back, with various others of the public buildings under his arms, and striking out boldly for St. Louis. He had discovered that that place was the geographical centre of the country, and the future centre of its population, and that it was to be the future great city of the world. This being the case, he desired to have the seat of government also removed thither without further delay.

The Capital-Mover did not succeed in his designs, and meanwhile the new War and Navy Departments and other costly improvements have more firmly anchored the government to Washington than ever; but this does not prevent St. Louis from being a vast and imposing city on its own account, without the aid of any such factitious resource. The title of "The Future Great City of the World," usually contracted to "The Future Great," given to it, half in derision, in these discussions, has stuck, and is quite generally recognized.

Dwellers on the Eastern sea-board find it hard to comprehend the great West—not so much the far West, of which they have some wild and fanciful ideas, but the central West, which presents a cultivated area, and a thickly populous civilization like their own. Get upon a railway train, and come a thousand miles across the country to the Mississippi River. It is lined with cities all along its course. The greater ones, in obedience to a law plainly in operation, are on the western bank. They have had their starting-point as depots of supplies for people who were moving further on, and as depots of supplies it

was fitting that they should be on the further shore, where the river need not be crossed. They burn a soft and inferior coal, yielded them by the region round about, and all are more or less enveloped in smoke. While the sun is shining on the Eastern sea-board we have left, these cities of the plain, artificers in iron and brass and every useful work, are pouring forth vapors as if they were but the mouth-pieces of some fiery subterranean activity.

But it is with St. Louis that we are to deal. I have seen it at different seasons, and from many points of view, but from no other can it be called so impressive as from the great bridge, of steel tubular arches, which forms the approach to it over the Mississippi, on a winter day when the river has moving ice in it. The bridge complete is a mile and a quarter long, and the part over the water about a third of a mile, which is divided into three vast spans. The cost, it may be said in passing, was some $10,000,000. The railway cars run within, and afterward through a tunnel a mile in length, under the city, which terminates at the Union Depot. Horse-car lines, vehicles, and pedestrians pass on the spacious top. Stand here and look off. The wide and turbid flood, coming resistlessly on around its curve, inspires with a sense of majesty and dread. Some ferry-boats with large stern wheels push through the broken ice, and leave clear tracks like roads behind them. The view, hemmed in by shrouding vapors, is but a hand's-breadth in any direction. A few features only of the life making up the eleven continuous miles of river-front appear. The sun strikes with a gleam on a bit of sand-bar on the opposite shore, emerging mysteriously from the smoke, as if it were only now that the chaos was beginning to give place to physical order. The city itself is barely visible. Of all

THE LEVEE.

the vast agglomeration of dwellings and industries which constitutes it what it is, no more than a dome or two, or the outlines of a shot-tower or an elevator, looms out vaguely. Or a row of red brick chimneys of a chemical works in the foreground makes a spot of color amid murky wreaths, to which their own belchings are every moment adding.

In summer the bridge is a breathing-place, and the temperature of a St. Louis summer is such that a breathing-place is much needed. In the summer nights lovers and others come out upon it, and sit on seats conveniently left at several points along its extent, and look down upon a much tamer and shallower river than that described.

But now for the city itself. Let us assume that we have entered it. It seems scarcely daybreak as we sit in the lobby of our hotel this dark morning, yet a glance at the dial shows that it is already ten o'clock. It is time to be moving. Whither first? Up into some high point, as the dome of the Court-house, for a general view of the whole? Ah, except upon some extremely rare occasion, that is useless to expect. The photographers take their pictures on Sundays, when the chimneys have stopped streaming for the time being, and then some partial prospects are to be had; but, as a rule, St. Louis is as invisible as London. When it is old and as large it is likely to be at least

as sooty. These Western cities exhale a tainted breath, stifle themselves in the fumes of their own prosperity. If there be philanthropists abroad, it would seem that they could aid them by no other possible boon so much as by that of resolving the problem how the waste product of decomposition of the bituminous coal may be carried off, or prevented from arising. Not that the inhabitants themselves object to it, more than in London. Oh dear no! They are rather proud of it, as they are of the clouded water of the Mississippi set upon the table to drink, and have theories of the benefit to health both of the one and the other.

No, St. Louis has got to be explored in detail. The essential things in American cities which distinguish them from one another, since they have so many things in common, are matters of local situation. As at Chicago it is the lake and prairie, and at Cincinnati the mountainous hills, so at St. Louis it is the river and its varied life which give the distinctive form and color to the place. This great waterway, with its eighteen miles of commercial frontage, margined with boats, and smoking with mills and foundries, is to be borne in mind as the basis of all that has grown up beside it.

A good share of the way is bordered with the levee—a very wide space prepared with Belgian pavement, and sloping like the glacis of a fort, which the river must

THE ST. LOUIS BRIDGE.

climb in its attacks upon the city. This space serves for the shipment and temporary storage of an incalculable bulk of goods of every kind. There are no regular wharfs, but landing-stages instead, moored by chains, so as to rise and fall with the water, and reached by small bridges. But of the river more anon: the stranger naturally plunges first into the thick of the town. Fourth Street may be called its Broadway, or Upper Broadway, devoted to an elegant retail trade, and the promenade of shoppers with full purses. Fifth Street tends to wholesale business. On Sixth are found close together Barr's, one of those mammoth emporiums of general merchandise, bustling like a bee-hive, which are growing into usage throughout the country, and a great handsome building, like a Renaissance palace, erected by the St. Louis Life-insurance Company. This latter has a row of statues along its roof of a really very creditable sort. Trade of the choicer kinds scatters a short way from these streets, which follow the general course of the river, westward on those which cross them at right angles. Up Olive Street is seen the imposing building, of gray granite, of the custom-house and post-office. It is not unlike the New York Post-office, and is among the best of those which the government has of late given to the great business centres of the country.

It will be seen that there is no change from the customary American lack of invention in the matter of street names. Why should we invariably have a series after the trees, Olive, Pine, Chestnut, and the like, even if those numerically named be defensible? Would it not be as well, for a change, to give them some such bold titles as those conferred upon race-horses, or to utilize science or fiction? Elsewhere, however, St. Louis has used the names of many of its early French pioneers, and is less open to the charge of triteness than some other places.

More good buildings are seen from about the corners of Fourth or Fifth street and Washington Avenue than almost anywhere else. They are five stories, of the best material, and the usual metropolitan patterns. Here are one or two without any signs put out, after the model of A. T. Stewart, of New York, on the theory that whoever does not know so well-known an establishment is of no consequence as a customer. Along Fourth Street an enter-

THE MERCHANTS' EXCHANGE.

prising person has erected a block with a very tall cupola, or tower, which is the most salient object upon which the eye catches. Across the way is the massive, dignified Court-house, in the classic style, and next this the Planter's Hotel, which has a Southern touch in its arches of an old-fashioned pattern, incised instead of raised upon its façade. In the matter of memories it must be much in advance of its more magnificent new rivals, the Lindell and Southern. The latter of these has made especial efforts, with what result remains to be seen, to be wholly and absolutely fire-proof.

On the steps of this Court-house slaves were once sold at auction. There are vestiges still of a Southern type of character in the passers in the street, as there may very well be where so large a traffic takes place with persons all the way down the river to New Orleans; but the general type is Northern, and the scenes, crowded, bustling, and metropolitan to a high degree.

There are persons now in middle life who remember when the whole present business centre was but a very shabby area. St. Louis is old historically, and the traditions of its early settlement and government by the French and Spanish in turn, according as one and then the other of these nations possessed the Mississippi Valley, are of a very romantic sort; but most of what it is it has become at a recent period. It shared liberally the great movement in immigration and city building in the West, dating from about 1835, and its real life, in the modern sense, is hardly more than contemporary with that of Chicago. Although founded in 1764, its population in 1810 was but 1400, and in 1836 but 10,000. The census of 1880 puts it at 350,522. By a curious mistake in the census of 1870, or the act of enumerators driven to unscrupulous lengths by morbid ambition in the race with rivals, about 100,000 names too many were added to the list. Until this error was rectified of late it was thus made to appear that the growth of St. Louis during the last decade was but thirteen per cent., while that of Chicago was sixty-eight, whereas, upon a proper estimate, the growth of St. Louis was sixty-nine per cent.

The building stone is largely a beautiful limestone, softly gray in color, and a sandstone, of later introduction, almost as red and cheerful as brick. The place is peculiarly fortunate in its building ma-

INTERIOR OF THE MERCHANTS' EXCHANGE.

ST. LOUIS FAIR GROUND.

terials, and they will be combined together in artistic effects to a much greater extent than now.

Of all the architectural monuments of the city the enthusiastic St. Louisan points with greatest pride, and deservedly, to the Merchants' Exchange. It is a grandly simple edifice for its purpose, in too narrow a street to be seen to the best advantage, but of a character to impress the most casual beholder. It is of granite and limestone, duly darkened by the prevailing smoke. It is the creditable boast that the whole of its material, including brick, iron, glass, lead, and paint, came from the bosom of the State itself. Three great porches give access as if to the abode of giants, as indeed its habitués may fairly be considered in commerce. If the exterior be somewhat approached by that of the Exchange at Chicago, there is nothing like the grand hall of the interior in this country, nor perhaps in the world. The figures can not express its air of vastness. It is not to the purpose to show that it is 226 feet long, 100 wide, and 79 high. I had the fortune to see it first in use for a national Presidential Convention. Faces could not be distinctly seen at the great distances. The acoustic properties are not good, though that is not important, as it is not for the accommodation of large general meetings, and the voices of but a few speakers could be heard. The delegations were ranged around the hall in a semicircle, a blue silken pennant marking the place of each. The spectators spread back in broad planes of mere shapeless humanity behind them, and clustered like flies in a gallery making a circuit of the room high above. It was a gallant and stirring spectacle.

"Pennsylvania gives seventy-nine votes" (or whatever the number may have been) "for Samuel J. Tilden," cried the chairman of that delegation, standing erect in his place. "Pennsylvania gives seventy-nine for Samuel J. Tilden," shouted the secretary at the right of the president's desk. "Pennsylvania seventy-nine for Tilden," echoed the secretary at the left, announcing the news to that side of the house; and these cries resounded down the hall like martial orders.

A gayer spectacle still is presented in the Exchange hall when it is given up, during Fair Week, in October, to the ball known as that of the Veiled Prophet. This is a costume ball, and all the vagaries of the Carnival are indulged in. Just now, however, its lower space is filled chiefly with marble-topped tables, on which are samples of grain and flour. Nonchalant dealers take pinches of the flour between thumb and fingers and scatter them over the floor. A couple of hundred brokers—seeming a mere handful—are clamoring wildly, after the manner of their business, near a handsome iron well-understood life, of such a portion of a great city.

The rest of the city is of a minor sort, with here and there some important monuments, remote from one another. The excellent Public High School, housed in a characteristic building, is one. The Four Courts, the central department of criminal correction, containing also the jail, is another. The latter follows somewhat the model of the Paris Hôtel de Ville, destroyed in the Commune. The jail is perhaps unique, consisting of a

VIEW OF ST. LOUIS, SHOWING THE FOUR COURTS.

fountain covered with classic divinities. The war, which was so poignantly a civil war on the borders, split up the commercial interests here represented, and up to 1875, when they reunited, there was both a Union Exchange and a Confederate Exchange.

All around this centre, at no great remove from the river, is a quarter of tall office buildings, intersected by narrow streets and alleys, and bustling with the great central cage of iron bars, upon which the cells open in tiers, and from which they are all equally under inspection. A keeper told me, on looking into this interior, that there was once a prisoner who had "dror'd it all off as natural as life"; but this accomplished criminal had disappeared, and his sketch was not extant.

Let us drop in at the place of a great dry-goods merchant on Washington Av-

A. STREET PROCESSION, ST. LOUIS.

enue, who may be called the A. T. Stewart of the town. He tells us of his first shop, which was a shabby old limestone house, put up by the early fur-traders on the levee, in contradistinction to his present palatial store. That was in 1835, and he brought a stock of goods there from Kentucky; and this is 1882. The contrast seems strongly enough marked, yet his talk has a certain unhopeful air, and is almost a constant pæan to Chicago. It is not enough that St. Louis has done so incredibly well, but there is an aggrieved tone, of which a good deal is heard in the place, if it can be made out that Chicago has done somewhat better.

Chicago may be more enterprising, he is inclined to admit. It is the centre of a more intelligent population. It is a reading and book-publishing place, while here there are no large book stores. The sluggish influence of slave days is not wholly outgrown here yet. Chicago has been artful in drawing to itself a sturdy Northern immigration, and especially during the war was it aided in this and every other way by the closing of the Mississippi to trade. This is in fact true. The blighting influence of the war on St. Louis, offset to some slight extent by its position as a centre of military supplies and troops, is so manifest in a study of the statistical tables that it almost seems that without it the inequality of populations in the two places would not have existed. In the decade from 1860 to 1870 St. Louis increased but 53,000, and Chicago 188,000. The summer climate, again, of St. Louis, our friend tells us, is relatively against it. Two-thirds of all the merchants have to go away to escape the extreme heat at what might otherwise be a favorable season. Finally, it is held that the railroads, or some of them, have been led to discriminate unfairly on freights in favor of Chicago.

This Machiavelian Chicago is capable of any shrewd and pushing schemes. It will send free railway passes to small traders in a commercial area which should not be tributary to it at all. It will draw grain from within forty miles of St. Louis, or make lower bids on iron-work in the town itself, though Carondelet, its southern section, is one congeries of mills and smelting furnaces. It will even throw doubts as to the local ownership of the great bridge which crosses from the Illinois side. An eye is deflected toward this crafty rival, upon any proposed course, even before it is considered in the scale of absolute benefit. The journals of the two are never done discussing, generally in the grimly humorous tone, questions of relative merits, from bank interest and grain receipts to size of feet and ears.

The calm outsider can not be expected to share in this lively contest, but may be content to admire a stupendous progress when it is under his eyes, irrespective of what may exist elsewhere. He may take leave also to doubt whether the greatest superiority consists in a mere augmentation of inhabitants, and whether that is not a more praiseworthy kind which has to do with the improved condition of those already on the ground. This talk of mere gross size sometimes becomes tiresome. "What is being done," one wearily asks, "for the greater happiness of man?"

There should be a number of first-class funerals, you are told by the ardent, before St. Louis can be expected to develop her full capacity. This is only another form of testimony, the judicious will perhaps find, to a conservatism and solidity in St. Louis business methods which have kept it out of wild-cat speculations to a greater extent than its neighbors, and render it a model for imitation rather than disparagement. One writer even finds fault that there is a less percentage of business failures here than elsewhere. It was but 5.4 per 1000 of business concerns, for a period named, as compared with 7.6 for Chicago. He ascribes it to stagnating caution and lack of aggressive spirit, and is not sure that a higher rate of bankruptcy may not be simply an indication of more active enterprise. It may be confidently said to this perverted mind that popula-

tion and wealth will grow in this fertile river valley and its capital even till the time shall come of some of those evils shown by Buckle as inhering in lands where the food supply is overabundant and men increase too rapidly; but at present it is of more importance that it should be a shining example of commercial honesty amid the corruptions of the times than have any possible acceleration.

The figures of the Capital-Mover, earlier adverted to, aim to show that in one hundred years our country is to have 600,000,000 of people, and St. Louis, the future great city of the world, 10,000,000 of them. Let us hope that its directing spirits in the mean time are not to be led, by a frenzied haste to overtake a destiny which they could not escape if they would, into corruptions of sentiment unworthy of their coming high estate.

St. Louis is probably central to a greater food-producing area than either Chica-

STATUE OF HUMBOLDT, IN TOWER GROVE PARK.

WASHINGTON AVENUE, CORNER OF GRAND AVENUE.

go, Cincinnati, or New Orleans. It must always be a great shipping market for grain, and has this advantage, that the Mississippi remains open so much longer in the winter than the northern route by the lakes. It appears to have been in the year 1881 the largest market for wheat and flour in the world, and in produce, provisions, and live stock second only to Chicago. Its central position makes it an eligible point for handling the products of both Northern and Southern States. Cotton and tobacco, to an enormous value, from the one join the cereals and lumber of the other. It is the largest purely inland cotton market in the world, though led in this respect by a number of seaports. It has received in a year very nearly half a million bales.

This marketing of supplies was the beginning, as it is the staple, of its prosperity, and is connected with its situation on the great river. St. Louis counts, in the Mississippi and 240 navigable tributaries, no less than 16,000 miles of waterway, to which steamboats from its levee penetrate, carrying articles up and down. Professor Waterhouse, of the Washington University, in an interesting pamphlet on the resources of Missouri, as far back as 1869, cited a solid mile and a half of steamboats lying at this levee, and what it has grown

to be since I have not space to show here. Upon this basis, later, has grown up a manufacturing interest of importance commensurate with the rest. Some 3000 varied establishments turn out an annual profit of $104,000,000, and put St. Louis seventh in the list of manufacturing cities. For the first time Cincinnati, which figures sixth in this list, leads her as a rival. There are points in which Cincinnati is very similar to St. Louis, and others in which it is much more wide-awake and advanced, though it has 100,000 less population. A study into the differences and resemblances of the two would be interesting to make, but it would be a matter of speculative interest merely, since the question of rivalry, at St. Louis, is directed at Chicago, and Chicago only.

Missouri is a State very rich in mineral resources. The Iron Mountain and Pilot Knob district is eighty miles by railroad below St. Louis. These mountains are of almost solid ore, so that it is estimated that they show enough above the surface to supply one million tons a year for two hundred years. Further in the southwest are great lead and zinc deposits. The west of the State is full of coal, perhaps not yet utilized enough to be sure that it is of the best quality; but nearer yet, across the river, on the Illinois side, is a sufficient supply, and of the best quality. The nearest coal is in St. Clair County, no more than seven or eight miles away, and the rest in Madison, Jackson, and Williamson, all close to the river, in Illinois.

This approximation of iron and coal to a leading transportation route has naturally resulted in the line of furnaces, mills, machine-shops, and boat-building yards, the clangor and smoke and lurid glare of which render the long precinct of Carondelet the beneficent sort of Pandemonium it is. More was expected from these than has really been accomplished, or, rather, there have been local set-backs of late which have prevented the favorable situation from exerting its full force. There are complaints of the high railroad freights on coal, so that, even at the short distance it has to come, it costs many times more than at some points less advantageously placed. There are times when it has cost as much to bring it hither as to mine it. If it be really due to any railway rapacity, it is an economic mistake akin to that of crippling the goose that laid the golden

eggs, and can not fail to be sharply repented of in the future.

It does not seem to the superficial observer that the railroads as a whole intend to neglect St. Louis, by any means. Thirteen separate trunk lines leave it, radiating to all points of the compass. The most considerable of these toward the East are the great Pennsylvania line, with its 6427 miles of road, and the Wabash, with 3348. To the West branches out the Missouri Pacific, with 5640 miles of track, and the St. Louis and San Francisco has al-

A BIT OF ST. LOUIS ARCHITECTURE.

HENRY SHAW.

was less than 1500 miles. And to show the rate at which it has been progressing in these later days, it may be said that there has been an increase of 8726 miles from 1880 to 1882, and about as much for each of the periods of five years preceding that, back to 1870.

To regulate more fairly the whole matter of railway freights, there has been lately organized a unique institution known as the "St. Louis Freight Bureau." It is maintained by the union of two hundred firms of leading merchants, each guaranteeing a payment of $100 per annum, and is in the hands of skilled railroad men. Its patriotic duty is to watch over the interests of St. Louis and of individual cases in an effectual way, which no mere private person unversed in the scope and technicalities of the subject could do. Much good is said to have already resulted to the city in the brief time of its establishment; and its officers say that they have found the railroads, with one or two exceptions, heartily in accord with them in clearing away misunderstandings.

ready laid down 1050 on its way across the continent, on the line of the thirty-fifth parallel. The total system gives the city 26,679 miles of railroad communications, in addition to the 16,000 by river, and makes it the second greatest railway centre in the world, Chicago leading with 33,199. The Union Depot, under these circumstances, with its long, orderly lines of waiting trains, and attendants standing ready to show the way to each, it may well be believed, is an imposing place. The Ohio and Mississippi, among these, will perhaps call to mind a commercial reminiscence now become historic. This stretch of beautiful road, 616 miles in all, across the rich States of Indiana and Illinois, from Cincinnati, was the immediate occasion of the panic of 1857. It was considered a Herculean undertaking at the time, and involved in failure its builders, the bankers Page and Bacon, and the disaster then spread to the rest of the country. Who would believe it now, sitting in its comfortable cars, as crowded with a multifarious, civilized travel as a city tramway? With this failure, railroad-building, said to be largely overdone then, as afterward in 1873, stopped; and most of the great enterprises named were not undertaken till after the war. In 1865, for example, the total mileage at St. Louis

Other characteristic institutions of St. Louis, to be named either for their early establishment as the first of their kind, or for their exceptional development, are the Pompier Corps, for life-saving at fires; the Kindergarten System; and the Manual Training School.

The Pompier Corps was organized in 1877 for life-saving and climbing to the tops of tall buildings where ladders will not reach, as a part of the truck service of the Fire Department. During its existence not a single accident has occurred. Exhibitions of its drill and efficiency have been given in many other cities of the country; and the leading cities, including New York and Boston, are rapidly adopting it as a model for themselves.

The St. Louis Kindergarten System, first installed at the urgent instance of a lady, Miss Susie Blow, daughter of a former Representative in Congress, has now attained such proportions as to number 8730 pupils and 87 paid teachers.

The Manual Training School, a department of Washington University, and under the excellent management of Professor Woodward, can not fail to inspire especial interest in all those upon whom our defective methods of education as a preparation for the duties of life are at times borne home. Its motto is, "The cultured mind, the skillful hand." Such schools are well known in continental Europe, and the writer remembers with pleasure the exhibits made by them at the Paris Exposition of 1878, from as far away as Russia, Italy, and Spain. But here all such aids to dignifying labor, investing the mechanical trades with the fascination that really belongs to them with the youthful mind when rightly approached, and preparing for a useful and paying livelihood a whole class, drawn now to worthless clerkships and the like on the ground of a petty respectability, are far too rare. The encouragement is devoutly to be wished for. A sufficient idea of the purposes of the Manual Training School is got from the articles establishing it. Its working during a four years' existence, the appearance of its shops, tools, and pupils, are material for an article in themselves. The ordinance of establishment declares: "Its object shall be instruction in mathematics, drawing, and the English branches of a high-school course, and instruction and practice in the use of tools. The tool instruction, as at present contemplated, shall include carpentry, wood-turning, pattern-making, iron clipping and filing, forge-work, brazing and soldering, the use of machine-shop tools, and such other instruction of a similar character as it may be deemed advisable to add to the foregoing from time to time. The students will divide their working hours, as nearly as possible, equally between mental and manual exercises. They shall be admitted, on examination, at not less than fourteen years of age, and the course shall continue three years."

The city rises gently from the river in three terraces, the last of which, at the suburb of Côte Brillante, is about two hundred feet high and four miles back. Westward, in this metropolis, as in so many others of the world, and in the world itself, the course of empire takes its way. The tendency of residences, and especially those of the fashionable sort, is to the west, and business follows them up. The rise of all the west-bound streets between Washington Avenue on the north and Pine Street on the south is lined with comfortable dwellings, improving in display toward the crest. Certain transverse avenues, as Garrison Avenue and Grand Avenue, assemble choice collections of these. A drive should be taken along

IN LAFAYETTE PARK.

STATUE OF BENTON, IN LAFAYETTE PARK.

a well - judged, really artistic sort, a particular in which Cincinnati, though smaller, is worthy of warm and especial commendation. A Frenchman, Narjoux, has written travels in which the basis of observations has been the character of the dwellings in which he found people living, and the idea might be a good one for the tourist through American cities. Among the houses of the better but secondary order, which have not grounds of some extent around them, what may be called the slice system prevails; that is to say, there are rows of houses of twenty or twenty-five feet, without side windows, and a space of about equal extent between each two, as if this was left vacant till a pressure should come for fi'ling up. The continuous block system of most large cities is not yet greatly in use. Space stands, for the time being, as a substitute for decoration.

There are probably more houses above the average in comfort, costing, say, from $10,000 to $30,000, and fewer proportionate palaces, than in any other city in the country. As to the matter of rents, they are less than in New York, more than in Philadelphia and Baltimore, and perhaps higher even than in Chicago. They are not as low as they ought to be; and the same may be said of the general expenses of living, which is somewhat unexpected here in the very heart of the food region, and so close to the sources of supply of fuel and building materials. It is ascribed to high taxation and high interest on money, which are both above the rates where they ought to remain.

Our drive may easily be extended a mile and a half further out to the King's Highway. If it sweep around then to the Jefferson Barracks, southward, it will have made a pretty complete circuit of the city. On the outskirts the sky is blue, the atmosphere clear. Whereas in the interior the sun may have shone, even on a pleasant day, in a wan, pale way, and cast furtive shadows on the pavement as if it

Grand Avenue, which is to sweep around a considerable portion of the city, somewhat after the manner of the exterior boulevards at Paris. It is still in a transition state. Handsome churches of the charming gray limestone are going up along it. At one point Vanderventer Place, an inclosure with a grass-plot in the centre, and somewhat recalling Hillhouse Avenue of New Haven, opens from it, and gives a view of the pleasant country beyond.

There are efforts at architectural adornment to be observed, but St. Louis houses in general are rather comfortable than ornate. The ornamentation is not often of

were no more than some very far off electric light, here we meet again with sunshine of the ordinary genial sort to which
we are used.   There are liberal vistas of
open country, and the fresh green of grass
and market-gardens on the nearer slopes.

St. Louis is a city without outside "resorts." In the hot summer nights, besides
the promenade on the bridge, much use

of a festival, awnings of the national banner, or of blue bunting sprinkled with
stars, put out from the restaurants, and
fronts of the fine buildings transformed
into the semblance of vast ensigns by
stretching the bunting behind the glass,
lights being placed behind this at night.
I should say that there was an especial
genius for these things at St. Louis.

PUBLIC HIGH SCHOOL.

is made of open-air gardens and theatres,
like the "Pickwick," and "Uhrig's Cave,"
conducted by the Germans after their
usual plan.   These are odd conglomera-
tions of buildings, both on Washington
Avenue, and are patronized by the best
people that remain in town.   There is at
the same time a good deal of gay street
life, recalling in its way that of the Paris
boulevards.   Little tables are put out in
front of the principal restaurants, and the
guests chatter and sip refreshments at
them, under the glowing gas-lights, till a
late hour.   I have seen, on the occasion

Of the regular spots repaired to by plea-
sure-seekers at all times indiscriminately,
most are touched in the route above indicated.   The Fair Ground at the proper
season draws great throngs, and especially on the Thursday of Fair Week, which is
an official and public holiday, and may be
counted a kind of Derby-day.   This is a
fair ground of no common order, but an
ornate park and zoological garden.   The
display in the midst of it when in progress
has the traits of a veritable Vanity Fair,
or of an international exposition.   An
amphitheatre for forty thousand people,

FRENCH CATHEDRAL.

and shaped like those for bull-fights in Spanish countries, holds a principal position. It is to the credit of the Fair Association that it should be so large, but one's opinion of the importance of forty thousand people is involuntarily lowered by seeing the space into which they could be put. At such a rate, the entire population of the country could be stood up in a small part of one of its towns, which is a reflection that does not often occur to the mind. All around is a congeries of chalets, put up by the newspaper press for the collection and dissemination of news, which indicates the scale of the occasion. Some of the prettiest are those of the German dailies. In some deep pits in the bottom of a kind of Gothic hunting-lodge, grizzlies, black and cinnamon bears, disport themselves after the manner of their kind, and invite the attention and fortuitous apples and cakes of the curious, like the bears of Berne.

Forest Park is a tract of nearly fifteen hundred acres, naturally wooded and diversified in surface, but not yet greatly improved. Having passed it, you come next to the vicinity of Shaw's Garden. No stranger will have failed to hear of Shaw's Garden. It was opened to the public by an amiable gentleman of wealth, Mr. Henry Shaw, in 1849, and has remained its permanent possession. It is a succession of conservatories of rare plants, and open-air spaces devoted to flower, fruit, and tree culture, and contains also a museum and botanical library. It is part of the owner's private domain. He has attained a venerable age now, occupying these later years in the pleasant pursuit of writing a treatise on the rose; and he will be buried, as he has lived, in the midst of his garden.

This same kindly citizen, exemplifying that "private initiative" which is so largely American, has also presented outright the long, handsome strip of Tower Grove Park, adjoining. It is a mile in length, and rather narrow. It offers a fine long vista down the centre, its whole length. A colossal bronze Shakespeare looks down a part of it toward a colossal bronze Humboldt, both the dignified work of Ferd. Müller, of Munich. He has made emblematic panels for the pedestals, and around that of the Humboldt is set a panegyric worth living and striving for indeed: "In honor of the most accomplished traveller of this or any other age."

Thence Lafayette Park may be touched on the return. It is a square of about the size and order of Boston Common, and encompassed by the most eminently respectable class of houses. A statue of Benton, draped in a cloak in Roman fashion, by Harriet Hosmer, rises in the midst of it. He is that Thomas H. Benton who spent thirty years in the United States Senate, and wrote a book about it. The motto on his statue is: "There is the East; there is India!"—a sentence from an eloquent speech advocating the Pacific Railroad in 1848. As early as 1818 Benton had predicted that the trade of the Orient would pass across this continent, probably carried by trains of camels, railroads not then having been invented. In the speech referred to he proposed that on the completion of the Pacific road a colossal statue of Columbus should be carved out of the Rocky Mountains, with one hand pointing westward, and the motto now given to Benton on the pedestal.

St. Louis is comprehended as a great

city, particularly in its river front, as has been said. Go to the extreme north, the quarter known as Baden. Observe the river-rats clustering about the groggeries, the negro roustabouts of the old plantation type unloading the boats, and hear the vigorous phraseology of the mates directing them in their labors. There are populations living by fishing and catching drift-wood. Near North Market Street a ferry crosses to a satirically named "Venice," which is largely a grain and cattle suburb. To the north all is lumber and cattle again. Here come the drovers from Kansas and Texas, and here the raftsmen

Nothing was known by the settlers of that, nor Arsenal Island, further down, nor any other of the islands in the river. Then toward 1780 it threatened to make the main channel, which had been seventy feet deep, pass behind it, and desert the city entirely; and again it returned to its proper place. It seems securely anchored down now both by the bridge and weighty storage establishments and depots which have grown up since the making of this so important a terminal point.

In the duelling days Benton fought here with Lucas, a leading lawyer. They met not once only but a second time, aft-

A BIT OF OLD ST. LOUIS.

floating down with their logs from the rivers of upper Wisconsin. They return by steamboat in high feather, with the cash proceeds in their pockets, and are apt to be lively customers on these return trips. There is at least one authentic instance of their throwing a captain of the Diamond Joe line overboard, and inspiring terror in all beholders, because denied permission to appear at table in their shirt sleeves.

"Bloody Island," across the river, once a famous duelling ground, has now become East St. Louis, and supports an end of the great bridge. It has been a chaotic piece of ground in its time, as most of that over which the Mississippi has had uninterrupted sway is likely to have been. In the earlier days it did not exist at all.

er an interval of a month. Lucas was wounded in the first encounter, and, not satisfied with the result, demanded a second, and was then killed. The moral of this, so far as Lucas was concerned, would seem to be to let bad enough alone. One Major Biddle, again, and Potter, a member of Congress, met here, at five paces, and both fell mortally wounded at the first fire. Stories of equally lurid interest might be multiplied, upon a social custom, now happily passed away, which seems to have been marked in this vicinity by a peculiar mingling of Western and Southern fierceness.

Take the Fifth Street line of cars, and examine the river front all the way southward. You get off at a stopping-place called the Wild Hunter Inn, and take an-

OLD SPANISH TOWER.

other car to Carondelet. The original settlers were French, as has been said, but little trace of them remains. A vast German invasion, on the other hand, has succeeded them, and put up its names on the shop signs, especially in the smaller trade. St. Louis is now one of the largest German cities of a West which is full of Germans, and from among them have sprung many most notable citizens.

There may be a broken-roofed old limestone warehouse or so along the levee from the French occupation, but nothing ornate. The French cathedral alone, on Walnut Street, has the interest of a certain quaint plainness, and even that is not very old.

Two vast German breweries of good red brick, really picturesque and imposing in their irregularity, are important features of the downward journey. The levee is packed with bags and bales, barrels and kegs, and the wagons that transport them. Alongside lie the boats. And such boats as they are!—side-wheelers and stern-wheelers, packets, barges, tugs, flat-boats, and dredge boats. Many of the packets bear the legend "U. S. Mail," and are still the quickest means of communication with the remote river points to which they ply. As a mass, they are many-decked, pavilionlike, and as ephemeral-looking as the piazzas of a summer hotel. The best of them are withdrawn for the winter, but sometimes they are simply laid up with the others. The accident has not been unfrequently seen that an ice-gorge forming in the river in the spring, and coming on with resistless force, has smashed and crunched whole fleets of them into shapeless ruin.

Carondelet is a main street of minor shops and houses, and the line of mills and furnaces before referred to along the river. The population in their grimy interiors, with streams of molten metal pouring, pigs and lengths of railroad iron at a cherry-red heat around them, and sparks flying on every side, seem not so much engaged in labor as in some demoniac play of fire-works, while over the whole presides the roar of air blasts, and circular saws, and the pounding of trip-hammers. It was here that the iron-clad gun-boats were built that did such good service during the war.

It is curious to remember that although the early constitution of St. Louis, so long as it was a foreign settlement, was essentially French, it was but for an extremely slight space of time under any legal French government. It made a part of the French province of Louisiana, and was established in 1763 by a fur-trader, Pierre Laclede Ligueste, under authority of the Governor-General at New Orleans, and was named after that gracious rococo sovereign, Louis XV. But it was precisely in 1763 that Louis XV., terminating by the Treaty of Paris his disastrous conflict known in Europe as the Seven Years' War, and here as the Old French War, was obliged to yield to Spain all of the French possessions on the west bank of the Mississippi, together with New Orleans, and to Great Britain those on the east bank.

The new domination, however, by no means began at once, not by reason of resistance to it, but for reasons connected with the sparsity of population, the vast distances to be traversed, and lack of physical ability in the new ownership to manifest its power. Four years afterward, or in 1768, some Spanish soldiers under Rios arrived at St. Louis, and completed the transfer, and it was not till 1780 that the first Spanish Governor, Pedro Piernas, was installed.

WAYMAN CROW.

Meanwhile many French settlers who had established themselves in a line of posts on the other side of the river, along a trail kept open from Canada, preferring, after the Treaty of Paris, a Latin domination at least to that of Great Britain, had crossed over and joined their compatriots. Principal among these was Captain St.-Ange de Bellerive, who had commanded at Fort Chartres, near where Kaskaskia now stands. He brought with him forty soldiers of his garrison. He was invested at St. Louis with the chief command, both military and civil, and continued to retain it, or something like it, by his personal influence, long after he was nominally superseded. He had great power, among other ways, over the Indian tribes, and made the famous Pontiac his intimate personal friend.

The Spanish *régime* continued peacefully under some five or six Governors, down to 1804, when the whole territory, having first been retransferred to France after the victories of Napoleon, was sold by Napoleon to the United States, in Jefferson's Presidency, for $15,000,000.

The Indian tribes in those days were an important auxiliary even in the wars of the Europeans. Just as French and Indians organized for the massacre of Braddock near Fort Du Quesne, or Pittsburgh, the British brought down Indians upon the French settlements of the West. In 1789, 1400 savages from the vicinity of Mackinaw, said to have been led by 140 British regulars, suddenly appeared before St. Louis, and made a fierce onslaught upon it. They were fortunately beaten off, and the approach of a body of Americans —for we aided our French allies where we could, as they aided us at Yorktown—completed their discomfiture. This was known as the year of the *Grand Coup*, just as the arrival of ten boats together at another time, for protection against robbers, an extraordinary prevalence of honey-bees, and the like, in the annals of the small settlement, caused distinctive appellations to be conferred on the years in which they took place.

When the American flag was first hoisted, in 1804, it floated over a little village of 150 houses and three streets, in one of which was a log church, under the jurisdiction, like all other ecclesiastical matters in the province, of the Bishopric of Cuba. Around the village was a line of stockade and stone fortresses, erected by the Spanish Governor Cruzat after the Indian invasion before mentioned. Up to a few years ago there was still standing on the river-bank an old round tower, somewhat like the disputed mill at Newport, which had once made part of these primitive fortifications.

The petty village of Cahokia, on the other side of the river, strange to state, was then the only post-office for St. Louis. A mail, carried on horseback, arrived there once a month. Now Cahokia has not even a post-office of its own, but has to go five miles, up to East St. Louis, for its letters.

It is worth while to go over to Cahokia, though let not the attempt be made unless the weather be good and the roads tolerably dry, under penalty of being hopelessly mired in the red-clay mud. St. Louis people recommend it enthusiastically to the seeker for antiquities. "Ah, yes, indeed," they say, "there you will find history to your heart's content; a quaint old French town, quite unchanged, and the inhabitants speaking their own language exclusively." But there is reason to believe that few of these eulogists have ever gone for themselves.

On that side we have still almost the wild and solemn Mississippi of Châteaubriand. We see the floating snags, deserted channels, a mass of tangled drift-wood, sand-bars, virgin islands overgrown with alders, and forming or in process of destruction. The powerful stream tears millions of acres yearly from the heart of the continent, to deposit in the Gulf of Mexico. Fortunately the jetties operated by Captain Eads now force it to scour its channels at the mouth, and in this way the blocking of navigation by this vast débris is prevented.

Father Marquette, the missionary, and Joliet, the merchant in his company, descended the Mississippi in 1673, having made their way to it from Quebec by the waters of Wisconsin. The Chevalier La Salle followed them five years later, and made a beginning of carrying out his statesman-like idea of binding the French possessions securely together by a chain of posts from Canada to the Gulf of Mexico. Detroit, Peoria, Vincennes, Cahokia, Kaskaskia, Natchez, may be mentioned as salient points in the series which soon came to be firmly established. These places have remained favorite ones with Canadians to this day. Evangeline, in Longfellow's lovely poem, stopped at one after another of them in her pathetic quest for Gabriel.

Cahokia can never have possessed structures of any great massiveness. Of what survive, the oldest is a tumble-down court-house of logs, weather-boarded. It has been a dwelling later, and a tavern; and the sign "Old Court Saloon" still adheres to it, though it is no longer even a saloon. Sheer indolence apparently prevents the sign from being taken down. There is no store, no post-office, no sidewalked street —no nothing. It is one of those places where the best-travelled road leads to the grave-yard. It is a poor hamlet now of less than twenty-five families, while in 1847 it had two hundred. The river has contributed to this decline by washing away a considerable part of its farming land. Of late, as if it had only engaged with a kind of malignant humor in a scheme to dislodge the inhabitants, it has begun to deliberately replace it.

The people speak creole French. I talked with an old farmer, patiently waiting at the slow ferry in one of those wagons painted with floriated work such as are still seen in Normandy and Canada. With his long gray locks and his shrewd face, he might have been himself a patriarch of 1793. He had come here from Canada, he said, in 1837, for the old French trail still remained, in a sense, open. He spoke of the disastrous floods, but had always been hoping for better things. "When one is settled on the land," he said, "it is so hard to get away."

These floods are a cruel, constantly recurring fact. Some time, no doubt, enormous as the cost must be, we shall see the great river running as in a great ditch through the heart of the continent, securely confined within its banks, like those streams of Switzerland which would be destructive torrents but for their well-ballasted margins of stone. At East St. Louis one day I fell in with an honest German whose home was a flat-boat, at present established high and dry on the sands. He was sunning himself near reels of fishing-nets, and his family and dogs were passing in and out of the cabin, while he smoked his pipe and the great city smoked opposite. He told me of the fish he took from the river, the "buffalo" and cat-fish, which are not unfrequently as large as a man, and weigh a hundred pounds. I could not help but congratulate him on his exceptionally good position in case of freshets. "Yes," he replied, "I have often been up near the tops of those steeples," pointing back to the thick of the settlement, "like Papa Noah,"

ST. LOUIS ART MUSEUM.

he added, seeming to appreciate the humors of his situation.

The early French were of the hardy race of trappers and explorers, and their vigorous blood has been a moving influence in the community throughout, though any distinctive trace of foreignness has passed away. The Chouteaus, lieutenants of Laclede, and others who have left their names to various streets and avenues of the city, were associated in the fur-trading companies with John Jacob Astor and the like, and made part of the choicest early bone and sinew of the country. The social influences descending from this source have been of a rather strict and severe sort.

St. Louis has no reason to be dissatisfied with the spirit of its individual citizens, both of this stock and others. We have seen what Henry Shaw has done. Of all the kindred benefactions none can be put higher than that of Wayman Crow, Esq., a leading merchant, who has established a beautiful Art Museum, which has been made a department of the flourishing Washington University. The building resembles that at Boston, though it is less finical, and more dignified and worthy of its purpose. It is made of the beautiful gray limestone, rough dressed, and topped with a roof of red slates. It was present-

ed as a memorial for a dead son, and in this aspect the idea seems more admirable than ever. Some two hundred students are found engaged in the department of fine arts. St. Louis has been a good market for pictures, and the comfortable houses at which we have glanced possess, say, a dozen collections comprising from twenty to a hundred each of the best modern works of the foreign school. The French taste chiefly prevails, though Munich and Düsseldorf too are not without representation. Along with the fashionable St. Louis Club, and the cultured University Club, there exists a well-attended Sketch Club as one of the institutions of the city.

Upon this basis have sprung up a number of young artists, who, after study abroad, represent their birth-place excellently well in the newer school. Of these the best-known are probably the two Chases, one in marine, the other in *genre* and portrait subjects. The academic work of Thomas Allen, and the vigorously humorous characterizations of Eichbaum, have also been favorably received at the East. Of the old school, the landscapists, Meeker and Marple, the painter of Indians, Wimar, and of animals, Tracy, and the portrait-painter, Conant, are the ablest.

ABRAHAM LINCOLN AT CINCINNATI

IN the summer of 1857 Mr. Lincoln made his first visit to Cincinnati. He was original counsel for the defendant in a patent reaper suit pending in the United States Circuit Court for Northern Illinois. The argument of the case was adjourned to Cincinnati, the home of Judge McLean, at his suggestion and for his accommodation.

Mr. Lincoln came to the city a few days before the argument took place, and remained during his stay at the house of a friend. The case was one of large importance pecuniarily, and in the law questions involved. Reverdy Johnson represented the plaintiff. Mr. Lincoln had prepared himself with the greatest care; his ambition was up to speak in the case, and to measure swords with the renowned lawyer from Baltimore. It was understood between his client and himself before his coming that Mr. Harding, of Philadelphia, was to be associated with him in the case, and was to make the "mechanical argument." Mr. Lincoln was a little surprised and annoyed, after reaching here, to learn that his client had also associated with him Mr. Edwin M. Stanton, of Pittsburgh, and a lawyer of our own bar, the reason assigned being that the importance of the case required a man of the experience and power of Mr. Stanton to meet Mr. Johnson. The Cincinnati lawyer was appointed "for his local influence." These reasons did not remove the slight conveyed in the employment, without consultation with him, of this additional counsel. He keenly felt it, but acquiesced. The trial of the case came on; the counsel for defense met each morning for consultation. On one of these occasions one of the counsel moved that only two of them should speak in the case. This motion was acquiesced in. It had always been understood that Mr. Harding was to speak to explain the mechanism of the reapers. So this motion excluded either Mr. Lincoln or Mr. Stanton from speaking—which? By the custom of the bar, as between counsel of equal standing, and in the absence of any action of the client, the original counsel speaks. By this rule Mr. Lincoln had precedence. Mr. Stanton suggested to Mr. Lincoln to make the speech. Mr. Lincoln answered, "No; do you speak." Mr. Stanton promptly replied, "I will," and, taking up his hat,

said he would go and make preparation. Mr. Lincoln acquiesced in this, but was deeply grieved and mortified; he took but little more interest in the case, though remaining until the conclusion of the trial. He seemed to be greatly depressed, and gave evidence of that tendency to melancholy which so marked his character. His parting on leaving the city can not be forgotten. Cordially shaking the hand of his hostess, he said: "You have made my stay here most agreeable, and I am a thousand times obliged to you; but in reply to your request for me to come again I must say to you I never expect to be in Cincinnati again. I have nothing against the city, but things have so happened here as to make it undesirable for me ever to return here."

Thus untowardly met the first time Mr. Lincoln and Mr. Stanton. Little did either then suspect that they were to meet again on a larger theatre, to become the chief actors in a great historical epoch.

While in the city he visited its lions, among other places of interest the grounds and conservatories of the late Nicholas Longworth, then living. The meeting of these remarkable men is worthy of a passing note. Nor can it be given without allusion to their dress and bearing. Mr. Lincoln entered the open yard, with towering form and ungainly gait, dressed in plain clothing cut too small. His hands and feet seemed to be growing out of their environment, conspicuously seen from their uncommon size. Mr. Longworth happened at the time to be near the entrance, engaged in weeding the shrubbery by the walk. His alert eye quickly observed the coming of a person of unusual appearance. He rose and confronted him.

"Will a stranger be permitted to walk through your grounds and conservatories?" inquired Mr. Lincoln.

"Y-e-s," haltingly, half unconsciously, was the reply, so fixed was the gaze of Mr. Longworth.

As they stood thus face to face the contrast was striking, so short in stature was the one that he seemed scarcely to reach the elbow of the other. If the dress of Mr. Lincoln seemed too small for him, the other seemed lost in the baggy bulkiness of his costume; the overflowing sleeves concealed the hands, and the extremities of the pantaloons were piled in heavy folds upon the open ears of the untied shoes. His survey of Mr. Lincoln was searching: beginning with the feet, he slowly raised his head, closely observing, until his upturned face met the eye of Mr. Lincoln. Thus for a moment gazed at each other in mutual and mute astonishment the millionaire pioneer and the now forever famous President. Mr. Lincoln passed on, nor did Mr. Longworth ever become aware that he had seen Mr. Lincoln.

The grounds and conservatories were viewed and admired. And so afterward the suburbs of the city—Walnut Hills, Mount Auburn, Clifton, and Spring Grove Cemetery. He lingered long in the grounds of Mr. Hoffner in study of the statuary. He sought to find out whom the statues represented, and was much worried when he found himself unable to name correctly a single one.

A day was given to the county and city courts. An entire morning was spent in Room No. 1 of the Superior Court, then presided over by Bellamy Storer, eccentric and versatile, in the maturity of his extraordinary powers. His manner of conducting the business of that room, miscellaneous, demurrers, motions, submitted docket, etc., was unique. The older members of the bar remember it well. To describe it literally would do gross injustice to that really great judge. To mingle in the same hour the gravity of the judge and the jest of the clown was a feat that only he could perform without loss of dignity, personal or judicial. On this morning the judge was in his happiest vein, in exuberant spirits, keeping the bar "in a roar," assisted much in this by the lively humor of poor Bob McCook.

Mr. Lincoln greatly enjoyed this morning, and was loath to depart when the curtain dropped. He said to the gentleman accompanying him: "I wish we had that judge in Illinois. I think he would share with me the fatherhood of the legal jokes of the Illinois bar. As it is now, they put them all on me, while I am not the author of one-half of them. By-the-way, however, I got off one last week that I think really good. I was retained in the defense of a man charged before a justice of the peace with assault and battery. It was in the country, and when I got to the place of trial I found the whole neighborhood excited, and the feeling was strong against my client. I saw the only way

was to get up a laugh, and get the people in a good humor. It turned out that the prosecuting witness was talkative; he described the fight at great length, how they fought over a field, now by the barn, again down to the creek, and over it, and so on. I asked him, on cross-examination, how large that field was; he said it was ten acres, he knew it was, for he and some one else had stepped it off with a pole. 'Well, then,' I inquired, 'was not that the smallest *crap* of a fight you have ever seen raised off of ten acres?' The hit took. The laughter was uproarious, and in half an hour the prosecuting witness was retreating amid the jeers of the crowd."

Mr. Lincoln remained in the city about a week. Freed from any care in the law case that brought him here, it was to him a week of relaxation. He was then not thinking of becoming President, and gave himself up to unrestrained social intercourse.

His conversation at this time related principally to the politics and politicians of Illinois—a theme of which he never seemed to weary. A strange chapter in the story of our country that is. What a crowd of great men arose with the first generation of white people on the broad Illinois prairie! There were Hardin, Logan the judge, Bissel, Trumbull, Douglas, Lincoln, and many other scarcely lesser names. Of these he discoursed as only he could. The Kansas-Nebraska agitation was at its height, and Douglas the prominent figure. Of him he spoke much.

Indeed, the story of Lincoln interlaces with that of Douglas. They are inseparable. It is the relation of antagonism. Parties might come and go—Whig, Know-Nothing, Union, Republican—they were never on the same side until, amid the throes of revolution, they met in the defense of the Union. Douglas was a perennial stimulus to Lincoln. Webster was wont to say, if he had attained any excellence in his profession, he owed it to his early conflicts with Jeremiah Mason. In his public speeches Lincoln seemed ever addressing Douglas; even to the last, as seen in his great speech at New York, when he made the words of Douglas his text.

When Lincoln was driving an ox-team at four dollars a month, and splitting rails, he first met Douglas, then teaching school in central Illinois.

Mr. Lincoln loved to tell the story of Douglas. It is indelibly written in my memory. Not in the very words can I repeat it, and yet even that in the salient points.

He said Douglas, when he first met him, was the smallest man he had ever seen—in stature under five feet, in weight under ninety pounds. He was teaching a country school, and lodging with a violent Democratic politician, a local celebrity. From him Douglas got his political bias. Douglas was his protégé. He encouraged Douglas in the study of the law, procured the books for him, had him admitted to the bar before a year, pushed him into the office of prosecuting attorney, and into the Legislature.

When Van Buren became President, the patron wanted the office of Register at the Land-office, and sent Douglas to Washington to procure the place for him. In due time Douglas returned with the commission in his pocket, but not for his patron. It was to himself. The old man was enraged at the ingratitude, and swore vengeance. He listened to no explanations. It was not long before he had an opportunity to gratify his feelings.

Douglas became the Democratic candidate for Congress, the whole State constituting one Congressional district. His opponent was Mr. Stewart—still living, a relative of Mrs. Lincoln. After an animated contest Douglas was defeated by one vote in a poll of 36,000. The old patron rejoiced in the belief that that one vote was his.

Mr. Douglas's sensitive nature was overwhelmed by this defeat. He gave way to uncontrollable grief, sought consolation in excessive drink, and his career seemed at an end. But time brought its accustomed relief, and he re-appeared in the arena, again the thunderer of the scene. The years to follow were to him years of unbroken prosperity. He became successively Judge of the Supreme Court, Representative in Congress, and Senator. The name and fame of the "Little Giant" overspread the land. These, however, were cheerless years to Mr. Lincoln, yet with unshaken fortitude he bore the banner of Whiggery. It was his custom to follow Mr. Douglas about the State, replying to him.

But a change came: the Kansas-Nebraska Bill awakened the moral sense of the State, and by common consent Mr.

Lincoln became its representative. Mr. Douglas, in Washington, was alarmed at the uprising, and hurried home to educate the people up to conquering their prejudice against slavery. He made a canvass of the State, Mr. Lincoln following him and replying to him. "After having spoken at a number of places," said Mr. Lincoln, "I was surprised one evening, before the speaking began, at Mr. Douglas entering my room at the hotel. He threw himself on the bed, and seemed in distress. 'Abe, the tide is against me,' said he. 'It is all up with me. I can do nothing. Don't reply to me this evening. I can not speak, but I must, and it is my last. Let me alone tonight.' I saw he was in great distress: he could not bear adversity; and I acquiesced in his request and went home."

They did not meet again in debate, if I mistake not, until the great contest of 1858.

Mr. Lincoln had a high admiration for the abilities of Mr. Douglas, and afterward was glad to have his aid in behalf of the Union, and commissioned him a major-general; but he thought him in debate and in politics adroit, unscrupulous, and of an amazing audacity. "It is impossible," said he, "to get the advantage of him; even if he is worsted, he so bears himself that the people are bewildered and uncertain as to who has the better of it."

"When I," said Thucydides, "in wrestling have thrown Pericles and given him a fall, by persisting that he had no fall he gets the better of me, and makes the bystanders, in spite of their own eyes, believe him." Thus doth man from age to age repeat himself; and yet not quite always. We hear of Gladstone felling trees, but it is not reported that he and Froude have wrestling matches.

Some weeks after this conversation with Mr. Lincoln I met Mr. Douglas, and drew from him his opinion of Mr. Lincoln. His very words, terse and emphatic as they were, I give: "Of all the —— —— Whig rascals about Springfield, Abe Lincoln is the ablest and most honest."

The Kansas-Nebraska Bill had indeed turned the tide against Douglas; the Republicans were successful, having a majority of one on joint ballot in the Legislature, thus securing the Senator.

With a common voice the Republicans of the State proclaimed Lincoln Senator. In caucus he received forty-nine votes out of the fifty-one Republican majority. If I recall the figures aright, Mr. Trumbull the other two. But these refused in any contingency to vote for Mr. Lincoln. "After balloting for some time, I learned from a trustworthy source," said Mr. Lincoln, "that on a certain future ballot these two men would cast their votes for the Democratic candidate, and elect him. I called a meeting of my friends, explained the situation to them, and requested them on the next ballot, after these two men had voted for Mr. Trumbull, to change their votes and elect him. At this there was a murmur of disapprobation and declarations never to do it. I resumed and said: 'Gentlemen, I am not here to play a part; you can not elect me; you can elect Mr. Trumbull, who is a good Republican. You put me in a false position if you use my name to the injury of the Republican party, and whoever does it is not my friend.' They then reluctantly acquiesced, and Mr. Trumbull was elected."

This is the most significant act in the merely personal history of Mr. Lincoln. It exhibited the self-control and equilibrium of his character, as well as his party fidelity. There is now before me a letter of his in which he announces his motto in political affairs, "Bear and forbear." This self-poise, self-abnegation, and forbearance enabled him to bring the ship of state safely through the stormy seas before him. He never labored for effect; there was nothing theatrical in him; he was not concerned about his personal relations to affairs; smiled when he was told that Seward was using him and getting all the glory. He sought nothing fantastical; but felt it to be his supreme duty to bring peace with honor to his distracted country.

A picturesque administration may please the unskillful, but it makes the judicious grieve. The machinery of government, like that of the human body, is usually working best when it is attracting no attention.

The bread thus thrown upon the waters by Mr. Lincoln in securing the election of Trumbull returned, and not after many days. But when he had these conversations it was unknown to him. To the suggestion he would certainly be selected as the next Senator, he quietly replied, "I don't know." But when the time came the Republican Convention unanimously nominated him for Senator—an act without precedent in our Senatorial history.

The debate followed. At that time, under the influence of a strong partisan enthusiasm, I felt that Lincoln had greatly the advantage. But upon reading the debate now, its moral bearings aside, as a mere intellectual feat, the advantage of either is not apparent. The argument of slavery is put with all the telling force of Douglas's vigorous mind and intense nature. He was a veritable "little giant."

Mr. Lincoln, as we have seen, remained in Cincinnati about a week, moving freely around. Yet not twenty men in the city knew him personally, or knew that he was here; not a hundred would have known who he was had his name been given them.

He came with the fond hope of making fame in a forensic contest with Reverdy Johnson. He was pushed aside, humiliated, and mortified. He attached to the innocent city the displeasure that filled his bosom, shook its dust from his feet, and departed never to return. How dark and impenetrable to him then was the thin veil soon to rise, revealing to him a resplendent future! He did return to the city, two years thereafter, with a fame wide as the continent, with the laurels of the Douglas contest on his brow, and the Presidency in his grasp. He returned, greeted with the thunder of cannon, the strains of martial music, and the joyous plaudits of thousands of citizens thronging the streets. He addressed a vast concourse on Fifth Street Market; was entertained in princely style at the Burnet House; and there received with courtesy the foremost citizens, come to greet this rising star.

The manner of the man was changed. The free conversation of unrestraint had given place to the vague phrase of the wary politician, the repose of ease to the agitation of unaccustomed elevation.

Two men have I known on the eve of a Presidential nomination, each expecting it—Chase and Lincoln. With each, but in different degrees, there was an all-absorbing egotism. To hear, every waking moment, one's hopes and prospects canvassed, develops in one the feeling that he is the most important thing in the universe. Accompanying this is a lofty exaltation of spirits; the blood mounts to the brain, and the mind reels in delirium. Pity the Presidential aspirant.

With high hope and happy heart Mr. Lincoln left Cincinnati after a three days' sojourn. But a perverse fortune attended him and Cincinnati in their intercourse. Nine months after Mr. Lincoln left us, after he had been nominated for the Presidency, when he was tranquilly waiting in his cottage home at Springfield the verdict of the people, his last visit to Cincinnati and the good things he had had at the Burnet House were rudely brought to his memory by a bill presented to him from its proprietors. Before leaving the hotel he had applied to the clerk for his bill; was told that it was paid, or words to that effect. This the committee had directed, but afterward neglected its payment. The proprietors shrewdly surmised that a letter to the nominee for the Presidency would bring the money.

The only significance in this incident is in the letter it brought from Mr. Lincoln, revealing his indignation at the seeming imputation against his honor, and his greater indignation at one item of the bill. "*As to wines, liquors, and cigars, we had none—absolutely none.* These last may have been in 'Room 15' by order of committee, but I do not recollect them at all."

Mr. Lincoln again visited Cincinnati on his way to Washington. His coming was not heralded by the roar of cannon, but it was greeted by an outpouring of the people such as no man here ever before or since has received; they thronged in countless thousands about the station, along the line of his march, covering the house-tops. They welcomed him with one continuous and unbroken storm of applause. Coming events were then casting their dark shadows before them. All men instinctively desired to look upon and cheer him who was to be their leader in the coming conflict.

There was an informal reception at the Burnet House, the people, in line, filing through and shaking his hand until a late hour in the evening. His manner was quiet, calm, resolute, and observant. All exaltation of feeling was gone. His reception amused and instructed him. As they passed before him, this one eagerly and enthusiastically grasped his hand, speaking out, "Be firm; don't back down." He was a good Republican. But this one takes his hand quietly, releases it slowly, while whispering, "The country expects a conservative administration." This is a Bell and Everett man. Another touches his hand with the tips of his fingers, and, with a curious gaze, passes on in silence. That is a Douglas man.

The reception over, Mr. Lincoln passes to his room to find his little son fretfully waiting his coming to be put to bed. The father lovingly takes him in his arms and retires to an adjoining room, undresses him, and puts him to bed. As he gazes upon the placid features of his sleeping child for a moment his mind turns from all around him and all before him, back to his quiet life and home, to the grave of the little one not with him. Its last sickness is before him; also the dream that warned him that his child could not live—the dream that ever came to him before coming calamity—that was once again to startle him, presaging his tragic end.

One may lift himself out of his early environment, but its impress is enduring.

About this weird and wonderful man—one of those unique characters that do not repeat themselves in history—is fast gathering a cloud of myth and legend, obscuring the real man. That we may retain some glimpses of this is the apology for these reminiscences.

THE AMERICAN COWBOY

DURING the last fifteen years the American cow-boy has occupied a place sufficiently important to entitle him to a considerable share of public attention. His occupation is unique. In the exercise of his function he is always a man on horseback. His duty as a worker in the cattle business is at times to ride over the range in order to see that straying cattle do not rove too far from the assigned limits of the herd of which he has charge; at times to drive the herd from one locality to another; and at times to "round up" the dispersed cattle, by which is meant to collect them together for the purpose of branding calves, or of selecting beef cattle, which latter are driven to railroad stations for shipment to market. The chief qualifications of efficiency in this calling are courage, physical alertness, ability to endure exposure and fatigue, horse-manship, and skill in the use of the lariat.

The original cow-boy of this country was essentially a creature of circumstance, and mainly a product of western and southwestern Texas. Armed to the teeth, booted and spurred, long-haired, and covered with the broad-brimmed sombrero—the distinctive badge of his calling—his personal appearance proclaimed the sort of man he was.

The Texas cow-boys were frontiersmen, accustomed from their earliest childhood to the alarms and the struggles incident to forays of Indians of the most ferocious and warlike nature. The section of the State in which they lived was also for many years exposed to incursions of bandits from Mexico, who came with predatory intent upon the herds and the homes of the people of Texas. The earrying of fire-arms and other deadly weapons was consequently a prevalent custom among them. And being scattered over vast areas, and beyond the efficient protection and restraints of civil law, they of necessity became a law unto themselves.

It is not a strange thing that such an occupation and such environment should have developed a class of men whom persons accustomed to the usages of cultivated society would characterize as ruffians of the most pronounced type. But among the better disposed of the Texas cow-boys, who constitute, it is believed, much more than a majority of them, there were true and trusty men, in whom the dangers and fortunes of their lives developed generous and heroic traits of character. The same experiences, however, led the viciously inclined to give free vent to the worst passions. Upon slight provocation they would shoot down a fellow-man with almost as little compunction as they fired upon the wild beasts.

But the peculiar characteristics of the Texas cow-boys qualified them for an important public service. By virtue of their courage and recklessness of danger, their excellent horsemanship, and skill in the use of fire-arms, and by virtue also of the influence which they have exerted upon their gentler brethren of the northern ranges, they have been an efficient instrumentality in preventing Indian outbreaks, and in protecting the frontier settlements of the entire range and ranch cattle area against predatory incursions and massacres by Indians. This has been a natural result of the fact that the cowboys constitute throughout that region a corps of mounted scouts, armed and equipped, twenty thousand strong. They traverse vast ranges, ford rivers, and search for cattle amid mountain fastnesses and in lurking-places of the river bottoms. No hostile movement could for a day escape their notice. It is certain that they have done much toward subduing a vast area to the arts of peace, and that an unarmed man may now travel alone throughout Wyoming, Dakota, Montana, and Idaho, and even in Texas, as safely as in the New England or the Middle States. As a pioneer of civilization the American cow-boy has therefore performed a public service which as fully entitles him to recognition as do the commercial results of his labors.

It is only twenty years since the discovery was made that between the line of settlement in Dakota, Nebraska, and Kansas at the east, and the Sierra Nevada and Coast ranges at the west, there was an area as large as the portion of the United States which is situated east of the Mississippi River, throughout which cattle could be raised and fattened on the open range, seeking their own food, water, and shelter without any aid from man, from the time they were dropped until they were in condition to be driven to a railroad station for shipment to market. This discovery, greater in its importance than the discovery of gold in California, or silver in Nevada, or petroleum in Pennsylvania, happened, according to the most reliable accounts, in this wise. Early in December, 1864, a government trader, with a wagon train of supplies drawn by oxen, was on his way west to Camp Douglas, in the Territory of Utah, but being overtaken on the Laramie Plains by an unusually severe snowstorm, he was compelled at once to go into winter-quarters. He turned his cattle adrift, expecting, as a matter of course, they would soon perish from exposure and starvation, but they remained about the camp, and as the snow was blown off the highlands the dried grass afforded them an abundance of forage. When the spring opened they were found to be in even better condition than when turned out to die four months previously. This at once led to the experiment of herding cattle on the northern ranges. But it was for years a slow and hazardous business. At that time it was the custom to allow the Indians upon the reservations to wander off during the summer months throughout the present range and ranch cattle area, in order that they might hunt buffaloes and other large game, and thus sustain themselves in their accustomed way until the approach of winter, when they returned to their reservations to be again provided for by the government. Permission to depart on these expeditions was always given upon the promise made to the military and civil officers of the United States that while absent they would be "good Indians." But as cattle were more easily caught than buffaloes, they found it greatly to their advantage to swoop down upon the herds, stampede them, and slaughter at their leisure as many as their needs re-

quired. Oftentimes, by way of amusement, they lifted the scalp of a stray cow-
boy. In many instances they massacred
whole camps of settlers, whose chief occupation was cattle herding. Occasionally
these "wards of the nation" so far forgot
themselves as to put on war-paint and set
the United States at defiance. The massacre of General Custer and his detachment, on the 25th of June, 1876, at Little
Big Horn, Dakota, near the present location of Fort Custer, led, however, to the
adoption of a more stringent policy on
the part of the United States government
with respect to requiring the Indians to
remain upon their reservations. During the five years following that tragic
event our valiant little army, widely
scattered over a vast area, had many
bloody encounters with the savages. At
last the spirit of resistance was broken,
and Montana, Idaho, and Dakota became
comparatively safe for the introduction
of the range cattle business, which had
already become known in Colorado and
Wyoming as a highly attractive enterprise and a speedy avenue to wealth. As
the work of the army drew nigh to completion the cow-boy galloped in, and became the mounted policeman of a vast
area, always on patrol.

But even after the red man had retired
to his reservation the lot of the cattle-
men was not entirely serene. From time
immemorial the horse-thief and the cattle-
thief seem to have been a sort of parasitic
growth upon frontier life, apparently begotten of its conditions. So it was on the
range. For several years the entire region from Kansas and Colorado at the
south to Montana and Dakota at the
north was infested by cattle-thieves. The
country afforded apparently illimitable
scope for this nefarious traffic. It seemed at one time somewhat a matter of doubt
as to which should prosper most, the
herdsmen or the cattle-thieves. As the
cattle of many proprietors intermingled
freely on vast ranges, it was comparatively easy and safe for a few marauders to
pounce down upon detached groups of
cattle here and there separated from the
main body of the herds, and drive them
off over some mountain range to a distant
valley or range where grazing was abundant, and there brand the calves with a
chosen hieroglyphic representative of a
separate ownership, and change the marks
of cattle already branded, by one or more

dashes with a red-hot iron. It was clearly seen that in order to stamp out this
new and threatening evil recourse must
be had to a drastic remedy. Accordingly
the various cattle associations organized
a detective service, composed mainly of
brave and trusty cow-boys, who were
charged with the duty of reconnoitring
the whole country in order to discover
the miscreants in their lairs, also to watch
for altered and surreptitious brands at the
railroad shipping stations. In this way a
large number of stolen cattle was recovered, and many cattle-thieves were apprehended. When the latter were arrested
within the limits of the efficient administration of the law, they were handed over
to the civil authorities. But when caught
beyond the limits of organized counties,
administrative justice was extemporized.
The cattle-men and the cow-boys themselves supplied judges, jurymen, witnesses, attorneys, constables, and execution-
ers. Sometimes a level-headed cow-boy
was placed upon the judicial bench. The
cattle-men assert that the extreme and
only penalty was never inflicted except
upon the clearest evidence of guilt.

When the verdict of guilty was pronounced, a short shrift, and a stout rope,
and a grave without a coffin or a winding-
sheet, ended the proceedings.

But a great change has taken place.
On the northern ranges cattle stealing
has become almost entirely a thing of the
past. States and Territories have enacted
laws requiring that all cattle shall be
branded, and that the brands shall be recorded in the office of the clerk of the
county in which the owner of each herd
resides. The brands are also published.
Thus the light of publicity is thrown upon
the whole range cattle business, and at
the same time it has acquired all those securities which characterize organized and
well-ordered commercial enterprises.

At first the raising of cattle on the
northern ranges was confined mainly to
settlers possessed of small means. But
soon men of enterprise and capital saw
that the placing of great herds on the
ranges of the north, as had been done for
years in Texas and in Mexico, would, under adequate protection, be attended with
great profit, for already railroads traversing or extending out into the Territories
afforded the facilities for transporting cattle to the three great primary cattle markets of the United States, viz., Chicago,

St. Louis, and Kansas City—Chicago being by far the largest—and thence to the markets of the world.

It was an enterprise which required both capital and courage. The State of Texas had for years been a prolific breeding ground for cattle. At that time cattle were worth on the ranges of that State but little more than their hides and tallow. Two-year-old steers could be purchased in almost unlimited numbers for from $3 50 to $4 50 a head. Besides, Texas had an army of cow-boys, who were acquainted with the Indian in all his ways, and who rather courted than refused a passage at arms with the savage. Here were therefore three material elements of success in a great undertaking—capital, cattle, and cow-boys. Intelligent enterprise came in and formed the combination, and not long afterward it became a matter of personal interest with the Indian to remain on his reservation all the year round. Speedily the Texas steer superseded the buffalo, and the cow-boy became the dominant power throughout New Mexico, Colorado, Wyoming, Montana, and the western portions of Dakota, Nebraska, and Kansas. Within the brief period of fifteen years the cordon of cattle interests was drawn so close around the Indian reservations that the monarch of the plains became "ye gentle savage."

As a general rule the ranch cattle business has, under good management, been wonderfully successful. Hundreds of men who a few years ago went into the business with exceedingly limited means have become "cattle kings," and now count their assets by hundreds of thousands and even by millions. In certain instances also women have embarked in the enterprise, and among the number are those who now rejoice in the sobriquet of "cattle queens."

The market value of the surplus product of the entire range and ranch cattle area during the year 1884 was about $40,000,000, aside from the consumption within that area. Besides, the increased value of herds during the year is estimated at quite as much more. Throughout that area the cattle business is the chief commercial enterprise; but as trade makes trade, it has been instrumental in creating important collateral and related trade interests. One of the most important results of this has been that the several transcontinental railroads have built up a large and profitable local traffic. The original conception of transcontinental traffic was that it would be confined almost entirely to "through business," but the local tonnage of the Northern Pacific Railroad during the year 1884 constituted ninety-five per cent. of its total tonnage, and the local tonnage of the Union Pacific Railroad constituted forty-three per cent. of its total tonnage.

The cow-boy of to-day, especially on the northern ranges, is of entirely different type from the original cow-boy of Texas. New conditions have produced the change. The range cattle business of Kansas, Nebraska, Colorado, Wyoming, Montana, and Dakota is, as already stated, a new business. Those engaged in it as proprietors are chiefly from the States situated east of the Missouri River and north of the Indian Territory. Among them are also many Englishmen, Scotchmen, Frenchmen, and Germans of large means, embracing titled men who have embarked in the business quite extensively. Many of these came to America originally as tourists or for the purpose of hunting buffaloes, but the attractiveness of the cattle business arrested them, and they have become virtually, if not through the act of naturalization, American herdsmen. Some of this class have, from the force of romantic temperament and the exhilaration of range life, themselves participated actively in the duties of the cowboy.

Organization, discipline, and order characterize the new undertakings on the northern ranges. In a word, the cattle business of that section is now and has from the beginning been carried on upon strictly business principles. Under such proprietorships, and guided by such methods, a new class of cow-boys has been introduced and developed. Some have come from Texas, and have brought with them a knowledge of the arts of their calling, but the number from the other States and the Territories constitutes a large majority of the whole. Some are graduates of American colleges, and others of collegiate institutions in Europe. Many have resorted to the occupation of cowboy temporarily and for the purpose of learning the range cattle business, with the view of eventually engaging in it on their own account, or in the interest of friends desirous of investing money in the enterprise.

The life of the cow-boy is always one of excitement and of romantic interest. His waking hours when "riding on trail" are spent in the saddle, and at night he makes his bed upon the lap of mother earth.

The great herds which are yearly driven out of Texas to the northern ranges usually embrace from 2500 to 4000 young cattle each, and the movement has since its beginning, about eighteen years ago, amounted to about 4,000,000 head, worth nearly $50,000,000. Each herd is placed in charge of a boss, with from eight to ten cow-boys, a provision wagon, and a cook. Four horses are supplied to each cow-boy, for the duty is an arduous one. The range cattle when away from their accustomed haunts are suspicious and excitable, and need to be managed with the greatest care to keep them from stampeding. When "on trail" they are "close herded" at nightfall, and all lie down within a space of about two acres. The cow-boys then by watches ride around them all night long. The sensible presence of man appears to give the animals a feeling of security.

The journey from southern Texas to Montana requires from four to six months. Herds are also driven from Oregon and Washington Territory to Wyoming and eastern Montana. It is impossible for one who has not had actual experience in "riding on trail" to imagine the difficulties involved in driving a large herd of wild cattle over mountain ranges, across desert lands where in some cases food and water are not found for many miles, and where streams must be crossed which are liable to dangerous freshets.

A large part of the northern ranges is embraced in the area which Silas Bent, an accomplished meteorologist, terms "the birthplace of the tornado." Thunder and lightning are here frequent, and they are especially terrifying to range cattle. The most thrilling incident in the life of the cow-boy occurs on the occasion of a thunder-storm at night. Such an occurrence is thus described from personal observation by Mr. William A. Baillie Grohman, an English writer:

"On the approach of one of these violent outbursts the whole force is ordered on duty; the spare horses—of which each man has always three, and often as many as eight or ten—are carefully fed and tethered, and the herd is 'rounded up,' that is, collected into as small a space as possible, while the men continue to ride around the densely massed herd. Like horses, cattle derive courage from the close proximity of man. The thunder peals, and the vivid lightning flashes with amazing brilliancy, as with lowered heads the herd eagerly watch the slow, steady pace of the cow-ponies, and no doubt derive from it a comforting sense of protection. Sometimes, however, a wild steer will be unable to control his terror, and will make a dash through a convenient opening. The crisis is at hand, for the example will surely be followed, and in two minutes the whole herd of 4000 head will have broken through the line of horsemen and be away, one surging, bellowing mass of terrified beasts. Fancy a pitch-dark night, a pouring torrent of rain, the ground not only entirely strange to the men, but very broken, and full of dangerously steep water-courses and hollows, and you will have a picture of cow-boy duty on such a night. They must head off the leaders. Once fairly off, they will stampede twenty, thirty, and even forty miles at a stretch, and many branches will stray from the main herd. Not alone the reckless rider, rushing headlong at breakneck pace over dangerous ground in dense darkness, but also the horses, small, insignificant beasts, but matchless for hardy endurance and willingness, are perfectly aware how much depends upon their speed that night, if it kills them. Unused till the last moment remains the heavy cowhide 'yuirt,' or whip, and the powerful spurs with rowels the size of five-shilling pieces. Urged on by a shout, the horses speed alongside the terrified steers until they manage to reach the leaders, when, swinging around, and fearless of horns, they press back the bellowing brutes till they turn them. All the men pursuing this manœuvre, the headlong rush is at last checked, and the leaders, panting and lashing their sides with their tails, are brought to a stand, and the whole herd is again 'rounded up.'"

Throughout the northern ranges sobriety, self-restraint, decent behavior, and faithfulness to duty are enjoined upon the cow-boys. A great improvement is also observable in the cow-boys of Texas. Deeds of violence among them are now few. The *morale* of the entire range and ranch cattle business of the United States now compares favorably with that of other large enterprises.

WITH THE BLUECOATS ON
THE BORDER

RIDE! on through the rush of the rain coming down in sheets from the unbroken gray of the sky; on over the dreary desolation of the prairie, now splashing through wide pools of water, now floundering ankle-deep through the thick, tenacious mud of the wide trail, not a living creature in sight, nothing but the brown grass of the plains stretching for miles to the misty horizon. Ride! down the slippery sides of the "coulees," through the foaming waters of the streams swirling and rushing along in yellow torrents. Up, good horses, up the steep banks, slipping and stumbling over rain-loosened stones; on over the prairie again. Ride! on toward the solitary ranch just looming through the mist away beyond there, the water streaming from our oil-skins, dripping from our soft, wide-brimmed hats, and running down the flanks of our tired horses. Ride! on up to the wide-open door of the rough mud-roofed cabin, its two lonely inhabitants—flannel-shirted, heavily booted government teamsters— standing expectantly in front. Rustle, boys, rustle! fresh horses to carry us on to the distant river and to the boat that is to take us back again to home and friends, our only chance, perhaps, for days, if not weeks, for the season is late, and the river falling in spite of the heavy rains. The brimming cup of sweet warm milk, handed to us with ready hospitality, fresh from the cows standing in the fenced-off space behind the ranch, we drink thankfully, and then on again through the steadily increasing downpour of the rain. Ride! through the rows of sage-brush, glistening silvery blue in the wet, onward and still onward, to the bare hills, miles in front of us, beyond which we know the river is swiftly flowing. Ride! guided by the endless line of poles supporting the military telegraph line that runs from the lonely frontier garrison we rode out from at daybreak this morning. Ride! past the long train of wagons, creeping slowly toward us, drawn by their patient long-horned "bull teams," and freighted with supplies for Uncle Sam's "boys in blue," some of whom, trudging along through the mud, or peering at us from under the canvas covering of the foremost wagon, wave their hats in greeting to us. A mounted officer—rubber-coated, glistening wet—hails us, and wheeling his horse about, gallops alongside of us, with polite request to forward a forgotten message to the little outpost we are bound for. Thanking us, and with hearty "good-by, good luck," he canters back again, riding with the free, easy, firm seat of the American cavalryman; and "slacking not speed nor

RIDE THROUGH THE STORM.

drawing rein," we turn and look back at the already distant wagons as they wind along the trail, their white covers almost melting into the prevailing moist gray of the atmosphere, and relieving only against the dark expanse of prairie. Ride! up through gently rising openings in the hills now, their bare, rugged sides rising high above us, the rills of water rushing down them seaming and scarring them, and spreading deep sloughs of red, sticky mud in our way. Ride! hour after hour, until with a final spurt we cross the butte in front of us, and there—broad, curving gracefully through the deep valley below, shining like purest silver in a sudden burst of light that breaks through the cloud masses above—there flows the "Wild Missouri." Hurrah! on once more! down the hill-side and out over the short stretch of green plain to the brink of the stream, and wet, dead tired, hungry, and thirsty, we pull up our smoking, panting horses at the log cabin of the soldier telegraph operator, beyond which, nestling in the shelter of cottonwood and willow trees, gleam the white walls of half a dozen tents, marking the camp of the little detachment of bluecoats, a solitary outpost of the garrison forty miles back of us over the prairie.

"No boat yet, but expect it every hour. Telegraphed at 4 A.M. from above. Probably stuck on a sand-bar. Water pretty low, and navigation slow. Come and take something!"—which hospitable offer of the young subaltern commanding the camp, wet and chilled through as we are, is gratefully accepted, and we make ourselves as comfortable as the prevailing dampness and the mosquitoes will permit. With the gathering shades of evening, and as the storm clouds are drifting away, a distant throbbing sound breaks through the calm air, and simultaneously with the long-drawn cry of "Stea-ea-eambo-o-oat!" from the blue-coated loungers on the bank, the long-expected stern-wheeler, its high chimneys rolling out volumes of smoke and showers of bright sparks, flashing like fire-flies in the gloaming, glides slowly into view, and with much ringing of bells from the pilot-house and much vociferation and hard cursing from a very energetic and hoarse-voiced mate, comes to a stop alongside the bank, and

is made fast by stout hawsers to convenient trees. Bidding farewell to our kindly young host, we seek "the seclusion that our cabin grants," and soon forget the fatigue and discomforts of the day in deep and refreshing slumber.

Early the next morning, with the first light of day, our journey down the great river begins. Onward, day after day, we steam through the wilderness, traversing scenes of weird desolation and savage beauty. On through the great high hills rising abruptly from the water's edge; on through the "Bad Lands," with the strange, fantastically shaped "buttes" and turreted heights, pile upon pile, brightly colored in bands of red, purple, black, and yellow, rising like walls of ancient and ruined fastnesses of some by-gone and long-forgotten race of giants. Down the river, now rushing rapidly through narrow banks, now spreading, broken with

A SOLDIER'S WELCOME.

shoals and sand-bars, far out on all sides, a mile or more in width; down the river, gradually opening up the bottom lands, the deep ravines and "coulees" running back into the hills; sometimes we see deer or antelope feeding on the banks, or rushing madly away in alarm at the approach of the noisy, smoking monster. At night we "tie up" at convenient places, for navigation is dangerous through a country where there are no light-houses or warning beacons, and on a river where the channel is so constantly changing. As the light fades away in the west we slacken speed and run under the high banks, where the "roosters," as the deck hands are called, scramble up through the loose sand, dragging the heavy ropes behind them, and making them fast to trees, or to spars buried deep in the soft earth. Sometimes we stop at a "wood-yard" where some "squaw-man"—i. e., white man with Indian wife—or some half-breed, solitary dwellers in the wilderness, turn an honest penny now and then by the sale of wood to the occasional passing steamer. Many of these "wood-hawks" are honest men, no doubt, but many of them are desperate characters, leading a lawless life, and as brutal in their instincts and as dangerous as the wild red men, their neighbors, and often connected with them by ties of blood through the rather loose marriage ties of savage life. At one of the little landing-places we hear rumors of a raid by Vigilants on the desperadoes and horse-thieves who have established their haunts along the banks of the river and its tributaries, and for a long time have endangered the lives and property of the honest settlers and travellers through the sparsely settled country south of the great stream. A band of them had carried their audacity to such an extent as to attack the escort of an army paymaster *en route* to a military post to pay the troops stationed there, and although they failed in their object, at least one of the soldiers guarding the treasure had met with his death in the discharge of his duty while protecting the property of the government.

Smoke has been seen rising over the trees down the river, vague rumors of a fight below seem to fill the air, and the feeling of excitement communicates itself to our little group of passengers, and as the boat swings out again into the swift yellow current and continues on her voyage down-stream, we gather along her low rails, looking out curiously and anxiously ahead at the high, sandy, tree-covered banks on either side. Rounding a long point of land running out into the river, a call from the pilot-house attracts our attention to a blackened, smoking heap of ashes on the left bank—all that is left of a ranch that had stood there—and a short distance further down we slow up a little at the still burning ruins of another house. "It's the Jones boys' ranch," says the mate. "By Jiminy the cow-boys is makin' a terrible clean sweep of the kentry." That they have not been long gone is evident. Two half-charred wagons stand in the "corral," the wooden fence of which is brightly burning, the flames licking the edge of a great wood-pile that even as we pass bursts into flames. In a small field of waving corn joining a potato patch the carcass of a mule is lying, while right on the bank, the red blood still flowing from a hole in its head, a large dog—a hound—is stretched lifeless. Near a pile of débris, which may have been a kitchen or other out-house of some kind, for a pot or two and a tin camp kettle are hanging from the low fire-seared branches of a tree hard by, a few chickens, shrilly cackling, are huddled together. No other sign of life is visible, and as we proceed, the quiet of the wilderness is broken only by the snort of our steam-pipes and the thump, thump, of our great wheel beating up the muddy waters. Suddenly there is a movement among the "roosters" on the deck below; they are gazing with bated breath and blanched faces at something on the river's bank. Follow the direction of their gaze, and peer into the dense thicket where, above the matted willows growing up from the black ooze, that dead tree raises its white, barkless branches like skeleton arms, as if in fearful exultation over the dreadful fruit it bears. Almost hidden from our sight by the tangle of underbrush and low trees, hanging there motionless and still, something formless and shadowy in the gloom of the jungle, something indistinct, but fearful in its mystery and silence, a silence rendered yet more appalling by the hoarse croaks of the black-winged ravens, ill-omened carrion birds, circling above the thicket, and fluttering on the topmost branches of the blasted tree.

"Look! look! down thar by them cottonwoods! that's them! that's the cow-

THE VIGILANTS.

boys!" Half hidden in a mass of wild rose-bushes, backed by the gray trunks and graceful feathery foliage of the poplars, a group of men and horses is standing. We gather close up to the rail, eager to see the dread horsemen, the result of whose avenging ride we have witnessed but a short half-hour ago. As the current takes the boat close inshore, and we approach nearer and nearer, they present an interesting tableau. Most of them have dismounted and are standing at their horses' heads waist-deep in the weeds and wild flowers, bronzed-faced, resolute-looking men, unconsciously picturesque in costume and attitude; bright-barrelled Winchesters swing across their high-pommelled saddles, on which is bound the scanty baggage of the cow-boy, while a few pack-mules quietly crop the grass a few paces in their rear under the care of their driver. They are evidently under some discipline, for no one else moves as a tall, handsome, blond-bearded man, flannel-shirted, high-booted, with crimson silk kerchief tied loosely, sailor fashion, around his sunburned neck, advances to the water's edge, and with courteous wave of broad-brimmed hat hails the boat. Clang! goes the gong; the big wheel stops. The stranger politely requests information about the purchase of some supplies, and inquires as to the news up the river. Many on board recognize him for a man of wealth and education well known in the Territory, but nothing is said as to the errand of himself and his men in this distant wild region. During our parley his men remain quietly at their posts, and when their leader, his questions answered, returns toward them, and we move on again, we can see them mount and ride off over the hills in a straggling, dust-enveloped little column.

Down the river, now slowly and cautiously scraping over the wide sand-bars, now swiftly gliding along, aided by the rapid-flowing current; down the river through the Country of Hell, with its broad desert plains and barren brown hills, inky black where the moving clouds cast their shadows; down the river past old abandoned Indian trading posts fast crumbling into ruins, past the lonely military telegraph station, where we learn of the passage of a "dug-out," with its crew of fugitive desperadoes flying from the wrath of the cow-boys; down the river between perpendicular sand-banks, crum-

bling away at the touch of the "rollers" caused by the passage of our boat, scaring up flocks of wild-geese and swift-flying, blue-winged heron; down the river through lovely prairies covered with waving grasses and gayly colored wild flowers, into the Indian country, until, looking across one of the long, flat, outrunning points of land that mark the constantly recurring curves of the river, there, shining in the morning sun, the distant buildings of the military post, our destination, gleam bright under the blue, white, and scarlet folds of the national standard floating gracefully out from its tall pole against the deep warm purple of the sky beyond. Hundreds of Indian tepees' are scattered over the wide plain, and at our approach we can see the inmates hurrying to the banks to watch the arrival of the great steamer. Wild-looking savages, their faces smeared with streaks of bright vermilion or orange, are watering their horses, their gaudily clothed forms reflecting straight down in the mirror-like surface of the water; some half-clad lads, who, lying prone upon their bellies, and leaning far over the high banks, have been fishing in the stream, pull in their lines and race along the shore, their coarse black hair floating out behind, and their bronze-colored naked limbs moving with untrammelled ease, as they easily keep pace with the boat; young bucks mounted on half-tamed ponies gallop along and mingle with the throng; the white sombreros and light blue uniforms of the Indian police contrast strangely with the party-colored rags of their fellow-savages. As we slowly paddle up to the landing we make our preparations to land, recognizing our acquaintances in the little group of shoulder-strapped bluecoats near the ambulance, which has just been drawn up to the bank by its team of four strong mules, and are soon exchanging greetings with our friends, who receive us with the frank, kindly, ready hospitality of the American soldier.

"Here, sergeant, this baggage to my quarters, please. Now, then, all aboard! Fire away, driver!" And with crack of long-thonged whip and simultaneous lashing out of four pair of iron-shod heels, away we go over the prairie to the post. Hi, mules! rattle along through the tepees, dusky faces peering through the dark openings in their sides; swing around the corner past the agent's house, into the broad road by the agency buildings, past the trader's stores with the lounging red-skins sunning themselves, leaning against the rough, mud-plastered walls, or going in and out of the open doorway; doff your hats, gentlemen, to smiling, prettily dressed ladies driving by in pony-cart. Rattle along, mules, past the log huts of the Indian scouts, with the little half-naked black-eyed children scurrying hastily away to the shelter of their roofs, to where the squaws are seated on the ground by the fires in the open air or engaged in some menial work—past the group of white-sheeted, painted-faced young bucks gambling for cartridges on the road-side—out again on the dusty plain through outlying tepees—up to the trim, clean "adobe" barracks of the soldiers, looking over the parade—past the many-barrelled Gatlings, grimly pointing toward the village, to the "adobe" houses of "The Row." Swing around! past the guard-house, the white-gloved sentry rattling his glittering rifle smartly to shoulder in salute, and bring up at the hospitably opened door of our genial host's quarters, where soon nearly all the officers of the little garrison are gathered, eager for news of what is going on in the outer world, and full of kindly offers of their services. The events that have taken place up the river are already known to them: four men had been killed, and their bodies consumed by the fire, at the fight at the Joneses' ranch, others had been captured and hung, and some—number unknown —had escaped. Orders have been received from below to look out for the fugitives, as some of them are suspected of being members of the band that "jumped" the paymaster some weeks ago. The scouts are out even now, but have not been heard from as yet, and these horse-thieves are so well acquainted with the country that, provided they don't get starved out somewhere, it will be a difficult matter to catch

them. In a low whitewashed room in a rough log cabin by the post-trader's stores dinner is served for the bachelors' mess, and we fall to heartily, and thoroughly enjoy the bountiful and palatable fare, after the monotony of the scanty *menu* of the boat with our sometimes not overnice table companions.

Retreat has been sounded; the flag, opening out its graceful folds, comes waving down the tall staff simultaneously with the thunder of the evening gun; and we cross the parade for a stroll out along the banks of the creek that flows tranquilly over its sandy bed in the deep ravine in rear of the post. Although the sun has disappeared, the western sky is all aglow with his light, and it is the pleasantest time of the day, this long hour of Northern twilight, before the shadows of night close in on the fair landscape before us. Down below us, where the

A "WOOD-HAWK."

creek spreads out into a wide and deep pool, some young Indian girls are bathing in its cool waters, and their laughing voices rise up melodiously in the still air. Some squaws are squatted along the edge filling their water jars or dipping their squalling little pappooses, clothes and all, into the stream.

Following the path along the bluff toward the high ground in our front, stopping for a moment at some graves fenced in with neat white palings, where some poor fellows are silently "awaiting the last reveille," as we see is inscribed in rude characters on the little head-boards, we climb to the top of the mound, and, turning, look back at the scene below us. At our feet lies the little fort, with its square parade-ground flanked by the "Officers' Row" opposite the barracks of the men, and at either end by the guard-house and quartermaster's stores and offices and the post hospital. We can see the soldiers gathered about the doors of their quarters, while in the open space between the fort and the agency buildings, standing white and straggling beyond, and rising above the tepees grouped near by, some young Indians are racing their horses, yelling and whooping like fiends. Still further beyond, where we can see the shining, curving river, and the creek emptying its waters into it, the village is lying, the smoke from its many fires melting into the air above. Very gradually the light fades, gray shadows are stealing over the prairie, where the great herd of agency cattle is slowly moving; the platforms on which the red-skins deposit the bodies of their dead stand out on the mounds black against the sky, and the weird, sobbing wail of mourning women strikes discordantly on our ears. Lights begin to twinkle in the barracks, and, ringing out clear and mellow, the bugle is sounding "first call" for tattoo.

A day or two pass quietly and uneventfully. We visit the range, and waste some ammunition at the big targets with the men, and sometimes, the regular practice over, some of the ladies—no mean shots—join us at the "butts." We roam about the village and agency, and scrape acquaintance with many of our red brethren, sometimes sitting in their tepees and endeavoring to learn as much as we can of the mysteries of the sign-language, and to master some of their guttural phrases.

One warm sunshiny afternoon, two or three days after our arrival at the post, as we lounge in a rocking-chair of the "sitting-room" of the quarters, enjoying a quiet smoke and discussing the news from a pile of journals just arrived by the semi-weekly mail, which has to be brought on horseback or by buckboard nearly a hundred miles over the prairie from the nearest stage station, the oft-repeated tap-tap-r-r-ratatattat of the drum over by the commandant's office, and a subdued sound of voices near the barracks, rouse us up from our half-reclining attitude, and we step to the window to see what reason there is for the unusual stir. Two sweat-covered horses stand with heaving flanks, heads bowed down, necks outstretched, before the door of the office, and an Indian scout squats on the ground beside them, holding the bridles loosely in his hand. In spite of his air of stolid indifference, his disordered dress—loose gray shirt, mud-splashed blue regulation trousers, bead-embroidered, yellow-fringed, and betasselled buckskin leggings—shows that he has ridden hard and fast. Through the open door, standing hat in hand by the commandant's desk, who, seated in his office chair, half turns around and looks up into the speaker's face, we see the half-breed chief of the scouts as he eagerly and somewhat excitedly makes his report. The door of the quarters next to ours opens, and a young officer, booted and in field dress, great-coat over his arm, revolver swinging in its leather holster at his side, comes forth and hurries across the parade, calling out to us in answer to our hail: "The scouts have corralled the thieves up on the Birdtail, and we're going to fetch them in."

Over by the barracks the men detailed for the duty are busily engaged preparing for the march, rolling up their great gray blankets, slinging on haversacks and canteens, and buckling the canvas prairie belts filled with brass-cylindered, leaden-headed cartridges. One by one they emerge from the doorways of their quarters, and, "falling in," rifle in hand, answer to their names as the roll is called by the sergeant. Rattling up from the corral come the wagons that are to convey the soldiers across the prairie to the place to which the bandits have been traced.

At dawn next morning, accompanying the commandant, we drive out to the scene of the hunt, for veritable hunt it is, and that after the noblest of all game —human beings imaged like ourselves. Where a high bluff overhangs for miles a wide morass, a thick, almost impenetrable jungle of dwarf willows, so matted and interlaced that the light of day scarcely can penetrate through the dense covering of their leaves, is the place where the scouts have first discovered signs of the fugitives. Beyond flows the river, so that their skiff, having been found and captured, under cover of the night, by the chief scout, who, swimming

for, with the exception of a bloody coat and a revolver, nothing more is found after the capture of some miserable, desperate wretches, who, making but slight resistance, surrender on recognizing the government uniform. Miserable-looking wretches

FAIR SHARP-SHOOTERS.

and wading the stream from the opposite shore, had towed the boat away from its hiding-place, the escape of the desperadoes is cut off by way of the water. We find the bluff picketed along its whole extent by the troops, some of whom stand, rifle in hand, looking out over the swamp, from which the mists of the morning are slowly rising, while others are gathered about an occasional small fire, warming their chilled frames and hastily cooking a frugal breakfast.

Down in the thickets the scouts and some of the soldiers, aided by their savage allies, are beating the bush, and scattering rifle-shots and a yell now and then from the Indians indicate that the trail is hot. Hot it may be, but the pursuit is soon given up,

they are, as, guarded by the vigilant soldiers, they are marched into the post. Wild-eyed and haggard, covered with mud and dirt, their brier-torn clothing hanging in shreds from their frames, emaciated with hunger, one of them with bullet-torn arm bound in blood-stained bandages, their abject appearance well proves that "the way of the transgressor is hard," as they are securely confined in the lock-up of the guard-house, there to await what fate has in store for them.

The ripple of excitement on the usually calm surface of life in the remote frontier fort caused by the raid has subsided, and the garrison settles down into the monotonous routine of its every-day work. Hay and wood for the coming long winter are being cut and brought in, quarters are repaired; sometimes we drive out for a shot at the prairie-chickens, or visit the agency, watching the distribution of rations to the Indians, or going about with the agent or his

assistants, studying the methods by which the savage is being schooled in the way of life of the
white man.   And a strange sight it is to see
one or two hundred fantastically attired
braves, working away under the hot sun
with pick and shovel at the great ir-
rigating ditch which is to convert
the grass-grown plain into a garden of plenty.

The time for our depart-
ure is at hand. From the
top of the guard-house
the lookout has sig-
nalled   "Smoke
'way up the riv-
er,"   where
the boat,

probably the last
one down this season,
is slowly making its way
through the now almost
unnavigable channel.   We
make our farewell calls on the
families of our kind entertain-
ers, and once more climbing
into the waiting ambulance,
rattle away to the landing-place.   It is late in the evening, and the river shines
like fluid gold under the bright light of the sky; before us the land opposite stretches
away flat to the round buttes on the far horizon; naked trees, where a fire has

A HOT TRAIL.

THE CAPTIVES.

scorched their limbs, rise up out of the purple undergrowth, and stand out against the sky in fantastic shapes; far out over the plain some figures, men and horses, are moving.

Patiently we wait near a huge pile of buffalo-robes and other freight; the usual curve in the river prevents a sight of the steamboat, but we can see her smoke rising over the trees where she seems to be stationary. "Stuck on the bar, I'll bet my boots!" says a great, long-limbed teamster, stretched at full length on the pile of skins. "Injin Charlie told me this mornin' that he an' Chicken waded the river at the P'int yesterday. I don't believe she'll git down as far as this to-night; the water is terrible low."

Deeper and deeper grow the shades of evening. The moon rises red and angry,

and casts long, quivering reflections down into the water. "She cometh not, he said," parodies a musical voice from the wagon. "You will have to put up with our rude frontier accommodations for another night, I fancy." It looks, indeed, as if it were useless to tarry any longer to-night, so, nothing loath, as far as enjoying "the rude frontier accommodations" for another night is concerned, we drive back to the post in the darkness. It is late on the following afternoon before the boat finally gets over the bar and steams up to the landing, and we once more bid farewell to our good friends, this time really to leave them.

Down the river once more, sometimes aground for hours on mud-banks and sand-bars, literally wading over them inch by inch with the help of our huge

GOOD-BY.

spars, sometimes running free and swift with the deep, fast-flowing current; down the river past more Indian villages and trading posts, past green hills, white-streaked where the gypsum crops through, reminding one of the English downs; across the reservation lines, past a "ranch" or two, outlying pioneer posts of westward-marching civilization; down the river into boundless tracts of oats and grain and great waving fields of corn; past large, prosperous-looking farms and great ranches, on under the iron railway bridge to the levee of the busy little frontier city.

And now as we stand on the rear platform of the "sleeper" on the Atlantic Express this fine evening, looking back over the long perspective of the rails as we fly over them homeward bound, we take back with us to the far East grateful remembrances of the kind and "comradely" treatment we have met with at the hands of the American soldier, and a thorough appreciation of the hardships and privations, the dangers and vicissitudes, of his life on the wild frontier—an honorable life of faithful performance of his arduous duties and of devotion to his colors.

GO WEST YOUNG MAN

NOT far from the Missouri River, in the northwestern corner of Iowa, is a colony of Englishmen who have undertaken, with moderate capital and infinite pluck, to build up their fortunes in this country. Their enterprise is new—just old enough, however, to furnish satisfactory evidence that agriculture is, when properly undertaken, one of the most profitable industries in this country. Their number at present is about three hundred, and many additional members are expected this spring.

This colony, often called the Close Colony, owes its origin to three enterprising brothers, respectively James, William, and Fred Close. One of these came out here in 1876 to row in the Cambridge boat crew at the Centennial Regatta. Some of the crew fell sick, however, and they were forced to leave Philadelphia and retire to Cape May to recuperate. There the young Englishman met his destiny, and closed his boating career by an engagement to marry. About this time the young lady's father advised young Close to take a trip West before returning to England, assuring him that if he should do so, he would be satisfied that this country offered stronger inducements to a young man than any across the water. Accordingly, he went West, and made up his mind to go into farming. He immediately drew his two brothers into the enterprise, and together they began on a large scale. At the same time they took steps to induce their friends in England to join them. Though the enterprise is not three years old, they control at present some two hundred thousand acres of land.

The young men who make up this community are, for the most part, graduates of Oxford or Cambridge. On one farm I met two tall and handsome young farmers whose uncle had been a distinguished member of Parliament. The last time I had seen them was in a London drawing-room. This time they tramped me through the mud and manure of the barn-yard to show me some newly bought stock. They were boarding with a Dutch farmer at three dollars per week in order to learn practical farming. Both were thoroughly contented, and looking forward to the future with pleasure.

Another young farmer whom I noticed on horseback with top-boots, flannel shirt, sombrero, and belt-knife, was pointed out to me as the grandson of the author of *Paley's Theology.* He was attending a cattle auction at Lemars, Iowa.

There, too, was a son of Thomas Bayley Potter, the distinguished honorary secretary of the Cobden Club, and M.P. for Rochdale, who had come out only to take a look at the place, but who so fell in love with the life that he decided to invest. One had been an admiral in the royal navy, another had been connected with a Shanghai bank. There was a brother to Lord Ducie, not to speak of future baronets, viscounts, and honorables. These young men had all been attracted here by their love of a free, active life, and the knowledge that they would enter a society congenial to their tastes and early associations.

Although differing widely from "Tom" Hughes's Tennessee colony, this Iowa community has accomplished (without any special agreement between the members) an undertaking which combines the profits of farming with the out-door sports so dear to an Englishman.

They have the very best ground for fox-hunting in the world—a rolling prairie with a creek here and there. Every colonist makes it his chief care, after buying his farm, to breed a good hunter for the steeple-chases. They have regular meets for fox or "paper" hunts, as the case may be. They last year opened a racing track, and wound up the races with a grand ball. The event was a grand success, and partners were brought even from St. Paul, 270 miles to the north, to grace the occasion.

Their relations with the Close Brothers are very simple, and entirely of a business nature. After a desire has been expressed to join the colony, and the firm have decided that they are worthy to be admitted, they are required to pay $250 as a species of initiation fee. This is about five per cent. on the first investment, and is a commission charged to each new colonist. In return, they contract for putting up houses, building wells, purchasing land and implements, etc., and furnishing advice whenever called upon. It is something in the nature of a lawyer's fee for future consultations. The tax is saved over and over again in the security the stranger obtains against all manner of exorbitant charges. Sharp as down-Easters are reputed to be, they are mere beginners compared to a Western land agent.

Thus we have an example of co-operation on a large scale that works perfectly, and has grown up from the conditions of the colony without any previous theorizing on the subject. The head of the colony buys for all at wholesale with a large discount. He sells at retail without charging the colonists anything but a nominal commission for his service. Herein lies one secret of the power and prosperity of this colony. They can combine for purchase; they can combine for contracts in working their estates on a large scale; they can combine for special rates in the shipment of their produce to Chicago, St. Paul, or St. Louis. The single colonist has not these advantages so pronounced, and above all does not enjoy the social advantage of being among people of his own tastes and home associations.

Now, then, for the dollars and cents of the matter. First locate the place on the map, to see what facilities Lemars and the northwestern section of Iowa have as a railroad centre. Note the Sioux City and St. Paul Railroad to St. Paul; note the Chicago, Milwaukee, and St. Paul, the Chicago and Northwestern, and the Illinois Central competing for the traffic to Chicago; note the convenience to the Missouri and St. Louis; note that it is on the edge of the cattle country on the west, and the grain on the east, lying on the line of thoroughfare between the Atlantic and Pacific. The soil is rich and deep, and there are no stones or tree stumps. You can run your furrow from the Missouri to the Mississippi if you choose, and find few impediments, except a house, and now and then a stream. Then take into account that the population of the vicinity is thrifty and peaceable, the labor market reasonable, and the ordinary conveniences of life in every store.

Here is a practical example of what can be done to-day in this neighborhood. I shall take a high figure for the price of land, and average figures for yield per acre:

Permanent Expenditure for Farm of 160 Acres, supposed to be started in 1880.

New land, 160 acres, at $5 per acre........		$800
House, 16 by 22, complete		300
Stabling, yards, and well		150
Farm implements:		
Two breaking ploughs..............	$35	
Two stirring ploughs	25	
Two corn cultivators	60	
Two harrows.....................	20	
Mower and reaper	100	
Other implements	85	325
Stove and other furniture................		100
Six good farm-horses....................		600
Two wagons and harnesses...............		200
		$2475

This, then, is the first cost of equipping 160 acres of excellent prairie land, about five miles at the most from the railroad. I have seen just such a farm, and can vouch for the figures. The house that is put up for $300 is a small frame one, with two rooms on the ground-floor, and two low-ceiling rooms up stairs. It is painted, and has, of course, windows and a chimney. I have made no charge for breaking land, because a man can break 140 acres for himself between May and July, and no doubt will do so.

Now, then, for the first year's expenses and returns:

Expenditure.

Seed for 40 acres put in flax............	$60 00
Seed for 20 acres put in corn...........	2 50
Labor and expense for sowing and reaping above...............................	100 00
Taxes on 160 acres	18 00
	$180 50

Returns.

40 acres flax, yielding 7 bushels per acre, at $1 per bushel	$280 00
20 acres corn, yielding 35 bushels, at 18 cents per bushel......................	126 00
Returns in 1880............	$406 00
Expenditure in 1880	180 50
	$225 50

Corn has yielded more than 100 bushels to the acre on older ground, and averages frequently sixty bushels to the acre. Flax has yielded as much as thirteen bushels to the acre. It is an exhausting crop, as a rule, but does no harm to the soil when sown on new breaking. But to continue:

Second Year (say 1881)—*Expenditure.*

174 bushels seed, for 100 acres wheat, at 85 cents per bushel..................	$147 90
Seed for 20 acres corn.................	2 50
50 bushels seed for 20 acres oats, at 25 cents per bushel.....................	12 50
Labor	175 00
Harvesting and threshing expenses......	170 00
Taxes................................	18 00
	$525 90

Returns.

100 acres wheat, yielding 17 bushels per acre, at 85 cents per bushel.........	$1445 00
20 acres corn, yielding 60 bushels per acre, at 20 cents per bushel.........	240 00
20 acres oats, yielding 40 bushels per acre, at 25 cents per bushel........	200 00
	$1885 00

At the end of the second year, the account stands thus:

Returns $1885 00
Expenditure (without counting cost of
living) 525 90
                                   —————
                                   $1359 10

—equivalent to 54 per cent. on the capital invested.

Now, then, you can go on putting in your wheat for the next year, and calculate your profits in the same way to five or ten years ahead. You must not be misled, however, by my figures, into supposing that any one can guarantee a big crop. I have taken average figures, neither very high nor very low, for yield and price. The profits, however, are so large, on an average crop, that a man can afford to suffer a bad harvest every ten years without feeling his loss very much. Then, again, crop or no crop, the value of his land is steadily increasing, so that in three years he may make enough from the sale of it to move somewhere else to advantage.

I have shown, in a rough way, the profit arising from farming in grain. The element of risk attending farming can be largely diminished by undertaking stock-raising at the same time. This is perhaps the most profitable business in the West to-day, and bids fair to become more so in the immediate future. There are two principal ways of making money in stock. The first is by raising the animal on your own account, and shipping it East; the other is by taking full-grown cattle from the plains, and fattening them for the market by contract. Both these methods are profitable, according to the surroundings.

The favorable conditions for stock-raising are as follows. The prairie grass is excellent in quality, being of the blue-joint species, and very abundant. I have driven through it when it has been higher than the heads of those sitting upon the seats of the wagon. It is cut, of course, when it is comparatively short, and you can have it stacked at one dollar a ton for winter use. There is plenty of free range for cattle all summer. There are no fences, and a boy with a pony and dogs can take care of 500 or 600 head, or 1500 sheep, for five dollars a month. There is absolutely no disease known among the herds of that region, as was well exhibited during the last year, when particular questioning upon that subject took place

all over the State. The estimate I give is based on actual experience, and includes all charges, such as rent for the use of farm, cost of keep and labor, salt, medicine, and interest at six per cent. on capital expended. I also make allowance for ordinary mortality. The profits deduced, therefore, are net.

Estimate of Expenses.

50 heifers, at $18 75, bought in spring.. $937 50
1 bull............................. 105 00
First year's expenses:
    Keep of 51 head, at $3 93 per head.. 200 43
    Keep of 40 calves, at $2 37 per head. 94 80
Second year's expenses:
    Keep of 51 head, at $3 93 per head.. 200 43
    Keep of 40 yearlings, at $3 93 per head. 157 20
    Keep of 40 calves, at $2 37 per head. 94 80
Third year's expenses:
    Keep of 71 head, at $3 93 per head.. 279 03
    Keep of 20 two-year-old steers, at
        $10 41 per head, fattened on grain. 208 20
    Keep of 40 yearlings, at $3 93 per head. 157 20
    Keep of 70 calves, at $2 37 per head. 166 2
                                         ————
                                         $2600 84

Value of Stock on First Day of Fourth Year.

70 cows, at $26...................... $1820 00
20 three-year-old steers, at $62 50, fat-
    tened for market.................. 1250 00
20 two-year-old steers, at $22 50 ...... 450 00
20 heifers, at $18 75 .... 375 00
70 yearlings, at $12 50............... 875 00
70 calves, at $2 50.................. 175 00
1 bull............................. 75 00
         Total value of stock....... $5020 00
         Expenses................. 2600 84
                                    ————
                                    $2419 16

This estimate takes no account of dairy produce, which of course forms an important factor in the problem. In the same way, while speaking of raising grain, I took no account of the enhanced value of land arising from cultivation and increasing immigration. The profits are so large that a large margin may be set aside for contingencies without materially affecting the result.

The freedom to pasture cattle on excellent grazing land, together with an accessible market, are the main reasons why at present stock-farming is particularly profitable. The first of these conditions is precarious, and it is evident that in ten years there will not be much good free range left east of the Missouri River. When immigration to that extent shall have shut him off from free pasturage, the stock man can either sell his farm at probably four times its present value, and move to Dakota or Montana, or else turn his attention to fattening stock on grain for other parties, as I have already suggested.

For instance, as a practical case, there is a cattle man of Council Bluffs who is said to own 100,000 head of cattle in Idaho. He has a range of sixty square miles of land not worth one cent to the acre for agriculture, yet affording excellent pasture for cattle. He has ten men employed at wages varying from twenty-four dollars to forty dollars per month to look after the stock. These men require 200 ponies to handle the cattle. An overseer is hired at $1200 a year. During the winter, however, four men can do all the work required, which is mainly breaking the ice in the streams that the cattle may have water. Streams serve as the great checks upon the cattle straying away, for they never will go far from water. In the spring of the year the cattle men of t⁻e plains have a grand "round up" (as it is called), the stock is picked out by means of the brand, and those cattle that are meant for the Eastern market are started for Omaha. They travel about ten miles a day, and generally take the whole season in the journey from the winter ground to the Missouri bottom. At Omaha the cattle are put on the train and shipped nominally to Chicago, but really to different points along the road, to be handed over to farmers for fattening. Mr. Stewart delivered over 1900 head to farmers last fall, and of these only eight were lost during the winter. The parties who receive the cattle agree to fatten them at the rate of five cents for every extra pound of weight they add to the animal. This seems small at first sight, but where cattle put on 250 extra pounds during a winter, and where two hogs are fed from the refuse of each ox, the farmer finds that the result to him is equivalent to selling his corn at 100 per cent. profit. The large cattle raisers, of course, have their inspectors, who travel from farm to farm to look after their property, and gather it together in the spring for shipment to Chicago, where they are either slaughtered or shipped to Europe. The cattle men have a great advantage over mere farmers, in that they are to a great extent independent of railways. If they are badly treated by one corporation, they have a simple remedy in driving their stock a few miles to the next road. The consequence is that east of Omaha rates for cattle are as favorable as could be desired, while west of this point, where one line has a monopoly of the business, the charges are exorbitant. From Wyoming to Council Bluffs a car-load of twenty head of cattle is charged $116. Consequently, cattle men will march their stock two thousand miles to Council Bluffs, and ship them from that point. They are allowed stop-over tickets, which give them the privilege of turning their stock out at any place for the winter, and then sending them on in the spring to market.

This northwestern section of Iowa is a good one on which to make studies in sheep-raising. There is a good run for sheep along the bluffs near the larger streams and rivers. Anybody who has seen the English "downs" will be reminded of them when he approaches the fine breezy bluffs of the Big Sioux River. I take some carefully prepared figures furnished by one of several Holstein farmers who have a settlement in this neighborhood. They came over here in 1874, most of them with very little ready money, but valuable experience as shepherds at home. They are now all well-to-do farmers. Their houses are far superior to those commonly seen on the prairies. They show their ancestry in the taste for flowers, and the care with which they breed their stock. The horses I saw in use among them were the best animals I have seen in this country for heavy work. I am told that they will not part with their stock at any price to strangers, and nobody who appreciates their circumstances will wonder at it. Here, then, is a

Practical Estimate for Sheep-Farming.

1875, September:

Cost of 500 ewes at $4 25 each..........$2125	
15 rams at $20.........................	300
Common prairie sheds for 1000 sheep.....	225
Grain and feed for winter..............	300
Herding and attendance per annum	250
Salt, medicine, etc.....................	50
	$3250

1876, September:

Cost of grain and feed for winter $500		
Herding and attendance............	250	
Salt, medicine, etc.................	50	800

1877:

Cost of grain and feed for winter $700		
Herding and attendance.............	250	
Salt, medicine, etc.................	50	1000

1878:

Cost of grain and feed for winter $700		
Attendance and herding............	250	
Medicine, salt, etc.	50	1000
		$6050

Adding now the annual interest:

1875—$3250 at 6 per cent..........$195
1876—$4050 " " 243
1877—$5050 " " 303
1878—$6050 " " 363 1104

Total cost of investment and keep......$7154

Returns.

May, 1876, sold 3348 pounds of wool at
20 cents per pound, clip of 515 sheep. $669 60
May, 1877, sold 6696 pounds of wool at
20 cents per pound, clip of 1030 sheep. 1,339 20
May, 1878, sold 6696 pounds of wool at
20 cents per pound, clip of 1030 sheep. 1,339 20
March, 1878, sold 515 fat sheep at $8 .. 4,120 00
May, 1879, sold 6696 pounds of wool at
20 cents per pound, clip of 1030 sheep. 1,339 20
March, 1879, sold 515 fat sheep at $8 .. 4,120 00
$12,927 20

May, 1879, on hand, 500 ewes
with lambs, at $4 ....$2000 00
May, 1879, on hand, 15 rams at
$20...................... 300 00
May, 1879, on hand, 515 year-
lings, at $1 75............ 901 25 3,201 25

Add for annual interest account:
1876--$669 60 at 6 per cent. $40 18
1877—$2008 80 at 6 per
cent................... 120 53
1878—$7468 00 at 6 per
cent................... 448 08
1879—$12,927 00 at 6 per
cent................... 775 62 1,384 41

Total returns..................$17,512 86
Total outlay.................... 7,154 00

Net profit in four years.......$10,358 86

This gives an idea of how profitable sheep-raising has been made to those who understand their business. While such large profits will not fall to the share of every tyro who experiments in shepherdizing, yet even to the most ignorant there will probably result a very much larger return for his money in this business than in any other for which he is not especially fitted.

As to wintering stock, this is a matter that costs very little. My estimate for sheds is small, for the reason that what out West is called a barn is merely a timber skeleton, over which is piled either the straw from the threshing machine or hay cut at one dollar a ton. Many farmers let their cattle go without winter shelter if they have any timber on the place, in which case the cattle take the lee side as a protection against the wind, and come out in the spring in good condition.

The last item in our money calculation is the ubiquitous hog. It would seem as though there were enough hogs in any one State out West to supply the world

with pork, and yet the hog-packing goes on, with no diminution in the demand, in spite of the tremendous supply. In the four months of the season of 1874-75, our packing houses disposed of five and a half million hogs. Last year they packed nearly seven million in the same time. Of these, Chicago alone appropriated two and a half million in the season of 1879-80. But to return to the hog in his natural condition, and as a subject for the capitalist.

Here is a carefully prepared estimate of what may be done with this invaluable adjunct of every farm. The profits are very great; but hogs are sometimes liable to an epidemic called lung disease, or hog cholera. Accordingly I have only allowed four pigs to each sow. These animals cost scarcely anything for keep. They fatten rapidly from the leavings about the barn-yard and the refuse of cattle. Two hogs can be counted to each head of cattle. I take a low figure in my estimate, including every expense, and allowing for the average mortality (including hog cholera):

Hog-Raising.

50 sows, averaging 75 pounds each, 25
young pigs, at three cents per pound... $175 77
First year's expense:
Cost of grain, and milk from cows, for
keeping 75 head.................. 100 20
Second year's expense:
Cost of keep for above, with increase of
200 pigs 183 33
Third year's expense:
75 old hogs, fattened from grain fed to
cattle, and keep of 350 pigs 235 41
$694 71

Valuation, Third Year.

75 old hogs, fattened for market, weighing 300 pounds each, at four cents per
pound $937 50
350 pigs, valued at................. 729 16

Total return.................. $1666 66
Total outlay.................. 694 71
$971 95

I have made these estimates apply to Northwestern Iowa. They are equally true for Southwestern Minnesota. The advantage which the section I have alluded to possesses is largely due to the fact that it is not dependent upon one railway system alone for shipment. This railroad question is so important a one out West that any one intending to buy land should carefully study the advantages of the place in connection with railroad facilities before even looking at the soil.

LADIES' DAY AT THE RANCH

"To river pastures of his flocks and herds
  Admetus rode, where sweet-breathed cattle grazed;
  Heifers and goats and kids and foolish sheep
  Dotted cool, spacious meadows with bent heads,
  And necks' soft wool broken in yellow flakes,
  Nibbling, sharp-toothed, the rich, thick-growing
      blades."

THERE was once a firm. It was in its way quite an ideal firm. Consisting as it did of a Millionaire blissfully indifferent to the manner in which his millions were being spent, a Man of Leisure with nothing to do but to travel, for the best interests of the "concern," between New York and Carneiro, and an Enthusiast who desired nothing but the privilege of doing all the work, I can not see that it lacked any element desirable in firms. For some time the Enthusiast was indulged in his passion for living and laboring at the ranch, for the Millionaire had a yacht, and the Man of Leisure had a family. The prairie was not supposed to be adapted to the yacht, and seemed equally unattractive to people who required schools, libraries, and the opera. But summer came, when school was not, and society palled.

Some of them were too young to be carried to Europe, and others were too old to start for California. Mount Desert was too crowded, and Montclair too lonely. They went to the Adirondacks last year, and were going to the Great Lakes next year. They know all about Newport and Nonquitt, and not enough about Tadousac. Where were they to go?

"Why not go out to the ranch?"

It was, of course, the young gentleman of the family who made the suggestion. He was gazed at.

Was he quite crazy? Did he remember that to live on a ranch meant to do without fish? Had he forgotten that they would be not only twelve miles from a lemon, but a thousand miles from a strawberry? Was he, perhaps, aware that it was hot in Kansas, and that there were undoubtedly mosquitoes? that there was never any breeze, though always too much wind? and that they would suffer from an utter dearth of trees and ice, and that it would not be a place where they could wear embroidered white dresses, and that the only things of which there would be a sufficient supply would be rattlesnakes and cyclones? A—— was also sure that there were no sunflowers, though this afterward proved to be a mistake. To all of which the young gentleman replied, stolidly, "Well, what is the use of having a ranch if you are never going to see it?"

The family reflected. After all, the Enthusiast had always said that life at the ranch was not only profitable but delightful. It was barely possible that he might be telling the truth. He was put upon his honor, and the following facts were elicited:

There were no mosquitoes, and occasionally it was cool. Sometimes the thermometer stood at 100° in the shade — or would if there were any shade—but in the rarer air they would not realize it. They would live through the cyclones, and forget all about the strawberries. Besides, there were melons. They could buy saddle-horses for from thirty to sixty dollars apiece, feed them all summer on the prairie, and sell them in the fall probably at a profit. Some of them didn't care for mountains, and so they would like it, and the rest of them didn't care for the sea, and so *they* would like it. The shooting was prime, and there were fifty acres of sunflowers. Moreover, there was a new ram, pure Atwood breed, and if they did not consider a mere journey of two days and three nights worth undertaking for the pleasure of seeing that ram alone, it was quite hopeless to think of presenting any farther attraction, and they were unworthy of possessing even a pecuniary interest in a ranch.

BUFFALO-GRASS.

They not only went, but they went in April; and they not only staid, but they staid till November. If the proof of the pudding is in the eating, it is sufficiently evident that ranch life was delightful.

Early as they had arrived, the flowers had come before them, and the barbaric splendor of the scenes in *Aïda* and *L'Africaine* seemed repeated as the glorious panorama of blossoming prairie unrolled day after day. , Can you picture to yourself ten acres of portulaca? or whole hill-sides curtained with what seems a superb variety of wistaria, except that it grows on a stalk instead of hanging from a vine? Do you know how it feels not to be able to step without crushing a flower, so that the little prairie-dogs, sitting contentedly with their intimate friends the owls on the little heaps of earth thrown up around their holes, have every appearance of having planted their own front yards with the choicest floral varieties? Think of driving into a great field of sunflowers, the horses trampling down the tall stalks, that spring up again behind the carriage, so that one outside the field would never know that a carriage-load of people were anywhere in it; or riding through a "grove" of them, the blossoms towering out of reach as you sit on horseback, and a tall hedge of them grown up as a barrier between you and your companion! Not a daisy, or a buttercup, or a clover, or a dandelion, will you see all summer; but new flowers too exquisite for belief; the great white prickly poppies, and the sensitive rose, with its leaves delicate as a maiden-hair fern, and its blossom a countless mass of crimson stamens tipped with gold, and faintly fragrant. Even familiar flowers are unfamiliar in size and pro-

fusion and color. What at home would be a daisy, is here the size of a small sunflower, with petals of delicate rose-pink, raying from a cone-shaped centre of rich maroon shot with gold. A—— had brought with her numerous packages of seeds and slips, nobly bent on having ribbon flower beds and mosaic *parterres* about the house; but she sat on the steps and threw them broadcas⁺, never knowing, in the profusion of flowers that would have been there anyway, whether hers ever came up or not. And how beautiful were the grasses—the most useful one the most beautiful of all; the delicate little "buffalo-grass," for which the prairie is famous, waving its tiny curled sickle of feathery daintiness as if its beauty were its only excuse for being, yet bravely "curing" itself into dry hay as it stands, when the autumn winds begin to blow, that the happy flocks may "nibble, sharp-toothed, the rich, thick-growing blades" all through the winter, without their being gathered into barns.

They raised their vases too. Bric-à-brac does not flourish in rooms whose doors and windows are open all day long to a Kansas breeze; so, when something was necessary for holding flowers, they would wander out over the prairie with a hammer, pick up a round stone, perhaps the size of a thimble, perhaps as big as a large bowl, crack it open, pour out the fine sand within it, and find a cavity as perfect as if hollowed out with an instrument, and as smooth as if lined with porcelain.

"My mother says that sand is splendid for cleaning knives," observed a small herder one day, watching their operations. Not eliciting any decided enthusiasm, he continued:

"I'm going to Chicago next week! Chicago's an awful big city."

"But not so big as New York, where we live, you know."

"Oh, I know all about York! it's down by the ocean. I've never seen an ocean, but I've heard one."

"Where?"

"In a shell."

"But we've been across the ocean! 'way over on the other side of it."

"Ho! that ain't nothin'. My mother was *born* over there. In Ireland."

Nor did they miss the flowers after dark; for then the prairie fires lit up the scene with rare magnificence of color. Not the deadly autumn fires, bringing with them, when the grass is dry, fear and desolation, but the fires set purposely in safe places in the spring, that the young grass may come up greener. There is nothing terrible in the sight; there are no falling buildings, and you hear no hissing, crackling flames. The low grass burns so quietly and steadily that the effect is simply that of great lighted cities in the distance.

"I suppose some of those fires must be in the next county," remarked A—— one evening.

"All our own fires on our own property, I can assure you," answered the proud Enthusiast.

It was long before they could accustom themselves to this magnificent scale of things; to realizing that they were living on ten thousand acres of their own; to the thought of caring for ten thousand sheep; to driving all the afternoon on their own "lawn," and making excursions for the day on their own property. Once, when they had ridden late and far, and had quite lost their way, they stopped at one of the adobe huts—wonderfully picturesque with flowers blossoming on the roof, and near by the "Kansas stable," with its one horse only sheltered as to its head—to ask their way. "And what property are we on now?" asked Admetus.

"The Monte Carneiro Ranch, sir."

"Thank you; good-day!" and Admetus rode on, to hide his smile at having to be told that he was on his own land. The sense of ownership was not slow to develop, however, and even the Baby became so imbued with the size of the ranch as to say sometimes, when they were driving fifteen or twenty miles from home, "Papa, I suppose you'll be cutting this grass pretty soon?"

In the middle of the summer came Colonel Higginson's article in the *Harper* on the Indian hieroglyphics, with illustrations to prove the similarity between the famous Dighton rock and many found at the West.

"They say that there are Indian hieroglyphics on our rocks at the Cave," remarked the Enthusiast, carelessly.

"Why *haven't* you told us before?"

"Because my enthusiasm is limited to sheep; but you can investigate, if you like."

Whereupon an imperative order was sent to the stable for "ponies for six, *immediately* after luncheon."

Many and many a time they had been to the Cave, which was quite the *pièce de résistance* of their excursions. It was no mere cavern in the side of a hill, but a cave so high that they could ride into it, with

KANSAS DAISIES.

two entrances on different sides, and a charming little oriel-window shaded by trees. Curiously enough, they had never happened to dismount and explore the op-

gave them long evenings of delicious restfulness; one was artistic, and preserved for them in the amber of her brush the delicate hue and fragile texture of the

INDIAN PICTURE WRITING OUTSIDE OF THE CAVE.

posite exit, but it was on the outer wall just beyond this that the hieroglyphics were said to be.

Truly it was a strange sensation, in that lonely spot, as they came out of the second entrance and crept carefully along the steep bluff overgrown with underbrush, to look up at the natural wall of rock towering above them, and see, clearly outlined on the space where it must have been singularly difficult to work at all, the crude and curious efforts of Indian drawing, and the full-length, life-size figure of a recumbent Indian chief.

There were many resources besides the never-failing ponies: hammocks and piazzas, lawn tennis, a piano, and a billiardroom. Of the ladies, one was musical, and

flowers that else they could have carried away with them only in memory; and one was literary, and kept them in the latest books and freshest magazines from New York; while one was a "reserve fund," drawn upon in every emergency. Then, for culture, there was the Professor, the genial, absorbed Professor, filling even the least scientific with something of his own enthusiasm for the splendid fossils of the region, the superb impressions of leaves, and the fossil shells picked up two thousand miles from either ocean. Who of them will ever forget the day when the first and only nautilus was found, just as they had decided that there were only clam shells; or the finding of the shark's tooth?

For those who sought in nature "no

charm unborrowed from the eye," there was fun enough in collecting the "freaks," the queer shapes into which accident had moulded the soft rock—shoes, boots, stock-

To see the sheep go in and out, night and morning, was a never-failing amusement. Sometimes the ladies wandered down to the corrals at sunset to see the

INDIAN PICTURE WRITING OUTSIDE OF THE CAVE.

ings, match-safes, and trinkets. Once a perfect sheep's head, even to the eyes, was picked up, like a curious bass-relief, not twenty feet from the front door.

By this time I can conceive of the gentle reader's saying, "I thought it was a sheep ranch?" in the tone of voice employed by Miss Betsy Trotwood when she asked, "Why do you call it a *Rookery*? I don't see any rooks." Sheep there were, indeed; thousands of them, objects of unfailing concern to the gentlemen and delight to the ladies.

"What is that stone wall?" asked, one afternoon, a lady sitting on the piazza with her opera-glass.

"That stone wall, madam," answered a Harvard graduate, politely, "is the sheep coming in to the corral."

herds come in, and you would have supposed them to be waiting for a Fourth-of-July procession with banners, from the eagerness with which they exclaimed, "Oh, here they come! there they are!" as the first faint tinkling of the bells was heard in the distance. If two herds appeared at once from opposite directions, the one with lambs had the "right of way," and Sly, the sheep-dog—not the only commander who has controlled troops by sitting down in front of them—would hold the other herd in check till the lambs were safely housed. The lambs born on the prairie during the day frisked back at night to the corral beside their mothers, a lamb four hours old being able to walk a mile.

When shearing-time came, they went

"COLUMBUS."

into the sheds expecting to see the thick wool fall in locks beneath the shears, like the golden curls of their own darlings: great was the amazement to see the whole woolly fleece taken off much as if it had been an overcoat, looking still, if it were rolled up in a ball, like a veritable sheep, and often quite as large as the shorn and diminished creature that had once been part of it. One very hot day they braved the heat themselves for the sake of going out on the prairie to see how sheep keep cool. Instead of scattering along the creek, seeking singly the shade of the bushes or the tall trees only to be found near the creek, they huddle together in the middle of the sunny field more closely than ever, hang their heads in the shadow of each other's bodies, and remain motionless for hours. Not a single head is to be seen as you approach the herd; only a broad level field of woolly backs, supported by a small forest of little legs.

"Like a banyan-tree," remarked Admetus.

A large part of the satisfaction of these simple pleasures was the charm of finding that they could be happy with such simple pleasures. To discover that you can not only live without the opera, but that you are really better amused than you ever were with the opera at your command, gives a sense of satisfaction with yourself very potent in the element of content. Yet they were not without their social excitements and their adventures. One Harvard graduate attracts another, and within a radius of thirty miles quite a colony of personal friends has formed itself, whose gatherings for little dinners or dances, tennis or whist, are most enjoyable. A hundred guests were entertained at Monte Carneiro alone "in the season"; ranch friends from all over the county, Eastern friends "stopping over" on their way to Colorado, or California, or Japan, and some who had learned even then that to "see the ranch" was really quite worth the trouble of two days and three nights in a Pullman car.

They thought little of driving or riding fifteen miles to a "neighbor's" for luncheon—always provided, however, that they knew the way. To find the way for yourself to a new ranch across the prairie, or to drive anywhere after dark, is a feat only attempted by the unwary. "Love will find out a way" through bolts and bars and parental interdiction; but Love itself would be baffled on the prairie, where the whole universe stretches in endless invitation, and where there is absolutely "nothing to hinder" from going in any direction that you please. "Foller a kind of a blind trail, one mile east and two mile south," is the kind of direction usually given in the vernacular; and so closely does one cultivate the powers of observation in a country where a bush may be a feature of the landscape, and a tall sunflower a landmark, that I am tempted to copy *verbatim* the written directions sent by a friend by which we were to find our way to her hospitable home:

"Cross the river at the Howards'; turn to the right, and follow a dim trail till you come to the ploughed ground, which you follow to the top of the hill. Follow the road on the west side of a corn field, and then a dim trail across the prairie to a wire fence. After you leave the wire fence, go up a little hill and down a little hill, then up another till you reach a road leading to the right, which angles across a section and leads into a road going south to Dr. Read's frame house with a wall of sod about it. Through his door-yard, and then through some corn. Leave the road after driving through the corn, and angle to the right to the corner of another corn field. Take the road to the west of this

ENTRANCE TO THE CAVE.

A KANSAS HOUSE.

going south, with corn field on the right, till you come to two roads. Follow the right-hand road (a dim trail at first) down the hill, past some hay-stacks, to the Osage-orange hedge. Follow that to the creek crossing, then through the grove of sun-flowers to a sod house. Go through the corn directly west, following the creek to the crossing near our house."

The distance was sixteen miles, but we took the letter with us, and found the way without the slightest difficulty, though a little puzzled at first by finding that "at the Howards'" meant anywhere within three miles of the Howards'.

As for adventures, some of them were thrilling. First, there was the rattle-snake under the piazza, its presence announced by the innocent Baby, who complained of it as disturbing his play, and "*whistlin' wid its tail.*" Then Admetus lost his way upon the prairie after dark,

corn, and go south, up a hill, then turn to the right and follow a *plain* road west; afterward south, past Mr. Dever's home-stead, a frame house on the right with a stone house unroofed. South, past a corn field and ploughed land on the right. The road turns to the right, toward the west, for a little way, then south, then a short distance east, and you reach the guide-post, which is near a thrifty-look-ing farm owned by Mr. Bryant; a frame house, corn field, wheat stacks, and melon patch. At the guide-post take the road and after two or three hours of riding in a circle, found on hastening to a friendly lighted window for information that by accident he had ridden up to his own front door. The Enthusiast had once ridden seven miles with his wife to make an afternoon call, only to find on their return that the creek had risen mysteriously so that it would be impossible to cross. A herd of sheep with the herder and a friend were waiting quietly at the same spot, within five minutes' walk of the house, *if they could only cross.* "You stay with the sheep," said E——, to his friend, "and C—— and I will ride down to find a better crossing." *They rode five miles*, and of course by the time they had retraced the five on the other bank it was too dark for their friend to attempt the

Then there were the grasshoppers. If you are quite sure that they are not intending to "'light," a flight of grasshoppers is a beautiful thing to see. All day they floated over us; millions upon millions upon millions of airy little creatures; with their white gauzy wings spread to the light, mounting steadily toward the sun; as it seemed. It was like a snow-storm in sunshine, if you can picture such a thing, with the flakes rising instead of falling.

The most terrible experience came with the least warning. It had been a lovely day, and the ladies were dressing for a tea at Elk Horn Ranch, four miles away, when some one exclaimed, "What a curious cloud!"

A perfectly cylindrical cloud, seemingly not more than two feet in diameter,

OLD EWE AND LAMBS.

same course. There was nothing to do but camp out for the night, with the bright windows of home shining just across the creek. Ropes were thrown over, supper and blankets slung across to the sufferers, and in the morning the creek had fallen again.

reached perpendicularly from the sky to the earth. The ladies grew a little anxious, as it did not change its aspect, but the Enthusiast, who had lived through one cyclone, and knew the signs, said, carelessly, as he sauntered up the avenue:

"Oh, you need not fear anything in that

A KANSAS BARN.

shape!—that is only a rain-cloud; no wind in that. A cyclone is spiral; very wide at the top, and tapering down to a mere point, as if it were boring into the earth. It's a horrid thing to see."

As he spoke, the cloud in question, as if mocking his depreciation of its power, began assuming the very shape described.

"It *is* a cyclone!" he said, quietly, but with whitening cheek. "You had better get your things. It is twenty-five miles away, but if the wind should change, it would be upon us in five minutes."

He shouted to the men at the corrals. Those who were busy in the wool-house came to the door, glanced at the sky, but went quietly back again. As one of them expressed it later, "If it was a-comin', I don't believe the spring-house would save us, and if it wasn't comin', we might as well finish the work."

The "things" which they were to secure received the usual foolish interpretations. A—— ran for a shawl to wrap Baby in, before she secured Baby himself; F—— ran to her chamber for a pocket-book with a precious fifty cents in it; some one wondered if she would not have time to change her boots, it was such a pity to wet her new ones running through the grass, for the rain was now falling heavily. The Enthusiast himself put on his best coat, laid

out for the "tea," and insisted that his wife should add to her incomplete toilet the touches of lace and jewels. "Why, my dear, you may never see your things again," was his explanation; but whether he hoped to rescue the things that were put on, or whether he was anxious for the family to be found beautifully dressed in case they were buried beneath the ruins, was not at all clear.

It had been previously arranged that in case of cyclone they were to run to the spring-house. To the feminine mind the cellar presented greater attractions; but the very strength and size of the great stone house would make it a terrible mass of ruins if it were blown over, and if it came in the path of the cyclone, its walls would be but a shaving before it. The small spring-house was built into a hill, and it was confidently hoped that cyclones would blow over it, instead of blowing it over.

A marked precursor of a cyclone is the appearance of the sky. It is not darkly terrible; it may even be of a clear and perfect blue, and the clouds may be dazzlingly white; but they shape themselves into immense cobble-stones, till the heavens look like an inverted pavement; what adds to the strangeness of this appearance is the apparent weight of the distinct, oval, egg-shaped clouds; it is impossible to conceive of them as ever dissipating in gentle rain, or even hail; if they fall, you feel that each one will fall heavily, crushing with terrible cruelty everything beneath it.

For an hour they watched and waited. Then the water-spout began to fade, and the cobble-stones disappeared. The horses were ordered, and the ladies finished their toilets, while the Baby was heard to murmur, in a tone of disappointment, "Papa, you *said* you were going to take me to the spring-house."

And at last they saw a genuine prairie fire.

"What are your precautions against fire?" Admetus had asked a few days before.

"Such as will delight your homœopathic soul," answered the Enthusiast. "A can of kerosene and a bundle of matches to set back fires with, though the fire-guards of ploughed ground that you have seen all round the ranch are the ounce of prevention, better than any cure. Then we always keep a hogshead full of water at the stable, ready for carting to the spot."

"A hogshead of water! What good can a hogshead of water do against a prairie fire?"

"Oh, we don't put it on with a hose, I assure you. My imagination gasps at the conception of managing a prairie fire with a hose. We dip old blankets and old clothes in it, or boughs of trees if we can get them, and beat the fire down with them."

The illustration followed soon. All day smoke had been drifting over Carneiro, and at night-fall the scouts reported that the whole force had better be put on. The "whole force" at the moment consisted of about twenty men who had just come in to supper, and who started at once in wagons and on horseback. Ponies were ordered after dinner for the entire household, even the ladies riding far enough to have a view of the exciting scene. There were no tumbling walls or blazing buildings, and there was no fear of lives being lost in upper stories; but there were miles upon miles, acres upon acres, of low grass burning like a sea of fire, while in the twilight shadows could be seen men galloping fiercely on swift ponies, while the slow wagons crept painfully, lest the precious water should be spilled, from every homestead, each with its one pitiful hogshead. It seemed incredible that such a mass of flame could ever be put out by such a handful of workers; and it was only, indeed, by each man's laboring steadily at his own arc of the great circle, trusting blindly that others were at work on the other side, as of course they always were, that the lurid scene darkened down at last.

As the season advanced, interest in the great crops almost overshadowed that in the "stock." The wild flowers had faded away, and no wonder, poor things! In their innocent joy at being admired—for none but sheep-men had ever visited the ranch before the ladies came, and what sheep-man ever stopped to look at a flower?—they had crowded close up to the

KANSAS THISTLE.

SENSITIVE ROSE.

And as the harvests were gathered in, the great labor-saving machines were as good as a circus: the "header," leaving all the stubble standing in the field, cutting off only the heads of the grain, which then walked solemnly up an inclined plane only to throw themselves from the top in despair into the wagon that rolled alongside; the "thresher," with its circular treadmill for a dozen horses, with their master on a revolving platform in the centre, from which he controlled them with his long-lashed whip; and the graceful "go-devil" rake, travelling idly over the hay fields and gathering up the hay with all the ease of a lady's carpet-sweeper.

This was the true glory of the year. At the East, people were hurrying back from the sea-shore or mountains; for them the summer was over and the harvest ended; but for us it had just begun. Some of us took the wonderful trip to Colorado—for we were only twelve hours from Denver—and some of us took to shooting prairie-chicken; but all of us were out-of-doors every day and all day long. Now began the season of the famous little duck suppers, when six or eight of us would start for a friend's ranch to spend the night, taking the precaution to eat our duck that night for fear the gentlemen *wouldn't* shoot any the next morning, but returning the next day laden with the spoils of the victors, shot in the cool gray of the misty dawn. Now it was that the Enthusiast discovered a method of rousing his rebellious comrades to the early breakfast that he himself affected: stationing himself in the billiard-room, he had only to shout, "Gentlemen, nineteen duck in the pond!" and in five minutes every man of the household, from the geological professor and the elegant young man from Chicago down to the boy who was "going to have" a gun next year, could be seen rushing down the hill in habiliments that brought back to these graduates of Harvard reminiscences of an early call to prayers.

And then it was in October that the Griffin came.

"Why, he's nothing but a gentleman!" exclaimed the Baby, who had insisted on

front door, and sprung up under the very horses' feet, vying with each other for the honor of being worn at a lady's belt, or painted on a panel, or pressed in a herbarium to be sent to the cultured East, or chosen to adorn an æsthetic parlor. But they had had quite enough of it, and had grown shy and sensitive. We can not believe that they will ever bloom at Carneiro in just such profusion again. They have crept away to more deserted places, and mayhap the day will come when they will only bloom for us in stately greenhouses, at a cost that shall insure for their loveliness respect as well as admiration.

But we hardly missed them, as the great grain fields took their places, and covered the land with the green shimmering of corn, the pale yellow of the wheat, the golden russet of rye, the stately rows of sorghum, like glorified cat-o'-nine-tails, the great pearly clusters of the rice-corn bending with their weight of rich loveliness, and, most beautiful of all, the golden millet. You do not know what millet is? Ah, no! but then you do not know what Kansas is. You do not know what it is to own a winding creek that would be worth its weight in gold to the commissioners of Central Park if they could buy it. You do not know what it is to have your landscape gardening done for you without a gardener.

going to the station, with many inquiries as to whether the expected arrival, which he took to be a flock of some rare kind of lambs, would be conveyed to the house "on legs or in wagons?"

I feel called upon to chronicle the noble zeal with which the Griffin immediately attacked his official duties. He did, indeed, wait a few moments to assuage the pangs of hunger with coffee and beefsteak; but almost immediately he remarked that it was a glorious day for sketching, and he must not lose such an opportunity. The ladies who put up the luncheon noticed that several gentlemen who had never been addicted to brush or pencil proposed to join this sketching expedition, and that the sketching materials seemed to consist largely of guns and cartridges; but the "studies" of prairie-chicken, duck, plover, and quail, "taken from life," which they brought back with them, made so valuable an addition to the next evening's dinner that no explanation was required, and no complaint made of a day of prolonged feminine solitude.

And the landscape only grew lovelier. The flowers had faded, and the great grain fields had been swept away; but the wild beautiful prairie, taking on the tawny coloring dear to the artist, with here and there a broad belt or mantle of the brilliant low red sumac, grew ever dearer. For the first time in my life I understood Emily Brontë's passion for her desolate brown moors. There is rare charm in a sense of isolation that you do not feel to be loneliness. And for the very reason that the undulating prairie offers so few salient points, the picture appeals to the eye and lingers in the mind more effectively than many a more impressive scene. The "values" count; every stroke "tells."

The identity of interests between master and men is a pleasant feature of ranch life. Occasionally, of course, there will be a disaffected laborer, who may even work up matters to a concentrated "strike"; but as a rule the men are happy and contented, proud of the ranch, and devoted to its success. They have their own cook at their own "quarters," from which, in the evening, come cheerful strains of Moody and Sankey or of native jollity, the chorus being not unfrequently,

"Oh, I'm a jolly herder,
    I want you for to know!
I herd the sheep for Wellington—
    For Wellington and Co."

When we asked a man who was putting "bunks" into a small house for some of the men to sleep in why he hadn't taken a larger one opposite, he replied, dryly:

"Oh, this one ain't near nice enough for the hens; so we took it. The hens are to have the other one."

There is something very enjoyable in the consciousness not only of controlling the movements of forty or fifty men, but of caring for all their interests, mental, physical, and moral. The men with families have separate houses, and to supply them with literature, see that their groceries are good, cure their sick children, and in fact administer everything they need, from advice to flannel, is not only an intense moral satisfaction to the ladies of the household with a taste for benevolence, but a source of much entertainment. Think, O *blasé* philanthropists, of getting up a Christmas tree for children who never saw one! A—— regarded as one of her pleasantest experiences of the summer the opportunity afforded her to make converts to homœopathy.

"You are as proud of having cured that child," remarked the Enthusiast, one day, "as if your little sugar pills had really done it some good."

"Oh no," said the lady, "I'm not proud of having cured it; I'm thankful for not having killed it. What is it, James?" as a new applicant presented himself.

"If you please, marm, I'd like some more medicine; the baby's almost well."

The delighted homœopathist, on the alert for "symptoms," proposed to change the prescription.

"Oh no, marm: I wouldn't make no change if I was you. Them other little pills was just boss."

Some of us, how-

KANSAS MILLET.

ever, still think that she owed her converts to the fact that she never sent in any bills.

"Why, I paid that other feller fifty cents for just one pill!" exclaimed the grateful recipient of medicine for ailments described as follows: "Well, my throat's sore, and my back aches, and my stomach's gin out, and my head's bad, and I don't feel very well *myself*."

What were our deprivations? Really, at the moment, I can not recall any. We had no "set tubs," but then we had no washing-day; once a week one of the teams going every day to Ellsworth took all the washing into town, where it was excellently done at the rate of thirty-seven cents a dozen, including the embroidered white dresses. We had no gas; but were we not using a duplex burner in our New York parlors, and carrying candles to our bed-chambers as the highest tribute to æstheticism? We had no door-bell; but do you know how pleasant it is not to have one? We had no mountains; but in that rarer air we had countless mountain effects on the low-lying hills—one slope crimson with the reflected glory of a superb sunset long after the others lay in violet shadow. We had no sea; but, strangely enough, of nothing is the prairie so suggestive as of the sea; no Eastern visitor ever failed to notice and to wonder at it. It seems incredible, but you have a constant impression that the sea is tossing just out of sight; perhaps because of doors and windows thrown wide open all day long to the soft glare of utterly unshaded sunshine, only tolerable on the prairie or at the sea-shore; perhaps because of the low murmur of the wind behind the hills, like the ceaseless monotone of surf. "Papa, it's just like the Point Road," was the criticism of one of the children as we drove rapidly across a favorite section—the "Point Road" being a drive of six miles along the sea, to which he had always been accustomed in summer.

A brisk walk on a cool morning or evening up and down the long and wide piazza, roofed over only at the porch, was pronounced by the Europeans fully equal to a promenade on the Atlantic steamers, and the gentleman who hesitated longest over the temporary parting from the yacht of his friend the Millionaire declared the scene to be fully equal to the deck of the *Peerless*, as he lay in the hammock swung gently by the cool clear breeze, with that moan of surf out of sight, the stars overhead, and the flag-staff over the porch creaking slightly in the wind like straining cordage. We had no groves, but there were plenty of trees, tall, beautiful elms, following the curves of the creeks. In other words, there were plenty of trees to *look at*, but we could always see over, or beyond, or through them, so that when, on our return trip to the East, we began to catch glimpses of prettily shaded lawns and cottages shut in by woods in the suburbs of Cincinnati, M—— expressed the feelings of us all when she said, wonderingly, "Somehow I'm not half so glad to see trees again as I thought I should be." We could not talk about the "lawn," or the "garden," or the "woods," but we soon knew the numbers of the sections by heart, so that we understood, when we asked the whereabouts of a new flower or fossil, if we were told that it had been found "over in Seven." "Ah!" said the lady of Elk Horn one day, "you really ought to come over and spend the night, just to see Twenty-one by moonlight."

But was it hot?

Certainly it was hot by the thermometer; but at the great elevation the heat was not felt to be so excessive as a lesser degree of it at home. Hardly a night did we sleep without a blanket, and there were evenings in August when it was too cool to sit on the piazza after dinner. Children play fearlessly bare-headed in the sun on the hottest days, and it is said that there has never been a case of sunstroke in Kansas. It was not a rare thing for us to drive into town in an open carriage with the thermometer at 100°, and without a particle of shade any of the way, the high wind making even parasols and broad-brimmed hats an impossibility.

As for our *menu*, I am glad of an opportunity to explain that the proverbial bacon and salt pork of the West have a *raison d'être* not suspected at the East. With chickens a dollar and a half a dozen, eggs ten cents a dozen, butter fifteen cents a pound, and quail, plover, duck, and prairie-chicken to be had for the shooting, the appetite of ranchmen becomes so satiated with what in New York would be the delicacies of the season, as to crave the stimulus of a bit of delicate bacon or a slice of rosy ham.

And now one word of warning. If you would see Kansas as we saw it, you must see it where we saw it. We refuse to be responsible for the Kansas seen from the car windows, in a frame of mind bordering on exasperation at the maddening slowness of a train of cars conscious of being a monopoly, and dragging its slow length along through a country so horribly level that you feel as if it would be some relief to spring to your feet and recite "Excelsior." No; you must leave the cars and the railroad and the dismal little railroad towns, and find your way to the big ranches where life and work are one long holiday. Should you choose Monte Carneiro, the Enthusiast will show you his corrals, and drive you round his corn fields; you can shoot your own quail for dinner, have a game of tennis and a *siesta* in the hammock after luncheon, and a game of billiards after dinner; then, as the little maid brings in the tray of tea, you can saunter into a parlor with great broad windows, full of rugs and *portières* and screens of Kensington embroidery, and the lady who pours your tea will afterward sing for you Schubert's "Serenade," or "I know that my Redeemer liveth." This is not the popular conception of ranch life; nor is it, I confess, the common mode of ranch life. Too many young ranchmen, eager to put all their capital into stock, think they can "manage" to live "any way" for a few years, and remain too long contented with ham and bacon in a "dugout"; but the little knot of friends who have gathered about Ellsworth believe that to make their homes not only comfortable but luxurious, to live not only de-

cently but æsthetically, to have not only a parlor but *portières*, is as much for their business interest as Tiffany undoubtedly considers his high rent and plate-glass windows.

Then, as your host steps out on the piazza to haul down the American flag—his only method of locking up for the night—you will catch a glimpse of the shifting lights of a train on the Union Pacific, pleasantly suggestive of a post-office, with two mails from the east and two from the west every day, a railroad station and telegraph office, within two miles. In the moonlight you can see the stablemen carefully housing for the night the choice Jersey and Swiss cattle; for our firm is quite too recently from New York to have lost its faith in blood and pedigree. Not yet has it been seriously affected by the Western passion for numbers rather than for quality, for so many "head" rather than so many "registered." Ten thousand sheep and five hundred cattle they will have, of course; but the Enthusiast insists upon "pure Atwoods," while the Millionaire and the Man of Leisure would scorn to belong to any firm that did not appreciate "registered" Jerseys.

When at last you seek the little Eastlake bedroom, it will be, I think, with the intention of leaving for the East by the earliest morning train; only, however, that you may gather together your Lares and Penates to return to Kansas as soon as possible, that you too may become an early settler before it is too late.

THE CITY OF COLUMBUS

The Capitol

At Olentangy Villa.

THE CITY OF COLUMBUS, OHIO.

BY DESHLER WELCH.

IF any one supposes that Amerigo Vespucci usurped all the honors belonging to Christopher Columbus, a glance at the atlas will show the mistake. That truth-teller, or even a school geography, offers abundant tribute to Columbus in teaching us that there are seventy-five towns, villages, and post-offices in the United States for which the immortal discoverer is sponsor. You will find them scattered to every point of the map; and large tracts of land in Oregon, Georgia, Pennsylvania, Arkansas, New York, Ohio, and Wisconsin are known as Columbia Counties. Columbus, the capital of the third largest State in the Union, is the most important and doubtless the most enduring establishment of the name. The city was laid out in 1812, and was incorporated as a borough in 1823, when it became the capital of the State. It was not incorporated as a city until 1834. The completion of the Erie Canal in 1825 had prepared the way for its rapid development. That canal revolutionized the course of trade. As if by magic, commerce swarmed on the

Lakes, and lifted a tide of settlers to the farthest woodland and prairie.

No striking features of natural scenery make Columbus a picturesque city. The Scioto is a muddy stream which serves the city only as a conduit for its sewage and the refuse of its factories. But though unambitious in its appearance, Columbus is built on one of the fairest spots of a rich alluvial plain, and is in itself a "solid" city, prosperous, wealthy, and conservative. Since the war it has had a develop-

promise a change of the most agreeable character.

The manufacturing interests of Columbus are very large and constantly increasing; the banks are heavy exchanges and depositories; and there is no Western city of its size that has a larger or sounder financial responsibility, and none whose citizens have more public spirit or enthusiastic enterprise.

In 1817 President Monroe and suite passed through Franklin County, in

PRESIDENT MONROE'S JOURNEY WEST, 1817.

ment which, if slow when compared with that of many other Western cities, has been sure and substantial. It has now a population of over 80,000, an increase of 30,000 since the census of 1880. It is laid out in regular squares; the streets are broad and beautiful. In 1871 the area of the city was extended to cover nearly eleven square miles. One of the disadvantages of the city has been the disagreeable effects of the smoke from the burning of soft coal; the advent of natural gas, however, and the recent resolutions of the younger and more ambitious element, formed into a "Board of Trade,"

which Columbus is situated, on his return to Detroit, after his northern tour of inspection of fortifications. They travelled on horseback, "generally escorted from one town to another by the military and distinguished citizens." They rode fast, and, as recorded, "in a canter." Mr. Monroe wore the old-fashioned three-cornered cocked hat, but otherwise in plain citizen dress, and his face was observed to be very much sunburnt from exposure.

At this time the number of people living in Columbus did not exceed 700, but the Franklin Bank had been incorporated, and the State offices had been removed from

LYNE STARLING.

en to manufacturing of lumber, spinning, etc., that the town began to show reason for existence. The men who worked then were hardy and industrious; doubtless few of them saw how great a town they were founding; for, like the diamond hunters, they subsequently scattered their accumulated wealth elsewhere. Of the four original projectors, Lyne Starling accomplished the most good; he liyed a bachelor, but when he died, in the fall of 1848, at the age of sixty-five years, he left $35,000—which was considered a large sum at that time—for the erection of the Starling Medical College—a noble and well-equipped institution, which has now a large museum and a first-class chemical laboratory, and has also associated with it an excellent hospital.

July 4, 1825, the celebration of the opening of the Ohio Canal took place at "Licking Summit," and Governor Clinton, of New York, accompanied by Solomon Van Rensselaer, and Messrs. Rathbone and Lord, who made the first loan to the State for the purposes of the canal, were present. Afterward, in Columbus, Governor Clinton declared that "ten years after the consummation of this work it will produce an annual revenue of at least a million dollars"; but the results were not as he predicted they would be. The history of the city from this time up to 1846 was uneventful, but then came an increased improvement. Speculation was not so wild

Chillicothe to Columbus, and on the first Monday in December, 1816, the Legislature had held its initial session in a State-house which cost $83,000, including the necessary adjunct of a penitentiary. Columbus had much to contend with, as it was thought to be a rough spot in the woods, and not near the important public roads; but settlers came from everywhere, and it grew with a strength that was of permanent value. About 1822 there was the usual result of hasty speculation, depression, and Henry Clay, who was then practising law, had his hands full in the defence of suits. But when the National Road was located, Columbus put on a cheerful face, and contrived a big impetus by a "feeder" to the Ohio Canal. Yet the people were like the fishes in the sea, living off one another, and it was not until serious attention was giv-

MEDICAL COLLEGE.

and foolish. Many new and substantial buildings were erected, and a great deal of capital was invested in railroads and banking concerns. The Columbus and Xenia Railway was constructed, and travel was opened to Cincinnati in 1850. In 1851 the Cleveland, Columbus, and Cincinnati Railroad was finished, and in 1852 the Central road to Zanesville; and the Columbus, Piqua, and Indiana was opened to Piqua in 1853. At this period the only prominent newspaper was the *Ohio Statesman*, which was founded by Samuel Medary in 1837, and was the leading organ of Democracy in the West. S. S. Cox was for many years its associate editor.

So much for the early history of a Western town. In these days the soil of progress of such cities is not turned over by any Pompeys, Ciceros, or Cæsars, and there are no remnants of early existence worth the trouble of handing down, except through the medium of the city's records on the public library shelf, and even there the dust is likely to remain undisturbed. But the pluck of the early settlers of Columbus was not especially inspired by any evidence of future greatness. In fact the location was selected in a rather hap-hazard way, without much reference to whether nature would do anything to assist; but in this particular the people builded better than they knew, for the seemingly inexhaustible coal-fields of the Hocking Valley were subsequently discovered at their very doors, and instantly made Columbus the *entrepôt* for a great distributing centre. Its position is in the midst of three great valleys, the Scioto, Muskingum, and Hocking, whose harvestings are in wonderful variance and abundance. The region of coal and iron has aroused and fed immense manufacturing interests, which have given employment and fortunes to thousands; its agricultural resources have stretched over a magnificent country of 8000 square miles, and the development, rapid as it has been, is really in its infancy. The cities, towns, and villages near it, such as Zanesville, Newark, Portsmouth, Chillicothe, Circleville, Ironton, Gallipolis, Logan, Lancaster, Athens, London, Washington C. H., Zenia, Springfield, Urbana, Piqua, Bellefontaine, Marion, Delaware, Akron, and Mount Vernon, help to sustain it by direct railroad communication, and are in a large measure dependent upon it for their supplies. Of course all this gives employment to the railroads, and a continually increasing interchange of traffic, which has excited such competition that now there are fourteen lines of railway which enter the city. It is very likely that Columbus may in time surpass both Cleveland and Cincinnati in the magnitude of its demands and supplies as a railroad centre. Fuel is cheap, freights are extremely low, and these, with many other advantages, offer unusual opportunities to merchants and manufacturers.

The records for the year 1886 show the value of real estate by tax duplicate to be nearly twenty-seven millions of dollars. The assessed value of new structures of the year is nearly a million and a half, and the rate of taxation on the $100 of valuation, $2 17. In the real estate sales the increase over the preceding year amounted to nearly two million dollars. Columbus now claims to be the wealthiest city of its size in the country, and has at least $190,000,000 of capital invested; about $18 000,000 is invested in incorporated manufacturing companies, $8,000,000 in individual manufacturing, $20,000,000 in the coal business, a like amount in the iron business, $35,000,000 in railroads, and the balance in real estate and wholesale and retail business and miscellaneous enterprises. The amount of business done last year in Columbus aggregated nearly $60,000,000, and it is stated by the local statisticians that the losses amounted to exactly $11,022 18.

Columbus has three great interests—coal, iron, and "buggies." On these three the city has shaped its ends and fashioned its hopes. The work of mining, selling, and shipping of coal gives employment to over ten thousand men. It is now the most important industry in the State. The report of the inspector indicates that 9,000,000 tons of coal were mined in Ohio last year, of which considerably over 2,000,000 tons were used by the city's own consumption. There are twenty-two firms and corporations engaged in mining and shipping coal.

The quality of the iron ore found in the Hocking Valley is said to be superior to even the Pennsylvania material. There are sixty-seven firms engaged in the business of buying the iron as it leaves the furnaces. The annual output averages 200,000 tons. This consumes about 400,000 tons of ore, and about 600,000 tons of coal, and 400,000 tons of

BUGGY FACTORIES.

limestone. Last year the business reached nearly $4,000,000. The railroad facilities enable Columbus to place iron anywhere at such prices and with such despatch as to dispel fear of annoying competition; and this, added to the fact that the coal and limestone used in the reduction of iron ore are found in the same soil, enables the manufacturer to produce iron cheaper than it can be done elsewhere. In conjunction with this the lumber trade is a very important factor in the interests of the city, reaching over 80,000,000 feet per year, and employing about fifteen hundred people in its handling. But the third principal industry of Columbus is the manufacture of "buggies" and carriages, which find their way not only to all parts of this country, but to some of the most obscure foreign places. There are eighteen manufacturers, employing about 2500 men and 300 women. Over three million feet of lumber and three thousand tons of iron are used annually in the construction of vehicles. It is also estimated that of other material used there are nearly four million feet of leather, equal to about seven thousand hides, and

about 75,000 yards of cloth, and 21,000 yards of Brussels carpet. These figures seem almost incredible, and to the reader who has up to this time wondered why Columbus is chiefly known as the residence of politicians and the seat of a very interesting State government, they will cause no little surprise. Last year the sale of over 20,000 carriages (buggies, etc.) indicates that, by counting ten hours to a day of work, one must have been made every nine minutes. One of the manufacturers made the statement that in the consumption of hides alone for this purpose, if the number of cattle killed were seen marching four abreast toward Columbus, there would be every year a procession over fifty miles long. The amount of capital employed is $2,500,000, and a yearly expenditure of $1,200,000, not including $825,000 for wages. Last year the receipts were about $3,000,000.

There are also in Columbus various other manufacturing enterprises—there are 365 in all—the most important of which is the making of machinery and agricultural implements. There are thirteen iron-founderies, two malleable-iron works, a steel-rail mill, a rolling-mill, and twelve galvanized-iron works. Almost every convenience of ordinary use to be obtained can be found of home make. The facilities for this are almost unequalled, and the trade has extended largely abroad.   There are 212 jobbing houses in Columbus, whose business last year exceeded $50,000,000.   It is claimed that there are very few cities where the maxim "pay as you go" is so rigidly adhered to.   There are not many pieces of property mortgaged to outside capitalists, and speculation is chiefly confined to the legitimate changes in the value of land and buildings.

houses which are solidly built, and without pretentious architecture.   The principal residence street is Broad Street, which does not belie its name, and is one of the most beautiful thoroughfares to be found in an American city.   It extends for a distance of several miles, and in the summer-time the four rows of shade trees form a bower of foliage which, while it may give to the avenue a rural beauty quite different from what a city street ought to be, according to the cold and

VIEW OF THE CITY FROM THE RIVER.

Most of the business buildings are large and substantial, ornamenting the streets upon which they are located. In this country, at least, conservatism is generally looked upon as provincialism. Columbus is "provincial" in that it is one of the most conservative cities in the land. Its upper ten thousand follow no fashions but their own. Things that are "New-Yorkish" have no following, except where they may aid for good and direct ends. The people are cultivated by refined instincts which do not lead to extravagance or display. The richest among them live quietly in comfortable homes, and in

uninteresting style of a Fifth Avenue resident, it is nevertheless a very lovely characteristic of Columbus, to which the householders are much attached. It runs at an angle with High Street, the leading business street, and at the juncture are formed the two sides of a huge square, in the centre of which stands the Capitol building, a bold and impressive structure, built of gray limestone quarried within four miles of the city. It is Doric in its style, and the time occupied in building was nearly fifteen years, by convict labor. This, of course, includes several suspensions of work. The cost when com-

BROAD STREET.

pleted amounted to $1,441,675. It is surrounded by immense colonnades and terraces, and the four porticoes are mounted by huge columns, 36 feet high and of 6 feet 2 inches base diameter. The height of the building to the pinnacle of the cupola is 158 feet. The interior of the building is elaborately fitted in different marbles, and the many rooms and offices open into a rotunda some 65 feet in diameter. The height from the floor to the eye of the dome is 120 feet. The first floor is devoted to State offices; the second, to the large chambers—the Senate, the State Library, the House of Representatives, and the Supreme Court Room. There are 53 rooms in the building, and 4892 pieces of American and foreign marbles were used in its construction. The rotunda floor is a mosaic of 4957 pieces of marble from Vermont and Portugal. The centre is a star of thirty-two points, formed by black, green, red, and white marbles. There are several pieces of art in the rotunda, and conspicuous among them are W. H. Powell's famous painting of "Commodore Perry's Victory on Lake Erie," owned by the State; four statues, import-

ed from Italy, representing "A Prophetess of the Future," "The Muse of History," "The Priestess of Bacchus," and the figure of "Innocence." The Lincoln Memorial is a historical group, cut from Italian marble, in *alto-rilievo*, the surface on which the figures are carved being 5 feet 2 inches in length, the height and width each being 3 feet 2 inches. The colossal bust surmounting the monument is of Carrara marble, and an exquisite piece of workmanship. The celebration of the opening of this building occurred January 1, 1856, and was made a great social event by Ohio. It was attended by the State Legislatures of Kentucky and Tennessee, and an old resident declares that the "house-warming" was made notable by the largest gathering of beauty and chivalry ever seen in the West.

It has always been said that if one wishes to meet a debtor or creditor, it was only necessary to take a position on the floor of the Capitol rotunda at noontime, for it would seem as if nearly everybody in Columbus made it a thoroughfare, connecting with one of the four streets. It has always been a great po-

DAVID W. DESHLER.

litical exchange. If the marbles of the walls and floors could speak, they would call forth the names of many whose reminiscences of early days in Columbus would interest a good-sized world. Salmon P. Chase, John Sherman, William Dennison, Allen G. Thurman, and Chief-Justice Waite have here fought their political battles. A silent listener often was Rutherford B. Hayes, who in his quiet home a few rods away never dreamed of being a future President of the United States. Perhaps no man in Ohio exhibited more of the true Northern grit and had more influence in Columbus affairs during the war than Salmon P. Chase, and his antislavery advocacy frequently brought him in contact with people who tested his bravery to no little extent. It is related that on one occasion, when he was announced to speak in a school-house somewhere between Columbus and Cincinnati, a notice was served on him that he would be mobbed if he attempted to utter a word. But he determined to fill his appointment. A crowd of his friends attended the meeting fully armed, but the enemies of the abolitionists startled the audience by a wild yell and a storm of eggs. The pistols put them to flight, but Mr. Chase, after quietly wiping a rotten egg from his shirt bosom, proceeded in the most unruffled way, amid the cheers of what was now a crowd of people. Mr. Chase was one of the leaders in organizing the Liberty Party in Columbus in December, 1841. He subsequently prepared an edition of the Statutes of Ohio, and was Governor from 1855 to 1859. His successor in this office was William Dennison, who afterward became Postmaster-General. Mr. Dennison held a sway which had a strong political effect, and some of his most earnest efforts were directed against the rebellion. The influence which such men as Chase, Dennison, and Thurman, with their families, exerted in the home affairs of Columbus had much to do, as can readily be imagined, in modelling all matters relative to social life. The constant interchange of hospitalities between the private citizens and statesmen who were drawn to the political centre fashioned its society, and made it not unmindful of its needs in education and science. This was followed by the establishment of a free public library, circulating libraries, a scientific association, and an art gallery. The Columbus Art Gallery was formed in 1879, and has now an average of about 200 scholars. It has had since its start about 1600 pupils. The studies pursued are in drawing from life, water-color, oil-painting, and decoration. The people have been slow, however, in expending any money for outward display in this direction, and doubtless it will not be until the rising generation are fully grown that there will be any elaborate architecture covering those things which mark the progress of thought. It was in Columbus that the novelist William D. Howells marked out a political career, first as an editor of the *Ohio State Journal*, and afterward as consul to Venice, where his literary abilities were developed with the strength that has since made him famous. Whitelaw Reid, now editor of the *Tribune*, although born and reared in Xenia, here first drew the encouragement which sent him to Virginia as a war correspondent. Nor has Columbus been wanting in other individuals who can lay claim to world-wide reputations outside of politics. The late William S. Sullivant made valuable contributions to botany; Professor Leo Lesquereux won considerable renown as a geologist; and Professor Dr. Theodore G. Wormley, now of the University of Pennsylvania, has been placed in the front rank of special chemists through his microscopical investigations in toxicology (his work on poisons, illustrated with steel - engravings by his wife, has excited much admiration and attention); Dr. James Hoge, father of the Ohio Presbytery, preached in Columbus for more than fifty years, and was a man of great eloquence;

VIEW IN THE CITY PARK.

Michael Sullivant resided in Columbus, but his Illinois farm was known as the largest in the world; David W. Deshler, at one time president of three banks, was the head of one of the oldest families in the State, and deeply interested himself in the good of the municipality and its private citizens; Dr. Samuel Mitchell Smith was Surgeon-General of Ohio during the war, for thirty years a professor in the Starling Medical College, and during the last twenty years of his life President of the Central Ohio Lunatic Asylum; Dr. Lin-

a place of enlistment and general rendezvous. In 1864 the United States barracks for that vicinity were established there, and the volunteers who went out from Columbus and the massing of State companies rendered the city's streets an active military scene which will never be forgotten. It was here also that the celebrated rebel John Morgan was confined, and from here that he made his escape. The barracks were occupied as an arsenal until November, 1875, when they were changed into a station for receiving and

VIEW ON THE RIVER.

coln Goodale gave to the city a beautiful park. During the war Columbus was in the midst of much activity as

organizing recruits, which are sent there
from Chicago, St. Louis, Cleveland, Cincinnati, Pittsburgh, and Detroit, and remain there several months. The expenditures amount to nearly $70,000 a year,
and the buildings have cost in the neighborhood of $400,000.

Columbus does much for charity. In
its organized work there are already the
Female Benevolent Association, the Industrial School, the Hannah Neil Mission,
the Women's Home, the Soldiers' Home,
the Hare Orphans' Home, the St. Francis
Hospital, and the House of the Good
Shepherd. During last year two gifts of
money were made to the Women's Associations by William G. Deshler, amounting to $133,000. One of these donations
consisted of $33,000 for the establishment
of a Protestant lying-in hospital. The alliance of charity and religion has always
been singularly strong in Columbus. The
various religious denominations have for
each other a praiseworthy regard. The
church edifices are not extravagant, but
they are substantial, and their work is
carried on quietly and effectively.

The State buildings located in Columbus are all architecturally beautiful, and
with the exception of Washington, no
other city can boast of larger structures
or so many. The State Insane Asylum
cost $2,000,000, and will accommodate
1300 patients. It has in connection with
it a farm of 300 acres. It is constructed
of cut stone and brick, and is situated
three miles west of the city, on rising
ground commanding a fine view of the
country. It has a complete armament
for its own use in private gas-works, water-works, engine-house, etc. There is
also an institution called the Idiot Asylum, which contains on the average about
800 inmates, and employs about 150 persons. The cost of this to the State is
$125,000 a year. The Ohio Penitentiary
was begun in 1833 and finished in 1835,

entirely by convict labor, and has cost
$800,000. The buildings are composed of
brick and stone, and now contain over
1300 prisoners. It is a model institution of the kind, with excellent system
and discipline. The prison shops are
large and commodious, and the convicts
are employed by manufacturers. The
annual expense of the prison maintenance
reaches on an average now to $250,000.
The Blind Asylum is of old English character in design, built of cut stone and
brick, and cost in the neighborhood of
$600,000. It will accommodate about 1000
people. The grounds surrounding the
asylum are beautiful, and tended with
jealous care. There are on an average
about 300 pupils being educated by the
State, employing about seventy persons as
instructors and help. The annual expenditures amount to about $50,000. The
Deaf and Dumb Asylum was erected at a
cost of $800,000. It is built of brick, and
elaborately trimmed with limestone and
sandstone. It is one of the finest structures in the State, and is surrounded by
extensive grounds. It has an average of
about 400 pupils, and the expenses reach
nearly $80,000 a year. A most important
and valuable adjunct to the business purposes of the city—because its ramifications
tend so largely to develop the resources
of the State—is the Ohio State University, which was founded by an act of
Congress in 1862. The United States
made a grant of 630,000 acres of public
land for the establishing of a college
"where the leading objects shall be to
teach such branches of learning as are
related to agriculture and the mechanic
arts"; this without excluding other scientific and classical studies, and including
military tactics. The total income of the
University has been over $60,000 a year
for some time past, and the value of the
endowment and property is estimated to
be about $1,200,000; this has been brought

THE INSANE ASYLUM.

THE CITY HALL.

about by the sale of land held in trust by the State, and the receipt of $300,000 from Franklin County, and $28,000 from the Columbus citizens. The University is located within the limits of the city, about three miles north of the "State-house," which seems to be the starting-point for local measurement. It is now surrounded by some 325 acres of land for agricultural uses, and a "campus" of forty acres is under constant improvement. There are four buildings; one containing the geological museum, art hall, laboratories, library, President's room, and chapel, and the office of the State meteorological bureau. Another contains the department of botany and horticulture, in conjunction with greenhouses and experimenting rooms. There are also in the other buildings the mechanical, chemical, and mining engineering; two dormitories for students, and the various rooms for class purposes. In the library are about 8000 books, which, with the convenience of the State library of over 60,000 volumes, gives the scholar all possible opportunity. Certain it is that Ohio is pursuing a most thorough and magnificent system, not only for the development of its natural resources, but for the education of its people. Opposite the southeast corner of the

State-house is the government building for the uses of the Post - office, United States courts, Signal Service Office, Internal Revenue Division, and the Pension Office. This building, recently completed, is one of the handsomest in Columbus; of modern style of architecture, and built of cut stone. Its cost was half a million dollars. It is perhaps worth saying that the Pension Office is the largest in the United States, paying out $1,675,000 a month. This provides for all the Ohio pensioners excepting those known as Navy pensioners, who draw from the Chicago agency. There are also nearly three thousand pensioners who reside in other States and Territories. The citizens of Columbus point with much pride to this new government building, because it was erected without any "jobbing" or corruption. The City Hall is an imposing building in Amherst stone. It is situated directly opposite the south side of the Capitol, and contains, besides the city offices, a public library, and at present the rooms of the Board of Trade. This organization has, however, arranged for an elaborate new building, a plan which was consummated by the more active young business men of the city as soon as the Columbus Club was formed. The Board of Trade now consists of about 500 active members. One of its aims is to offer and provide entertainment for strangers, especially for members of the Legislature, who are for a time residents in the city. It has already accomplished much good by its strong co-operation of influential citizens in the improvement of streets and lighting the city. Building operations in Columbus recently have been so numerous as to prevent a detailed mention here. It is said no city of less than twice its size can show such a building record.

In regard to its municipal matters, Columbus is fully abreast with the times. Its police and fire departments are thoroughly adequate, and its public-school system, numbering twenty-two buildings, and providing for the education of 10,000 children, is in the hands of thoughtful and progressive people. The sanitary condition of the city is excellent. It is supplied with water from living springs through the "Holly" engine-works. The sewerage is particularly good, as Columbus is built on high rolling ground, that makes desirable surface drainage. There are two very handsome parks. Goodale Park was presented to the city in 1851 by Lincoln Goodale, and contains about forty acres of undulating ground, filled with a natural growth of forest trees, a pretty lake, and gravelled walks. The City Park, lying in the southern part of the city, is a place of frequent resort, handsomely laid out, and ornamented by fountains and garden shrubbery. Franklin Park is another convenient breathing-place.

Green Lawn Cemetery contains nearly eighty-five acres of land, and lies about a mile and a half southwesterly from the State-house. The greater portion of the grounds is covered by native forest trees, and is laid out in many graceful avenues, which are lined by handsome monuments and well-kept burial lots. The street railroad facilities of Columbus are extensive and in excellent order. There is also a large Union Depot, very commodious and substantial, in which over one hundred passenger trains daily arrive and depart.

There are four daily papers published in the city, and several weeklies and monthlies. The *Ohio State Journal* and *Daily Times* are morning papers, and the *Dispatch* is published in the evening. There is also a German daily, the *West-bote*. The *Ohio State Journal* was published before the city of Columbus was laid out, and its early history justifies the figure of speech that "it rocked the cradle of the infant capital." Its history is really older than its present name, it being a direct descendant of the *Western Intelligencer*, which was established by Colonel James Kilbourne in 1811, in the village of Worthington, nine miles from the "high bank on the Scioto." It was removed to Columbus in 1814. In 1825 its present name was adopted. Governor John Greiner, famous the country over in the singing campaigns of the '40's, was one of its editors. General William Schouler was identified with it from 1856 to 1858, and Dr. Isaac J. Allen was the editor during the early part of the war. Later editors were William D. Howells and General James M. Comly. The present editor is S. J. Flickenger.

Rustic reminders of early days are the old Scioto River bridge and the turnpike-road to Cincinnati, travelled by the Ohio Stage Company, and owned by Neil Sullivant, Tallmadge, and Deshler—men who afterward looked upon the enterprise as a most gratifying foundation to their success in life.

Among the memories of early Columbus is "the old Eagle Tavern," where, if there were such things in those days—and there must have been since the time of Cæsar — many political rings were formed. At any rate, it was a famous resort in the '20's, and was situated on High Street, opposite the public offices. Among those who frequented the place were Henry Stanbery, Thomas Ewing, James M. Bell, Lyne Starling, and scores of others who became prominent in the political history of Ohio. The proprietor of the place was a John Young, who was noted for the excellence of his mint-juleps, the elegance of his wardrobe, and his being the greatest gambler in Ohio. Perhaps it was to this latter fact that Bell, who was at one time Speaker of the House, owed his passion for gambling, which afterward proved his ruin. Ewing was considered the epicure of the clique, caring little for drink, and Stanbery never forgot the delights of many cozy hours at the old Eagle, even after he became a member of Johnson's cabinet, from which, it will be remembered, he resigned to defend the impeachment. Nothing now remains of this old "Eagle Coffee-House."

WISCONSIN AND MINNESOTA

A VISITOR at a club in Chicago was pointed out a table at which usually lunched a hundred and fifty millions of dollars! This impressive statement was as significant in its way as the list of the men, in the days of Emerson, Agassiz, and Longfellow, who dined together as the Saturday Club in Boston. We cannot, however, generalize from this that the only thing considered in the Northwest is money, and that the only thing held in esteem in Boston is intellect.

The chief concerns in the Northwest are material, and the making of money, sometimes termed the "development of resources," is of the first importance. In Minneapolis and St. Paul, social position is more determined by money than it is in most Eastern cities, and this makes social life more democratic, so far as traditions and family are concerned. I desire not to overstate this, for money is potent everywhere; but I should say that a person not devoted to business, or not succeeding in it, but interested rather in intellectual pursuits—study, research, art (not decorative), education, and the like—would find less sympathy there than in Eastern cities of the same size, and less consideration. Indeed, I was told, more than once, that the spirit of plutocracy is so strong in these cities as to make a very disagreeable atmosphere for people who value the higher things in life more than money and what money only will procure, and display which is always more or less vulgar. But it is necessary to get closer to the facts than this statement.

The materialistic spirit is very strong in the West; of necessity it is, in the struggle for existence and position going on there, and in the unprecedented opportunities for making fortunes. And hence arises a prevailing notion that any education is of little value that does not bear directly upon material success. I should say that the professions, including divinity and the work of the scholar and the man of letters, do not have the weight there that they do in some other places. The professional man, either in the college or the pulpit, is expected to look alive and keep up with the procession. Tradition is weak; it is no objection to a thing that it is new, and in the general strain "sensations" are welcome. The general motto is, "Be alive; be practical." Naturally, also, wealth recently come by desires to assert itself a little in display, in ostentatious houses, luxurious living, dress, jewelry, even to the frank delight in the diamond shirt stud.

But we are writing of Americans, and the Americans are the quickest people in the world to adapt themselves to new situations. The Western people travel much, at home and abroad, and they do not require a very long experience to know what is in bad taste. They are as quick as anybody—I believe they gave us the phrase—to "catch on" to quietness and a low tone. Indeed, I don't know but they would boast that if it is a question of subdued style, they can beat the world. The revolution which has gone all over the country since the Exposition of 1876 in house-furnishing and decoration is quite as apparent at the West as in the East. The West has not suffered more than the East from eccentricities of architecture in the past twenty years. Violations of good taste are pretty well distributed, but of new houses the proportion of handsome, solid, good structures is as large in the West as in the East, and in the cities I think the West has the advantage in variety. It must be frankly said that if the Easterner is surprised at the size, cost, and palatial character of many of their residences, he is not less surprised by the refinement and good taste of their interiors. There are cases where money is too evident, where the splendor has been ordered, but there are plenty of other cases where individual taste is apparent, and love of harmony and beauty. What I am trying to say is that the East undervalues the real refinement of living going along with the admitted cost and luxury in the West. The art of dining is said to be a test of civilization—on a certain plane. Well, dining, in good houses (I believe that is the phrase), is much the same East and West as to appointments, service, cuisine, and talk, with a trifle more freedom and sense of newness in the West : No doubt there is a difference in tone, appreciable but not easy to define. It relates less to the things than the way the things are considered. Where a family has had "things" for two or three generations they are less an object than an unregarded matter of course; where things and a manner of living are newly acquired, they have more importance in themselves. An old community, if it is really civilized (I mean a state in which intellectual concerns are paramount), values less and less, as an end, merely material refinement. The tendency all over the United States is for wealth to run into vulgarity.

In St. Paul and Minneapolis one thing notable is the cordial hospitality, another is the public spirit, and another is the intense devotion to business, the forecast and alertness in new enterprises. Where society is fluid and on the move, it seems comparatively easy to interest the citizens in any scheme for the public good. The public spirit of those cities is admirable. One notices also an uncommon power of organization, of devices for saving time. An illustration of this is the immense railway transfer ground here. Midway between the cities is a mile square of land where all the great railway lines meet, and by means of communicating tracks easily and cheaply exchange freight cars, immensely increasing the facility and lessening the cost of transportation. Another illustration of system is the State office of Public Examiner, an office peculiar to Minnesota, an office supervising banks, public institutions, and county treasuries, by means of which a uniform system of accounting is enforced for all public funds, and safety is insured.

There is a large furniture and furnishing store in Minneapolis, well sustained by the public, which gives one a new idea of the taste of the Northwest. A community that buys furniture so elegant and chaste in design, and stuffs and decorations so æsthetically good, as this shop offers it, is certainly not deficient either in material refinement or the means to gratify the love of it.

What is there besides this tremendous energy, very material prosperity, and undeniable refinement in living? I do not know that the excellently managed public-school system offers anything peculiar for comment. But the High-School in St. Paul is worth a visit. So far as I could judge, the method of teaching is admirable, and produces good results. It

has no rules, nor any espionage. Scholars are put upon their honor. One object of education being character, it is well to have good behavior consist, not in conformity to artificial laws existing only in school, but to principles of good conduct that should prevail everywhere. There is system here, but the conduct expected is that of well-bred boys and girls anywhere. The plan works well, and there are very few cases of discipline. A manual training school is attached—a notion growing in favor in the West, and practised in a scientific and truly educational spirit. Attendance is not compulsory, but a considerable proportion of the pupils, boys and girls, spend a certain number of hours each week in the workshops, learning the use of tools, and making simple objects to an accurate scale from drawings on the black-board. The design is not at all to teach a trade. The object is strictly educational, not simply to give manual facility and knowledge in the use of tools, but to teach accuracy, the mental training that there is in working out a definite, specific purpose.

The State University is still in a formative condition, and has attached to it a preparatory school. Its first class graduated only in 1872. It sends out on an average about twenty graduates a year in the various departments, science, literature, mechanic arts, and agriculture. The bane of a State university is politics, and in the West the hand of the Granger is on the college, endeavoring to make it "practical." Probably this modern idea of education will have to run its course, and so long as it is running its course the Eastern colleges which adhere to the idea of intellectual discipline will attract the young men who value a liberal rather than a material education. The State University of Minnesota is thriving in the enlargement of its facilities. About one-third of its scholars are women, but I notice that in the last catalogue, in the Senior Class of twenty-six there is only one woman. There are two independent institutions also that should be mentioned, both within the limits of St. Paul, the Hamline University, under Methodist auspices, and the McAllister College, under Presbyterian. I did not visit the former, but the latter, at least, though just beginning, has the idea of a classical education foremost, and does not adopt co-education. Its library is well begun by the gift of a miscellaneous collection, containing many rare and old books, by the Rev. E. D. Neill, the well-known antiquarian, who has done so much to illuminate the colonial history of Virginia and Maryland. In the State Historical Society, which has rooms in the Capitol in St. Paul, a vigorous and well-managed society, is a valuable collection of books illustrating the history of the Northwest. The visitor will notice in St. Paul quite as much taste for reading among business men as exists elsewhere, a growing fancy for rare books, and find some private collections of interest. Though music and art cannot be said to be generally cultivated, there are in private circles musical enthusiasm and musical ability, and many of the best examples of modern painting are to be found in private houses. Indeed, there is one gallery in which is a collection of pictures by foreign artists that would be notable in any city. These things are mentioned as indications of a liberalizing use of wealth.

Wisconsin is not only one of the most progressive, but one of the most enlightened, States in the Union. Physically it is an agreeable and beautiful State, agriculturally it is rich, in the southern and central portions at least, and it is overlaid with a perfect net-work of railways. All this is well known. I wish to speak of certain other things which give it distinction. I mean the prevailing spirit in education and in social-economic problems. In some respects it leads all the other States.

There seem to be two elements in the State contending for the mastery, one the New England, but emancipated from tradition, the other the foreign, with ideas of liberty not of New England origin. Neither is afraid of new ideas nor of trying social experiments. Co-education seems to be everywhere accepted without question, as if it were already demonstrated that the mingling of the sexes in the higher education will produce the sort of men and women most desirable in the highest civilization. The success of women in the higher schools, the capacity shown by women in the management of public institutions and in reforms and charities, have perhaps something to do with the favor to woman suffrage. It may be that, if women vote there in general elections as well as school matters, on the ground that every public office

"relates to education," prohibition will be agitated as it is in most other States, but at present the lager-bier interest is too strong to give prohibition much chance. The capital invested in the manufacture of beer makes this interest a political element of great importance.

Milwaukee and Madison may be taken to represent fairly the civilization of Wisconsin. Milwaukee, having a population of about 175,000, is a beautiful city, with some characteristics peculiar to itself, having the settled air of being much older than it is, a place accustomed to money and considerable elegance of living. The situation on the lake is fine, the high curving bluffs offering most attractive sites for residences, and the rolling country about having a quiet beauty. Grand Avenue, an extension of the main business thoroughfare of the city, runs out into the country some two miles, broad, with a solid road, a stately avenue, lined with fine dwellings, many of them palaces in size and elegant in design. Fashion seems to hesitate between the east side and the west side, but the east or lake side seems to have the advantage in situation, certainly in views, and contains a greater proportion of the American population than the other. Indeed, it is not easy to recall a quarter of any busy city which combines more comfort, evidences of wealth and taste and refinement, and a certain domestic character, than this portion of the town on the bluffs, Prospect Avenue and the adjacent streets. With the many costly and elegant houses there is here and there one rather fantastic, but the whole effect is pleasing, and the traveller feels no hesitation in deciding that this would be an agreeable place to live. From the avenue the lake prospect is wonderfully attractive—the beauty of Lake Michigan in changing color and variety of lights in sun and storm cannot be too much insisted on—and this is especially true of the noble Esplanade, where stands the bronze statue (a gift of two citizens) of Solomon Juneau the first settler of Milwaukee in 1818. It is a very satisfactory figure, and placed where it is, it gives a sort of foreign distinction to the open place which the city has wisely left for public use. In this part of the town is the house of the Milwaukee Club, a good building, one of the most tasteful internally, and one of the best appointed, best arranged, and comfortable club-houses in the country. Near this is the new Art Museum (also the gift of a private citizen), a building greatly to be commended for its excellent proportions, simplicity, and chasteness of style, and adaptability to its purpose. It is a style that will last, to please the eye, and be more and more appreciated as the taste of the community becomes more and more refined.

In this quarter are many of the churches, of the average sort, but none calling for special mention except St. Paul's, which is noble in proportions and rich in color, and contains several notable windows of stained glass, one of them occupying the entire end of one transept, the largest, I believe, in the country. It is a copy of Doré's painting of Christ on the way to the Crucifixion, an illuminated street scene, with superb architecture of marble and porphyry, and crowded with hundreds of figures in colors of Oriental splendor. The colors are rich and harmonious, but it is very brilliant, flashing in the sunlight with magnificent effect, and I am not sure but it would attract the humble sinners of Milwaukee from a contemplation of their little faults which they go to church to confess.

The city does not neglect education, as the many thriving public schools testify. It has a public circulating library of 42,000 volumes, sustained at an expense of $22,000 a year by a tax; is free, and well patronized. There are good private collections of books also, one that I saw large and worthy to be called a library, especially strong in classic English literature.

Perhaps the greatest industry of the city, certainly the most conspicuous, is brewing. I do not say that the city is in the hands of the brewers, but with their vast establishments they wield great power. One of them, the largest in the country, and said to equal in its capacity any in the world, has in one group seven enormous buildings, and is impressive by its extent and orderly management, as well as by the rivers of amber fluid which it pours out for this thirsty country. Milwaukee, with its large German element —two-thirds of the population, most of whom are freethinkers—has no Sunday except in a holiday sense; the theatres are all open, and the pleasure-gardens, which are extensive, are crowded with merrymakers in the season. It is, in short, the Continental fashion, and while the church-es and church-goers are like churches and church-goers everywhere, there is an air of general Continental freedom.

The general impression of Milwaukee is that it is a city of much wealth and a great deal of comfort, with a settled, almost conservative feeling, like an Eastern city, and charming, cultivated social life, with the grace and beauty that are common in American society anywhere. I think the men generally would be called well-looking, robust, of the quiet, assured manner of an old community. The women seen on the street and in the shops are of good physique and good color and average good looks, without anything startling in the way of beauty or elegance. I speak of the general aspect of the town, and I mention the well-to-do physical condition because it contradicts the English prophecy of a physical decadence in the West, owing to the stimulating climate and the restless pursuit of wealth. On the train to Madison (the line runs through a beautiful country) one might have fancied that he was on a local New England train: the same plain, good sort of people, and in abundance the well-looking, domestic sort of young women.

Madison is a great contrast to Milwaukee. Although it is the political and educational centre, has the Capitol and the State University, and a population of about 15,000, it is like a large village, with the village habits and friendliness. On elevated, hilly ground, between two charming lakes, it has an almost unrivalled situation, and is likely to possess, in the progress of years and the accumulation of wealth, the picturesqueness and beauty that travellers ascribe to Stockholm. With the hills of the town, the gracefully curving shores of the lakes and their pointed bays, the gentle elevations beyond the lakes, and the capacity of these two bodies of water as pleasure resorts, with elegant music pavilions and fleets of boats for the sail and the oar—why do we not take a hint from the painted Venetian sail?—there is no limit to what may be expected in the way of refined beauty of Madison in the summer, if it remains a city of education and of laws, and does not get up a "boom," and set up factories, and blacken all the landscape with coal smoke!

The centre of the town is a big square, pleasantly tree-planted, so large that the facing rows of shops and houses have a remote and dwarfed appearance, and in the middle of it is the great pillared State-house, American style. The town itself is one of unpretentious, comfortable houses, some of them with elegant interiors, having plenty of books and the spoils of foreign travel. In one of them, the old-fashioned but entirely charming mansion of Governor Fairchild, I cannot refrain from saying, is a collection which, so far as I know, is unique in the world— a collection to which the helmet of Don Quixote gives a certain flavor; it is of barbers' basins, of all ages and countries.

Wisconsin is working out its educational ideas on an intelligent system, and one that may be expected to demonstrate the full value of the popular method—I mean a more intimate connection of the university with the life of the people than exists elsewhere. What effect this will have upon the higher education in the ultimate civilization of the State is a question of serious and curious interest. Unless the experience of the ages is misleading, the tendency of the "practical" in all education is a downward and material one, and the highest civilization must continue to depend upon a pure scholarship, and upon what are called abstract ideas. Even so practical a man as Socrates found the natural sciences inadequate to the inner needs of the soul. "I thought," he says, "as I have failed in the contemplation of true existence (by means of the sciences), I ought to be careful that I did not lose the eye of the soul, as people may injure their bodily eye by gazing on the sun during an eclipse....That occurred to me, and I was afraid that my soul might be blinded altogether if I looked at things with my eyes, or tried by the help of the senses to apprehend them. And I thought I had better have recourse to ideas, and seek in them the truth of existence." The intimate union of the university with the life of the people is a most desirable object, if the university does not descend and lose its high character in the process.

The graded school system of the State is vigorous, all working up to the university. This is a State institution, and the State is fairly liberal to it, so far as practical education is concerned. It has a magnificent new science building, and will have excellent shops and machinery for the sciences (especially the applied) and the mechanic arts. The system is elective. A small per cent. of the students take Greek, a larger number Latin, French, and German, but the university is largely devoted to science. In all the departments, including law, there are about six hundred students, of whom above one hundred are girls. There seems to be no doubt about co-education as a practical matter in the conduct of the college, and as a desirable thing for women. The girls are good students, and usually take more than half the highest honors on the marking scale. Notwithstanding the testimony of the marks, however, the boys say that the girls don't "know" as much as they do about things generally, and they (the boys) have no doubt of their ability to pass the girls either in scholarship or practical affairs in the struggle of life. The idea seems to be that the girls are serious in education only up to a certain point, and that marriage will practically end the rivalry.

The distinguishing thing, however, about the State University is its vital connection with the farmers and the agricultural interests. I do not refer to the agricultural department, which it has in common with many colleges, nor to the special short agricultural course of three months in the winter, intended to give farmers' boys, who enter it without examination or other connection with the university, the most available agricultural information in the briefest time, the intention being not to educate boys away from a taste for farming, but to make them better farmers. The students must be not less than sixteen years old, and have a common-school education. During the term of twelve weeks they have lectures by the professors and recitations on practical and theoretical agriculture, on elementary and agricultural chemistry, on elemental botany, with laboratory practice, and on the anatomy of our domestic animals and the treatment of their common diseases. But what I wish to call special attention to is the connection of the university with the farmers' institutes.

A special act of the Legislature, drawn by a lawyer, Mr. C. E. Estabrook, authorized the farmers' institutes, and placed them under the control of the regents of the university, who have the power to select a State superintendent to control them. A committee of three of the regents has special charge of the institutes. Thus the farmers are brought into direct relation with the university, and while, as a prospectus says, they are not actually non-resident students of the university, they receive information and instruction directly from it. The State appropriates twelve thousand dollars a year to this work, which pays the salaries of Mr. W. H. Morrison, the superintendent, to whose tact and energy the success of the institutes is largely due, and his assistants, and enables him to pay the expenses of specialists and agriculturists who can instruct the farmers and wisely direct the discussions at the meetings. By reason of this complete organization, which penetrates every part of the State, subjects of most advantage are considered, and time is not wasted in merely amateur debates.

I know of no other State where a like system of popular instruction on a vital and universal interest of the State, directed by the highest educational authority, is so perfectly organized and carried on with such unity of purpose and detail of administration; no other in which the farmer is brought systematically into such direct relations to the university. In the current year there have been held eighty-two farmers' institutes in forty-five counties. The list of practical topics discussed is 279, and in this service have been engaged one hundred and seven workers, thirty-one of whom are specialists from other States. This is an "agricultural college," on a grand scale, brought to the homes of the people. The meetings are managed by local committees in such a way as to evoke local pride, interest, and talent. I will mention some of the topics that were thoroughly discussed at one of the institutes: clover as a fertilizer; recuperative agriculture; bee-keeping; taking care of the little things about the house and farm; the education for farmers' daughters; the whole economy of sheep husbandry; egg production; poultry; the value of thought and application in farming; horses to breed for the farm and market; breeding and management of swine; mixed farming; grain-raising; assessment and collection of taxes; does knowledge pay? (with illustrations of money made by knowledge of the market); breeding and care of cattle, with expert testimony as to the best sorts of cows; points in corn culture; full discussion of small-fruit cul-

ture; butter-making as a fine art; the dairy; our country roads; agricultural education. So, during the winter, every topic that concerns the well-being of the home, the profit of the farm, the moral welfare of the people and their prosperity, was intelligently discussed, with audiences fully awake to the value of this practical and applied education. Some of the best of these discussions are printed and widely distributed. Most of them are full of wise details in the way of thrift and money-making, but I am glad to see that the meetings also consider the truth that as much care should be given to the rearing of boys and girls as of calves and colts, and that brains are as necessary in farming as in any other occupation.

As these farmers' institutes are conducted, I do not know any influence comparable to them in waking up the farmers to think, to inquire into new and improved methods, and to see in what real prosperity consists. With prosperity, as a rule, the farmer and his family are conservative, law-keeping, church-going, good citizens. The little appropriation of twelve thousand dollars has already returned to the State a hundredfold financially and a thousandfold in general intelligence.

I have spoken of the habit in Minnesota and Wisconsin of depending mostly upon one crop—that of spring wheat—and the disasters from this single reliance in bad years. Hard lessons are beginning to teach the advantage of mixed farming and stock-raising. In this change the farmers' institutes of Wisconsin have been potent. As one observer says, "They have produced a revolution in the mode of farming, raising crops, and caring for stock." The farmers have been enabled to protect themselves against the effects of drought and other evils. Taking the advice of the institute in 1886, the farmers planted 50,000 acres of ensilage corn, which took the place of the short hay crop caused by the drought. This provision saved thousands of dollars' worth of stock in several counties. From all over the State comes the testimony of farmers as to the good results of the institute work, like this: "Several thousand dollars' worth of improved stock have been brought in. Creameries and cheese factories have been established and well supported. Farmers are no longer raising grain exclusively as heretofore. Our hill-sides are covered with clover. Our farmers are encouraged to labor anew. A new era of prosperity in our State dates from the farmers' institutes."

There is abundant evidence that a revolution is going on in the farming of Wisconsin, greatly assisted, if not inaugurated, by this systematic popular instruction from the university as a centre. It may not greatly interest the reader that the result of this will be greater agricultural wealth in Wisconsin, but it does concern him that putting intelligence into farming must inevitably raise the level of the home life and the general civilization of Wisconsin. I have spoken of this centralized, systematic effort in some detail because it seems more efficient than the work of agricultural societies and sporadic institutes in other States.

In another matter Wisconsin has taken a step in advance of other States; that is, in the care of the insane. The State has about 2600 insane, increasing at the rate of about 167 a year. The provisions in the State for these are the State Hospital (capacity of 500), Northern Hospital (capacity of 600), the Milwaukee Asylum (capacity of 255), and fifteen county asylums for the chronic insane, including two nearly ready (capacity 1220). The improvement in the care of the insane consists in several particulars—the doing away of restraints, either by mechanical appliances or by narcotics, reasonable separation of the chronic cases from the others, increased liberty, and the substitution of wholesome labor for idleness. Many of these changes have been brought about by the establishment of county asylums, the feature of which I wish specially to speak. The State asylums were crowded beyond their proper capacity, classification was difficult in them, and a large number of the insane were miserably housed in county jails and poor-houses. The evils of great establishments were more and more apparent, and it was determined to try the experiment of county asylums. These have now been in operation for six years, and a word about their constitution and perfectly successful operation may be of public service.

These asylums, which are only for the chronic insane, are managed by local authorities, but under constant and close State supervision; this last provision is absolutely essential, and no doubt accounts for the success of the undertaking.

It is not necessary here to enter into details as to the construction of these buildings. They are of brick, solid, plain, comfortable, and of a size to accommodate not less than fifty nor more than one hundred inmates: an institution with less than fifty is not economical; one with a larger number than one hundred is unwieldy, and beyond the personal supervision of the superintendent. A farm is needed for economy in maintenance and to furnish occupation for the men; about four acres for each inmate is a fair allowance. The land should be fertile, and adapted to a variety of crops as well as to cattle, and it should have woodland to give occupation in the winter. The fact is recognized that idleness is no better for an insane than for a sane person. The house-work is all done by the women; the farm, garden, and general out-door work by the men. Experience shows that three-fourths of the chronic insane can be furnished occupation of some sort, and greatly to their physical and moral well-being. The nervousness incident always to restraint and idleness disappears with liberty and occupation. Hence greater happiness and comfort to the insane, and occasionally a complete or partial cure.

About one attendant to twenty insane persons is sufficient, but it is necessary that these should have intelligence and tact; the men capable of leading in farm-work, the women to instruct in house-work and dress-making, and it is well if they can play some musical instrument and direct in amusements. One of the most encouraging features of this experiment in small asylums has been the discovery of so many efficient superintendents and matrons among the intelligent farmers and business men of the rural districts, who have the practical sagacity and financial ability to carry on these institutions successfully.

These asylums are as open as a school; no locked doors (instead of window-bars, the glass-frames are of iron painted white), no pens made by high fences. The inmates are free to go and come at their work, with no other restraint than the watch of the attendants. The asylum is a home and not a prison. The great thing is to provide occupation. The insane, it is found, can be trained to regular industry, and it is remarkable how little restraint is needed if an earnest effort is made to do without it. In the county asylums of Wisconsin about one person in a thousand is in restraint or seclusion each day. The whole theory seems to be to treat the insane like persons in some way diseased, who need occupation, amusement, kindness. The practice of this theory in the Wisconsin county asylums is so successful that it must ultimately affect the treatment of the insane all over the country.

And the beauty of it is that it is as economical as it is enlightened and humane. The secret of providing occupation for this class is to buy as little material and hire as little labor as possible; let the women make the clothes, and the men do the farm-work without the aid of machinery. The surprising result of this is that some of these asylums approach the point of being self-supporting, and all of them save money to the counties, compared with the old method. The State has not lost by these asylums, and the counties have gained; nor has the economy been purchased at the expense of humanity to the insane; the insane in the county asylums have been as well clothed, lodged, and fed as in the State institutions, and have had more freedom, and consequently more personal comfort and a better chance of abating their mania. This is the result arrived at by an exhaustive report on these county asylums in the report of the State Board of Charities and Reforms, of which Mr. Albert O. Wright is secretary. The average cost per week per capita of patients in the asylums by the latest report was, in the State Hospital, $4 39; in the Northern Hospital, $4 33; in the county asylums, $1 89.

The new system considers the education of the chronic insane an important part of their treatment; not specially book-learning (though that may be included), but training of the mental, moral, and physical faculties in habits of order, propriety, and labor. By these means wonders have been worked for the insane. The danger, of course, is that the local asylums may fall into unproductive routine, and that politics will interfere with the intelligent State supervision. If Wisconsin is able to keep her State institutions out of the clutches of men with whom politics is a business simply for what they can make out of it (as it is with those who oppose a civil service not based upon partisan dexterity and subserviency), she will carry her enlightened ideas into the making of a model State. The working out of such a noble reform as this in the treatment of the insane can only be intrusted to men specially qualified by knowledge, sympathy, and enthusiasm, and would be impossible in the hands of changing political workers. The systematized enlightenment of the farmers in the farmers' institutes by means of their vital connection with the university needs the steady direction of those who are devoted to it and not to any party success. As to education generally, it may be said that while for the present the popular favor to the State University depends upon its being "practical" in this and other ways, the time will come when it will be seen that the highest service it can render the State is by upholding pure scholarship, without the least material object.

Another institution of which Wisconsin has reason to be proud is the State Historical Society—a corporation (dating from 1853) with perpetual succession, supported by an annual appropriation of five thousand dollars, with provisions for printing the reports of the society and the catalogues of the library. It is housed in the Capitol. The society has accumulated interesting historical portraits, cabinets of antiquities, natural history, and curiosities, a collection of copper, and some valuable MSS. for the library. The library is one of the best historical collections in the country. The excellence of it is largely due to Lyman C. Draper, LL.D., who was its secretary for thirty-three years, but who began as early as 1834 to gather facts and materials for border history and biography, and who had in 1852 accumulated thousands of manuscripts and historical statements, the nucleus of the present splendid library, which embraces rare and valuable works relating to the history of nearly every State. This material is arranged by States, and readily accessible to the student. Indeed, there are few historical libraries in the country where historical research in American subjects can be better prosecuted than in this. The library began in January, 1854, with fifty volumes. In January, 1887, it had 57,935 volumes and 60,731 pamphlets and documents, making a total of 118,666 titles.

There is a large law library in the State-house, the university has a fair special library for the students, and in the city is a good public circulating library, free, supported by a tax, and much used. For a young city, it is therefore very well off for books.

Madison is not only an educational centre, but an intelligent city; the people read and no doubt buy books, but they do not support book-stores. The shops where books are sold are variety shops, dealing in stationery, artists' materials, cheap pictures, bric-à-brac. Books are of minor importance, and but few are kept "in stock." Indeed, bookselling is not a profitable part of the business; it does not pay to "handle" books, or to keep the run of new publications, or to keep a supply of standard works. In this the shops of Madison are not peculiar. It is true all over the West, except in two or three large cities, and true perhaps not quite so generally in the East; the book-shops are not the literary and intellectual centres they used to be.

There are several reasons given for this discouraging state of the book trade. Perhaps it is true that people accustomed to newspapers full of "selections," to the flimsy publications found on the cheap counters, and to the magazines, do not buy "books that are books," except for "furnishing"; that they depend more and more upon the circulating libraries for anything that costs more than an imported cigar or half a pound of candy. The local dealers say that the system of the great publishing houses is unsatisfactory as to prices and discounts. Private persons can get the same discounts as the dealers, and can very likely, by ordering a list, buy more cheaply than of the local bookseller, and therefore, as a matter of business, he says that it does not pay to keep books; he gives up trying to sell them, and turns his attention to "varieties." Another reason for the decline in the trade may be in the fact that comparatively few booksellers are men of taste in letters, men who read, or keep the run of new publications. If a retail grocer knew no more of his business than many booksellers know of theirs, he would certainly fail. It is a pity on all accounts that the book trade is in this condition. A bookseller in any community, if he is a man of literary culture, and has a love of books and knowledge of them, can do a great deal for the cultivation of the public taste. His shop becomes a sort of intellectual centre of the town. If the public find there an atmosphere of books, and are likely to have their wants met for publications new or rare, they will generally sustain the shop. At least this is my observation. Still I should not like to attempt to say whether the falling off in the retail book trade is due to want of skill in the sellers, to the publishing machinery, or to public indifference. The subject is worthy the attention of experts. It is undeniably important to maintain everywhere these little depots of intellectual supply. In a town new to him the visitor is apt to estimate the taste, the culture, the refinement, as well as the wealth of the town, by its shops. The stock in the dry-goods and fancy stores tells one thing, that in the art stores another thing, that in the book-stores another thing, about the inhabitants. The West, even on the remote frontiers, is full of magnificent stores of goods, telling of taste as well as luxury; the book-shops are the poorest of all.

The impression of the Northwest, thus far seen, is that of tremendous energy, material refinement, much open-mindedness, considerable self-appreciation, uncommon sagacity in meeting new problems, generous hospitality, the Old Testament notion of possessing this world, rather more recognition of the pecuniary as the only success than exists in the East and South, intense national enthusiasm, and unblushing and most welcome "Americanism."

In these sketchy observations on the Northwest nothing has seemed to me more interesting and important than the agricultural changes going on in eastern Dakota, Minnesota, and Wisconsin. In the vast wheat farms, as well as in the vast cattle ranges, there is an element of speculation, if not of gambling, of the chance of immense profits or of considerable loss, that is neither conducive to the stable prosperity nor to the moral soundness of a State. In the breaking up of the great farms, and in the introduction of varied agriculture and cattle raising on a small scale, there will not be so many great fortunes made, but each State will be richer as a whole, and less liable to yearly fluctuations in prosperity. But the gain most worth considering will be in the home life and the character of the citizens. The best life of any community depends upon varied industries. No part of the United States has ever prospered, as regards the well-being of the mass of the people, that relied upon the production of a single staple.

ST LOUIS AND KANSAS

S T. LOUIS is eighty years old. It was incorporated as a town in 1808, thirteen years before the admission of Missouri into the Union as a State. In 1764 a company of thirty Frenchmen made a settlement on its site and gave it its distinguished name. For nearly half a century, under French and Spanish jurisdiction alternately, it was little more than a trading post, and at the beginning of this century it contained only about a thousand inhabitants. This period, however, gave it a romantic historic background, and as late as 1853, when its population was a hundred thousand, it preserved French characteristics and a French appearance—small brick houses and narrow streets crowded down by the river. To the stranger it was the Planters' Hotel and a shoal of big steam-boats moored along an extensive levee roaring with river traffic. Crowded, ill-paved, dirty streets, a few country houses on elevated sites, a population forced into a certain activity by trade, but hindered in municipal improvement by French conservatism, and touched with the rust of slavery—that was the St. Louis of thirty-five years ago.

Now everything is changed as by some magic touch. The growth of the city has always been solid, unspeculative, conservative in its business methods, with some persistence of the old French influence, only gradually parting from its ancient traditions, preserving always something of the aristocratic flavor of "old families," accounted "slow" in the impatience of youth. But it has burst its old bounds, and grown with a rapidity that would be marvellous in any other country. The levee is comparatively deserted, although the trade on the lower river is actually very large. The traveller who enters the city from the east passes over the St. Louis Bridge, a magnificent structure and one of the engineering wonders of the modern world, plunges into a tunnel under the business portion of the old city, and emerges into a valley covered with a network of railway tracks, and occupied by apparently interminable lines of passenger coaches and freight-cars, out of the confusion of which he makes his way with difficulty to a carriage. impressed at once by the enormous railway traffic of the city. This is the site of the proposed Union Depot, which waits upon the halting action of the Missouri Pacific system. The eastern outlet for all this growing traffic is over the two tracks of the bridge; these are entirely inadequate, and during a portion of the year there is a serious blockade of freight. A second bridge over the Mississippi is already a necessity to the commerce of the city, and is certain to be built within a few years.

St. Louis, since the war, has spread westward over the gentle ridges which parallel the river, and become a city vast in territory and most attractive in appearance. While the business portion has expanded into noble avenues with stately business and public edifices, the residence parts have a beauty, in handsome streets and varied architecture, that is a continual surprise to one who has not seen the city for twenty years. Its extent is coincident with the county, whose governmental functions it has absorbed. I had set down the length of the city along the river front as thirteen miles, with a depth of about six miles; but the official statistics are: length of river front, 19.15 miles: length of western limits, 21.27; extent north and south in an air line, 17: and length east and west on an air line, 6.62. This gives an area of 61.37 square miles, or 39,276 acres. This includes the public parks (containing 2095 acres), and is sufficient room for the population of 450,000, which the city doubtless has in 1888. By the United States census of 1870 the population was reported much larger than it was, the figures having no doubt been manipulated for political purposes. Estimating the natural increase from this false report, the city was led to claim a population far beyond the actual number, and unjustly suffered a little ridicule for a mistake for which it was not responsible. The United States census of 1880 gave it 350,522. During the eight years from 1880 there were erected 18,574 new dwelling-houses, at a cost of over fifty millions of dollars.

The great territorial extension of the city in 1876 was for a time a disadvantage, for it threw upon the city the care of enormous street extensions, made a sporadic movement of population beyond Grand Avenue, which left hiatuses in improvement, and created a sort of furor of fashion for getting away from what to me is still the most attractive residence portion of the town, namely, the elevated ridges west of Fourteenth Street, crossed by Lucas Place and adjoining avenues. In this quarter, and east of Grand Avenue, are fine high streets, with detached houses and grounds, many of them both elegant and comfortable, and this is the region of the Washington University, some of the finest club-houses, and handsomest churches. The movements of city populations, however, are not to be accounted for. One of the finest parts of the town, and one of the oldest of the better residence parts, that south of the railways, containing broad, well-planted avenues, and very

stately old homes, and the exquisite Lafayette Park, is almost wholly occupied now by Germans, who make up so large a proportion of the population.

One would have predicted at an early day that the sightly bluffs below the city would be the resort of fashion, and be occupied with fine country houses. But the movement has been almost altogether westward and away from the river. And this rolling, wooded region is most inviting, elevated, open, cheerful. No other city in the West has fairer suburbs for expansion and adornment, and its noble avenues, dotted with conspicuously fine residences, give promise of great beauty and elegance. In its late architectural development, St. Louis, like Chicago, is just in time to escape a very mediocre and merely imitative period in American building. Beyond Grand Avenue the stranger will be shown Vandeventer Place, a semi-private oblong park, surrounded by many pretty and some notably fine residences. Two of them are by Richardson, and the city has other specimens of his work. I cannot refrain from again speaking of the effect that this original genius has had upon American architecture, especially in the West, when money and enterprise afforded him free scope. It is not too much to say that he created a new era, and the influence of his ideas is seen everywhere in the work of architects who have caught his spirit.

The city has addressed itself to the occupation and adornment of its great territory and the improvement of its most travelled thoroughfares with admirable public spirit. The rolling nature of the ground has been taken advantage of to give it a nearly perfect system of drainage and sewerage. The old pavements of soft limestone, which were dust in dry weather and liquid mud in wet weather, are being replaced by granite in the business parts and asphalt and wood blocks (laid on a concrete base) in the residence portions. Up to the beginning of 1888 this new pavement had cost nearly three and a half million dollars, and over thirty-three miles of it were granite blocks. Street railways have also been pushed all over the territory. The total of street lines is already over one hundred and fifty-four miles, and over thirty miles of these give rapid transit by cable. These facilities make the whole of the wide territory available for business and residence, and give the poorest the means of reaching the parks.

The park system is on the most liberal scale, both public and private; the parks are already famous for extent and beauty, but when the projected connecting boulevards are made they will attain world-wide notoriety. The most extensive of the private parks is that of the combined Agricultural Fair Grounds and Zoological Gardens. Here is held annually the St. Louis Fair, which is said to be the largest in the United States. The enclosure is finely laid out and planted, and contains an extensive park, exhibition buildings, cottages, a race-track, an amphitheatre, which suggests in size and construction some of the largest Spanish bull rings, and picturesque houses for wild animals. The zoological exhibition is a very good one. There are eighteen public parks. One of the smaller (thirty acres) of these, and one of the oldest, is Lafayette Park, on the south side. Its beauty surprised me more than almost anything I saw in the city. It is a gem; just that artificial control of nature which most pleases—forest trees, a pretty lake, fountains, flowers, walks planned to give everywhere exquisite vistas. It contains a statue of Thomas H. Benton, which may be a likeness, but utterly fails to give the character of the man. The largest is Forest Park, on the west side, a tract of 1372 acres, mostly forest, improved by excellent drives, and left as much as possible in a natural condition. It has ten miles of good driving roads. This park cost the city about $850,000, and nearly as much more has been expended on it since its purchase. The surface has great variety of slopes, glens, elevations, lakes, and meadows. During the summer music is furnished in a handsome pagoda, and the place is much resorted to. Fronting the boulevard are statues of Governor Edward Bates and Frank P. Blair, the latter very characteristic.

Next in importance is Tower Grove Park, an oblong of 276 acres. This and Shaw's Garden, adjoining, have been given to the city by Mr. Henry Shaw, an Englishman who made his fortune in the city, and they remain under his control as to care and adornment during his life. Those who have never seen foreign parks and pleasure gardens can obtain a very good idea of their formal elegance and impressiveness by visiting Tower Grove Park and the Botanical Gardens. They will see the perfection of lawns, avenues ornamented by statuary, flower beds, and tasteful walks. The entrances, with stone towers and lodges, suggest similar effects in France and in England. About the music stand are white marble busts of six chief musical composers. The drives are adorned with three statues in bronze, thirty feet high, designed and cast in Munich by Frederick Müller. They are figures of Shakespeare, Humboldt, and Columbus, and so nobly conceived and executed that the patriotic American must wish they had been done in this country. Of Shaw's Botanical Garden I need to say little, for its fame as a comprehensive and classified collection of trees, plants, and flowers is world-wide. It has no equal in this country. As a place for botanical study no one appreciated it more highly than the late Professor Asa Gray. Sometimes a peculiar classification is followed; one locality is devoted to economic plants —camphor, quinine, cotton, tea, coffee, etc.; another to "Plants of the Bible." The space of fifty-four acres, enclosed by high stone walls, contains, besides the open garden and *allées* and glass houses, the summer residence and the tomb of Mr. Shaw. This old gentleman, still vigorous in his eighty-eighth year, is planning new adornments in the way of statuary and busts of statesmen, poets, and scientists. His plans are all liberal and cosmopolitan. For over thirty years his botanical knowledge, his taste, and abundant wealth and leisure have been devoted to the creation of this wonderful garden and park, which all bear the stamp of his strong individuality, and of a certain pleasing foreign formality. What a source of unfailing delight it must have been to him! As we sat talking with him I thought how other millionnaires, if they knew how, might envy a matured life, after the struggle for a competency is over, devoted to this most rational enjoyment, in an occupation as elevating to the taste as to the character, and having in mind always the public good. Over the entrance gate is the inscription, "Missouri Botanical Gardens." When the city has full control of the garden the word "Missouri" should be replaced by "Shaw."

The money expended for public parks gives some idea of the liberal and far-sighted provision for the health and pleasure of a great city. The parks originally cost the city $1,309,944, and three millions more have been spent upon their improvement and maintenance. This indicates an enlightened spirit, which we shall see characterizes the city in other things, and is evidence of a high degree of culture.

Of the commerce and manufactures of the town I can give no adequate statement without going into details, which my space forbids. The importance of the Mississippi River is much emphasized, not only as an actual highway of traffic, but as a regulator of railway rates. The town has by the official reports been discriminated against, and even the Inter-State Act has not afforded all the relief expected. In 1887 the city shipped to foreign markets by way of the Mississippi and the jetties 3,973,000 bushels of wheat and 7,365,000 bushels of corn—a larger exportation than ever before except in the years 1880 and 1881. An outlet like this is of course a check on railway charges. The trade of the place employs a banking capital of fifteen millions. The deposits in 1887 were thirty-seven millions; the clearings over $894,527,731—the largest ever reached, and over ten per cent. in excess of the clearings of 1886. To whatever departments I turn in the report of the Merchants' Exchange for 1887 I find a vigorous growth—as in building—and in most articles of commerce a great increase. It appears by the tonnage statements that, taking receipts and shipments together, 12,060,995 tons of freight were handled in and out during 1886, against 14,359,059 tons in 1887—a gain of nineteen and a half per cent. The buildings in 1886 cost $7,030,819; in 1887, $8,162,914. There were $44,740 more stamps sold at the post-office in 1887 than in 1886. The custom-house collections were less than in 1886, but reached the figures of $1,414,747. The assessed value of real and personal property in 1887 was $217,142,320, on which the rate of taxation in the old city limits was $2 50.

It is never my intention in these papers to mention individual enterprises for their own sake, but I do not hesitate to do so when it is necessary in order to illustrate some peculiar development. It is a curious matter of observation that so many Western cities have one or more specialties in which they excel—houses of trade or manufacture larger and more important than can be found elsewhere. St. Louis finds itself in this category in regard to several establishments. One of these is a wooden-ware company, the largest of the sort in the country, a house which gathers its peculiar goods from all over the United States, and distributes them almost as widely—a business of gigantic proportions and bewildering detail. Its annual sales amount to as much as the sales of all the houses in its line in New York, Chicago, and Cincinnati together. Another is a hardware company, wholesale and retail, also the largest of its kind in the country, with sales annually amounting to six millions of dollars, a very large amount when we consider that it is made up of an infinite number of small and cheap articles in iron, from a fish-hook up—indeed, over fifty thousand separate articles. I spent half a day in this establishment, walking through its departments, noting the unequalled system of compact display, classification, and methods of sale and shipment. Merely as a method of system in business I have never seen anything more interesting. Another establishment, important on account of its central position in the continent and its relation to the Louisiana sugar fields, is the St. Louis Sugar Refinery. The refinery proper is the largest building in the Western country used for manufacturing purposes, and, together with its adjuncts of cooper shops and warehouses, covers five entire blocks and employs 500 men. It has a capacity of working up 400 tons of raw sugar a day, but runs only to the extent of about 200 tons a day, making the value of its present product $7,500,000 a year.

During the winter and spring it uses Louisiana sugars; the remainder of the year, sugars of Cuba and the Sandwich Islands. Like all other refineries of which I have inquired, this reckons the advent for the Louisiana crop as an important regulator of prices. This establishment, in common with other industries of the city, has had to complain of business somewhat hampered by discrimination in railway rates. St. Louis also has what I suppose, from the figures accessible, to be the largest lager-beer brewing establishment in the world; its solid, gigantic, and architecturally imposing buildings lift themselves up like a fortress over the thirty acres of ground they cover. Its manufacture and sales in 1887 were 456,511

barrels of beer—an increase of nearly
100,000 since 1885-6. It exports largely
to Mexico, South America, the West In-
dies, and Australia. The establishment
is a marvel of system and ingenious devices. It employs 1200 laborers, to whom
it pays $500,000 a year. Some of the de-
tails are of interest. In the bottling department we saw workmen filling, cork-
ing, labelling, and packing at the rate of
100,000 bottles a day. In a year 25,000,000
bottles are used, packed in 400,000 barrels
and boxes. The consumption of barley
is 1,100,000 bushels yearly, and of hops
over 700,000 pounds, and the amount of
water used for all purposes is 250,000,000
gallons—nearly enough to float our navy.
The charges for freight received and
shipped by rail amount to nearly a million dollars a year. There are several
other large breweries in the city. The
total product manufactured in 1887 was
1,383,361 barrels, equal to 43,575,872 gallons—more than three times the amount
of 1877. The barley used in the city and
vicinity was 2,932,192 bushels, of which
340,335 bushels came from Canada. The
direct export of beer during 1887 to foreign countries was equal to 1,924,108 quart
bottles. The greater part of the barley
used comes from Iowa, Minnesota, and
Wisconsin.

It is useless to enumerate the many railways which touch and affect St. Louis.
The most considerable is the agglomeration known as the Missouri Pacific, or
Southwestern System, which operated 6994
miles of road on January 1, 1888. This
great aggregate is likely to be much diminished by the surrender of lines, but
the railway facilities of the city are constantly extending.

There are figures enough to show that
St. Louis is a prosperous city, constantly
developing new enterprises with fresh energy; to walk its handsome streets and
drive about its great avenues and parks is
to obtain an impression of a cheerful town
on the way to be most attractive; but its
chief distinction lies in its social and intellectual life, and in the spirit that has
made it a pioneer in so many educational
movements. It seems to me a very good
place to study the influence of speculative
thought in economic and practical affairs.
The question I am oftenest asked is, whether the little knot of speculative philosophers accidentally gathered there a few
years ago, and who gave a sort of fame

to the city, have had any permanent influence. For years they discussed abstractions; they sustained for some time a very
remarkable periodical of speculative philosophy, and in a limited sphere they
maintained an elevated tone of thought
and life quite in contrast with our general
materialism. The circle is broken, the
members are scattered. Probably the
town never understood them, perhaps
they did not altogether understand each
other, and may be the tremendous conflict of Kant and Hegel settled nothing.
But if there is anything that can be demonstrated in this world it is the influence
of abstract thought upon practical affairs
in the long-run. And although one may
not be able to point to any definite thing
created or established by this metaphysical
movement, I think I can see that it was
a leaven that had a marked effect in the
social, and especially in the educational,
life of the town, and liberalized minds, and
opened the way for the trial of theories in
education. One of the disciples declares
that the State Constitution of Missouri and
the charter of St. Louis are distinctly
Hegelian. However this may be, both
these organic laws are uncommonly wise
in their provisions. A study of the evolution of the city government is one of
the most interesting that the student can
make. Many of the provisions of the
charter are admirable, such as those securing honest elections, furnishing financial
checks, and guarding against public debt.
The mayor is elected for four years, and
the important offices filled by his appointment are not vacant until the beginning
of the third year of his appointment, so
that hope of reward for political work is
too dim to affect the merits of an election.
The composition and election of the school
board is also worthy of notice. Of the
twenty-one members, seven are elected on
a general ticket, and the remaining fourteen by districts, made by consolidating
the twenty-eight city wards, members to
serve four years, divided into two classes.
This arrangement secures immunity from
the ward politician.

St. Louis is famous for its public schools,
and especially for the enlightened methods, and the willingness to experiment in
improving them. The school expenditures for the year ending June 30, 1887,
were $1,095,773; the school property in
lots, buildings, and furniture in 1885 was
estimated at $3,445,254. The total num-

ber of pupils enrolled was 56,936. These required about 1200 teachers, of whom over a thousand were women. The actual average of pupils to each teacher was about 42. There were 106 school buildings. with a seating capacity for about 50,000 scholars. Of the district schools 13 were colored, in which were employed 78 colored teachers. The salaries of teachers are progressive, according to length of service. As for instance, the principal of the High-School has $2400 the first year, $2500 the second, $2600 the third, $2750 the fourth; a head assistant in a district school, $650 the first year, $700 the second, $750 the third, $800 the fourth, $850 the fifth.

The few schools that I saw fully sustained their public reputation as to methods, discipline, and attainments. The Normal School, of something over 100 pupils, nearly all the girls being graduates of the High-School, was admirable in drill, in literary training, in calisthenic exercises. The High-School is also admirable, a school with a thoroughly elevated tone and an able principal. Of the 600 pupils at least two-thirds were girls. From appearances I should judge that it is attended by children of the most intelligent families, for certainly the girls of the junior and senior classes, in manner, looks, dress, and attainments, compared favorably with those of one of the best girls' schools I have seen anywhere, the Mary Institute, which is a department of the Washington University. This fact is most important, for the excellence of our public schools (for the product of good men and women) depends largely upon their popularity with the well-to-do classes. One of the most interesting schools I saw was the Jefferson, presided over by a woman, having fine fire-proof buildings and 1100 pupils, nearly all of whom are of foreign parentage—German, Russian, and Italian, with many Hebrews also—a finely ordered, wide-awake school of eight grades. The kindergarten here was the best I saw; good teachers, bright and happy little children, with natural manners, throwing themselves gracefully into their games with enjoyment and without self-consciousness, and exhibiting exceedingly pretty fancy and kindergarten work. In St. Louis the kindergarten is a part of the public-school system, and the experiment is one of general interest. The question cannot be called settled. In

the first place the experiment is hampered in St. Louis by a decision of the Supreme Court that the public money cannot be used for children out of the school age, that is, under six and over twenty. This prevents teaching English to adult foreigners in the evening schools, and, rigidly applied, it shuts out pupils from the kindergarten under six. One advantage from the kindergarten was expected to be an extension of the school period; and there is no doubt that the kindergarten instruction ought to begin before the age of six, especially for the mass of children who miss home training and home care. As a matter of fact many of the children I saw in the kindergartens were only constructively six years old. It cannot be said, also, that the Froebel system is fully understood or accepted. In my observation the success of the kindergarten depends entirely upon the teacher; where she is competent, fully believes in and understands the Froebel system, and is enthusiastic, the pupils are interested and alert; otherwise they are listless, and fail to get the benefit of it. The Froebel system is the developing the concrete idea in education, and in the opinion of his disciples this is as important for children of the intelligent and well-to-do as for those of the poor and ignorant. They resist, therefore, the attempt which is constantly made, to introduce the primary work into the kindergarten. But for the six years' limit the kindergarten in St. Louis would have a better chance in its connection with the public schools. As the majority of children leave school for work at the age of twelve or fourteen, there is little time enough given for book education; many educators think time is wasted in the kindergarten, and they advocate the introduction of what they call kindergarten features in the primary classes. This is called by the disciples of Froebel an entire abandonment of his system. I should like to see the kindergarten in connection with the public school tried long enough to demonstrate all that is claimed for it in its influence on mental development, character, and manners, but it seems unlikely to be done in St. Louis, unless the public-school year begins at least as early as five, or, better still, is specially unlimited for kindergarten pupils.

Except in the primary work in drawing and modelling, there is no manual training feature in the St. Louis public schools. The teaching of German is recently dropped from all the district schools (though retained in the High), in accordance with the well-founded idea of Americanizing our foreign population as rapidly as possible.

One of the most important institutions in the Mississippi Valley, and one that exercises a decided influence upon the intellectual and social life of St. Louis, and is a fair measure of its culture and the value of the higher education, is the Washington University, which was incorporated in 1853, and was presided over until his death, in 1887, by the late Chancellor William Greenleaf Eliot, of revered memory. It covers the whole range of university studies, except theology, and allows no instruction either sectarian in religion or partisan in politics, nor the application of any sectarian or party test in the election of professors, teachers, or officers. Its real estate and buildings in use for educational purposes cost $625,000; its libraries, scientific apparatus, casts, and machinery cost over $160,000, and it has investments for revenue amounting to over $650,000. The University comprehends an undergraduate department, including the college (a thorough classical, literary, and philosophical course, with about sixty students), open to women, and the polytechnic, an admirably equipped school of science; the St. Louis Law School, of excellent reputation; the Manual Training School, the most celebrated school of this sort, and one that has furnished more manual training teachers than any other; the Henry Shaw School of Botany; the St. Louis School of Fine Arts; the Smith Academy, for boys; and the Mary Institute, one of the roomiest and most cheerful school buildings I know, where 400 girls, whose collective appearance need not fear comparison with any in the country, enjoy the best educational advantages. Mary Institute is justly the pride of the city.

The School of Botany, which is endowed and has its own laboratory, workshop, and working library, was, of course, the outgrowth of the Shaw Botanical Garden; it has usually from twenty to thirty special students.

The School of Fine Arts, which was reorganized under the university in 1879, has enrolled over 200 students, and gives a wide and careful training in all the departments of drawing, painting, and modelling, with instructions in anatomy, perspective, and composition, and has life classes for both sexes, in drawing from draped and nude figures. Its lecture, working rooms, and galleries of paintings and casts are in its Crow Art Museum—a beautiful building, well planned and justly distinguished for architectural excellence. It ranks among the best art buildings in the country.

The Manual Training School has been in operation since 1880. It may be called the most fully developed pioneer institution of the sort. I spent some time in its workshops and schools, thinking of the very interesting question at the bottom of the experiment, namely, the mental development involved in the training of the hand and the eye, and the reflex help to manual skill in the purely intellectual training of study. It is, it may be said again, not the purpose of the modern manual training to teach a trade, but to teach the use of tools as an aid in the symmetrical development of the human being. The students here certainly do beautiful work in wood turning and simple carving, in iron-work and forging. They enjoy the work; they are alert and interested in it. I am certain that they are the more interested in it in seeing how they can work out and apply what they have learned in books, and I doubt not they take hold of literary study more freshly for this manual training in exactness. The school exacts close and thoughtful study with tools as well as in books, and I can believe that it gives dignity in the opinion of the working student to hand labor. The school is large, its graduates have been generally successful in practical pursuits and in teaching, and it has demonstrated in itself the correctness of the theory of its authors, that intellectual drill and manual training are mutually advantageous together. Whether manual training shall be a part of all district-school education is a question involving many considerations that do not enter into the practicability of this school, but I have no doubt that manual training schools of this sort would be immensely useful in every city. There are many boys in every community who cannot in any other way be awakened to any real study. This training school deserves a chapter by itself, and as I have no space for details, I take the liberty of referring those interested to a volume on its aims and methods by Dr. C. M. Woodward, its director.

Notwithstanding the excellence of the public-school system of St. Louis, there is no other city in the country, except New Orleans, where so large a proportion of the youths are being educated outside the public schools. A very considerable portion of the population is Catholic. There are forty-four parochial schools, attended by nineteen thousand pupils, and over a dozen different Sisterhoods are engaged in teaching in them. Generally each parochial school has two departments —one for boys and one for girls. They are sustained entirely by the parishes. In these schools, as in the two Catholic universities, the prominence of ethical and religious training is to be noted. Seven-eighths of the schools are in charge of thoroughly trained religious teachers. Many of the boys' schools are taught by Christian Brothers. The girls are almost invariably taught by members of religious Sisterhoods. In most of the German schools the girls and smaller boys are taught by Sisters, the larger boys by lay teachers. Some reports of school attendance are given in the Catholic Directory: SS. Peter and Paul's (German), 1300 pupils; St. Joseph's (German), 957; St. Bridget's, 950; St. Malachy's, 756; St. John's, 700; St. Patrick's, 700. There is a school for colored children of 150 pupils, taught by colored Sisters.

In addition to these parochial schools there are a dozen academies and convents of higher education for young ladies, all under charge of Catholic Sisterhoods, commonly with a mixed attendance of boarders and day scholars, and some of them with a reputation for learning that attracts pupils from other States, notably the Academy of the Sacred Heart, St. Joseph's Academy, and the Academy of the Visitation, in charge of cloistered nuns of that order. Besides these, in connection with various reformatory and charitable institutions, such as the House of the Good Shepherd and St. Mary's Orphan Asylum, there are industrial schools in charge of the Sisterhoods, where girls receive, in addition to their education, training in some industry to maintain themselves respectably when they leave their temporary homes. Statistics are wanting, but it will be readily inferred from these statements that there are in the city a great number of single women devoted for life, and by

special religious and intellectual training, to the office of teaching.

For the higher education of Catholic young men the city is distinguished by two remarkable institutions. The one is the old St. Louis University, and the other is the Christian Brothers' College. The latter, which a few years ago outgrew its old buildings in the city, has a fine pile of buildings at Côte Brillante, on a commanding site about five miles out, with ample grounds, and in the neighborhood of the great parks and the Botanical Garden. The character of the school is indicated by the motto on the façade of the building—*Religio, Mores, Cultura*. The institution is designed to accommodate a thousand boarding students. The present attendance is 450, about half of whom are boarders, and represent twenty States. There is a corps of thirty-five professors, and three courses of study are maintained —the classical, the scientific, and the commercial. As several of the best parochial schools are in charge of Christian Brothers, these schools are feeders of the college, and the pupils have the advantage of an unbroken system with a consistent purpose from the day they enter the primary department till they graduate at the college. The order has, at Glencoe, a large Normal School for the training of teachers. The fame and success of the Christian Brothers as educators in elementary and the higher education, in Europe and the United States, is largely due to the fact that they labor as a unit in a system that never varies in its methods of imparting instruction, in which the exponents of it have all undergone the same pedagogic training, in which there is no room for the personal fancy of the teacher in correction, discipline, or scholarship, for everything is judiciously governed by prescribed modes of procedure, founded on long experience, and exemplified in the co-operative plan of the Brothers. In vindication of the exceptional skill acquired by its teachers in the thorough drill of the order, the Brotherhood points to the success of its graduates in competitive examinations for public employment in this country and in Europe, and to the commendation its educational exhibits received at London and New Orleans.

The St. Louis University, founded in 1829 by members of the Society of Jesus, and chartered in 1834, is officered and controlled by the Jesuit Fathers. It is an

mendowed institution. depending upon
fees paid for tuition. Before the war its
students were largely the children of
Southern planters, and its graduates are
found all over the South and Southwest;
and up to 1881 the pupils boarded and
lodged within the precincts of the old
buildings on the corner of Ninth Street
and Washington, where for over half a
century the school has vigorously flourished. The place, which is now sold and
about to be used for business purposes,
has a certain flavor of antique scholarship,
and the quaint buildings keep in mind the
plain but rather pleasing architecture of
the French period. The University is in
process of removal to the new buildings
on Grand Avenue, which are a conspicuous ornament to one of the most
attractive parts of the city. Soon nothing will be left of the institution on
Ninth Street except the old college
church, which is still a favorite place of
worship for the Catholics of the city.
The new buildings, in the early decorated English Gothic style, are ample and
imposing; they have a front of 270 feet,
and the northern wing extends 325 feet
westward from the avenue. The library,
probably the finest room of the kind in
the West, is sixty-seven feet high, amply
lighted, and provided with three balco-
nies. The library, which was packed for
removal, has over 25,000 volumes, is said
to contain many rare and interesting
books, and to fairly represent science and
literature. Besides this, there are special
libraries, open to students, of over 6000
volumes. The museum of the new building is a noble hall, one hundred feet by
sixty feet, and fifty-two feet high, without columns, and lighted from above
and from the side. The University has
a valuable collection of ores and minerals,
and other objects of nature and art that
will be deposited in this hall, which will
also serve as a picture-gallery for the
many paintings of historical interest.
Philosophical apparatus, a chemical laboratory, and an astronomical observatory
are the equipments on the scientific side.

The University has now no dormitories
and no boarders. There are twenty-five
professors and instructors. The entire
course, including the preparatory, is sev-
en years. A glance at the catalogue
shows that in the curriculum the institution keeps pace with the demands of the
age. Besides the preparatory course (89

pupils), it has a classical course (143 pupils), an English course (82 pupils), and
85 post-graduate students, making a total
of 399. Its students form societies for
various purposes; one, the Sodality of
the Blessed Virgin Mary, with distinct
organizations in the senior and junior
classes, is for the promotion of piety and
the practice of devotion toward the Blessed Virgin; another is for training in public speaking and philosophic and literary disputation; there is also a scientific
academy, to foster a taste for scientific
culture; and there is a student's library
of 4000 volumes, independent of the religious books of the Sodality societies.

In a conversation with the president I
learned that the prevailing idea in the
courses of study is the gradual and healthy
development of the mind. The classes
are carefully graded. The classics are
favorite branches, but mental philosophy,
chemistry, physics, astronomy, are taught
with a view to practical application. Much
stress is laid upon mathematics. During
the whole course of seven years, one hour
each day is devoted to this branch. In
short, I was impressed with the fact that
this is an institution for mental training.
Still more was I struck with the prominence in the whole course of ethical and
religious culture. On assembling every
morning, all the Catholic students hear
mass. In every class in every year
Christian doctrine has as prominent a
place as any branch of study; beginning in the elementary class with the
small catechism and practical instructions
in the manner of reciting the ordinary
prayers, it goes on through the whole
range of doctrine—creed, evidences, ritu-
al, ceremonial, mysteries—in the minutest
details of theory and practice; ingraining,
so far as repeated instruction can, the
Catholic faith and pure moral conduct in
the character, involving instructions as
to what occasions and what amusements
are dangerous to a good life, on the reading of good books and the avoiding bad
books and bad company.

In the post-graduate course, lectures
are given and examinations made in ethics, psychology, anthropology, biology,
and physics; and in the published ab-
stracts of lectures for the past two years
I find that none of the subjects of modern doubt and speculation are ignored
—spiritism, psychical research, the cell
theory, the idea of God, socialism, ag-

nosticism, the Noachian deluge, theories of government, fundamental notions of physical science, unity of the human species, potency of matter, and so on. During the past fifty years this faculty has contained many men famous as pulpit orators and missionaries, and this course of lectures on philosophic and scientific subjects has brought it prominently before the cultivated inhabitants of the town.

Another educational institution of note in St. Louis is the Concordia Seminar of the Old Lutheran, or the Evangelical Lutheran, Church. This denomination, which originated in Saxony, and has a large membership in our Western States, adheres strictly to the Augsburg Confession, and is distinguished from the general Lutheran Church by greater strictness of doctrine and practice, or, as may be said, by a return to primitive Lutheranism; that is to say, it grounds itself upon the literal inspiration of the Scriptures, upon salvation by faith alone, and upon individual liberty. This Seminar is one of several related institutions in the Synod of Missouri, Ohio, and other States: there is a college at Fort Wayne, Indiana, a Progymnasium at Milwaukee, a Seminar of practical theology at Springfield, Illinois, and this Seminar at St. Louis, which is wholly devoted to theoretical theology. This Church numbers, I believe, about 200,000 members.

The Concordia Seminar is housed in a large, commodious building, effectively set upon high ground in the southern part of the city. It was erected and the institution is sustained by the contributions of the congregations. The interior, roomy, light, and commodious, is plain to barrenness, and has a certain monastic severity, which is matched by the discipline and the fare. In visiting it one takes a step backward into the atmosphere and theology of the sixteenth century. The ministers of the denomination are distinguished for learning and earnest simplicity. The president, a very able man, only thirty-five years of age, is at least two centuries old in his opinions, and wholly undisturbed by any of the doubts which have agitated the Christian world since the Reformation. He holds the faith "once for all" delivered to the saints. The Seminar has a hundred students. It is requisite to admission, said the president, that they be perfect Latin, Greek, and Hebrew scholars. A large

proportion of the lectures are given in Latin, the remainder in German and English, and Latin is current in the institution, although German is the familiar speech. The course of study is exacting, the rules are rigid, and the discipline severe. Social intercourse with the other sex is discouraged. The pursuit of love and learning are considered incompatible at the same time; and if a student were inconsiderate enough to become engaged, he would be expelled. Each student from abroad may select or be selected by a family in the communion, at whose house he may visit once a week, which attends to his washing, and supplies to a certain extent the place of a home. The young men are trained in the highest scholarship and the strictest code of morals. I know of no other denomination which holds its members to such primitive theology and such strictness of life. Individual liberty and responsibility are stoutly asserted, without any latitude in belief. It repudiates prohibition as an infringement of personal liberty, would make the use of wine or beer depend upon the individual conscience, but no member of the communion would be permitted to sell intoxicating liquors, or to go to a beer garden or a theatre. In regard to the sacrament of communion, there is no authority for altering the plain directions in the Scripture, and communion without wine, or the substitution of any concoction for wine, would be a sin. No member would be permitted to join any labor union or secret society. The sacrament of communion is a mystery. It is neither transubstantiation nor consubstantiation. The president, whose use of English in subtle distinctions is limited, resorted to Latin and German in explanation of the mystery, but left the question of real and actual presence, of spirit and substance, still a matter of terms; one can only say that neither the ordinary Protestant nor the Catholic interpretation is accepted. Conversion is not by any act or ability of man; salvation is by faith alone. As the verbal inspiration of the Scriptures is insisted on in all cases, the world was actually created in six days of twenty-four hours each. When I asked the president what he did with geology, he smiled and simply waved his hand. This communion has thirteen flourishing churches in the city. In a town so largely German, and with so many freethinkers as well as free-livers, I cannot but consider this strict sect, of a simple unquestioning faith and high moral demands, of the highest importance in the future of the city. But one encounters with surprise, in our modern life, this revival of the sixteenth century, which plants itself so squarely against so much that we call "progress."

As to the institutions of charity, I must content myself with saying that they are many, and worthy of a great and enlightened city. There are of all denominations 211 churches; of these the Catholics lead with 47; the Presbyterians come next with 24; and the Baptists have 22; the Methodists North, 4; and the Methodists South, 8. The most interesting edifices, both for associations and architecture, are the old Cathedral; the old Christ Church (Episcopalian), excellent Gothic; and an exquisite edifice, the Church of the Messiah (Unitarian), in Locust Street.

The city has two excellent libraries. The Public Library, an adjunct of the public-school system, in the Polytechnic Building, has an annual appropriation of about $14,000 from the School Board, and receives about $5000 more from membership and other sources. It contains about 67,000 volumes, and is admirably managed. The Mercantile Library is in process of removal into a magnificent six-story building on Broadway and Locust Street. It is a solid and imposing structure, the first story of red granite, and the others of brick and terra-cotta. The library and reading-rooms are on the fifth story, the rest of the building is rented. This association, which is forty-two years old, has 3500 members, and had an income in 1887 of $120,000, nearly all from membership. In January, 1888, it had 68,732 volumes, and in a circulation of over 168,000 in the year, it had the unparalleled distinction of reducing the fiction given out to 41.95 per cent. Both these libraries have many treasures interesting to a book lover, and though neither is free, the liberal, intelligent management of each has been such as to make it a most beneficent institution for the city.

There are many handsome and stately buildings in the city, the recent erections showing growth in wealth and taste. The Chamber of Commerce, which is conspicuous for solid elegance, cost a million and a half dollars. There are 3295 members

of the Merchants' Exchange. The Court-house, with its noble dome, is as well-proportioned a building as can be found in the country. A good deal may be said for the size and effect of the Exposition Building, which covers what was once a pretty park at the foot of Lucas Place, and cost $750,000. There are clubs many and flourishing. The St. Louis Club (social) has the finest building, an exceedingly tasteful piece of Romanesque architecture on Twenty-ninth Street. The University Club, which is like its namesake in other cities, has a charming old-fashioned house and grounds on Pine Street. The Commercial Club, an organization limited in its membership to sixty, has no club-house, but, like its namesake in Chicago, is a controlling influence in the prosperity of the city. Representing all the leading occupations, it is a body of men who, by character, intellect, and wealth, can carry through any project for the public good, and which is animated by the highest public spirit.

Of the social life of the town one is permitted to speak only in general terms. It has many elements to make it delightful—long use in social civilities, interest in letters and in education, the cultivation of travel, traditions, and the refinement of intellectual pursuits. The town has no academy of music, but there is a good deal of musical feeling and cultivation: there is a very good orchestra, one of the very best choruses in the country, and Verdi's *Requiem* was recently given splendidly. I am told by men and women of rare and special cultivation that the city is a most satisfactory one to live in, and certainly to the stranger its society is charming. The city has, however, the Mississippi Valley climate—extreme heat in the summer, and trying winters.

There is no more interesting industrial establishment in the West than the plate-glass works at Crystal City, thirty miles south on the river. It was built up after repeated failures and reverses—for the business, like any other, had to be learned. The plant is very extensive, the buildings are of the best, the machinery is that most approved, and the whole represents a cash investment of $1,500,000. The location of the works at this point was determined by the existence of a mountain of sand, which is quarried out like rock, and is the finest and cleanest silica known in the country. The production is confined entirely to plate-glass, which is cast in great slabs, twelve feet by twelve and a half in size, each of which weighs, before it is reduced half in thickness by grinding, smoothing, and polishing, about 750 pounds. The product for 1887 was 1,200,000 feet. The coal used in the furnaces is converted into gas, which is found to be the most economical and most easily regulated fuel. This industry has drawn together a population of about 1500. I was interested to learn that labor in the production of this glass is paid twice as much as similar labor in England, and from three to four times as much as similar labor in France and Belgium. As the materials used in making plate-glass are inexpensive, the main cost, after the plant, is in labor. Since plate-glass was first made in this country, eighteen years ago, the price of it in the foreign market has been continually forced down, until now it costs the American consumer only half what it cost him before, and the jobber gets it at an average cost of 75 cents a foot, as against the $1 50 a foot which we paid the foreign manufacturer before the establishment of American factories. And in these eighteen years the government has had from this source a revenue of over seventeen millions, at an average duty, on all sizes, of less than 59 per cent.

Missouri is one of the greatest of our States in resources and in promise, and it is conspicuous in the West for its variety and capacity of interesting development. The northern portion rivals Iowa in beautiful rolling prairie, with high divides and park-like forests; its water communication is unsurpassed; its mineral resources are immense; it has noble mountains as well as fine uplands and fertile valleys, and it never impresses the traveller as monotonous. So attractive is it in both scenery and resources that it seems unaccountable that so many settlers have passed it by. But, first slavery, and then a rural population disinclined to change, have stayed its development. This state of things, however, is changing, has changed marvellously within a few years in the northern portion, in the iron regions, and especially in larger cities of the west, St. Joseph and Kansas City. The State deserves a study by itself, for it is on the way to be a great empire of most varied interests. I can only

mention here one indication of its moral progress. It has adopted a high license and local option law. Under this the saloons are closed in nearly all the smaller villages and country towns. A shaded map shows more than three-fourths of the area of the State, including three-fifths of the population, free from liquor-selling. The county court may grant a license to sell liquor to a person of good moral character on the signed petition of a majority of the tax-paying citizens of a township or of a city block; it must grant it on the petition of two-thirds of the citizens. Thus positive action is required to establish a saloon. On the map there are 76 white counties free of saloons, 14 counties in which there are from one to three saloons only, and 24 shaded counties which have altogether 2263 saloons, of which 1450 are in St. Louis and 520 in Kansas City. The revenue from the saloons in St. Louis is about $800,000, in Kansas City about $375,000, annually. The heavily shaded portions of the map are on the great rivers.

Of all the wonderful towns in the West none has attracted more attention in the East than Kansas City. I think I am not wrong in saying that it is largely the product of Eastern energy and capital, and that its closest relations have been with Boston. I doubt if ever a new town was from the start built up so solidly or has grown more substantially. The situation, at the point where the Missouri River makes a sharp bend to the east, and the Kansas River enters it, was long ago pointed out as the natural centre of a great trade. Long before it started on its present career it was the great receiving and distributing point of Southwestern commerce, which left the Missouri River at this point for Santa Fé and other trading marts in the Southwest. Aside from this river advantage, if one studies the course of streams and the incline of the land in a wide circle to the westward, he is impressed with the fact that the natural business drainage of a vast area is Kansas City. The city was therefore not fortuitously located, and when the railways centred there, they obeyed an inevitable law. Here nature intended, in the development of the country, a great city. Where the next one will be in the Southwest is not likely to be determined until the Indian Territory is open to settlement. To the north, Omaha, with reference to

Nebraska and the West, possesses many similar advantages, and is likewise growing with great vigor and solidity. Its situation on a slope rising from the river is commanding and beautiful, and its splendid business houses, handsome private residences, and fine public schools give ample evidence of the intelligent enterprise that is directing its rapid growth.

It is difficult to analyze the impression Kansas City first makes upon the Eastern stranger. It is usually that of immense movement, much of it crude, all of it full of purpose. At the Union Station, at the time of the arrival and departure of trains, the whole world seems afloat; one is in the midst of a continental movement of most varied populations. I remember that the first time I saw it in passing, the detail that most impressed me was the racks and rows of baggage-checks; it did not seem to me that the whole travelling world could need so many. At that time a drive through the city revealed a chaos of enterprise—deep cuts for streets, cable roads in process of construction over the sharp ridges, new buildings, hills shaved down, houses perched high up on slashed knolls, streets swarming with traffic and roaring with speculation. A little more than a year later the change toward order was marvellous: the cable roads were running in all directions; gigantic buildings rising upon enormous blocks of stone gave distinction to the principal streets; the great residence avenues had been beautified, and showed all over the hills stately and picturesque houses. And it is worthy of remark that while the "boom" of speculation in lots had subsided, there was no slacking in building, and the reports showed a steady increase in legitimate business. I was confirmed in my theory that a city is likely to be most attractive when it has had to struggle heroically against natural obstacles in the building.

I am not going to describe the city. The reader knows that it lies south of the river Missouri, at the bend, and that the notable portion of it is built upon a series of sharp hills. The hill portion is already a beautiful city; the flat part, which contains the railway depot and yards, a considerable portion of the manufactories and wholesale houses, and much refuse and squatting population (white and black), is unattractive in a high degree. The Kaw or Kansas River would seem to be the natural western boundary, but it is not the boundary; the city and State line runs at some distance east of Kansas River, leaving a considerable portion of low ground in Kansas City. Kansas, which contains the larger number of the great packing houses and the great stock-yards. This identity of names is confusing. Kansas City (Kansas), Wyandotte, Armourdale, Armstrong, and Riverview (all in the State of Kansas) have been recently consolidated under the name of Kansas City, Kansas. It is to be regretted that this thriving town of Kansas, which already claims a population of 40,000, did not take the name of Wyandotte. In its boundaries are the second largest stock-yards in the country, which received last year 670,000 cattle, nearly 2,500,000 hogs, and 210,000 sheep, estimated worth $51,-000,000. There also are half a dozen large packing houses, one of them ranking with the biggest in the country, which last year slaughtered 195,933 cattle, and 1,907,164 hogs. The great elevated railway, a wonderful structure, which connects Kansas City, Missouri, with Wyandotte, is owned and managed by men of Kansas City, Kansas. The city in Kansas has a great area of level ground for the accommodation of manufacturing enterprises, and I noticed a good deal of speculative feeling in regard to this territory. The Kansas side has fine elevated situations for residences, but Wyandotte itself does not compare in attractiveness with the Missouri city, and I fancy that the controlling impetus and capital will long remain with the city that has so much the start.

Looking about for the specialty which I have learned to expect in every great Western city, I was struck by the number of warehouses for the sale of agricultural implements on the flats, and I was told that Kansas City excels all others in the amount of sales of farming implements. The sale is put down at $15,000,000 for the year 1887—a fourth of the entire reported product manufactured in the United States. Looking for the explanation of this, one largely accounts for the growth of Kansas City, namely, the vast rich agricultural regions to the west and southwest, the development of Missouri itself, and the facilities of distribution. It is a general belief that settlement is gradually pushing the rainy belt further and further westward over the prairies and plains, that the breaking up of the sod by the plough and the tilling have increased evaporation and consequently rainfall. I find this questioned by competent observers, who say that the observation of ten years is not enough to settle the fact of a change of climate, and that, as not a tenth part of the area under consideration has been broken by the plough, there is not cause enough for the alleged effect, and that we do not yet know the cycle of years of drought and years of rain. However this may be, there is no doubt of the vast agricultural yield of these new States and Territories, nor of the quantities of improved machinery they use. As to facility of distribution, the railways are in evidence. I need not name them, but I believe I counted fifteen lines and systems centring there. In 1887, 4565 miles of railway were added to the facilities of Kansas City, stretching out in every direction. The development of one is notable as peculiar and far-sighted, the Fort Scott and Gulf, which is grasping the East as well as the Southwest; turning eastward from Fort Scott, it already reaches the iron industries of Birmingham, pushes on to Atlanta, and seeks the seaboard. I do not think I overestimate the importance of this quite direct connection of Kansas City with the Atlantic.

The population of Kansas City, according to the statistics of the Board of Trade, increased from 41,786 in 1877 to 165,924 in 1887, the assessed valuation from $9,370,287 in 1877 to $53,017,290 in 1887, and the rate of taxation was reduced in the same period from about 22 mills to 14. I notice also that the banking capital increased in a year—1886 to 1887—from $3,873,000 to $6,950,000, and the Clearing-house transactions in the same year from $251,963,441 to $353,895,458. This, with other figures which might be given, sustains the assertion that while real-estate speculation has decreased in the current year, there was a substantial increase of business. During the year ending June 30, 1886, there were built 4054 new houses, costing $10,393,207; during the year ending June 30, 1887, 5889, costing $12,839,868. An important feature of the business of Kansas City is in the investment and loan and trust companies, which are many, and aggregate a capital of $7,773,000. Loans are made on farms in Kansas, Missouri, Nebraska, and Iowa, and also for city improvements.

Details of business might be multiplied, but enough have been given to illustrate the material prosperity of the city. I might add a note of the enterprise which last year paved (mainly with cedar blocks on concrete) thirteen miles of the city; the very handsome churches in process of erection, and one or two (of the many) already built, admirable in plan and appearance; the really magnificent building of the Board of Trade—a palace, in fact; and other handsome, costly structures on every hand. There are thirty-five miles of cable road. I am not sure but these cable roads are the most interesting—certainly the most exciting—feature of the city to a stranger. They climb such steeps, they plunge down such grades, they penetrate and whiz through such crowded, lively thoroughfares, their trains go so rapidly, that the rider is in a perpetual exhilaration. I know no other locomotion more exciting and agreeable. Life seems a sort of holiday when one whizzes through the crowded city, up and down and around amid the tall buildings, and then launches off in any direction into the suburbs, which are alive with new buildings. Independence Avenue is shown as one of the finest avenues, and very handsome it and that part of the town are, but I fancied I could detect a movement of fashion and preference to the hills southward.

In the midst of such a material expansion one has learned to expect fine houses, but I was surprised to find three very good book-stores (as I remember, St. Louis has not one so good), and a very good start for a public library, consisting of about 16,000 well-arranged and classified books. Members pay $2 a year, and the library receives only about $2500 a year from the city. The citizens could make no better-paying investment than to raise this library to the first rank. There is also the beginning of an art school in some pretty rooms, furnished with casts and autotypes, where pupils practice drawing under direction of local artists. There are two social clubs—the University, which occupies pleasant apartments, and the Kansas City Club, which has just erected a handsome club-house. In these respects, and in a hundred refinements of living, the town, which has so largely drawn its young, enterprising population from the extreme East, has little the appearance of a frontier place; it is the push, the public spirit, the mixture of fashion and slouching negligence in street attire, the mingling of Eastern smartness with border emancipation in manner, and the general restlessness of movement, that proclaim the newness. It seems to me that the incessant stir, and especially the clatter, whir, and rapidity of the cable cars, must have a decided effect on the nerves of the whole population. The appearance is certainly that of an entire population incessantly in motion.

I have spoken of the public spirit. Besides the Board of Trade there is a Merchants' and Manufacturers' Bureau, which works vigorously to bring to the city and establish mercantile and manufacturing enterprises. The same spirit is shown in the public schools. The expenditures in 1887 were, for school purposes, $226,923; for interest on bonds, $18,408; for grounds and buildings, $110,087; in all, $355,418. The total of children of school age was, white, 31,667; colored, 4204. Of these in attendance at school were, white, 12,933; colored, 1975. There were 25 schoolhouses and 212 teachers. The schools which I saw—one large grammar-school, a colored school, and the High-School of over 600 pupils—were good all through, full of intelligent emulation, the teachers alert and well equipped, and the attention to literature, to the science of government, to what, in short, goes to make intelligent citizens, highly commendable. I find the annual reports, under Professor J. M. Greenwood, most interesting reading. Topics are taken up and investigations made of great public interest. These topics relate to the even physical and mental development of the young in distinction from the effort merely to stuff them with information. There is a most intelligent attempt to remedy defective eyesight. Twenty per cent. of school children have some anomaly of refraction or accommodation which should be recognized and corrected early; girls have a larger per cent. of anomalies than boys. Irish, Swedish, and German children have the highest percentage of affections of the eyes; English, French, Scotch, and Americans the lowest. Scientific observations of the eyes are made in the Kansas City schools, with a view to remedy defects. Another curious topic is the investigation of the Contents of Children's Minds—that is, what very small children know about common things. Professor Stanley Hall published recently the result of examinations made of very little folks in Boston schools. Professor Greenwood made similar investigations among the lowest grade of pupils in the Kansas City schools, and a table of comparisons is printed. The per cent. of children ignorant of common things is astonishingly less in Kansas City schools than in the Boston; even the colored children of the Western city made a much better showing. Another subject of investigation is the alleged physical deterioration in this country. Examinations were made of hundreds of school children from the age of ten to fifteen, and comparisons taken with the tables in Mulhall's *Dictionary of Statistics*, London, 1884. It turns out that the Kansas City children are taller, taking sex into account, than the average English child at the age of either ten or fifteen, weigh a fraction less at ten, but upward of four pounds more at fifteen, while the average Belgian boy and girl compare favorably with American children two years younger. The tabulated statistics show two facts, that the average Kansas City child stands fully as tall as the tallest, and that in weight he tips the beam against an older child on the other side of the Atlantic. With this showing, we trust that our American experiment will be permitted to go on.

In reaching the necessary limit of a paper too short for its subject, I can only express my admiration of the indomitable energy and spirit of that portion of the West which Kansas City represents, and congratulate it upon so many indications of attention to the higher civilization, without which its material prosperity will be wonderful but not attractive.

NOTE.—In the number for July I quoted the remarks of several commercial travellers, contrasting their ability to sell goods, mainly luxuries, in Illinois and Iowa, attributing the falling off of their trade in the latter State to restrictive legislation. In regard to the general effect upon prosperity of prohibitory legislation, I had personally no opinion to express, and certainly should not attempt to form one without observation. As to the railway companies, there is no question that they should be held to their charter rights and responsibilities; but, on the other hand, there is no doubt that much of the agitation and attempted legislation against them is against the best development of the State, and inspired by a notion of what will be popular with the masses. As to the Iowa farmers, their prosperity, their surplus for luxuries and for advanced education, I have received several letters from intelligent correspondents in the State, denying, and by statistics disproving, the inferences of the commercial travellers. I am more than glad to acknowledge them, because it ought to be true that if less money is spent for liquor, there should be more for general purposes of civilization and comfort.

CINCINNATI AND LOUISVILLE

CINCINNATI is a city that has a past. As Daniel Webster said, that at least is secure. Among the many places that have been and are the Athens of America, this was perhaps the first. As long ago as the first visit of Charles Dickens to this country it was distinguished as a town of refinement as well as cultivation; and the novelist, who saw little to admire, though much to interest him in our raw country, was captivated by this little village on the Ohio. It was already the centre of an independent intellectual life, and produced scholars, artists, writers, who subsequently went east instead of west. According to tradition, there seems to have been early a tendency to free thought, and a response to the movement which, for lack of a better name, was known in Massachusetts as transcendentalism.

The evolution of Cincinnati seems to have been a little peculiar in American life. It is a rich city, priding itself on the solidity of its individual fortunes and business, and the freedom of its real property from foreign mortgages. Usually in our development the pursuit of wealth comes first, and then all other things are added thereto, as we read the promise. In Cincinnati there seems to have been a very considerable cultivation first in time, and we have the spectacle of what wealth will do in the way of the sophistication and materialization of society. Ordinarily we have the process of an uncultivated community gradually working itself out into a more or less ornamented and artistic condition as it gets money. The reverse process we might see if the philosophic town of Concord, Massachusetts, should become the home of rich men engaged in commerce and manufacturing. I may be all wrong in my no-

tion of Cincinnati, but there is a sort of tradition, a remaining flavor of old-time culture before the town became commercially so important as it was before the war.

It is difficult to think of Cincinnati as in Ohio. I cannot find their similarity of traits. Indeed, I think that generally in the State there is a feeling that it is an alien city; the general characteristics of the State do not flow into and culminate in Cincinnati as its metropolis. It has had somehow an independent life. If you look on a geologic map of the State, you see that the glacial drift, I believe it is called, which flowed over three-fourths of the State and took out its wrinkles did not advance into the southwest. And Cincinnati lies in the portion that was not smoothed into a kind of monotony. When a settlement was made here it was a good landing-place for trade up and down the river, and was probably not so much thought of as a distributing and receiving point for the interior north of it. Indeed, up to the time of the war, it looked to the South for its trade, and naturally, even when the line of war was drawn, a good deal of its sympathies lay in the direction of its trade. It had become a great city, and grown rich both in trade and manufactures, but in the decline of steam-boating and in the era of railways there were physical difficulties in the way of adapting itself easily to the new conditions. It was not easy to bring the railways down the irregular hills and to find room for them on the landing. The city itself had to contend with great natural obstacles to get adequate foothold, and its radiation over, around, and among the hills produced some novel features in business and in social life.

What Cincinnati would have been, with its early culture and its increasing wealth, if it had not become so largely German in its population, we can only conjecture. The German element was at once conservative as to improvements and liberalizing, as the phrase is, in theology and in life. Bituminous coal and the Germans combined to make a novel American city. When Dickens saw the place it was a compact, smiling little city, with a few country places on the hills. It is now a scattered city of country places, with a little nucleus of beclouded business streets. The traveller does not go there to see the city, but to visit the suburbs, climbing into them, out of the smoke and grime, by steam "inclines" and grip railways. The city is indeed difficult to see. When you are in it, by the river, you can see nothing; when you are outside of it you are in any one of half a dozen villages, in regions of parks and elegant residences, altogether charming and geographically confusing; and if from some commanding point you try to recover the city idea, you look down upon black roofs half hid in black smoke, through which the fires of factories gleam, and where the colored Ohio rolls majestically along under a dark canopy. Looked at in one way, the real Cincinnati is a German city, and you can only study its true character "Over the Rhine," and see it successfully through the bottom of an upturned beer glass. Looked at another way, it is mainly an affair of elegant suburbs, beautifully wooded hills, pleasure-grounds, and isolated institutions of art or charity. I am thankful that there is no obligation on me to depict it.

It would probably be described as a city of art rather than of theology, and one of rural homes rather than metropolitan society. Perhaps the German element has had something to do in giving it its musical character, and the early culture may have determined its set more toward art than religion. As the cloud of smoke became thicker and thicker in the old city, those who disliked this gloom escaped out upon the hills in various directions. Many, of course, still cling to the solid ancestral houses in the city, but the country movement was so general that church-going became an affair of some difficulty, and I can imagine that the church-going habit was a little broken up while the new neighborhoods were forming on the hills and in the winding valleys, and before the new churches in the suburbs were erected. Congregations were scattered, and society itself was more or less disintegrated. Each suburb is fairly accessible from the centre of the city, either by a winding valley or by a bold climb up a precipice, but, owing to the configuration of the ground, it is difficult to get from one suburb to another without returning to the centre and taking a fresh start. This geographical hinderance must necessarily interfere with social life, and tend to isolation of families, or to merely neighborhood association.

Although much yet remains to be done in the way of good roads, nature and art have combined to make the suburbs of the city wonderfully beautiful. The surface is most picturesquely broken, the forests are fine, from this point and that there are views pleasing, poetic, distant, perfectly satisfying in form and variety, and in advantageous situations taste has guided wealth in the construction of stately houses, having ample space in the midst of manorial parks. You are not out of sight of these fine places in any of the suburbs, and there are besides, in every direction, miles of streets of pleasing homes. I scarcely know whether to prefer Clifton, with its wide sweeping avenues rounding the hills, or the perhaps more commanding heights of Walnut, nearer the river, and overlooking Kentucky. On the East Walnut Hills is a private house worth going far to see for its color. It is built of broken limestone, the chance find of a quarry, making the richest walls I have anywhere seen, comparable to nothing else than the exquisite colors in the rocks of the Yellowstone Falls, as I recall them in Mr. Moran's original studies.

If the city itself could substitute gas fuel for its smutty coal, I fancy that, with its many solid homes and stately buildings, backed by the picturesque hills, it would be a city at once curious and attractive to the view. The visitor who ascends from the river as far as Fourth Street is surprised to find room for fair avenues, and many streets and buildings of mark. The Probasco fountain in another atmosphere would be a thing of beauty, for one may go far to find so many groups in bronze so good. The Post-office building is one of the best of the Mullet-headed era of our national architecture—so good generally that one wonders that the architect thought it expedient to destroy the effect of the monolith columns by cutting them to resemble superimposed blocks. A very remarkable building also is the new Chamber of Commerce structure, from Richardson's design, massive, mediaeval, challenging attention, and compelling criticism to give way to genuine admiration. There are other buildings, public and private, that indicate a city of solid growth; and the activity of its strong Chamber of Commerce is a guarantee that its growth will be maintained with the enterprise common to American cities. The effort is to make manufacturing take the place in certain lines of business that, as in the item of pork-packing, has been diverted by various causes. Money and effort have been freely given to regain the Southern trade interrupted by the war, and I am forced to believe that the success in this respect would have been greater if some of the city newspapers had not thought it all-important to manufacture political capital by keeping alive old antagonisms and prejudices. Whatever people may say, sentiment does play a considerable part in business, and it is within the knowledge of the writer that prominent merchants in at least one Southern city have refused trade contracts that would have been advantageous to Cincinnati, on account of this exhibition of partisan spirit, as if the war were not over. Nothing would be more contemptible than to see a community selling its principles for trade, but it is true that men will trade, other things being equal, where they are met with friendly cordiality and toleration, and where there is a spirit of helpfulness instead of suspicion. Professional politicians, North and South, may be able to demonstrate to their satisfaction that they should have a chance to make a living, but they ask too much when this shall be at the expense of free-flowing trade, which is in itself the best solvent of any remaining alienation, and the surest disintegrator of the objectionable political solidity, and to the hinderance of that entire social and business good feeling which is of all things desirable and necessary in a restored and compacted Union. And it is as bad political as it is bad economic policy. As a matter of fact, the politicians of Kentucky are grateful to one or two Republican journals for aid in keeping their State "solid." It is a pity that the situation has its serious as well as its ridiculous aspect.

Cincinnati in many respects is more an Eastern than a Western town; it is developing its own life, and so far as I could see, without much infusion of young fortune-hunting blood from the East. It has attained its population of about 275,000 by a slower growth than some other Western cities, and I notice in its statistical reports a pause rather than excitement since 1878-79-80. The valuation of real and personal property has kept about the same for nearly ten years (1886, real estate about $129,000,000, personal about $42,000,000), with a falling off in the personalty, and a noticeable decrease in the revenue from taxation. At the same time manufacturing has increased considerably. In 1880 there was a capital of $60,523,350, employing 74,798 laborers, with a product of $148,957,280. In 1886 the capital was $76,248,200, laborers 93,103, product $190,722,153. The business at the Post-office was a little less in 1886 than in 1883. In the seven years ending with 1886 there was a considerable increase in banking capital, which reached in the city proper over ten millions, and there was an increase in clearings from 1881 to 1886.

It would teach us nothing to follow in detail the fluctuations of the various businesses in Cincinnati, either in appreciation or decline, but it may be noted that it has more than held its own in one of the great staples—leaf tobacco—and still maintains a leading position. Yet I must refer to one of the industries for the sake of an important experiment made in connection with it. This is the experiment of profit-sharing at Ivorydale, the establishment of Messrs. Proctor and Gamble, now, I believe, the largest soap factory in the world. The soap and candle industry has always been a large one in Cincinnati, and it has increased about seventy-five per cent. within the past two years. The proprietors at Ivorydale disclaim any intention of philanthropy in their new scheme—that is, the philanthropy that means giving something for nothing, as a charity: it is strictly a business operation. It is an experiment that I need not say will be watched with a good deal of interest as a means of lessening the friction between the interests of capital and labor. The plan is this: Three trustees are named who are to declare the net profits of the concern every six months; for this purpose they are to have free access to the books and papers at all times, and they are to permit the employés to designate a book-keeper to make an examination for them also. In determining the net profits, interest on all capital invested is calculated as an expense at the rate of six per cent., and a reasonable salary is allowed to each member of the firm who gives his entire time to the business. In order to share in the profits the employé must have been at work for three consecutive months, and must be at work when the semiannual account is made up. All the men share whose wages have exceeded $5 a week, and all the women whose wages have exceeded $4 25 a week. The proportion divided to each employé is determined by the amount of wages earned; that is, the employés shall share as between themselves in the profits exactly as they have shared in the entire fund paid as wages to the whole body, excluding the first three months' wages. In order to determine the profits for distribution, the total amount of wages paid to all employés (except travelling salesmen, who do not share) is ascertained. The amount of all expenses, including interest and salaries, is ascertained, and the total net profits shall be divided between the firm and the employés sharing in the fund. The amount of the net profit to be distributed will be that proportion of the whole net profit which will correspond to the proportion of the wages paid as compared with the entire cost of production and the expense of the business. To illustrate: If the wages paid to all employés shall equal twenty per cent. of the entire expenditure in the business, including interest and salaries of members of the firm, then twenty per cent. of the net profit will be distributed to employés.

It will be noted that this plan promotes steadiness in work, stimulates to industry, and adds a most valuable element of hopefulness to labor. As a business enterprise for the owners it is sound, for it makes every workman an interested party in increasing the profits of the firm—interested not only in production, but in the marketableness of the thing produced. There have been two divisions under this plan. At the declaration of the first the workmen had no confidence in it; many of them would have sold their chances for a glass of beer. They expected that "expenses" would make such a large figure that nothing would be left to divide.

When they received, as the good workmen did, considerable sums of money, life took on another aspect to them, and we may suppose that their confidence in fair dealing was raised. The experiment of a year has been entirely satisfactory; it has not only improved the class of employés, but has introduced into the establishment a spirit of industrial cheerfulness. Of course it is still an experiment. So long as business is good, all will go well; but if there is a bad six months, and no profits, it is impossible that suspicion should not arise. And there is another consideration: the publishing to the world that the business of six months was without profit might impair credit. But, on the other hand, this openness in legitimate business may be contagious, and in the end promotive of a wider and more stable business confidence. Ivorydale is one of the best and most solidly built industrial establishments anywhere to be found, and doubly interesting for the intelligent attempt to solve the most difficult problem in modern society. The first semiannual dividend amounted to about an eighth increase of wages. A girl who was earning five dollars a week would receive as dividend about thirty dollars a year. I think it was not in my imagination that the laborers in this establishment worked with more than usual alacrity, and seemed contented. If this plan shall prevent strikes, that alone will be as great a benefit to the workmen as to those who risk capital in employing them.

Probably to a stranger the chief interest of Cincinnati is not in its business enterprises, great as they are, but in another life just as real and important, but which is not always considered in taking account of the prosperity of a community—the development of education and of the fine arts. For a long time the city has had an independent life in art and in music. Whether a people can be saved by art I do not know. The pendulum is always swinging backward and forward, and we seem never to be able to be enthusiastic in one direction without losing something in another. The art of Cincinnati has a good deal the air of being indigenous, and the outcome in the arts of carving and design and in music has exhibited native vigor. The city has made itself a reputation for wood-carving and for decorative pottery. The Rockwood pottery, the private enterprise of Mrs. Bellamy Storer, is the only pottery in this country in which the instinct of beauty is paramount to the desire of profit. Here for a series of years experiments have been going on with clays and glazing, in regard to form and color, and in decoration purely for effect, which have resulted in pieces of marvellous interest and beauty. The effort has always been to satisfy a refined sense rather than to cater to a vicious taste, or one for startling effects already formed. I mean that the effort has not been to suit the taste of the market, but to raise that taste. The result is some of the most exquisite work in texture and color anywhere to be found, and I was glad to learn that it is gaining an appreciation which will not in this case leave virtue to be its own reward.

The various private attempts at art expression have been consolidated in a public Museum and an Art School, which are among the best planned and equipped in the country. The Museum Building in Eden Park, of which the centre pavilion and west wing are completed (having a total length of 214 feet from east to west), is in Romanesque style, solid and pleasing, with exceedingly well-planned exhibition-rooms and picture-galleries, and its collections are already choice and interesting. The fund was raised by the subscriptions of 455 persons, and amounts to $316,501, of which Mr. Charles R. West led off with the contribution of $150,000, invested as a permanent fund. Near this is the Art School, also a noble building, the gift of Mr. David Sinton, who in 1855 gave the Museum Association $75,000 for this purpose. It should be said that the original and liberal endowment of the Art School was made by Mr. Nicholas Longworth, in accordance with the wish of his father, and that the association also received a legacy of $40,000 from Mr. R. R. Springer. Altogether the association has received considerably over a million of dollars, and has in addition, by gift and purchase, property valued at nearly $200,000. The Museum is the fortunate possessor of one of the three Russian Reproductions, the other two being in the South Kensington Museum of London and the Metropolitan of New York. Thus, by private enterprise, in the true American way, the city is graced and honored by art buildings which give it distinction, and has a school of art so well equipped and con-

ducted that it attracts students from far and near, filling its departments of drawing, painting, sculpture, and wood-carving with eager learners. It has over four hundred scholars in the various departments. The ample endowment fund makes the school really free, there being only a nominal charge of about five dollars a year.

In the collection of paintings, which has several of merit, is one with a history, which has a unique importance. This is B. R. Haydon's "Public Entry of Christ into Jerusalem." This picture of heroic size, and in the grand style which had a great vogue in its day, was finished in 1820, sold for £170 in 1831, and brought to Philadelphia, where it was exhibited. The exhibition did not pay expenses, and the picture was placed in the Academy as a companion piece to Benjamin West's "Death on the Pale Horse." In the fire of 1845 both canvases were rescued by being cut from the frames and dragged out like old blankets. It was finally given to the Cathedral in Cincinnati, where its existence was forgotten until it was discovered lately and loaned to the Museum. The interest in the picture now is mainly an accidental one, although it is a fine illustration of the large academic method, and in certain details is painted with the greatest care. Haydon's studio was the resort of English authors of his day, and the portraits of several of them are introduced into this picture. The face of William Hazlitt does duty as St. Peter; Wordsworth and Sir Isaac Newton and Voltaire appear as spectators of the pageant—the cynical expression of Voltaire is the worldly contrast to the believing faith of the disciples—and the inspired face of the youthful St. John is that of John Keats. This being the only portrait of Keats in life, gives this picture extraordinary interest.

The spirit of Cincinnati, that is, its concern for interests not altogether material, is also illustrated by its College of Music. This institution was opened in 1878. It was endowed by private subscription, the largest being $100,000 by Mr. R. R. Springer. It is financially very prosperous; its possessions in real estate, buildings—including a beautiful concert hall—and invested endowments amount to over $300,000. Its average attendance is about 550, and during the year 1887 it had about 650 different scholars. From tuition alone about $45,000 were received, and although the expenditures were liberal, the college had at the beginning of 1888 a handsome cash balance. The object of the college is the development of native talent, and to evoke this the best foreign teachers obtainable have been secured. In the departments of the voice, the piano, and the violin, American youth are said to show special proficiency, and the result of the experiment thus far is to strengthen the belief that out of our mixed nationality is to come most artistic development in music. Free admission is liberally given to pupils who have talent but not the means to cultivate it. Recognizing the value of broad culture in musical education, the managers have provided courses of instruction in English literature, lectures upon American authors, and for the critical study of Italian. The college proper has forty teachers, and as many rooms for instruction. Near it, and connected by a covered way, is the great Music Hall, with a seating capacity of 5400, and the room to pack in nearly 7000 people. In this superb hall the great annual musical festivals are held. It has a plain interior, sealed entirely in wood, and with almost no ornamentation to impair its resonance. The courage of the projectors who dared to build this hall for a purely musical purpose and not for display is already vindicated. It is no doubt the best auditorium in the country. As age darkens the wood, the interior grows rich, and it is discovered that the effect of the seasoning of the wood or of the musical vibrations steadily improves the acoustic properties, having the same effect upon the sonorousness of the wood that long use has upon a good violin. The whole interior is a magnificent sounding-board, if that is the proper expression, and for fifty years, if the hall stands, it will constantly improve, and have a resonant quality unparalleled in any other auditorium.

The city has a number of clubs, well housed, such as are common to other cities, and some that are peculiar. The Cuvier Club, for the preservation of game, has a very large museum of birds, animals, and fishes, beautifully prepared and arranged. The Historical and Philosophical Society has also good quarters, a library of about 10,000 books and 44,000 pamphlets, and is becoming an important depository of historical manuscripts.

The Literary Society, composed of 100 members, who meet weekly, in commodious apartments, to hear an essay, discuss general topics, and pass an hour socially about small tables, with something to eat and drink, has been vigorously maintained since 1848.

An institution of more general importance is the Free Public Library, which has about 150,000 books and 18,000 pamphlets. This is supported in part by an accumulated fund, but mainly by a city tax, which is appropriated through the Board of Education. The expenditures for it in 1887 were about $50,000. It has a notably fine art department. The Library is excellently managed by Mr. A. W. Whelpley, the librarian, who has increased its circulation and usefulness by recognizing the new idea that a librarian is not a mere custodian of books, but should be a stimulator and director of the reading of a community. This office becomes more and more important now that the good library has to compete for the attention of the young with the "cheap and nasty" publications of the day. It is probably due somewhat to direction in reading that books of fiction taken from the Library last year were only fifty-one per cent. of the whole.

An institution established in many cities as a helping hand to women is the Women's Exchange. The Exchange in Cincinnati is popular as a restaurant. Many worthy women support themselves by preparing food which is sold here over the counter, or served at the tables. The city has for many years sustained a very good Zoological Garden, which is much frequented except in the winter. Interest in it is not, however, as lively as it was formerly. It seems very difficult to keep a "zoo" up to the mark in America.

I do not know that the public schools of Cincinnati call for special mention. They seem to be conservative schools, not differing from the best elsewhere, and they appear to be trying no new experiments. One of the high-schools which I saw with 600 pupils is well conducted, and gives good preparation for college. The city enumeration is over 87,000 children between the ages of six and twenty-one, and of these about 36,000 are reported not in school. Of the 2300 colored children in the city, about half were in school. When the Ohio Legislature repealed the law establishing separate schools for colored people, practically creating mixed schools, a majority of the colored parents in the city petitioned and obtained branch schools of their own, with colored teachers in charge. The colored people everywhere seem to prefer to be served by teachers and preachers of their own race.

The schools of Cincinnati have not adopted manual training, but a Technical School has been in existence about a year, with promise of success. The Cincinnati University under the presidency of Governor Cox shows new vitality. It is supported in part by taxation, and is open free to all resident youth, so that while it is not a part of the public-school system, it supplements it.

Cincinnati has had a great many discouragements of late, turbulent politics and dishonorable financial failures. But, for all that, it impresses one as a solid city, with remarkable development in the higher civilization.

In its physical aspect Louisville is in every respect a contrast to Cincinnati. Lying on a plain, sloping gently up from the river, it spreads widely in rectangular uniformity of streets—a city of broad avenues, getting to be well paved and well shaded, with ample spaces in lawns, houses detached, somewhat uniform in style, but with an air of comfort, occasionally of elegance and solid good taste. The city has an exceedingly open, friendly, cheerful appearance. In May, with its abundant foliage and flowery lawns, it is a beautiful city: a beautiful, healthful city in a temperate climate, surrounded by a fertile country, is Louisville. Beyond the city the land rises into a rolling country of Blue-Grass farms, and eastward along the river are fine bluffs broken into most advantageous sites for suburban residences. Looking northward across the Ohio are seen the Indiana "Knobs." In high-water the river is a majestic stream, covering almost entirely the rocks which form the "Falls," and the beds of "cement" which are so profitably worked. The canal, which makes navigation round the rapids, has its mouth at Shipping-port Island. About this spot clusters much of the early romance of Louisville. Here are some of the old houses and the old mill built by the Frenchman Tarascon in the early part of the century. Here in a weather-beaten wooden tenement, still

standing, Tarascon offered border hospitality to many distinguished guests; Aaron Burr and Blennerhasset were among his visitors, and General Wilkinson, the projector of the canal, then in command of the armies of the United States; and it was probably here that the famous "Spanish conspiracy" was concocted. Corn Island, below the rapids, upon which the first settlement of Louisville was made in 1778, disappeared some years ago, gradually washed away by the swift river.

Opposite this point, in Indiana, is the village of Clarksville, which has a unique history. About 1785 Virginia granted to General George Rogers Clark, the most considerable historic figure of this region, a large tract of land in recognition of his services in the war. When Virginia ceded this territory to Indiana the township of Clarksville was excepted from the grant. It had been organized with a governing board of trustees, self-perpetuating, and this organization still continues. Clarksville has therefore never been ceded to the United States, and if it is not an independent community, the eminent domain must still rest in the State of Virginia.

Some philosophers say that the character of a people is determined by climate and soil. There is a notion in this region that the underlying limestone and the consequent succulent Blue-Grass produce a race of large men, frank in manner, brave in war, inclined to oratory and ornamental conversation, women of uncommon beauty, and the finest horses in the Union. Of course a fertile soil and good living conduce to beauty of form and in a way to the free graces of life. But the contrast of Cincinnati and Louisville in social life and in the manner of doing business cannot all be accounted for by Blue-Grass. It would be very interesting, if one had the knowledge, to study the causes of this contrast in two cities not very far apart. In late years Louisville has awakened to a new commercial life, as one finds in it a strong infusion of Western business energy and ambition. It is jubilant in its growth and prosperity. It was always a commercial town, but with a dash of Blue-Grass leisure and hospitality, and a hereditary flavor of manners and fine living. Family and pedigree have always been held in as high esteem as beauty. The Kentuckian of society is a great contrast to the Virginian, but it may be only the development of the tide-water gentleman in the freer, wider opportunities of the Blue - Grass region. The pioneers of Kentucky were backwoodsmen, but many of the early settlers, whose descendants are now leaders in society and in the professions, came with the full-blown tastes and habits of Virginia civilization, as their spacious colonial houses, erected in the latter part of the last century and the early part of this, still attest. They brought and planted in the wilderness a highly developed social state, which was modified into a certain freedom by circumstances. One can fancy in the abundance of a temperate latitude a certain gayety and joyousness in material existence, which is contented with that, and has not sought the art and musical development which one finds in Cincinnati. All over the South, Louisville is noted for the beauty of its women, but the other ladies of the South say that they can always tell one from Louisville by her dress, something in it quite aware of the advanced fashion, something in the "cut"—a mystery known only to the feminine eye.

I did not intend, however, to enter upon a disquisition of the different types of civilization in Cincinnati and in Louisville. One observes them as evidences of what has heretofore been mentioned, the great variety in American life, when one looks below the surface. The traveller enjoys both types, and is rejoiced to find such variety, culture, taking in one city the form of the worship of beauty and the enjoyment of life, and in the other greater tendency to the fine arts. Louisville is a city of churches, of very considerable religious activity, and of pretty staunch orthodoxy. I do not mean to say that what are called modern ideas do not leaven its society. In one of its best literary clubs I heard the Spencerian philosophy expounded and advocated with the enthusiasm and keenness of an emancipated Eastern town. But it is as true of Louisville as it is of other Southern cities that traditional faith is less disturbed by doubts and isms than in many Eastern towns. One notes here also, as all over the South, the marked growth of the temperance movement. The Kentuckians believe that they produce the best fluid from rye and corn in the Union, and that they are the best judges of it. Neither proposition will be disputed, nor will one

trifle with a legitimate pride in a home production ; but there is a new spirit abroad, and both Bourbon and the game that depends quite as much upon the knowledge of human nature as upon the turn of the cards are silently going to the rear. Always Kentuckians have been distinguished in politics, in oratory, in the professions of law and of medicine; nor has the city ever wanted scholars in historical lore, men who have not only kept alive the traditions of learning and local research, like Colonel John Mason Brown, but have exhibited the true antiquarian spirit of Colonel H. T. Durrett, whose historical library is worth going far to see and study. It will be a great pity if his exceedingly valuable collection is not preserved to the State to become the nucleus of a Historical Society worthy of the State's history. When I spoke of art it was in a public sense ; there are many individuals who have good pictures, and especially interesting portraits, and in the early days Kentucky produced at least one artist, wholly self-taught, who was a rare genius. Matthew H. Jouett was born in Mercer County in 1780, and died in Louisville in 1820. In the course of his life he painted as many as three hundred and fifty portraits, which are scattered all over the Union. In his mature years he was for a time with Stuart in Boston. Some specimens of his work in Louisville are wonderfully fine, recalling the style and traditions of the best masters, some of them equal if not superior to the best by Stuart, and suggesting in color and solidity the vigor and grace of Vandyck. He was the product of no school but nature and his own genius. Louisville has always had a scholarly and aggressive press, and its traditions are not weakened in Mr. Henry Watterson. On the social side the good-fellowship of the city is well represented in the Pendennis Club, which is thoroughly home-like and agreeable. The town has at least one book-store of the first class, but it sells very few American copyright books. The city has no free or considerable public library. The Polytechnic Society, which has a room for lectures, keeps for circulation among subscribers about 38,000 books. It has also a geological and mineral collection, and a room devoted to pictures, which contains an allegorical statue by Canova.

In its public schools and institutions of

charity the city has a great deal to show that is interesting. In medicine it has always been famous. It has four medical colleges, a college of dentistry, a college of pharmacy, and a school of pharmacy for women. In nothing, however, is the spirit of the town better exhibited than in its public-school system. With a population of less than 180,000, the school enrolment, which has advanced year by year, was in 1887 21,601, with an aggregate belonging of 17,392. The amount expended on schools, which was in 1880 $197,699, had increased to $323,943 in 1887 —a cost of $18 62 per pupil. Equal provision is made for colored schools as for white, but the number of colored pupils is less than 3000, and the colored high-school is small, as only a few are yet fitted to go so far in education. The negroes all prefer colored teachers, and so far as I could learn, they are quite content with the present management of the School Board. Coeducation is not in the Kentucky idea, nor in its social scheme. There are therefore two high-schools—one for girls and one for boys—both of the highest class and efficiency, in excellent buildings, and under most intelligent management. Among the teachers in the schools are ladies of position, and the schools doubtless owe their good character largely to the fact that they are in the fashion: as a rule, all the children of the city are educated in them. Manual training is not introduced, but all the advanced methods in the best modern schools, object-lessons, word-building, moulding, and drawing, are practised. During the fall and winter months there are night schools, which are very well attended. In one of the intermediate schools I saw an exercise which illustrates the intelligent spirit of the schools. This was an account of the early settlement, growth, and prosperity of Louisville, told in a series of very short papers—so many that a large number of the pupils had a share in constructing the history. Each one took up connectively a brief period or the chief events in chronological order, with illustrations of manners and customs, fashions of dress and mode of life. Of course this mosaic was not original, but made up of extracts from various local histories and statistical reports. This had the merit of being a good exercise as well as inculcating an intelligent pride in the city.

Nearly every religious denomination is represented in the 142 churches of Louisville. Of these 9 are Northern Presbyterian and 7 Southern Presbyterian, 11 of the M. E. Church South and 6 of the M. E. Church North, 18 Catholic, 7 Christian, 1 Unitarian, and 31 colored. There are seven convents and monasteries, and a Young Men's Christian Association. In proportion to its population, the city is preeminent for public and private charities: there are no less than thirty-eight of these institutions, providing for the infirm and unfortunate of all ages and conditions. Unique among these in the United States is a very fine building for the maintenance of the widows and orphans of deceased Freemasons of the State of Kentucky, supported mainly by contributions of the Masonic lodges. One of the best equipped and managed industrial schools of reform for boys and girls is on the outskirts of the city. Mr. P. Caldwell is its superintendent, and it owes its success, as all similar schools do, to the peculiar fitness of the manager for this sort of work. The institution has three departments. There were 125 white boys and 79 colored boys, occupying separate buildings in the same enclosure, and 41 white girls in their own house in another enclosure. The establishment has a farm, a garden, a greenhouse, a library building, a little chapel, ample and pleasant play-yards. There is as little as possible the air of a prison about the place, and as much as possible that of a home and school. The boys have organized a very fair brass band. The girls make all the clothes for the establishment; the boys make shoes, and last year earned $8000 in bottoming chairs. The school is mainly sustained by taxation and city appropriations; the yearly cost is about $26,000. Children are indentured out when good homes can be found for them.

The School for the Education of the Blind is a State institution, and admits none from outside the State. The fine building occupies a commanding situation on hills not far from the river, and is admirably built, the rooms spacious and airy, and the whole establishment is well ordered. There are only 79 scholars, and the few colored are accommodated by themselves in a separate building, in accordance with an act of the Legislature in 1884 for the education of colored blind children. The distinction of this institution is that it has on its premises the United States printing-office for furnishing publications for the blind asylums of the country. Printing is done here both in letters and in points, by very ingenious processes, and the library is already considerable. The space required to store a library of books for the blind may be reckoned from the statement that the novel of *Ivanhoe* occupies three volumes each larger than Webster's Unabridged Dictionary. The weekly *Sunday-school Times* is printed here. The point writing consists entirely of dots in certain combinations to represent letters, and it is noticed that about half the children prefer this to the alphabet. The preference is not explained by saying that it is merely a matter of feeling.

The city has as yet no public parks, but the very broad streets—from sixty to one hundred and twenty feet in width—the wide spacing of the houses in the residence parts, and the abundant shade make them less a necessity than elsewhere. The city spreads very freely and openly over the plain, and short drives take one into lovely Blue-Grass country. A few miles out on Churchill Downs is the famous Jockey Club Park, a perfect racing track and establishment, where world-wide reputations are made at the semiannual meetings. The limestone region, a beautifully rolling country, almost rivals the Lexington plantations in the raising of fine horses. Driving out to one of these farms one day, we passed, not far from the river, the old Taylor mansion and the tomb of Zachary Taylor. It is in the reserved family burying-ground, where lie also the remains of Richard Taylor, of Revolutionary memory. The great tomb and the graves are overrun thickly with myrtle, and the secluded irregular ground is shaded by forest trees. The soft wind of spring was blowing sweetly over the fresh green fields, and there was about the place an air of repose and dignity most refreshing to the spirit. Near the tomb stands the fine commemorative shaft bearing on its summit a good portrait statue of the hero of Buena Vista. I liked to linger there, the country was so sweet; the great river flowing in sight lent a certain grandeur to the resting-place, and I thought how dignified and fit it was for a President to be buried at his home.

The city of Louisville in 1888 has the unmistakable air of confidence and buoyant prosperity. This feeling of confidence is strengthened by the general awakening of Kentucky in increased immigration of agriculturists, and in the development of extraordinary mines of coal and iron, and in the railway extension. But locally the Board of Trade (an active body of 700 members) has in its latest report most encouraging figures to present. In almost every branch of business there was an increase in 1887 over 1886; in both manufactures and trade the volume of business increased from twenty to fifty per cent. For instance, stoves and castings increased from 16,574,547 pounds to 19,386,808; manufactured tobacco, from 12,729,421 pounds to 17,059,006; gas and water pipes, from 56,083,380 pounds to 63,745,216; grass and clover seed, from 4,240,908 bushels to 6,601,451. A conclusive item as to manufactures is that there were received in 1887 951,767 tons of bituminous coal, against 204,221 tons in 1886. Louisville makes the claim of being the largest tobacco market in the world in bulk and variety. It leads largely the nine principal leaf-tobacco markets in the West. The figures for 1887 are—receipts, 123,569 hogsheads; sales, 135,192 hogsheads; stock in hand, 36,431 hogsheads, against the corresponding figures of 62,074, 65,924, 13,972 of its great rival, Cincinnati. These large figures are a great increase over 1886, when the value of tobacco handled here was estimated at nearly $20,000,000. Another great interest always associated with Louisville, whiskey, shows a like increase, there being shipped in 1887 119,637 barrels, against 101,943 barrels in 1886. In the Louisville collection district there were registered one hundred grain distilleries, with a capacity of 80,000 gallons a day. For the five years ending June 30, 1887, the revenue taxes on this product amounted to nearly $30,000,000. I am not attempting a conspectus of the business of Louisville, only selecting some figures illustrating its growth. Its manufacture of agricultural implements has attained great proportions. The reputation of Louisville for tobacco and whiskey is widely advertised, but it is not generally known that it has the largest plough factory in the world. This is one of four which altogether employ about 2000 hands, and make a product valued at $2,275,000. In 1880 Louisville made 80,000 ploughs; in 1886, 190,000. The capacity of manufacture in 1887 was increased by the enlargement of the chief factory to a number not given, but there were shipped that year 11,005,151 pounds of ploughs. There is a steadily increasing manufacture of woollen goods, and the production of the mixed fabric known as Kentucky jeans is another industry in which Louisville leads the world, making annually 7,500,000 yards of cloth, and its four mills increased their capacity twenty per cent. in 1887. The opening of the hard-wood lumber districts in eastern Kentucky has made Louisville one of the important lumber markets: about 125,000,000 feet of lumber, logs, etc., were sold here in 1887. But it is unnecessary to particularize. The Board of Trade think that the advantages of Louisville as a manufacturing centre are sufficiently emphasized from the fact that during the year 1887 seventy-three new manufacturing establishments, mainly from the North and East, were set up, using a capital of $1,290,500, and employing 1621 laborers. The city has twenty-two banks, which

had, July 1, 1887, $8,200,200 capital, and $19,927,138 deposits. The clearings for 1887 were $281,110,402—an increase of nearly $50,000,000 over 1886.

Another item which helps to explain the buoyant feeling of Louisville is that its population increased over 10,000 from 1886 to 1887, reaching, according to the best estimate, 177,000 people. I should have said also that no city in the Union is better served by street railways, which are so multiplied and arranged as to "correspondences" that for one fare nearly every inhabitant can ride within at least two blocks of his residence. In these cars, as in the railway cars of the State, there is the same absence of discrimination against color that prevails in Louisiana and in Arkansas. And it is an observation hopeful, at least to the writer, of the good time at hand when all party lines shall be drawn upon the broadest national issues, that there seems to be in Kentucky no social distinction between Democrats and Republicans.

CHICAGO — THE MAIN EXHIBIT

CHICAGO will be the main exhibit at the Columbian Exposition of 1893. No matter what the aggregation of wonders there, no matter what the Eiffel-Tower-like chief exhibit may be, the city itself will make the most surprising presentation. Those who go to study the world's progress will find no other result of human force so wonderful, extravagant, or peculiar. Those who carry with them the prejudices begotten out of political rivalry or commercial envy will discover that, however well founded some of the criticism has been—especially as to the spirit of the Chicagoans—the development of the place has not followed the logical deductions. Those who go clear-minded, expecting to see a great city, will find one different from that which any precedent has led them to look for.

While investigating the management and prospects of the Columbian Exposition, I was a resident of Chicago for more than a fortnight. A born New-Yorker, the energy, roar, and bustle of the place were yet sufficient to first astonish and then to fatigue me. I was led to examine the city, and to cross-examine some of its leading men. I came away compelled to acknowledge its possession of certain forceful qualities which I never saw exhibited in the same degree anywhere else. I got a satisfactory explanation of its growth and achievements, as well as proof that it must continue to expand in population and commercial influence. Moreover, without losing a particle of pride or faith in New York—without perceiving that New York was affected by the consideration—I acquired a respect for Chicago such as it is most likely that any American who makes a similar investigation must share with me.

The city has been thought intolerant of criticism. The amount of truth there is in this is found in its supervoluminous civicism. The bravado and bunkum of the Chicago newspapers reflect this quality, but do it clumsily, because it proceeds from a sense of business policy with the editors, who laugh at it themselves. But underlying the behavior of the most able and enterprising men in the city is this motto, which they constantly quoted to me, all using the same words, "We are for Chicago first, last, and all the time." To define that sentence is, in a great measure, to account for Chicago. It explains the possession of a million inhabitants by a city that practically dates its beginning after the war of the rebellion. Its adoption by half a million men as their watchword means the forcing of trade and manufactures and wealth; the getting of the World's Fair, if you please. In order to comprehend Chicago, it is best never to lose sight of the motto of its citizens.

I have spoken of the roar and bustle and energy of Chicago. This is most noticeable in the business part of the town, where the greater number of the men are crowded together. It seems there as if the men would run over the horses if the drivers were not careful. Everybody is in such a hurry and going at such a pace that if a stranger asks his way, he is apt to have to trot along with his neighbor to gain the information, for the average Chicagoan cannot stop to talk. The whole business of life is carried on at high pressure, and the pithy part of Chicago is like three hundred acres of New York Stock Exchange when trading is active. European visitors have written that there are no such crowds anywhere as gather on Broadway, and this is true most of the time; but there is one hour on every week-day when certain streets in Chicago are so packed with people as to make Broadway look desolate and solitudinous by comparison. That is the hour between half past five and half past six o'clock, when the famous tall buildings of the city vomit their inhabitants upon the pavements. Photographs of the principal corners and crossings, taken at the height of the human torrent, suggest the thought that the camera must have been turned on some little-known painting by Doré. Nobody but Doré ever conceived such pictures. To those who are in the crowds, even Chicago seems small and cramped; even her street cars, running in breakneck trains, prove far too few; even her streets that connect horizon with horizon seem each night to roar at the city officials for further annexation in the morning.

We shall see these crowds simply and

satisfactorily accounted for presently; but they exhibit only one phase of the high-pressure existence; they form only one feature among the many that distinguish the town. In the tall buildings are the most modern and rapid elevators, machines that fly up through the towers like glass balls from a trap at a shooting contest. The slow-going stranger, who is conscious of having been "kneaded" along the streets, like a lump of dough among a million bakers, feels himself loaded into one of those frail-looking baskets of steel netting, and the next instant the elevator-boy touches the trigger, and up goes the whole load as a feather is caught up by a gale. The descent is more simple. Something lets go, and you fall from ten to twenty stories as it happens. There is sometimes a jolt, which makes the passenger seem to feel his stomach pass into his shoes, but, as a rule, the mechanism and management both work marvellously toward ease and gentleness. These elevators are too slow for Chicago, and the managers of certain tall buildings now arrange them so that some run "express" to the seventh story without stopping, while what may be called accommodation cars halt at the lower floors, pursuing a course that may be likened to the emptying of the chambers of a revolver in the hands of a person who is "quick on the trigger." It is the same everywhere in the business district. Along Clark Street are some gorgeous underground restaurants, all marble and plated metal. Whoever is eating at one of the tables in them will see the ushers standing about like statues until a customer enters the door, when they dart forward as if the building were falling. It is only done in order to seat the visitor promptly. Being of a sympathetic and impressionable nature, I bolted along the streets all the time I was there as if some one on the next block had picked my pocket.

In the Auditorium Hotel the guests communicate with the clerk by electricity, and may flash word of their thirst to the bar-tender as lightning dances from the top to the bottom of a steeple. A sort of annunciator is used, and by turning an arrow and pressing a button, a man may in half a minute order a cocktail, towels, ice-water, stationery, dinner, a bootblack, and the evening newspapers. Our horse-cars in New York move at the rate of about six miles an hour. The cable-cars of Chicago make more than nine miles an hour in town, and more than thirteen miles an hour where the population is less dense. They go in trains of two cars each, and with such a racket of gong-ringing and such a grinding and whir of grip-wheels as to make a modern vestibuled train seem a waste of the opportunities for noise. But these street cars distribute the people grandly, and while they occasionally run over a stray citizen, they far more frequently clear their way by lifting wagons and trucks bodily to one side as they whirl along. It is a rapid and a business-like city. The speed with which cattle are killed and pigs are turned into slabs of salt pork has amazed the world, but it is only the ignorant portion thereof that does not know that the celerity at the stock-yards is merely an effort of the butchers to keep up with the rest of the town. The only slow things in Chicago are the steam railway trains. Farther on we will discover why they are so.

I do not know how many very tall buildings Chicago contains, but they must number nearly two dozen. Some of them are artistically designed, and hide their height in well-balanced proportions. A few are mere boxes punctured with window-holes, and stand above their neighbors like great hitching-posts. The best of them are very elegantly and completely appointed, and the communities of men inside them might almost live their lives within their walls, so multifarious are the occupations and services of the tenants. The best New York office buildings are not injured by comparison with these towering structures, except that they are not so tall as the Chicago buildings, but there is not in New York any office structure that can be compared with Chicago's so-called Chamber of Commerce office building, so far as are concerned the advantages of light and air and openness and roominess which its tenants enjoy. In these respects there is only one finer building in America, and that is in Minneapolis. It is a great mistake to think that we in New York possess all the elegant, rich, and ornamental outgrowths of taste, or that we know better than the West what are the luxuries and comforts of the age. With their floors of deftly laid mosaic-work, their walls of marble and onyx, their balustrades of copper worked into arabesquerie, their artistic lanterns, elegant electric fixtures, their costly and luxurious public rooms, these Chicago office buildings force an exclamation of praise, however unwillingly it comes.

They have adopted what they call "the Chicago method" in putting up these steepling hives. This plan is to construct the actual edifice of steel framework, to which are added thin outer walls of brick or stone masonry, and the necessary partitions of fire-brick, and plaster laid on iron lathing. The buildings are therefore like enclosed bird-cages, and it is said that, like bird-cages, they cannot shake or tumble down. The exterior walls are mere envelopes. They are so treated that the buildings look like heaps of masonry, but that is homage paid to custom more than it is a material element of strength. These walls are to a building what an envelope is to a letter, or a postage-stamp is to that part of an envelope which it covers. The Chicago method is expeditious, economical, and in many ways advantageous. The manner in which the great weight of houses so tall as to include between sixteen and twenty-four stories is distributed upon the ground beneath them is ingenious. Wherever one of the principal upright pillars is to be set up, the builders lay a pad of steel and cement of such extent that the pads for all the pillars cover all the site. These pads are slightly pyramidal in shape, and are made by laying alternate courses of steel beams crosswise, one upon another. Each pair of courses of steel is filled in and solidified with cement, and then the next two courses are added and similarly treated. At last each pad is eighteen inches thick, and perhaps eighteen feet square; but the size is governed by the desire to distribute the weight of the building at about the average of a ton to the square foot.

This peculiar process is necessitated by the character of the land underneath Chicago. Speaking widely, the rule is to find from seven to fourteen feet of sand superimposed upon a layer of clay between ten and forty feet in depth. It has not paid to puncture this clay with piling. The piles sink into a soft and yielding substance, and the clay is not tenacious enough to hold them. Thus the Chicago Post-office was built, and it not only settles continuously, but it settles unevenly. On the other hand, the famous Rookery

Building, set up on these steel and cement pads, did not sink quite an inch, though the architect's calculation was that, by squeezing the water out of the clay underneath, it would settle seven inches. Very queer and differing results have followed the construction of Chicago's biggest buildings, and without going too deep into details, it has been noticed that while some have pulled neighboring houses down a few inches, others have lifted adjoining houses, and still others have raised buildings that were at a distance from themselves. The bed of clay underneath Chicago acts when under pressure like a pan of dough, or like a blanket tautened at the edges and held clear of underneath support. Chicago's great office buildings have basements, but no cellars.

I have referred to the number of these stupendous structures. Let it be known next that they are all in a very small district, that narrow area which composes Chicago's office region, which lies between Lake Michigan and all the principal railroad districts, and at the edges of which one-twenty-fifth of all the railroad mileage of the world is said to terminate, though the district is but little more than half a mile square or 300 acres in extent. One of these buildings—and not the largest—has a population of 4000 persons. It was visited and its elevators were used on three days, when a count was kept, by 19,000, 18,000, and 20,000 persons. Last October there were 7000 offices in the tall buildings of Chicago, and 7000 more were under way in buildings then undergoing construction. The reader now understands why in the heart of Chicago every work-day evening the crowds convey the idea that our Broadway is a deserted thoroughfare as compared with, say, the corner of Clark and Jackson streets.

These tall buildings are mainly built on land obtained on 99 year leasehold. Long leases rather than outright purchases of land have long been a favorite preliminary to building in Chicago, where, for one thing, the men who owned the land have not been those with the money for building. Where very great and costly buildings are concerned, the long leases often go to corporations or syndicates, who put up the houses. It seems to many strangers who visit Chicago that it is reasonable to prophesy a speedy end to the feverish impulse to swell the number of these giant piles, either through legislative ordinance or by the fever running its course. Many prophesy that it must soon end. This idea is bred of several reasons. In the first place, the tall buildings darken the streets, and transform the lower stories of opposite houses into so many cellars or damp and dark basements. In the next place, the great number of tall and splendid office houses is depreciating the value of the humbler property in their neighborhoods. Four-story and five-story houses that once were attractive are no longer so, because their owners cannot afford the conveniences which distinguish the greater edifices, wherein light and heat are often provided free, fire-proof safes are at the service of every tenant, janitors officer a host of servants, and there are barber shops, restaurants, cigar and news stands, elevators, and a half-dozen other conveniences not found in smaller houses. It would seem, also, that since not all the people of Chicago spend their time in offices, there must soon come an end of the demand for these chambers. So it seems, but not to a thoroughbred Chicagoan. One of the foremost business men in the city asserts that he can perceive no reason why the entire business heart of the town—that square half-mile of which I have spoken—should not soon be all builded up of cloud-capped towers. There will be a need for them, he says, and the money to defray the cost of them will accompany the demand. The only trouble he foresees will be in the solution of the problem what to do with the people who will then crowd the streets as never streets were clogged before.

This prophecy relates to a little block in the city, but the city itself contains 181½ square miles. It has been said of the many annexations by which her present size was attained that Chicago reached out and took to herself farms, prairie land, and villages, and that of such material the great city now in part consists. This is true. In suburban trips, such as those I took to Fort Sheridan and Fernwood, for instance, I passed great cabbage farms, groves, houseless but plotted tracts, and long reaches of the former prairie. Even yet Hyde Park is a separated settlement, and a dozen or more villages stand out as distinctly by themselves as ever they did. If it were true, as her rivals insist, that Chicago added all this tract

merely to get a high rank in the census reports of population, the folly of the action would be either ludicrous or pitiful, according to the stand-point from which it was viewed. But the true reason for her enormous extension of municipal jurisdiction is quite as peculiar. The enlargement was urged and accomplished in order to anticipate the growth and needs of the city. It was a consequence of extraordinary foresight, which recognized the necessity for a uniform system of boulevards, parks, drainage, and water provision when the city should reach limits that it was even then seen must soon bound a compact aggregation of stores, offices, factories, and dwellings. To us of the East this is surprising. It might seem incredible were there not many other evidences of the same spirit and sagacity not only in Chicago, but in the other cities of the West, especially of the Northwest. What Minneapolis, St. Paul, and Duluth are doing toward a future park system reveals the same enterprise and habit of looking far ahead. And Chicago, in her park system, makes evident her intentions. In all these cities and in a hundred ways the observant traveller notes the same forehandedness, and prepares himself to understand the temper in which the greatest of the Western capitals leaned forth and absorbed the prairie. Chicago expects to become the largest city in America—a city which, in fifty years, shall be larger than the consolidated cities that may form New York at that time.

Now on what substance does Chicago feed that she should foresee herself so great? What manner of men are those of Chicago? What are the whys and the wherefores of her growth?

It seems to have ever been, as it is now, a city of young men. One Chicagoan accounts for its low death rate on the ground that not even its leading men are yet old enough to die. The young men who drifted there from the Eastern States after the close of the war all agree that the thing which most astonished them was the youthfulness of the most active business men. Marshall Field, Potter Palmer, and the rest, heading very large mercantile establishments, were young fellows. Those who came to Chicago from England fancied, as it is said that Englishmen do, that a man may not be trusted with affairs until he has lost half his hair and all his teeth. Our own Eastern men were apt to place wealth and success at the middle of the scale of life. But in Chicago men under thirty were leading in commerce and industry. The sight was a spur to all the young men who came, and they also pitched in to swell the size and successes of the young men's capital. The easy making of money by the loaning of it and by handling city realty—sources which never failed with shrewd men—not only whetted the general appetite for big and quick money-making, but they provided the means for the establishment and extension of trade in other ways and with the West at large.

It is one of the peculiarities of Chicago that one finds not only the capitalists but the storekeepers discussing the whole country with a familiarity as strange to a man from the Atlantic coast as Nebraska is strange to most Philadelphians or New-Yorkers. But the well-informed and "hustling" Chicagoan is familiar with the differing districts of the entire West, North, and South, with their crops, industries, wants, financial status, and means of intercommunication. As in London we find men whose business field is the world, so in Chicago we find the business men talking not of one section or of Europe, as is largely the case in New York, but discussing the affairs of the entire country. The figures which garnish their conversation are bewildering, but if they are analyzed, or even comprehended, they will reveal to the listener how vast and how wealthy a region acknowledges Chicago as its market and its financial and trading centre.

Without either avowing or contesting any part of the process by which Chicago men account for their city's importance or calculate its future, let me repeat a digest of what several influential men of that city said upon the subject. Chicago, then, is the centre of a circle of 1000 miles diameter. If you draw a line northward 500 miles, you find everywhere arable land and timber. The same is true with respect to a line drawn 500 miles in a northwesterly course. For 650 miles westward there is no change in the rich and alluring prospect, and so all around the circle, except where Lake Michigan interrupts it, the same conditions are found. Moreover, the lake itself is a valuable element in commerce. The rays or spokes in all these directions

become materialized in the form of the tracks of 35 railways which enter the city. Twenty-two of these are great companies, and at a short distance sub-radials made by other railroads raise the number to 50 roads. As said above, in Chicago one-twenty-fifth of the railway mileage of the world terminates, and serves 30 millions of persons, who find Chicago the largest city easily accessible to them. Thus is found a vast population connected easily and directly with a common centre, to which everything they produce can be brought, and from which all that contributes to the material progress and comfort of man may be economically distributed.

A financier who is equally well known and respected in New York and Chicago put the case somewhat differently as to what he called Chicago's territory. He considered it as being 1000 miles square, and spoke of it as "the land west of the Alleghanies and south of Mason and Dixon's line." This region, the richest agricultural territory in the world, does its financiering in Chicago. The rapid increase in wealth of both the city and the tributary region is due to the fact that every year both produce more, and have more to sell and less to buy. Not long ago the rule was that a stream of goods ran eastward over the Alleghanies, and another stream of supplies came back, so that the West had little gain to show. But during the past five years this back-setting current has been a stream of money returned for the products the West has distributed. The West is now selling to the East and to Europe and getting money in return, because it is manufacturing for itself, as well as tilling the soil and mining for the rest of the world. It therefore earns money and acquires a profit instead of continuing its former process of toiling merely to obtain from the East the necessaries of life.

The condition in which Nebraska and Kansas find themselves is the condition in which a great part of the West was placed not long ago—a condition of debt, of being mortgaged, and of having to send its earnings to Eastern capitalists. That is no longer the case of the West in general. The debtor States now are Kansas, Nebraska, the two Dakotas, and western Minnesota; but Iowa, Illinois, Ohio, Indiana, Missouri, Wisconsin, and

Michigan (the States most closely tributary to Chicago) have paid off their mortgages, and are absorbing money and investing it in local improvements. What they earn is now their own, and it comes back to them in the form of money. This money used to be shipped to the East, to which these States were in debt, but now it is invested where it is earned, and the consequence has been that in the last five or six years the West has rarely shipped any currency East, but has been constantly drawing it from there.

In this change of condition is seen an explanation of much that has made Chicago peculiar. She has been what she would call "hustling." For years, in company with the entire Western country, she has been making money only to pay debts with. That, they say, is why men in Chicago have talked only "business"; that is why Chicago has had no leisure class, no reservoir of home capital seeking investment. The former conditions having changed, now that she is producing more and buying less, the rest will change also.

When we understand what are the agricultural resources of the region for which Chicago is the trading-post, we perceive how certain it was that its debt would be paid, and that great wealth would follow. The corn lands of Illinois return a profit of $15 to the acre, raising 50 to 60 bushels at 42½ cents a bushel last year, and at a cost for cultivation of only $7 an acre. Wheat produces $22.50 an acre, costs a little less than corn, and returns a profit of from $12 to $15. Oats run 55 bushels to the acre, at 27 cents a bushel, and cost the average farmer only, say, $6 an acre, returning $8 or $9 an acre in profit. These figures will vary as to production, cost, and profit, but it is believed that they represent a fair average. This midland country, of which Chicago is the capital, produces two thousand million bushels of corn, seven hundred million bushels of oats, fifty million hogs, twenty-eight million horses, thirty million sheep, and so on, to cease before the reader is wearied; but in no single instance is the region producing within 50 per cent. of what it will be made to yield before the expiration of the next twenty years. Farming there has been haphazard, rude, and wasteful; but as it begins to pay well, the methods

begin to improve. Drainage will add new lands, and better methods will swell the crops, so that, for instance, where 60 bushels of corn to the acre are now grown, at least 100 bushels will be harvested. All the corn lands are now settled, but they are not improved. They will yet double in value. It is different with wheat; with that the maximum production will soon be attained.

Such is the wealth that Chicago counts up as tributary to her. By the railroads that dissect this opulent region she is riveted to the midland, the southern, and the western country between the Rockies and the Alleghanies. She is closely allied to the South, because she is manufacturing and distributing much that the South needs, and can get most economically from her. Chicago has become the third manufacturing city in the Union, and she is drawing manufactures away from the East faster than most persons in the East imagine. To-day it is a great Troy stove-making establishment that has moved to Chicago; the week before it was a Massachusetts shoe factory that went there. Many great establishments have gone there, but more must follow, because Chicago is not only the centre of the midland region in respect of the distribution of made-up wares, but also for the concentration of raw materials. Chicago must lead in the manufacture of all goods of which wood, leather, and iron are the bases. The revolution that took place in the meat trade when Chicago took the lead in that industry affected the whole leather and hide industry. Cattle are dropping 90,000 skins a week in Chicago, and the trade is confined to Chicago, St. Louis, Kansas City, Omaha, and St. Paul. It is idle to suppose that those skins will be sent across the Alleghanies to be turned into goods and sent back again. Wisconsin has become the great tanning State, and all over the district close around Chicago are factories and factory towns where hides are turned into leather goods. The West still gets its finer goods in the East, but it is making the coarser grades, and to such an extent as to give a touch of New England color to the towns and villages around Chicago.

This is not an unnatural rivalry that has grown up. The former condition of Western dependence was unnatural. The science of profitable business lies in the practice of economy. Chicago has in abundance all the fuels except hard coal. She has coal, oil, stone, brick—everything that is needed for building and for living. Manufactures gravitate to such a place for economical reasons. The population of the north Atlantic division, including Pennsylvania and Massachusetts, and acknowledging New York as its centre, is 17,401,000. The population of the northern central division, trading with Chicago, is 22,362,279. Every one has seen each succeeding census shift the centre of population farther and farther West, but not every one is habituated to putting two and two together.

"Chicago is yet so young and busy," said he who is perhaps the leading banker there, "she has no time for anything beyond each citizen's private affairs. It is hard to get men to serve on a committee. The only thing that saves us from being boors is our civic pride. We are fond, proud, enthusiastic in that respect. But we know that Chicago is not rich, like New York. She has no bulk of capital lying ready for investment and reinvestment; yet she is no longer poor. She has just got over her poverty, and the next stage, bringing accumulated wealth, will quickly follow. Her growth in this respect is more than paralleled by her development into an industrial centre."

So much, then, for Chicago's reasons for existence. The explanation forms not merely the history of an American town, and a town of young men, it points an old moral. It demonstrates anew the active truth that energy is a greater force than money. It commands money. The young founders of Chicago were backed in the East by capitalists who discounted the energy they saw them display. And now Chicago capitalists own the best street railway in St. Louis, the surface railway system of Toledo, a thousand enterprises in hundreds of Western towns.

Chicago has been as crude and rough as any other self-creating entity engaged in a hard struggle for a living. And latterly confidence in and exultation over the inevitable success of the battle have made her boastful, conceited, and noisy. But already one citizen has taken to building houses for rental and not for sale. He has arranged an imitation Astor estate as far ahead as the law will permit, which is to say to one generation unborn. Already, so they boast in Chi-

cago, you may see a few tables in the Chicago Club surrounded by whist-players with gray locks and semispherical waistcoats *in the afternoons during business hours!* — a most surprising thing, and only possible at the Chicago Club, which is the old club of the "old rich." These partially globular old whist-players are still in business, of course, as everybody is, but they let go with one hand, as it were, in the afternoons, and only stroll around to their offices at four or five o'clock to make certain that the young members of the other clubs have not stolen their trade while they were playing cards. The other clubs of Chicago merely look like clubs, as we understand the word in New York. They are patronized as our dining-clubs are, with a rush at luncheon-time, although at both ends of the town, in the residence districts, there are clubs to which men drift on Sundays.

And here one is brought to reflect that Chicago is distinctly American. I know that the Chicagoans boast that theirs is the most mixed population in the country, but the makers and movers of Chicago are Americans. The streets of the city are full of strange faces of a type to which we are not used in the East — a dish-faced, soft-eyed, light-haired people. They are Scandinavians; but they are as malleable as lead, and quickly and easily follow and adopt every Americanism. In return, they ask only to be permitted to attend a host of Lutheran churches in flocks, to work hard, live temperately, save thriftily, and to pronounce every *j* as if it were a *y*. But the dominating class is of that pure and broad American type which is not controlled by New England or any other tenets, but is somewhat loosely made up of the overflow of the New England, the Middle, and the Southern States. It is as mixed and comprehensive as the West Point school of cadets. It calls its city "She-caw-ger." It inclines to soft hats, and only once in a great while does a visitor see a Chicagoan who has the leisure or patience to carry a cane. Its signs are eloquent of its habits, especially of its habit of freedom. "Take G——'s candy to the loved ones at home," stares from hundreds of walls. "Gentlemen all chew Fraxy because it sweetens the breath after drinking," one manufacturer declares; then he adds, "Ladies who play tennis chew it because it lubricates the throat." A bottler of spring water advertises it as "God's own liver remedy." On the bill-boards of a theatre is the threat that "If you miss seeing Peter Peterson, half your life will be gone." In a principal street is a characteristic sign product, "My fifteen-cent meals are world-beaters"; yet there are worse terrors for Chicago diners-out, as is shown by the sign, "Business lunch — quick and cheap."

But the visitor's heart warms to the town when he sees its parks and its homes. In them is ample assurance that not every breath is "business," and not every thought commercial. Once out of the thicket of the business and semi-business district, the dwellings of the people reach mile upon mile away along pleasant boulevards and avenues, or facing noble parks and parkways, or in a succession of villages green and gay with foliage and flowers. They are not cliff dwellings like our flats and tenements; there are no brown-stone cañons like our uptown streets; there are only occasional hesitating hints there of those Philadelphian and Baltimorean mills that grind out dwellings all alike, as nature makes pease and man makes pins. There are more miles of detached villas in Chicago than a stranger can easily account for. As they are not only found on Prairie Avenue and the boulevards, but in the populous wards and semi-suburbs, where the middle folk are congregated, it is evident that the prosperous moiety of the population enjoys living better (or better living) than the same fraction in the Atlantic cities.

Land in New York has been too costly to permit of these villa-like dwellings, but that does not alter the fact that existence in a home hemmed in by other houses is at best but a crippled living. There never has been any valid excuse for the building of these compressed houses by New York millionaires. It sounds like a Celtic bull, but, in my opinion, the poorer millionaires of Prairie Avenue are better off. A peculiarity of the buildings of Chicago is in the great variety of building-stones that are employed in their construction. Where we would build two blocks of brown-stone, I have counted thirteen varieties of beautiful and differing building material. Moreover, the contrasts in architectural design

evidence among Chicago house-owners a complete sway of individual taste. It is in these beautiful homes that the people, who do not know what to do with their club-houses, hold their card parties; it is to them that they bring their visitors and friends; in short, it is at home that the Chicagoan recreates and loafs.

It is said, and I have no reason to doubt it, that the clerks and small tradesmen who live in thousands of these pretty little boxes are the owners of their homes; also that the tenements of the rich display evidence of a tasteful and costly garnering of the globe for articles of luxury and *virtu*. A sneering critic, who wounded Chicago deeply, intimated that theirs must be a primitive society where the rich sit on their door-steps of an evening. That really is a habit there, and in the finer districts of all the Western cities. To enjoy themselves the more completely, the people bring out rugs and carpets, always of gay colors, and fling them on the steps—or stoops, as we Dutch legatees should say—that the ladies' dresses may not be soiled. As these step clothings are as bright as the maidens' eyes and as gay as their cheeks, the effect may be imagined. For my part, I think it argues well for any society that indulges in the trick, and proves existence in such a city to be more human and hearty and far less artificial than where there is too much false pride to permit of it. In front of many of the nice hotels the boarders lug out great arm-chairs upon the portal platforms or beside the curbs. There the men sit in rows, just as I can remember seeing them do in front of the New York Hotel and the old St. Nicholas Hotel in happy days of yore, to smoke in the sunless evening air, and to exchange comments on the weather and the passers-by. If the dead do not rise until the Judgment-day, but lie less active than their dust, then old Wouter Van Twiller, Petrus Stuyvesant, and the rest of our original Knickerbockers will be sadly disappointed angels when they come to, and find that we have abandoned these practices in New York, after the good example that our first families all set us.

It is in Chicago that we find a great number of what are called boulevarded streets, at the intersections of which are signs bearing such admonitions as these: "For pleasure driving. No traffic wagons allowed;" or, "Traffic teams are not allowed on this boulevard." Any street in the residence parts of the city may be boulevarded and turned over to the care of the park commissioners of the district, provided that it does not lie next to any other such street, and provided that a certain proportion of the property-holders along it are minded to follow a simple formula to procure the improvement. Improved road-beds are given to such streets, and they not only become neat and pretty, but enhance the value of all neighboring land. One boulevard in Chicago penetrates to the very heart of its bustling business district. By means of it men and women may drive from the southern suburbs or parks to the centre of trade, perhaps to their office doors, under the most pleasant conditions. By means of the lesser beautified avenues among the dwellings men and women may sleep of nights, and hide from the worst of the city's tumult among green lawns and flower beds.

Chicago's park system is so truly her crown, or its diadem, that its fame may lead to the thought that enough has been said about it. That is not the case, however, for the parks change and improve so constantly that the average Chicagoan finds some of them outgrowing his knowledge, unless he goes to them as he ought to go to his prayers. It is not in extent that the city's parks are extraordinary, for, all told, they comprise less than two thousand acres. It is the energy that has given rise to them, and the taste and enthusiasm which have been expended upon them, that cause our wonder. Sand and swamp were at the bottom of them, and if their surfaces now roll in gentle undulations, it is because the earth that was dug out for the making of ponds has been subsequently applied to the forming of hills and knolls. The people go to some of them upon the boulevards of which I have spoken, beneath trees and beside lawns and gorgeous flower beds, having their senses sharpened in anticipation of the pleasure-grounds beyond, as the heralds in some old plays prepare us for the action that is to follow. Once the parks are reached, they are found to be literally for the use of the people who own them. I have a fancy that a people who are so largely American would not suffer them to be otherwise. There are no signs warning the public off the grass, or announcing that they "may look, but

mustn't touch" whatever there is to see. The people swarm all over the grass, and yet it continues beautiful day after day and year after year. The floral displays seem unharmed; at any rate, we have none to compare with them in any Atlantic coast parks. The people even picnic on the sward, and those who can appreciate such license find, ready at hand, baskets in which to hide the litter which follows. And, O ye who manage other parks we wot of, know that these Chicago play-grounds seem as free from harm and eyesore as any in the land.

The best parks face the great lake, and get wondrous charms of dignity and beauty from it. At the North Side the Lincoln Park commissioners, at great expense, are building out into the lake, making a handsome paved beach, sea-wall, esplanade, and drive to enclose a long, broad body of the lake water. Although the great blue lake is at the city's edge, there is little or no sailing or pleasure-boating upon it. It is too rude and treacherous. Therefore these commissioners of the Lincoln Park are enclosing, behind their new-made land, a watercourse for sailing and rowing, for racing, and for more indolent aquatic sport. The Lake Shore Drive, when completed, will be three miles in length, and will connect with yet another notable road to Fort Sheridan twenty-five miles in length. All these beauties form part of the main exhibit at the Columbian Exposition. Realizing this, the municipality has not only voted five millions of dollars to the Exposition, but has set apart $3,500,000 for beautifying and improving the city in readiness for the Exposition and its visitors, even as a bride bedecketh herself for her husband. That is well; but it is not her beauty that will most interest the visitors to Chicago.

I have an idea that all this is very American; but what is to be said of the Chicago Sunday, with its drinking shops all wide open, and its multitudes swarming out on pleasure bent? And what of the theatres opening to the best night's business of the week at the hour of Sunday evening service in the churches? I suspect that this also is American—that sort of American that develops under Southern and Western influences not dominated by the New England spirit. And yet the Puritan traditions are not without honor and respect in Chicago, witness the fact that the city spent seventeen and a quarter millions of dollars during the past five years upon her public schools.

Another thing that I suspect is American, though I am sorry to say it, is the impudence of the people who wait on the public. It is quite certain that the more intelligent a man is, the better waiter he will make; but your free-born American acknowledges a quality which more than offsets his intelligence. In pursuit of knowledge I went to a restaurant, which was splendid if it was not good, and the American who waited on me lightened his service with song in this singular manner: "Comrades, com—you said coffee, didn't yer?—ever since we were boys; sharing each other's sor—I don't think we've got no Roquefort—sharing each other's joys. Brie, then—keerect!" (I recall all this against my country, not against Chicago restaurants. A city which possesses Harvey's, Kinsley's, or the Wellington need not be tender on that point.) But it is as much as a man's self-respect is worth to hazard a necessary question of a ticket-seller in a theatre or railroad depot. Those *bona fide* Americans, the colored men, are apt to try their skill at repartee with the persons they serve; and while I cannot recall an instance when a hotel clerk was impudent, I several times heard members of that fraternity yield to a sense of humor that would bankrupt a Broadway hotel in three weeks. In only one respect are the servitors of the Chicago public like the French: they boast the same motto—"Liberty, equality, fraternity."

There is another notable thing in Chicago which, I am certain, is a national rather than a merely local peculiarity. I refer to dirty streets. In our worst periods in New York we resort to a Latin trick of tidying up our most conspicuous thoroughfares, and leaving the others to the care of—I think it must be the Federal Weather Bureau to whose care we leave them. However, nearly all American cities are disgracefully alike in this respect, and until some dying patriot bequeathes the money to send every Alderman (back) to Europe to see how streets should and can be kept, it is, perhaps, idle to discuss the subject. But these are all comparative trifles. Certainly they will seem such to whoever shall look into the situation of Chicago closely enough to discover the great problems that lie before the people as a corporation.

She will take up these questions in their turn and as soon as possible, and, stupendous as they are, no one who understands the enterprise and energy of Chicago will doubt for a moment that she will master them shrewdly.

These problems are of national interest, and one is a subject of study throughout Christendom. They deal with the disciplining of the railroads, which run through the city at a level with the streets, and with the establishment of an efficient system of drainage or sewage. A start has been made for the handling of the sewage question. The little Chicago River flows naturally into the great lake; but years ago an attempt to alter its course was made by the operation of pumping-works at Bridgeport, within the city limits, whereby 40,000 gallons of water per minute are pumped out of the river, and into a canal that connects with the Illinois River, and thence with the Mississippi and the Gulf of Mexico. At most times this causes a sluggish flow of the river southward away from the lake. Water from the lake is also pumped into the river to dilute its waters, but it remains a noisome stream, a sewer in fact, whose waters at times flow or are driven into Lake Michigan to pollute the city's water supply. "Measures have been taken to construct a large gravity channel as an outlet for the sewage into the Illinois River. The Chicago Sanitary District has been formed by act of Legislature; nine trustees have been elected to supervise the construction of the channel, engineers have been set at work upon surveys," and perhaps the channel which will result will serve the double purpose of disposing of the sewage and establishing a navigable waterway connecting Chicago and her commerce with the Mississippi River. It is said that this will cost Chicago twenty millions of dollars. Honestly done, it will certainly be worth whatever it costs.

Chicago's water supply has been linked with this sewage problem. It does not join with it. Once the sewage matter were settled, the old two-mile crib in Lake Michigan would bring to town water than which there is none more pure on earth. The five-mile tunnel and crib now in course of construction (that is to say, the tunnel and gate pushed five miles out into the lake) certainly will leave nothing to be desired, even as the sewage is now ordered.

The railroad question is more bothersome. Chicago is criss-crossed by a grid-iron of railway tracks. Practically all of them enter the city and dissect the streets at grade; that is to say, at the level of the city's arteries. Speaking not too loosely, the locomotives and cars mangle or kill two persons on every week-day in the year, or six hundred persons annually. The railroad officials argue that they invented and developed Chicago, and that her people are ungrateful to protest against a little thing like a slaughter which would depopulate the average village in a year. In so far as it is true that they created the city, they will but repeat the experience of that fabled inventor whose monstrous mechanical off-spring claimed him for its victim, for, in a wholesome public-spirited sense, that is what must become their fate. Chicago is ten miles deep and twenty-four miles wide, and the railroads (nearly all using a number of tracks) all terminate within 4000 feet of the Rookery Building. I rely on the accuracy of a noted Chicagoan for that measurement. The Rookery is situated very much as the Bank of England is in London and as the City Hall is in New York, so that it will be seen that Chicago is at the mercy of agencies that should be her servants, and not her masters.

Some railroad men, looking from their stand-point, assert that it will cost Chicago one hundred millions of dollars to overcome this injury to her comfort and her safety. This assertion is often echoed in Chicago by men not in the railroad business. On the other hand, I shall be surprised if the railroads do not have to bear a large share of the cost, whatever it may prove to be, because I take it that Chicago will not fail to profit by the experiences of other cities where this problem has already been dealt with, and where it has not been so lightly taken for granted that when railroads are in the way of the people, it is the people, and not the railroads, who must pay to move them out of the way. The sum of present human judgment seems to be that the cost is divisible, and that the railroads should look after their tracks, and the people after their streets.

The entire nation will observe with keen interest the manner in which Chicago deals with this problem, not with any anticipation of an unjust solution that will trespass on the popular rights, but to note the determination of the lesser question, whether the railroads shall be compelled to sink their tracks in trenches or to raise them on trusses, or whether, as has also been suggested, all the roads shall combine to build and terminate at a common elevated structure curving around the outside of the thick of the city, and capable of transferring passengers from road to road, as well as of distributing them among points easily accessible from every district.

One would think it would be to the advantage of the principal railway corporations to try at once to effect an agreement among themselves and with the city for this reform, because, as I have said, the railroads are now the slowest of Chicago's institutions. The reduced speed at which the municipality obliges them to run their trains must be still further modified, and even the present headway is hindered by the frequent delays at the numerous crossings of the tracks. This is a nuisance. Every occasional traveller feels it, and what must it be to the local commuters who live at a distance from their business? They move by slow stages a quarter of an hour or more before the cars in which they ride are able to get under the scheduled headway. But it is more than a local question. It is one of the peculiarities of Chicago that she arrests a great proportion of the travelling public that seeks destinations beyond her limits in either direction. They may not want to go to Chicago at all, but it is the rule of most roads that they must do so. They must stop, transfer baggage, and change railroads. Often a stay at a hotel is part of the requirement. If this is to continue, the public might at least have the performance expedited. Both the local and the general nuisance will, in all likelihood, be remedied together. It is the aim of all progressive railroad managers to shorten time and prevent transfers wherever possible; and delays against which the entire travelling public protests cannot long avoid remedy.

In interviews with Chicago men the newspapers have obtained many estimates of the number of visitors who will attend the Columbian Exposition. One calculation, which is called conservative, is that ten million persons will see the display, and will leave three hundred millions of dollars in the city. It is not easy to judge of such estimates, but we know that there is a wider interest in this Exposition than in any that was ever held. We know also that in the foremost countries of Europe workmen's clubs and popular lotteries have been established or projected for the purpose of sending their most fortunate participants to Chicago— a few of many signs of an uncommon desire to witness the great exhibition.

Whatever these visitors have heard or thought of Chicago, they will find it not only an impressive but a substantial city. It will speak to every understanding of the speed with which it is hastening to a place among the world's capitals. Those strangers who travel farther in our West may find other towns that have builded too much upon the false prospects of districts where the crops have proved uncertain. They may see still other showy cities, where the main activity is in the direction of "swapping" real estate. It is a peculiar industry, accompanied by much bustle and lying. But they will not find in Chicago anything that will disturb its tendency to impress them with a solidity and a degree of enterprise and prosperity that are only excelled by the almost idolatrous faith of the people in their community. The city's broad and regular thoroughfares will astonish many of us who have imbibed the theory that streets are first mapped out by cows; its alley system between streets will win the admiration of those who live where alleys are unknown; its many little homes will speak volumes for the responsibility and self-respect of a great body of its citizens.

The discovery that the city's harbor is made up of forty-one miles of the banks of an internal river will lead to the satisfactory knowledge that it has preserved its beautiful front upon Lake Michigan as an ornament. This has been bordered by parks and parkways in pursuance of a plan that is interrupted to an important extent only where a pioneer railway came without the foreknowledge that it would eventually develop into a nuisance and an eyesore. Its splendid hotels, theatres, schools, churches, galleries, and public works and ornaments will commend the city to many who will not study its commercial side. In short, it will be found that those who visit the exposition will not afterward reflect upon its assembled proofs of the triumphs of man and of civilization without recalling Chicago's contribution to the sum.

THREE CAPITALS

TO one travelling over this vast country, especially the northern and western portions, the superficial impression made is that of uniformity, and even monotony: towns are alike, cities have a general resemblance, State lines are not recognized, and the idea of conformity and centralization is easily entertained. Similar institutions, facility of communication, a disposition to stronger nationality, we say, are rapidly fusing us into one federal mass.

But when we study a State at its centre, its political action, its organization, its spirit, the management of its institutions of learning and of charity, the tendencies, restrictive or liberal, of its legislation, even the tone of social life and the code of manners, we discover distinctions, individualities, almost as many differences as resemblances. And we see—the saving truth in our national life—that each State is a wellnigh indestructible entity, an empire in itself, proud and conscious of its peculiarities, and jealous of its rights. We see that State boundaries are not imaginary lines, made by the geographers, which could be easily altered by the central power. Nothing, indeed, in our whole national development, considering the common influences that have made us, is so remarkable as the difference of the several States. Even on the lines of a common settlement, say from New England and New York, note the differences between northern Ohio, northern Indiana, northern Illinois, Wisconsin, and Minnesota. Or take another line, and see the differences between southern Ohio, southern Indiana, southern Illinois, and northern Missouri. But each State, with its diverse population, has a certain homogeneity and character of its own. We can understand this where there are great differences of climate, or when one is mountainous and the other flat. But why should Indiana be so totally unlike the two States that flank it, in so many of the developments of civilized life or in retarded action: and why should Iowa, in its entire temper and spirit, be so unlike Illinois? One State copies the institutions of another, but there is always something in its life that it does not copy from any other. And the perpetuity of the Union rests upon the separateness and integrity of this State life. I confess that I am not so much impressed by the magnitude of our country as I am by the wonderful system of our complex government in unity, which permits the freest development of human nature, and the most perfect adaptability to local conditions. I can conceive of no greater enemy to the Union than he who would by any attempt at further centralization weaken the self-dependence, pride, and dignity of a single State. It seems to me that one travels in vain over the United States if he does not learn that lesson.

The State of Illinois is geographically much favored both for agriculture and commerce. With access to the Gulf by two great rivers that bound it on two sides, and communicating with the Atlantic by Lake Michigan, enterprise has aided these commercial advantages by covering it with railways. Stretching from Galena to Cairo, it has a great variety of climate; it is well watered by many noble streams, and contains in its great area scarcely any waste land. It has its contrasts of civilization. In the northern half are the thriving cities; the extreme southern portion, owing in part to a more debilitating, less wholesome, climate, and in part to a less virile, ambitious population, still keeps its "Egyptian" reputation. But the railways have already made a great change in southern Illinois, and education is transforming it. The establishment of a normal school at Carbondale in 1874–5 has changed the aspect of a great region. I am told by the State Superintendent of Education that the contrast in dress, manners, cultivation, of the country crowd which came to witness the dedication of the first building, and those who came to see the inauguration of the new school, twelve years later, was something astonishing.

Passing through the central portion of the State to Springfield, after an interval of many years, let us say a generation, I was impressed with the transformation the country had undergone by tree-planting and the growth of considerable patches of forest. The State is generally prosperous. The farmers have money, some surplus to spend in luxuries, in the education of their children, in musical instruments, in the adornment of their homes. This is the universal report of the Commercial Travellers, those modern couriers of business and information, who run in swarms to and fro over the whole land. In this respect they always contrast the State with Iowa, which they say has no money, and where trade, to their apprehension, stands still, except in the river towns. They attribute this difference to intermeddling and prohibitory legislation. It seems unaccountable otherwise, for Iowa, with its rolling prairies and park-like timber, loved in the season of birds and flowers, is one of the most fertile and lovely States in the West.

Springfield, which spreads its 30,000 people extensively over a plain on the Sangamon River, is prosperous, and in the season when any place can be agreeable, a beautiful city. The elm grows well in the rich soil, and its many broad, well-shaded streets, with pretty detached houses and lawns, make it very attractive, a delightful rural capital. The large Illinois towns are slowly lifting themselves out of the slough of rich streets, better adapted to crops than to trade; though good material for pavement is nowhere abundant. Springfield has recently improved its condition by paving, mostly with cedar blocks, twenty-five miles of streets. I notice that in some of the Western towns tile pavement is being tried. Manufacturing is increasing—there is a prosperous rolling-mill and a successful watch factory—but the overwhelming interest of the city is that it is the centre of the political and educational institutions—of the life emanating from the State-house.

The State-house is, I believe, famous. It is a big building, a great deal has been spent on it in the way of ornamentation, and it enjoys the distinction of the highest State-house dome in the country—350 feet. It has the merit also of being well placed on an elevation, and its rooms are spacious and very well planned. It is an incongruous pile externally, mixing many styles of architecture, placing Corinthian capitals on Doric columns, and generally losing the impression of a dignified mass in details. Within, it is especially rich in wall casings of beautiful and variegated marbles, each panel exquisite, but all together tending to dissipate any idea of unity of design or simplicity. Nothing whatever can be said for many of the scenes in relief, or the mural paintings (except that they illustrate the history of the State), nor for most of the statues in the corridors, but the decoration of the chief rooms, in mingling of colors and material, is frankly barbarous.

Illinois has the reputation of being slow in matters of education and reform. A day in the State offices, however, will give the visitor an impression of intelligence and vigor in these directions. The office of the State Board of Pharmacy in the Capitol shows a strict enforcement of the law in the supervision of drugs and druggists. Prison management has also most intelligent consideration. The two great penitentiaries, the Southern, at Chester (with about 800 convicts), and the Northern, at Joliet (with about 1600 convicts), call for no special comment. The one at Joliet is a model of its kind, with a large library, and such schooling as is practicable in the system, and is well administered; and I am glad to see that Mr. McClaughry, the warden, believes that incorrigibles should be permanently held, and that grading, the discipline of labor and education, with a parole system, can make law-abiding citizens of many convicts.

In school education the State is certainly not supine in efforts. Out of a State population of about 3,500,000, there were, in 1887, 1,627,841 under twenty-one years, and 1,096,464 between the ages of six and twenty-one. The school age for free attendance is from six to twenty-one; for compulsory attendance, from eight to fourteen. There were 749,994 children enrolled, and 506,197 in daily attendance. Those enrolled in private schools numbered 87,725. There were 2258 teachers in private schools, and 22,925 in public schools; of this latter, 7462 were men and 15,463 women. The average monthly salary of men was $51 48, and of women $42 17. The sum available for school purposes in 1887 was $12,896,515, in an assessed value of taxable property of $797,752,888. These figures are from Dr. N. W. Edwards, Superintendent of Public Instruction, whose energy is felt in every part of the State.

The State prides itself on its institutions of charity. I saw some of them at Jacksonville, an hour's ride west of Springfield. Jacksonville is a very pretty city of some 15,000, with elm-shaded avenues that suggest but do not rival New Haven—one of those intellectual centres that are a continual surprise to our English friends in their bewildered exploration of our monotonous land. In being the Western centre of Platonic philosophy, it is more like Concord than like New Haven. It is the home of a large number of people who have travelled, who give intelligent attention to art, to literary study in small societies and clubs—its Monday Evening Club of men long antedated most of the similar institutions at the East—and to social problems. I certainly did not expect to find, as I did, water-colors by Turner in Jacksonville, besides many other evidences of a culture that must modify many Eastern ideas of what the West is and is getting to be.

The Illinois College is at Jacksonville. It is one of twenty-five small colleges in the State, and I believe the only one that adheres to the old curriculum, and does not adopt co-education. It has about sixty students in the college proper, and about one hundred and thirty in the preparatory academy. Most of the Illinois colleges have preparatory departments, and so long as they do, and the various sects scatter their energies among so many institutions, the youth of the State who wish a higher education will be obliged to go East. The school perhaps the most vigorous just now is the University of Illinois, at Urbana, a school of agriculture and applied science mainly. The Central Hospital for the Insane (one of three in the State), under the superintendence of Dr. Henry F. Carriel, is a fine establishment, a model of neatness and good management, with over nine hundred patients, about a third of whom do some light work on the farm or in the house. A large conservatory of plants and flowers is rightly regarded as a remedial agency in the treatment of the patients. Here also is a fine school for the education of the blind.

The Institution for the Education of Deaf-Mutes, Dr. Philip H. Gillette, superintendent, is, I believe, the largest in the world, and certainly one of the most thoroughly equipped and successful in its purposes. It has between five hundred and six hundred pupils. All the departments found in many other institutions are united here. The school has a manual train-

ing department; articulation is taught; the art school exhibits surprising results in aptitude for both drawing and painting; and industries are taught to the extent of giving every pupil a trade or some means of support—shoemaking, cabinetmaking, printing, sewing, gardening, and baking.

Such an institution as this raises many interesting questions. It is at once evident that the loss of the sense of hearing has an effect on character, moral and intellectual. Whatever may be the education of the deaf-mute, he will remain, in some essential and not easily to be characterized respects, different from other people. It is exceedingly hard to cultivate in them a spirit of self-dependence, or eradicate the notion that society owes them perpetual care and support. The education of deaf-mutes, and the teaching them trades, so that they become intelligent and productive members of society, of course induce marriages among them. Is not this calculated to increase the number of deaf-mutes? Dr. Gillette thinks not. The vital statistics show that consanguineous marriages are a large factor in deaf-muteism; about ten per cent., it is estimated, of the deaf-mutes are the offspring of parents related by blood. Ancestral defects are not always perpetuated in kind; they may descend in physical deformity, in deafness, in imbecility. Deafness is more apt to descend in collateral branches than in a straight line. It is a striking fact in a table of relationships prepared by Dr. Gillette that, while the 450 deaf-mutes enumerated had 770 relationships to other deaf-mutes, making a total of 1220, only twelve of them had deaf-mute parents, and only two of them one deaf-mute parent, the mother of these having been able to hear, and that in no case was the mother alone a deaf-mute. Of the pupils who have left this institution, 251 have married deaf-mutes, and 19 hearing persons. These marriages have been as fruitful as the average, and among them all only sixteen have deaf-mute children; in some of the families having a deaf child there are other children who hear. These facts, says the report, clearly indicate that the probability of deaf offspring from deaf parentage is remote, while other facts may clearly indicate that a deaf person probably has or will have a deaf relation other than a child.

Springfield is old enough to have a historic flavor and social traditions; perhaps it might be called a Kentucky flavor, so largely did settlers from Kentucky determine it. There was a leisurely element in it, and it produced a large number of men prominent in politics and in the law, and women celebrated for beauty and spirit. It was a hospitable society, with a certain tone of "family" that distinguished it from other frontier places, a great liking for the telling of racy stories, and a hearty enjoyment of life. The State has provided a Gubernatorial residence which is at once spacious and pleasant, and is a mansion, with its present occupants, typical in a way of the old *régime* and of modern culture.

To the country at large Springfield is distinguished as the home of Abraham Lincoln to an extent perhaps not fully realized by the residents of the growing capital, with its ever new interests. And I was perhaps unreasonably disappointed in not finding that sense of his personality that I expected. It is, indeed, emphasized by statues in the Capitol and by the great mausoleum in the cemetery—an imposing structure, with an excellent statue in bronze, and four groups, relating to the civil war, of uncommon merit. But this great monumental show does not satisfy the personal longing of which I speak. Nor is the Lincoln residence much more satisfactory in this respect. The plain two-story wooden house has been presented to the State by his son Robert, and is in charge of a custodian. And although the parlor is made a show-room and full of memorials, there is no atmosphere of the man about it. On Lincoln's departure for Washington the furniture was sold and the house rented, never to be again occupied by him. There is here nothing of that personal presence that clings to the Hermitage, to Marshfield, to Mount Vernon, to Monticello. Lincoln was given to the nation, and—a frequent occurrence in our uprooting business life —the home disappeared. Lincoln was honored and beloved in Springfield as a man, but perhaps some of the feeling toward him as a party leader still lingers, although it has disappeared almost everywhere else in the country. Nowhere else was the personal partisanship hotter than in this city, and it is hardly to be expected that political foes in this generation should quite comprehend the elevation of

Lincoln, in the consenting opinion of the world, among the greatest characters of all ages. It has happened to Lincoln that every year and a more intimate knowledge of his character have added to his fame and to the appreciation of his moral grandeur. There is a natural desire to go to some spot pre-eminently sacred to his personality. This may be his birthplace. At any rate, it is likely that before many years Kentucky will be proud to distinguish in some way the spot where the life began of the most illustrious man born in its borders.

When we come to the capital of Indiana we have, in official language, to report progress. One reason assigned for the passing of emigrants through Indiana to Illinois was that the latter was a prairie country, more easily subdued than the more wooded region of Indiana. But it is also true that the sluggish, illiterate character of its early occupants turned aside the stream of Western emigration from its borders. There has been a great deal of philosophic speculation upon the acknowledged backwardness of civilization in Indiana, its slow development in institutions of education, and its slow change in rural life, compared with its sister States. But this concerns us less now than the awakening which is visible at the capital and in some of the northern towns. The forests of hard timber which were an early disadvantage are now an important element in the State industry and wealth. Recent developments of coal-fields and the discovery of natural gas have given an impetus to manufacturing, which will powerfully stimulate agriculture and traffic, and open a new career to the State.

Indianapolis, which stood still for some years in a reaction from real estate speculation, is now a rapidly improving city. with a population of about 125,000. It is on the natural highway of the old National Turnpike, and its central location in the State, in the midst of a rich agricultural district, has made it the centre of fifteen railway lines, and of active freight and passenger traffic. These lines are all connected for freight purposes by a belt road, over which pass about 5000 freight cars daily. This belt road also does an enormous business for the stock-yards, and its convenient line is rapidly filling up with manufacturing establishments. As a consequence of these facilities the trade of the city in both wholesale and retail houses is good and increasing. With this increase of business there has been an accession of banking capital. The four national and two private banks have an aggregate capital of about three millions, and the Clearing-house report of 1887 showed a business of about one hundred millions, an increase of nearly fifty per cent. over the preceding year. But the individual prosperity is largely due to the building and loan associations, of which there are nearly one hundred, with an aggregate capital of seven millions, the loans of which exceed those of the banks. These take the place of savings-banks, encourage the purchase of homesteads, and are preventives of strikes and labor troubles in the factories.

The people of Indianapolis call their town a Park City. Occupying a level plain, its streets (the principal ones with a noble width of ninety feet) intersect each other at right angles; but in the centre of the city is a Circle Park of several acres, from which radiate to the four quarters of the town avenues ninety feet broad that relieve the monotony of the right lines. These streets are for the most part well shaded, and getting to be well paved, lined with pleasant but not ambitious residences, so that the whole aspect of the city is open and agreeable. The best residences are within a few squares of the most active business streets, and if the city has not the distinction of palaces, it has fewer poor and shabby quarters than most other towns of its size. In the Circle Park, where now stands a statue of Governor Morton, is to be erected immediately the Soldiers' Monument, at a cost of $250,000.

The city is fortunate in its public buildings. The County Court-house (which cost $1,600,000) and City Hall are both fine buildings; in the latter are the city markets, and above, a noble auditorium with seats for 4000 people. But the State Capitol, just finished within the appropriation of $2,000,000, is pre-eminent among State Capitols in many respects. It is built of the Bedford limestone, one of the best materials both for color and endurance found in the country. It follows the American plan of two wings and a dome; but it is finely proportioned; and the exterior, with rows of graceful Corinthian columns above the basement story, is altogether pleasing. The interior is spacious and impressive, the Chambers fine, the furnishing solid and in good taste, with nowhere any over-ornamentation or petty details to mar the general noble effect. The State Library contains, besides the law books, about 20,000 miscellaneous volumes.

When Matthew Arnold first came to New York the place in the West about which he expressed the most curiosity was Indianapolis; that he said he must see, if no other city. He had no knowledge of the place, and could give no reason for his preference except that the name had always had a fascination for him. He found there, however, a very extensive book-store, where his own works were sold in numbers that pleased and surprised him. The shop has a large miscellaneous stock, and does a large jobbing and retail business, but the miscellaneous books dealt in are mostly cheap reprints of English works, with very few American copyright books. This is a significant comment on the languishing state of the market for works of American authors in the absence of an international copyright law.

The city is not behind any other in educational efforts. In its five free public libraries are over 70,000 volumes. The city has a hundred churches and a vigorous Young Men's Christian Association, which cost $75,000. Its private schools have an excellent reputation. There are 20,000 children registered of school age, and 11,000 in daily attendance in twenty-eight free-school houses. In methods of efficacy these are equal to any in the Union, as is shown by the fact that there are reported in the city only 325 persons between the ages of six and twenty-one unable to read and write. The average cost of instruction for each pupil is $19 64 a year. In regard to advanced methods and manual training, Indianapolis schools claim to be pioneers.

The latest reports show educational activity in the State as well as in the capital. In 1886 the revenues expended in public schools were about $5,000,000. The State supports the Indiana University at Bloomington, with about 300 students, the Agricultural College at Lafayette, with over 300, and a Normal School at Terre Haute, with an attendance of about 500. There are, besides, seventeen private colleges and several other normal schools. In 1886 the number of school-children enrolled in the State was 506,000, of whom 346,000 were in daily attendance. To those familiar with Indiana these figures show a greatly increased interest in education.

Several of the State benevolent institutions are in Indianapolis: a hospital for the insane, which cost $1,200,000, and accommodates 1600 patients; an asylum for the blind, which has 132 pupils; and a school for deaf-mutes, which cost $500,000, and has about 400 scholars. The novel institution, however, that I saw at Indianapolis is a Reformatory for Women and Girls, controlled entirely by women. The board of trustees are women, the superintendent, physician, and keepers are women. In one building, but in separate departments, were the female convicts, 42 in number, several of them respectable-looking elderly women who had killed their husbands, and about 150 young girls. The convicts and the girls—who are committed for restraint and reform —never meet except in chapel, but it is more than doubtful if it is wise for the State to subject girls to even this sort of contiguity with convicts, and to the degradation of penitentiary suggestions. The establishment is very neat and well ordered and well administered. The work of the prison is done by the convicts, who are besides kept employed at sewing and in the laundry. The girls in the reformatory work half a day, and are in school the other half.

This experiment of the control of a State-prison by women is regarded as doubtful by some critics, who say that women will obey a man when they will not obey a woman. Female convicts, because they have fallen lower than men, or by reason of their more nervous organization, are commonly not so easily controlled as male convicts, and it is insisted that they indulge in less "tantrums" under male than under female authority. This is denied by the superintendent of this prison, though she has incorrigible cases who can only be controlled by solitary confinement. She has daily religious exercises, Bible reading and exposition, and a Sunday-school; and she doubts if she could control the convicts without this religious influence. It not only has a daily quieting effect, but has resulted in several cases in "conversion." There are in the institution several girls and women of color, and I asked the su-

perintendent if the white inmates exhibited any prejudice against them on account of their color. To my surprise, the answer was that the contrary is the case. The whites look up to the colored girls, and seem either to have a respect for them or to be fascinated by them. This surprising statement was supplemented by another, that the influence of the colored girls on the whites is not good; the white girl who seeks the company of the colored girl deteriorates, and the colored girl does not change.

Indianapolis, which is attractive by reason of a climate that avoids extremes, bases its manufacturing and its business prosperity upon the large coal beds lying to the west and south of it, the splendid and very extensive quarries of Bedford limestone contiguous to the coal-fields, the abundant supply of various sorts of hard wood for the making of furniture, and the recent discovery of natural gas. The gas-field region, which is said to be very much larger than any other in the country, lies to the northwest, and comes within eight miles of the city. Pipes are already laid to the city limits, and the whole heating and manufacturing of the city will soon be done by the gas. I saw this fuel in use in a large and successful pottery, where are made superior glazed and encaustic tiles, and nothing could be better for the purpose. The heat in the kilns is intense; it can be perfectly regulated; as fuel the gas is free from smoke and smut, and its cost is merely nominal. The excitement over this new agent is at present extraordinary. The field where it has been found is so extensive as to make the supply seem inexhaustible. It was first discovered in Indiana at Eaton, in Delaware County, in 1886. From January 1, 1887, to February, 1888, it is reported that 1000 wells were opened in the gas territory, and that 245 companies were organized for various manufactures, with an aggregate capital of $25,000,000. Whatever the figures may be, there are the highest expectations of immense increase of manufactures in Indianapolis and in all the gas region. Of some effects of this revolution in fuel we may speak when we come to the gas wells of Ohio.

I had conceived of Columbus as a rural capital, pleasant and slow, rather a village than a city. I was surprised to find a city of 80,000 people, growing with a rapidity astonishing even for a Western town, with miles of prosperous business blocks (High Street is four miles long), and wide avenues of residences extending to suburban parks. Broad Street, with its four rows of trees and fine houses and beautiful lawns, is one of the handsomest avenues in the country, and it is only one of many that are attractive. The Capitol Square, with several good buildings about it, makes an agreeable centre of the city. Of the Capitol building not much is to be said. The exterior is not wholly bad, but it is surmounted by a truncated something that is neither a dome nor a revolving turret, and the interior is badly arranged for room, light, and ventilation. Space is wasted, and many of the rooms, among them the relic-room and the flag-room, are inconvenient and almost inaccessible. The best is the room of the Supreme Court, which has attached a large law library. The general State Library contains about 54,000 volumes, with a fair but not large proportion of Western history.

Columbus is a city of churches, of very fine public schools, of many clubs, literary and social, in which the intellectual element predominates, and of an intelligent, refined, and most hospitable society. Here one may study the educational and charitable institutions of the State, many of the more important of which are in the city, and also the politics. It was Ohio's hard fate to be for many years an "October State," and the battle-field and corruption-field of many outside influences. This no doubt demoralized the politics of the State, and lowered the tone of public morality. With the removal of the cause of this decline, I believe the tone is being raised. Recent trials for election frauds, and the rehabilitation of the Cincinnati police, show that a better spirit prevails.

Ohio is growing in wealth as it is in population, and is in many directions an ambitious and progressive State. Judged by its institutions of benevolence and of economies, it is a leading State. No other State provides more liberally for its unfortunates, in asylums for the insane, the blind, the deaf-mutes, the idiotic, the young waifs and strays, nor shows a more intelligent comprehension of the legitimate functions of a great commonwealth, in the creation of boards of education and of charities and of health, in a State inspection of workshops and factories, in establishing bureaus of meteorology and of forestry, and a fish commission, and an agricultural experiment station. The State has thirty-four colleges and universities, a public-school system which has abolished distinctions of color. and which by the reports is as efficient as any in the Union. Cincinnati, the moral tone of which, the Ohio people say, is not fairly represented by its newspapers, is famous the world over for its cultivation in music and its progress in the fine and industrial arts. It would be possible for a State to have and be all this and yet rise in the general scale of civilization only to a splendid mediocrity, without the higher institutions of pure learning, and without a very high standard of public morality. Ohio is in no less danger of materialism, with all its diffused intelligence, than other States. There is a recognizable limit to what a diffused level of education, say in thirty-four colleges, can do for the higher life of a State. I heard an address in the Capitol by ex-President Hayes on the expediency of adding a manual-training school to the Ohio State University at Columbus. The comment of some of the legislators on it was that we have altogether too much book-learning; what we need is workshops in our schools and colleges. It seems to a stranger that whatever first-class industrial and technical schools Ohio needs, it needs more the higher education, and the teaching of philosophy, logic, and ethics. In 1886 Governor Foraker sent a special message to the Legislature pointing out the fact that notwithstanding the increase of wealth in the State, the revenue was inadequate to the expenditure, principally by reason of the undervaluation of taxable property (there being a yearly decline in the reported value of personal property), and a fraudulent evasion of taxes. There must have been a wide insensibility to the wrong of cheating the State to have produced this state of things, and one cannot but think that it went along with the low political tone before mentioned. Of course Ohio is not a solitary sinner among States in this evasion of duty, but she helps to point the moral that the higher life of a State needs a great deal of education that is neither commercial nor industrial nor simply philanthropic.

It is impossible and unnecessary for the purposes of this paper to speak of many of the public institutions of the State, even of those in the city. But educators everywhere may study with profit the management of the public schools under the City Board of Education, of which Mr. R. W. Stevenson is superintendent. The High-School, of over 600 pupils, is especially to be commended. Manual training is not introduced into the schools, and the present better sentiment is against it; but its foundation, drawing, is thoroughly taught from the primaries up to the High-School, and the exhibits of the work of the schools of all grades in modelling, drawing, and form and color studies, which were made last year in New York and Chicago, gave these Columbus schools a very high rank in the country. Any visitor to them must be impressed with the intelligence of the methods employed, the apprehension of modern notions, and also the conservative spirit of common-sense.

The Ohio State University has an endowment from the State of over half a million dollars, and a source of ultimate wealth in its great farm and grounds, which must increase in value as the city extends. ◦ It is a very well equipped institution for the study of the natural sciences and agriculture, and might easily be built up into a university in all departments, worthy of the State. At present it has 335 students, of whom 150 are in the academic department, 41 in special practical courses, and 143 in the preparatory school. All the students are organized in companies, under an officer of the United States, for military discipline; the uniform, the drill, the lessons of order and obedience, are invaluable in the transforming of carriage and manners. The university has a museum of geology which ranks among the important ones of the country. It is a pity that a consolidation of other State institutions with this cannot be brought about.

The Ohio Penitentiary at Columbus is an old building, not in keeping with the modern notions of prison construction. In 1887 it had about 1300 convicts, some 100 less than in the preceding year. The management is subject to political changes, and its officers have to be taken from various parts of the State at the dictation of political workers. Under this system the best management is liable to be upset by an election. The special interest in the prison at this time was in the observation of the working of the parole law. Since the passage of the act in

May, 1885, 283 prisoners have been paroled, and while several of the convicts have been returned for a violation of parole, nearly the whole number are reported as law-abiding citizens. The managers are exceedingly pleased with the working of the law; it promotes good conduct in the prison, and reduces the number in confinement. The reduction of the number of convicts in 1887 from the former year was ascribed partially to the passage of the general sentence law in 1884, and the habitual crimes act in 1885. The criminals dread these laws, the first because it gives no fixed time to build their hopes upon, but all depends upon their previous record and good conduct in prison, while the latter affects the incorrigible, who are careful to shun the State after being convicted twice, and avoid imprisonment for life. The success of these laws and the condition of the State finances delay the work on the Intermediate Prison, or Reformatory, begun at Mansfield. This Reformatory is intended for first offenders, and has the distinct purpose of prevention of further deterioration, and of reformation by means of the discipline of education and labor. The success of the tentative laws in this direction, as applied to the general prisons, is, in fact, a strong argument for the carrying out of the Mansfield scheme.

There cannot be a more interesting study of the "misfits" of humanity than that offered in the Institution for Feebleminded Youth, under the superintendence of Dr. G. A. Doren. Here are 715 imbeciles in all stages of development from absolute mental and physical incapacity. There is scarcely a problem that exists in education, in the relation of the body and mind, in the inheritance of mental and physical traits, in regard to the responsibility for crime, in psychology or physiology, that is not here illustrated. It is the intention of the school to teach the idiot child some trade or occupation that will make him to some degree useful, and to carry him no further than the common branches in learning. The first impression, I think, made upon a visitor is the almost invariable physical deformity that attends imbecility — ill-proportioned, distorted bodies, dwarfed, misshapen gelatinoids, with bones that have no stiffness. The next impression is the preponderance of the animal nature, the persistence of the lower passions, and the absence of moral qualities in the general immaturity. And perhaps the next impression is of the extraordinary effect that physical training has in awakening the mind, and how soon the discipline of the institution creates the power of self-control. From almost blank imbecility and utter lack of self-restraint the majority of these children, as we saw them in their school-rooms and work-shops, exhibited a sense of order, of entire decency, and very considerable intelligence. It was demonstrated that most imbeciles are capable of acquiring the rudiments of an education and of learning some useful occupation. Some of the boys work on the farm, others learn trades. The boys in the shoe-shop were making shoes of excellent finish. The girls do plain sewing and house-work apparently almost as well as girls of their age outside. Two or three things that we saw may be mentioned to show the scope of the very able management and the capacities of the pupils. There was a drill of half a hundred boys and girls in the dumb-bell exercise, to music, under the leadership of a pupil, which in time, grace, and exact execution of complicated movements would have done credit to any school. The institution has two bands, one of brass and one of strings, which perform very well. The string band played for dancing in the large amusement hall. Several hundred children were on the floor dancing cotillons, and they went through the variety of changes not only in perfect time and decorum, but without any leader to call the figures. It would have been a remarkable performance for any children. There were many individual cases of great and deplorable interest. Cretins, it was formerly supposed, were only born in mountainous regions. There are three here born in Ohio. There were five imbeciles of what I should call the ape type, all of one Ohio family. Two of them were the boys exhibited some years ago by Barnum as the Aztec children—the last of an extinct race. He exhibited them as a boy and a girl. When they had grown a little too large to show as children, or the public curiosity was satisfied about the extinct race, he exhibited them as wild Australians.

The humanity of so training these imbeciles that they can have some enjoyment of life, and be occasionally of some use to their relations, is undeniable. But since the State makes this effort in the survival of the unfittest, it must go further and provide a permanent home for them. The girls who have learned to read and write and sew and do house-work, and are of decent appearance, as many of them are, are apt to marry when they leave the institution. Their offspring are invariably idiots. I saw in this school the children of mothers who had been trained here. It is no more the intention of the State to increase the number of imbeciles than it is the number of criminals. Many of our charitable and penal institutions at present do both.

I should like to approach the subject of Natural Gas in a proper spirit, but I have neither the imagination nor the rhetoric to do justice to the expectations formed of it. In the restrained language of one of the inhabitants of Findlay, its people "have caught the divine afflatus which came with the discovery of natural gas." If Findlay had only natural gas, "she would be the peer, if not the superior, of any municipality on earth"; but she has much more, "and in all things has no equal or superior between the oceans and the lakes and the gulf, and is marching on to the grandest destiny ever prepared for any people, in any land, or in any period, since the morning stars first sang together, and the flowers in the garden of Eden budded and blossomed for man." In fact, "this she has been doing in the past two years in the grandest and most satisfactory way, and that she will continue to progress is as certain as the stars that hold their midnight revel around the throne of Omnipotence."

Notwithstanding this guarded announcement, it is evident that the discovery of natural gas has begun a revolution in fuel, which will have permanent and far-reaching economic and social consequences, whether the supply of gas is limited or inexhaustible.

Those who have once used fuel in this form are not likely to return to the crude and wasteful heating by coal. All the cities and large towns west of the Alleghanies are made disagreeable by bituminous coal smoke. The extent of this annoyance and its detraction from the pleasure of daily living cannot be exaggerated. The atmosphere is more or less vitiated, and the sky obscured, houses, furniture, clothing, are dirty, and clean linen and clean hands and face are not expected. All this is changed where gas is used for fuel. The city becomes cheerful, and the people can see each other. But this is not all. One of the great burdens of our Northern life, fire building and replenishing, disappears, house-keeping is simplified, the expense of servants reduced, cleanliness restored. Add to this that in the gas regions the cost of fuel is merely nominal, and in towns distant some thirty or forty miles it is not half that of coal. It is easy to see that this revolution in fuel will make as great a change in social life as in manufacturing, and that all the change may not be agreeable. This natural gas is a very subtle fluid, somewhat difficult to control, though I have no doubt that invention will make it as safe in our houses as illuminating gas is. So far as I have seen its use, the heat from it is intense and withering. In a closed stove it is intolerable; in an open grate, with a simulated pile of hard coal or logs, it is better, but much less agreeable than soft coal or wood. It does not, as at present used, promote a good air in the room, and its intense dryness ruins the furniture. But its cheapness, convenience, and neatness will no doubt prevail, and we are entering upon a gas age, in which, for the sake of progress, we shall doubtless surrender something that will cause us to look back to the more primitive time with regret. If the gas wells fail, artificial gas for fuel will doubtless be manufactured.

I went up to the gas-fields of northern Ohio in company with Professor Edward Orton, the State Geologist, who has made a study of the subject, and pretty well defined the fields of Indiana and Ohio. The gas is found at a depth of between 1100 and 1200 feet, after passing through a great body of shale and encountering salt-water, in a porous Trenton limestone. The drilling and tubing enter this limestone several feet to get a good holding. This porous limestone holds the gas like a sponge, and it rushes forth with tremendous force when released. It is now well settled that these are reservoirs of gas that are tapped, and not sources of perpetual supply by constant manufacture. How large the supply may be in any case cannot be told, but there is a limit to it. It can be exhausted, like a vein of coal. But the fields are so large, both in Indiana and Ohio, that it seems probable that by sinking new wells the supply will be continued for a long time. The evidence that it is not inexhaustible in any one well is that in all in which the flow of gas has been tested at intervals the force of pressure is found to diminish. For months after the discovery the wells were allowed to run to waste, and billions of feet of gas were lost. A better economy now prevails, and this wastefulness is stopped. The wells are all under control, and large groups of them are connected by common service pipes. The region about Fostoria is organized under the Northwestern Gas Company, and controls a large territory. It supplies the city of Toledo, which uses no other fuel, through pipes thirty miles long, Fremont, and other towns. The loss per mile in transit through the pipes is now known, so that the distance can be calculated at which it will pay to send it. I believe that this is about fifty to sixty miles. The gas when it comes from the well is about the temperature of 32° Fahr., and the common pressure is 400 pounds to the square inch. The velocity with which it rushes, unchecked, from the pipe at the mouth of the well may be said to be about that of a minie-ball from an ordinary rifle. The Ohio area of gas is between 2000 and 3000 square miles. The claim for the Indiana area is that it is 20,000 square miles, but the geologists make it much less.

The speculation in real estate caused by this discovery has been perhaps without parallel in the history of the State, and, as is usual in such cases, it is now in a lull, waiting for the promised developments. But these have been almost as marvellous as the speculation. Findlay was a sleepy little village in the black swamp district, one of the most backward regions of Ohio. For many years there had been surface indications of gas, and there is now a house standing in the city which used gas for fuel forty years ago. When the first gas well was opened, ten years ago, the village had about 4500 inhabitants. It has now probably 15,000, it is a city, and its limits have been extended to cover an area six miles long by four miles wide. This is dotted over with hastily built houses, and is rapidly being occupied by manufacturing establishments. The city owns all the gas wells, and supplies fuel to factories and private houses at the simple cost of maintaining the service-pipes. So rapid has been the growth and the demand for gas that there has not been time to put all the pipes underground, and they are encountered on the surface all over the region. The town is pervaded by the odor of the gas, which is like that of petroleum, and the traveller is notified of his nearness to the town by the smell before he can see the houses. The surface pipes, hastily laid, occasionally leak, and at these weak places the gas is generally ignited in order to prevent its tainting the atmosphere. This immediate neighborhood has an oil field contiguous to the gas, plenty of limestone (the kilns are burned by gas), good building stone, clay fit for making bricks and tiles, and superior hard-wood forests. The cheap fuel has already attracted here manufacturing industries of all sorts, and new plants are continually made. I have a list of over thirty different mills and factories which are either in full operation or getting under way. Among the most interesting of these are the works for making window-glass and table glass. The superiority of this fuel for the glass furnaces seems to be admitted.

Although the wells about Findlay are under control, the tubing is anchored, and the awful force is held under by gates and levers of steel, it is impossible to escape a feeling of awe in this region at the subterranean energies which seem adequate to blow the whole country heavenward. Some of the wells were opened for us. Opening a well is unscrewing the service-pipe and letting the full force of the gas issue from the pipe at the mouth of the well. When one of these wells is thus opened the whole town is aware of it by the roaring and the quaking of the air. The first one exhibited was in a field a mile and a half from the city. At the first freedom from the screws and clamps the gas rushed out in such density that it was visible. Although we stood several rods from it, the roar was so great that one could not make himself heard shouting in the ear of his neighbor. The geologist stuffed cotton in his ears and tied a shawl about his head, and, assisted by the chemist, stood close to the pipe to measure the flow. The chemist, who had not taken the precaution to protect himself, was quite deaf for some time after the experiment. A four-inch pipe, about sixty feet in length, was then screwed on, and the gas ignited as it issued from the end on the ground. The roaring was as before. For several feet from the end of the tube there was no flame, but beyond was a sea of fire sweeping the ground and rioting high in the air—billows of red and yellow and blue flame, fierce and hot enough to consume everything within reach. It was an awful display of power.

We had a like though only a momentary display at the famous Karg well, an eight-million-feet well. This could only be turned on for a few seconds at a time, for it is in connection with the general system. If the gas is turned off, the fires in houses and factories would go out, and if it were turned on again without notice, the rooms would be full of gas, and an explosion follow an attempt to relight it. This danger is now being removed by the invention of an automatic valve in the pipe supplying each fire, which will close and lock when the flow of gas ceases, and admit no more gas until it is opened. The ordinary pressure for house service is about two pounds to the square inch. The Karg well is on the bank of the creek, and the discharge-pipe through which the gas (though not in its full force) was turned for our astonishment extends over the water. The roar was like that of Niagara; all the town shakes when the Karg is loose. When lighted, billows of flame rolled over the water, brilliant in color and fantastic in form, with a fury and rage of conflagration enough to strike the spectator with terror. I have never seen any other display of natural force so impressive as this. When this flame issues from an upright pipe, the great mass of fire rises eighty feet into the air, leaping and twisting in fiendish fury. For six weeks after this well was first opened its constant roaring shook the nerves of the town, and by night its flaming torch lit up the heaven and banished darkness. With the aid of this new agent anything seems possible.

The feverishness of speculation will abate; many anticipations will not be realized. It will be discovered that there is a limit to manufacturing, even with fuel that costs next to nothing. The supply of natural gas no doubt has its defined limits. But nothing seems more certain to me than that gas, manufactured if not natural, is to be the fuel of the future in the West, and that the importance of this economic change in social life is greater than we can at present calculate.

THE ARCHITECTURE OF MINNESOTA
AND ST PAUL

IT is just thirty years since Anthony Trollope ascended the Mississippi to the head of navigation and the Falls of St. Anthony, and recorded his impressions of the works of nature and of man along the shores of that river. As might perhaps have been expected, he admired with enthusiasm the works of nature, and as might certainly have been expected, he found little to admire in the handiwork of man. "I protest that of all the river scenery that I know, that of the upper Mississippi is by far the finest and the most continued. One thinks, of course, of the Rhine; but, according to my idea of beauty, the Rhine is nothing to the upper Mississippi . . . The idea constantly occurs that some point on every hill-side would form the most charming site ever yet chosen for a noble residence." Thus Trollope wrote of the upper Mississippi; and thus again of the "twin cities" that are the subject of our present inquisition: "St. Paul contains about 14,000 inhabitants, and, like all other American towns, is spread over a surface of ground adapted to the accommodation of a very extended population. As it is belted on one side by the river, and on the other by the bluffs which accompany the course of the river, the site is pretty and almost romantic." The other "twin" is so much the later born that to few Minneapolitans does it ever occur that it had even seen the light in 1861. "Going on from Minnehaha, we came to Minneapolis, at which place there is a fine suspension-bridge across the river, just above the Falls of St. Anthony, and leading to the town of that name. Till I got there I could hardly believe that in these days there should be a living village called Minneapolis by living men. I presume I should describe it as a town, for it has a municipality and a post-office, and of course a large hotel. The interest of the place, however, is in the saw-mills."

I do not mean to celebrate again the growth of St. Paul and Minneapolis from these small beginnings, which is the marvel even of the marvellous West. But for our immediate purpose it is necessary to bear in mind not only the rapidity of the growth of the two cities, but the intensity of the rivalry between them—a rivalry which the stranger hardly comprehends, however much he may have heard of it, until he has seen the workings of it on the spot. Indeed, it is scarcely accurate to describe the genesis of Minneapolis, in particular, as a growth at all. St. Paul has been developed from the frontier trading-post of the earlier days by an evolution the successive stages of which have left their several records, but Minneapolis has risen like an exhalation, or, to adopt even a mustier comparison, has sprung from the heads of its projectors full-panoplied in brick and mortar. There are traces of the village that Trollope saw, and there are the towering structures of a modern city, and there is nothing between. In this electric air, where there is so little "precipitation" in the atmosphere and so much in everything else, where "the flux of mortal things" is not a generalization of the mind, but a palpable fact of daily experience, where antiquity means the day before yesterday, and posterity the day after to-morrow, the present is the most contemptible of tenses, and men inevitably come to think and live and build in the future-perfect. A ten-story building in a ten-acre lot requires explanation, and this seems to be the explanation;—this, and the adjacency of the hated rival. In St. Paul the elevator came as a needed factor in commercial architecture, since the strip of shore to which the town was confined in Trollope's time still limits and cramps the business quarter, and leaves only the vertical dimension available for expansion. Towering buildings are the normal outcome of such a situation. Minneapolis, on the other hand, occupies a table-land above the river, which at present is practically unlimited. Although, of course, every growing or grown town must have a most frequented part—a centre where land is costlier than elsewhere and buildings rise higher—the altitude of the newest and tallest structures of Minneapolis could scarcely be explained without reference to the nearness of St. Paul, and the intensity of the local pride born of that nearness. If the physical necessities of the case prescribed ten-story buildings in St. Paul, the moral necessity of not being outdone would prescribe twelve-story buildings for Minneapolis.

Evidently there could be no better places than the twin cities to study the development of Western architecture, or rather to ascertain whether there is any such thing. There seems to be among the Western lay populations a faith that there is, which is none the less firm for being a trifle vague, and this faith is shared by some of the practitioners of architecture in the West. In the inscrutable workings of our official architecture one of these gentlemen came to be appointed a few years ago the supervising architect of the Treasury. It is a measure of the extent and intelligence of the national interest in the art that this functionary, with little more than the official status of a clerk, and with no guarantee that he has any professional status whatever, has little less than the ædiliary powers of an Augustus. To have found a city of brick and to have left a city of marble is a boast that more than one supervising architect could have paraphrased in declaring that he found the government architecture Renaissance and he left it Gothic, or that he found it Gothic and he left it nondescript, while each successive incumbent could have declared that he found it and left it without architectural traditions and without architectural restraints. The ambition of the architect immediately in question was not sectarian so much as sectional. To him it seemed that a bureau had too many traditions which to other students seemed to have none at all. Not personally addicted to swearing to the words of any master, he considered that the influence of authority in his office was much too strong. He was himself from the remote West, and in an interview setting forth his hopes and purposes, shortly after he came into the office from which he was shortly to go out, he explained that "Eastern" conventionalities had had altogether too much sway in the previous conduct of the office, and that he meant to embody "Western ideas" in the public buildings. In the brief interval before his retirement he designed many monuments, from which one should be able to derive some notion of Western architectural ideas, and one of these is the government building at Minneapolis. This edifice is mainly remarkable for the multitude of ill-assorted and unadjusted features which it exhibits, especially for the "grand choice" of pediments which its fronts present—pediments triangular and curved, pediments closed and broken —and for the variety and multiplicity of the cupolas and lanterns and crestings by which the sky-line is tormented into violent agitation. The features themselves cannot be "Western," since they are by no means novel, the most recent of them dating back to Sir Christopher Wren, and it must be the combination or the remarkable profusion of "things" that constitutes the novelty and the Westernness which it was the mission of the author to introduce into our public architecture. The City Hall and Court-house in St. Paul is a large and conspicuous building, the more conspicuous for being isolated in the midst of an open square, and it is unfortunate in design, or the absence of it, the arrangement of its voids and solids being quite unstudied and casual, and the aggregation quite failing to constitute a whole. There are by no means so many features in it as in the government building at Minneapolis, nor are they classic; but the architect has introduced more "things" than he was able to handle, and they are equally irrelevant to the pile and to each other, especially the tower that was intended to be the culminating feature of the composition, but which fails to fulfil its purpose from any point of view, crowning as it does a recessed angle of the front. This also is a congeries of unrelated and unadjusted parts, and in the light of the illustrations of his meaning furnished by our official spokesman, this also may be admitted to be characteristically W——n. The same admission may reluctantly be made concerning the similar Chamber of Commerce, which consists architecturally of two very busy and bustling fronts, compiled of "features" that do not make up a physiognomy, and which stands upon a massive sash frame of plate-glass. As a matter of fact, these things have their counterparts in the East, only there they are not referred to the geography, but to the illiteracy or insensibility of the designer, and this classification seems simpler, and, upon the whole, more satisfactory.

Minneapolis has a compensation for its newness in the fact that when its public buildings came to be projected, the fashion of such edifices as these had passed away. If the work of Mr. Richardson has been much misunderstood, as I tried to point out in speaking of the domestic architecture of Chicago, if its accidents have been mistaken by admiring disciples for its essence, even if its essential and admirable qualities do not always suffice to make it available as a model, it is necessary only to consider such buildings as have just been mentioned to perceive how beneficial, upon the whole, his influence has been, for it has at least sufficed to make such buildings impossible—impossible, at least, to be done by architects who have any pretensions to be "in the movement"—and it is hard to conceive that they can be succeeded by anything so bad. The City Hall of Minneapolis, for instance, was projected but a few years later than its government building, but in the interval Richardson's influence had been at work. That influence is betrayed both in the accepted design now in course of executi n and in the other competitive designs, and it has resulted in a specific resemblance to the public building at Pittsburg which its author professed his hope to make "a dignified pile of rocks." The variations which the authors of the Minneapolis City Hall have introduced in the scheme they have reproduced in its general massing and in its most conspicuous features are not all improvements. By the introduction of grouped openings into its solid shaft the tower of Pittsburg is shorn of much of its power; nor can the substitution be commended in its upper stage of a modification of the motive employed by Richardson in Trinity, Boston, and derived by him from Salamanca, for the simpler treatment used in the prototype of this building as the culminating feature of a stark and lofty tower. The far greater elaboration of the corner pavilions of the principal fronts, also, though in part justified by the greater tractability of the material here employed, tends rather to confusion than to enrichment. On the other hand, the more subdued treatment of the curtain wall between the tower and the pavilions gives greater value and detachment to both, and is thus an advance upon the prototype; and the central gable of the subordinate front is distinctly more successful than the corresponding feature of Pittsburg, the archway, withdrawn between two protecting towers, of which the suggestion comes from mediæval military architecture. Observe, however, that

the derivation of the general scheme of the building and of its chief features from an earlier work is by no means an impeachment of the architect's originality, provided the precedent he chooses be really applicable to his problem, and provided he analyze it instead of reproducing it without analysis. In what else does progress consist than in availing one's self of the labor of one's predecessors? If the Grecian builders had felt the pressure of the modern demand for novelty, and had endeavored to comply with it by making dispositions radically new, instead of refining upon the details of an accepted type, or if the mediæval builders had done the same thing, it is manifest that the typical temple or the typical cathedral would never have come to be built, that we should have had no Parthenon and no Cologne. The requirements of the Minneapolis building, a court-house and town-hall, are nearly enough alike to those of the county building at Pittsburg to make it credible that the general scheme of the earlier work may by force of merit have imposed itself upon the architect of the later. The general difference of treatment is the greater richness and elaboration of the newer structure, and this is a legitimate consequence of the substitution of freestone for granite, while the differences of detail and the introduction at Minneapolis of features that have no counterpart at Pittsburg suffice to vindicate the designer from the reproach of having followed his model thoughtlessly or with servility. So far as can be judged from the drawings, the municipal building of Minneapolis, when it comes to be finished, will be a monument of which the Minneapolitans will have a right to be proud for better reasons than mere magnitude and costliness.

Another work, this time completely executed, by the designers of the City Hall, the public library of Minneapolis, betrays also the influence of Richardson. The motive of the principal front, an arcade bounded by round towers and surmounted by a story of blank wall, was pretty evidently suggested by his unexecuted design for a similar building at Buffalo. The precedent here is perhaps not so directly in point, seeing that the effectiveness of an arcade increases with its length, and in a much greater ratio, and that the arcade here is not only much shorter than

in the projected building,
but is still further short-
ened to the eye by being
heightened and carried
through two stories. The
towers, too, would have
been more effective had it
been practicable to give
greater solidity to their
lower stages. Yet the
building is distinctly successful, and its most happy feature, the gabled centre that includes the en-
trance, is one which illustrates the inventiveness of
the designers, as well as
their power of judicious selection and modification.

As was remarked in the
paper on Chicago, the ar-
chitectural activity of the
West is not largely ecclesiastical, and the churches
are for the most part as
near to traditional models
as their designers have the
knowledge to bring them.
In the Eastern States a
great many interesting essays have been made tow-
ards solving the modern
problem of a church in
which the pulpit and not
the altar is the central

ENTRANCE TO PUBLIC LIBRARY, MINNEAPOLIS.
Long and Kees, Architects.

point of design, while yet retaining an
ecclesiastical expression. There is an edifice in St. Paul called "The People's
Church," in which the designer seems
purposely to have avoided an ecclesiastical expression, and to have undertaken to
typify in brick and stone the wild, free theology of the West. He has so far succeeded
that nobody could possibly take the result
of his labors for a church in the usual acceptation of the term, but this negative
attainment does not yet constitute a positive architectural success. It may be that
Western ideas in theology are thus far
somewhat too sketchy to form a basis for
the establishment of an architectural type,
since mere negation is insusceptible of
architectural expression. The People's
Church does not lack, however, many of
the qualities that should belong to every
building as a building, apart from its
destination. In spite of such unhappy
freaks as that by which the stone basement merges into the brick superstructure

with no architectural mark of the transition, and cuts the openings quite at random, or as that by which the brick wall,
for a considerable but indefinite extent, is
quite promiscuously aspersed with irregular bits of stone, it shows a considerable
skill in the placing and detailing of features, and the disposition of the openings
gives the principal front a grateful sense
of stability and repose. The ample entrances designate it as a place of popular
assembly, and possibly its religious purpose may be taken to be confessed, though
somewhat shamefacedly, in the wheel-
window at the centre of one front, and
the tall traceried opening at the centre of
the other, which are the only relics of ecclesiastical architecture that are suffered
to appear. It is evident that it is a "People's" something, and possibly this is as
near to a specification of its purpose as the
neo-theologians have attained. In this
case, as it is notoriously difficult for a
man to give expression to an idea of which

position and in the design of the features, especially in the open fenestration of the transept gable, and its strong contrast with the solider flanks of wall pierced only by the smaller openings that indicate the gallery staircases, the slope of which is also expressed in the masonry of the wall itself; and the low polygonal tower effectually unites and dominates the two fronts. The innovation in the treatment of detail, by which what is commonly the "wrought work" of a building in facile sandstone is left rough-faced, is a caprice that seems also to proceed from the pursuit of novelty, and that gains nothing in vigor for what it loses in refinement. A rough-faced moulding seems to be a contradiction in terms, yet here not only are the mouldings rough-faced, but also the columns and colonnettes, and the corbelled pinnacles that detach the tower and the gables, and it is only in the copings of these that the asperities of the sandstone are mitigated. Slovenliness is

THE PEOPLE'S CHURCH, ST. PAUL.
J. W. Stevens, Architect.

he is not possessed, the architectural ambiguity is assuredly not to be imputed to the architect:

A Unitarian church in Minneapolis is also an unconventional specimen of church architecture, though it could not be taken for anything but a church, and it is undeniably a vigorous performance, consisting of massive, well-divided, and "well-punched" walls in a monochrome of dark red sandstone. The novelty and the unconventionality, however, seem, both in composition and in detail, to have been sought rather than to have proceeded from the conditions of the problem, and the effect is so far marred by the loss of the naturalness and straightforwardness that justify a departure from convention. For example, even in a galleried church the division into two stories can scarcely be considered the primary fact of the building, though this division is the primary fact of this design, and is emphasized by the torus that is the most conspicuous moulding. For all that, there is much felicity in the general dis-

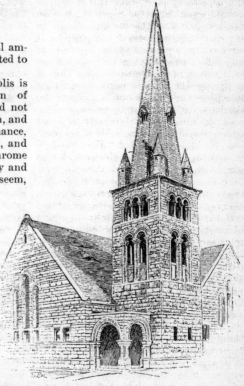

PRESBYTERIAN CHURCH, ST. PAUL.—Gilbert and Taylor, Architects.

not vigor, and in the coarsening of this detail the designer, in spite of having produced a vigorous and interesting work, exposes himself to the critical amenity bestowed by Dryden upon Elkanah Settle, that "his style is boisterous and roughhewn."

A more conventional and a quite unmistakable example of church building is a Presbyterian church in St. Paul, which follows the established ecclesiastical type, albeit with a recognition of the modern demand that a church shall be a good place in

PUBLIC LIBRARY, MINNEAPOLIS.—Long and Kees, Architects.

which to preach and to be preached to —a demand which here, as often elsewhere, is met by shortening the arms of the cruciform plan until the church is virtually limited to the crossing. It is no disparagement to the present design to say that in its general composition it seems to have been suggested by,—and at any rate it suggests,—an early and interesting work of Mr. Richardson's, a church in Springfield, Massachusetts, upon which it improves at some points, notably in the emphatic exposition of the masonic structure. At other points the variation is not so successful. The tower at Springfield with its attached turret, the entrance arch at its base, and the broach-spire with pinnacle detached over the squinches, is a very vigorous piece of design. In the corresponding feature at St. Paul the relation between the two superposed open stages is not rhythmic or felicitous, though each in itself is well modelled, and the transition from the tower to the shingled spire, marked by shingled pinnacles without a parapet, is distinctly unfortunate. For all that, the church is a studied and scholarly performance.

In the material and materializing development of the West it is not surprising that the chief object of local pride should not be the local church, but the local hotel. "Of course a large hotel" is now, as in Trollope's time, a necessary ingredient of a local "boom." In respect of architecture the large hotel of Minneapolis has a decided advantage over the

large hotel of St. Paul. For the caravansary of the older town is an example of the kind of secular Victorian Gothic that was stimulated by the erection of Sir Gilbert Scott's Midland Hotel in London, than which a less eligible model could scarcely be put before an untrained designer, since there is little in it to redeem an uneasy and uninteresting design except carefully studied and carefully adjusted detail. This careful study and adjustment being omitted, as they are in the Hotel Ryan, and a multiplicity of features retained and still further confused by a random introduction of color, the result is a bewildering and saltatory edifice which has nothing of interest except the banded piers of the basement. The West House in Minneapolis is a much more considerable structure. It has a general composition, both vertically and laterally, consisting in the former case of three divisions, of which the central is rather the most important, and in the latter of an emphasis of the centre and the ends in each front and of a subordination of the intervening wall. Here also there is a multiplicity of features, but they are not so numerous or distributed so much at random as to prevent us from seeing the countenance,—for undeniably the building has a physiognomy, and that is in itself an attainment. In artistic quality the features are very various, and the one trait they seem to have in common is a disregard for academic correctness or for purity of style. This is

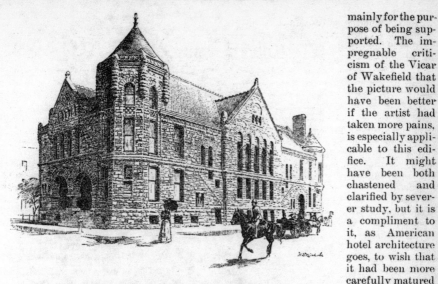

UNITARIAN CHURCH, MINNEAPOLIS.—L. S. Buffington, Architect.

mainly for the purpose of being supported. The impregnable criticism of the Vicar of Wakefield that the picture would have been better if the artist had taken more pains, is especially applicable to this edifice. It might have been both chastened and clarified by severer study, but it is a compliment to it, as American hotel architecture goes, to wish that it had been more carefully matured by its designer before being irretrievably executed. The interior presents several interesting points of design as well as of arrangement, but perhaps it owes its chief attractiveness to the rich and quiet

conspicuous in the main entrance, which is perhaps the most effective and successful of them, being a massive and powerful *porte cochère*, in which, however, an unmistakably Gothic dwarf column adjoins a panelled pilaster, which as unmistakably owes its origin to the Renaissance, and a like freedom of eclecticism may be observed throughout the building. In its degree this freedom may be Western, though a European architect would be apt to dismiss it indiscriminately as American, whereas an American architect would be more apt to ask himself, with respect to any particular manifestation of it, whether it was really, and not only conventionally, a solecism. In this place the conjunction does not strike one as incongruous, but there are other features in which the incongruity is real, such as the repeated projections of long and ugly corbels to support things that are pretty evidently there

WEST HOTEL, MINNEAPOLIS.—L. S. Buffington, Architect.

decoration of those of its rooms that have been intrusted to Mr. Bradstreet, who for many years has been acting as an evangelist of good taste to the two cities, and who for at least the earlier of those years must have felt that he was an evangelist *in partibus.* The interior design and decoration of the Opera - house at Minneapolis are a yet more important illustration of his skill; but interiors are beyond the scope of this paper. For public works other than public buildings the two cities are not as yet very notable. The site of St. Paul makes

LUMBER EXCHANGE, MINNEAPOLIS.—Long and Kees, Architects.

a bridge across the river at this point a very conspicuous object, and perhaps nowhere in the world would a noble and monumental bridge be more effective. The existing bridges, however, are works of the barest utility, apparently designed by railroad engineers with no thought of anything beyond efficiency and economy, and they are annoying interruptions to the panorama unrolled to the spectators from the hill-side in the shining reach of the great river. Minneapolis has been more fortunate in this respect, although the river by no means plays so important a part in its landscape. The suspension-bridge of Trollope's time has, of course, long since disappeared, having been replaced by another, built in 1876 from the designs of Mr. Griffith, which was a highly picturesque object, and was perhaps the most satisfactory solution yet attained, though by no means a completely satisfactory solution, of the artistic problem involved in the design of a suspension-bridge—a problem which to most designers of such bridges does not appear to be involved in it at all. It is unfortunate that, although the Minneapolitans appre-

ciated this structure as one of their chief municipal ornaments, they should have sacrificed it, whereas there could scarcely have been any insuperable difficulty in locating the site of the new bridge where the new exigencies demanded so that the old might be preserved. In another respect Minneapolis has derived a great advantage from the necessity of taking long views that is imposed upon her people by the conditions of their lives. This is the reservation, at the instigation of a few provident and public-spirited citizens, of the three lakes that lie in the segment of a circle a few miles inland from the existing city, and of the strip of land connecting them. Even now, with little improvement beyond road-making, the circuit of the future parks is a delightful drive, and when Minneapolis shall have expanded until they constitute a bounding boulevard, the value of them as a municipal possession will be quite incalculable.

The aspect of the commercial quarters of the two cities has more points of difference than of resemblance. The differences proceed mainly from the fact already noted that the commercial quarter of St. Paul is cramped as well as limited by the topography, and that it is all coming to be occupied by a serried mass of lofty buildings, whereas the lofty buildings of Minneapolis are still detached objects erected in anticipation of the pressure for room that has not yet begun to be felt. It is an odd illustration of the local rivalry that although the cities are so near together, the architects are confined to their respective fields, and it is very unusual, if not unexampled, that an ar-

ENTRANCE TO BANK OF COMMERCE, MINNEAPOLIS.
Harry W. Jones, Architect.

chitect of either is employed in the other. Such an employment would very likely be resented as incivism. Eastern architects are admitted on occasion as out of the competition, but in the main each city is built according to the plans of the local designers. The individual characteristics of the busiest and most successful architects are thus impressed upon the general appearance of the towns, and go to widen the difference due to natural

causes. The best examples of commercial architecture in Minneapolis, such as the Bank of Commerce, and the Lumber Exchange before its extension and heightening, have the same straightforward and severely business-like character as the buildings designed by Mr. Root in Chicago, and indeed they seem to owe not a little to suggestions derived from him. The entrance to the Lumber Exchange pretty distinctly recalls some of his entrances, and the manner in which the centre of the longer front is signalized also indicates an admiring study of Mr. Root's work. Here this is managed by projecting shallow oriels, carried through the five central stories of the building on each side of the ample opening in each story directly over the entrance, and by flanking this central bay in the upper division with narrow and solid turrets, corbelled and pinnacled. The scheme is not so effectively wrought out as it deserves to be, and as it might be. The central feature is not developed into predominance, and the main divisions of the building are no more emphasized in treatment than the divisions between the intermediate stories. The observer may recur to the Vicar of Wakefield to express his regret that the promise of so promising a scheme should not have been fulfilled, although, in spite of its shortcomings, the result is a very respectable "business block." These remarks apply to the original building, and not to the building as it has since been reconstructed by the addition of two stories, which throw out the relations of its parts, and make it difficult to decipher the original scheme. The Bank of Commerce is as frankly utilitarian as the Lumber Exchange, the designer having relaxed the restraint imposed upon him by the prosaic and pedestrian character of his problem only in the design of the scholarly and rather ornate entrances. For the rest, the architecture is but the expression of the structure, which is expressed clearly and with vigor. The longer front shows the odd notion of emphasizing the centre by withdrawing it, a procedure apparently irrational, which has, however, the compensation of giving value and detachment to the entrance at its base. The problem was much more promising than that of the Lumber Exchange, seeing that here, with an ample area, there are but six stories against ten, and it is out of all comparison better solved. The four central stories are grouped by piers continued through them and connected by round arches above the fifth, while the first and sixth are sharply separated in treatment, the former as an unmistakable basement, with a plain segment-headed opening in each bay, and the latter as an unmistakable attic, with a triplet of lintelled and shafted openings aligned over each of the round arches. The fronts are, moreover, distinguished, without in the least compromising the utilitarian purpose of the structure, by the use of the architectural devices the lack of which one deplores in the other building, inso-much that the difference be-tween the two is the difference between a building merely blocked out and a finished building, and suggests again that the Lumber Exchange must have been designed under pressure. The building of the *Globe* newspaper in Minneapolis is a vigorous composition in Richardsonian Romanesque, excessively broken and diversified, doubtless, for its extent, but with interesting pieces of detail, and with a picturesque angle tower that comes in very happily from several points of view of the business quarter. The emphatic framing of this tower between two plain piers is a noteworthy point of design, and so is the use of the device that emphasizes the angles throughout their whole extent, while still keeping the vertical lines in subordination to the horizontal.

Among the business blocks of St. Paul the building of the *Pioneer Press* newspaper is eminent for the strictness with

CORNER OF BANK OF COMMERCE, MINNEAPOLIS.

which the design conforms itself to the utilitarian conditions of the structure, and the impressiveness of the result attained, not in spite of those apparently forbidding conditions, but by means of them. Here also Mr. Root's buildings, to which this praise belongs in so high a degree, have evidently enough inculcated their lesson upon the designer of the present structure. An uncompromising parallel-opiped of brown brick rears itself to the height of twelve stories, with no break at all in its outline, and with no architecture that is not evolved directly from the requirements of the building. One does not seem to be praising a man very highly to praise him for talking prose when he has a prosaic subject. A mere incompetency to poetry would apparently suffice to earn this moderate eulogy. Yet, in fact, nothing is much rarer in our architecture than the power to deny one's

THE GLOBE BUILDING, MINNEAPOLIS.
E. Townsend Mix, Architect.

self irrelevant beauties. The *Pioneer Press* building is a basement of three stories, the first story of the brick-work counting in with the two-story substructure of masonry, carrying a superstructure of seven, crowned with an attic of two. This latter feature proceeds, doubtless, from the special requirement of a newspaper office superposed upon a business block, and it may be inferred that to this requirement is due the greater enrichment of the lower of the two attic stories—contrary to the usual arrangement, and testifying the architect's belief, mistaken or not, that the editorial function is of more dignity and worthier of celebration than the typographical. At any rate, the unusual disposition is architecturally fortunate, since it provides, in the absolutely plain openings of what is presumably the composing-room, a grateful interval between the comparative richness of the arcades beneath and of the cornice above. In the main front, the ample entrance at the centre supplies a visible motive for the vertical as well as for the subordinate lateral division. It is developed through the three stories of the basement, and it is recognized in a prolongation upward of its flanking piers through the central division, which is completed by round arches, the spandrels of which are decorated, and through the attic, so as to effect a triple division for the front. The unostentatious devices are highly effective by which the monotony that would result from an identical treatment of the seven central stories is relieved, while the impression made by the magnitude of such a mass is retained. The terminal piers are left entirely unbroken throughout all their extent, except for a continuous string course above the eighth story, which might better have been omitted, since it cuts the intermediate piers very awkwardly, and detracts from the value of the heavier string course only one story higher, that has an evident reason of being as the springing course of the arcade, while the intermediate piers are crossed by string courses above the fifth and the ninth stories, so as to give to the central and dominant feature of the main

ENTRANCE TO " PIONEER PRESS " BUILDING, ST. PAUL.
S. S. Beman, Architect.

composition a triple division of its own into a beginning, a middle, and an end.

The building is very successful, and the more successful because the designer has shirked nothing and blinked nothing, but out of this nettle, commercial demands, has plucked this flower, commercial architecture. The same praise of an entire relevancy to its purpose belongs to the Bank of Minnesota, a well-proportioned and well-divided piece of masonry, in spite of more effort at variety in outline, and of somewhat more of fantasy in detail. The former is manifested in the treatment of the roof, in which the gables of the upper story are relieved against a low mansard; and the latter in the design of these gables and of the rich and effective entrance. The problem, as one of composition, is very much simplified here, since the building is of but six stories, and the dilemma of monotony or miscellany which so awfully confronts the designers of ten and twelve story buildings does not present itself. The lower two stories, though quite differently detailed, are here grouped into an architectural basement, the grouping being emphasized in the main front by the extension of the entrance through both. The superstructure is of three stories, quite identical and very plain in treatment, and above is the lighter and more open fenestration of the gabled attic.

Of far more extent and pretension than this, being indeed perhaps the costliest and most "important" of all the business blocks of St. Paul, is the building of the New York Life-Insurance Company. In saying that the total impression of this edifice is one of picturesque quaintness, one seems to deny its typicalness, if not its appropriateness as a housing and an expression of the local genius, for assuredly there is nothing quaint about the Western business man or his procedures during business hours, however quaint and

even picturesque one may find him when relaxing into anecdote in his hours of ease. The building owes its quaintness in great part to the division of its superstructure into two unequal masses flanking a narrow court, at the base of which is the main entrance. The general arrangement is not uncommon in the business blocks of New York. The unequal division into masses of which one is just twice as wide as the other looks capricious in the present detached condition of the building, though when another lofty building abuts upon it the inequality will be seen to be a sensible precaution to secure the effective lighting of the narrower mass, the light for the wider being secured by a street upon one side and by the court upon the other. Even so, this will not be so intuitively beheld as the fact of the inequality itself, and as the differences of treatment to which it gives rise and by which it is emphasized; for the quaintness resulting from the asymmetry is so far from being ungrateful to the designer that he has seized upon it with avidity, and developed it by all the means in his power. Quaintness is the word that everybody uses spontaneously to express the character of the Dutch and Flemish Renaissance, and the treatment of these unequal gables is obviously derived from Flemish examples. The origin of their crow steps and ailerons is unmistakable, and the treatment of the grouped and somewhat huddled openings, and their rounded pediments and bull's-eyes, rich-

CORNER OF "PIONEER PRESS" BUILDING.

BANK OF MINNESOTA, ST. PAUL.—Wilcox and Johnson, Architects.

with the bulbous pictur-esqueness of the gables. The care with which its detail is studied is evident, and also the elegance of the detail in its kind and in its place, but it does not seem to be in its place anywhere out-of-doors, and still less as applied to the entrance of a business block to which it is merely applied, and from which it is not developed. Its extreme delicacy, indeed, almost gives the impression that it is meant to be a still small voice of protest on the part of an "Eastern" architect against a "boisterous and roughhewn" Westernness. A still smaller voice of scholarly protest seems to be emitted by the design of the neighboring Endicott arcade, the voice of one crying, very softly, in the wilderness. So ostentatiously discreet is the detail of this building, indeed, so minute the scale of it, and so studious the avoidance of anything like stress, and the effort for understatement, that the very quietness of its remonstrance gives it the effect of vociferation.

"He who, in quest of quiet, 'Silence!' hoots,
Is apt to make the hubbub he imputes."

It seems to be a distinct expostulation, for example, with the architect of the Guaranty Loan building in Minneapolis, which has many striking details, not without ingenuity, and certainly not without "enterprise," but as certainly without the refinement that comes of a studied and affectionate elaboration, insomuch that this also may be admitted to be W——n, and to invite the full force of Dryden's criticism. The building in the exterior of which this mild remonstrance is made has an interior feature that is noteworthy for other qualities than the avoidance of indiscretion and over-statement, the "arcade," so called, from which it takes its name, a broad cor-ridor, sumptuous in material and treat-

ly and heavily framed in terra-cotta, is equally characteristic, to the point of being *baroque*. This character and the picturesqueness that results from it, although confined to the gables, give the building its prevailing expression. A massive basement of two stories in masonry carries the five stories of brick-work heavily quoined in stone that constitute the body of the building, and this is itself subdivided by slight but sufficient differences, the lower story being altogether of masonry and the upper arcaded. An intermediate story, emphatically marked off above and below, separates this body from the two-story roof, the gables of which we have been considering. The main entrance, which gives access to a stately and sumptuous corridor, seems itself extraneous to the building, having little congruity either with the straightforward and structural treatment of the main building, or ment to the "palatial" point, one's admiration for which is not destroyed, though it is abated, by a consideration of its irrelevancy to a business block. The building of the New York Life in Minneapolis, by the same architects as the building of the same corporation in St. Paul, is more readily recognizable by a New-Yorker as their work. It

TOP OF NEW YORK LIFE-INSURANCE BUILDING, ST. PAUL.
Babb, Cook, and Willard, Architects.

is a much more commonplace and a much more utilitarian composition—a basement of four stories, of which two are in masonry, carrying a central division also of four and an attic of two, the superstructure being of brick-work. The two principal divisions are too nearly equal, nor does the change of material effected by building the upper two stories of the basement in brick-work achieve the rhythmic relation for the attainment of which it was doubtless introduced, but the structure is nevertheless a more satisfactory example of commercial architecture than the St. Paul building. Its entrance, of four fluted and banded columns of a very free Roman Doric, with the platform on consoles above, has strength and dignity, and is a feature that can evidently be freely exposed to the weather, and that is not incongruous as the portal of a great commercial building. A very noteworthy feature of the interior is the double spiral staircase in metal, that has apparently been inspired by the famous rood screen of St. Étienne du Mont in Paris, and that is a very taking and successful design, in which the treatment of the material is ingenious and characteristic.

We have seen that the huddled condition of the business quarter of St. Paul, practically a disadvantage in comparison

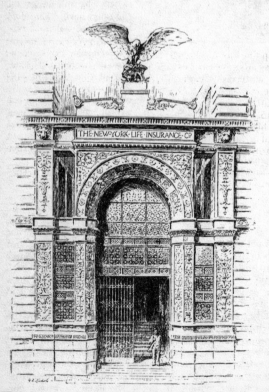

ENTRANCE TO NEW YORK LIFE BUILDING, ST. PAUL.

NEW YORK LIFE BUILDING, MINNEAPOLIS.
Babb, Cook, and Willard, Architects.

dences" have come to crown the hill-side, and really noble residences many of them are. There are perhaps as skilfully designed houses in the younger city, and certainly there are houses as costly; but there is nothing to be compared with the massing of the handsome houses of St. Paul upon the ridge above the river. Indeed, there are very few streets in the United States that give in as high a degree as Summit Avenue the sense of an expenditure liberal without ostentation, directed by skill, and restrained by taste. What mainly strikes a pilgrim from the East is not so much the merit of the best of these houses as the fact that there are no bad ones; none, at least, so bad as to disturb the general impression of richness and refinement, and none that make the crude display of "new money" that is to be seen in the fashionable quarters of cities even richer and far older. The houses rise, to borrow one of Ruskin's eloquent phrases, "in fair fulfilment of domestic service and modesty of home seclu-

with the spaciousness of Minneapolis, has become architecturally a positive advantage. The natural advantages with respect to the quarters of residence seem to be strongly on the side of St. Paul. The river-front at Minneapolis is not available for house-building, nor is there any other topographical indication of a fashionable quarter, except what is furnished by the slight undulations of the plateau. The more pretentious houses are for the most part scattered, and, of course, much more isolated than the towering commercial buildings. On the other hand, the fashionable quarter of St. Paul is distinctly marked out by nature. It could not have been established anywhere but at the edge of the bluff overhanging the town and commanding the Mississippi. Surely this height must have been one of those eminences that struck the imagination of Trollope when they were yet unoccupied. And now the "noble resi-

DWELLING IN MINNEAPOLIS.
Harry W. Jones, Architect.

VESTIBULE OF NEW YORK LIFE BUILDING, MINNEAPOLIS.

sion." The air of completeness, of finish, of "keeping," so rare in American towns, is here as marked as at Newport. In the architecture there is a wide variety, which does not, however, suffice to destroy the homogeneousness of the total effect. Suggestions from the Romanesque perhaps prevail, and testify anew to the influence of Richardson, though there are suggestions from the Renaissance and from pointed architecture that show scholarship as well as invention. The cleverness and ingenuity of a *porte cochère* of two pointed arches are not diminished by the likelihood that it was suggested by a canopied tomb in a cathedral. But, indeed, from whatever source the inspiration of the architects may have come, it is everywhere plain that they have had no intention of presenting "examples" of historical architecture, and highly unlikely that they would be disturbed by the detection in their work of solecisms that were such merely from the academic point of view. It is scarcely worth while to go into specific criticism of their domestic work. To illustrate it is to show that the designers of the best of it are quite abreast of the architects of the older parts of the country, and that they are able to command an equal skill of craftsmanship in the execution of their designs.

This does not answer our question whether there is any such thing as Western architecture, or whether these papers should not rather have been entitled, "Glimpses of Architecture in the West." The interest in this art throughout the West is at least as general as the interest in it throughout the East, and it is attested in the twin cities by the existence of a flourishing and enterprising periodical, the *Northwestern Architect*, to which I am glad to confess my obligations. It is natural that this interest, when joined to an intense local patriotism, should lead to a magnifying of the Westernness of such structures as are the subjects of local pride. It is common enough to hear the same local patriot who declaims to you in praise

DWELLING IN ST. PAUL.
Mould and McNichol, Architects.

of Western architecture explain also that the specimens of it which he commends to your admiration are the work of architects of "Eastern" birth or training. Now, if not in Dickens's time, the "man of Boston raisin'" is recognized in the West to have his uses. The question whether there is any American architecture is not yet so triumphantly answered that it is other than provincial to lay much stress on lo-cal differences. The general impression that the Eastern observer derives from Western architecture is the same that American architecture in general makes upon the European observer, and that is that it is a very much emancipated archi-tecture. Our architects are assuredly less trammelled by tradition than those of any older countries, and the architects of the West are even less trammelled than those of the East. Their character-istic buildings show this char-acteristic equal-ly, whether they be good or bad. The tow-ering commer-cial structures that are forced upon them by new conditions and facilities are very seldom spe-cimens of any historical style. and the best and the worst of them, the most and the least studied, are apt to be equally hard to classify. To be emancipated is not a merit,

PORTE COCHÈRE, ST. PAUL.—Wilcox and Johnson, Architects.

and to judge whether or not it is an advantage, one needs to examine the performances in which the emancipation is exhibited. "That a good man be 'free,' as we call it," says Carlyle, in one of his most emphatic jeremiads—"be permitted to unfold himself in works of goodness and nobleness—is surely a blessing to him, immense and indispensable; to him and to those about him. But that a bad man be 'free'—permitted to unfold himself in *his* particular way—is, contrariwise, the

the ecclesiologists operated, during the period of modern Gothic at least, with equal force, though without any official sanction. To be "ungrammatical," not to adopt a particular phase of historical architecture, and not to confine one's self to it in a design, was there the unforgivable offence, even though the incongruities that resulted from transcending it were imperceptible to an artist and obvious only to an archæologist. A designer thoroughly trained under either of these systems, and

PORCH IN ST. PAUL.—Mould and McNichol, Architects.

fatalest curse you could inflict upon him; curse, and nothing else, to him and all his neighbors."

There is here not a question of morals, but of knowledge and competency. The restraints in architecture of a recognized school, of a prevailing style, are useful and salutary in proportion to the absence of restraint that the architect is capable of imposing upon himself. The secular tradition of French architecture, imposed by public authority and inculcated by official academies, is felt as a trammel by many architects, who, nevertheless, have every reason to feel grateful for the power of design which this same official curriculum has trained and developed. In England the fear of the archæologists and of

then transferred to this country as a practitioner, must feel, as many such a practitioner has in fact felt, that he was suddenly unshackled, and that his emancipation was an unmixed advantage to him; but it is none the less true that his power to use his liberty wisely came from the discipline that was now relaxed. The academic prolusions of the Beaux Arts, or the exercises of a draughtsman, have served their purpose in qualifying him for independent design. The advocates of the curriculum of the English public schools maintain that, obsolete as it seems, even the practice of making Latin verses has its great benefits, in imparting to the pupil the command of literary form and of beauty of diction. There are many

FROM A DWELLING IN ST. PAUL.
Gilbert and Taylor, Architects.

cy. Evidently the progress of American architecture will not be promoted by the labors of designers, whether they be "Western" or "Eastern," who have merely "lived in the alms basket" of architectural forms, and whose notion of architecture consists in multiplying "features," as who should think to enhance the expressiveness of the human countenance by adorning it with two noses.

One cannot neologize with any promise of success unless he knows what is already in the dictionary, and a professional equipment that puts its owner really in posses-

examples to sustain this contention, as well as the analogous contention that a faithful study and reproduction of antique or of mediæval architecture are highly useful, if not altogether indispensable, to cultivate an architect's power of design. Only it may be pointed out that the use of these studies is to enable the student to express himself with more power and grace in the vernacular, and that one no longer reverts to Latin verse when he has really something to say. The monuments that are accepted as models by the modern world are themselves the results of the labors of successive generations. It was by a secular process that the same structural elements employed at Thebes and Karnac were developed to the perfection of the Parthenon. In proportion to the newness of their problems it is to be expected that the efforts of our architects will be crude; but there is a vast difference between the crudity of a serious and matured attempt to do a new thing and the crudity of mere ignorance and self-sufficien-

DWELLINGS IN ST. PAUL.
Wilcox and Johnson, Architects.

PORCH IN ST. PAUL.—A. H. Stem, Architect.

sion of the best that has been done in the world is indispensable to successful eclecticism in architecture. On the other hand, it is equally true that no progress can result from the labors of architects whose training has made them so fastidious that they are more revolted by the crudity of the forms that result from the attempt to express a new meaning than by the failure to make the attempt, and so conceal what they are really doing behind a mask of historical architecture, of which the elegance is quite irrelevant. This latter fault is that of modern architecture in general. The history of that architecture indicates that it is a fault even more unpromising of progress than the crudities of an emancipated architecture, in which the discipline of the designer fails to supply the place of the artificial check of a historical style. It is more feasible to

tame exuberances than to create a soul under the ribs of death. The emancipation of American architecture is thus ultimately more hopeful than if it were put under academic bonds to keep the peace. It may freely be admitted that many of its manifestations are not for the present joyous, but grievous, and that to throw upon the individual designer the responsibility withheld from a designer with whom fidelity to style is the first duty is a process that fails when his work, as has been wittily said, "shows no more self-restraint than a bunch of fire-crackers." But these papers have also borne witness that there are among the emancipated practitioners of architecture in the West men who have shown that they can use their liberty wisely, and whose work can be hailed as among the hopeful beginnings of a national architecture.

CHICAGO ARCHITECTURE

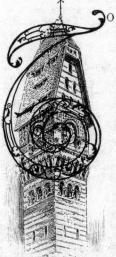

CLOCK TOWER; DEARBORN
STATION.
C. L. W. Eidlitz, Architect.

O begin with a para-dox, the feature of Chicago is its fea-turelessness. There is scarcely any cap-ital, ancient or modern, to which the site supplies so little of a visible reason of being. The prairie and the lake meet at a level, a liquid plain and a plain of mud that cannot prop-erly be called solid, with nothing but the change of ma-terial to break the expanse. Indeed, when there is a breeze, the sur-face of Lake Mich-igan would be dis-tinctly more diversified than that of the adjoining land, but for the handiwork of man. In point of fact, Chicago is, of course, explained by the confluence here of the two branches of the Chicago River. These have determined the site, the plan, and the building of the town, but one can scarcely describe as natural features the two sinuous ditches that drain the prairie into the lake, apparently in defiance of the law that water runs, and even oozes, down hill. Streams, however narrow and sluggish they may be, so they be them-selves available for traffic, operate an ob-struction to traffic by land; and it is the fact that for some distance from the junc-tion the south fork of the river flows parallel with the shore of the lake and within a half-mile of it, which establishes in this enclosure the commercial centre of Chicago. Even the slight obstacle in-terposed to traffic by the confluent streams, bridged and tunnelled as they are, has sufficed greatly to raise the cost of land within this area in comparison with that outside, and to compel here the erection of the towering structures that are the most characteristic and the most impres-sive monuments of the town.

In character and in impressiveness these

by no means disappoint the stranger's expectations, but in number and extent they do, rather. For what one expects of Chicago before anything else is modernness. In most things one's expectations are fully realized. It is the most contemporaneous of capitals, and in the appearance of its people and their talk in the streets and in the clubs and in the newspapers it fairly palpitates with "actuality." Nevertheless the general aspect of the business quarter is distinctly old-fashioned, and this even to the effete Oriental from New York or Boston. The elevator is nearly a quarter of a century old, and the first specimens of "elevator architecture," the Western Union and the *Tribune* buildings in New York, are very nearly coeval with the great fire in Chicago. One would have supposed that the rebuilders of Chicago would have seized upon this hint with avidity, and that its compressed commercial quarter would have made up in altitude what it lacked in area. In fact, not only are the great modern office buildings still exceptional in the most costly and most crowded district, but it is astonishing to hear that the oldest of them is scarcely more than seven years of age. "Men's deeds are after as they have been accustomed," and the first impulse of the burnt-out merchants of Chicago was not to seize the opportunity the clean sweep of the fire had given them to improve their warehouses and office buildings, but to provide themselves straightway with places in which they could find shelter and do business. The consequence was that the new buildings of the burnt district were planned and designed, as well as built, with the utmost possible speed, and the rebuilding was for the most part done by the same architects who had built the old Chicago, and who took even less thought the second time than they had taken the first, by reason of the greater pressure upon them. The American commercial Renaissance, commonly expressed in cast-iron, was in its full efflorescence just before the fire. The material was discredited by that calamity, but unhappily not the forms it had taken, and in Chicago we may see, what is scarcely to be seen anywhere else in the world, fronts in cast-iron, themselves imitated from lithic architecture, again imitated in masonry, with the modifications reproduced that had been made necessary by the use of the less trustworthy

material. This ignoble process is facilitated by the material at hand, a limestone of which slabs can be had in sizes that simulate exactly the castings from which the treatment of them is derived. After the exposure of a few months to the bituminous fumes, it is really impossible to tell one of these reproductions from the original, which very likely adjoins it. Masonry and metal alike appear to have come from a foundry rather than from a quarry, and to have been moulded according to the stock patterns of some architectural iron-works. The lifelessness and thoughtlessness of the iron-founders' work predominate in the streets devoted to the retail trade, and the picturesque tourist in Chicago is thus compelled to traverse many miles of street fronts quite as dismal and as monotonous as the commercial architecture of any other modern town.

Even if the old-fashioned architects who rebuilt Chicago had been anxious to reconstruct it according to the best and newest lights, it would have been quite out of their power to do so unaided. The erection of a twelve-story building anywhere involves an amount of mechanical consideration and a degree of engineering skill that are quite beyond the practitioners of the American metallic Renaissance. In Chicago the problem is more complicated than elsewhere, because these towering and massive structures ultimately rest upon a quagmire that is not less but more untrustworthy the deeper one digs. The distribution of the weight by carrying the foundations down to a trustworthy bottom, and increasing the area of the supporting piers as they descend, is not practicable here, nor, for the same reason, can it be done by piling. It is managed in the heaviest buildings by floating them upon a raft of concrete and railroad iron spread a few feet below the surface, so that there are no cellars in the business quarter, and the subterranean activities that are so striking in the elevator buildings of New York are quite unknown. If the architects of the old Chicago, to whom their former clients naturally applied to rear the phœnix of the new, had been seized with the ambition of building Babels, they would doubtless have made as wild work practically as they certainly would have made artistically in the confusion of architectural tongues that would have fallen upon them. It is in every point of view fortunate that the moderni-

zation of the town was reserved for the better-trained
designers of a younger generation.

It might be expected that
the architecture of Chicago
would be severely utilitarian in purpose if not in
design, and this is the case.
The city may be said to
consist of places of business and places of residence.
There are no churches, for
example, that fairly represent the skill of the architects. The best of them
are scarcely worthy of illustration or discussion
here, while the worst of
them might suitably illustrate the work projected
by a ribald wit on "The
Comic Aspects of Chris-
tianity." Among other
things it follows from this
deficiency that Chicago
lacks almost altogether, in
any general view that can be
had of it, the variety and ani-
mation that are imparted to the
sky line of a town seen from the
water or from an eminence by a
"tiara of proud towers," even when
these are not specially attractive in
outline or in detail, nor especially fortunate in their grouping. There is nothing, for example, in the aspect of Chicago from the lake, or from any attainable point of view, that is comparable to
the sky line of the Back Bay of Boston as
seen from the Cambridge bridge, or of
lower New York from either river. The
towering buildings are almost wholly
flat - roofed, and their stark, rectangular
outlines cannot take on picturesqueness,
even under the friendly drapery of the
smoke that overhangs the commercial
quarter during six days of the week.
The architect of the Dearborn Station
was very happily inspired when he relieved the prevailing monotony with the
quaint and striking clock tower that adjoins that structure.

The secular public buildings of Chicago are much more noteworthy than the
churches, but, upon the whole, they bear
scarcely so large a relation to the mass of
private buildings as one would expect from
the wealth and the public spirit of the

FROM THE CITY AND COUNTY BUILDING.
J. W. Egan and J. R. Mullett, Architects.

town, and, with one or two very noteworthy exceptions, recent as many of
them are, they were built too early. The
most discussed of them is the City and
County Building, and this has been discussed for reasons quite alien to its architecture, the halves of what was originally
a single design having been assigned to
different architects. The original design
has been followed in the main, and the
result is an edifice that certainly makes
a distinctive impression. A building,
completely detached, 340 feet by 280 in
area, and considerably over 100 feet high,
can scarcely fail to make an impression
by dint of mere magnitude, but there is
rather more than that in the City and
County Building. The parts are few and
large, but five stories appearing, the

THE ART INSTITUTE.

substitutions as that of an Indian's head for the antique mask in a frieze of conventionalized American foliage. He has attained what must be in such an attempt the gratifying success of converting his modern material to a result as dull and lifeless and uninteresting as his prototype. It does not, however, impair the grandiosity of the general effect. This is impaired not merely by the poverty of design already noted in the attic, but also by the niggardliness shown in dividing the polished granite columns of the porticoes into several drums, though monoliths are plainly indicated by their dimensions, and by the general scale of the masonry. The small economy is the more injurious because a noble regardlessness of expense is of the essence of the architecture, and an integral part of its effectiveness. The most monumental feature of the projected building has never been supplied —a huge arch in the centre of each of the shorter fronts giving access to the central court, and marking the division between the property of the city and that of the county. It is possible that the failure to finish this arch has proceeded from the political conflict that has left its scars upon the building elsewhere. There is an obvious practical difficulty in intrusting the two halves of an arch to rival architects and rival contractors. However that may be, the arch is unbuilt, and the entrance to the central court is a mere rift in the wall. The practical townsfolk have seized the opportunity thus presented by the unoccupied space of free quarters for the all-pervading buggy. With a contempt for the constituted authorities that it must be owned the constituted authorities have gone far to justify, they tether their horses in the shadow of their chief civic monument, like so many Arabs under the pillars of Palmyra or Persepolis, and heighten the impression of being the relic of an extinct race that is given to the pile not only by its unfin-

masonry is massive, and the projecting and pedimented porticoes are on an ample scale. These things give the building a certain effect of sumptuosity and swagger that allies it rather to the Parisian than to the Peorian Renaissance. The effect is marred by certain drawbacks of detail, and by one that is scarcely of detail, the extreme meanness and baldness of the attic, in which, for the only time in the building, the openings seem to be arranged with some reference to their uses, and in which, accordingly, they have a painfully pinched and huddled appearance. In the decorative detail there is apparent a divergency of views between the two architects appointed to carry out the divided halves of the united design. The municipal designer—or possibly it is the county gentleman—has been content to stand upon the ancient ways, and to introduce no detail for which he has not found Ludovican precedent, while his rival is of a more aspiring mind, and has endeavored to carry out the precepts of the late Thomas Jefferson, by classicising things modern. His excursions are not very daring, and consist mainly in such ished state and by the stains of smoke, undistinguishable from those of time, but by its entirely exotic architecture. This single example of Ludovican architecture recalls, as most examples of it do, Thackeray's caricature of its Mæcenas. Despoiled of its periwig and its high heels, that is to say, of its architecture, which is easily separable from it, the building would merely lose all its character without losing anything that belongs to it as a building.

Nevertheless this municipal building has its character, and in comparison with the next most famous public building of Chicago it vindicates the wisdom of its architect in subjecting himself to the safeguard of a style, of which, moreover, his work shows a real study. The style may be absolutely irrelevant both to our needs and to our ideas, as irrelevant as the political system of Louis XIV., which it recalls. Its formulas may seem quite empty, but they gather dignity if not meaning when contrasted with the work of an avid "swallower of formulas," like the architect of the Board of Trade. His work is of no style — a proposition that is not invalidated by the probability that he himself would call it "American eclectic Gothic." We all know what the untutored and aboriginal architect stretches that term to cover. There is no doubt about its being characteristically modern and American—one might say characteristically Western if he did not recall equally free and untrammelled exuberances in the Atlantic States. But it is impossible to ascribe to it any architectural merit, unless a complete disregard for precedent is to be imputed for righteousness, whether it proceed from ignorance or from contempt. And indeed there are not many other structures in the United States of equal cost and pretension which equally with this combine the dignity of a commercial traveller with the bland repose of St. Vitus. It is difficult to contemplate its bustling and uneasy façade without feeling a certain sympathy with the mob of anarchists that "demonstrated" under its windows on the night of its opening. If they were really anarchists, it was very ungrateful of them, for one would go far to find a more perfect expression of anar-

ENTRANCE TO THE ART INSTITUTE.
Burnham and Root, Architects.

chy in architecture, and it is conceivable that they were instigated by an outraged architectural critic in disguise. If that ringleader had been caught and arraigned, he could have maintained, with much better reason, the plea that Gustave Courbet made for his share in the destruction of the column of the Place Vendôme, that his opposition to the monument was not political but æsthetic.

Fortunately there is no other among the public or quasi-public buildings of Chicago of which the architecture is so

BALCONY OF AUDITORIUM.
Adler and Sullivan, Architects.

It owes its effectiveness to the clearness of its division into the three main parts of base and superstructure and roof, to the harmonious relation between them, and to the differences in the treatment of them that enhance this harmony. The Aristotelian precept that a work of art must have a beginning, a middle, and an end is nowhere more conspicuously valid than in architecture, and nowhere does the neglect of it entail more unfortunate consequences. The severity of the basement, with its plain rectangular openings, is an effective introduction to the somewhat lighter and more open fenestration of the second and third stories, which are grouped to form the second term in the proportion, and this in turn to the range of openings in the gable of the shorter front, and to the row of peaked dormers in the longer that animate the sky line and complete the composition. It may be significant, with reference to the tendency of Western architecture, that this admirable building, admirable in the sobriety and moderation that are facilitated by its moderate size, is precisely what one would not expect to find in Chicago, so little is there evident in it of an intention to "collar the eye," or to challenge the attention it so very well repays.

In part, as we have just intimated, this modesty may be ascribed to the modest dimensions of the building. At any rate, it was out of the question in another public or quasi-public building, which is the latest and, at this writing, the loudest of the lions of Chicago—the Auditorium. Whatever else a ten-story building, nearly 200 feet by more than 350 in area and 140 in height, with a tower rising 80 feet further, may happen to be, it must be conspicuous, and it is nowise possible that its designer should make it appear bashful or unobtrusive. Of however re-

hopeless and so irresponsible ; no other that would so baffle the palæontological Paley who should seek in it evidences of design, and that does not exhibit at least an architectural purpose, carried out with more or less of consistency and success. At the very centre of the commercial water-front there was wisely reserved from traffic in the rebuilding of the town the Lake Park, a mile in extent and some hundreds of feet in depth, which not only serves the purpose of affording a view of the lake from the business quarter, but also secures an effective foreground for the buildings that line its landward edge. One of the oldest of these, young as all of them are, is the Art Institute. This is of a moderate altitude, and suffers somewhat from being dwarfed by the elevator buildings erected since, being of but three stories and a roof; but no neighbors could make it other than a vigorous and effective work. It is extremely simple in composition, as will be seen, and it bears very little ornament, this being for the most part concentrated upon the ample and deeply moulded archway of the entrance.

tiring a disposition he may be, in such a situation he must brazen it out. It is in his power to adopt a very simple or a very elaborate treatment, and to imperil the success of his work by making it dull on the one hand or unquiet on the other. Messrs. Adler and Sullivan, the architects of the Auditorium, have chosen the better part in treating their huge fronts with great severity, insomuch that the building can scarcely be said to exhibit any "features," except the triple entrance on the lake front, with its overhanging balcony, and the square tower that rises over the southern front to a height of 225 feet. A place of popular entertainment constructed upon a scale and with a massiveness to which we can scarcely find a parallel since Roman days would present one of the worthiest and most interesting problems a modern architect could have, if he were left to solve it unhampered. It is quite difficult enough to tax the power of any designer without any complications. The problem of design in the Chicago Auditorium is much complicated with requirements entirely irrelevant to its main purpose. The lobbies, the auditorium, and the stage of a great theatre, which are its essential parts, are all susceptible of an exterior expression more truthful and more striking than has yet been attained, in spite of many earnest and interesting essays. In the interior of the Auditorium, where the architects were left free, they have devoted themselves to solving their real problem with a high degree of success, and have attained an impressive simplicity and largeness. We are not dealing with interiors, however, and they were required to envelop the outside of their theatre in a shell of many-storied commercial architecture, which forbade them even to try for a monumental expression of their great hall. In the main, their exterior appears and must be judged only as a "business block." They have their exits and their entrances, and it is really only in these features that the exterior betrays the primary purpose of the building. The tower even is evidently not so much monumental as utilitarian. It is pre-

pared for in the substructure only by a slight and inadequate projection of the wall and a slight and inadequate thickening of the piers, while it is itself obviously destined for profitable occupancy, being a small three-story business block, superimposed upon a huge ten-story business block. Such a structure cannot be converted into a monumental feature by making it more massive at the top than it is

TOWER OF AUDITORIUM.
Adler and Sullivan, Architects.

at the bottom, even though the massiveness be as artistically accentuated as it is in the tower of the Auditorium by the powerful open colonnade and the strong machicolated cornice in which it culminates. Waiving, as the designers have been compelled to do, the main purpose of the structure, and considering it as a commercial building, the Auditorium does not leave very much to be desired. The basement especially, which consists of three stories of granite darker than the limestone of the superstructure, and appropriately rough-faced, is a vigorous and dignified performance, in which the expression of rugged strength is enhanced by the small and deep openings, and in

THE FIELD BUILDING.
H. H. Richardson, Architect.

which the necessarily large openings of the ground-floor are prevented from enfeebling the design by the massiveness of the lintels and flat arches that enclose them, and of the piers and pillars by which these are supported. The superstructure is scarcely worthy of this basement. The triple vertical division of the wall is effectively proportioned, but a much stronger demarcation is needed between the second and third members than is furnished by the discontinuous sill course of the eighth story, while a greater projection, a greater depth, and a more vigorous modelling of the main cornice, and an enrichment of the attic beneath, would go far to relieve the baldness and monotony that are the defects of the design, and that are scarcely to be condoned because there are other architectural faults much worse and much more frequent which the designers have avoided. It is only, as has been said, in the entrances that they have been permitted to exhibit the object of the building. Really it is

only in the entrance on the lake front, for the triplet of stilted arches at the base of the tower is not a very felicitous or a very congruous feature. The three low arches of the lake front are of a Roman largeness—true *vomitoria*—and their effectiveness is increased by the simplicity of their treatment, by the ample lateral abutment provided for them, and by the long and shallow balcony that overhangs them. With the arches themselves this makes a very impressive feature, albeit the balcony is a questionable feature. Even to the layman there must be a latent contradiction in the intercalation of a pillar to relieve the bearing of a lintel, when the pillar is referred to an unsupported plinth obviously lighter and weaker than the lintel itself. This contradiction is not explained away by the vigor and massiveness of the shallow corbels that really account for the alternate columns, and it suggests that the construction so exhibited is not the true construction at all, and leaves this latter to be inferred without any help from the architecture. Even if one waives his objection to architectural forms that do not agree with the structural facts, it is surely not pedantic to require that the construction asserted by the forms shall be plausible to the extent of agreeing with itself. It is a pity that there should be such a drawback from a feature so effective; but the drawback does not prevent the feature from being effective, nor do the shortcomings we have been considering in the design of the Auditorium, nor even the much more serious drawback that was inherent in the problem and imposed upon the architects, prevent it from being a very impressive structure, and justifying the pride with which it is regarded by all patriotic Chicagoans.

But, as has been intimated, it is not in monumental edifices that the characteristic building of Chicago is to be looked for. The "business block," strictly utilitarian in purpose, and monumental only in magnitude and in solidity of construction, is the true and typical embodiment in building of the Chicago idea. This might be said, of course, of any American city. Undoubtedly the most remarkable achievements of our architects and the most creditable have been in commercial architecture. But in this respect Chicago is more American than any of the Eastern cities, where there are signs, even in the commercial quarters, of division of interest and infirmity of purpose. In none of them does the building bespeak such a singleness of devotion, or indicate that life means so exclusively a living. Even the exceptions prove the rule by such tokens as the modest dimensions of the Art Institute and the concealment of the Auditorium in the heart of a business block. It does not by any means follow that the business blocks are uninteresting. There are singularly few exceptions to the rule of dismalness in the buildings that were hurriedly run up after the fire. One of these exceptions, the American Express Company, has an extrinsic interest as being the work of Mr. Richardson, and as being, so far as it need be classified, an example of Victorian Gothic, although its openings are all lintelled, instead of the Provençal Romanesque to which its author afterward addicted himself with such success. So successful an example is it that an eminent but possibly bilious English architect who visited Chicago at an early stage of the rebuilding declared it to be the only thing in the town worth looking at—a judgment that does not seem so harsh to the tourist of to-day who compares it with its thus disesteemed contemporaries. It is a sober and straightforward performance in a safe monochrome of olive sandstone, and it thus lacks the note of that variety of Victorian Gothic that Mr. Ruskin's eloquence stimulated untrained American designers to

produce, in which the restlessness of unstudied forms is still further tormented by the spotty application of color. Upon the whole, it is a matter for congratulation that the earlier rebuilders of Chicago, being what they were, should have been so ignorant or careless of what was going on elsewhere, which, had they been aware of it, they would have been quite certain to misapply. Not only did they thus escape the frantic result that came of Victorian Gothic in untutored hands, but they escaped also the pettiness and puerility that resulted of "Queen Anne," even when it was done by designers who ought to have known better. The present writer had the honor of disparaging in these pages that curious mode of building when it was dressed in its little brief authority, and playing its most fantastic tricks. Now it is so well recognized that Queen Anne is dead that it seems strange educated architects ever could have fancied they detected the promise and potency of architectural life in her cold remains. This most evanescent of fashions seems never to have prevailed in Chicago at all.

One of the earliest of the more modern and characteristic of the commercial structures of Chicago, the Field building, is by Mr. Richardson also—a huge warehouse covering a whole square, and seven stories high. With such an opportunity Mr. Richardson could be trusted implicitly at least to make the most of his dimensions; and large as the building is in fact, it looks interminably big. Its bigness is made apparent by the simplicity of its treatment and the absence of any lateral division whatever. Simplicity, indeed, could scarcely go further. The vast expanses of the fronts are unrelieved by any ornament except a leaf in the cornice, and a rudimentary capital in the piers and mullions of the colonnaded attic. The effect of the mass is due wholly to its magnitude, to the disposition of its openings, and to the emphatic exhibition of the masonic structure. The openings, except in the attic, and except for an ample pier reserved at each corner, are equally spaced throughout. The vertical division is limited to a sharp separation from the intermediate wall of the basement on one hand, and of the attic on the other. It must be owned that there is even a distinct infelicity in the arrangement of the five stories of this intermediate wall, the two superposed arcades, the upper of which, by rea-

ARCADE FROM THE STUDEBAKER BUILDING.
S S. Beman, Architect.

son of its multiplied supports, is the more solid of aspect, and between which there is no harmonious relation, but, contrariwise, a competition. Nevertheless, the main division is so clear and the handling throughout so vigorous as to carry off even a more serious defect. Nothing of its kind could be more impressive than the rugged expanse of masonry, of which the bonding is expressed throughout, and which in the granite basement becomes Cyclopean in scale, and in the doorway especially Cyclopean in rude strength. The great pile is one of the most interesting, as it is one of the most individual, examples of American commercial buildings. In it the vulgarity of the "commercial palace " is gratefully conspicuous by its absence, and it is as monumental in its massiveness and durability as it is grimly utilitarian in expression.

It is in this observance of the proprieties of commercial architecture, and in this self-denying rejection of an ornateness improper to it, that the best of the commercial architecture of Chicago is a welcome surprise to the tourist from the East. When the rebuilding of the business quarter of Boston was in progress, and while that city was, for the most part, congratu-lating itself upon the display of the skill of its architects, for which the fire had opened a field, Mr. Richardson observed to the author of these remarks that there was more character in the plain and solid warehouses that had been destroyed than in the florid edifices by which they had been replaced. The saying was just; for the burned Boston was as unmistakably commercial as much of the rebuilt Boston is irrelevantly palatial. In the warehouse just noticed, Mr. Richardson himself resisted this besetting temptation of the architect, and his work certainly loses nothing of the simplicity which with the uninstructed builders of old Boston was in large part mere ignorance and unskilfulness, but emphasizes it by the superior power of distributing his masses that belonged to him as a trained and sensitive designer; for the resources of an artist are required to give an artistic and poignant impression even of rudeness. The rebuilt commercial quarter of Boston is by no means an extreme example of misplaced ornateness. Within the past three or four years Wall Street has been converted from the humdrum respectability of an old-fashioned business thoroughfare to a street of commercial palaces, the aspect of which must contain an element of grievousness to the judicious, who see that the builders have lavished their repertory of ornament and variety in buildings to which nobody resorts for pleasure, but everybody for business alone, and that they have left themselves nothing further in the way of enrichment when they come to do temples and palaces properly so called. Mr. Ruskin has fallen into deep, and largely into deserved, discredit as an architectural critic by promulgating rhapsodies as dogmas. His intellectual frivolity is even more evident and irritating by reason of the moral earnestness that attends it, recalling that perfervid pulpiteer of whom a like-minded eulogist affirmed that "he wielded his prurient imagination like a battle-axe in the service of the Lord of Hosts." All the same, lovers of architecture owe him gratitude for his eloquent inculcation of some of the truths that he arrived at by feeling, however inconclusive is the reasoning by which he endeavors to support them; and one of these is the text so much preached from in the *Seven Lamps*, that "where rest is forbidden, so is ornament." In the best of the commercial buildings of Chicago there is nothing visible of the conflict of which we hear so much from architects between the claims of "art" and the claims of utility, nor any evidence of a desire to get the better of a practical client by smuggling architecture upon him, and deceiving him for his own good and the glory of his architect. It is a very good lesson to see how the strictly architectural success of the commercial buildings is apt to be directly in proportion to the renunciation by the designers of conventional "architecturesqueness," and to their loyal acceptance at all points of the utilitarian conditions under which they are working.

The Studebaker building is one of the show buildings of Chicago, but it cannot be said to deserve this particular praise in so high a degree as several less celebrated structures. It partakes—shall we say?—too much of the palatial character of Devonshire Street and Wall Street to be fairly representative of the severity of commercial architecture in Chicago. It is

very advantageously placed, fronting the Lake Park, and it is in several respects not unworthy of its situation. The arrangement of the first five stories is striking, and the arcade that embraces the upper three of these is a notable and well-studied feature, with detail very good in itself, and very well adjusted in place and in scale. It is the profusion of this detail, and the lavish introduction of

carved marble and of polished granite shafts, that first impress every beholder with its palatial rather than commercial character; but this character is not less given to the front, or to that part of it which

THE OWINGS BUILDING.
Cobb and Frost, Architects.

has character, by the very general composition that makes the front so striking. An arcade superposed upon two colonnades, which are together of less than its own height, can scarcely fail of impressiveness; but here it loses some of its impressiveness in losing all its significance by reason of its subdivision into three equal stories, none of them differing in purpose from any other or from the colonnade below, and the larger grouping that simulates a lofty hall above two minor stories is thus seen to be merely capricious. Of course pretty much the same criticism may be passed upon most American works of commercial architecture, and upon the best not less than upon the worst, but that it cannot be passed upon the best commercial buildings of Chicago is their peculiar praise. Moreover, the Studebaker building has some marked defects peculiar to its design. The flanking piers of the building, in spite of the effort made to increase their apparent massiveness by a solid treatment of the terminal arches at the base, are painfully thin and inadequate, and their tenuity is emphasized by the modelling into nook shafts of their inner angles in the second story. These are serious blemishes upon the design of the first five stories, and these stories exhaust the architectural interest of the building. There is something even ludicrous in the sudden and complete collapse of the architecture above the large arcade, as if the ideas of the designer had all at once given out, or rather as if an untrained builder had been called upon to add three stories to the unfinished work of a scholarly architect. If the substructure be amenable to the criticism that it is not commercial architecture, the superstructure is amenable to the more radical criticism that it is not architecture at all.

The Owings building is another conspicuous commercial structure that invites the same criticism of not being strictly commercial, but in a very different way. There is here no prodigality of ornament, and no irrelevant preciousness of material. A superstructure of grayish brick surmounts a basement of gray stone, and the decoration is reserved for the main entrance, which it is appropriate to signalize and render conspicuous even in works of the barest utility. This is attained here by the lofty gable, crocketed and covered with carving, that rises above the plain archway which forms the entrance itself. The lintelled openings of the basement elsewhere are of a Puritanical severity, and so are the arched openings of the brick superstructure. Neither is there the least attempt to suggest the thing that is not in the interior arrangement by way of giving va-

riety and interest to the exterior. In the treatment of the wall space the only one of the "unnecessary features" in which Mr. Ruskin declares architecture to consist is the corniced frieze above the fourth story of the superstructure, with its suggested support of tall and slim pilasters; and this is quite justifiable as giving the building a triple division, and distinguishing the main wall from the gable. For this purpose, however, obviously enough, the dividing feature should be placed between the two parts it is meant to differentiate; and in the present instance this line is two stories higher than the point actually selected, and is now marked only by a light string-course. If the emphatic horizontal belt had been raised these two stories, the division it creates would not only have corresponded to an organic division of the building, but another requisite of architectural composition would have been fulfilled, inasmuch as one of the three members would visibly have predominated over the others, whereas now the three are too nearly equal. It is quite true that the prolongation of the pilasters through two more stories would have made them spindle quite intolerably, but in any case they are rather superfluous and impertinent, and it would have decorated the fronts to omit them. The accentuation of vertical lines by extraneous features is not precisely what is needed in a twelve-story building of these dimensions. In these points, however, there is no departure from the spirit of commercial architecture. That occurs here not in detail, but in the general scheme that gives the building its picturesqueness of outline. The corbelled turret at the angle makes more eligible the rooms its openings light; but the steep gabled roofs which this turret unites and dominates plainly enough fail to utilize to the utmost the spaces they enclose, and so far violate the conditions of commercial architecture. It seems ungracious to find fault with them on that account, they are so successfully studied in mass and in detail, and the group they make with the turret is so spirited and effective, but nevertheless they evidently do not belong to an office building, and, to borrow the expression of a Federal judge upon a famous occasion, their very picturesqueness is *aliunde*.

THE MONTANA CITIES

I.—HELENA.

THE Territory of Montana is in itself an empire. It was given Territorial rights in 1864, and since then has increased rapidly both in wealth and population. Fabulously rich in mines, already having an annual output of nearly $26,000,000, it is famous for its vast areas of grazing land, and is becoming widely known as an agricultural country. With a total area of 93,000,000 acres of land, of which 16,000,000 are agricultural, 38,000,000 grazing, 12,000,000 timber, 5,000,000 mineral, and 22,000,000 mountainous, it is the source of the Columbia and the Missouri, and has an almost innumerable number of smaller streams, whose presence in the mountain cañons and in the valleys gives the Territory a charming picturesqueness. Within a distance of from twenty to forty miles of Helena are thousands of mining claims yet to be developed, any one of which may prove as rich as the richest of those that are now productive. If the several agricultural valleys were placed in a continuous line, they would form a belt 4000 miles long, and averaging four miles in width. Every year the number of farms increases. In the Gallatin, Prickly-Pear, Yellowstone, Bitter Root, Sun River, and other valleys, one no longer sees neglected fields.

But if one were to write in detail of Montana and its resources, he would find the task an arduous one. There are so many valleys, each with its own claims and characteristics, so many mines and towns and districts, that a volume might be devoted to each. There is great and general buoyancy among the people, and local prejudice runs high.

Regarding Helena and Butte, however, there is almost a unanimity of feeling. The two places are looked upon as perfect illustrations of what has been accomplished in the Territory since the age of development began.

To the younger generation Helena is a Parisian-like centre which he hopes in time to see. Capitalists may make their money at Butte or elsewhere, but are moderately sure to spend it at Helena; and the miner or ranchman is never so happy as when he finds himself in what, without question, is the metropolis of the Territory. I know of no city in the extreme middle West that could so well satisfy one who had learned to appreciate Western life as Helena. Its climate, its surroundings, even its society, largely composed of Eastern and college-bred men and young wives fresh from

HELENA, LOOKING DOWN BROADWAY.

older centres, are delightfully prominent features. The city has a population of nearly 15,000, and considering its great wealth, it is not surprising that it should have electric lights, a horse-car line, and excellent schools.

Thanks to the railways, which have had and are continuing to have so important an effect upon the country overlooked by the Rocky Mountains, Montana's isolation is now a thing of the past. Two railroad routes connect it with the East and Pacific West, and there is still the Missouri, navigable from St. Louis to the Great Falls, within easy reach of Helena.

The early history of Helena, which fortunately may still be gathered from living witnesses, is a striking illustration of the fact that chance and luck were once the two most important factors of ultimate success in the Territory. None who came into Montana in early days were systematic discoverers. The majority of them knew little of the theory of mining. What success they had was due to luck. The paying properties they found were nearly all discovered by chance. When John Cowan and Robert Stanley grew dissat-

isfied with the amount of room afforded them in the overcrowded camps of Alder Gulch, they resolved to push northward to Kootanie, where rich diggings had been reported. In July, 1864, the two men and their friends reached a tributary of the Prickly-Pear. There the supply of food they had brought ran low, and further progress northward was impossible. In despair, the party made camp and began to dig for gold. Luckily finding it, they named their diggings the Last Chance Mines, and their district Rattlesnake, the latter word being suggested, no doubt, by the presence of earlier settlers than they themselves. In September Cowan and Stanley built their cabins, and thus had the honor of being the first residents of a camp that in after-years became the present city of Helena.

From the very first, Last Chance Gulch fulfilled its first promise. Soon after Cowan's cabin was completed a Minnesota wagon train reached the valley, and brought an increase of population to the young camp, the fame of which had gone broadcast over the land. Fabulous stories were told of its great wealth, and during the winter of 1864–5 there was a wild stampede to it from all directions. But still the infant Helena was without a name. The first Territorial election had already been held, and on the 12th of December the first Legislature assembled at Bannack. In view of this progress, the miners of Last Chance decided that their camp must no longer go unchristened. At a meeting held in the cabin of Uncle John Somerville the name Helena was accepted, and given without dissent to the collection of rudely built huts in which the miners lived.

Helena then entered upon its eventful and prosperous career. Discovery followed discovery, and the town, unsightly with its main streets occupied by sluice-boxes and gravel heaps, became the centre of a mining district that proved richer every day. In the summer of 1865 the first newspaper was printed. The press was brought in over the mountains on the backs of pack-mules, and many of the earlier editions were printed on yellow wrapping paper.

In 1869 the township of Helena was entered from the general government. In a period of seven years the placer claims near Helena yielded $20,000,000, and although far removed from the outside world, the city, as a mining centre, was of great importance, and may be said to have enjoyed an uninterrupted period of success.

Helena, regarded from a local standpoint, is the geographical, commercial, monetary, political, railroad, and social centre of Montana. Its trade is larger and more extended than that of any other city or town in the Territory, and therefore its commercial supremacy is unquestioned. The Helena banks, rich in deposits and many in number, may well entitle the city to its claim as the monetary centre. The terminus of the lately completed Manitoba system, and having the Northern Pacific as an outlet to the east, west, and south, it has several branch roads to the important mining camps of Wickes, Marysville, and Rimini, and is promised others which are to aid in developing the rich districts scattered about the surrounding country.

Helena, in the truest sense of the word, is cosmopolitan. Let one walk the streets at any hour of the day or night, and he will be sure to notice the peculiarity. Crowding the sidewalks are miners, picturesque in red shirts and top-boots; long-haired Missourians, waiting, like Micawber, for something to "turn up"; ranchmen, standing beside their heavily loaded wagons; trappers; tourists; men of business. Chinamen and Indians, Germans and Hebrews, whites and blacks, the prosperous and the needy, the representatives of every State in the Union, Englishmen and Irishmen, all make Helena their home. No traditions, no old family influence, no past social eminence, hamper the restless spirit of the busy workers. There is a long list of daily visitors, and the city is never without its sight-seers. Invalids seek it for its climatic advantages.

The site of Helena, though the railway station is a mile from the heart of the town, was most happily chosen. It could not have been better had Cowan and his *confrères* foreseen the future size and importance of the camp they founded. The city faces toward the north. Behind it rise the mountains of the main range, the noble isolated peaks, bare, brown, and of every varying shape and size, forming a background of which one never tires. The old camp was gathered into the narrow quarters of the winding gulch that extends from the mountains to the open valley of the Prickly-Pear. The present city has outgrown

POURING GOLD—ASSAY OFFICE, HELENA.

COUNTY COURT-HOUSE, HELENA.

nearer to the railway that has come from the outside world to lend Helena a helping hand.

Leaving the hotel in the very heart of the town, and following Main Street to its upper end, we find ourselves in the oldest part of the city. Nothing here is modern or suggestive of wealth. At your side are rudely built log cabins, with gravel roofs and dingy windows. They are time-stained and weather-beaten now. Chickens scratch upon the roofs; half-fed dogs slink away at your approach. A Chinaman has taken this for his home, and has hung his gaudy red sign of " Wah Sing" over the low doorway; and in this live those who have failed to find in Helena their El Dorado, and now are reduced to living Heaven only knows how. But in years gone past, when the city was a camp, who scoffed at a cabin of logs? These huts were the homes of future capitalists.

We pass once more into Main Street, and from it into Broadway, that climbs a steep hill-slope, and brings us to the government Assay Office. It is a plain two-storied brick building with stone trimmings, and occupies a little square by itself. Within, all is order and neatness. To the right of the main hall are the rooms where the miners' gold-dust and silver ore are melted and poured in molten streams from the red-hot crucibles. Bars and bricks of the precious metals

such limitations, and from the gulch, down which the leading business street runs, has spread over the confining hills, and to-day proudly looks out upon the broad valley, and far beyond it, to the peaks that mark the course of the great Missouri. Directly overshadowing the city is Mount Helena. From it the view is broadest, grandest, most complete. At one's feet is the town of rapid growth. You can see the houses scattered at random over the low, bare elevations, and in the old ravine, the source of so much wealth, the scene of such strange stories, are the flat-roofed business blocks in which Helena takes such justifiable pride. It is no mere frontier town that you look upon. It is a city rather—a city compactly built, and evidently vigorous and growing. On its outskirts, crowning sightly eminences or clinging to the steep hill-sides, are the new houses of those upon whom fortune has smiled, and far out upon the levels are scattered groups of buildings that every day draw

TWO OLD-TIMERS, HELENA.

are shown, and in the vaults they are stacked in glittering array. Every room has its interest. In one the accounts are kept by the assayer; in another are rows of delicate scales, in which the smallest particles of ore are weighed to determine the purity of the moulds packed away in the strongly guarded vaults.

As the ore is received it is tested, weighed, and melted. From the retorts it is run

cellaneous), the Historical Society, and the Legislature. The walls are of Montana granite, quarried near Helena, and the trimmings, of red sandstone, came from Bayfield, on Lake Superior. The building is 132 feet long by 80 wide, and with the basement is three stories high.

To the left of the main entrance is a Norman tower. From it is had one of those views for which Helena is so fa-

A STREET SCENE IN WICKES.

into moulds, which, after being properly valued and marked, are placed in vaults or shipped to the government Mint at Philadelphia. An ordinary gold brick is a trifle larger than the common clay brick. One was shown us which measured 9 inches long, $3\frac{1}{4}$ wide, and $2\frac{1}{2}$ high. Its actual weight was $509\frac{25}{100}$ ounces, the component parts being (basis 1000) 667.2 gold, 294 silver, and 29.2 baser metals. The cash value of the mould was $7373.

The County Court-house, costing $200,-000, is one of the most conspicuous objects of the city. Besides affording accommodation for all the courts and officers of the county, it has rooms for the Governor and other Territorial officials, the Montana Library (both law and mis-

mous—a view of city, valley, mountains. We are nearly 5000 feet above sea-level, and the air is clear and rarefied. Swiftly flows the blood through our veins, and our lungs are all expanded. No wonder the people love their city. Never is the weather sultry, never is the heat oppressive. In winter, a month of snow and terrible cold; then an early spring, with wild flowers in March, and green grasses in April.

From the Court-house our way is through a succession of residence streets. All are wide, long, and straight. On either side grows a row of cotton-wood-trees, the leaves turning now, and some of them dropping to the ground, on this September day. Behind the trees are cottages, some of wood, others of bright red brick; and before and around each house is a bit of lawn, with a few shade trees, and a flower bed tucked away in some sunny corner. Here a riding party is ready for a canter out into the valley or to the mountain trails; and there stands a pony phaeton, upstart successor of the old canvas-covered wagons that twenty years ago were the only vehicles to be seen in this far-off land.

The newer and more pretentious houses in Helena are on Madison Avenue, a wide thoroughfare nearly parallel to Main will descend the hill to Main Street once more, and crossing the city, climb to this popular boulevard. Far away, across the valley, are seen the purple peaks of the Beet Range, out of which rises a huge cone known as Bear's Tooth. At its base the Missouri takes its plunge into the Gate of the Mountains. For more than a hundred miles the view is unobstructed. Mountains are everywhere; piled together here; broken, snow-capped, and isolated in other directions. No wonder that the people have selected the plateau as the site of their best houses. In no other city of the

SMELTING-WORKS, WICKES.

Street, but having a much higher elevation and more commanding outlook. A few years ago the plateau which may now be regarded as the "court end" of Helena was without a tree or house. It now presents an entirely different appearance. Madison Avenue in itself would claim attention in any city, while the residences that face it afford striking evidence of the fact that Helena is fast outgrowing all provincialism, and to-day deserves the encomiums that one is inclined to bestow upon it.

Leaving the cottage-lined streets, we far West is there to be had a more extended or a more interesting view.

Benton Avenue is another favorite residence street. Walking down its shaded length, passing the houses that are springing into existence as though by magic, we gain a still deeper insight into the life and attractions of the city. Are we interested in churches? If so, they are here, Episcopal and Congregationalist, Baptist, Methodist, and Catholic. Scattered at random about the city, and in no instance being more than well suited to present needs, they still give Helena its proper tone, and show by their presence that a new life has crept into the old camp of reckless mining days.

The Helena Board of Trade was organized in 1887, and on the 1st of January, 1888, issued its first annual report. Many interesting facts regarding the growth of the city are given in the pamphlet. The assessable wealth of Helena in 1887, according to the Secretary of the Board, is $8,000,000, or, estimating the population at 13,000, over $615 *per capita*. The assessed valuation of Lewis and Clarke County for 1887 was $11,000,000, while its actual wealth was $75,000,000. There were 388 new buildings erected in Helena and its several additions in 1886 and '87, the total cost of which was $2,037,000.

The chief social organization in Helena is the Helena Club. Among its members are men prominent in all business circles, and in such industries as cattle-raising and mining. The club-rooms are fully supplied with current literature, and are the popular resort during the late afternoon and early evening. A stranger in Helena is moderately sure of finding whomsoever he wishes to meet at the club, and I am sure the hospitalities of the organization are always gladly extended.

In her schools and other public institutions Helena is fully abreast of the times. There are five brick school-houses in the city, and money for their support is raised by direct taxation on property. School lands cannot be sold in Montana until the Territory becomes a State. Then, however, there will be 5,000,000 acres available for the establishment of a fund that will relieve the tax-payers from their present burden.

Besides the public schools there are other institutions, maintained by the Catholic sisters, and a business college with an enrolment already of nearly 500 scholars.

The two library associations of Helena, namely, the City Library and the Historical Society's Library, were both destroyed by fire in 1874, but have since been replaced by collections that are large, varied, and valuable. The Law Library contains neary 4000 volumes of reports, text-books, and laws. The last Legislature appropriated $3000 to its use. The Historical Society's Library consists of original MSS., old historical works, home pamphlets and maps, and contains 5000 volumes. The society occupies two rooms in the Court-house, and last year

THOMAS CRUSE.
From photograph by R. H. Beckwith, Helena.

was given $400 by the Legislature. The object of the officers is to collect and preserve such original letters, diaries, and accounts of travel in Montana as shall serve as the material from which a comprehensive history of the Territory may be gathered. The Helena Free Library contains 2500 carefully selected books of miscellaneous reading, and is supported by a city tax of one-half mill on each dollar of valuation. The income from such source was $2600 in 1886. Still another library is that belonging to the Young Men's Christian Association.

Sufferers from pulmonary troubles are often greatly benefited by living at Helena. The air is dry and bracing, and acts as a tonic to those who have not much natural energy. It would be unwise to advise all who are ill to try living at Helena. No one can select a new home for a patient without first knowing his particular trouble. But I have no doubt that one who takes his case in hand before disease does more than suggest its presence, and goes to Montana prepared to live in the open air, will be able to build up his constitution and begin life anew.

But having seen the city, let us now visit Wickes, and glance for a moment at one of the regions from which the people draw the revenue that they have poured so freely forth for the public good. Making an early start, we will drive down Main Street to the station, and taking the train there, ride down the Prickly-Pear Valley to the Junction, and then on toward the southeast to our destination. On one side rise the mountains, with cool, inviting-looking cañons, hemmed in by high hills, and leading into the heart of the range; on the other is the valley, extending far away to the hills in the east. Grasses are brown, and the pines deep green. For an hour the Montana of old is ours to enjoy: isolated, quiet, just as nature fashioned it.

And then comes Wickes: an unsightly town; a mining camp; a place with many saloons and no churches; wooden shanties; wavering streets; groups of men, flannel-shirted, unshaven; a background of mountains. This is the picture. We can hear the heavy pounding of the crushers in the works; the air at times is heavy with the smoke of the furnaces. The town is not inviting. It is, as Helena once was, rough, uncouth, repellent almost; but it is rich.

Not rich in itself perhaps, but unquestionably so in its surroundings. The largest works at Wickes are those of the Helena Mining and Reduction Company. The town is the creation of this company, and the works bring together the throng that greets us. The product of the smeltery in 1886 had a money value of $1,105,190 76. Nearly 500 men are employed, and ore from Idaho as well as from the mines near the town is treated. Standing anywhere in the main street, we look upon a country fairly riddled with mines. Some of them are famous producers; others are but just opened. One can scarcely realize the possible future of the region. Every day brings its progress; every year the output is greater. As we walk through the dimly lighted buildings, stopping now to watch the crushers and again to listen while the guide explains the process of reduction, one begins to form a just estimate of Helena's claims, for all this district is at her very doors, and the more money Wickes produces, the more brilliant become the prospects of the Territorial capital.

Marysville, nearly thirty miles from Helena, is a second Wickes in appearance, but when one remembers the wealth of the mines which have created the town, he forgets the ugliness of the streets, and ceases to notice the dilapidation of the rudely built cabins. Marysville is chiefly famous as the site of the Drum Lummon, but does not depend on this mine alone for its support. The town is the chief seat of an extremely rich district, already well developed, and is an important suburb of Helena. It is connected by rail with the latter city, and will eventually be the terminus of a branch of the Manitoba road.

The discoverer of the Drum Lummon was Mr. Thomas Cruse. In the days before he sold his property and returned to Helena a much honored millionnaire, Mr. Cruse was locally known as "old Tommy," and was looked upon as a somewhat visionary man. None questioned after a time that his mine, where he lived and labored alone, was valuable, but few placed its worth so high as did the patient owner. When he refused half a million for his mine, the people of Helena called him foolish, and when he turned away from the offer of a million, they called him a fool. But the miner was wiser than his friends, and eventually received his price, $11,500,000, and a goodly number of shares in the new company. Then, as so often is the case, the old familiarity was dropped, and the "Tommy" of by-gone days became Mr. Thomas Cruse, "capitalist." A kind, thoroughly honest man, of whom all who know him are ready to say a good word, he is a familiar figure on the streets of Helena, and to-day is president of a savings-bank in the city where a few years ago he was not sure of getting trusted for enough to keep himself alive. As an illustration of the ups and downs of a miner's life he is a notable example.

Mining, fascinating as it seems to one who learns only its brighter side, must not be thought the only industry from which Helena derives its revenue. It is undoubtedly the chief occupation of the people, but fortunes have been made and are now being made in that other great Montana industry, stock-raising. In his last report, the Governor of Montana estimated that there were then in the Territory:

Cattle	1,400,000
Horses	190,000
Sheep	2,000,000

Sheep-raising is a most profitable business. The Montana grasses are abundant and nutritious, and a vast area of country is available for pasturage. Montana wool has a ready sale in Eastern markets. The clip for 1887 is estimated at 5,771,420 pounds. Cattle suffered severely in the winter of 1886-7, and the industry was badly crippled, although not by any means annihilated. Millions of Helena capital are invested both in sheep and cattle, and it is an open question which have been the more successful, the miners or the stockmen. "Cattle kings," as the men who have made fortunes out of stock are facetiously called, are by no means a rarity in the city. The possessions of many of them are enormous. I doubt if even the men themselves know exactly how many sheep or cattle they own.

east Helena is seen nestled in its winding gulch, and creeping out upon the low-browed hills. The air is so clear that objects fifty miles away seem close at hand. By degrees the grade becomes steeper, and leaving the valley, one finds himself among the gigantic cliffs and buttresses

STREET IN BUTTE, AND COURT-HOUSE.

II.—BUTTE.

From Helena to Butte is only a half-day's ride. Leaving the one early in the morning, you are at the other by noon. The journey is extremely interesting. The route is westward, by the Northern Pacific, over the main divide of the Rocky Mountains to Garrison, and from there southward, through the fertile Deer Lodge Valley, to the city of mines, smelteries, and steep hills. For an hour after leaving Helena the road traverses the Prickly-Pear Valley. Westward rise the Rockies, seemingly impossible, and in the south-

of granite that form the foundations of the huge natural wall that stretches north and south from British Columbia to the borders of old Mexico. Then comes the Mullan Tunnel, long and dark, through which the train passes to the western side of the divide, where the slopes have a pastoral beauty in strange contrast to the appearance of those on the east. At last we are literally among the mountains. Tall peaks surround us; the pines choke the winding valleys that we follow; clear streams of water flow past us; we enter park after park. The coloring is exquisite, and so varied that one cries out with delight. Strangely fashioned monuments of red and yellow sandstone, grim cliffs of dark basaltic rock, rich green masses of firs and pines, surrounded by dull brown grasses, and scattered over the slopes the bright patches of the quaking-asp, colored by the early frosts, and as beautiful as the New England maples after their first encounter with the chilly nights of fall.

The Deer Lodge Valley is of varying width, and contains a large area of agricultural and natural hay lands. The chief towns are Deer Lodge and Anaconda, the latter having a population of 5000. The smelting-works at Anaconda are said to be the largest in the world, and cover nearly fifteen acres of land.

The city of Butte does not claim to be picturesque. It is an interesting place, however, as one so rich and productive and energetic must be, and from the top of its high hills the view of distant mountains does much toward making one forget the disagreeable features of the city itself. The very activity of Butte is sometimes wearisome. It never ceases. By day and night the tall chimneys at the mills are pouring forth their smoke and flame; the streets at all hours of the day and night are filled with moving throngs. Money-making is the evident passion of the day. In the race for it all else is forgotten. The city covers the slope of a steep, rocky hill, overlooked by a bare butte, from which the town derives its name, and for the most part the houses are set down at random, and present a heterogeneous collection of wooden cabins and high brick blocks. There is everywhere a sign of haste and uncertainty. No trees are to be seen; the streets take a bold plunge from heights above to the levels below. There is nothing soft or winning to the side which nature shows. By some great convulsion the hills have been created, and man has occupied them with all their crudities.

Silver Bow County, of which Butte is the county-seat, has the smallest superficial area, but the largest population, of any county in Montana. It was originally a part of Deer Lodge County, but in 1881 achieved its independence by reason of the discovery of the great copper and silver leads at Butte and vicinity. Mining is the main industry in the county, which so early as 1870 contained the locations of 981 gulch claims and 226 bar and hill claims. The total cost of ditches at that time was $106,000. Gulch mining prospered until 1871, when it collapsed.

Butte is the centre of what is known as the Summit Mountain District, and has an elevation of 5800 feet. The city is virtually the county of Silver Bow. Under the general title of Butte are included Butte proper, South Butte, Walkerville, Centreville, and Meadesville; the several towns form the largest and richest mining camp in the world. The district of which Butte is the natural centre is three miles square, and contains more than 5000 mineral claims, 2000 of which are held under United States patents. The product of the camp for 1886 was $13,246,500, divided as follows:

Fine bullion per express	$5,856,500
Copper (55,000,000 pounds, at 10 cents)	5,500,000
Silver ore shipments	650,000
Silver in matte	1,240,000
Total	$13,246,500

In 1881 the output amounted to only $1,247,600. For 1887 the returns show an increase over the product of 1886 of over $3,000,000. Nearly 5000 men are employed in the various stamp-mills and smelteries, and the monthly pay-roll amounts to $500,000.

The post-office at Butte pays a net profit to the government of $23,000 a year. The city is well supplied with banks, carrying check deposits aggregating over $2,000,000, and has an assessed property valuation of from $8,000,000 to $9,000,000. On the business streets are a number of buildings of great size and solidity, and elsewhere are several private houses built by those who have made princely fortunes since coming to Butte. Particularly noticeable are the public buildings, such as the schools and Court-house. The latter cost $150,000, and on the former more than $100,000 have been expended. Gas and electricity are used in lighting; the retail trade is large; and as a rule Butte is a well-regulated city, enjoying a majority of the modern improvements, and happy in the knowledge that its fame is world-wide, and its prestige as a mining centre undisputed.

Quartz locations were made on and near the present site of Butte as early as 1864. In 1867 the town site was laid out, and Butte had a population of nearly 500 souls. The early comers were only moderately successful in their ventures, however, and in time the placer claims were exhausted.

THE PANS.

In 1875 came the startling discovery that the "black ledges of Butte" were rich with silver. The news spread rapidly. Old claims were relocated, and smelteries and mills erected. The camp grew rapidly. In a year the Utah and Northern road reached the place, and the present era of wealth and progress was fully inaugurated. This, in brief, is the history of Butte. All its trials and disappointments came at an early day, and when once overcome, never returned. To-day the Utah and Northern furnishes its southern outlet, and the Montana, Union, and Northern Pacific its eastern and western. Before another year passes the Manitoba will give it still another direct connection with the outside world, and with other local lines will bring it into closer communication with Helena and the various districts of Montana.

The mines of Butte are of two classes—one silver, the other copper-bearing. The silver ores vary in richness from fifteen to eighty ounces of silver per ton. Most of the silver veins also contain from $4 to $12 per ton gold. Some of the copper mines carry silver, but the percentage is small. The principal copper ores are copper glance, erubescite, and pyrites. The rough ore assays from 8 to 60 per cent copper, and most of it bears a concentration from two to two

and one-half tons into one, with a small loss in lastings.

The process of mining as practised at Butte is of too complicated a nature to be properly described by a layman, and I therefore quote from an expert. "The silver ores," he says, "are either free or base. In the first the silver contents are extracted after the ore has been stamped by simply mixing it with mercury in water, the precious metal amalgamating readily with the quicksilver. In base ores, however, the process is more expensive and complex. After the ore has been hoisted from the mine, it is conveyed in hand-cars to the upper part of the mill, where it is put through large iron crushers, which reduce it to about the size of walnuts. From the crushers it drops to the drying floor, where all the moisture it contains is evaporated, and where it is mixed with a proportion of salt varying from 8 to 10 per cent. of its weight, the amount of salt depending on the baseness of the ore. When thoroughly dried it is shovelled under the stamps—large perpendicular iron bars weighing 900 pounds—which are raised by machinery and permitted to drop on the ore below at the rate of about fifty strokes per minute. The effect, of course, is to crush the ore to powder, in which condition it is taken automatically to the roasters. These are huge hollow cylinders, revolving slowly,

THE SETTLERS.

and filled with flames of intense heat, conveyed from the furnaces below by means of a draught. As the cylinders revolve, the action of the heat drives off the sulphur in the ore, liberates the chlorine in the salt, and a chemical change takes place in the nature of the silver in the ore, making a chloride of what was formerly a sulphide of silver, and rendering it susceptible of amalgamation with quicksilver, just like the silver in the ' free' ore mentioned. From the roasters the pulp is then conveyed by tramway to the pans— large tubs filled with water, in which quicksilver is placed with the pulp. The mass is then violently agitated, so that every particle of the silver chloride comes in contact with the quicksilver, by which it is taken up. The whole is then conveyed to the settlers—another series of tubs in which the water settles, and from which the metal is drawn in the form of amalgam. This is afterward subjected to heat, volatilizing the quicksilver, which is afterward condensed for use again by means of cold-water pipes, leaving the silver in a pure metallic state, to be melted into bars and shipped for coinage."

Copper ores are somewhat more simply smelted. They are of a sulphurous composition, and must be roasted before the metal contents are put in marketable shape. They are either desulphurized by "heat roasting," or by being run through "reverberatory furnaces." After this initial treatment, the ore, previously crushed and rolled to the fineness of sand, is dumped into the matting furnaces, whence, so far as possible, the worthless ingredients are reduced to a molten state to separate them from the metal base. The metal is then drawn off into sand cavities, similar to the drawing off of pig-iron, where the metal cools and becomes copper matte. This matte usually assays from 55 to 65 per cent. of copper, besides the silver it contains. Silver-copper matte is a desirable matte. The Parrott Company, by an adaptation of the Bessemer converter process, produces a copper matte carrying only two per cent. of impurities. The process is a very interesting one, and probably the cheapest in use in this camp, all things considered. Some of the Butte companies, whose ore carries from 49 to 79 per cent. of copper, ship their product in a crude state—some to Eastern smelters, others to England

and Wales. The high per cent. of copper returns a handsome profit.

Our hotel at Butte was in nearly the centre of the city. Close by ran the main street, with its ever-changing pictures, and from the upper end of which we could look down upon the famous camp. The sight was novel in the extreme. On every hand were tall smoke-stacks pouring forth smoke and flames like miniature volcanoes, and great heaps of mineral refuse were scattered around promiscuously. There was nothing to see but stamp-mills and smelteries, nothing to do but visit them. Mines and mining were the talk of the hour. No one thought of anything else. The very ground seemed honey-combed, and we knew that by day and night an army of men was at work in the dimly lighted " cross-cuts," industriously searching for the treasures nature so long refused to disclose. Rough-looking, pale, worn, and haggard are these miners of Butte. Many of them have lived the greater part of their lives in the horrible chambers that, lined as they are with precious metals, have still no charm for their inmates. Life in the mines is modern slavery. The looks of the men prove this; the wan faces of the children bear painful evidence of the fact.

Above the city proper, on the road to Walkerville, were grouped the cabins of these laborers. Nothing more desolate than their appearance can be imagined. Perched on rocky ledges, crowded into narrow gulches, unpainted, blacked by the smoke, unrelieved by tree or shrub or grass - plot, they bore not even the suggestion of home, but were more like hovels—untidy, neglected, and oppressive to look upon.

There are 340 stamps in operation at Butte, and the amount of ore treated every day amounts to 500 tons, or 15,000 tons per month. Besides the stamp-mills there are seven smelteries, with a capacity of 1250 tons.

A majority of the mines have their own mills and smelteries, equipped with every modern appliance for the rapid and saving reduction of ore, and all are rich producers. Viewing the many properties, acquainted with their figures, one wonders how copper can ever be "cornered," and how long it will be before silver is a drug upon the market.

INDIAN TERRITORY

BETWEEN the broad and fertile acres of Kansas and the broad and only less fertile acres of Texas lies a wild and beautiful region known as the Indian Territory. The imaginary lines which divide it from the neighboring States have been strengthened by national law into strong walls, which, if not actually impassable, have yet proved substantial barriers. Even the inhabitants of the contiguous States have little personal knowledge of the people or the land, beyond a strong hatred of the one, born of an undue lust for the other. The eastern part of this Territory is inhabited by what are called the "five civilized tribes" — the Cherokees, Creeks, Seminoles, Choctaws, and Chickasaws. Each of them lives a life absolutely separate from the rest, with its own peculiarities, its own institutions, and its own national characteristics, for each—let it not be forgotten—each is a nation. But certain things are true of them all. Common circumstances and common needs have wrought upon common traits of race and character to produce like results. The government of each nation is republican, with frequently recurring elections, legislatures, executives, and systems of judiciary. Each nation supports common schools and high-schools, provides charitable institutions, and fosters churches. Whether Choctaw or Cherokee, these Indians carry on large business interests, and live intelligent and valuable lives.

The traveller who leaves St. Louis at night wakes to find himself in the prairie country, strewn thick with villages of the peculiar, unthrifty, huddled appearance of Southwestern hamlets. He has scarcely breakfasted before, on a sudden, he discovers the prairie roll away before him unvexed with hut or herd, and mile after mile the railway strides on through the luxuriant acres, past the fertile bottoms. The mysterious silence and space explain themselves. This is Indian land, and the Cherokee people have as yet found no better use for this northern country than to keep an unoccupied strip between themselves and their white neighbors. When at last a town appears, it is still a Southwestern town, but it is a brick and mortar city, with shops and newspapers and a busy life of its own. It is a considerable tax

on credulity to discover that this town of Vinita is also Indian, and altogether Indian; that its business life is full and active and reaching out widely; that its citizens have private interests in many other regions, and affect the public affairs of two nations, moving sometimes the destinies of an alien and mightier race than their own. Its men and women have their life in books and thought and music, brave men marry fair women, and children play about the streets, whose future holds happiness and prosperity.

This is the most commercial town of this nation, but not its most representative settlement. "Have you seen Tahlequah?" is the instant question asked of him who professes a knowledge of the Indian Territory, and not without reason. Located in the interior of the country, among the mountains, the approach by the all-day ride among the wooded hills, over the grassy uplands, and through the forest glades threaded everywhere with rushing creeks, serves to heighten the effect. Beginning the journey with many miles of illimitable prairie stretching out to vast horizons, and reaching the first definite point at the ford of the Arkansas, where that lordly river is joined by two others only less large, an impression of space and distance and bigness is at once produced, upon which the imagination builds the future of a fairy tale. This effect is increased by hour after hour through great trees in beautiful virgin forests, and from frequent heights by far-reaching prospect of river and wooded hill. Eastern readers will find similar effects of distance in Pennsylvania, but the nearer view, the woods and fields and little creeks, are those of the middle South, of Alabama, or the more fertile portions of eastern North Carolina. To that State also must be compared the wilder scenery of the Chickasaw territory, and to the South belong the lupins and the lilies and the veil of fairy daisies, pink and white, that broider over the whole scene, mingling in a thousand forms the flora of the woods and the prairie, the South and the West. Tahlequah first discovers itself afar off, across one of the most beautiful of these prospects, in a large and somewhat imposing brick building, standing out

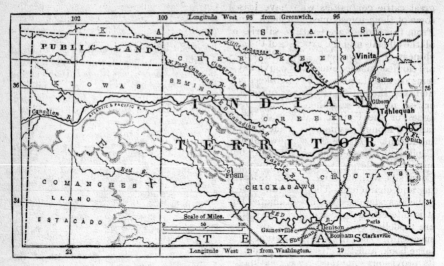

MAP OF INDIAN TERRITORY.

alone upon a swelling height. Unneighbored, and yet requiring a considerable population to fill it, it seems something of a mystery; and when the winding road comes face to face with its simplicity and its size, it proves no less mysterious, although in a different way, since it is a public college for Indian boys and young men. Three miles' further ride, still in the open country, though no longer through an altogether uncultivated region, brings the traveller suddenly into the long main street of a large town. Here sits in serene and self-centred isolation the capital of a nation, containing in itself every element of such a capital except those metropolitan products which belong to crowded centres of the world's life.

In the very middle of Tahlequah is its Capitol, a large brick structure surrounded by an open square filled with locust-trees. The size and relative importance of this building mark the feeling that this is a nation. Here meets a Legislature composed of two Houses, retaining traces of the common Indian and white influence over their origin, in their titles of Council and Senate. The Council is presided over by a Speaker, and the Senate by the Assistant Chief. Bills must pass both Houses, and require the signature of the Executive. This officer possesses much power, and is a man of many titles, since he is actually President, and is better known as Principal Chief, while in common conversation

he is usually addressed as Governor. Under him is an Assistant-Chief answering to our Vice-President, a Secretary of State, a Treasurer, a Superintendent of Public Instruction, and several other officers. All are elected directly by the people, and for terms of four years. These hotly contested elections occur every two years, when half of the Council are chosen, and in August, a month of agricultural vacation, thus marking the chief occupation of the people. All the affairs of the nation—very nearly literally all of them—are debated and settled by this Legislature. The establishment and support of schools, questions of finance, permissions or licenses to railways or telegraphs, the admission of religious teachers to the privileges of the nation—all these matters are decided as of old in council; but neither the hereditary right of Indian custom on the one hand, nor the Anglo-Saxon condition of age on the other, admits to this body. Every lad among the Cherokees may vote and be voted for. In the Capitol are the various offices of the President, the Treasurer, and the other officers of state, and here they spend busy days, for it is no trifling matter to administer the affairs of this little nation of 25,000 souls. If it be little, it is also rich: $95,000 come every year into the hands of its Treasurer in good drafts of the United States, interest on the funds held by us in trust for these Indians, and as much more from the great cattle companies who have leased some of their unoccupied northern land. From this money are paid the salaries of all the officials and the expenses of the machinery of government, the public works are carried on, the school and convict systems are maintained. The Cherokees pay no taxes, the nation is so rich; quite otherwise, for now and then, when a need arises, or the United States rents fresh lands, a money payment is made to each inhabitant. Out of the windows of the Capitol may be seen the less imposing but spacious building where the Supreme Court sits, with its three judges, of learning and character. The particulars of a judicial system are seldom dramatic, but it is interesting to learn that the courts are modelled on our own, and are very successful. The laws of this nation fill a large book, and the strictness of some of its provisions—notably those relating to intoxication—would make a Puritan envious. The code in general would do credit to any community, and its laws are well enforced by mounted police—a body of men so much honored that positions in its ranks are greatly coveted; and if crime is somewhat too frequent in this region, it must not be forgotten that the nation is burdened with a class of most disreputable white men, entirely exempt from its own law, and difficult to reach by any other. If its convict system is not as elaborate as that of Crofton or Elmira, it seems to be effectual in its results, since its convicts may be seen making its roads, under a slight guard, or, wholly unguarded, doing the janitor's work in its Capitol. A well-appointed asylum holds the indigent blind and other unfortunates of various kinds. The notable fact is remarked in Tahlequah that a crazy man may actually be seen there by the curious.

It has been already mentioned that the state maintains a school system. This includes small local schools all over the nation, and the two highest institutions at the capital, known to its inhabitants as the male and female seminaries. It is not a part of this survey to describe the various and flourishing missions which are to be found all over the Territory, with large and important schools and churches, varying in size and favor according to the denomination caring for them, but any candid historian cannot leave them out of account in determining either causes or results of this civilization.

Our present purpose, however, is with the national life, and that pays much attention to education. These two seminaries were originally counterparts of each other, but in March, 1887, the building used for the girls was destroyed by fire. It is already nearly if not quite restored, according to modern ideas of convenience, at a cost to the nation of many thousands of dollars. These two schools are located three miles from the town and three miles apart, yet it is said that hollow trees grow midway here as well as elsewhere, and that divided lads and lassies find ways to meet even in this far-away land. Indian hearts are the hearts of men, and Indian eyes are the eyes of fair maids. Looking off over the fields, the visitor to the girls' seminary is shown the spot where was buried Samuel Wooster, its founder and first head, the man who suggested much which other men wise in state-craft worked out. It is not often given to a nation to rise up complete in fifty years, and this school, educating and training mothers, has had much to do with what we see. Here Indian girls learn Latin, literature, mathematics, the sciences, mental and moral philosophy, rhetoric, and the various lesser branches usually supposed to lead up to these scholastic heights. The catalogue gives curious evidence that this is a strange land. We find pupils from "Seguoyah," and "Cooweescoowee," and "Going Snake," but the girls who answer to the least civilized names are very likely to bear no other resemblance to their red forefathers.

The teachers are largely of Indian descent, many of them alumnæ of this very school, but one who listens to recitations on the familiar problems in ethics, or reads the familiar regulation, "Pupils must bring their own bedding and towels," finds it hard to realize that this is an establishment of an Indian tribe. The first class graduated more than forty years ago, and to-day nearly two hundred Indian girls gather here for instruction. In the Male Seminary nearly as many boys are drilled daily in practice at arms, and study a somewhat more elaborate curriculum. Greek as well as Latin is taught here, and a wider range of science, while trigonometry and surveying are made much of. "Discipline can add nothing to the mental or moral capacities," says the catalogue of this Cherokee school, "but can bring them under such a process of training as to develop the latent energies of mind and body, and direct them to a course of right action, so that the future citizen and lawgiver may be fitted for his great work." To this end, doubtless, the national legislature has passed a statute law forbidding the use of intoxicating liquors and gambling. A law of the commonwealth as an enforcer of the faculty is a suggestion that some Eastern colleges might like to borrow! In one sort of school or another, three-quarters of the children are taught, some of the district schools containing more than seventy - five scholars. In these the young Cherokees learn geography, grammar, spelling, arithmetic, and history, and their teachers frequently meet in institutes and conventions to compare methods. All are free schools, except the two seminaries, which charge a moderate tuition. When any pupil is unable to pay this, however, he is taught, and even clothed, out of the national treasury. A student proving himself more than usually apt at letters, after going through their own schools, if anxious for further education, is often sent to some college at the East, and that at the expense of the nation, for this little people has the strange idea that a good citizen is of value to the state, and that it can well afford to produce such a result at some public cost. Other students go on with their education at their own cost, and the aristocracy among this people knows much of cities and schools in the United States—*of foreign ways*, in their patriotic colloquialism.

Up and down the streets of Tahlequah walks a population industrious and well-to-do, busy about the daily affairs of shop and farm and school and state. Its outward aspect and many of its habits are those of the Southwest, to which it belongs by choice as well as by situation, while even its deficiencies are to a great extent those of the surrounding States. Its women, dressed in the fashions and perhaps the goods of the metropolitan market, sit down in their elaborately decorated parlors, or in their more humble homes, to discuss the food and clothes of the nursery, or the last magazine, or the gossip of the town, according to their tastes and habits, much as do their sisters across the border. Their fathers and husbands are occupied as are their kind in any centre of a farming district which is

also the legal and legislative centre. According to the testimony given in 1885 to a committee of the United States Senate, the 5000 men of this nation were 3500 of them farmers, not 200 of them professional men, 133 were mechanics, and—in an Indian tribe it must be remembered—only 23 were hunters and fishermen. Their flocks and herds numbered 67,000 cattle, 123,000 hogs and sheep, and 136,000 horses;* 89,000 acres were under cultivation, and 100,000 enclosed. The 6000 families lived in 5000 dwellings, and the 3600 farmers owned more than 4000 farms. They had no taxes to pay—except, indeed, the few merchants—there was no currency to depreciate, for there was no scrip, and all payments were in cash. There was no public debt, but, on the other hand, a public revenue; and from that fairy purse came all the public expenses, divided 50 per cent. for the expenses of government itself, 35 per cent. for the national schools, and 15 per cent. for the support of the asylums.

All this elaborate life goes on among a people only half of whom speak English, and presenting the problem of a nation divided into two sharply opposed classes—the highly civilized class of the towns; and the peasant farmers of the open country, or "natives," as it is the fashion to call them, in amusing disregard of a common origin. The dweller in the town, whose life has been described, has usually, but not always, a large admixture of white blood in his ancestry; the other is likely to be a "full-blood" Indian. He lives in a cabin on his farm, in entire comfort, though certainly not in luxury. He cultivates his ground himself, or rents it, sends his children—since he must—to the nearest school, eats, drinks, sleeps, and wakes to live the same round. He knows no ambitions and no progress. He retains many of the Indian habits, is usually dirty, and often ignorant. The laws of his nation furnish him a home, a little work furnishes him clothes and food, such learning as he has he receives for nothing, his land is at his disposal forever, and he knows no further wants. Law is the only uncertain fact in his life, and his chief interest in that is to see that it does not change. To prevent any such untoward happening he arouses

* These figures were based on the census of 1880, and it was stated that the number of cattle had trebled since that time.

himself to take part, and an active part, in the elections, and it is not improbable that he tries his hand at law-making for himself; for another curious fact about this curious population is that no distinction of governing class and governed can be made between the Cherokee of the town and the Cherokee of the field. The full-blood is always present in the national Legislature, the Council being usually almost entirely of that complexion, and it is invariably an obstructive element in all effort for closer contact with the white man's civilization. It may be objected that this is too sweeping a condemnation of the full-bloods, and indeed there are notable exceptions—individuals full of the strength and power and character of the best of the race, though living remote from the towns and speaking no English; but unhappily they do not represent the mass of their fellows.

To the student of land problems the Cherokee land title is a most interesting feature of their life, and the inferences to be drawn from its workings are many and valuable. The Cherokee is usually known as a communist, and in some sense of the word this is true; in some prominent particulars it is not true; but the peculiar situation is such that what he lacks in legal communism he makes up through other circumstances. In so far as the ideal of the communist will be realized when every man lives on his own land, and finds his wants as a member of the community supplied by the central government—in so far as this is the communistic ideal, the Cherokee presents to-day an illustration of national land-holding.

On the first day of August, 1838, the Cherokee tribe, assembled in camp at Oquohee, Indian Territory, began their proceedings with this somewhat grandiloquent claim:

"Whereas the title of the Cherokee people to their lands is the most ancient and absolute known to man, its date is beyond the recall of human record, its validity confirmed and illustrated by possession and enjoyment antecedent to all pretence of claim by any other portion of the human race."

On this basis the remarkable men assembled in this Council proceeded to form the wonderful constitution under which the tribe has lived and prospered so signally, and from which were copied in a measure the constitutions of the other nations. Probably influenced by the Indian idea of property in land—the idea of socialism—they held that the land belonged to the Cherokee tribe, and not to the individuals thereof. Land, says the Indian, like his communistic brother, is as air and water, the property of all; it cannot be given away to the few. Pursuing this theory, the Cherokee constitution secured the nationalization of land in the Cherokee state in these words:

"The land of the Cherokee nation shall remain the common property, but the improvements made thereon and in the possession of the citizens of the nation are the exclusive and indefeasible property of the citizens respectively who made and may be rightfully in possession thereof."

These improvements therefore descend to the heirs of the citizen, or they may be sold by him, but the land, occupy it as long as he will, can never be his. He may occupy as much land as he can cultivate, provided he does not come within one-quarter of a mile of his neighbor. This prohibition does not, of course, refer to the towns. He must establish a claim to this land by proving it to be unoccupied, and at the proper distance from his neighbor, and when he shall have fenced it, or put upon it fifty dollars' worth of improvements, he has the right to occupy as long as he chooses; but if he fails to so occupy it for two years, it reverts to the nation again. There is absolutely no limit to the amount he may thus use if he can cultivate it; but if he wishes to possess himself of two different farms, they must be the required quarter of a mile apart. To be sure that speculation does not interfere with the common right of all to her land, the Cherokee nation through her Legislature has laid certain restrictions upon her people. The valuable black-walnut and pecan timber belongs to the nation; the individual may neither cut it nor sell it. The possible mines of her rocky hills may not be opened, for an old statute makes the discovery of a mine punishable with death. The remembrance of their cruel ejectment from their rich mineral lands in Georgia is thus curiously embalmed in the law. And while there is no limit to the amount which a citizen may cultivate, he can take up for pasturage but fifty acres, thus effectually preventing the absorption of the land by great grazing firms. Thus the Cherokee has his land held for him forever by his state. He may sell his improvements, and he and his family may practically reside in the same place permanently, since the right of occupancy may be devised. This right may also be sold. But the individualizing of the land that would seem to be thus brought about is neutralized by the vast tracts of rich unoccupied territory waiting the industrious hand. How thoroughly this plan has worked as its sanguine modern advocates would have us believe it always will work, is shown by the exact correspondence between the number of male inhabitants and the number of dwellings (5000 each), and the nearly similar number of farmers and farms—3500 farmers on 4000 farms. Moreover, the right of a woman to the land is the same as that of a man; and her husband, although not a Cherokee nor even an Indian, may acquire her rights by marriage, and be adopted into the tribe. This is the only door for alien proprietorship, and "Cherokee rights," joined to the pretty faces gained from a mixed Indian and white ancestry, have proved a strong attraction to many a wanderer, and a heritage of joy or sorrow, as it might be, to many an Indian woman.

What has been said in detail of the Cherokees is true to some extent of the other four nations. There is the same mixed population of town and country dweller, with the same characteristics of enterprise and obstruction. The northernmost of these tribes, a small fragment of the Creeks, who have come most into contact with the white men of the border, have suffered rather than gained in the encounter. The *morale* of the people is lower, although their civilization is more complex. The body of this tribe, however, is in the interior. Their government has many features like that of the Cherokees, with some difference in the number of judges, the length of terms of office, and such minor points. The Indian glamour seems to still cover a people ruled by a House of Warriors and a House of Kings; but the more prosaic virtues are added thereunto in the boast under oath that they have no paupers, no insane, that every family in the nation has a home, that $40,000 is spent each year for schools, of which there are four hundred common schools, with five of a higher grade. Corn, cotton, and oats are raised, and the Creeks have some manufactures. The little tribe of Seminoles is perhaps the most nearly pure

democracy we have on the continent. Its Council, composed of three members from each town, votes directly on the ratification of all its laws by a standing vote. A democratic Assembly drafts these laws and submits them to this hardly less democratic Council. Here the commune has but one restriction, and that a right of occupancy, and the little population has no less care taken of it than its larger neighbors, for here also are day schools and boarding-schools, and here the *blacksmiths* are paid by the government. The laws of this nation are Spartan in their character. The murderer is "killed," as they succinctly put it, and the thief is whipped three times for as many offences, but the fourth time he is "killed" also.

The Chickasaws live in the magnificent hill country on the borders of Texas, and have been retarded rather than helped by contact with their border neighbors. Their government is much like the others, and here is again the curious division of feeling and action between the full-bloods and the half-breeds. Their capabilities are great, and there is the intense pride in their nation and its privileges and successes found in the others. This pride of race is no small element of character in all the five tribes. It is most extreme, and it suits well the handsome Spanish-looking men. It was a Chickasaw governor who refused to meet a committee of the United States Senate outside his own nation. Other governors had been visited among their people, and with a certain fine sense of what was due his position, he would not sacrifice national dignity to convenience. The Choctaws also live on the borders of Texas, but in this case to the advantage rather than the detriment of the people. The student of aboriginal races will find it an interesting problem why the close contact in blood and life with white civilization has told for good among the Cherokees and Choctaws, and, except in isolated instances, far otherwise among the Creeks and Chickasaws. The constitution of the Choctaw nation is somewhat more elaborate than the others. We have here a veto power, requiring a two-thirds vote to override it; one of the requirements for office is a belief in a future state; third-term difficulties are effectually prevented by a provision that no Principal Chief shall hold his office more than four years out of six, the term being two years. The judicial system works so smoothly that thirty-eight cases out of forty are convicted; and it is the custom to release a murderer after his conviction until the time of his execution arrives, when he always returns of his own accord to suffer the extreme penalty. Land tenure is the same as with the Cherokees, except that it must yield an *annual* income; and the school system, with its appendix of Eastern colleges, is equally elaborate. With an income from government bonds of $62,000, and of $50,000 from the leases of mines already opened in its incalculable deposits of coal, copper, iron, and lead, it is little wonder that the Choctaws can see nothing better for them in the civilization and government of the States around them.

The tremendous pressure for the unoccupied lands possessed by all these nations has led the border States to a hope of forcible possession by the government at Washington; or, failing of this, of a federation of these nations into a single Indian State, thus opening up the agricultural and mineral treasures of this almost unknown region. The first hope is not altogether without warrant even in high places, unjust and legally impossible as it would be. Much local jealousy among the different tribes somewhat hinders the latter plan, but a greater obstacle is the natural fear of white influence and action. What security have these favored and perfectly satisfied commonwealths that any of their possessions and privileges would remain to them in the face of the white man's greed? At present they are held by patents as definite and distinct as legal phrasing can make them, and protected by carefully kept up barriers of bad roads and unoccupied country. But once make this land a possible home of possible Oklahoma associations, and what would become of land title or Indian law? Perhaps the Mission Indians of California could answer. Already the Missouri, Kansas, and Texas Railway, which runs through the eastern part of the Territory from north to south, has a grant of a tract of land ten miles wide on each side of its track (60,000,000 acres in all), all the way from Kansas to Texas. This grant becomes operative the day that "the Indian title is extinguished." Is it any wonder that the dwellers along its route are not eager to have the land thrown open?

What may be in the future for these remarkable peoples it is not quite easy to say, but meanwhile what they have already accomplished has a direct bearing upon two different questions. We see in their history and achievement the key to the Indian problem. Education, religion, a good system of law and government, self-help and self-responsibility, an understanding of their relations to the world at large — these things have made the Cherokees and their sister nations what we find them. And in passing it may be remarked that the men who taught them these things lived among them and made themselves of them. To be thrown out among white men is *not* absolutely necessary to the Indian: witness the difference between the border nations and those of the interior. It may be better that the red man should work out his problem by himself. His ability to do it, and the progress he will make under favorable circumstances, are proved by the five civilized tribes. The large unprogressive element, with its laziness and dirt, is no argument against this conclusion. Nor is the admixture of white blood the only enterprising quality in these nations, as is sometimes somewhat superficially charged. Where education and religion and responsibility have joined hands, their pupil has been raised to the extent of his possibility, be he white or red; and when these have been wanting, the white blood has only added crime to stupidity. It is in this last element—the presence or absence of responsibility—that much of the secret lies. The Indian who finds all his wants supplied through no act of his own, regards neither education nor progress as any factor in his scheme of existence. But in him who finds himself pressed with multiplied necessities constant effort is required, and development is forced upon him.

And here we have the other answer that the Indian Territory gives to the student—the answer to certain questions of land tenure. You have here the national ownership of land in favorable conditions. A young nation, under most fortunately strong and able leadership, isolated from contaminating influence, in a country neither too warm nor too cold for productive labor, with a fine system of laws and government, and a good measure of civilization already achieved at the beginning and since developed. The land is held by the nation from the first, and there is more than enough. If it is true that it can be in a sense transferred, this is not absolutely true, and the fact that there is such an abundance of it prevents any disturbance of the scheme by this fact. And on the other hand a national revenue, sufficient and inalienable, does away with the usual necessity of taxing the land by providing for all the requirements of popular need. The most ardent communist could hardly want more than this: land held perpetually for him, as much as he desires, and every public want supplied. What is the result? Half the nation sits down content to eat and drink, a great unprogressive animal class, a weight upon the community, failing of every end of civilization or any comprehension of its advantages. Those others who have discovered for themselves individual wants, and who have learned to supply them each man for himself, have found the meaning of progress and civilization. They have

done away with the much-talked-of equality, and practically, if not ostensibly, achieved the destruction of the communistic scheme. They, and they alone, have developed anything further than the brute beast. And if as a people they have lost in the process something of simplicity and strength, a glance at the two halves of the nation will answer the question of the value of the experiment. Land, and the wisest provisions of law, and elaborate schemes of ready-made well-being furnished by the government, will not bring real welfare. The proletariat might eat and drink and sleep, perhaps, if they could realize their present dream, but life would hardly be what they imagine. No better than the beasts that perish, they might well question if it were worth the living. Not because its people are Indians, but because of their communism, is civilization but a partial success—a sort of half-baked loaf—in the Indian Territory.

CHICAGO'S GENTLE SIDE

WHEN I wrote my first paper upon Chicago, I supposed myself well equipped for the task. I saw Chicago day after day, lived in its hotels and clubs, met its leading business men and officials, and got a great deal which was novel and striking from what I saw around me, and from what I heard of the commercial and other secrets of its marvellous growth and sudden importance. It is customary to ridicule the travellers who found books upon short visits to foreign places, but the ridicule is not always deserved. If the writers are travelled and observant spectators, if they ask the right questions of the right men, and if they set down nothing of which they are not certain, the probability is that what they write will be more valuable in its way than a similar work from the pen of one who is dulled to the place by familiarity. And yet I know now that my notes upon Chicago only went half-way. They took no heed of a moiety of the population, the women, with all that they stand for.

I saw the rushing trains of cable-cars in the streets and heard the clang-clang of their gongs. It seemed to me then (and so it still seems, after many another stay in the city) that the men in the streets leap to the strokes of those bells; there is no escaping their sharp din; it sounds incessantly in the men's ears. It seems to jog them, to keep them rushing along, like a sort of Western conscience, or as if it were a goad, or the perpetual prod of a bayonet. It is as if it might be the voice of the Genius of the West crying, "Clang-clang (hustle)!—clang-clang (be lively)!" And it needs no wizard sight to note the effect upon the men as they are kept up to their daily scramble, and forge along the thoroughfares—more often talking to themselves when you pass them than you have ever noticed that men in other cities are given to do. I saw all that; but how stupid it was not to notice that the women escaped the relentless influence!

They appear not to hear the bells. The lines of the masculine straining are not furrowed in their faces. They remain composed and unmoved. They might be the very same women we see in Havana or Brooklyn, so perfectly undisturbed and at ease are they—even when they pass the Board of Trade, which I take to be the dynamo that surcharges the air for the men.

I went into the towering office buildings, nerving myself for the moment's battle at the doors against the outpouring torrent and the missilelike office-boys, who shoot out as from the mouths of cannon. I saw the flying elevators, and at every landing heard the bankers and architects and lawyers shout "Down!" or "Up, up!" and saw them spring almost out of their clothes, as if each elevator was the only one ever built, and would make only one trip before it vanished like a bubble. The office-girls were as badly stricken with this *St. Vitus hustle* as the men, which must account for my not noticing that the main body of women, when they came to these buildings to visit husbands or brothers, were creatures apart from the confusion—reposeful, stylish, carefully toileted, serene, and unruffled.

I often squeezed into the luncheon crowd at the Union League Club, and got the latest wheat quotation with my roast, and the valuation of North Side lots with my dessert; but I did not then know that there was a ladies' side entrance to the club-house, leading to parlors and dining-rooms as quiet as any in Philadelphia, where impassive maids in starched caps sat like bits of majolica-ware, and the clang-clang of the car bells sounded faintly, like the antipodean echoes in a Japanese sea-shell. I smoked at the Chicago Club with Mayor Washburne, and the softening influence of women in public affairs happened not to come into our talk; with Mr. Burnham, the leading architect, and heard nothing of the buildings put up for and by women. Far less was there any hint, in the crush at that club, of the Argonauts—those leisurely Chicago Club men who haunt a separate house where they loaf in flannels, and the women add the luxurious, tremulous shiver of silk to the sounds of light laughter and elegant dining.

And every evening, while that first study of the city went on, the diurnal stampede from the tall buildings and the choking of the inadequate streets around them took place. The cable-cars became loaded and incrusted with double burdens, in which men clung to one another like caterpillars. Thus the crowded business district was emptied and the homes were filled. Any one could see that, and I wrote that there were more home-going and home-staying there than in any large Eastern city in this country. But who could guess what that meant? Who could know the extent of the rulership of the women at night and in the homes, or how far it went beyond those limitations? Who would dream that—in Chicago, of all places—all talk of business is tabooed in the homes, and that the men sink upon thick upholstering, in the soft shaded light of silk-crowned lamps, amid lace-work and bric-à-brac, and in the blessed atmosphere of music and gentle voices—all so soothing and so highly esteemed that it is there the custom for the men to gather accredited strangers and guests around them at home for the enjoyment of dinner, cigars, and cards, rather than at the clubs and in the hotel lobbies? I could not know it, and so, for one reason and another, the gentle side of Chicago was left out of that article.

"Great as Chicago is, the period of her true greatness is yet to come," writes Mr. James Dredge, the editor of London *Engineering*, and one of the British commissioners to our Columbian Exposition. "Its commencement will dawn when her inhabitants give themselves time to realize that the object of life is not that of incessant struggle; that the race is not always to the swift, but rather to those who understand the luxury and advantage of repose, as well as sustained effort." In whichever of our cities an Englishman stays long enough to venture an opinion of it, that is what he is sure to say. It is true of all of them, and most true of Chicago. But to discover that there is a well-spring of repose there requires a longer acquaintance than to note the need of it. There is such a reservoir in Chicago. It is in the spirit of the women, and it is as notable a feature of Chicago homes as of those of any American city. But the women contribute more than this, for from the polish of travel and trained minds their leaders reflect those charms which find expression in good taste and manners, a love of art and literature, and in the ability to discern what is best, and to distinguish merit and good-breeding above mere wealth and pedigree.

What the leaders do the others copy, and the result is such that I do not believe that in any older American city we shall find fashionable women so anxious to be considered patrons of art and of learning, or so forward in works of public improvement and governmental reform as well as of charity. Indeed, this seems to me quite a new character for the woman of fashion, and whether I am right in crediting her with it the reader will discover before he finishes this paper. It is necessary to add that not all the modish women there belong in this category. There is a wholly gay and idle butterfly set in Chicago, but it is small, and the distinctive peculiarity of which I speak lies in the fact that in nearly all the societies and movements of which I am going to write we see the names of rich and stylish women. They entertain elegantly, are accustomed to travel, and rank with any others in the town, yet are associated with those forceful women whose astonishing activity has worked wonders in that city. The Chicago woman whose name is farthest known is Mrs. Potter Palmer. She is the wife of a man who is there not altogether improperly likened, in his relation to that city, to one of our Astors in New York. Yet she is at the head of the Woman's Department or Commission of the exposition, and is active in perhaps a score of women's organizations of widely differing aims. Her name, therefore, may stand as illustrating what has been here said upon this subject.

There is no gainsaying the fact that, in the main, Chicago society is crude; but I am not describing the body of its people; it is rather that reservoir from which are to spring the refinement and graces of the finished city that is here to be considered. If it is true that hospitality is a relic of barbarism, it still must be said that it flourishes in Chicago, which is almost as open-armed as one of our Southern cities. As far as the men are concerned, the hospitality is Russian; indeed, I was again and again reminded of what I have read of the peculiarities of the Russians in what I saw of the pleasures of the younger generation of wealthy men in Chicago. They attend to business with all their hearts by day, and to fun with all their might after dark. They are mainly college men and fellows of big physique, and if ever there were hearty, kindly, jolly, frank fellows in the world, these are the ones. They eat and drink like Russians, and from their fondness for surrounding themselves with bright and elegant women, I gather that they love like Russians. In like manner do they spend their money. In New York heavy drinking in the clubs is going out of fashion, and there is less and less high play at cards; but in Chicago, as in St. Petersburg, the wine flows freely, the stakes are high. Though the pressure is thus greater than with us in New York, I saw no such effects of the use of stimulants as would follow Chicago freedom were it indulged in the metropolis.

But enough of what is exceptional and unrepresentative. The Chicago men are very proud of the women, and the most extravagant comments which Max O'Rell makes upon the prerogatives of American ladies seem very much less extravagant in Chicago than anywhere else. Their husbands and brothers tell me that there is a keen rivalry among the women who are well-to-do for the possession of nice houses, and for the distinction of giving good and frequent dinner parties, and of entertaining well. "They spend a great deal of money in this way," I was told; "but they are not mercenary; they do not worship wealth, and nag their husbands to get more and more, as do the

women of the newer West. Their first question about a new-comer is neither as to his wealth nor his ancestry. Even more than in Washington do the Chicago women respect talent, and vie with one another to honor those who have any standing in the World of Intellect." In the last ten years the leading circles of women there have undergone a revolution. Women from the female colleges, and who have lived abroad or in the Eastern cities, have displaced the earlier leaders, have married and become the mistresses of the homes, as well as the mothers of daughters for whose future social standing they are solicitous.

The noted men and women who have visited Chicago, professionally or from curiosity, in recent years, have found there the atmosphere of a true capital. They have been welcomed and honored in delightful circles of cultivated persons assembled in houses where are felt the intangible qualities that make charming the dwellings of true citizens of the world. For costliness and beauty the numerous fine residences of Chicago are celebrated. Nowhere is there seen a greater variety in the display of cultivated taste in building. All over Christendom fine houses are put up in homage to women, and we shall see, if I mistake not, that these Chicago women deserve the palaces in which they rule. But, to return to the interiors of the homes, what I find to praise most highly there is the democracy of the men and women. It is genuine. The people's hearts are nearer their waistcoats and bodices out there. They aren't incrusted with the sediment of a century of caste-worship and pride and distrust. They are genuine and natural and frank.

I have seen a thing in Chicago—and have seen it several more times than once—that I never heard of anywhere else, and that looked a little awkward at first, for a few moments. I refer to a peculiar freedom of intercourse between the sexes after a dinner or on a rout—*camaraderie* and perfect accord between the men and the women. In saying this I refer to very nice matrons and maidens in very nice social circles who have nevertheless staid after the coffee, and have taken part in the flow of fun which such a time begets, quite as if they liked it and had a right to. In one case the men had withdrawn to the library, and a noted entertainer was in the full glory of his career, reciting a poem or giving a dialect imitation of a conversation he had overheard on a street car. The wife of the host trespassed, with a little show of timidity, to say that the little girls, her daughters, were about to go to bed, and wanted the noted entertainer to "make a face" for them—apparently for them to dream upon.

"Why, come in," said the host.

"Oh, may we?" said the wife, very artlessly, and in came all the ladies of the party, who, it seems, had gathered in the hallway. The room was blue with smoke, but all the ladies "loved smoke," and so the evening wore on gayly.

The next occasion was in a mansion on the lake-side. An artist and a poet, well known in both hemispheres, were the especial guests, and the company generally would have been welcome in the best circles in any of the world's capitals, except, possibly, in New York, where it is said that an ultra swell personage told the Lord Chief Justice of England that he had met no explorers, historians, poets, scholars, generals, or naval heroes, "because none of them is in society." Of the ladies one was literary, one was a philanthropist and reformer, and the others were just wives, but wives of the brilliant fellows, and all able to coach the men and to tell queer little bits of their own experiences. When the coffee was brought on, on this occasion, there was no movement on the part of the women towards leaving the table. No suggestion was made that they do so; there was no apology offered for their not doing so; the subject was not mentioned. There were glasses of "green mint" for all, and cigars for the men. Then the stories flowed and the laughter bubbled. The queer thing was that there was no apparent strain; all were at perfect ease—the ladies being as much so as other men would have been without them. One of the women told two long stories of a comical character, imitating the dialect and mannerisms of different persons precisely as a man given to after-dinner entertaining would have done. Once there was a pause and a little hesitation, and a story-teller said, "I think I can tell this here, can't I?" "Why, of course, go on," said his wife. So he told whatever it was, the point being so pretty and sentimental that it was a little difficult to determine why he had hesitated, unless it was that it had "a big, big D" in one sentence.

I have been present on at least a dozen occasions when the men smoked and drank and the women kept with them, being—otherwise than in the drinking and smoking—in perfect fellowship with them. Such conditions are Arcadian. They are part and parcel of the kinship that permits the Chicagoans to bring their rugs out and to sit on the stoops in the evenings.

Their stylishness is the first striking characteristic of the women of Chicago. It is a Parisian quality, apparent in New York first and in Chicago next, among all our cities. The number of women who dress well in Chicago is very remarkable, and only there and in New York do the shop-girls and working-women closely follow the prevailing modes. Chicago leads New York in the employment of women in business. It is not easy to find an office or a store in which they are not at work as secretaries, accountants, cashiers, type-writers, saleswomen, or clerks. It has been explained to me that women who want to do for themselves are more favored there than anywhere else. The awful fire of twenty years ago wrecked so many families, and turned so many women from lives of comfort to paths of toil, that the business men have from that day to this shown an inclination to help every woman who wants to help herself.

The influence of the homes is felt everywhere. It is even more truly a city of homes than Brooklyn, for its flats and tenements are comparatively few. Such makeshifts are not true homes, and do not carry household pride with them in anything like the degree that it is engendered in those who live in separate houses which they own.

One of the famous towering office buildings of Chicago is, in the main, the result of a woman's financiering. I refer to "the Temple" of the Woman's Christian Temperance Union, an enormous and beautiful pile, which is, in a general way, like the great Mills Building in Broad Street, New York. It is thirteen stories high, it cost more than a million of dollars, and the scheme of it, as well as the execution thereof, from first to last, was the work of women and children. Mrs. Matilda B. Carse, who is grandiloquently spoken of in the Chicago newspapers as "the chief business woman of the continent," inspired and planned the raising of the money. For ten years she advocated the great work, and in the course of that time she formed a corporation, called "The Woman's Temple Building Association," for carrying forward the project. She was elected its first president, in July, 1887, and it was capitalized at $600,000. Frances Willard, of the National organization of the Union, cooperated towards enlisting the interest and aid of the entire Temperance Union sisterhood, which adopted the building as its headquarters or "Temple." Four hundred thousand dollars' worth of the stock was purchased with what is referred to as "the outpouring of 100,000 penny banks," and bonds were issued for $600,-000. The building is expected to yield $250,000 a year in rentals. The income is to be divided, one-half to the National organization, and the rest *pro rata* to the various State organizations, according to the amount each subscribed to the fund. Mrs. Carse's was the mind which planned the financial operation, but the credit of carrying it out rests with Miss Willard, the several other leaders of the Union, and the good women everywhere who have faith in them.

Mrs. Carse is the woman to whom the members of the Chicago Woman's Club refer all plans for raising funds. The Chicago Woman's Club is the mother of woman's public work in that city. An explanation of what that means seems to me to rank among the most surprising of the chapters which I have had occasion to write as the result of my Western studies. I know of no such undertakings or cooperation by women elsewhere in our country. This very remarkable Woman's Club has five hundred members and six great divisions, called the committees on Reform, Philanthropy, Education, Home, Art and Literature, Science and Philosophy. The club has rooms in the building of the famous Art Institute. It holds literary meetings every two weeks, each committee or division furnishing two topics in a year. The members write the papers and the meetings discuss them. Each committee officers and manages its own meetings, the chairwoman of the committee being in charge, and opening as well as arranging the discussions. The Art and Literature and the Science and Philosophy committees carry on classes, open to all members of the club. They

engage lecturers, and perform an educational work. Apart from these class meetings, the club rooms are in use every day as a headquarters for women. They include a kitchen, a dining-room, and a tea-room — tea, by-the-way, being served at all the committee meetings.

The membership is made up of almost every kind of women, from the ultra-fashionable society leaders to the working-women, and includes literary and other professional women, business women, and plain wives and daughters. "And," say the members, "women who never hear anything anywhere else, hear everything that is going on in the world by attending the club meetings." It is impossible to name all the women who are conspicuous in the club. Of the fashionable women, such ones as Mrs. Potter Palmer, Mrs. Dunlap, a brilliant society leader, and Mrs. Charles Henrotin are active members. Frances Willard, the head of the Temperance Union, is a member, and so is Mrs. Carse. She is a wealthy woman also, as well as one of great force of mind. Mrs. Caroline K. Sherman, a writer widely known for her energetic pursuit of philosophical studies, is active in the Science and Philosophy classes. Mrs. George E. Adams, wife of the member of Congress of that name from Illinois, is a social ruler, and yet is very active in the hard work the club undertakes. She helped raise the University Fund, of which I shall speak. A very active personage, not of the fashionable class, is Miss Ada C. Sweet, who was disbursing officer at Chicago for the Pension Bureau under four Presidents, and paid out something more than a million of dollars a year. She devotes her right hand to the defence of her sex, and her left hand to her own support. Of other leaders on the gentle side of that robust city there will be mention as their works here are considered. So far as any one can see, the wealthy and fashionable women are as active as any others. Those who are referred to as representative of the riches and refinement of the town not only have given of their wealth, but of their sympathy and time in the various movements I am about to describe.

Each woman on entering the club designates which division she wishes to enter. Her name is catalogued accordingly, and she works with that committee. Each committee holds periodic meetings, at which subjects are given out for papers and discussion at the next session. The Home Committee, for instance, deals with the education and rearing of children, domestic service, dress reform, decorative art, and kindred subjects. That has always been the method in the club, but a result of that and other influences has been that "Chicago ladies have been papered to death," as one of them said to me, and in the last few years the development of a higher purpose and more practical work has progressed. It began when the Reform Committee undertook earnest work, and ceased merely to hear essays, to discuss prison reform, to go "slumming," and to pursue all the fads that were going. This committee began its earnest work with the County Insane Asylum, where it was found that hundreds of women were herded without proper attention, three in a bed, sometimes; with insufficient food, with only a counterpane between them and the freezing winter air at night, and no flannels by day. The root of the trouble was the old one—the root of all public evil in this country—the appointment of public servants for political reasons and purposes. The first step of the Reform Committee was to ask the county commissioners to appoint a woman physician to the asylum. Dr. Florence Hunt was so appointed, and went there at $25 a month. She found that the nurses made up narcotics by the pailful to give to the patients at night so as to stupefy them, in order that they might themselves be free for a good time. The new doctor stopped that and the giving of all other drugs, except upon her order. Then she insisted upon the employment of fit nurses. She and the women doctors who followed her there suffered much petty persecution, but a complete reform was in time accomplished, and the woman physician became a recognized necessity there. To-day, as a consequence, the asylums at Kankakee, Jackson, and Elgin—all Illinois institutions—have women physicians also. I am assured that no one except a physician can appreciate how great a reform it was to establish the principle that women suffering from mental diseases should be put in charge of women. Mrs. Helen S. Shedd was at the front of the asylum reform work, which is still going on.

She next led the Reform Committee

into the Poor-house, where they went, as they always do, with the plea, "There are women there; we want a share in the charge of that place for the sake of our sex." They have adopted the motto, "What are you doing with the women and children?" and they find that the politicians cannot turn aside so natural and proper an inquiry. The politicians try to frighten the women. They say, "You don't want to pry into such things and places; you can't stand it." But the Chicago ladies have proved that they can stand a very great deal, as we shall see, on behalf of humanity; especially feminine humanity. "You are using great sums of money for the care of the poor, the sick, the insane, and the vicious," they say. "One-half of these are women; and we, as women, insist upon knowing how you are performing your task. We do not believe you bring the motherly or the sisterly element to your aid; we know that you do not understand women's requirements." That line of argument has always proved irresistible.

While I was in Chicago in August some of the women were looking over the plans for four new police stations. It transpired as they talked that they have succeeded in establishing a Woman's Advisory Board of the Police, consisting of ten women appointed by the Chief of Police, and in charge of the quarters of all women and children prisoners, and of the station-house matrons, two of whom are allotted to each station where women are taken. Through the work of her women, Chicago led in this reform, which is now extending to the chief cities of the country. Now, all women and juveniles are separated from the men in nine of the Chicago precinct stations, to one of which every such prisoner must be taken, no matter at what time or on what charge such a person is arrested. The chief matron is Mrs. Jane Logan, a woman who came to Chicago from Toronto and became conspicuous in the Woman's Club and in the Household Art Association. Miss Sweet "coaxed her into the police work," and the Mayor appointed her chief matron. She has an office in a down-town station, where the worst prisoners are taken, as well as the friendless girls and waifs who drift in at the railway stations. The waifs are all taken to her, and she never leaves them until they are on the way back to their homes, or to

CHICAGO'S GENTLE SIDE   433

better guardianship. She maintains an "annex," kept clean and sweet, with homelike beds and pictures, and to this place are taken any first offenders and others of saving whom she thinks there is a chance. Female witnesses are also kept there instead of in the prisoners' cells, and all who go to the annex are entirely secluded from reporters as well as all others. Two of the best matrons of the force are in charge day and night. All women and girl prisoners are attended at court, even the drunken women being washed and dressed and made to look respectable. Mrs. Logan always goes herself with the young girls to see that they are not approached, and in order that, if it is just and advantageous that they should escape punishment, she may plead with the court for their release. Formerly, every woman who was arrested was searched by men, and thrown into a cell in the same jail room with the male prisoners. Lost children, homeless girls, and abandoned women were all huddled together. The women of the city "couldn't stand it," they say. They worked eight years, led by Miss Sweet, to bring about the now accomplished reform.

In all cases in which women complain of abuse or mistreatment by the police or others, Mrs. Logan sits on the Police Trial Board, "to show the unfortunate woman that she has a friend." The Board is composed of five inspectors and the assistant chief of police, and the president asked her to join its sessions whenever a woman is involved in any case that comes before it. The police do not oppose the work of the women. Desperate and abandoned females used to make fearful charges against the patrolmen and others on the force under the old *régime.*

Mrs. Logan is described as beautiful and refined, as gentle and unassuming in the highest degree, as about thirty-five years of age, and as having humanity for her propelling force—almost for her religion. Her work is a prolonged effort of patience, kindness, and justice. Last Christmastime seventy-five girls were arrested for shoplifting. She found one, eighteen years of age, flat on her face on a cell floor. She took her to the annex, away from the sight of prison bars, and got her story from her. It was that she was of a respectable family, and had come to town to work as a stenographer, but could get no employment. Her brother sent money

for her board in a quiet household, but she had little other money, and in time she spent her last cent. She mended her gloves until they were mended all over, and then her stockings gave out. She drifted into a store, saw the profusion of things there, and stole three handkerchiefs, thinking she would sell them. She was caught in the act. As she could not go to trial until morning, Mrs. Logan went to her boarding-house and explained that she was "going to spend the night with friends." Next day, to oblige the chief matron, the court released the girl, and then Mrs. Logan told the police reporters the whole story, and got their promise that they would not publish a word of it. Mrs. Howe, the president of the Advisory Board, sent ten dollars to the girl, and she returned five dollars "for the next girl who needed it." She is nicely situated now, through the efforts of the women. I heard many such stories of Mrs. Logan's work. She is incessantly rushing about, getting passes and money, sending for the ladies of the Advisory Board to go to court or to the station-houses; telegraphing to parents to take back runaway girls and boys; and speaking for those who have no one else to say a kind word for them.

Mrs. R. C. Clowry, wife of the manager of the Western Union Telegraph Office, is a member of the Police Advisory Board; she is also on the Woman's Commission of the World's Fair, and is a music composer of some celebrity. She and Miss Sweet are the representatives of the Woman's Club on the Board. From the Woman's Protective Agency to the Board came Mrs. Fanny Howe, the president of the Board, and Mrs. Flora P. Tobin.

Mrs. Howe is also president of the Protective Agency, one of the most remarkable humanitarian organizations in the city. Its founder, Mrs. J. D. Harvey, is the daughter of Judge Plato, who was distinguished among the early settlers of town; but one of the greatest workers in it, and the person who has done the most towards developing it, is Mrs. Charlotte Cushing Holt. She is tenderly described by her friends as "a very small, short, pretty, doll-like woman, in a Quakerish reform dress"; and it is added that "the amount of work she can do is astounding." She is studying law just now, because she needs that branch of knowledge in order to advise the poor. The Protective Agency protects women and children in all their rights of property and person, gives them legal advice, recovers wages for servants, sewing-women, and shop-girls who are being swindled; finds guardians for defenceless children; procures divorces for women who are abused or neglected; protects the mothers' right to their children. It has obtained heavy sentences against men in cases of outrage—so very heavy that this crime is seldom committed. In a matter akin to this, the women of this society perform what seems to me a most extraordinary work. It is a part of the belief of these ladies that all women have rights, no matter how bad or lost to decency some of them may be. Therefore they stand united against the ancient custom, among criminal lawyers, of destroying a woman's testimony by showing her bad character. This these women call "a many-century-old trick to throw a woman out of court and deny her justice."

As an instance of the manner in which they display their zeal on behalf of the principle that no matter how bad a woman is she should have fair play, there was this state of affairs: Five mistresses of disorderly resorts had brought as many young girls to Mrs. Logan, and had said they wanted them saved. The girls were pure, but had been brought to the houses in question by men who had pretended that they were taking them to restaurants or respectable dwellings. The Agency caused the arrest of the men implicated; and when the first case came up for trial, the Agency sent for fourteen or sixteen married women of fine social position to come to court and sit through the trial to see fair play. When the bagnio-keeper, who was the chief witness against the prisoner, took the stand, she testified that the girl had been told that her house was a restaurant where she was to have supper. Undeceived, she was greatly frightened, and the woman took charge of her. Then the counsel for the defence began to draw out the story of the woman's evil life and habits. He was rebuked from the Bench, and was told that the woman's character for chastity could not affect her testimony, and that when counsel asked such questions of women witnesses the Court would insist that similar questions be put to all male witnesses in each case, with the same intent to destroy the force of their depositions. Thus was established

a new principle in criminal practice. In the other cases prosecuted by the Agency the same array of matrons in silks, laces, and jewels was conspicuous in the court-rooms. The police and court officials are said to have been astonished at this proceeding by women of their standing. But the women have not only gained a step towards perfect justice for their sex, they say that their presence in court has put an end to the ribaldry that was always a feature of trials of the kind. Not far removed from this work has been the successful effort of the women to raise what is called "the age of consent" from twelve to sixteen years.

The Philanthropy Committee of the Woman's Club began its active work in the county jail, where it found a shocking state of affairs. There was only one woman official in the jail, and at four o'clock every afternoon she locked up the women and went away. When she had gone the men were free to go in, and they did. The women of the committee demanded the appointment of a night matron, and the sheriff said he required an order from certain judges who were nominally in charge. This they obtained, and then they were told they must secure from the county an appropriation for the proposed matron's salary. The county officials granted the money conditionally upon the nomination for the place being made by the Woman's Club. The matron was appointed, the work of reform was begun, and it was as if a fresh lake breeze had blown through the unwholesome place. The men cannot intrude upon the women now, and little vagrant girls of ten to fourteen years of age are no longer locked up with hardened criminals. The children have a separate department, where toys and books and a kindly matron brighten their lives while they are awaiting trial. Still another department in the jail is a school for the boys, who are sometimes kept there three or four months before being tried. It was after this work in the jail that the Philanthropy Committee took up the police-station reforms. The first matrons who were put in charge of the stations were political appointees, except a few who were nominally recommended by the Woman's Christian Temperance Union. The whole system was a sham; the matrons had to have political backing; they were not in sympathy with the movement, and were not competent. They were "just poor," and had large families, and merely wanted the money. There are twenty-five satisfactory matrons now.

A few years ago there was a movement among Chicago men for the foundation of an Industrial School for Homeless Boys who were not criminals. The idea was to train the boys and put them out for adoption. The plan languished and was about to be abandoned, when the Woman's Club took hold of it. Mr. George, a farmer, had promised to give three hundred acres of land worth $40,000 if any one would raise $40,000 for the buildings. The Woman's Club rose "as one man," got the money in three months, and turned it over to the men, who then founded the Illinois Manual Training School at Glenwood, near the city. An advisory board of women in the club attends to the raising of money, the provision of clothing, and the exercise of a general motherly interest in the institution, which is exceptionally successful.

This list of gentle reforms and revolutions is but begun. The Education Committee of this indomitable club discovered, a few years since, that the statute providing for compulsory education was not enforced. The ladies got up a tremendous agitation, and many leading men, as well as women, went to the Capitol at Springfield and secured the passage of a mandatory statute insuring the attendance at school of children of from six to fourteen years during a period of sixteen weeks in each year. Five women were appointed among the truant officers, and the law was strictly carried out. It is found that it works well to employ women in this capacity. They are invited into the houses by the mothers, who tell them, as they would not tell men, the true reasons for keeping their children from school, as, for instance, that they have but one pair of shoes for six children. A beautiful charity resulted from this work. There was established in the club an aid society. Mrs. Murray F. Tuley, the wife of Judge Tuley, a woman long identified with free kindergarten work, became very active in establishing this society. She interested all classes, obtained the use of a room in the City Hall, recruited workers from the Church societies, the Woman's Club, and from almost everywhere else, to sew for the children. She got the merchants to

send great rolls of flannels, and shoes and stockings by the hundreds of pairs. These are stored in the room in the City Hall, and when the truant officers discover a case of need they report it, and the Board of Education orders relief granted through the truant agency.

Some members of the Woman's Club are physicians, such as Dr. Sarah Hackett Stevenson, Dr. Julia Holmes Smith, Dr. Mary A. Mixer, Dr. Marie J. Mergler, Dr. Julia Ross Low, Dr. Frances Dickinson, Dr. Elizabeth L. Chapin, Dr. Sarah H. Brayton, Dr. Rose S. Wright Bryan, and Dr. Leila G. Bedell. There are between 200 and 250 women doctors in Chicago, by-the-way, and in the club are two women preachers.

Mrs. Dr. Julia Ross Low came to the club one day with a solemn tale of the need of a hospital for sufferers from contagious diseases. There was none in the city. No hospital would take such cases, and they were kept at home to endanger whole neighborhoods. She told of the fearful results of contagion in places where whole families occupied one room, and where, when disease came, two or three must die. Her words made a great impression. A woman who had lost two children by some dread disease offered to give ten thousand dollars towards founding such a hospital; but it was discovered that under the law the hospital must be a public institution. Therefore a monster mass-meeting was held. The county and city officials attended, and so did many physicians and a host of influential persons. Franklin Head presided, under the rule the women have adopted of asking men to preside on such occasions so as not to offend ultra-conservative minds. Strong resolutions were adopted, and later the press helped the movement enthusiastically. The women say that the Chicago newspapers always co-operate with them gallantly and ardently. The county commissioners then appropriated thirty thousand dollars and put up a building, the planning of which was supervised by the women.

In this case, as whenever a committee has more than it can do, the whole club took hold. "Now, everybody pull for the contagious hospital," was the signal, and every woman in the club dropped everything else, went home, enlisted the husbands, fathers, and brothers, and so quickly stirred all Chicago.

Last May one of the committees invited President Harper, of the Chicago University, to deliver an address on the Higher Education of Women, and particularly upon the plans of the university in that respect. He made it evident that the university plans were very liberal; that women were to have the same advantages as men, the same examinations, the same classes, the same professors, and that they would be eligible to the same professorships. Considering the great endowment of the institution, this was seen to be the fullest and richest opportunity that American women enjoy for the pursuit of learning; but it also came out that, although there had been five hundred applications from the graduates of other female schools and colleges, there were to be no accommodations whatever for them. The donations to the university had come in such a way that no money could be set apart for the construction of dormitories. The chairman of the Education Committee (all the heads of committees in the club are called "chairmen") proposed that the club pledge itself to raise $150,000 for a Woman's Building for the university. The motion was carried unanimously, and a committee was appointed, and in sixty days (on July 10, 1892) it had collected $168,000. Three different women gave $50,000 each, so that when the committee had time to count what it had, there was $18,000 more than was needed. Of course dollars never go begging for a use to which to be put, and these will be used for interior appointments. Another committee was appointed to insure the planning of a building satisfactory to women, and to furnish the apartments, which are not to be merely bedrooms, but are to include a large assembly-room, dining-rooms and parlors, a gymnasium, library, baths, and whatever, the parlors being common to every two or three bedrooms, and all the appointments being homelike and inviting.

Mrs. Dr. Stevenson was in the chair when this great movement was set on foot, and she has since interested Chicago anew by demanding bath-houses on the lake front for the boys, and afterwards for the poor in general.

A very remarkable member of the Woman's Club is Jane Addams, of whose gentle character it is sufficient to say that her friends are fond of referring to her as "Saint Jane." She is not robust in health, but, after doing more than ten men would want to do, she usually explains that it is something she has found "in which an invalid can engage." She is a native of Illinois, is wealthy, and while on a visit to London, becoming interested in Toynbee Hall, evolved a theory which has brightened her own and very many other lives. It is that "the rich need the poor as much as the poor need the rich"; that there is a vast number of girls coming out of the colleges for whom there is not enough to do to interest them in life, and who grow *ennuyée* when they might be active and happy. It is her idea that when they interest themselves in their poor brothers and sisters they find the pure gold of happiness. She asked the aid of many ladies of leisure, and went to live in one of the worst quarters of Chicago, taking with her Miss Ellen Starr, a teacher, and a niece of Eliza Allen Starr, the writer. She found an old-time mansion with a wide hall through the middle and large rooms on either side. It had been built for a man named Hull, as a residence, but it had become an auction-house, and the district around it had decayed into a quarter inhabited by poor foreigners. The woman who had fallen heir to it gave it to Miss Addams rent free until 1893. She and Miss Starr lived in it, filled it plainly, but with fine taste, with pictures and ornaments as well as suitable furniture and appointments for the purposes to which it was to be put. A piano was put in the large parlor or assembly-room, which is used every morning for a kindergarten. A beautiful young girl, Miss Jennie Dow, gave the money for the kindergarten, and taught it for a year. Miss Fanny Garry, a daughter of Judge Garry, organized a cooking-school, and, with her young friends to assist her, teaches the art of cooking to poor girls.

A great many of the best-known young men and ladies in North Side circles contribute what they can to the success of this charity, now known as Hull House, and the subject of general local pride. These young persons teach Latin classes, maintain a boys' club, and instruct the lads of the neighborhood in the methods of boyish games; support a modelling class, a class in wood-carving, and another in American history. Every evening in the week some club meets in Hull House—a political economy club, a German club, or what not. Miss Addams's idea is that the poor have no social life, and few if any of the refinements which gild the intercourse that accompanies it. Therefore on one night in each week a girls' club meets in Hull House. The girls invite their beaux and men friends, and play games and talk and dance, refreshing themselves with lemonade and cake. The young persons who devote their spare time to the work go right in with the girls and boys and help to make the evenings jolly, one who is spoken of as "very swell" bringing his violin to furnish the dance music. The boys' club has one of the best gymnasiums in the city. The boys prepare and read essays and stories, and engage in improving tasks. There is a *crèche* in the Hull House system, and the sick of the district all go there for relief. College extension classes are also in the scheme, and public-school teachers attend the classes with college graduates, who enlist for the purpose of teaching them.

One of the new undertakings of the Chicago women is the task set for itself by the Municipal Reform League. It was organized in March, 1892, by the ladies who were connected with the World's Fair Congresses, a comprehensive work, for the description of which I have no space. A large committee was studying municipal reform when they decided to found an independent society, to endure long after the World's Fair, and to devote itself to local municipal reform, and especially to the promotion of cleanliness in the streets. A mass-meeting was held in Music Hall, and Judge Gresham presided. Many of the city officials and the local judges came, and the hall was crammed. Among the speakers were the Mayor, the Commissioner of Public Works, and the health commissioners. A clergyman arraigned them as responsible for the sorry state of the streets, and was followed by Miss Ada C. Sweet and Dr. Stevenson. A public meeting was held next day in the Woman's Club to organize the new society. Miss Sweet was elected president, and the other offices were filled by women. A constitution was adopted to admit everybody to membership who would express a desire to assist in the work and to keep their own premises in order. Six hundred members are on the rolls, and these include one hundred men, among whom are millionaires and working-men. Money has been contributed liberally, but only the secretary receives compensation.

The work performed is all in the direction of forcing the public officials to do their duty. The Health Department is in charge of the alleys, and the Street Department of the streets. To keep these departments up to their work, all the members of Miss Sweet's society are constituted volunteer inspectors, pledged to report once a week whatever remissness they discover. Thus the society has the eyes of Argus to scan the entire city. Where these eyes are kept wide open the greatest improvement is already apparent. Miss Sweet knows what every contractor is doing, as well as who is negligent and who is faithful, and she says she knows that there is not a single contractor whose contract could not be annulled to-morrow. She insists that the plan adopted by her society, if pursued, will transform Chicago into the model city of the world so far as public tidiness is concerned. Already many wealthy ladies drive down the alleys instead of the streets, and even walk through the byways, and so do many influential men, for the purpose of detecting negligence and reporting it. The complaints are forwarded, in the society's formal manner, to the responsible commissioners, and they do all they can, Miss Sweet admits, yet are rendered measurably impotent because they cannot appoint proper inspectors. The reformers will not stop until they have destroyed the entire contract system, and have made the police do the work of inspection. Already ten policemen are detailed to do this work, and eighteen more are to extend the system. An amazing and disheartening discovery attended the beginning of this undertaking. The garbage of the city was supposed to be burned as it accumulated; instead, it was being dumped in a circle of hillocks around the outskirts of the town. A plan for disposing of it by fire had failed, and the officials sat helplessly down and gave up the job. The women took up the task, and last year three methods were undergoing trial, and 180 tons a day were being burned. That mere incident in the history of this movement for clean streets is a grand return for the investment of interest in the project which the public has made.

Miss Sweet is no beginner at these almost superhuman tasks of awakening a great community to a perception of its rights and requirements. Three years ago she found that the police patrol wagons were the only vehicles in Chicago for the transportation of the sick and injured. Men and women, falling ill or meeting with disabling accidents, were picked up by the police and carted home or to the hospitals in heavy open patrol wagons built with springs fitted to bear a load of two dozen patrolmen. She first tried to get the officials to buy and equip ambulances and organize an ambulance corps in the Police Department. Failing in this, she raised money among her friends, and had an ambulance made and fitted with necessary appliances for the sick and desperately injured. She presented it to the city, requesting that it be put into immediate use in the Central District. Last year the Police Department had six of these ambulances in use, each carrying a medical man. It also maintains a corps of men trained to the care of the sick and injured. More of the wagons are promised, and a perfect ambulance system extending over the whole city is not a far-distant consummation.

Mrs. James M. Flower, a member of the School Board, and of a family of great social distinction, should be mentioned here as having, with other noble dames, organized and pushed to success a training-school for nurses. The Art and Literature Committee of the Woman's Club also deserves credit and mention for raising money for a scholarship at the Chicago Art Institute, the prize being given each year to the girl or boy graduate of the public schools who shows the most artistic talent.

These unusual activities and undertakings are but a part of what the women are doing, and are in addition to the kindly and humane efforts which the reader had doubtless expected to hear about, and which but parallel those which interest and occupy American ladies everywhere. There are proportionately as many workers in the hospitals, schools, and asylums, as many noble founders and supporters of refuges and hospitals, as many laborers in church and mission work, in Chicago as in New York or Boston. If the reader understand that those of which I have told are all added, like jewels upon a crown, to all the usual benefactions, the force of this chapter will be appreciated.

There are in Chicago, as elsewhere, Browning and Ibsen and Shakespearian circles and clubs, and if the city boasts few *littérateurs* or artists of celebrity, there is no lack of lovers and students of the work of those who live elsewhere. The Twentieth Century Club, founded, I believe, by the brilliant Mrs. George Rowswell Grant, is the most ambitious literary club, and has a large and distinguished membership. It meets in the houses of wealthy ladies, and is at times addressed by distinguished visitors whom it invites to the city. The Chicago Literary Club is another such organization, and of both these men as well as women are members. The Chicago Folk-lore Society, a new aspirant to such distinction, was organized in December, 1891, the first meeting being called by Mrs. Fletcher S. Bassett at the Chicago Woman's Club rooms. Eugene Field, of whose verse and of whose delightful personality Chicago cannot be too proud, George W. Cable, General and Mrs. Miles, Mr. and Mrs. Potter Palmer, Dr. Sarah Hackett Stevenson, Charles W. Deering, Mr. and Mrs. C. Henrotin, and Mr. and Mrs. Franklin MacVeagh are among the members. The motto of this society illumines its field of work. It is, "Whence these legends and traditions?" It has started a museum of Indian and other relics and curios, and may make an exhibition during the World's Fair. It will certainly distinguish itself during the congress of folk-lore scholars to be held in Chicago in 1893. The president of the society is Dr. S. H. Peabody. The directors are all women—Mrs. S. S. Blackwelder, Mrs. Fletcher S. Bassett, and Mrs. Potter Palmer; and the treasurer is Helen G. Fairbank.

I had a most interesting talk with one of the women active in certain of the public works I have described, and she told me that one reason why the women succeeded so well with the officials and politicians is that they are not voters, are not in politics, and ask favors (or rights) not for themselves, but for the public. That, she thought, sounded like an argument against granting the suffrage to women; but she said she would have to let it stand, whatever it sounded like. She said that the Chicago men not only spring to the help of a woman who tries to get along, "but they hate to see her fail, and they won't allow her to fail if they can help it." She remarked that the reason that active Chicago women do not show the aggressive, harsh spirit and lack of graceful femininity which are often associated with women who step out of the domestic sphere is because the Chicago women have not had to fight their way. The men have helped them. She gloried in the strides the women have made towards independence in Chicago.

"A fundamental principle with us," she said, " is that a girl may be dependent, but a woman must be independent in order to perform all her functions. She must be independent in order to wisely make a choice of her career—whether she will be a wife and mother, and, if so, whose wife and mother she will be."

GLIMPSES OF WESTERN ARCHITECTURE

WE have been speaking, of course, of the better commercial edifices, and it is by no means to be inferred that Chicago does not contain "elevator buildings" as disunited and absurd and restless as those of any other American town. About these select few, also, there is nothing especially characteristic. It is otherwise with the commercial buildings designed by Messrs. Burnham and Root. With the striking exception of Mr. Richardson's Field building, the names of these designers connote what there is of characteristically Chicagoan in the architecture of the business streets, so that, after all, the individuality is not local, but personal. The untimely and deplora-

perception. This is the quality that such towering structures as the Insurance Exchange, the Phœnix Building, and "The Rookery" have in common, and that clearly distinguishes them from the mass of commercial palaces in Chicago or elsewhere. There is no sacrifice to picturesqueness of the utilitarian purpose in their general form, as in the composition of the Owings building, and no denial of it in detail, as in the irrelevant arcade of the Studebaker building. Their flat roofs are not tormented into protuberances in order to animate their skylines, and those of them that are built around

CORNER OF INSURANCE EXCHANGE.
Burnham and Root, Architects.

ble death of John Wellborn Root makes it proper to say that the individuality was mainly his. It consists largely in a clearer perception than one finds elsewhere of the limitations and conditions of commercial architecture, or in a more austere and self-denying acting upon that

an interior court are frankly hypæthral. Nor is there in any of them any incongruous preciousness of material. They are of brick, brown or red, upon stone basements, and the ornament is such, and gle piers, upon the visible sufficiency of which the effectiveness, especially of a lofty building, so largely depends, never fail in this sufficiency, and the superior solidity that the basement of any building needs as a building, when it cannot be attained in fact by reason of commercial exigencies, is suggested in a more rugged and more massive treatment not less than in the employment of a visibly stronger material. These dispositions are aided by the devices at the command of the architect. The angle piers are weighted to the eye by the solid corbelled pinnacles at the top, as in the Insurance Exchange and the Rookery, or stiffened by a slight

ENTRANCE TO THE PHŒNIX BUILDING.
Burnham and Root, Architects.

only such, as is needed to express and to emphasize the structural divisions and dispositions. These are negative merits, it is true, but, as our commercial architecture goes, they are not less meritorious on that account, and one is inclined to wish that the architects of all the commercial palaces might attend to the preachments upon the fitness of things that these edifices deliver; for they have very positive merits also. They are all architectural compositions, and not mere walls promiscuously pierced with openings, or, what is much commoner, mere ranges of openings scantily framed in strips of wall. They are sharply and unmistakably divided into the parts that every building needs to be a work of architecture, the members that mark the division are carefully and successfully adjusted with reference to their place and their scale, and the treatment of the different parts is so varied as to avoid both monotony and miscellany. The an-

withdrawal that gives an additional vertical line on each side of the arris, as in the Phœnix, while the same purpose is partly subserved in the Rookery by the projection from the angle of the tall metallic lantern standards that repeat and enforce this line. The lateral division of the principal fronts is similar in all three structures. A narrow central compartment is distinguished in treatment, by an actual projection or by the thickening of the pier, from the longer wings, while the coincidence of this central division with the main entrance relieves the arrangement from the unpleasant look of an arrangement obviously forced or arbitrary. In the Insurance Exchange the centre is signalized by a balconied projection over the entrance, extending through the architectural basement — the dado, so to speak, which is here the principal division — by a widening of the piers and a concentration of the central openings in the second division, and above by an interruption of the otherwise unbroken arcade that traverses the attic. In the Rookery it is marked by a slight projection, which above is still further projected into tall corbelled pinnacles, and the wall thus bounded is slightly bowed, and its openings diminished and multiplied. In the Phœnix Building this bowing is carried so much further as to result in a corbelled oriel extending through four stories, and repeated on a smaller scale at each end of the principal front and in the centre of each shorter front. This feature may perhaps be excepted from the general praise the buildings deserve of a strict adherence to their utilitarian purpose. Not that, even in Chicago, a business man may not have occasion to look out of the window, nor that, if he does, he may not be pardoned for desiring to extend his view beyond the walls and windows of over the way. An oriel-window is not necessarily an incongruity in a "business block," but the treatment of these oriels is a little fantastic and a little ornate for their destination, and it is not in any case fortunate. The entrances, to be sure, are enriched with a decoration beyond the mere expression of the structure which has elsewhere been the rule, but they do not appear incongruous. The entrance to a building that houses the population of a considerable village must be wide, and if its height were regulated by that of the human figure, it would resemble the burrow by which the Esquimau gains access to his snow hut, and become a manifest absurdity as the portal of a ten-story building. It must be large and conspicuous, and it should be stately, and it were a "very cynical asperity" to deny to the designer the privilege of enhancing by ornament the necessary stateliness of the one feature of his building which must arrest, for a moment at least, the attention of the most preoccupied visitor. It cannot be said that such a feature as the entrance of the Phœnix Building is intensely characteristic of a modern "business block," but it can be said that in its place it does not in the least disturb the impression the structure makes of a modern "business block." If beauty be its own excuse for being, this entrance needs no other, for assuredly it is one of the most beautiful and artistic works that American architecture has to show, so admirably propor-

tioned it is, and so admirably detailed, so clear and emphatic without exaggeration in the expression of the structure, and so rich and refined the ornament. Upon the whole these buildings, by far the most successful and impressive of the business buildings of Chicago, not merely attest the skill of their architects, but reward their self-denial in making the design for

ORIEL, PHŒNIX BUILDING.
Burnham and Root, Architects.

a commercial building out of its own elements, however unpromising these may seem — in permitting the building, in a word, to impose its design upon them, and in following its indications, rather than in imposing upon the building a design derived from anything but a consideration of its own requirements. Hence it

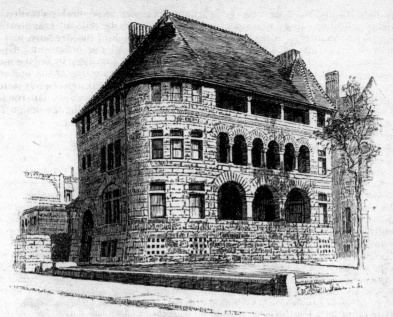

DWELLING ON LAKE SHORE DRIVE.
H. H. Richardson, Architect.

is that, without showing anywhere any strain after originality, these structures are more original than structures in which such a strain is evident. "The merit of originality is not novelty; it is sincerity." The designer did not permit himself to be diverted from the problem in hand by a consideration of the irrelevant beauties of Roman theatres or Florentine palaces or Flemish town-halls, and accordingly the work is not reminiscent of these nor of any previous architectural types, of which so many contemporary buildings have the air of being adaptations under extreme difficulties. It is to the same directness and sincerity in the attempt to solve a novel problem that these buildings owe what is not their least attraction, in the sense they convey of a reserved power. The architect of a commercial palace seems often to be discharging his architectural vocabulary and wreaking his entire faculty of expression upon that contradiction in terms. Some of the buildings of which we have been speaking exhibit this prodigality. There is something especially grateful and welcome in turning from one of them to a building like one of those now in question, which sug-

gests by comparison that after he had completed the design of it the architect might still have had something left in his portfolios and in his intellect.

In considering the domestic architecture of Chicago it is necessary to recur to the topographical conditions, for these have had as marked an influence upon it as they have had upon the commercial quarter, although this influence operates in almost the opposite direction. The commercial centre—the quarter of wholesale traffic and of "high finance"—is huddled into the space between the lake and the river. But when this limit is once passed there is no natural limit. No longer pent up, the whole boundless continent is Chicago's, and the instinct of expansion is at liberty to assert itself in every direction but the east, where it is confronted by Lake Michigan. There is thus no east side in Chicago to supplement the north and the west and the south sides, among which the dwellings of the people are divided, but there is no natural obstacle whatsoever to the development of the city in these three directions, and no natural reason why it should expand in one rather than in another, except what is

again furnished by the lake. To the minority of people who live where they will
and not where they must, this is a considerable exception, and one would suppose
that the fashionable quarter would be that
quarter from which the lake is most accessible. This is distinctly enough the
north side, which a stranger, without the
slightest interest, present or prospective,
in Chicago real estate, may be pardoned
for inferring to be the most desirable for
residence. For it happens that the dwellers upon the south side are cut off from
any practical or picturesque use of the
lake by the fact that the shore to the
south of the city is occupied by railroad
tracks, and the nearest houses of any pretensions are turned away from the water,
of which only the horses stabled in the
rear are in a position to enjoy the view.
The inference that the north is the most
eligible of the sides one finds to be violently combated by the residents of the
south and the west, and he finds also that
instead of one admittedly fashionable
quarter, as in every other city, Chicago
has three claimants for that distinction,
to the conflict between whose claims may
be ascribed the otherwise not very ex-
plicable delay in fixing a site for the
World's Fair. Each of these quarters
has its centre and its dependencies, and
between each two there is a large area either unoccupied, or occupied with dwellings very much humbler than those that
line the avenues that are severally the
boasts of the competing sides. The three
appear to have received nearly equal
shares of municipal attention, for there is

a park for each—nay, there are three parks
for the west side, though these are thus
far well beyond the limit of fashion if not
of population, and nominally two for the
south side, though even these bear more
the relation to the quarter for which they
were provided that the Central Park bore
to New York in 1870 than that which it
bears in 1891; they are still, that is to
say, rather outlying pleasure-grounds accessible to excursionists than parks in actual public use. Lincoln Park, the park
of the north side, is the only one of the
parks of Chicago that as yet deserves this
description, and the north side is much to
be congratulated upon possessing such a
resort. It has the great advantage of an
unobstructed frontage upon the lake, and
it is kept with the same skill and propriety with which it was planned.

It will be evident from all this that in
the three residential quarters of Chicago
there is plenty of room, and it is this spaciousness that gives a pervading characteristic to its domestic architecture. The
most fashionable avenues are not filled
with the serried ranks of houses one expects to see in a city of a million people.
On the contrary, in Michigan Avenue
and Prairie Avenue, on the south side,
and in the corresponding streets in the
other quarters, there is commonly a considerable strip of sward in front of the
house, and often at the sides as well. The
houses are often completely or partly detached, and they are frequently of a generous breadth, and always of a moderate
height. Three stories is the limit, which
is rarely exceeded even in the costliest

DWELLING IN PRAIRIE AVENUE.
H. H. Richardson, Architect.

JANUA RICHARDSONIENSIS.
N'Importe Qui, Architect.

does not very often offend in this particular direction. The commercial palace against which we have been inveighing is by no means so offensive as the domestic sham palace, and from this latter offence Chicago is much freer than most older American cities. The grateful result is that the houses in the best quarters are apt to look eminently "livable"; and though inequalities of fortune are visible enough, there is not so visible as to be conspicuous any attempt of the more fortunate to force them on the notice of the less fortunate. In other words, Chicago is, in its outward aspect at least, the most democratic of great American cities, and its aspect increases one's wonder that anarchism should have sprung up in this rich and level soil — to which, of course, the answer is that it didn't, being distinctly an exotic.

Another characteristic of the domestic architecture of Chicago there is—less prevalent than this absence of pretentiousness and mere display, but still prevalent enough to be very noteworthy—and that is the evidence it affords of an admiration for the work of Mr. Richardson, which, if not inordinate, is at least undiscriminating and misapplied. What region of our land, indeed, is not full of his labors, done vicariously, and with a zeal not according to knowledge? In Chicago his misunderstood example has fructified much more in the quarters of residence than in the business quarters, insomuch that one can scarcely walk around a square either in the north or in the south side without seeing some familiar feature or detail, which has often been borrowed outright from one of his works, and is reproduced without reference to its context. Now the great and merited success of Richardson was as personal and incommunicable as any artistic success can be. It was

dwellings. Conditions so different prevail in all the Eastern cities, even in Philadelphia, the roominess of which is one of its sources of local pride, that to the inhabitant of any one of them the domestic building of Chicago indicates a much less populous city than Chicago is, and its character seems rather suburban than urban. In the main this character of suburbanity is heightened by the architectural treatment of the dwellings. There are exceptions, and some of them are conspicuous and painful exceptions; but the rule is that the architect attempts to make the house even of a very rich man look like a home rather than like a palace, and that there is very little of the mere ostentation of riches. Even upon the speculative builder this feeling seems to have imposed itself; and however crude and violent his work may be in other ways, it

due to his faculty of reducing a complicated problem to its simplest and most
forcible expression. More specifically, it
was due to his faculty for seizing some
feature of his building, developing it into
predominance, and skilfully subordinat-
ing the rest of his composition to it, until
this feature became the building. It was
his power of disposing masses, his insist-
ence upon largeness and simplicity, his
impatience of niggling, his straightforward and virile handling of his tasks,
that made his successes brilliant,
and even his failures interesting.
Very much of all this is a matter
of temperament, and Richardson's
best buildings were the express
image of that impetuous and exuberant personality that all who
knew him remember. He used to
tell of a tourist from Holland in
whom admiration for his art had
induced a desire to make his acquaintance, and who upon being
introduced to him exclaimed,
" Oh, Mr. Richardson, how you
are like your work!" "Now
wasn't that a Dutch remark?"
Richardson concluded the story.
Indeed the tact of the salutation
must be admitted to have been
somewhat Batavian, but it was
not without critical value. One
cannot conceive of Richardson's
work as having been done by an
anæmic architect, or by a self-dis-
trustful architect, or by a profess-
or of architecture, faithful as his
own professional preparation had
been. There is a distinction well
recognized in the art to which
architecture has more or less
plausibly been likened that is no
less valid as applied to architecture itself—the distinction between
" school music " and " bravura
music." If we adopt this distinction, Richardson must be classed
among the bravura performers in
architecture, who are eligible rather for admiration than for study.
Assuredly designers will get nothing but good from his work if
they learn from it to try for largeness
and simplicity, to avoid niggling, and
to consider first of all the disposition of
their masses. But these are merits that
cannot be transferred from a photograph. They are quite independent of

a fondness for the Provençal Romanesque, and still more of an exaggeration
of the depth of voussoirs and of the dwarf-
ishness of pillars. These things are readily enough imitable, as nearly every block
of dwellings in Chicago testifies, but
they are scarcely worth imitating. In
Richardson's best work there is apt to be
some questionable detail, since the success
or failure of his building is commonly
decided before the consideration of detail
arises, and it is this questionable detail

ORIEL OF DWELLING.
R. M. Hunt, Architect.

that the imitators are apt to reproduce
without asking it any questions. Moreover, it will probably be agreed by most
students that Richardson's city houses are,
upon the whole, and in spite of some
noteworthy exceptions, the least success-

FRONT IN DEARBORN AVENUE.
John Addison, Architect.

not be said to have been developed effectively; nay, it can hardly be said to have been developed in an architectural sense at all, and the result proves that though a skilful disposition of masses is much, it is not everything. We have just been saying that the success or failure of Richardson's work was in a great degree independent of the merit of the detail, but this dwelling scarcely exhibits any detail.

This is the more a drawback because the loggia is a feature of which lightness and openness are the essential characteristic, and which seems, therefore, to demand a certain elegance of treatment, as was rec-

ful of his works. As it happens, there are two of them in Chicago itself, one on the north side and one on the south, and if their author had done nothing else, it is likely that they would be accepted rather as warnings than as examples. The principal front of the former has the simple leading motive that one seldom fails to find in the work of its architect, in the central open loggia of each of its three stories, flanked on each side by an abutment of solid wall, and the apportionment of the front between voids and solids is just and felicitous. Three loggie seem an excessive allowance for the town house of a single family; but if we waive this point as an affair between the architect and his client exclusively, it must be owned that the arrangement supplies a motive susceptible of very effective development. In this case it can-

ognized alike by the architects of the Gothic and the Renaissance palaces in Italy, from which we derive the feature and the name. It is, indeed, in the contrast between the lightened and enriched fenestration of the centre and the massiveness of the flanking walls that the potential effectiveness of the arrangement resides. Here, however, there are no lightening and no enrichment. Rude vigor characterizes as much the enclosed arcades as the enclosing walls, and becomes as much the predominant expression of the front of a dwelling of moderate dimensions as of the huge façades of the Field warehouse. Such modelling as is introduced tends rather to enforce than to mitigate this expression, for the piers of the lower arcade are squared, and the intercalated shafts of the upper are doubled perpendicularly to the front, as are the shafts of the colonnade above, so as to lay an additional stress upon the thickness of a wall that is here manifestly a mere screen. The continuation of the abacus of the arcade through the wall and its re-appearance as the transom of the flanking windows is an effective device that loses some of its effectiveness from its introduction into both arcades. It scarcely modifies the impression the front makes of lacking detail altogether. The double-dentilled string-course that marks off and corbels out the attic is virtually the only moulding the front shows. Yet the need of mouldings is not less now than it was in the remote antiquity when a forgotten Egyptian artist perceived the necessity of some expedient to subdivide a wall, to mark a level, to sharpen or to soften a transition. For three thousand years his successors have agreed with him, and for a modern architect to abjure the use of these devices is to deny himself the rhetoric of his art. The incompleteness that comes of this abjuration in the present instance must be apparent to the least-trained layman, who vaguely feels that "something is the matter" with the building thus deprived of a source of expression, for which the texture given to the whole front by the exhibition of the bonding of the masonry, skilful and successful as this is in itself, by no means compensates. The sensitive architect must yearn to set the stone-cutters at work anew to bring out the expression of those parts that are especially in need of rhetorical exposition, to accentuate the sills of the arcades, to define and refine their arches, to emphasize the continuous line of the abacus, and especially to mark the summit of the sloping basement, which now is merged into the plane of the main wall without the suggestion of a

plinth. It is conceivable that an architect might by the skilful employment of color so treat a front, without the least projection or recess from top to bottom or from end to end, as to make us forget to deplore the absence of mouldings. Some interesting attempts in that direction have, in fact, been made, and complete success in such an attempt would be entitled to the praise of a *tour de force*. But when in a monochromatic wall the designer omits the members that should express and emphasize and adorn his structural dispositions without offering any substitute for them, his building will appear, as this dwelling appears, a work merely "blocked out" and left unfinished; and if it be the work of a highly endowed and highly accomplished designer like Richardson, the deficiency must be set down merely as an unlucky caprice. We have been speaking exclusively of the longer front, since it is manifest that the shorter shares its incompleteness, without the partial compensation of a strong and striking composition, which would carry off much unsuccessful detail, though it is not strong enough to carry off the lack of detail, even with the powerful and simple roof that covers the whole—in itself an admi-

A HOUSE OF BOWLDERS.
Burnham and Root, Architects.

A BYZANTINE CORBEL.
Henry Ives Cobb, Architect.

having no counterpart upon the other, and serving to weaken at a critical point the wall the emphasis of whose massiveness and lateral expanse may be said to be the whole purport of the design, to which everything else is quite ruthlessly sacrificed. For this the building is kept as low as possible, insomuch that the ridge of its rather steep roof reaches only the level of the third story of the adjoining house. For this the openings are diminished in size upon both sides, insomuch that they become mere orifices for the admission of light; and in number upon the long side, insomuch that the designer seems to regard them as annoying interruptions to his essay in the treatment of blank wall. A granite wall over a hundred and fifty feet long, as in the side of this dwelling, almost unbroken, and with its structure clearly exhibited, is sure enough to arrest and strike the beholder; and so is the shorter front, in which the same treatment prevails, with a little more of ungracious concession to practical needs in the more numerous openings;

rable and entirely satisfactory piece of work.

Capriciousness may with as much justice be charged upon the only other example of Richardson's domestic architecture in Chicago, which, even more than the house we have been considering, arrests attention and prevents apathy, but which seems even more from the purpose of domestic architecture. Upon the longer though less conspicuous front it lacks any central and controlling motive; and on the shorter and more conspicuous, this motive, about which the architect so seldom leaves the beholder in any doubt, is obscured by the addition at one end of a series of openings irrelevant to it,

but the beholder could scarcely accept the result as an eligible residence. The treatment is even more strictly than in the house on the north side an exposition of masonry. There is here, to be sure, some decorative detail in the filling of the head of the doorway and in the sill above it, but this detail is so minute, in the case of the egg-and-dart that adorns the sill so microscopic, that it does not count at all in the general effect. A moulding that does count in the general effect, and that vindicates itself at the expense of the structural features not thus developed, is the main cornice, an emphatic and appropriate profile. In this building there seems to be a real attempt to

supply the place of mouldings by modifications of the masonry, which in the other
forms an unvaried reticulation over the
whole surface. In this not only are the
horizontal joints accentuated, and the vertical joints slurred so as to assist very
greatly in the emphasis of length, but the
courses that are structurally of unusual
importance, the sills and lintels of the
openings, are doubled in width, thus
strongly belting the building at their several levels. Here again a device that
needs only to be expressed in modelling to
answer an artistic purpose fails to make
up for the absence of modelling. The
merits of the building as a building,
however, are much effaced when it is
considered as a dwelling, and the structure ceases to be defensible, except, indeed,
in a military sense. The whole aspect of
the exterior is so gloomy and forbidding
and unhomelike that, but for its neighborhood, one would infer its purpose to be
not domestic, but penal. Lovelace has
assured us that "stone walls do not a
prison make," but when a building consists as exclusively as possible of bare
stone walls, it irresistibly suggests a place
of involuntary seclusion, even though
minds especially "innocent and quiet"
might take it for a hermitage. Indeed,
if one were to take it for a dwelling expressive of the character of its inmates, he
must suppose it to be the abode of a re-
cluse or of a misanthrope, though when
Timon secures a large plot upon a fashionable avenue, and erects a costly building to show his aversion to the society of
his kind, he exposes the sincerity of his
misanthropical sentiments to suspicion.
Assuming that the owner does not profess such sentiments, but is much like his
fellow-citizens, the character of his abode
must be referred to a whim on the part
of his architect—a Titanic, or rather a Gar-
gantuan freak. For there is at least nothing petty or puerile about the design of
these houses. They bear an unmistakably
strong and individual stamp, and failures
as, upon the whole, they must be called,
they really increase the admiration aroused
by their author's successes for the power
of design that can make even wilful error
so interesting.

That romantic architecture is not in-
consistent with the suggestion of a home,
or with the conditions of a modern town-
house, is shown, if it needed any showing, by a dwelling that adjoins the first

of the Richardson houses, and that nobody who is familiar with Mr. W. K. Vanderbilt's house or with the Marquand
houses in New York would need to be
told was the work of Mr. Hunt. It recalls particularly the Vanderbilt house,
being in the same monochrome of light
gray, and repeating, though with a wide
variation, some of the same features, especially the corbelled tourelle. This is
here placed to much better advantage at
a salient instead of a re-entrant angle; it
is more happily proportioned; the corbel-
ling, not continuous, but broken by the
wall of the angle, is very cleverly managed, and the whole feature is as picturesque and spirited as it is unmistakably
domestic in expression. The house does
not exhibit the same profusion of sculp-
tural ornament as the earlier work it recalls, nor is there so much of strictly architectural detail. By this comparison,
indeed, one would be inclined to call this
treatment severe; but it is prodigality itself in comparison with its neighbor.
This latter comparison is especially instructive because in the block, as a matter of mere mass and outline, Mr. Richardson's composition, considerably simpler, is also pretty distinctly more forcible than that of Mr. Hunt, by reason of
its central and dominating feature, and
especially by reason of the completeness
with which it is united by the simple and
unbroken roof; whereas the criticism often passed upon the Vanderbilt house,
that it grows weak above the cornice-
line, is applicable, though in a less degree, to its author's later work. The various roofs required by the substructure,
and carried to the same height, have been
imperfectly brought into subjection, and
their grouping does not make a single or
a total impression. Taking the fronts by
themselves, considering them with reference to the distribution of voids and solids, we must omit the minor front of Mr.
Richardson's work as scarcely showing
any composition; but the principal front
is much more striking and memorable,
assuredly, tha. either elevation of Mr.
Hunt's design, carefully and successfully
as both of them have been studied. Yet
there is no question at all that the latter
is by far the more admirable and effective
example of domestic architecture, because
the possibilities of expression that inhere
in the masses are in the one case brought
out, and left latent in the other.

Of course Mr. Hunt's work is no more characteristically Chicagoan than Mr. Richardson's, and, of course, the dwellings we have been considering are too large and costly to be fairly representative of the domestic architecture of any city. The rule, to which there are as few exceptions in Chicago as elsewhere, is that architecture is regarded as a superfluity that only the rich can afford; whereas a genuine and general interest in it would require the man who was able to own a house at all to insist upon what the tailors call a "custom-made" dwelling, and would lead him equally to reject a ready-made residence and a misfit. In that case we should see in single houses of moderate size and moderate cost the same evidence of affectionate study as in houses of greater pretensions, even though the design might be evinced only in the careful and thoughtful proportioning and adjustment of the parts. Chicago has its share, but no more than its share, of instances in which the single street front of a modest dwelling has been thought worthy of all the pains that could be given to it. Of one such instance in Chicago an illustration is given, and it is somewhat saddening to one who would like to find in it an evidence of intelligent lay interest in architecture to be informed that it is the residence of its architect.

Upon the whole, the domestic architecture of the town has few local characteristics, besides those already mentioned, which are due to local conditions rather than to local preferences. The range of building material is wide, and includes a red sandstone from Lake Superior that has not yet made its way into the Eastern cities, of a more positive tint than any in general use there. On the other hand, the whole continent has been laid under tribute for Chicago. The green "Chester serpentine" which one encounters so often in Philadelphia—and generally with regret, though in combination it may become very attractive—almost unknown in New York as it is, is not uncommon in the residential quarters of Chicago. Another material much commoner here than elsewhere is the unhewn bowlder that Mr. Richardson employed in the fantastic lodge at North Easton, which was one of his happiest performances. In a long and low structure like that the defects of the material are much less manifest than

when it is attempted to employ it in a design of several stories. The architect, in the example shown in our illustration, has wisely simplified his design to the utmost to conform to the intractability of his material, and with equal wisdom has marked with strong belts the division of his stories. But in spite of its ruggedness the wall looks weak, since it is plain that there is no bonding, and that it is not properly a piece of masonry, but a layer of highly magnified concrete, which owes its stability only to the cohesion of the cement, and to give the assurance of being a trustworthy wall needs to be framed in a conspicuous quoining of unquestionable masonry.

One other trait is common enough among such of the dwellings of Chicago as have architectural pretensions to be remarked, and that is the prevalence of Byzantine carving. This is not really a Chicagoan characteristic. If it is especially noticeable here, it is because Chicago is so new, and it is in the newer quarters of older towns that it is to be seen. It is quite as general on the west side of New York. Its prevalence is again in great part due to the influence of Richardson, and one is inclined to welcome it as at least tending to provide a common and understood way of working for architectural carvers, and the badge of something like a common style for buildings that have little else in common. The facility with which its spiky leafage can be used for surface decoration tempts designers to provide surfaces for its decoration, in such structural features as capitals and corbels, at the cost of the modelling which is so much more expressive and so much more troublesome, when a mere cushion will do better as a basis for Byzantine ornament.

For the rest, the clever and ingenious features which one often comes upon in the residential streets of Chicago, and the thoroughly studied fronts that one comes upon so much more seldom, would excite neither more nor less surprise if they were encountered in the streets of any older American town. But from what has been said it will be seen that in every department of building, except only the ecclesiastical, Chicago has already examples to show that should be of great value to its future growth in stimulating its architects to produce and in teaching its public to appreciate.

COMMENTS ON KENTUCKY

ALL Kentucky, like Gaul, is divided into three parts. This division, which may not be sustained by the geologists or the geographers, perhaps not even by the ethnologists, is, in my mind, one of character: the east and southeast mountainous part, the central blue-grass region, and the great western portion, thrifty in both agriculture and manufactures. It is a great self-sustaining empire, lying midway in the Union, and between the North and the South (never having yet exactly made up its mind whether it is North or South), extending over more than seven degrees of longitude. Its greatest length east and west is 410 miles; its greatest breadth, 178 miles. Its area by latest surveys, and larger than formerly estimated, is 42,283 square miles. Within this area prodigal nature has brought together nearly everything that a highly civilized society needs: the most fertile soil, capable of producing almost every variety of product for food or for textile fabrics; mountains of coals and iron ores and limestone; streams and springs everywhere; almost all sorts of hard-wood timber in abundance. Nearly half the State is still virgin forest of the noblest trees, oaks, sugar-maple, ash, poplar, black walnut, linn, elm, hickory, beech, chestnut, red cedar. The climate may honestly be called temperate: its inhabitants do not need to live in cellars in the summer, nor burn up their fences and furniture in the winter.

Kentucky is loved of its rivers. It can be seen by their excessively zigzag courses how reluctant they are to leave the State, and if they do leave it they are certain to return. The Kentucky and the Green wander about in the most uncertain way before they go to the Ohio, and the Licking and Big Sandy exhibit only a little less reluctance. The Cumberland, after a wide detour in Tennessee, returns; and Powell's River, joining the Clinch and entering the Tennessee, finally persuades that river, after it has looked about the State of Tennessee and gladdened northern Alabama, to return to Kentucky.

Kentucky is an old State, with an old civilization. It was the pioneer in the great western movement of population after the Revolution. Although it was first explored in 1770, and the Boone trail through the wilderness of Cumberland Gap was not marked till 1775, a settlement had been made in Frankfort in 1774, and in 1790 the territory had a population of 73,677. This was a marvellous growth, considering the isolation by hundreds of miles of wilderness from Eastern communities, and the savage opposition of the Indians, who slew fifteen hundred white settlers from 1783 to 1790. Kentucky was the home of no Indian tribe, but it was the favorite hunting and fighting ground of those north of the Ohio and south of the Cumberland, and they united to resent white interference. When the State came into the Union in 1792—the second admitted—it was the equal in population and agricultural wealth of some of the original States that had been settled a hundred and fifty years, and in 1800 could boast 220,759 inhabitants, and in 1810, 406,511.

At the time of the settlement, New York west of the Hudson, western Pennsylvania, and western Virginia were almost unoccupied except by hostile Indians; there was only chance and dangerous navigation down the Ohio from Pittsburgh, and it was nearly eight hundred miles of a wilderness road, which was nothing but a bridle-path, from Philadelphia by way of the Cumberland Gap to central Kentucky. The majority of emigrants came this toilsome way, which was, after all, preferable to the river route, and all passengers and produce went that way eastward, for the steam-boat had not yet made the ascent of the Ohio feasible.

In 1779 Virginia resolved to construct a wagon-road through the wilderness, but no road was made for many years afterward, and indeed no vehicle of any sort passed over it till a road was built by action of the Kentucky Legislature in 1796. I hope it was better then than the portion of it I travelled from Pineville to the Gap in 1888.

Civilization made a great leap over nearly a thousand miles into the open garden spot of central Kentucky, and the exploit is a unique chapter in our frontier development. Either no other land ever lent itself so easily to civilization as the blue-grass region, or it was exceptionally fortunate in its occupants. They formed almost immediately a society distinguished for its amenities, for its political influence, prosperous beyond precedent in farming, venturesome and active in trade, developing large manufactures, especially from hemp, of such articles as could be transported by river, and sending annually through the wilderness road to the East and South immense droves of cattle, horses, and swine. In the first necessity, and the best indication of superior civilization, good roads for transportation, Kentucky was conspicuous in comparison with the rest of the country. As early as 1825 macadam roads were projected, the turnpike from Lexington to Maysville on the Ohio was built in 1829, and the work went on by State and county co-operation until the central region had a system of splendid roads, unexcelled in any part of the Union. In 1830 one of the earliest railways in the United States, that from Lexington to Frankfort, was begun; two years later seven miles were constructed, and in 1835 the first locomotive and train of cars ran on it to Frankfort, twenty-seven miles, in two hours and twenty-nine minutes. The structure was composed of stone sills, in which grooves were cut to receive the iron bars. These stone blocks can still be seen along the line of the road, now a part of the Louisville and Nashville system. In all internal improvements the State was very energetic. The canal around the Falls of the Ohio at Louisville was opened in 1831, with some aid from the general government. The State expended a great deal in improving the navigation of the Kentucky, the Green, and other rivers in its borders by an expensive system of locks and dams; in 1837 it paid $19,500 to engineers engaged in turnpike and river improvement, and in 1839 $31,675 for the same purpose.

The story of early Kentucky reads like a romance. By 1820 it counted a population of over 516,000, and still it had scarcely wagon-road communication with the East. Here was a singular phenomenon, a prosperous community, as one might say a garden in the wilderness, separated by natural barriers from the great life of the East, which pushed out north of it a connected, continuous development; a community almost self-sustaining, having for its centre the loveliest agricultural region in the Union, and evolving a unique social state so gracious and attractive that it was thought necessary to call in the effect of the blue-grass to explain it, unaided human nature being inadequate, it was thought, to such a result. Almost from the beginning fine houses attested the taste and prosperity of the settlers; by 1792 the blue-grass region was dotted with neat and commodious dwellings, fruit orchards and gardens, sugar groves, and clusters of villages; while, a little later, rose, in the midst of broad plantations and park-like forests, lands luxuriant with wheat and clover and corn and hemp and tobacco, the manorial dwellings of the colonial period, like the stately homes planted by the Holland Land Company along the Hudson and the Mohawk and in the fair Genesee, like the pillared structures on the James and the Staunton, and like the solid square mansions of old New England. A type of some of them stands in Frankfort now, a house which was planned by Thomas Jefferson and built in 1796, spacious, permanent, elegant in the low relief of its chaste ornamentation. For comfort, for the purposes of hospitality, for the quiet and rest of the mind, there is still nothing so good as the colonial house, with the slight modifications required by our changed conditions.

From 1820 onward the State grew by a natural increment of population, but without much aid from native or foreign emigration. In 1860 its population was only about 919,000 whites, with some 225,000 slaves and over 10,000 free colored persons. It had no city of the first class, nor any villages specially thriving. Louisville numbered only about 68,000, Lexington less than 15,000, and Frankfort, the capital, a little over 5000. It retained the lead in hemp and a leading position in tobacco; but it had fallen away behind its much younger rivals in manufactures and the building of railways, and only feeble efforts had been made in the development of its extraordinary mineral resources.

How is this arrest of development accounted for? I know that a short way of accounting for it has been the presence of slavery. I would not underestimate this. Free labor would not go where it had to compete with slave labor; white labor now does not like to come into relations with black labor; and capital also was shy of investment in a State where both political economy and social life were disturbed by a color line. But this does not wholly account for the position of Kentucky as to development at the close of the war. So attractive is the State in most respects, in climate, soil, and the possibilities of great wealth by manufactures, that I doubt not the State would have been forced into the line of Western progress and slavery become an unimportant factor long ago, but for certain natural obstacles and artificial influences.

Let the reader look on the map, at the ranges of mountains running from the northeast to the southwest—the Blue Ridge, the Alleghanies, the Cumberland, and Pine mountains, continuous rocky ridges, with scarcely a water gap, and only at long intervals a passable mountain gap—and notice how these would both hinder and deflect the tide of emigration. With such barriers the early development of Kentucky becomes ten times a wonder. But about 1825 an event occurred that placed her at a greater disadvantage in the competition. The Erie Canal was opened. This made New York, and not Virginia, the great commercial highway. The railway development followed. It was easy to build roads north of Kentucky, and the tide of settlement followed the roads, which were mostly aided by land grants; and in order to utilize the land grants the railways stimulated emigration by extensive advertising. Capital and population passed Kentucky by on the north. To the south somewhat similar conditions prevailed. Comparatively cheap roads could be built along the eastern slope of the Alleghanies, following the great valley from Pennsylvania to Alabama; and these southwestwardly roads were also aided by the gen-

eral government. The North and South
Railway of Alabama, and the Alabama and
Great Southern, which cross at Birming-
ham, were land-grant roads. The roads
which left the Atlantic seaboard passed
naturally northward and southward of
Kentucky, and left an immense area in
the centre of the Union—all of western
and southwestern Virginia and eastern
Kentucky—without transportation facilities. Until 1880 here was the largest area
east of the Mississippi unpenetrated by
railways.

The war removed one obstacle to the
free movement of men desiring work and
seeking agreeable homes, a movement
marked in the great increase of the industrial population of Louisville and the
awakening to varied industries and trade
in western Kentucky. The offer of cheap
land, which would reward skilful farming
in agreeable climatic conditions, has attracted foreign settlers to the plateau south
of the blue-grass region; and scientific investigation has made the mountain district in the southeast the object of the
eager competition of both domestic and
foreign capital. Kentucky, therefore, is
entering upon a new era of development.
Two phases of it, the Swiss colonies, and
the opening of the coal, iron, and timber
resources, present special points of interest.

This incoming of the commercial spirit
will change Kentucky for the better and
for the worse, will change even the tone
of the blue-grass country, and perhaps
take away something of that charm about
which so much has been written. So
thoroughly has this region been set forth
by the pen and the pencil and the lens
that I am relieved of the necessity of
describing it. But I must confess that
all I had read of it, all the pictures I had
seen, gave me an inadequate idea of its
beauty and richness. So far as I know,
there is nothing like it in the world.
Comparison of it with England is often
made in the use of the words "garden"
and "park." The landscape is as unlike
the finer parts of Old England as it is unlike the most carefully tended parts of New
England. It has neither the intense green,
the subdivisions in hedges, the bosky
lanes, the picturesque cottages, the nice-
ness of minute garden culture, of England, nor the broken, mixed lawn gardening and neglected pastures and highways,
with the sweet wild hills, of the Berkshire

region. It is an open, elevated, rolling
land, giving the traveller often the most
extended views over wheat and clover,
hemp and tobacco fields, forests and blue-
grass pastures. One may drive for a hundred miles north and south over the splendid macadam turnpikes, behind blooded
roadsters, at an easy ten-mile gait, and see
always the same sight—a smiling agricultural paradise, with scarcely a foot,
in fence corners, by the road-side, or in
low grounds, of uncultivated, uncared-
for land. The open country is more
pleasing than the small villages, which
have not the tidiness of the New England small villages; the houses are for
the most part plain; here and there is a
negro cabin, or a cluster of them, apt to
be unsightly, but always in view somewhere is a plantation-house, more or less
pretentious, generally old-fashioned and
with the colonial charm. These are frequently off the main thoroughfare, approached by a private road winding
through oaks and ash-trees, seated on
some gentle knoll or slope, maybe with a
small flower-garden, but probably with
the old sentimental blooms that smell
good and have reminiscences, in the
midst of waving fields of grain, blue-grass
pastures, and open forest glades watered
by a clear stream. There seems to be
infinite peace in a house so surrounded.
The house may have pillars, probably a
colonial porch and doorway with carving
in bass-relief, a wide hall, large square
rooms, low studded, and a general air of
comfort. What is new in it in the way
of art, furniture, or bric-à-brac may not
be in the best taste, and may "swear" at
the old furniture and the delightful old
portraits. For almost always will be
found some portraits of the post-Revolu-
tionary period, having a traditional and
family interest, by Copley or Jouett, perhaps a Stuart, maybe by some artist who
evidently did not paint for fame, which
carry the observer back to the colonial
society in Virginia, Philadelphia, and
New York. In a country house and in
Lexington I saw portraits, life-size and
miniature, of Rebecca Gratz, whose loveliness of person and character is still a
tender recollection of persons living. She
was a great beauty and toast in her day.
It was at her house in Philadelphia, a
centre of wit and gayety, that Washington
Irving and Henry Brevoort and Gulian
C. Verplanck often visited. She shone not

less in New York society, and was the most intimate friend of Matilda Hoffman, who was betrothed to Irving; indeed it was in her arms that Matilda died, fadeless always to us as she was to Irving, in the loveliness of her eighteenth year. The well-founded tradition is that Irving, on his first visit to Abbotsford, told Scott of his own loss, and made him acquainted with the beauty and grace of Rebecca Gratz, and that Scott, wanting at the moment to vindicate a race that was aspersed, used her as a model for Rebecca in *Ivanhoe*.

One distinction of the blue-grass region is the forests, largely of gigantic oaks, free of all undergrowth, carpeted with the close-set, luscious, nutritive blue-grass, which remains green all the season when it is cropped by feeding. The blue-grass thrives elsewhere, notably in the upper Shenandoah Valley, where somewhat similar limestone conditions prevail; but this is its natural habitat. On all this elevated rolling plateau the limestone is near the surface. This grass blooms toward the middle of June in a bluish, almost a peacock blue, blossom, which gives to the fields an exquisite hue. By the end of the month the seed ripens into a yellowish color, and while the grass is still green and lush underneath, the surface presents much the appearance of a high New England pasture in August. When it is ripe, the top is cut for the seed. The limestone and the blue-grass together determine the agricultural pre-eminence of the region, and account for the fine breeding of the horses, the excellence of the cattle, the stature of the men, and the beauty of the women; but they have social and moral influence also. It could not well be otherwise, considering the relation of the physical condition to disposition and character. We should be surprised if a rich agricultural region, healthful at the same time, where there is abundance of food, and wholesome cooking is the rule, did not affect the tone of social life. And I am almost prepared to go further, and think that blue-grass is a specific for physical beauty and a certain graciousness of life. I have been told that there is a natural relation between Presbyterianism and blue-grass, and am pointed to the Shenandoah and to Kentucky as evidence of it. Perhaps Presbyterians naturally seek a limestone country. But the relation, if it exists, is too subtle and the facts are too few to build a theory on.

Still, I have no doubt there is a distinct variety of woman known as the blue-grass girl. A geologist told me that once when he was footing it over the State with a geologist from another State, as they approached the blue-grass region from the southward they were carefully examining the rock formation and studying the surface indications, which are usually marked on the border line, to determine exactly where the peculiar limestone formation began. Indications, however, were wanting. Suddenly my geologist looked up the road and exclaimed, "We are in the blue-grass region now." "How do you know?" asked the other. "Why, there is a blue-grass girl."

There was no mistaking the neat dress, the style, the rounded contours, the gracious personage. A few steps further on the geologists found the outcropping of the blue limestone.

Perhaps the people of this region are trying to live up to the thorough-bred. A pedigree is a necessity. The horse is of the first consideration, and either has or gives a sort of social distinction: first, the running horse, the thoroughbred, and now the trotting horse, which is beginning to have a recognizable descent, and is on the way to be a thorough-bred. Many of the finest plantations are horse farms; one might call them the feature of the country. Horse-raising is here a science, and as we drive from one estate to another, and note the careful tillage, the trim fences, the neat stables, the pretty paddocks, and the houses of the favorites, we see how everything is intended to contribute to the perfection in refinement of fibre, speed, and endurance of the noble animal. Even persons who are usually indifferent to horses cannot but admire these beautiful high-bred creatures, either the famous ones displayed at the stables, or the colts and fillies, which have yet their reputations to make, at play in the blue-grass pastures; and the pleasure one experiences is a refined one in harmony with the landscape. Usually horse-dealing carries with it a lowering of the moral tone, which we quite understand when we say of a man that he is "horsy." I suppose the truth is that man has degraded the idea of the horse by his own evil passions, using him to gamble and cheat with. Now the visitor will find little of these degrading associations in the blue-grass region. It is an orthodox and a moral region. The best and most successful horse-breeders have nothing to do with racing or betting. The yearly product of their farms is sold at auction, without reserve or favor. The sole business is the production of the best animals that science and care can breed. Undeniably where the horse is of such importance he is much in the thought, and the use of "horsy" phrases in ordinary conversation shows his effect upon the vocabulary. The recital of pedigree at the stables, as horse after horse is led out, sounds a little like a chapter from the Book of Genesis, and naturally this Biblical formula gets into a conversation about people.

And after the horses there is whiskey. There are many distilleries in this part of the country, and a great deal of whiskey is made. I am not defending whiskey, at least any that is less than thirty years old and has attained a medicinal quality. But I want to express my opinion that this is as temperate as any region in the United States. There is a wide-spread strict temperance sentiment, and even prohibition prevails to a considerable degree. Whiskey is made and stored, and mostly shipped away; rightly or wrongly, it is regarded as a legitimate business, like wheat raising, and is conducted by honorable men. I believe this to be the truth, and that drunkenness does not prevail in the neighborhood of the distilleries, nor did I see anywhere in the country evidence of a habit of dram-drinking, of the traditional matter-of-course offering of whiskey as a hospitality. It is true that mint grows in Kentucky, and that there are persons who would win the respect of a tide-water Virginian in the concoction of a julep. And no doubt in the mind of the born Kentuckian there is a rooted belief that if a person needed a stimulant, the best he can take is old hand-made whiskey. Where the manufacture of whiskey is the source of so much revenue, and is carried on with decorum, of course the public sentiment about it differs from that of a community that makes its money in raising potatoes for starch. Where the horse is so beautiful, fleet, and profitable, of course there is intense interest in him, and the general public take a lively pleasure in the races; but if the reader has been accustomed to associate this part of Kentucky with horse-racing and drinking as prominent

characteristics, he must revise his opinion.

Perhaps certain colonial habits lingered longer in Kentucky than elsewhere. Travellers have spoken about the habit of profanity and gambling, especially the game of poker. In the West generally profane swearing is not as bad form as it is in the East. But whatever distinction central Kentucky had in profanity or poker, it has evidently lost it. The duel lingered long, and prompt revenge for insults, especially to women. The blue-grass region has "histories"—beauty has been fought about; women have had careers; families have run out through dissipation. One may hear stories of this sort even in the Berkshire Hills, in any place where there have been long settlement, wealth, and time for the development of family and personal eccentricities. And there is still a flavor left in Kentucky; there is still a subtle difference in its social tone; the intelligent women are attractive in another way from the intelligent New England women—they have a charm of their own. May Heaven long postpone the day when, by the commercial spirit and trade and education, we shall all be alike in all parts of the Union! Yet it would be no disadvantage to anybody if the graciousness, the simplicity of manner, the refined hospitality, of the blue-grass region should spread beyond the blue limestone of the Lower Silurian.

In the excellent State Museum at Frankfort, under the charge of Professor John R. Procter,* who is State geologist and also director of the Bureau of Immigration, in addition to the admirable exhibit of the natural resources of Kentucky, are photographs, statistics, and products showing the condition of the Swiss and other foreign farming colonies recently established in the State, which were so interesting and offered so many instructive points that I determined to see some of the colonies.

This museum and the geological department, the intelligent management of which has been of immense service to the commonwealth, is in one of the detached buildings which make up the present Cap-

* Whatever value this paper has is so largely due to Professor Procter that I desire to make to him the most explicit acknowledgments. One of the very best results of the war was keeping him in the Union.

itol. The Capitol is altogether antiquated, and not a credit to the State. The room in which the Lower House meets is shabby and mean, yet I noticed that it is fairly well lighted by side windows, and debate can be heard in it conducted in an ordinary tone of voice. Kentucky will before many years be accommodated with new State buildings more suited to her wealth and dignity. But I should like to repeat what was said in relation to the Capitol of Arkansas. Why cannot our architects devise a capitol suited to the wants of those who occupy it? Why must we go on making these huge inconvenient structures, mainly for external display, in which the legislative Chambers are vast air-tight and water-tight compartments, commonly completely surrounded by other rooms and lobbies, and lighted only from the roof, or at best by high windows in one or two sides that permit no outlook—rooms difficult to speak or hear in, impossible to ventilate, needing always artificial light? Why should the Senators of the United States be compelled to occupy a gilded dungeon, unlighted ever by the sun, unvisited ever by the free wind of heaven, in which the air is so foul that the Senators sicken? What sort of legislation ought we to expect from such Chambers? It is perfectly feasible to build a legislative room cheerful and light, open freely to sun and air on three sides. In order to do this it may be necessary to build a group of connected buildings, instead of the parallelogram or square, which is mostly domed, with gigantic halls and stairways, and, considering the purpose for which it is intended, is a libel on our ingenuity and a burlesque on our civilization.

Kentucky has gone to work in a very sensible way to induce immigration and to attract settlers of the right sort. The Bureau of Immigration was established in 1880. It began to publish facts about the State, in regard to the geologic formation, the soils, the price of lands, both the uncleared and the lands injured by slovenly culture, the kind and amount of products that might be expected by thrifty farming, and the climate; not exaggerated general proclamations promising sudden wealth with little labor, but facts such as would attract the attention of men willing to work in order to obtain for themselves and their children comfortable homes and modest independence. Invitations were

made for a thorough examination of lands—of the different sorts of soils in different counties—before purchase and settlement. The leading idea was to induce industrious farmers who were poor, or had not money enough to purchase high-priced improved lands, to settle upon lands that the majority of Kentuckians considered scarcely worth cultivating, and the belief was that good farming would show that these neglected lands were capable of becoming very productive. Eight years' experience has fully justified all these expectations. Colonies of Swiss, Germans, Austrians, have come, and Swedes also, and these have attracted many from the North and Northwest. In this period I suppose as many as ten thousand immigrants of this class, thrifty cultivators of the soil, have come into the State, many of whom are scattered about the State, unconnected with the so-called colonies. These colonies are not organized communities in any way separated from the general inhabitants of the State. They have merely settled together for companionship and social reasons, where a sufficiently large tract of cheap land was found to accommodate them. Each family owns its own farm, and is perfectly independent. An indiscriminate immigration has not been desired or encouraged, but the better class of laboring agriculturists, grape-growers, and stock-raisers. There are several settlements of these, chiefly Swiss, dairy-farmers, cheese-makers, and vine-growers, in Laurel County; others in Lincoln County, composed of Swiss, Germans, and Austrians; a mixed colony in Rock Castle County; a thriving settlement of Austrians in Boyle County; a temperance colony of Scandinavians in Edmonson County; another Scandinavian colony in Grayson County; and scattered settlements of Germans and Scandinavians in Christian County. These settlements have from one hundred to over a thousand inhabitants each. The lands in Laurel and Lincoln counties, which I travelled through, are on a high plateau, with good air and temperate climate, but with a somewhat thin, loamy, and sandy soil, needing manure, and called generally in the State poor land—poor certainly compared with the blue-grass region and other extraordinarily fertile sections. These farms, which had been more or less run over by Kentucky farming, were sold at from one to five dollars an acre. They are farms that a man cannot live on in idleness. But they respond well to thrifty tillage, and it is a sight worth a long journey to see the beautiful farms these Swiss have made out of land that the average Kentuckian thought not worth cultivating. It has not been done without hard work, and as most of the immigrants were poor, many of them have had a hard struggle in building comfortable houses, reducing the neglected land to order, and obtaining stock. A great attraction to the Swiss was that this land is adapted to vine culture, and a reasonable profit was expected from selling grapes and making wine. The vineyards are still young; experiment has not yet settled what kind of grapes flourish best, but many vine-growers have realized handsome profits in the sale of fruit, and the trial is sufficient to show that good wine can be produced. The only interference thus far with the grapes has been the unprecedented late freeze last spring.

At the recent exposition in Louisville the exhibit of these Swiss colonies—the photographs showing the appearance of the unkempt land when they bought it, and the fertile fields of grain and meadow and vineyards afterward, and the neat plain farm cottages, the pretty Swiss chalet with its attendants of intelligent comely girls in native costumes offering articles illustrating the taste and the thrift of the colonies, wood-carving, the products of the dairy, and the fruit of the vine—attracted great attention.

I cannot better convey to the reader the impression I wish to in regard to this colonization and its lesson for the country at large than by speaking more in detail of one of the Swiss settlements in Laurel County. This is Bernstadt, about six miles from Pittsburg, on the Louisville and Nashville road, a coal-mining region, and offering a good market for the produce of the Swiss farmers. We did not need to be told when we entered the colony lands; neater houses, thrifty farming, and better roads proclaimed it. It is not a garden spot; in some respects it is a poor-looking country; but it has abundant timber, good water, good air, a soil of light sandy loam, which is productive under good tillage. There are here, I suppose, some two hundred and fifty families, scattered about over a large area, each on its farm. There is no collection of houses;

the church (Lutheran), the school-house, the store, the post-office, the hotel, are widely separated; for the hotel-keeper, the store-keeper, the postmaster, and I believe the school-master and the parson, are all farmers to a greater or less extent. It must be understood that it is a primitive settlement, having as yet very little that is picturesque, a community of simple working people. Only one or two of the houses have any pretension to taste in architecture, but this will come in time— the vine-clad porches, the quaint gables, the home-likeness. The Kentuckian, however, will notice the barns for the stock, and a general thriftiness about the places. And the appearance of the farms is an object-lesson of the highest value.

The chief interest to me, however, was the character of the settlers. Most of them were poor, used to hard work and scant returns for it in Switzerland. What they have accomplished, therefore, is the result of industry, and not of capital. There are among the colonists skilled laborers in other things than vine-growing and cheese-making — watch-makers and wood-carvers and adepts in various trades. The thrifty young farmer at whose pretty house we spent the night, and who has saw-mills at Pittsburg, is of one of the best Swiss families; his father was for many years President of the republic, and he was a graduate of the university at Lucerne. There were others of the best blood and breeding and schooling, and men of scientific attainments. But they are all at work close to the soil. As a rule, however, the colonists were men and women of small means at home. The notable thing is that they bring with them a certain old civilization, a unity of simplicity of life with real refinement, courtesy, politeness, good-humor. The girls would not be above going out to service, and they would not lose their self-respect in it. Many of them would be described as "peasants," but I saw some, not above the labors of the house and farm, with real grace and dignity of manner and charm of conversation. Few of them as yet speak any English, but in most houses are evidences of some German culture. Uniformly there was courtesy and frank hospitality. The community amuses itself rationally. It has a very good brass band, a singing club, and in the evenings and holidays it is apt to assemble at the hotel and take a little wine and sing the songs of fatherland. The hotel is indeed at present without accommodations for lodgers—nothing but a *Wirthshaus*, with a German garden where dancing may take place now and then. With all the hard labor, they have an idea of the simple comforts and enjoyments of life. And they live very well, though plainly. At a house where we dined, in the colony Strasburg, near Bernstadt, we had an excellent dinner, well served, and including delicious soup. If the colony never did anything else than teach that part of the State how to make soup, its existence would be justified. Here, in short, is an element of homely thrift, civilization on a rational basis, good-citizenship, very desirable in any State. May their vineyards flourish! When we departed early in the morning—it was not yet seven—a dozen Switzers, fresh from the dewy fields, in their working dresses, had assembled at the hotel, where the young landlady also smiled a welcome, to send us off with a song, which ended, as we drove away, in a good-by *yodel*.

A line drawn from the junction of the Scioto River with the Ohio southwest to a point in the southern boundary about thirty miles east of where the Cumberland leaves the State defines the eastern coal-measures of Kentucky. In area it is about a quarter of the State—a region of plateaus, mountains, narrow valleys, cut in all directions by clear, rapid streams, stuffed, one may say, with coals, streaked with iron, abounding in limestone, and covered with superb forests. Independent of other States a most remarkable region, but considered in its relation to the coals and iron ores of West Virginia, western Virginia, and eastern Tennessee, it becomes one of the most important and interesting regions in the Union. Looking to the southeastern border, I hazard nothing in saying that the country from the Breaks of Sandy down to Big Creek Gap (in the Cumberland Mountain), in Tennessee, is on the eve of an astonishing development—one that will revolutionize eastern Kentucky, and powerfully affect the iron and coal markets of the country. It is a region that appeals as well to the imagination of the traveller as to the capitalist. My personal observation of it extends only to the portion from Cumberland Gap to Big Stone Gap, and the head waters of the Cumberland between Cumberland Mountain and Pine Mountain,

but I saw enough to comprehend why eager purchasers are buying the forests and the mining rights, why great companies, American and English, are planting themselves there and laying the foundations of cities, and why the gigantic railway corporations are straining every nerve to penetrate the mineral and forest heart of the region. A dozen roads, projected and in progress, are pointed toward this centre. It is a race for the prize. The Louisville and Nashville, running through soft-coal fields to Jellico and on to Knoxville, branches from Corbin to Barboursville (an old and thriving town) and to Pineville. From Pineville it is under contract, thirteen miles, to Cumberland Gap. This gap is being tunnelled (work going on at both ends) by an independent company, the tunnel to be open to all roads. The Louisville and Nashville may run up the south side of the Cumberland range to Big Stone Gap, or it may ascend the Cumberland River and its Clover Fork, and pass over to Big Stone Gap that way, or it may do both. A road is building from Knoxville to Cumberland Gap, and from Johnson City to Big Stone Gap. A road is running from Bristol to within twenty miles of Big Stone Gap; another road nears the same place—the extension of the Norfolk and Western—from Pocahontas down the Clinch River. From the northwest many roads are projected to pierce the great deposits of coking and cannel coals, and find or bore a way through the mountain ridges into southwestern Virginia. One of these, the Kentucky Union, starting from Lexington (which is becoming a great railroad centre), has reached Clay City, and will soon be open to the Three Forks of the Kentucky River, and on to Jackson, in Breathitt County. These valley and transridge roads will bring within short hauling distance of each other as great a variety of iron ores of high and low grade, and of coals, coking and other, as can be found anywhere—according to the official reports, greater than anywhere else within the same radius. As an item it may be mentioned that the rich, pure, magnetic iron ore used in the manufacture of Bessemer steel, found in East Tennessee and North Carolina, and developed in greatest abundance at Cranberry Forge, is within one hundred miles of the superior Kentucky coking coal. This contiguity (a contiguity of coke, ore, and limestone) in this region points to the manufacture of Bessemer steel here at less cost than it is now elsewhere made.

It is unnecessary that I should go into details as to the ore and coal deposits of this region: the official reports are accessible. It may be said, however, that the reports of the Geological Survey as to both coal and iron have been recently perfectly confirmed by the digging of experts. Aside from the coal-measures below the sandstone, there have been found above the sandstone, north of Pine Mountain, 1650 feet of coal-measures, containing nine beds of coal of workable thickness, and between Pine and Cumberland mountains there is a greater thickness of coal-measures, containing twelve or more workable beds. Some of these are coking coals of great excellence. Cannel-coals are found in sixteen of the counties in the eastern coal fields. Two of them at least are of unexampled richness and purity. The value of a cannel-coal is determined by its volatile combustible matter. By this test some of the Kentucky cannel-coal excels the most celebrated coals of Great Britain. An analysis of a cannel-coal in Breathitt County gives 66.28 of volatile combustible matter; the highest in Great Britain is the Boghead, Scotland, 51.60 per cent. This beautiful cannel-coal has been brought out in small quantities *via* the Kentucky River; it will have a market all over the country when the railways reach it. The first coal identified as coking was named the Elkhorn, from the stream where it was found in Pike County. A thick bed of it has been traced over an area of 1600 square miles, covering several counties, but attaining its greatest thickness in Letcher, Pike, and Harlan. This discovery of coking coal adds greatly to the value of the iron ores in northeastern Kentucky, and in the Red and Kentucky valleys, and also of the great deposits of ore on the southeast boundary, along the western base of the Cumberland, along the slope of Powell's Mountain, and also along Wallin's Ridge, three parallel lines, convenient to the coking coal in Kentucky. This is the Clinton or red fossil ore, stratified, having from 45 to 54 per cent. of metallic iron. Recently has been found on the north side of Pine Mountain, in Kentucky, a third deposit of rich "brown" ore, averaging 52 per cent. of metallic iron. This is the same as the celebrated brown ore

used in the furnaces at Clifton Forge; it makes a very tough iron. I saw a vein of it on Straight Creek, three miles north of Pineville, just opened, at least eight feet thick.

The railway to Pineville follows the old wilderness road, the trail of Boone, and the stage road, along which are seen the ancient tavern stands where the jolly story-telling travellers of fifty years ago were entertained and the droves of horses and cattle were fed. The railway has been stopped a mile west of Pineville by a belligerent property owner, who sits there with his Winchester rifle, and will not let the work go on until the courts compel him. The railway will not cross the Cumberland at Pineville, but higher up, near the great elbow. There was no bridge over the stream, and we crossed at a very rough and rocky wagon ford. Pineville, where there has long been a backwoods settlement on the south bend of the river just after it breaks through Pine Mountain, is now the centre of a good deal of mining excitement and real estate speculation. It has about five hundred inhabitants, and a temporary addition of land buyers, mineral experts, engineers, furnace projectors, and railway contractors. There is not level ground for a large city, but what there is is plotted out for sale. The abundant iron ore, coal, and timber here predict for it a future of some importance. It has already a smart new hotel, and business buildings and churches are in process of erection. The society of the town had gathered for the evening at the hotel. A wandering one-eyed fiddler was providentially present who could sing and play "The Arkansas Traveller" and other tunes that lift the heels of the young, and also accompany the scream of the violin with the droning bagpipe notes of the mouth-harmonica. The star of the gay company was a graduate of Annapolis, in full evening dress uniform, a native boy of the valley, and his vis-à-vis was a heavy man in a long linen duster and carpet slippers, with a palm-leaf fan, who crashed through the cotillon with good effect. It was a pleasant party, and long after it had dispersed, the troubadour, sitting on the piazza, wiled away sleep by the break-downs, jigs, and songs of the frontier.

Pineville and its vicinity have many attractions; the streams are clear, rapid, rocky, the foliage abundant, the hills picturesque. Straight Creek, which comes in along the north base of Pine Mountain, is an exceedingly picturesque stream, having along its banks fertile little stretches of level ground, while the gentle bordering hills are excellent for grass, fruit orchards, and vineyards. The walnut-trees have been culled out, but there is abundance of oak, beech, poplar, cucumber, and small pines. And there is no doubt about the mineral wealth.

We drove from Pineville to Cumberland Gap, thirteen miles, over the now neglected Wilderness Road, the two mules of the wagon unable to pull us faster than two miles an hour. The road had every variety of badness conceivable—loose stones, ledges of rock, bowlders, sloughs, holes, mud, sand, deep fords. We crossed and followed up Clear Creek (a muddy stream) over Log Mountain (full of coal) to Cañon Creek. Settlements were few—only occasional poor shanties. Climbing over another ridge, we reached the Yellow Creek Valley, through which the Yellow Creek meanders in sand. This whole valley, lying very prettily among the mountains, has a bad name for "difficulties." The hills about, on the sides and tops of which are ragged little farms, and the valley itself, still contain some lawless people. We looked with some interest at the Turner house, where a sheriff was killed a year ago, at a place where a "severe" man fired into a wagon-load of people and shot a woman, and at other places where in recent times differences of opinion had been settled by the revolver. This sort of thing is, however, practically over. This valley, close to Cumberland Gap, is the site of the great city, already plotted, which the English company are to build as soon as the tunnel is completed. It is called Middleborough, and the streets are being graded and preparations made for building furnaces. The north side of Cumberland Mountain, like the south side of Pine, is a conglomerate, covered with superb oak and chestnut trees. We climbed up to the mountain over a winding road of ledges, bowlders, and deep gullies, rising to an extended pleasing prospect of mountains and valleys. The pass has a historic interest, not only as the ancient highway, but as the path of armies in the civil war. It is narrow, a deep road between overhanging rocks. It is easily defended. A light bridge thrown over the road, leading to rifle-pits and

breastworks on the north side, remains to attest the warlike occupation. Above, on the bald highest rocky head on the north, guns were planted to command the pass. Two or three houses, a blacksmith's shop, a drinking tavern, behind which on the rocks four men were playing old sledge, made up the sum of its human attractions as we saw it. Just here in the pass Kentucky, Tennessee, and Virginia touch each other. Virginia inserts a narrow wedge between the other two. On our way down the wild and picturesque road we crossed the State of Virginia and went to the new English hotel in Tennessee. We passed a magnificent spring, which sends a torrent of water into the valley, and turns a great millwheel—a picture in its green setting—saw the opening of the tunnel with its shops and machinery, noted the few houses and company stores of the new settlement, climbed the hill to the pretty hotel, and sat down on the piazza to look at the scene. The view is a striking one. The valley through which the Powell River runs is pleasant, and the bold, bare mountain of rock at the right of the pass is a noble feature in the landscape. With what joy must the early wilderness pilgrims have hailed this landmark, this gateway to the Paradise beyond the mountains! Some miles north in the range are the White Rocks, gleaming in the sun and conspicuous from afar, the first signal to the weary travellers from the east of the region they sought. Cumberland Gap is full of expectation, and only awaits the completion of the tunnel to enter upon its development. Here railways from the north, south, and west are expected to meet, and in the Yellow Creek Valley beyond, the English are to build a great manufacturing city. The valleys and sides of these mountain ranges (which have a uniform elevation of not much more than 2000 to 2500 feet) enjoy a delightful climate, moderate in the winter and temperate in the summer. This whole region, when it is accessible by rail, will be attractive to tourists.

We pursued our journey up the Powell River Valley, along the base of the Cumberland, on horseback—one day in a wagon in this country ought to satisfy anybody. The roads, however, are better on this side of the mountain: all through Lee County, in Virginia, in spots very good. This is a very fine valley, with good water, cold and clear, growing in abundance oats and corn, a constant succession of pretty views. We dined excellently at a neat farm-house on the river, and slept at the house of a very prosperous farmer near Boon's Path post-office. Here we are abreast the White Rocks, the highest point of the Cumberland (3451 feet), that used to be the beacon of immigration. The valley grows more and more beautiful as we go up, full fields of wheat, corn, oats, friendly to fruit of all sorts, with abundance of walnut, oak, and chestnut timber—a fertile, agreeable valley, settled with well-to-do farmers. The next morning, beautifully clear and sparkling, we were off at seven o'clock through a lovely broken country, following the line of Cumberland (here called Stone) Mountain, alternately little hills and meadows, cultivated hill-sides, stretches of rich valley, exquisite views—a land picturesque and thriving. Continuing for nine miles up Powell Valley, we turned to the left through a break in the hills into Poor Valley, a narrow, wild, sweet ravine among the hills, with a swift crystal stream overhung by masses of rhododendrons in bloom, and shaded by magnificent forest trees. We dined at a farm-house by Pennington's Gap, and had a swim in the north fork of Powell River, which here, with many a leap, breaks through the bold scenery in the gap. Further on, the valley was broader and more fertile, and along the wide reaches of the river grew enormous beech-trees, the russet foliage of which took on an exquisite color toward evening. Indeed the ride all day was excitingly interesting, with the great trees, the narrow rich valleys, the frequent sparkling streams, and lovely mountain views. At sunset we came to the house of an important farmer who has wide possessions, about thirteen miles from Big Stone Gap. We have nothing whatever against him except that he routed us out at five o'clock of a foggy Sunday morning, which promised to be warm—July 1st—to send us on our way to "the city." All along we had heard of "the city." In a radius of a hundred miles Big Stone Gap is called nothing but "the city," and our anticipations were raised.

That morning's ride I shall not forget. We crossed and followed Powell River. All along the banks are set the most remarkable beech-trees I have ever seen—great, wide-spreading, clean-boled trees,

overshading the stream, and giving under their boughs, nearly all the way, ravishingly lovely views. This was the paradisiacal way to Big Stone Gap, which we found to be a round broken valley, shut in by wooded mountains, covered more or less with fine trees, the meeting-place of the Powell River, which comes through the gap, and its south fork. In the round elevation between them is the inviting place of the future city. There are two Big Stone Gaps—the one open fields and forests, a settlement of some thirty to forty houses, most of them new and many in process of building, a hotel, and some tents: the other, the city on the map. The latter is selling in small lots, has wide avenues, parks, one of the finest hotels in the South, banks, warehouses, and all that can attract the business man or the summer lounger.

The heavy investments in Big Stone Gap and the region I should say were fully justified by the natural advantages. It is a country of great beauty, noble mountain ranges, with the valleys diversified by small hills, fertile intervales, fine streams, and a splendid forest growth. If the anticipations of an important city at the gap are half realized, the slopes of the hills and natural terraces will be dotted with beautiful residences, agreeable in both summer and winter. It was the warmest time of the year when we were there, but the air was fresh and full of vitality. The Big Stone Gap Improvement Company has the city and its site in charge; it is a consolidation of the various interests of railway companies and heavy capitalists, who have purchased the land. The money and the character of the men behind the enterprise insure a vigorous prosecution of it. On the west side of the river are the depot and switching-grounds which the several railways have reserved for their use, and here also are to be the furnaces and shops. When the city outgrows its present site it can extend up valleys in several directions. We rode through fine forests up the lovely Powell Valley to Powell Mountain, where a broad and beautiful meadow offers a site for a suburban village. The city is already planning for suburbs. A few miles south of the city a powerful stream of clear water falls over precipices and rocks seven hundred feet in continuous rapids. This is not only a charming addition to the scenic attractions of the region, but the stream will supply the town with excellent water and unlimited "power." Beyond, ten miles to the northeast, rises High Knob, a very sightly point, where one gets the sort of view of four States that he sees on an atlas. It is indeed a delightful region; but however one may be charmed by its natural beauty, he cannot spend a day at Big Stone Gap without being infected with the great enterprises brooding there.

We forded Powell River and ascended through the gap on its right bank. Before entering the gorge we galloped over a beautiful level plateau, the counterpart of that where the city is laid out, reserved for railways and furnaces. From this point the valley is seen to be wider than we suspected, and to have ample room for the manufacturing and traffic expected. As we turned to see what we shall never see again—the virgin beauty of nature in this site—the whole attractiveness of this marvellously picturesque region burst upon us—the great forests, the clear swift streams, the fertile meadows, the wooded mountains that have so long secluded this beauty and guarded the treasures of the hills.

The pass itself, which shows from a distance only a dent in the green foliage, surprised us by its wild beauty. The stony road, rising little by little above the river, runs through a magnificent forest, gigantic trees growing in the midst of enormous bowlders, and towering among rocks that take the form of walls and buttresses, square structures like the Titanic ruins of castles ; below, the river, full and strong, rages over rocks and dashes down, filling the forest with its roar, which is echoed by the towering cliffs on either side. The woods were fresh and glistening from recent rains, but what made the final charm of the way was the bloom of the rhododendron, which blazed along the road and illuminated the cool recesses of the forest. The time for the blooming of the azalea and the kalmia (mountain-laurel) was past, but the pink and white rhododendron was in full glory, masses of bloom, not small stalks lurking like underbrush, but on bushes attaining the dignity of trees, and at least twenty-five feet high. The splendor of the forest did not lessen as we turned to the left and followed up Pigeon Creek to a high farming region, rough but fer-

tile, at the base of Black Mountain. Such a wealth of oak, beech, poplar, chestnut, and ash, and, sprinkled in, the pretty cucumber-magnolia in bloom! By sunset we found our way, off the main road, to a lonely farm-house hidden away at the foot of Morris Pass, secluded behind an orchard of apple and peach trees. A stream of spring-water from the rocks above ran to the house, and to the eastward the ravine broadened into pastures. It seemed impossible to get further from the world and its active currents. We were still in Virginia.

Our host, an old man over six feet in height, with spare, straight, athletic form, a fine head, and large clear gray eyes, lived here alone with his aged spouse. He had done his duty by his country in raising twelve children (that is the common and orthodox number in this region), who had all left him except one son, who lived in a shanty up the ravine. It was this son's wife who helped about the house and did the milking, taking care also of a growing family of her own, and doing her share of field-work.) I had heard that the women in this country were more industrious than the men. I asked this woman, as she was milking that evening, if the women did all the work. No, she said ; only their share. Her husband was all the time in the field, and even her boys, one only eight, had to work with him; there was no time to go to school, and indeed the school didn't amount to much anyway—only a little while in the fall. She had all the care of the cows. "Men," she added, "never notice milking;" and the worst of it was that she had to go miles around in the bush night and morning to find them. After supper we had a call from a bachelor who occupied a cabin over the pass, on the Kentucky side, a loquacious philosopher, who squatted on his heels in the door-yard where we were sitting, and interrogated each of us in turn as to our names, occupations, residence, ages, and politics, and then gave us as freely his own history and views of life. His eccentricity in this mountain region was that he had voted for Cleveland and should do it again. Mr. Morris couldn't go with him in this; and when pressed for his reasons he said that Cleveland had had the salary long enough, and got rich enough out of it. The philosopher brought the news, had heard it talked about on

Sunday, that a man over Clover Fork way had killed his wife and brother. It was claimed to be an accident; they were having a game of cards and some whiskey, and he was trying to kill his son-in-law. Was there much killing round here? Well, not much lately. Last year John Cone, over on Clover Fork, shot Mat Harner in a dispute over cards. Well, what became of John Cone? Oh, he was killed by Jim Blood, a friend of Harner. And what became of Blood? Well, he got shot by Elias Travers. And Travers? Oh, he was killed by a man by the name of Jacobs. That ended it. None of 'em was of much account. There was a pleasing naïveté in this narrative. And then the philosopher, whom the milkmaid described to me next morning as "a simlar sort of man," went on to give his idea about this killing business. "All this killing in the mountains is foolish. If you kill a man, that don't aggravate him; he's dead and don't care, and it all comes on you."

In the early morning we crossed a narrow pass in the Black Mountain into "Canetucky," and followed down the Clover Fork of the Cumberland. All these mountains are perfectly tree-clad, but they have not the sombreness of the high regions of the Great Smoky and the Black Mountains of North Carolina. There are few black balsams, or any sort of evergreens, and the great variety of deciduous trees, from the shining green of the oak to the bronze hue of the beech, makes everywhere soft gradations of color most pleasing to the eye. In the autumn, they say, the brilliant maples in combination with the soberer bronzes and yellows of the other forest trees give an ineffable beauty to these ridges and graceful slopes. The ride down Clover Fork, all day long, was for the most part through a virgin world. The winding valley is at all times narrow, with here and there a tiny meadow, and at long intervals a lateral opening down which another sparkling brook comes from the recesses of this wilderness of mountains. Houses are miles apart, and usually nothing but cabins half concealed in some sheltered nook. There is, however, hidden on the small streams, on mountain terraces, and high up on the slopes, a considerable population, cabin dwellers, cultivators of corn, on the almost perpendicular hills. Many of these corn fields are so steep that

it is impossible to plough them, and all the cultivation is done with the hoe. I heard that a man was recently killed in this neighborhood by falling out of his corn field. The story has as much foundation as the current belief that the only way to keep a mule in the field where you wish him to stay is to put him into the adjoining lot. But it is true that no one would believe that crops could be raised on such nearly perpendicular slopes as these unless he had seen the planted fields.

In my limited experience I can recall no day's ride equal in simple natural beauty — not magnificence — and splendor of color to that down Clover Fork. There was scarcely a moment of the day when the scene did not call forth from us exclamations of surprise and delight. The road follows and often crosses the swift, clear, rocky stream. The variegated forest rises on either hand, but all along the banks vast trees without underbrush dot the little intervales. Now and then, in a level reach, where the road wound through these monarch stems, and the water spread in silver pools, the perspective was entrancing. But the color! For always there were the rhododendrons, either gleaming in masses of white and pink in the recesses of the forest, or forming for us an *allée*, close set, and uninterrupted for miles and miles; shrubs like trees, from twenty to thirty feet high, solid bouquets of blossoms, more abundant than any cultivated parterre, more brilliant than the finest display in a horticultural exhibition. There is an avenue of rhododendrons half a mile long at Hampton Court, which is world-wide famous. It needs a day to ride through the rhododendron avenue on Clover Fork, and the wild and free beauty of it transcends all creations of the gardener.

The inhabitants of the region are primitive and to a considerable extent illiterate. But still many strong and distinguished men have come from these mountain towns. Many families send their children away to school, and there are fair schools at Barbersville, Harlan Court House, and in other places. Long isolated from the moving world, they have retained the habits of the early settlers, and to some extent the vernacular speech, though the dialect is not specially marked. They have been until recently a self-sustaining people, raising and manufacturing nearly everything required by their limited knowledge and wants. Not long ago the women spun and wove from cotton and hemp and wool the household linen, the bed-wear, and the clothes of the family. In many houses the loom is still at work. The colors used for dyeing were formerly all of home make except, perhaps, the indigo; now they use what they call the "brought in" dyes, bought at the stores; and prints and other fabrics are largely taking the places of the home-made. During the morning we stopped at one of the best houses on the fork, a house with a small apple orchard in front, having a veranda, two large rooms, and a porch and kitchen at the back. In the back porch stood the loom with its web of half-finished cloth. The farmer was of the age when men sun themselves on the gallery and talk. His wife, an intelligent, barefooted old woman, was still engaged in household duties, but her weaving days were over. Her daughters did the weaving, and in one of the rooms were the linsey-woolsey dresses hung up, and piles of gorgeous bed coverlets, enough to set up half a dozen families. These are the treasures and heirlooms handed down from mother to daughter, for these handmade fabrics never wear out. Only eight of the twelve children were at home. The youngest, the baby, a sickly boy of twelve, was lounging about the house. He could read a little, for he had been to school a few weeks. Reading and writing were not accomplishments in the family generally. The other girls and boys were in the corn field, and going to the back door. I saw a line of them hoeing at the top of the field. The field was literally so steep that they might have rolled from the top to the bottom. The mother called them in, and they lounged leisurely down, the girls swinging themselves over the garden fence with athletic ease. The four eldest were girls: one, a woman of thirty-five, had lost her beauty, if she ever had any, with her teeth; one, of thirty, recently married, had a stately dignity and a certain nobility of figure; one, of sixteen, was undeniably pretty — almost the only woman entitled to this epithet that we saw in the whole journey. This household must have been an exception, for the girls usually marry very young. They were all, of course, barefooted. They were all laborers, and evidently took life seriously, and however much their knowledge of the world was limited, the household evidently respected itself. The elder girls were the weavers, and they showed a taste and skill in their fabrics that would be praised in the Orient or in Mexico. The designs and colors of the coverlets were ingenious and striking. There was a very handsome one in crimson, done in wavy lines and bizarre figures, that was called the Kentucky Beauty, or the Ocean Wave, that had a most brilliant effect. A simple, hospitable family this. The traveller may go all through this region with the certainty of kindly treatment, and in perfect security—if, I suppose, he is not a revenue officer, or sent in to survey land on which the inhabitants have squatted.

We came at night to Harlan Court House, an old shabby hamlet, but growing and improving, having a new courthouse and other signs of the awakening of the people to the wealth here in timber and mines. Here in a beautiful valley three streams—Poor, Martin, and Clover forks—unite to form the Cumberland. The place has fourteen "stores" and three taverns, the latter a trial to the traveller. Harlan has been one of the counties most conspicuous for lawlessness. The trouble is not simply individual wickedness, but the want of courage of public opinion, coupled with a general disrespect for authority. Plenty of people lament the state of things, but want the courage to take a public stand. The day before we reached the Court House the man who killed his wife and his brother had his examination. His friends were able to take the case before a friendly justice instead of the judge. The facts sworn to were that in a drunken dispute over cards he tried to kill his son-in-law, who escaped out of the window, and that his wife and brother opposed him, and he killed them with his pistol. Therefore their deaths were accidental, and he was discharged. Many people said privately that he ought to be hung, but there was entire public apathy over the affair. If Harlan had three or four resolute men who would take a public stand that this lawlessness must cease, they could carry the community with them. But the difficulty of enforcing law and order in some of these mountain counties is to find proper judges, prosecuting officers, and sheriffs. The officers are as likely as not to be the worst men in the community, and if they are not, they are likely to use their authority for satisfying their private grudges and revenges. Consequently men take the "law" into their own hands. The most personally courageous become bullies and the terror of the community. The worst citizens are not those who have killed most men, in the opinion of the public. It ought to be said that in some of the mountain counties there has been very little lawlessness, and in some it has been repressed by the local authorities, and there is great improvement on the whole. I was sorry not to meet a well-known character in the mountains, who has killed twenty-one men. He is a very agreeable "square" man, and I believe "high-toned," and it is the universal testimony that he never killed a man who did not deserve killing, and whose death was a benefit to the community. He is called, in the language of the country, a "severe" man. In a little company that assembled at the Harlan tavern were two elderly men, who appeared to be on friendly terms enough. Their sons had had a difficulty, and two boys out of each family had been killed not very long ago. The fathers were not involved in the vendetta. About the old Harlan court-house a great many men have been killed during court week in the past few years. The habit of carrying pistols and knives, and whiskey, are the immediate causes of these deaths, but back of these is the want of respect for law. At the ford of the Cumberland at Pineville was anchored a little house-boat, which was nothing but a whiskey shop. During our absence a tragedy occurred there. The sheriff with a posse went out to arrest some criminals in the mountain near. He secured his men, and was bringing them into Pineville, when it occurred to him that it would be a good plan to take a drink at the house-boat. The whole party got into a quarrel over their liquor, and in it the sheriff was killed and a couple of men seriously wounded. A resolute surveyor, formerly a general in our army, surveying land in the neighborhood of Pineville, under a decree of the United States court, has for years carried on his work at the personal peril of himself and his party. The squatters not only pull up his stakes and destroy his work day after day, but it was reported that they had shot at his corps from the bushes. He can only go on with his work by employing a large guard of armed men.

This state of things in eastern Kentucky will not be radically changed until the railways enter it, and business and enterprise bring in law and order. The State government cannot find native material for enforcing law, though there has been improvement within the past two years. I think no permanent gain can be expected till a new civilization comes in, though I heard of a bad community in one of the counties that had been quite subdued and changed by the labors of a devout and plain-spoken evangelist. So far as our party was concerned, we received nothing but kind treatment, and saw little evidences of demoralization, except that the young men usually were growing up to be "roughs," and liked to lounge about with shot-guns rather than work. But the report of men who have known the country for years was very unfavorable as to the general character of the people who live on the mountains and in the little valleys—that they were all ignorant; that the men generally were idle, vicious, and cowardly, and threw most of the hard labor in the field and house upon the women; that the killings are mostly done from ambush, and with no show for a fair fight. This is a tremendous indictment, and it is too sweeping to be sustained. The testimony of the gentlemen of our party, who thoroughly know this part of the State, contradicted it. The fact is there are two sorts of people in the mountains, as elsewhere.

The race of American mountaineers occupying the country from western North Carolina to eastern Kentucky is a curious study. Their origin is in doubt. They have developed their peculiarities in isolation. In this freedom stalwart and able men have been from time to time developed, but ignorance and freedom from the restraints of law have had their logical result as to the mass. I am told that this lawlessness has only existed since the war; that before, the people, though ignorant of letters, were peaceful. They had the good points of a simple people, and if they were not literate, they had abundant knowledge of their own region. During the war the mountaineers were carrying on a civil war at home. The opposing parties were not soldiers, but bushwhackers. Some of the best citizens were run out of the country, and never returned. The majority were Unionists, and in all the mountain region of eastern

Kentucky I passed through there are few to-day who are politically Democrats. In the war, home-guards were organized, and these were little better than vigilance committees for private revenge. Disorder began with this private and partly patriotic warfare. After the war, when the bushwhackers got back to their cabins, the animosities were kept up, though I fancy that politics has little or nothing to do with them now. The habit of reckless shooting, of taking justice into private hands, is no doubt a relic of the disorganization during the war.

Worthless, good-for-nothing, irreclaimable, were words I often heard applied to people of this and that region. I am not so despondent of their future. Railways, trade, the sight of enterprise and industry, will do much with this material. Schools will do more, though it seems impossible to have efficient schools there at present. The people in their ignorance and their undeveloped country have a hard struggle for life. This region is, according to the census, the most prolific in the United States. The girls marry young, bear many children, work like galley-slaves, and at the time when women should be at their best they fade, lose their teeth, become ugly, and look old. One great cause of this is their lack of proper nourishment. There is nothing unhealthy in out-door work in moderation if the body is properly sustained by good food. But healthy, handsome women are not possible without good fare. In a considerable part of eastern Kentucky (not I hear in all) good wholesome cooking is unknown, and civilization is not possible without that. We passed a cabin where a man was very ill with dysentery. No doctor could be obtained, and perhaps that, considering what the doctor might have been, was not a misfortune. But he had no food fit for a sick man, and the women of the house were utterly ignorant of the diet suitable to a man in his state. I have no doubt that the abominable cookery of the region has much to do with the lawlessness, as it visibly has to do with the poor physical condition.

The road down the Cumberland, in a valley at times spreading out into fertile meadows, is nearly all the way through magnificent forests, along hill-sides fit for the vine, for fruit, and for pasture, while frequent outcroppings of coal testify to the abundance of the fuel that has been so long stored for the new civilization. These mountains would be profitable as sheep pastures did not the inhabitants here, as elsewhere in the United States, prefer to keep dogs rather than sheep.

I have thus sketched hastily some of the capacities of the Cumberland region. It is my belief that this central and hitherto neglected portion of the United States will soon become the theatre of vast and controlling industries.

I want space for more than a concluding word about western Kentucky, which deserves, both for its capacity and its recent improvements, a chapter to itself. There is a limestone area of some 10,000 square miles, with a soil hardly less fertile than that of the blue-grass region, a high agricultural development, and a population equal in all respects to that of the famous and historic grass country. Seven of the ten principal tobacco-producing counties in Kentucky and the largest Indian corn and wheat raising counties are in this part of the State. The western coal field has both river and rail transportation, thick deposits of iron ore, and more level and richer farming lands than the eastern coal field. Indeed, the agricultural development in this western coal region has attracted great attention.

Much also might be written of the remarkable progress of the towns of western Kentucky within the past few years. The increase in population is not more astonishing than the development of various industries. They show a vigorous, modern activity for which this part of the State has not, so far as I know, been generally credited. The traveller will find abundant evidence of it in Owensborough, Henderson, Hopkinsville, Bowling Green, and other places. As an illustration: Paducah, while doubling its population since 1880, has increased its manufacturing 150 per cent. The town had in 1880 twenty-six factories, with a capital of $600,000, employing 950 men; now it has fifty factories, with a cash capital of $2,000,000, employing 3250 men, engaged in a variety of industries—to which a large iron furnace is now being added. Taking it all together—variety of resources, excellence of climate, vigor of its people—one cannot escape the impression that Kentucky has a great future.

IOWA

THE State of Iowa occupies a space on the earth's surface between the fortieth and forty-fourth parallels of north latitude, and between the ninetieth and ninety-seventh parallels of longitude west of Greenwich. It is surrounded by the State of Minnesota on the north, by the State of Missouri on the south, and by Illinois and Wisconsin on the east, and Nebraska and Dakota on the west. The Mississippi River washes its entire eastern border, and the Missouri River its western.

Its area is about 55,000 square miles. It was organized as a Territory by an act of Congress on June 12, 1838, and it was admitted into the Union as a State under another act of Congress passed March 3, 1845.

The political power and sovereignty of this region was acquired by the United States by virtue of a treaty with France in 1803, called the "treaty for the purchase of Louisiana." Although it afterward became attached, for the purpose of local government, to the Territory of Michigan, and subsequently constituted a part of the Territory of Wisconsin, it never belonged to that large part of the country known as the "Northwestern Territory," or as the territory lying northwest of the Ohio River which had at one time belonged to Great Britain, and was ceded by Great Britain to the United States by the treaty of peace of 1783. The State of Virginia, which claimed this sovereignty, afterward relinquished her right also to the United States.

This "Northwestern Territory," which was the subject of the ordinance of 1787 concerning slavery and other rights granted to the people of that Territory, and out of which were subsequently created the States of Ohio, Indiana, Illinois, Michigan, and Wisconsin, did not include any territory west of the Mississippi River, as was distinctly shown by treaties between Great Britain and France, and between the United States and Great Britain. So far as the title of the United States to this part of the country is concerned, it rests upon the treaty for the purchase of Louisiana in 1803, made by Mr. Jefferson on behalf of the United States, and Napoleon, First Consul, on behalf of France.

The whole of this region called Louisiana had been the subject of contest between France and Spain in an early day, when the French claimed it as part of that territory discovered by Marquette and Hennepin, French explorers from the Canadian country, and the Spaniards as appertaining to their conquest of Mexico. Spain had had undisputed possession and control of it for many years prior to 1803, and about a year before the treaty between France and the United States she had ceded it to France.

The city of New Orleans, about one hundred and five miles above the mouth of the Mississippi River, had become a place of much importance by reason of its control, in the hands of Spain, of the navigation of that river, and the interests of the people of the United States living east of the Mississippi in that navigation was very large. Meanwhile we purchased all that was called the Louisiana country, by which the United States obtained entire control of both sides of the Mississippi River to its mouth.

Of course at that early day there was very little settlement of white people west of the river. The only point of any note to which that phrase can be applied was St. Louis, situated about twenty miles below the confluence of the Mississippi and Missouri rivers. During all the period of this controversy and of the transfers of the country embraced in the Louisiana Purchase, that portion of it now constituting the State of Iowa was in the undisturbed control of various bands of unciv-ilized Indians. The names of these tribes are numerous, and they do not seem to have established among themselves any distinct geographical lines separating their various possessions, but to have roamed at will over the whole extent of the wild prairies of this region.

The State derives its name from the tribe known now as the Iowa tribe. Much learning, or at least research, has been wasted in the attempt to show the orthog-raphy and definition of this word among the Indians themselves. While Wash-ington Irving, with the license allowable to an imaginative writer, states that the meaning of the word is "beautiful," and recounts the incident by which that phrase was first applied to the country, saying that the tribe who in their wanderings arrived at the highest point in the Iowa prairies, looking over the vast expanse of country uninterrupted by hills or swamps, involuntarily uttered the word "Iowa," meaning "beautiful." But probably a better authority for the meaning of the word was Mr. Antoine Le Claire, a half-breed of the "Sac" and "Fox" nations, who always asserted humorously that he was the first white man born in Iowa, though his mother was an Indian. He was employed for many years by the United States as an interpreter in their dealings with the various Indian tribes. His definition of the word was, "Here is the spot—this is the place—to dwell in peace." It is very certain, however, that the name of the State and the name of one of its secondary rivers, running through a large part of the centre of the State, is derived from the name of the tribe.

The earliest settlements made by any white persons within the limits of this region were on the Mississippi River, one in the northern part, the other in the southern part. Julian Dubuque, who was a native of Canada, and who had follow-ed a French emigration from Canada into the Northwestern Territory to Prairie du Chien, where the United States had estab-lished a military post on the east bank of the river, obtained permission of the Fox Indians about 1788 to work mines of lead which had been discovered at a point where is now the city of Dubuque. On the opposite side of the river, in what is now the State of Illinois, valuable lead mines had been discovered about twelve miles east of Dubuque. And the city of Galena,

deriving its name from the ore in which lead is found, has been built up by the mining interests there developed. The corresponding mines, worked and estab-lished by Dubuque after their discovery, became the nucleus of the first settlement in what is now the State of Iowa. The privilege granted him by the Indian tribe was confirmed by the Spanish Governor, Carondelet, and Dubuque spent his life in mining and trade at that point until his death in the year 1810.

At a point on the Mississippi River about twelve or fifteen miles north of the southern boundary of the State of Iowa, where is now the town of Montrose, in the county of Lee, Louis Honoré Tesson es-tablished a trading post. It will be per-ceived that both of these points of early settlements within the boundaries of Iowa were by Frenchmen, and were on the Mis-sissippi River some two hundred miles apart, and were in the latter part of the last century, before any organized civil government, su h as Spain might have pretended to assert, was established.

The country remained under the actual control of various tribes of Indians, main-ly the Sacs and Foxes, until the period of the celebrated Black Hawk war in 1832. This war grew out of controversies be-tween the chiefs of the Sac and Fox na-tions, led by Black Hawk, and white peo-ple on the Illinois side of the river, about the construction and validity of a treaty made between the United States and these Indians for the occupation of lands by the settlers.

As the white people began to settle up the country which it was supposed was obtained by that treaty (of 1828), they came in contact with the Indians, who re-fused to give up their lands. This result-ed in a bloody war, carried on on the Illi-nois side of the river by the Indians, who mainly crossed over from the Iowa side at or near Rock Island to assist their breth-ren in Illinois. The result of that war was the utter subjugation of the tribes, and a new treaty, made in 1832, by which they ceded to the United States the larger part of what is now the State of Iowa. An-other result of this war was that Black Hawk, the great warrior and principal chief of the Sac and Fox tribes, was de-posed by order of the government of the United States, and Keokuk, a subordinate chief who had opposed the action of the Indians, was made principal chief of the tribes. At the place on the Mississippi River where Keokuk had his home, a city has risen of sixteen or eighteen thousand population, which bears his name, and in memory of his friendship and service to the United States the people of that city have recently erected a monument, which adorns one of the handsomest public parks in the State.

With the ratification of this treaty of purchase the Western pioneers began to make settlements in the country, and a form of civilized government was established by attaching the few people that were first in the country west of the Mississippi River to the Territory of Michigan for judicial purposes. In 1837 the Territory of Wisconsin was organized by an act of Congress, and included the region west of the Mississippi River of which Iowa was a part; and the first Legislature of this new Territory was held at Burlington, on the west bank of that river, in the southern part of what is now the State of Iowa. In the next year, 1838, Iowa was constituted a separate Territory, and the seat of government established at Burlington. There were also, about this time, land-offices established for the sale of public lands, and surveys were made of these lands preparatory to such sales.

These sales were by law first made at public auction—any person having means to do so being at liberty to bid for any lands of the government subject to sale at that time. There did not exist then any of those statutes afterward passed by Congress by which the first settler upon the public lands was protected by priority of right in making this purchase. Nor was there any protection for the buildings, fences, and other improvements made upon the soil by the labor of the actual settler. It was only in 1842 that Congress for the first time passed a law which was the beginning of that wise and salutary system since come to be known as the "pre-emption laws of the United States," which granted to a man who settled upon and cultivated any land of the United States a priority of purchase, at a fixed price, under proper circumstances.

It cannot properly be omitted, in any attempt to give an account of the progress of the State of Iowa from the organized Territory of 40,000 people to a State with a population of 2,000,000, to advert to the generosity displayed by the Congress of the United States in granting its lands to

GEORGE W. JONES.

States for various purposes of public use —of charity, of education, and of internal improvements.

One of the earliest of these magnificent gifts was the donation to the then Territory of Iowa of alternate sections of public lands for five miles on each side of the Des Moines River for the improvement of the navigation of that river by slackwater. Under this statute 322,392 acres of land have been certified to the State.

It is true that, so far as regards locking and damming smaller streams is concerned, the suggestion seems to have proved a failure, after a vast expenditure of money. But while this was the prevailing idea, and while Iowa was in a state of Territorial organization, the Congress of the United States made the donation above referred to. When we consider that the Des Moines River runs through the entire length of the State of Iowa, from its northwest to its southeast corner, and that the lands through which it runs were then, and are to this day, as fine a body of rich soil as any in the world, the generosity of the grant cannot be questioned. Iowa has also shared largely in the grants of land made by Congress for railroad purposes. Not to consume our space by minute descriptions of these grants, it will suffice to say that four roads

AUGUSTUS C. DODGE.

across the State of Iowa from east to west,
from the Mississippi to the Missouri River, had each the same grant of every alternate section within five miles on each
side of its line, to aid in its construction.
And to these, with other railroads in the
State, Congress has given an aggregate of
4,708,400 acres of land of similar quality. It may be safely said that the rapid
growth of the State in wealth and in population is largely due to the construction
of these roads, and would otherwise have
been delayed for a period of time which
can only be conjectured.

This control and conduct of the sales
of the public lands introduced into the
history of Iowa two of its early men of
influence and distinction. One of these
was the Hon. George W. Jones, who,
while living in the State of Wisconsin,
was for many years Surveyor-General
of the district of public lands which
included Iowa, and who supervised the
government surveys of these lands. The
other was Augustus Cæsar Dodge, who, it
is believed, was the first land-officer appointed to conduct sales of these lands in
the Iowa district; and he and General
Jones were the first Senators of the State
in the Congress of the United States.

General George Wallace Jones was
born in Vincennes, Indiana, April 12, 1804.
His earliest introduction to Iowa was in
connection with the mining business in
the region of Dubuque, where he erected
the first reverberating furnace in the
State, and where he was the first to open
a store for mercantile business. He was
an aide to General Dodge, and took an
active part in the Black Hawk war. He
was appointed by President Buchanan
in 1860 as Minister to Bogota, in South
America, from which place, after the
breaking out of the recent civil war in the
autumn of 1861, he was recalled. He has
since resided in Dubuque, where he now
lives, at the advanced age of eighty-five
years, held in honorable esteem by his
neighbors and by the citizens of the State
which he so long and so faithfully served.

General Jones occupied a prominent
position in the Senate of the United States
during the twelve years of his service
there. He was unwearied in his efforts
at serving his State and promoting the interests of its citizens. In obtaining appropriations for public buildings, in securing
land grants which we have already mentioned, in establishing a general system of
liberal donations for public purposes, in
the efforts to improve the navigation of
the Mississippi River, and in ways too numerous, though important, to be recited
here, he proved himself a valuable and
faithful public servant. He was second
to Mr. Cilley, of New Hampshire, in the
unfortunate duel with Mr. Graves, of Kentucky, which resulted in the death upon
the ground of the former.

Augustus Cæsar Dodge was born at St.
Genevieve, Missouri, on January 2, 1812.
He was the son of General Henry Dodge,
a great Indian fighter of the Northwest,
who took a most efficient part in the Black
Hawk war, in which also his son Augustus served in a minor capacity. Mr.
Dodge was raised in his father's family
in northern Illinois and Wisconsin, the
family, like many others, being gathered
around the lead mines found at Galena
and Dubuque. When the sale of public
lands in Iowa required the establishment
of offices for that purpose, one was located at Dubuque and another at Burlington at the same time. In 1838 Mr.
Dodge was appointed by President Van
Buren register of the land-office at the
latter place, and he then removed to that
town, which became his home for the rest
of his life. In the summer of 1840 he was
elected Delegate to Congress from Iowa.
On the 2d day of September Mr. Dodge

took his seat in the Twenty-seventh Congress, then convened in an extra session, and on the 7th of December he welcomed his father to a seat by his side as the Delegate from the Territory of Wisconsin. It also occurred, very singularly, that the father and son afterward served together in the Congress of the United States as Senators, the one from the State of Wisconsin and the other from the State of Iowa. Augustus Dodge continued by re-elections to serve as Delegate for the Territory of Iowa from that period until its admission as a State into the Union, December 28, 1846. The service of General Dodge as Senator continued from the 26th of December, 1848, until March 4, 1855. This period covered the exciting incidents of the contest in 1850 concerning the admission of the States created out of the territory ceded to us by Mexico, and on this subject our Senator, though strong in his Democratic sentiments, followed generally the lead of Mr. Benton. And in the great Kansas-Nebraska struggle of 1854 he sided with Mr. Douglas in the passage of what has been since known as the "Kansas-Nebraska Bill." The effect in Iowa of the passage of this bill was the utter overthrow of the Democratic party, which had, since the organization of the Territory, been under the control and leadership of General Jones and General Dodge.

General Dodge was, on the 8th of February, 1855, appointed by President Pierce Minister to the court of Spain. He discharged faithfully and creditably the duties of that high position. He died at Burlington, November 20, 1883.

It is proper also in this connection to revert to the first Delegate who represented the Territory of Iowa in the Congress of the United States. This was W. W. Chapman, a native of Clarksburg, Virginia, where he was born in August, 1808, and who is now living, at the age of eighty years, in vigorous health, mental and bodily, in the State of Oregon.

A distinguished Kentuckian, John Chambers, was made Governor of the Territory of Iowa by President Harrison in 1841. He was born in the State of New Jersey in 1779. While Governor of the Territory his success in managing the relations of the country with the Indians was very great. On his retirement from public service Governor Chambers

W. W. CHAPMAN.

returned to his home in Kentucky, where he died, beloved by every one, at an advanced age, on the 21st of September, 1852.

The growth of the State of Iowa in population, in wealth, and in all elements of high civilization and prosperity, from the period of its admission into the Union, or rather from its organization as a Territory, is almost unparalleled. For a period of twenty years, from 1840 to 1860, probably no State ever exceeded that of Iowa in the rapidity of its increase. If you take another short period, from the census of 1850 to the census of 1870, and consider that this included the time of the civil war, both the ratio of the growth and absolute increase is wonderful. The census of 1840 represents the Territory of Iowa as having 43,112 souls, and that of 1850 gave her 192,214. At this latter period she was the twenty-seventh State in the scale of population; and in 1860, numbering 674,913, she was the twentieth. In 1870, with a population of 1,194,020, she was the eleventh.

It only remains to add that by the census of 1880 she was tenth in the Union, with a population of 1,624,615. And the State of Michigan, which was ninth, and Kentucky, which was eighth, had only eight or ten thousand more than the State of Iowa.

JOHN CHAMBERS.

There are no means at hand of ascertaining with precision the present population of the State, but taking such evidence as there is, it may safely be estimated that it is in excess of 1,850,000, and that the census of 1890 will show that over 2,000,000 of people inhabit the State of Iowa. This growth is the more remarkable because it was unaided by any adventitious circumstances. It was the regular overflow of the population from the States east and southeast of Iowa. Like all new Northern or Free States bordering upon the Southern or Slave States, and especially like Indiana and Illinois, Iowa received large accessions to her population from these bordering States, and especially from Kentucky, Missouri, Virginia, and Tennessee.

There were, in the early days of Iowa, very few men of wealth, and still fewer who had any surplus capital to aid themselves or their neighbors in the cultivation of the soil. And even to this day, though a very prosperous State in many respects, there are few if any individuals in the State entitled to be called rich or wealthy, and there are no great organizations of banks or other associations with large surplus means.

There were, during this period of growth, no large cities, nor are there now, to which population was attracted, and which swelled the aggregate census of the State. If

it be a misfortune, which may be doubted, to Iowa that she has no St. Louis nor Chicago, nor even cities to compare with Omaha, with Denver, with St. Paul and Minneapolis, in States much younger, it is one to which she must submit, as the largest city in the State, the seat of its official government, the city of Des Moines, does not perhaps at the present day number 40,000 population. At the periods of the rapid progress to which we have heretofore referred, some three or four towns on the Mississippi River struggled up in 1860 to populations varying from twelve to twenty thousand. These were Dubuque, Davenport, Burlington, and Keokuk; but it must be conceded that while the growth of the interior of the State has displayed such wonderful rapidity, these towns seem to have attained almost a stationary position at about the beginning of the recent civil war.

The State of Iowa is now and always has been essentially an agricultural State. There are few manufacturing establishments within its boundaries, although struggles have been made to establish them; and while in some instances a partial success has followed, it cannot be said that these amounted to much. The rate of interest for the loan of money which could be had in Iowa up to the close of the civil war was largely in excess of that which could be profitably used by those engaged in manufacturing. The ease with which persons who were dependent upon their own labor for the support of themselves and families could secure in Iowa land sufficient to support that family in comfort, with prospects of increasing wealth and happiness, created a source of competition for the labor necessary to carry on manufacturing establishments which almost forbade the attempt. These conditions are now rapidly changing, and it may be hoped that our infant manufactures will be more successful.

Nor should it be a matter of surprise that the present population of Iowa should be mainly a population of farmers; for no country exists upon the face of the globe where the soil is at once so fertile, so cheap, and the climate so favorable. We hazard nothing in saying that the 55,000 square miles, or the 35,000,000 of acres, of land constituting the area of this State has no equal in capacity for profitable cultivation, for salubrity of climate, for variety of productions, and for all that goes to make up a happy, a prosperous, and contented community, whose wealth and support grow out of the cultivation of the soil. In other words, it may well be doubted whether any civil or political subdivision of the globe, of a similar or nearly similar extent of surface, is capable of supporting a heavier population than the State of Iowa. It is destitute of deserts, of swamps, of mountains, which interfere with this purpose.

The land, though almost exclusively prairie, by which we mean large bodies of it without trees, produces the richest kind of native grass, on which herds of cattle grow and fatten for the market. It is gently undulating, and nowhere presents any large tracts of flat or undrained soil. There are several rivers which run through the State into the Mississippi and Missouri of such size as to furnish ample drainage of the earth's surface, and water for all needed purposes. Among these are the Des Moines, which runs from the northwestern corner of the State to the Mississippi River at the southeastern corner, a distance of more than 300 miles, which, until railroads superseded its use, was navigated by steamboats for 150 miles. The Iowa River and the Cedar are also very considerable streams in the interior of the State. At any point in the midst of the prairies farthest from a river a well dug down into the soil from ten to fifteen feet always supplies sufficient water of the purest quality. And though wood and timber were scarce, there was sufficient for the days of early settlement; and beds of fine coal, underlying the surface of one-third and perhaps one-half of the State, render this scarcity of wood immaterial for purposes of fuel.

The forty-second parallel north latitude runs almost through the centre of the State of Iowa, and the climate of the State is very similar to that of Indiana and Illinois east of it. West of it, if you go 150 miles from the Missouri River, the country where, for want of rain, the land is unprofitable for cultivation, begins. And as you go farther west it becomes altogether impossible to cultivate it without irrigation.

The Iowa climate and the nature of the soil are propitious for as great variety of the fruits of the earth as any part of the world. The cereals which it produces in abundance are wheat and rye and oats

and Indian-corn; and in the reports of the census of 1880 it was found that Iowa produced in that year 31,154,205 bushels of wheat. Still later it has been reported to be the third State in the Union in regard to the quantity of wheat produced.

Perhaps the most important crop, next to wheat, is that of Indian-corn. The animals to which the farmer turns his attention successfully are cattle and hogs and horses. Sheep do not seem to thrive very well in Iowa, owing to the want of moun-

JAMES W. GRIMES.

tain-sides, to the general level surface of the country, and to other circumstances. As in most new countries West, hog-raising was in the early days the most profitable business of the farmers. The animal which is fed, when it is to be fatted for market, on Indian-corn, is in fact the means of converting that article into bacon, lard, and pork. Gradually this business, originally predominant in Kentucky, Indiana, and the States near to Cincinnati, which for years was the great market where the hog was bought and slaughtered and converted into the products mentioned, has receded farther west.

So also the raising of beef cattle, which until very recently was one of the most profitable pursuits in Iowa, by reason of the vast unoccupied meadows of natural prairie grass on which they were fed and fattened without much expense, has yielded to the successful cultivation of the soil, by which these prairies have been converted into fields of corn and wheat and other grain, and devoted to the production of potatoes and fruits, so that the cattle business has been largely transferred to the wild regions of the Territories bordering on the Rocky Mountains.

These are not indications of decaying prosperity, but they are the necessary results of an increased population and the cultivation of the earth in the production of more profitable crops. This soil and climate are also very favorable to fruits, the apple, the cherry, the pear, the strawberry, the raspberry, all of which are successfully raised throughout the entire State. And the records of agricultural expositions show that Iowa rivals many of the best of the States in the production of the apple, both in regard to its quality and its quantity. In this growth of the State an element hard to be computed, but easily appreciated by one who has travelled through it at periods of twenty-five years apart, is the increased comfort, beauty, and salubrity of the homes of the people. Handsome houses, sometimes expensive, well painted, well ventilated, with barns rivalling those of Pennsylvania in service and extent, gardens in which the vegetables for the table and the flowers which decorate the homestead are cultivated with success, present themselves now where formerly the turf cabin or the slight effort to make a house which would pass with the land-office for a lawful settlement was only to be seen.

The condition of these farmers has been very much improved financially by the cheapness of money growing out of its great increase in the United States since the termination of the civil war. The money which the farmer, fifteen or twenty years ago, for the purpose of improving his land, building his house, and stocking his farm, had to borrow at the rate of ten and twelve per cent. per annum, he has been enabled to obtain and pay off, if not wholly, in part, by the productions of his farm, and by the use of industry and economy. Or if not entirely free of this debt, he can now borrow the same money at six per cent., with increased prospects of rapidly discharging it. It would be difficult to find in any equal number of farmers to those living in the State of Iowa a more prosperous, happy, and contented population.

The system of education of Iowa, which has been a matter of earnest attention since the Territorial government was organized, may be considered under two aspects—the common-school system and the collegiate system. The liberality of Congress in granting lands for the purposes of education in all Western States where the soil primarily belonged to the government cannot be too highly commended. In addition to grants like 500,000 acres to aid in the establishing of a university, Congress granted later to each State in the Union a large amount for the establishment of an agricultural college, and a provision in the act for the admission of the State of Iowa gave to her five per cent. of all sales by the United States of the public lands within the State, to aid the university. But there was the grandest gift of all in the provision in the same act that the sixteenth and thirty-sixth sections of every township of the public land should be appropriated for the purposes of common schools, under the supervision of the State. In some respects perhaps the State has not managed these various grants in the way to realize the highest amount of money and the greatest benefits for the cause of education. But the State herself has supplemented these gifts with contributions of her own, and with taxes levied on the people of each locality for the support of schools, so that these contributions and provisions have created a system by which every child in the State of Iowa, from the age of six to sixteen years, may pass six to eight months of each year of his life in attendance on school without charge.

The rigid enforcement of this system has dotted the whole surface of the State with comfortable school - houses. And while, perhaps, teachers are not paid very compensatory salaries, and therefore are not always the most capable for the business, yet as a system calculated to educate every human being in the State up to a certain degree of attainment, it is difficult to see how it could be much improved. One of the incidents of this system is that most of the teachers are females, to whom the compensation is quite a blessing, who are generally better adapted to the education and training of children in their early youth than men, and who have, in the State of Iowa at least, done credit to the sex by their skill, their diligence, and good conduct.

The purpose of this school system was primarily to educate the youth in the elements of an English education—reading, writing, arithmetic, orthography, geography, grammar, history. In some of the more ambitious towns and cities there has been engrafted upon this, and paid for from the same source, what is often called the high-school or grammar-school, in which are taught, in addition to the subjects just mentioned, the dead languages, often Latin, sometimes Greek, and German and French. These high-schools in the larger cities are to some extent the equivalents of lower grades of colleges, and no doubt better education is frequently obtained in them than can be had in poorly endowed and struggling colleges, which perhaps should never have been started. It is, however, becoming a question, and a grave one, in the State, whether these high-schools are not a violation of the spirit and purpose found in the statutes, which were intended to establish what we understand by the words a "common-school system."

In regard to the other class of educational institutions—colleges and universi-

WILLIAM B. ALLISON.

ties—Iowa has suffered in common with nearly all the Western States, and perhaps some of the Eastern States, by the efforts to create a college in every town of any size, and for every religious denomination, as well as the college and university established by the State. There is no more unfortunate delusion than that which possesses some men who desire to leave their property at their death to charitable and benevolent institutions than to devise a sum for the creation of a college, the amount of which will barely suffice to erect the first building necessary for such institutions, leaving the support of the professors, the establishment of scholarships, the purchase of laboratories, globes, and maps, necessary to the conducting of any college, to chance or to solicitation, or to any of the means which may be supposed to supply these necessities of college instruction.

In addition to colleges thus projected, almost every Christian denomination in the State of Iowa has attempted to establish one of its own. And the Methodists, the early pioneers of civilization and religion, possessing the largest membership

JAMES HARLAN.

of any Christian Church in the State, have thought it necessary to attempt the establishment of a college for each of its four Conferences. The result of this has been, in the State of Iowa, that the efforts of the friends of liberal education have been divided and paralyzed. The colleges are unable to give salaries sufficient to command the services of competent professors; none of them have the philosophical apparatus which should be provided; all of them are struggling inefficiently, with one or two exceptions. The Congregationalists have in "Cornell University," at Grinnell, a fairly successful college. "Iowa State University," at Iowa City, has not been without reasonable endowments by the proceeds of lands given by the Federal government and by some contributions from the State treasury, but has not been very fortunate in the manner in which it has been conducted by the trustees appointed by the State.

It is now, however, placed upon a footing which promises success, and with a new and efficient President (Schaefer), and with the confidence of the public, with an efficient medical department and a still more successful law department, it may be said to be fairly deserving the name of "university."

The agricultural college organized by the State five or six years ago, and supported by the proceeds from the sale of land donated by the government, has not developed great capacity for instruction in agricultural labor and science, either because no sufficient system of instruction has been devised, or because the intestine controversies among the trustees, presidents, and professors have retarded its growth and obstructed its usefulness. The latter circumstance has been a source of regret to all who are interested in the institution.

With regard to religion in the State of Iowa, we have already stated that the Methodists are quite numerous, having four separate Conferences in the State. The other forms of the Protestant religions, as the Baptists, the Presbyterians, the Congregationalists, and Episcopalians, have their numbers in about the order in which the denominations are here named. The Catholics, as might be inferred from the absence of a large city population, are not as numerous as in other States. The numbers of the church membership of each denomination, which cannot be here given, make the State a marked one for its religious character. And as might be supposed from the sources from whence its population came, and the advantages for education which it has had for now nearly fifty years, the population is a highly moral and educated one.

With regard to its material prosperity, its wealth, and the extent of the cultivation of the soil and the profitable products of that soil, in place of any specific statistics in regard to the various classes into which the wealth of the State may be divided and its producing capacity estimated, we will give, as the best general indication of all this, a statement of the number of miles of railroad within the State completed and in profitable operation.

This statement, with a comparison with other States, is taken from a statistical account for the year 1882. In that year Iowa had 6113 miles of completed railroad. The four States which exceeded her in the number of miles within their borders were Illinois, 8326 miles; Pennsylvania, 6690 miles; Ohio, 6664 miles; and New York, 6279 miles. Of the five principal kingdoms of Europe, including Great Britain and Ireland, the number of miles given for the same year in the same table was, for Germany, 22,563; Great Britain and Ireland, 18,186; France, 17,027; Russia, 14,067; Austria and Hungary, 11,738. To make striking the wonderful progress of the State of Iowa, as shown by these figures, it may be stated that in 1850, with a population of 192,000, there was not a mile of railroad within the State. In 1880, with a population of 1,624,615, there were, two years later, 6113 miles of railroad in actual use.

At this latter period she was the fifth in the Union in the number of miles of railroad in active use. And only five of the great kingdoms of Europe exceeded her in this respect. When we consider that these roads are all running now at a profit on the cost of construction, at a period when that construction cost nearly twice as much as it would now, and that the State itself produces but little for transportation which is not the growth of the soil, some estimate may be made of the wealth of the State in that soil, and of the industry of her population.

The situation of Iowa with regard to its finances is probably as favorable as that of any State in the Union. Her public debt as funded in bonds does not amount to $300,000. And this would long since have been paid off but for the fact that it was created at a time when a high rate of interest was necessary to secure the loan. As all these bonds bear eight per cent. interest, payable in the city of New York, the holders refuse to accept the par value of the bonds not yet due, and the State has not felt inclined to purchase them at a premium, as the government of the United States is doing in regard to its bonds. Something of a drawback on this financial condition of the State exists in the amount of indebtedness of counties and cities, contracted mainly to aid in the construction of railroads.

This sketch of the State would be very incomplete without some reference to the part which she played in the civil war which we still call recent, though over twenty years have elapsed since its close.

The State sent into the actual service of that war, from its beginning in April, 1861, to its close in 1865, 76,242 soldiers. Of these, all except the First Regiment were enlisted for three years or for the duration

JOHN A. KASSON.

of the war, if that should be less than three years. This First Regiment was hastily called out for ninety days' service by the Governor, and took part in the battle of Wilson's Creek, at which the commander of the Federal force, General Lyon, was killed, while marching at the head of the Iowa regiment, whose colonel was too ill to be on the field of battle.

At the time when the existence of the war was recognized by Congress, and the President made his first call for troops, Iowa had two Representatives in the Lower House of Congress, both of whom came home and were made colonels of Iowa regiments, leaving the halls of Congress for that purpose, and serving through to the end of the war. These were General Curtis, of Keokuk, and General Vandever, of Dubuque, the latter of whom is now, at the age of seventy-one years, a member of the same body, from the State of Cali-

SAMUEL J. KIRKWOOD.

ward became the Republican party of the State. From 1854 to 1858 he was a wise and judicious Governor, a careful conservator of all the best interests of the State; and when, upon the expiration of General Jones's term of service and his retirement from the Senate of the United States, Governor Grimes was elected by the Legislature to fill his place, it was recognized at once as the necessary result of his standing with his party and of his abilities as a statesman. His service as chairman of the Committee on Naval Affairs was of the greatest value to the nation. Few men during the period of the war, and during the enactment of what are called the "reconstruction measures" of Congress, including the amendments of the Constitution, exercised a more potent and favorable influence than Senator Grimes. Cool, clear-headed, sagacious, his opinion was often solicited and always listened to with great consideration. His independence of spirit and his profound statesmanship were strongly evidenced in his vote for the acquittal of President Johnson at the impeachment trial. Some two years after this trial was over, Governor Grimes, whose health had failed so as to render him unable to attend to his duties in the Senate, resigned, and left public life; and after a short trip to Europe, returning to his home in Burlington, he died of the paralysis from which he had been suffering for three or four years. It may be doubted whether any man has ever possessed the confidence and respect of the people of Iowa more unreservedly than Governor Grimes.

fornia. Of the part which the State of Iowa and her gallant soldiers took in this bloody struggle it is impossible, within the limits of this article, to speak at any length. Their bodies were strewn upon every battle-field of the war, from Wilson's Creek and Donelson and Shiloh to its close by the capture of General Johnston's army in North Carolina.

It would be impossible to select for special mention, without an invidious distinction, and within the narrow range of this article, those whose names are covered with glory, many of whom died upon the field of battle or while in service in the army. With regard to those who occupied positions in civil life during this eventful period, and indeed from the period anterior to this by six or eight years, when the subject of controversy which led to the war was ripening to the issue which terminated in that event, we cannot omit to speak of several of the most distinguished.

Mr. James W. Grimes, placing himself at the head of the party which made the issue in 1854 on the repeal of the Missouri Compromise by the Kansas-Nebraska Act of Congress, led it to a victory which included his own election as Governor. Governor Grimes came to Iowa from the State of New Hampshire. After the election of 1854, and indeed during that election, he took the leadership of what after-

The Legislature of the State which was elected at the time that Grimes was elected Governor, elected the Hon. James Harlan as Senator to succeed General Dodge. Mr. Harlan, a native of Indiana, migrated to Iowa during the Territorial stage of its existence. He served in the Senate of the United States until March 4, 1873, with the exception of a short period when he was Secretary of the Interior under President Johnson.

Mr. Harlan's services, like Mr. Grimes's, during this period of the war and of reconstruction, were by his colleagues and by the country appreciated very highly. Since his retirement from the Senate he has held the office of president of the commission for distributing the award of the arbitration in regard to the *Alabama* claims, in which he has given universal satisfaction. He is now living in retirement at Mount Pleasant, Iowa, in a lonely age, his wife and children, except one, being dead.

Another distinguished man of civil life, mainly of this period, but whose services have been since continued, is the Hon. J. A. Kasson. Mr. Kasson was an active and efficient political worker in the canvass which led to the election of Mr. Lincoln in 1860. He was made First Assistant Postmaster-General under the Hon. Montgomery Blair, and in that capacity, or by virtue of his experience in that position, he was appointed our representative to the European conference which established the system of international postage, where his services were invaluable. He was, during the war, elected to the Congress of the United States from the Congressional district of Iowa which includes the capital of the State. He served in that capacity during a large part of the war, and during the closing scenes of the "reconstruction measures," and after a year or two of retirement was made Minister to Austria, which place he filled with distinction. He has since that time been a member of Congress. One of his more recent public services was two years ago, as chairman of the organization which had charge of the celebration at Philadelphia on the 17th of September of the centennial of the adoption of the Constitution of the United States. He has recently been appointed by President Harrison one of the commissioners to the Berlin Conference on the Samoan question.

One other figure prominent during the war, but in civil life, is that of Governor Kirkwood, who migrated from the State of Ohio. Shortly after the formation of the State he settled in Iowa, and after several terms of service in the State Legislature was Governor when the war broke out in 1861. His efficient services in raising and collecting troops, and devising means of clothing and equipment, secured for him the sobriquet of the "war Governor" of the State, having been re-elected in the midst of the war to the same office with an overwhelming majority. He has since served in the Senate of the United States, and as Secretary of the Interior by the appointment of President Garfield. He has now retired from public life, and is enjoying a well-deserved rest, with a popularity not surpassed among the citizens of the State.

Among the men of distinction of Iowa who entered the public service about the beginning of the war was one of the present Senators, the Hon. James F. Wilson, a native of Ohio. He was a member of the Convention to amend the Constitution of Iowa in 1856, and he succeeded General S. R. Curtis in 1861 as one of the two members of Congress to which the State was entitled. Afterward he was re-elected, and served in the House of Representatives until March 3, 1869. As a member of the Judiciary Committee, and as chairman of that committee for several years preceding the end of his service, he took a prominent part in the legislation in support of the war, and in the enactment of the "reconstruction measures." The country is indebted to him for the statutory provision which permitted negroes to testify as witnesses in the courts of the United States, and which did away with the rule of exclusion with regard to parties to the suit and persons interested in the event of the suit which had previously prevailed under the common law. At the close of his term in March, 1869, he was offered by General Grant, on his inauguration as President, the place of Secretary of State in his cabinet. This he was compelled to decline on account of the condition of his private affairs, which imperatively demanded his personal attention. After remaining in

JAMES F. WILSON.

private life, except as one of the board of directors of the Union Pacific Railroad, he was elected to the Senate of the United States, December, 1883. He has since been re-elected, and has a full term of six years yet to serve. Mr. Wilson has always been and is to-day one of the strongest men presented by the State of Iowa to the public service, and has the unlimited confidence of the voters of that State.

Another Senator who served as Representative, and who is now serving in the

GEORGE W. McCRARY.

Senate, is the Hon. William B. Allison, also a native of Ohio. He was elected Representative to the Thirty-eighth, Thirty-ninth, Fortieth, and Forty-first Congresses, in which as an industrious and sagacious statesman he soon attained prominence, being for some years before he left that body chairman of the Committee on Appropriations. On March 4, 1873, he took his seat as Senator, and has been twice re-elected. In the Senate he has for many years held the position of chairman of the Appropriations Committee, which, from the responsibility it imposes and the power it gives, has long been considered as the highest post of honor in that body after that of President of the Senate. The estimate which the people of Iowa and the public generally place upon the services of Mr. Allison, and the confidence which he inspires amongst his

friends and associates, cannot be more strongly evinced than by the simple statement that at the recent Republican Convention for the nomination of a candidate for the approaching election of President, Mr. Allison was presented by his own State with entire unanimity, and was supported by sufficient votes of the other States to make them amount to 99 at the beginning of the contest.

During the war one man from Iowa attained great distinction, and has since been in the civil service of the nation in high position. This is the Hon. W. W. Belknap, the son of Major-General Belknap, of the war with Mexico and the war of 1812. Residing at Keokuk, Iowa, at the outbreak of the war in the spring of 1861, he was appointed Major of the Fifteenth Regiment of Iowa Volunteers, and took part, soon after the organization of the regiment, in the battle of Shiloh, April 6 and 7, 1862. From that period to the end of the war his services were most valuable, attracting the attention of the country and of his superior officers. He was rapidly promoted to Brigadier-General and Brevet Major-General of the volunteer army. An act of distinguished gallantry on his part during one of the battles around Atlanta cannot be here omitted. The enemy, in attacking the barricades behind which General Belknap and his troops were fighting, approached so close that General Belknap reached over and caught a major of the rebel army by his coat collar and dragged him inside and made him a prisoner. At the close of the war General Belknap was made Collector of Internal Revenue for the first district of Iowa, and while holding that position he was invited by General Grant to take the place of Secretary of War in his cabinet upon the death of General Rawlins.

This position he occupied four or five years, and in the administration of the affairs of the army, which presented many troublesome questions growing out of the dissolution of the army and the reconstruction of that which remained, General Belknap was found most efficient. It is true that in the House of Representatives articles of impeachment were preferred against him, charging him with improper conduct in the disposal of a sutlership or post-tradership in the army. He was, however, acquitted on trial before the Senate, and has ever since retained the undiminished confidence of those who knew him well and were best qualified to judge of his character.

Another public man of Iowa of high reputation was made a member of his cabinet by President Hayes upon its organization. This was the Hon. George W. McCrary, who after eight years of distinguished service in Congress, where he rose to be a leading member of that body, entered the cabinet of Mr. Hayes as Secretary of War, and remained there until he was appointed a Circuit Judge of the United States. Here, after four or five years of service, having a large family and struggling with comparative poverty, he accepted the offer of a railroad company in the West to serve as its attorney and counsellor, at a salary of $10,000 per annum, in which he is now engaged.

JOHN F. DILLON.

It is thus that by a niggardly policy and insufficient salaries the best offices of the country, especially its judicial offices, are abandoned for the pursuits of private life. Another very remarkable illustration of this truth is that of Hon. J. F. Dillon, who, after serving in the State of Iowa as judge of the local court, and then as judge of the Supreme Court of the State, and afterward as Circuit Judge for the same circuit afterward occupied by Judge McCrary, also resigned in the height of his usefulness and of his reputation as a great judge, and accepted the place of professor in the Columbia College law school in New York, and of counsel and attorney for the Union Pacific Railroad Company, in which two places alone his compensation was three times as large as that which he received from the government of the United States as Circuit Judge.

There remains to be noticed one other remarkable figure in the history of Iowa, distinguished both in the military and civil service of the country. This was General Samuel R. Curtis, who was born in the State of Ohio, February 3, 1807, and was educated at the Military Academy at West Point in 1827. After serving as second lieutenant in the Seventh Infantry for a short time he resigned, and en-

gaged in civil engineering in his native State. Upon the outbreak of the Mexican war, after assisting the Governor of Ohio to organize troops sent forward by that State, he was made Colonel of the Third Regiment. With this regiment he marched to the Rio Grande, where he was too late to take part in any of the distinguished battles fought by General Taylor. But when General Taylor left the Rio Grande Colonel Curtis was left in command, and also to act as civil Governor in that region. In 1847 he accepted the office of chief engineer of the Des Moines River improvement in Iowa, and he removed to Keokuk in that year, where he established the home which he occupied from that time until his death. In 1850 he was made chief engineer of the city of St. Louis, and under his direction a general system of sewerage was established throughout the city, and the ponds which had been the sources of trouble were drained, and an invaluable service rendered to one of the finest cities of the United States. He was elected Mayor of Keokuk in 1855. In 1856 he was elected to represent the first district of Iowa in the Thirty-fifth Congress, and was re-elected to the same place in the Thirty-sixth and Thirty-seventh Congresses.

During this last Congress he was chair-

SAMUEL R. CURTIS.

as they were assembled in St. Louis. He was finally sent with an army of eighteen or twenty thousand men in pursuit of Price and others in southwestern Missouri. He dispersed and followed these into the Boston Mountains in Arkansas, and at Pea Ridge, where the enemy rallied and gave him battle, he won one of the most remarkable victories of the war. It is very true that this battle, in the numbers of men engaged in it and in the practical effect it had upon the war, cannot be compared to such great victories as the capture of Vicksburg, the battles of Gettysburg, Chickamauga, and others that might be mentioned, but if the comparison is to be made with regard to the tactical skill displayed, by which the Federal army was enabled to contest the field with twice its numbers, and also considering the overwhelming defeat of the enemy, it must be conceded that it presents features of ability and capacity for command in battle and in arrangements preliminary to it of the highest order. Yet General Curtis has not received at the hands of his countrymen in any public form even the scant justice which would show the measure of gratitude and consideration to which his eminent services entitle him.

After the battle of Pea Ridge he continued in command in the Southwest until he was superseded by other commanders. He died December 26, 1866.

The level prairie in the northern part of the State, about half-way between the Mississippi and Missouri rivers, at a point near Spirit Lake, attains an elevation of 1700 feet above the sea. This rise from these rivers is so gradual that it was not suspected until some enterprising engineer tested it by his instrument. A lover of his State, gazing from this point over the broad reach within his vision of wheat and rye and oats and corn, and the cattle grazing on its natural meadows, might paraphrase Mr. Webster's eloquent allusion to Massachusetts, and say of Iowa: "She needs no eulogium from me. There she is; she speaks for herself."

man of the Committee on the Pacific Railroad, and while the honor of suggesting the practicability of that work and the best route of its construction may be contested, as it is, by many persons, it is impossible to deny to him the honor, so well merited, that by his tact, his energy, and his familiarity with that class of subjects he did more than any one person to pass through Congress the law under which this great work was completed, and also that of the Central Pacific Railroad, the two making a complete connection of the Pacific coast with the rest of the country. Upon the outbreak of the late civil war, though one of the only two members to which the State was entitled in Congress, he at once returned to Iowa, assisted in organizing troops, and was elected Colonel of the Second Iowa Regiment, the First Regiment being merely ninety-day volunteers, who were disbanded shortly after the battle of Wilson's Creek.

From that time on General Curtis's career was a distinguished one in the annals of the civil war. He at once suppressed the rebellion and protected the railroads from east to west in northern Missouri. He was placed in command of the troops

ST CLAIR'S DEFEAT

THE attitude of the United States and Great Britain, as they faced each other in the Western wilderness at the beginning of the year 1791, was one of scarcely veiled hostility. The British held the lake posts at Detroit, Mackinaw, and Niagara, and more or less actively supported the Indians in their efforts to bar the Americans from the Northwest. Nominally they held the posts because the Americans had themselves left unfulfilled some of the conditions of the treaty of peace; but this was felt not to be the real reason, and the Americans loudly protested that their conduct was due to sheer hatred of the young republic. The explanation was simpler. The British had no far-reaching design to prevent the spread and growth of the English-speaking people on the American continent. They cared nothing, one way or the other, for that spread and growth, and it is unlikely that they wasted a moment's thought on the ultimate future of the race. All that they desired was to preserve the very valuable fur trade of the region round the Great Lakes for their own benefit. They were acting from the motives of self-interest that usually control nations; and it never entered their heads to balance against these immediate interests the future of a nation many of whose members were to them mere foreigners.

The majority of the Americans on their side were exceedingly loath to enter into aggressive war with the Indians, but were reluctantly forced into the contest by the necessity of supporting the backwoodsmen. The frontier was pushed westward not because the leading statesmen of America or the bulk of the American people foresaw the continental greatness of this country or strove for such greatness, but because the bordermen of the West and the adventurous land-speculators of the East were personally interested in acquiring new territory, and because, against their will, the governmental representatives of the nation were finally forced to make the interests of the Westerners their own. The people of the seaboard, the leaders of opinion in the coast towns and old-settled districts, were inclined to look eastward rather than westward. They were interested in the quarrels of the Old World nations; they were immediately concerned in the rights of the fisheries they jealously shared with England, or the trade they sought to secure with Spain. They did not covet the Indian lands. They had never heard of the Rocky Mountains—nobody had as yet; they cared as little for the Missouri as for the Congo, and they thought of the Pacific slope as a savage country, only to be reached by an ocean voyage longer than the voyage to India. They believed that they were entitled, under the treaty, to the country between the Alleghanies and the Great Lakes; but they were quite content to see the Indians remain in actual occupancy, and they had no desire to spend men and money in driving them out. Yet they were even less disposed to proceed to extremities against their own people, who in very fact were driving out the Indians; and this was the only alternative, for in the end they had to side with one or the other set of combatants. The governmental authorities of the newly created republic shared these feelings. They felt no hunger for the Indian lands; they felt no desire to stretch their boundaries, and thereby add to their already heavy burdens and responsibilities. They wished to do strict justice to the Indians; the treaties they held with them were carried on with scrupulous fairness, and were honorably lived up to by the United States officials. They strove to keep peace, and made many efforts to persuade the frontiersmen to observe the Indian boundary lines, and not to intrude on the territory in dispute; and they were quite unable to foresee the rapidity of the nation's westward growth. Like the people of the Eastern seaboard, the men high in governmental authority were apt to look upon the frontiersmen with feelings dangerously kin to dislike and suspicion. Nor were these feelings wholly unjustifiable. The men who settle in a new country and begin subduing the wilderness plunge back into the very conditions from which the race has raised itself by the slow toil of ages. The conditions cannot but tell upon them. Inevitably, and for more than one lifetime —perhaps for several generations—they tend to retrograde, instead of advancing. They drop away from the standard which highly civilized nations have reached. As with harsh and dangerous labor they bring the new land up towards the level of the old, they themselves partly revert to their ancestral conditions; they sink back towards the state of their ages-dead barbarian forefathers. Few observers can see beyond this temporary retrogression into the future for which it is a preparation. There is small cause for wonder in the fact that so many of the leaders of Eastern thought looked with coldness upon the effort of the Westerners to push north of the Ohio.

Yet it was these Western frontiersmen who were the real and vital factors in the solution of the problems which so annoyed the British monarchy and the American republic. They eagerly craved the Indian lands; they would not be denied entrance to the thinly peopled territory, wherein they intended to make homes for themselves and their children. Rough, masterful, lawless, they were neither daunted by the prowess of the red warriors whose wrath they braved, nor awed by the displeasure of the government whose solemn engagements they violated. The enormous extent of the frontier dividing the white settler from the savage, and the tangled inaccessibility of the country in which it everywhere lay, rendered it as difficult for the national authorities to control the frontiersmen as it was to chastise the Indians. If the separation of interests between the thickly settled East and the sparsely settled West had been complete, it may be that the East would have refused outright to support the West, in which case the advance would have been very slow and halting. But the separation was not complete. The frontiersmen were numerically important in some of the States, as in Virginia, Georgia, and even Pennsylvania and New York, and under a democratic system of government this meant that these States were more or less responsive to their demands. It was greatly to the interest of the frontiersmen that their demands should be gratified, while other citizens had no very concrete concern in the matter one way or the other. In addition to this, and even more important, was the fact that there were large classes of the population everywhere who felt much sense of identity with the frontiersmen, and sympathized with them. The fathers or grandfathers of these people had themselves been frontiersmen, and they were still under the influences of the traditions which told of a constant march westward through the vast forests, and a no less constant warfare with a hostile savagery. Moreover, in many of the communities there were people whose kinsmen or friends had gone to the border, and the welfare of these adventurers was a matter of more or less interest to those who had staid behind. Finally, and most important of all, though the nation might be lukewarm originally, and might wish to prevent the settlers from trespassing on the Indian lands or entering into an Indian war, yet when the war had become of real moment, and when victory was doubtful, the national power was sure to be used in favor of the hard-pressed pioneers. At first the authorities at the national capital would blame the whites, and try to temporize and make new treaties, or even threaten to drive back the settlers with a strong hand; but when the ravages of the Indians had become serious, when the bloody details were sent to homes in every part of the Union by letter after letter from the border, when the little newspapers began to publish accounts of the worst atrocities, when the county lieutenants of the frontier counties were clamoring for help, when the Congressmen from the frontier districts were appealing to Congress, and the Governors of the States whose frontiers were molested were appealing to the President —then the feeling of race and national kinship rose, and the government no longer hesitated to support in every way the hard-pressed wilderness vanguard of the American people.

The situation had reached this point by the year 1791. For seven years the Federal authorities had been vainly endeavoring to make some final settlement of the question by entering into treaties with the Northwestern and Southwestern tribes. In the earlier treaties the delegates from the Continental Congress asserted that the United States were invested with the fee of all the land claimed by the Indians. In the later treaties the

Indian proprietorship of the lands was conceded. This concession at the time seemed important to the whites; but the Indians probably never understood that there had been any change of attitude; nor did it make any practical difference, for, whatever the theory might be, the lands had eventually to be won, partly by whipping the savages in fight, partly by making it better worth their while to remain at peace than to go to war.

The Federal officials under whose authority these treaties were made had no idea of the complexity of the problem. In 1789 the Secretary of War, the New-Englander Knox, solemnly reported to the President that if the treaties were only observed and the Indians conciliated, they would become attached to the United States, and the expense of managing them for the next half-century would be only some fifteen thousand dollars a year. He probably represented not unfairly the ordinary Eastern view of the matter. He had not the slightest conception of the rate at which the settlements were increasing. Though he expected that tracts of Indian territory would from time to time be acquired, he made no allowance for a growth so rapid that within the half-century a dozen populous States were to stand within the Indian-owned wilderness of his day. He utterly failed to grasp the central feature of the situation, which was that the settlers needed the land, and were bound to have it within a few years, and that the Indians would not give it up, under no matter what treaty, without an appeal to arms.

As a matter of fact the red men were as little disposed as the white to accept a peace on any terms that were possible. The Secretary of War, who knew nothing of Indians by actual contact, wrote that it would be indeed pleasing "to a philosophic mind to reflect that, instead of exterminating a part of the human race by our modes of population .... we had imparted our knowledge of cultivation and the arts to the aboriginals of the country," thus preserving and civilizing them; and the public men who represented districts remote from the frontier shared these views of large though vague beneficence. But neither the white frontiersmen nor their red antagonists possessed "philosophic minds." They represented two stages of progress, ages apart, and it would have needed many centuries to bring the lower to the level of the higher. Both sides recognized the fact that their interests were incompatible, and that the question of their clashing rights had to be settled by the strong hand.

In the Northwest matters culminated sooner than in the Southwest. The Georgians and the settlers along the Tennessee and Cumberland were harassed rather than seriously menaced by the Creek war parties; but in the North the more dangerous Indians of the Miami, the Wabash, and the lakes gathered in bodies so large as fairly to deserve the name of armies. Moreover, the pressure of the white advance was far heavier in the North. The pioneers who settled in the Ohio basin were many times as numerous as those who settled on the lands west of the Oconee or north of the Cumberland, and were fed from States much more populous. The advance was stronger, the resistance more desperate ; naturally the open break occurred where the strain was most intense.

There was fierce border warfare in the South. In the North there were regular campaigns, and pitched battles were fought between Federal armies as large as those commanded by Washington at Trenton or Greene at Eutaw Springs, and bodies of Indian warriors more numerous than had ever yet appeared on any single field.

The newly created government of the United States was very reluctant to make formal war on the Northwestern Indians. Not only were President Washington and the national Congress honorably desirous of peace, but they were hampered for funds, and dreaded any extra expense. Nevertheless, they were forced into war. Throughout the years 1789 and 1790 an increasing volume of appeals for help came from the frontier countries. The Governor of the Northwestern Territory, the Brigadier - General of the troops on the Ohio, the members of the Kentucky Convention, all the county lieutenants of Kentucky, the lieutenants of the frontier counties of Virginia proper, the representatives from the counties, the field-officers of the different districts, the General Assembly of Virginia—all sent bitter complaints and long catalogues of injuries to the President, the Secretary of War, and the two Houses of Congress— complaints which were redoubled after

Harmar's failure. With heavy hearts the national authorities prepared for war.

Their decision was justified by the redoubled fury of the Indian raids during the early part of 1791. Among others, the settlements near Marietta were attacked, a day or two after the new year began, in bitter winter weather. A dozen persons, including a woman and two children, were killed, and five men were taken prisoners. The New England settlers, though brave and hardy, were unused to Indian warfare. They were taken by surprise, and made no effective resistance; the only Indian hurt was wounded with a hatchet by the wife of a frontier hunter. There were some twenty-five Indians in the attacking party; they were Wyandots and Delawares, who had been mixing on friendly terms with the settlers throughout the preceding summer, and so knew how best to deliver the assault. The settlers had not only treated these Indians with much kindness, but had never wronged any of the red race, and had been lulled into a foolish feeling of security by the apparent good-will of the treacherous foes. The assault was made in the twilight on the 2d of January, the Indians crossing the frozen Muskingum, and stealthily approaching a block-house and two or three cabins. The inmates were frying meat for supper, and did not suspect harm, offering food to the Indians; but the latter, once they were within-doors, dropped the garb of friendliness, and shot or tomahawked all save a couple of men who escaped, and the five who were made prisoners. The captives were all taken to the Miami or Detroit, and, as usual, were treated with much kindness and humanity by the British officers and traders with whom they came in contact. McKee, the British Indian agent, who was always ready to incite the savages to war against the Americans as a nation, but who was quite as ready to treat them kindly as individuals, ransomed one prisoner; the latter went to his Massachusetts home to raise the amount of his ransom, and returned to Detroit to refund it to his generous rescuer. Another prisoner was ransomed by a Detroit trader, and worked out his ransom in Detroit itself. Yet another was redeemed from captivity by the famous Iroquois chief Brant, who was ever a terrible and implacable foe, but a greathearted and kindly victor. The fourth prisoner died, while the Indians took so great a liking to the fifth that they would not let him go, but adopted him into the tribe, made him dress as they did, and in a spirit of pure friendliness pierced his ears and nose. After Wayne's treaty he was released, and returned to Marietta to work at his trade as a stone-mason, his bored nose and slit ears serving as mementos of his captivity.

The squalid little town of Cincinnati also suffered from the Indian war parties in the spring of this year, several of the townsmen being killed by the savages, who grew so bold that they lurked through the streets at nights, and lay in ambush in the gardens where the garrison of Fort Washington raised their vegetables. One of the Indian attacks, made upon a little palisaded "station" which had been founded by a man named Dunlop, some seventeen miles from Cincinnati, was noteworthy because of an act of not uncommon cruelty by the Indians. In the station there were some regulars. Aided by the settlers, they beat back their foes; whereupon the enraged savages brought one of their prisoners within ear-shot of the walls and tortured him to death. The torture began at midnight, and the screams of the wretched victim were heard until daylight.

Until this year the war was not general. One of the most bewildering problems to be solved by the Federal officers on the Ohio was to find out which tribes were friendly and which hostile. Many of the inveterate enemies of the Americans were as forward in professions of friendship as the peaceful Indians, and were just as apt to be found at the treaties, or lounging about the settlements; and this widespread treachery and deceit made the task of the army officers puzzling to a degree. As for the frontiersmen, who had no means whatever of telling a hostile from a friendly tribe, they followed their usual custom, and lumped all the Indians, good and bad, together, for which they could hardly be blamed. Even St. Clair, who had small sympathy with the backwoodsmen, acknowledged that they could not and ought not to submit patiently to the cruelties and depredations of the savages: "they are in the habit of retaliation, perhaps without attending precisely to the nations from which the injuries are received." A long course of such aggressions and retaliations result-

ed, by the year 1791, in all the Northwestern Indians going on the war-path. The hostile tribes had murdered and plundered the frontiersmen; the vengeance of the latter, as often as not, had fallen on friendly tribes; and these justly angered friendly tribes usually signalized their taking the red hatchet by some act of treacherous hostility directed against settlers who had not molested them.

In the late winter of 1791 the hitherto friendly Delawares, who hunted or traded along the western frontiers of Pennsylvania and Virginia proper, took this manner of showing that they had joined the open foes of the Americans. A big band of warriors spread up and down the Alleghany for about forty miles, and on the 9th of February attacked all the outlying settlements. The Indians who delivered this attack had long been on intimate terms with the Alleghany settlers, who were accustomed to see them in and about their houses; and as the savages acted with seeming friendship to the last moment, they were able to take the settlers completely unawares, so that no effective resistance was made. Some settlers were killed and some captured. Among the captives was a lad named John Brickell, who, though at first maltreated, and forced to run the gauntlet, was afterwards adopted into the tribe, and was not released until after Wayne's victory. After his adoption he was treated with the utmost kindness, and conceived a great liking for his captors, admiring their many good qualities, especially their courage and their kindness to their children. Long afterwards he wrote down his experiences, which possess a certain value as giving from the Indian stand-point an account of some of the incidents of the forest warfare of the day.

The warriors who had engaged in this raid on their former friends, the settlers along the Alleghany, retreated two or three days' journey into the wilderness to an appointed place, where they found their families. One of the Girtys was with the Indians. No sooner had the last of the warriors come in, with their scalps and prisoners, including the boy Brickell, than ten of their number deliberately started back to Pittsburg, to pass themselves as friendly Indians, and trade. In a fortnight they returned, laden with goods of various kinds, including whiskey. Some of the inhabitants, sore from disaster, suspected that these Indians were only masquerading as friendly, and prepared to attack them; but one of the citizens warned them of their danger, and they escaped. Their effrontery was as remarkable as their treachery and duplicity. They had suddenly attacked and massacred settlers by whom they had never been harmed, and with whom they preserved an appearance of entire friendship up to the very moment of the assault. Then, their hands red with the blood of their murdered friends, they came boldly into Pittsburg, among the near neighbors of these same murdered men, and staid there several days to trade, pretending to be peaceful allies of the whites. With savages so treacherous and so ferocious it was a mere impossibility for the borderers to distinguish the hostile from the friendly, as they hit out blindly to revenge the blows that fell upon them from unknown hands. Brutal though the frontiersmen often were, they never employed the systematic and deliberate bad faith which was a favorite weapon with even the best of the red tribes.

The people who were out of reach of the Indian tomahawk, and especially the Federal officers, were often unduly severe in judging the borderers for their deeds of retaliation. Brickell's narrative shows that the parties of seemingly friendly Indians who came in to trade were sometimes —and, indeed, in this year 1791 it is probable they were generally—composed of Indians who were engaged in active hostilities against the settlers, and who were always watching for a chance to murder and plunder. On March 9th, a month after the Delawares had begun their attacks, the grim backwoods Captain Brady, with some of his Virginian rangers, fell on a party of them who had come to a block-house to trade, and killed four. The Indians asserted that they were friendly, and both the Federal Secretary of War and the Governor of Pennsylvania denounced the deed and threatened the offenders; but the frontiersmen stood by them. Soon afterwards a delegation of chiefs from the Seneca tribe of the Iroquois arrived at Fort Pitt and sent a message to the President complaining of the murder of these alleged friendly Indians. On the very day these Seneca chiefs started on their journey home another Delaware war party killed nine settlers, men, women, and children, within twenty miles

of Fort Pitt, which so enraged the people of the neighborhood that the lives of the Senecas were jeopardized. The United States authorities were particularly anxious to keep at peace with the Six Nations, and made repeated efforts to treat with them; but the Six Nations stood sullenly aloof, afraid to enter openly into the struggle, and yet reluctant to make a firm peace or cede any of their lands.

The intimate relations between the Indians and the British at the lake posts continued to perplex and anger the Americans. While the frontiers were being mercilessly ravaged, the same Indians who were committing the ravages met in council with the British agent, Alexander McKee, at the Miami Rapids, the council being held in this neighborhood for the special benefit of the very towns which were most hostile to the Americans, and which had been partially destroyed by Harmar the preceding fall. The Indian war was at its height, and the murderous forays never ceased throughout the spring and summer. McKee came to Miami in April, and was forced to wait nearly three months, because of the absence of the Indian war party, before the principal chiefs and head men gathered to meet him. At last, on July 1st, they were all assembled; not only the Shawnees, Delawares, Wyandots, Ottawas, Pottawattamies, and others who had openly taken the hatchet against the Americans, but also representatives of the Six Nations, and tribes of savages from lands so remote that they carried no guns, but warred with bows, spears, and tomahawks, and were clad in buffalo-robes instead of blankets. McKee in his speech to them did not incite them to war. On the contrary, he advised them, in guarded language, to make peace with the United States, but only upon terms consistent with their "honor and interest." He assured them that, whatever they did, he wished to know what they desired, and that the sole purpose of the British was to promote the welfare of the confederated Indians. Such very cautious advice was not of a kind to promote peace; and the goods furnished the savages at the council included not only cattle, corn, and tobacco, but also quantities of powder and balls.

The chief interest of the British was to preserve the fur trade for their merchants, and it was mainly for this reason that they clung so tenaciously to the lake posts. For their purposes it was essential that the Indians should remain lords of the soil. They preferred to see the savages at peace with the Americans, provided that in this way they could keep their lands; but, whether through peace or war, they wished the lands to remain Indian, and the Americans to be barred from them. While they did not at the moment advise war, their advice to make peace was so faintly uttered and so hedged round with conditions as to be of no weight, and they furnished the Indians not only with provisions, but with munitions of war. While McKee and other British officers were at the Miami Rapids, holding councils with the Indians and issuing to them goods and weapons, bands of braves were continually returning from forays against the American frontier, bringing in scalps and prisoners; and the wilder subjects of the British King, like the Girtys, and some of the French from Detroit, went off with the war parties on their forays. The authorities at the capital of the new republic were deceived by the warmth with which the British insisted that they were striving to bring about a peace; but the frontiersmen were not deceived, and they were right in their belief that the British were really the mainstay and support of the Indians in their warfare.

Peace could only be won by the unsheathed sword. Even the national government was reluctantly driven to this view. As all the Northwestern tribes were banded in open war, it was useless to let the conflict remain a succession of raids and counter-raids. Only a severe stroke delivered by a formidable army could cow the tribes. It was hopeless to try to deliver such a crippling blow with militia alone, and it was very difficult for the infant government to find enough money or men to equip an army composed exclusively of regulars. Accordingly preparations were made for a campaign with a mixed force of regulars, special levies, and militia; and St. Clair, already Governor of the Northwestern Territory, was put in command of the army as Major-General.

Before the army was ready the Federal government was obliged to take other measures for the defence of the border. Small bodies of rangers were raised from among the frontier militia, being paid at the usual rate for soldiers in the army—a

net sum of about two dollars a month while in service. In addition, on the repeated and urgent request of the frontiersmen, a few of the most active hunters and best woodsmen, men like Brady, were enlisted as scouts, being paid six or eight times the ordinary rate. These men, because of their skill in woodcraft and their thorough knowledge of Indian fighting, were beyond comparison more valuable than ordinary militia or regulars, and were prized very highly by the frontiersmen.

Besides thus organizing the local militia for defence, the President authorized the Kentuckians to undertake two offensive expeditions against the Wabash Indians, so as to prevent them from giving aid to the Miami tribes, whom St. Clair was to attack. Both expeditions were carried on by bands of mounted volunteers, such as had followed Clark on his various raids. The first was commanded by Brigadier-General Charles Scott; Colonel John Hardin led his advance-guard, and Wilkinson was second in command. Towards the end of May, Scott crossed the Ohio at the head of eight hundred horse-riflemen, and marched rapidly and secretly towards the Wabash towns. A mounted Indian discovered the advance of the Americans, and gave the alarm, and most of the Indians escaped just as the Kentucky riders fell on the towns. But little resistance was offered by the surprised and outnumbered savages. Only five Americans were wounded, while of the Indians thirty-two were slain, as they fought or fled, and forty-one prisoners, chiefly women and children, were brought in, either by Scott himself, or by his detachments under Hardin and Wilkinson. Several towns were destroyed, and the growing corn cut down. There were not a few French living in the towns, in well-finished log houses, which were burned with the wigwams. The second expedition was under the command of Wilkinson, and consisted of over five hundred men. He marched in August, and repeated Scott's feat, again burning down two or three towns, and destroying the goods and the crops. He lost three or four men killed or wounded, but killed ten Indians and captured some thirty. In both expeditions the volunteers behaved well, and committed no barbarous act, except that in the confusion of the actual onslaught a few non-combatants were slain. The Wabash Indians were cowed and disheartened by their punishment, and in consequence gave no aid to the Miami tribes; but beyond this the raids accomplished nothing, and brought no nearer the wished-for time of peace.

Meanwhile St. Clair was striving vainly to hasten the preparations for his own far more formidable task. There was much delay in forwarding him the men and the provisions and munitions. Congress hesitated and debated; the Secretary of War, hampered by a newly created office and insufficient means, did not show to advantage in organizing the campaign, and was slow in carrying out his plans, while there was positive dereliction of duty on the part of the quartermaster, and the contractors proved both corrupt and inefficient. The army was often on short commons, lacking alike food for the men and fodder for the horses; the powder was poor, the axes useless, the tents and clothing nearly worthless, while the delays were so extraordinary that the troops did not make the final move from Fort Washington until mid-September.

St. Clair himself was broken in health; he was a sick, weak, elderly man, high-minded, and zealous to do his duty, but totally unfit for the terrible responsibilities of such an expedition against such foes. The troops were of wretched stuff. There were two small regiments of regular infantry, the rest of the army being composed of six months levies and of militia ordered out for this particular campaign. The pay was contemptible. Each private was given three dollars a month, from which ninety cents were deducted, leaving a net payment of two dollars and ten cents a month. Sergeants netted three dollars and sixty cents, while the lieutenants received twenty-two, the captains thirty, and the colonels sixty dollars. The mean parsimony of the nation in paying such low wages to men about to be sent on duties at once very arduous and very dangerous met its fit and natural reward. Men of good bodily powers and in the prime of life, and especially men able to do the rough work of frontier farmers, could not be hired to fight Indians in unknown forests for two dollars a month. Most of the recruits were from the streets and prisons of the seaboard cities. They were hurried into a campaign against peculiarly formidable foes before they had acquired the rudiments of a soldier's training, and of course they never even understood what woodcraft meant. The officers were men of courage, as in the end most of them showed by dying bravely on the field of battle, but they were utterly untrained themselves, and had no time in which to train their men. Under such conditions it did not need keen vision to foretell disaster. Harmar had learned a bitter lesson the preceding year; he knew well what Indians could do and what raw troops could not, and he insisted with emphasis that the only possible outcome to St. Clair's expedition was defeat.

As the raw troops straggled to Pittsburg they were shipped down the Ohio to Fort Washington; and St. Clair made the headquarters of his army at a new fort some twenty-five miles northward, which he christened Fort Hamilton. During September the army slowly assembled— two small regiments of regulars, two of six months levies, a number of Kentucky militia, a few cavalry, and a couple of small batteries of light guns. After wearisome delays, due mainly to the utter inefficiency of the quartermaster and contractor, the start for the Indian towns was made on October the 4th.

The army trudged slowly through the deep woods and across the wet prairies, cutting out its own road, and making but five or six miles a day. On October 13th a halt was made to build another little fort, christened in honor of Jefferson. There were further delays, caused by the wretched management of the commissariat department, and the march was not resumed until the 24th, the numerous sick being left in Fort Jefferson. Then the army once more stumbled northward through the wilderness. The regulars, though mostly raw recruits, had been reduced to some kind of discipline, but the six months levies were almost worse than the militia. Owing to the long delays, and to the fact that they had been enlisted at various times, their terms of service were expiring day by day, and they wished to go home, and tried to, while the militia deserted in squads and bands. Those that remained were very disorderly. Two who attempted to desert were hanged, and another, who shot a comrade, was hanged also; but even this severity in punishment failed to stop the demoralization.

"A MOUNTED INDIAN DISCOVERED THE ADVANCE OF THE AMERICANS."

With such soldiers there would have been grave risk of disaster under any commander, but St. Clair's leadership made the risk a certainty. There was Indian sign, old and new, all through the woods, and the scouts and stragglers occasionally interchanged shots with small parties of braves, and now and then lost a man killed or captured. It was therefore certain that the savages knew every movement of the army, which, as it slowly neared the Miami towns, was putting itself within easy striking range of the most formidable Indian confederacy in the Northwest. The density of the forest was such that only the utmost watchfulness could prevent the foe from approaching within arm's-length unperceived. It behooved St. Clair to be on his guard, and he had been warned by Washington, who had never forgotten the scenes of Braddock's defeat, of the danger of a surprise. But St. Clair was broken down by the worry and by continued sickness; time and again it was doubtful whether he could do so much as stay with the army. The second in command, Major-General Richard Butler, was also sick most of the time, and, like St. Clair, he possessed none of the qualities of leadership save courage. The whole burden fell on the Adjutant-General, Colonel Winthrop Sargent, an old Revolutionary officer; without him the expedition would probably have failed in ignominy even before the Indians were reached; and he showed not only cool courage, but ability of a good order: yet in the actual arrangements for battle he was of course unable to remedy the blunders of his superiors.

St. Clair should have covered his front and flanks for miles around with scouting parties; but he rarely sent any out, and, thanks to letting the management of those that did go devolve on his subordinates, and to not having their reports made to him in person, he derived no benefit from what they saw. He had twenty Chickasaws with him, but he sent these off on an extended trip, lost touch of them entirely, and never saw them again until after the battle. He did not seem to realize that he was himself in danger of attack. When some fifty miles or so from the Miami towns, on the last day of October, sixty of the militia deserted; and he actually sent back after them one of his two regular regiments, thus weakening by one-half the only trustworthy portion of his force.

On November 3d the doomed army, now reduced to a total of about fourteen hundred men, camped on the eastern fork of the Wabash, high up, where it was but twenty yards wide. There was snow on the ground, and the little pools were skimmed with ice. The camp was on a narrow rise of ground, where the troops were cramped together, the artillery and most of the horse in the middle. On both flanks and along most of the rear the ground was low and wet. All about the wintry woods lay in frozen silence. In front the militia were thrown across the creek, and nearly a quarter of a mile beyond the rest of the troops. Parties of Indians were seen during the afternoon, and they skulked around the lines at night, so that the sentinels frequently fired at them; yet neither St. Clair nor Butler took any adequate measures to ward off the impending blow. It is improbable that, as things actually were at this time, they could have won a victory over their terrible foes, but they might have avoided overwhelming disaster.

On November 4th the men were under arms, as usual, by dawn, St. Clair intending to throw up intrenchments and then make a forced march in light order against the Indian towns. But he was forestalled. Soon after sunrise, just as the men were dismissed from parade, a sudden assault was made upon the militia, who lay unprotected beyond the creek. The unexpectedness and fury of the onset, the heavy firing, and the wild whoops and yells of the throngs of painted savages threw the militia into disorder. After a few moments' resistance they broke and fled in wild panic to the camp of the regulars, among whom they drove in a frightened herd, spreading dismay and confusion.

The drums beat, and the troops sprang to arms as soon as they heard the heavy firing at the front, and their volleys for a moment checked the onrush of the plumed woodland warriors. But the check availed nothing. The braves filed off to one side and the other, completely surrounded the camp, killed or drove in the guards and pickets, and then advanced close to the main lines.

A furious battle followed. After the first onset the Indians fought in silence, no sound coming from them save the incessant rattle of their fire as they crept from log to log, from tree to tree, ever closer and closer. The soldiers stood in close order in the open; their musketry and artillery fire made a tremendous noise, but did little damage to a foe they could hardly see. Now and then, through the hanging smoke, terrible figures flitted, painted black and red, the feathers of hawk and eagle braided in their long scalp locks; but, save for these glimpses, the soldiers knew the presence of their sombre enemy only from the fearful rapidity with which their comrades fell dead and wounded in the ranks. They never even knew the numbers or leaders of the Indians. At the time it was supposed that they outnumbered the whites; but it is probable that the reverse was the case, and it may even be that they were not more than half as numerous. It is said that the chief who led them, both in council and battle, was Little Turtle the Miami. At any rate there were present all the chiefs and picked warriors of the Delawares, Shawnees, Wyandots, and Miamies, and all the most reckless and adventurous young braves from among the Iroquois and the Indians of the upper lakes, as well as many of the ferocious whites and half-breeds who dwelt in the Indian villages.

The Indians fought with the utmost boldness and ferocity, and with the utmost skill and caution. Under cover of the smoke of the heavy but harmless fire from the army they came up so close that they shot the troops down as hunters slaughter a herd of standing buffalo. Watching their chance, they charged again and again with the tomahawk, gliding in to close quarters, while their bewildered foes were still blindly firing into the smoke-shrouded woods. The men saw no enemy as they stood in the ranks to load and shoot; in a moment, without warning, dark faces frowned through the haze, the war-axes gleamed, and on the frozen ground the weapons clattered as the soldiers fell. As the comrades of the fallen sprang forward to avenge them, the lithe warriors vanished as rapidly as they had appeared, and once more the soldiers saw before them only the dim forests and the shifting smoke wreaths, with vague half-glimpses of the hidden foe, while the steady singing of the Indian bullets never ceased, and on every hand the bravest and steadiest fell, one by one.

At first the army, as a whole, fought firmly; indeed, there was no choice, for it was ringed by a wall of flame. The officers behaved very well, cheering and encouraging their men, but they were the special targets of the Indians, and fell rapidly. St. Clair and Butler, by their cool fearlessness in the hour of extreme peril, made some amends for their shortcomings as commanders. They walked up and down the lines from flank to flank, passing and repassing one another; for the two lines of battle were facing outward, and each general was busy trying to keep his wing from falling back. St. Clair's clothes were pierced by eight bullets, but he was himself untouched. He wore a blanket coat with a hood; he had a long queue, and his thick gray hair flowed from under his three-cornered hat; a lock of his hair was carried off by a bullet. Several times he headed the charges, sword in hand. General Butler had his arm broken early in the fight, but he continued to walk to and fro along the line, his coat off, and the wounded arm in a sling. Another bullet struck him in the side, inflicting a mortal wound, and he was carried to the middle of the camp, where he sat propped up by knapsacks. Men and horses were falling around him at every moment. St. Clair sent an aide, Lieutenant Ebenezer Denny, to ask how he was; he displayed no anxiety, and answered that he felt well. While speaking, a young cadet, who stood near by, was hit on the knee-cap by a spent ball, and at the shock cried aloud, whereat the general laughed so that his wounded side shook. The aide left him, and there is no further certain record of his fate, except that he was slain; but it is said that in one of the Indian rushes a warrior bounded towards him and sunk the tomahawk in his brain before any one could interfere.

Instead of being awed by the bellowing artillery, the Indians made the gunner a special object of attack. Man after man was picked off, until every officer was killed but one, who was wounded, and most of the privates also were slain or disabled. The artillery was thus almost silenced; and the Indians, emboldened by success, swarmed forward and seized the guns, while at the same time a part of the left wing of the army began to shrink back. But the Indians were now on comparatively open ground, where the regulars could see them and get at them, and under St. Clair's own leadership the troops rushed fiercely at the savages with fixed bayonets, and drove them back to cover. By this time the confusion and disorder were great, while from every hollow and grass-patch, from behind every stump and tree and fallen log, the Indians continued their fire. Again and again the officers led forward the troops in bayonet charges, and at first the men followed them with a will. Each charge seemed for a moment to be successful, the Indians rising in swarms and running in headlong flight from the bayonets. In one of the earliest, in which Colonel Darke led his battalion, the Indians were driven several hundred yards across the branch of the Wabash; but when the colonel halted and rallied his men he found that the savages had closed in behind him, and he had to fight his way back, while the foe he had been driving at once turned and harassed his rear. He was himself wounded, and lost most of his command. On re-entering camp he found the Indians again in possession of the artillery and baggage, from which they were again driven; they had already scalped the slain who lay about the guns. Major Thomas Butler had his thigh broken by a bullet, but he continued on horseback in command of his battalion until the end of the fight, and led his men in one of the momentarily successful bayonet charges. The only regular regiment present lost every officer, killed or wounded. The commander of the Kentucky militia, Colonel Oldham, was killed early in the action, while trying to rally his men.

The charging troops could accomplish nothing permanent. The men were too clumsy and ill trained in forest warfare to overtake their fleet, half-naked antagonists. The latter never received the shock; but though they fled, they were nothing daunted, for they turned the instant the battalion did, and followed firing. They skipped out of reach of the bayonets and came back as they pleased, and they were only visible when raised by a charge.

Among the pack-horse men were some who were accustomed to the use of the the bands of his musket flew off; he picked up another just as two levy officers ordered a charge, and followed the charging party at a run. By this time the battalions were broken, and only some thirty men followed the officers. The Indians fled before the bayonets, until they reached a ravine filled with down timber, whereupon they halted behind the impenetrable tangle of fallen logs.

"AGAIN AND AGAIN THE OFFICERS LED FORWARD THE TROOPS."

rifle and to life in the woods, and these fought well. One named Benjamin Van Cleve kept a journal, in which he described what he saw of the fight. He had no gun, but five minutes after the firing began he saw a soldier near him with his arm swinging useless, and he borrowed the wounded man's musket and cartridges. The smoke had settled to within three feet of the ground, so he knelt, covering himself behind a tree, and only fired when he saw an Indian's head, or noticed one running from cover to cover. He fired away all his ammunition, and The soldiers also halted, and were speedily swept away by the fire of the Indians, whom they could not reach; but Van Cleve, showing his skill as a woodsman, covered himself behind a small tree, and gave back shot for shot, until all his ammunition was gone. Before this happened his less skilful companions had been slain or driven off, and he ran at full speed back to camp. Here he found the artillery had been taken and retaken again and again. Stricken men lay in heaps everywhere, and the charging troops were once more driving the Indians across the creek in front of the camp. Van Cleve noticed that the dead officers and soldiers who were lying about the guns had all been scalped, and that "the Indians had not been in a hurry, for their hair was all skinned off." Another of the packers who took part in the fight, one Thomas Irwin, was struck with the spectacle offered by the slaughtered artillerymen, and with grewsome homeliness. compared the reeking heads to pumpkins in a December corn-field.

As the officers fell, the soldiers, who at first stood up bravely enough, gradually grew disheartened. No words can paint the hopelessness and horror of such a struggle as that in which they were engaged. They were hemmed in by foes who showed no mercy, and whose blows they could in no way return. If they charged they could not overtake the Indians, and the instant the charge stopped the Indians came back. If they stood, they were shot down by an unseen enemy; and there was no stronghold, no refuge, to which to flee. The Indian attack was relentless, and could neither be avoided, parried, nor met by counter-assault. For two hours or so the troops kept up a slowly lessening resistance, but by degrees their hearts failed. The wounded had been brought towards the middle of the lines, where the baggage and tents were, and an ever-growing proportion of new wounded men joined them. In vain the officers tried, by encouragement, by jeers, by blows, to drive them back to the fight. They were unnerved. As in all cases where large bodies of men are put in imminent peril of death, whether by shipwreck, plague, fire, or violence, numbers were swayed by a mad panic of utterly selfish fear, and others became numbed and callous, or snatched at any animal gratification during their last moments. Many soldiers crowded round the fires and stood stunned and confounded by the awful calamity; many broke into the officers' marquees and sought for drink, or devoured the food which the rightful owners had left when the drums beat to arms.

There was but one thing to do. If possible the remnant of the army must be saved, and it could only be saved by instant flight, even at the cost of abandoning the wounded. The broad road by which the army had advanced was the only line of retreat. The artillery had already been spiked and abandoned. Most of the horses had been killed, but a few were still left, and on one of these St. Clair mounted. He gathered together those fragments of the different battalions which contained the few men who still kept heart and head, and ordered them to charge and regain the road from which the savages had cut them off. Repeated orders were necessary before some of the men could be roused from their stupor sufficiently to follow the charging party, and they were only induced to move when told that it was to retreat.

Colonel Darke and a few officers placed themselves at the head of the column, the coolest and boldest men drew up behind them, and they fell on the Indians with such fury as to force them back well beyond the road. This made an opening, through which, said Van Cleve the packer, the rest of the troops "pressed like a drove of bullocks." The Indians were surprised by the vigor of the charge, and puzzled as to its object; they opened out on both sides, and half the men had gone through before they fired more than a chance shot or two. They then fell on the rear and began a hot pursuit. St. Clair sent his aide, Denny, to the front to try to keep order, but neither he nor any one else could check the flight. Major Clark tried to rally his battalion to cover the retreat, but he was killed and the effort abandoned.

There never was a wilder rout. As soon as the men began to run, and realized that in flight there lay some hope of safety, they broke into a stampede, which became uncontrollable. Horses, soldiers, and the few camp-followers and the women who had accompanied the army were all mixed together. Neither command nor example had the slightest weight; the men were abandoned to the terrible selfishness of utter fear. They threw away their weapons as they ran. They thought of nothing but escape, and fled in a huddle, the stronger and the few who had horses trampling their way to the front through the old, the weak, and the wounded, while behind them raged the Indian tomahawk. Fortunately the attraction of plundering the camp was so overpowering that the savages only followed the army about four miles; otherwise hardly a man would have escaped.

St. Clair was himself in much danger.

for he tried to stay behind and stem the torrent of fugitives; but he failed, being swept forward by the crowd; and when he attempted to ride to the front to rally them, he failed again, for his horse could not be pricked out of a walk. The packer Van Cleve in his journal gives a picture of the rout. He was himself one of the few who lost neither courage nor generosity in the rout.

Among his fellow-packers were his uncle and a young man named Bonham, who was his close and dear friend. The uncle was shot in the wrist, the ball lodging near his shoulder; but he escaped. Bonham, just before the retreat began, was shot through both hips, so that he could not walk. Young Van Cleve got him a horse, on which he was with difficulty mounted; then, as the flight began, Bonham bade Van Cleve look to his safety, as he was on foot, and the two separated. Bonham rode until the pursuit had almost ceased; then, weak and crippled, he was thrown off his horse and slain. Meanwhile Van Cleve ran steadily on foot. By the time he had gone two miles most of the mounted men had passed him. A boy, on the point of falling from exhaustion, now begged his help, and the kind-hearted backwoodsman seized the lad and pulled him along nearly two miles farther, when he himself became so worn out that he nearly fell. There were still two horses in the rear, one carrying three men and one two; and behind the latter Van Cleve, summoning his strength, threw the boy, who escaped. Nor did Van Cleve's pity for his fellows cease with this, for he stopped to tie his handkerchief around the knee of a wounded man. His violent exertions gave him a cramp in both thighs, so that he could barely walk; and in consequence the strong and active passed him, until he was within a hundred yards of the rear, where the Indians were tomahawking the old and wounded men. So close were they that for a moment his heart sunk in despair; but he threw off his shoes, the touch of the cold ground seemed to revive him, and he again began to trot forward. He got round a bend in the road, passing half a dozen other fugitives; and long afterwards he told how well he remembered thinking that it would be some time before they would all be massacred and his own turn come. However, at this point the pursuit ceased, and a few miles farther on he had gained the

middle of the flying troops, and, like them, came to a walk. He fell in with a queer group, consisting of the sole remaining officer of the artillery, an infantry corporal, and a woman called Red-headed Nance. The latter two were crying, the corporal for the loss of his wife, the woman for the loss of her child. The worn-out officer hung on the corporal's arm, while Van Cleve "carried his fusee and accoutrements and led Nance, and in this sociable way arrived at Fort Jefferson a little after sunset."

Before reaching Fort Jefferson the wretched army encountered the regular regiment which had been so unfortunately detached a couple of days before the battle. The most severely wounded were left in the fort, and then the flight was renewed, until the disorganized and half-armed rabble reached Fort Washington and the mean log huts of Cincinnati. Six hundred and thirty men had been killed, and over two hundred and eighty wounded; less than five hundred, only about a third of the whole number engaged in the battle, remained unhurt. But one or two were taken prisoners, for the Indians butchered everybody, wounded or unwounded, who fell into their hands. There is no record of the torture of any of the captives, but there was one singular instance of cannibalism. The savage Chippewas from the far-off North devoured one of the slain soldiers, probably in a spirit of ferocious bravado; the other tribes expressed horror at the deed. The Indians were rich with the spoil. They got horses, tents, guns, axes, powder, clothing, and blankets — in short, everything their hearts prized. Their loss was comparatively slight; it may not have been one-twentieth that of the whites. They did not at the moment follow up their victory, each band going off with its own share of the booty. But the triumph was so overwhelming and the reward so great that the war spirit received a great impetus in all the tribes. The bands of warriors that marched against the frontier were more numerous, more formidable, and bolder than ever.

In the following January Wilkinson with a hundred and fifty mounted volunteers marched to the battle-field to bury the slain. The weather was bitterly cold; snow lay deep on the ground, and some of the volunteers were frost-bitten. Four miles from the scene of the battle, where

"ON THE BATTLE-FIELD ITSELF THE SLAIN LAY THICK."

the pursuit had ended, they began to find the bodies on the road, and close alongside in the woods, whither some of the hunted creatures had turned at the last to snatch one more moment of life. Many had been dragged from under the snow and devoured by wolves. The others lay where they had fallen, showing as mounds through the smooth white mantle that covered them. On the battle-field itself the slain lay thick, scalped, and stripped of all their clothing which the conquerors deemed worth taking. The bodies, blackened by frost and exposure, could not be identified, and they were buried in a shallow trench in the frozen ground. The volunteers then marched home.

When the remnant of the defeated army reached the banks of the Ohio, St. Clair sent his aide, Denny, to carry the news to Philadelphia, at that time the national capital. The river was swollen, there were incessant snow-storms, and ice formed heavily, so that it took twenty days of toil and cold before Denny reached Wheeling and got horses. For ten days

more he rode over the bad winter roads, reaching Philadelphia with the evil tidings on the evening of December 19th. It was thus six weeks after the defeat of the army before the news was brought to the anxious Federal authorities.

The young officer called first on the Secretary of War; but as soon as the Secretary realized the importance of the information he had it conveyed to the President. Washington was at dinner, with some guests, and was called from the table to listen to the tidings of ill fortune. He returned with unmoved face, and at the dinner and at the reception which followed he behaved with his usual stately courtesy to those whom he was entertaining, not so much as hinting at what he had heard. But when the last guest had gone, his pent-up wrath broke forth in one of those fits of volcanic fury which sometimes shattered his iron outward calm. Walking up and down the room, he burst out in wild regret for the rout and disaster, and bitter invective against St. Clair, reciting how in that very room he had wished the unfortunate commander success and honor, and had bidden him above all things beware of a surprise. "He went off with that last solemn warning thrown into his ears," spoke Washington, as he strode to and fro, "and yet to suffer that army to be cut to pieces, hacked, butchered, tomahawked, by a surprise, the very thing I guarded him against! Oh God! Oh God! he's worse than a murderer! How can he answer it to his country?" Then, calming himself by a mighty effort, "General St. Clair shall have justice ... he shall have full justice." And St. Clair did receive full justice, and mercy too, from both Washington and Congress. For the sake of his courage and honorable character they held him guiltless of the disaster, for which his lack of capacity as a general was so largely accountable.

HOW KENTUCKY BECAME A STATE

IT is not Kentucky's fault if the centennial of her admission into the Union comes in 1892, right alongside of the fourth centennial of the discovery of America. Congress is to blame for that. But, even a contrast with the tremendous achievement of the incomparable Columbus cannot divest of its absorbing interest the romantic story of the founding of our first interior commonwealth.

Its very beginning was unique. The rise of a State and the establishment of the magnificent empire of the West were decreed when, on the 7th of June, 1769,

Daniel Boone looked out upon "the beautiful level of Kentucky," which so impressed him with the abundance and splendid development of its animal life, with the astonishing fertility of its virgin soil, and the lavishness of its natural gifts, still clothed with all the charms of primeval freshness, that he afterwards described it as "a second paradise."

Kentucky, in the manner of her founding, illustrated the new era that had just dawned upon the world. Unlike any of the States of the old Confederation, she had never actually experienced the dominion of a foreign power, nor felt the authority of a royal master. She was born free. Boone brought with him into the depths of the Western wild a coal of that sacred fire which burned so brightly upon the banks of the Yadkin, and in the same month of May, 1775, when the heroic North Carolinians adopted the immortal declaration of Mecklenburg, the pioneers of Kentucky gathered in solemn conclave under a mighty elm in the now famous blue-grass region, and they also virtually proclaimed their independence of Great Britain. For this alone could be the meaning of the attempted establishment of the colony of Transylvania upon no other authority than that of occupancy and of a deed from the Cherokees, and with the bold announcement specifically and deliberately made that "all power is originally in the people."

Such was the spirit of the men who laid the foundation of Kentucky, and built upon it under circumstances that seemed a defiance of the impossible itself. They did this in a land which they found devoid of every product of human art, and while cut off from civilization and from human aid by hundreds of miles and by ranks of mountains. It was one of the most remarkable feats of the Anglo-Saxon race, and in some respects is without a parallel. It opened the way for results the importance of which is already beyond all calculation.

But swallowed up as they were in this vast solitude, the pioneers were not too remote for savage vengeance, nor too far away to bear a glorious part in the war of the Revolution. Few minor events of American history are more thrilling or more widely known than the successes of "the Hunters of Kentucky" over the British and the Indians at the sieges of Boonsborough and of Bryant's Station,

their massacre at the deadly ambuscade of the Blue Licks, and the swift and wonderful campaigns of George Rogers Clark, the Stonewall Jackson of the early West.

It was in 1780, in the very midst of the harassments and distractions of this war, that Virginia, to her everlasting credit, took time to perfect a bill and make a donation for education in Kentucky that resulted in the founding of Transylvania University. Jefferson, whose broad culture was second only to his superb statesmanship, was then at the helm in the Old Dominion, and he had linked his enduring name with that of Kentucky long before he had penned "the Resolutions of '98."

To fully appreciate the situation of the Kentucky pioneers, it must be remembered that while the close of the Revolution meant peace to the seaboard States, it did not mean peace to them. Savage depredations and burnings and slaughters continued through all the years from the surrender of Yorktown until the British gave up the military posts in the Northwest, and to these aggravations, from which the old government could not protect them, must be added the trying vexations through which they went before they could secure the separation of the district from Virginia, and its admission into the Union. It was during these unsettled times that General Wilkinson, the soldier of fortune who afterwards became the commander-in-chief of the American army, cut such a figure; that the Spanish conspiracy and the question of the free navigation of the Mississippi so agitated the people; and that the jealousy of the North and the South over the balance of power had an early demonstration in the long-delayed reception of Kentucky with her slaves as a member of the Union.

The old Confederation had ample time to crumble leisurely to pieces, and Kentucky to consume years in holding separation conventions before the object she so patiently sought was gained. It was not until the 4th of February, 1791, that Congress passed the bill admitting her into the Union, but the event was put off for more than a year, for the bill stipulated that it was not to occur until the 1st of June, 1792. This act was the first of its kind ever adopted by the Congress of the United States, and was signed by Washington when New York city was the capital of the country, and when the present Federal government was only three years old. An eloquent evidence of the patriotic feeling existing in Kentucky at this time, in spite of her neglect by the government, is seen in the date of the adoption of her first Constitution—the 19th of April, 1792—the anniversary of the battle of Lexington. This document, which was evidently modelled after the then new Constitution of the United States, seems to have been for the most part the work of George Nicholas, an associate of Madison and Patrick Henry, a student of the backwoods who would have done credit to the Middle Temple, and the leading legal light of his day in the district. It was a College of Electors, as required by this Constitution, which convened shortly after its adoption, and in regular national style made choice of Isaac Shelby as Governor.

And it came to pass that Friday, the 1st of June, 1792, rolled around, and on that day, a hundred years ago, Kentucky became a member of the Union, with Lexington, the most central of her settlements, as the capital of the new-born State.

It is curious that "Lexington," the title of a British Lord, should have become the slogan of the American Revolution, but not more curious than the fact that the first spot of ground on this continent named to commemorate the opening battle of that struggle should have been located beyond the confines of civilization, and in the heart of the far-distant wilderness of Kentucky. Lexington, the metropolis of the blue-grass region, is to-day the oldest public monument in existence to the first dead of the war of independence, and she was toasted as the first namesake of Lexington, Massachusetts, at the centennial celebration of that battle. The beautiful incident of the naming of Lexington, Kentucky, which occurred early in June, 1775, was witnessed by Simon Kenton and other noted pioneers. Longfellow was urged to make it the subject of a poem, and corresponded with the writer in regard to it, but he died, unfortunately, too soon for the story to be embalmed by him in immortal verse.

When Lexington became the capital of Kentucky in 1792, she had a thousand inhabitants, and was the largest and most important town in the State, in spite of mud roads and of thieving Indians, who carried off the settlers' negroes and sold them at Detroit for whiskey. Her stores were filled with heavy stocks of goods; manufactories flourished, and especially powder-mills, as one might naturally imagine, considering the exposed condition of her customers; her sales of pack-horses were large and constant; her schools were growing; traders were coming and going all the time; and altogether she was a busy town, furnishing an immense area of the Western country, including Cincinnati, with supplies of every kind.

Such was the settlement, crowded with strangers, where on Monday the 4th of June, 1792, commenced the first session of the Kentucky Legislature, and the organization of the State government. On that day Governor Shelby arrived from Danville, where all the conventions had been held, and as he came on horseback down the hill which overlooked the little capital, the citizens made the valley of the Elkhorn resound with the cracking of their flint-lock rifles, and with the roar of an old six-pounder which the explosive and emphatic Mad Anthony Wayne requested the use of a short time after. The Governor, provided with leggins, saddlebags, and holsters, was halted with his escort at the intersection of the two principal streets of the village, where he was received with military honors by the largest and most picturesque procession that the Western country had ever seen. There, with all the formality and punctiliousness that Sir Charles Grandison himself could have desired, he was presented with a written address of welcome in behalf of Lexington by Mr. John Bradford, or "Old Wisdom," as he was admiringly called, the chairman of the town Board of Trustees, the editor of the only newspaper in the commonwealth, and a gentleman of substantial scientific attainments. The oath of office was then administered to the Governor, who, after more salutes had been indulged in, took his place in the procession, which immediately began to move, and to the sound of drum and fife and ten village bells, he was escorted through the main street, past the printing-office, the site of the old block-house, the prosperous-looking stores, and the liberty pole, the pillory, and the stocks, the court-house yard, where the settlers hitched their horses, and on to the Sheaf of Wheat inn, where he "lighted" from his tired nag and lodged. The "Light Infantry" and the "Troop of Horse" then paraded the unpaved public square, where the inaugural ceremonies were concluded by the firing of fifteen rounds—one for each of the States then in the Union—and a general discharge of rifles in honor of the new Governor.

The General Assembly met in the State House, a gloomy but substantial two-story log building of the regular old pioneer type, above whose gabled roof on Main Street floated the American flag. It met, however, mainly to elect officers, after which it adjourned, and the rest of the day was spent in rejoicings, in the announcement of appointments by the Governor, and in the interchange of courtesies between the citizens and their guests. On the 6th of June, after the Legislature had been fully organized, the members of both Houses assembled in the Senate Chamber of the State House to formally receive the Governor's message, which was delivered in person, after the elaborate Federal style of the day, which was followed in Kentucky up to the time of Governor Scott, when it was changed to the present simple one in accordance with a precedent established by President Jefferson. Exactly at noon the Governor entered the plain and unpretentious room attended by the Secretary of State, and was immediately conducted to a position on the right of the Speaker of the Senate, when, after respectfully addressing first the Senate and then the House, he proceeded to read the communication he had prepared. At the close of the address he delivered to each Speaker a copy of the manuscript, and retired as solemnly and as formally as he had entered. The two Houses then separated, and after gravely voting an address in reply to that of his Excellency, adjourned. It was a curious sight, that first session of the Kentucky Legislature, where an imitation of a kingly custom of Great Britain appeared in such striking contrast to the natural and unaffected ways of early Western life: the pomp of the House of Lords in a log cabin; the royal ermine and the republican 'coon-skin.

Kentucky literally fought her way to Statehood through seventeen such years as mark the calendar of no other American commonwealth. She had never known the fostering care of the general government, which, even as late as 1792, had accomplished nothing in the way of opening the Mississippi to her trade, nor had done anything to free her from that serious obstacle to her progress, the retention of the Northwestern posts by England. The presence of British troops encouraged the Indians to violence; and the State was admitted to the Union during the murdering and marauding that followed St. Clair's defeat. But the self-made commonwealth remained true to the government which so many of her sons had fought and suffered to establish. The very motto of the State seal is a reminder of the patriotic sentiments which animated Kentucky a hundred years ago. It was suggested by a couplet from a popular air that was sung by the Sons of Liberty during the Revolution:

"Come, join hand in hand, Americans all;
  By uniting we stand, by dividing we fall."

WESTERN OUTLOOK FOR SPORTSMEN

TO all who delight in the manly and invigorating recreations of the shooting field it must be a matter of great regret that among the framers of our Constitution there was no one so far-seeing as to incorporate a general law for the protection of the big game of this country. Had such provision existed—even during the past twenty years—we would not have witnessed the wanton extermination of the buffalo, and the threatened annihilation of the giant of the North American *Cervidæ*—the elk. It is only the observant and practical sportsman who for the past twenty-five years has spent months at a time in the haunts of the game of this country who can claim a right to discuss the Western game outlook intelligently. For the most part, the fashionable hunter's chief aim is to simply kill for the sake of killing, resorting to all manner of unworthy artifices to accomplish this end; to slaughter, even when his game cannot be utilized, that he may boast of numbers slain, and to wantonly destroy, that he may show on his return the trophies torn from his victims. At the present time the West is overrun yearly by trophy-hunters from all parts of the world. Unable, in the majority of cases,

from lack of endurance and skill and a knowledge of wood-craft, to procure their own antlers and pelts, they employ native hunters at high wages to lead them to the game, and, if they fail to hit the game, to do the killing for them. These men are induced, therefore, to slaughter vast quantities of game when it is not in season, when otherwise they would have reserved it for their own maintenance, and permitted the noble animals to perpetuate their kind. In this way thousands of heads of game are annually destroyed, but their number is comparatively small when compared with that killed by skin-hunters, ranchmen, and by reckless stockmen, who, just for the fun of it, never miss an opportunity to employ their repeating rifles at all kinds of game.

This unnecessary destruction of game could have been prevented, or at least checked, had adequate laws existed, and their enforcement been made a matter of national consideration. But on looking Westward we find that the great decrease of game other than the buffaloes and the elk is mainly consequent on the settlement of what but a short time ago were the natural homes of the animals. Within a few years the country between the Mississippi and the Pacific coast has become traversed by railroads, and the grassy plains and fertile valleys on which countless herds of buffalo, elk, and antelope used to roam without molestation have become cattle ranges and stock farms. In fact the whole Western country may now be described as one huge stock ranch covered with cattle-men and settlers, before which the different varieties of big game are retiring.

Sixteen years back no man could go amiss in searching for game in the West. He had only to strike into the mountains, ten to one hundred miles from the railroad, to get all the hunting he wanted. The mountains were covered with elk and white and black tail deer, and the plains with antelope. At that time mountain-sheep were very numerous in the Bad Lands of the Missouri, Little Missouri, and Yellowstone. Bear, both grizzlies and black, were common in the mountain ranges, while buffaloes were plentiful in Montana, very abundant in Texas, and fairly numerous in northern Nebraska, Kansas, and the Indian Territory.

Even then the Union Pacific Railroad had cut the great buffalo herd in two. The skin-hunters had already begun, and in the course of two or three years they had exterminated the buffaloes in Kansas and Nebraska. The destruction was not completed in Texas and the Indian Territory until 1880, while the last important killing in Montana and Dakota was in 1883.

At the present time, outside of the National Park, where about two hundred and sixty buffaloes are now harbored, there are not over three hundred, probably not as many, left in the whole United States. The survivors of this magnificent race of animals are scattered in little bunches in several localities. There are about one hundred in Montana, or at least there were a year ago, some at the head of Dry Creek and the remainder at the head of Porcupine Creek. In Wyoming there are a few stragglers from the National Park, which, when chased, run back there for protection. In the mountains of Colorado last summer there were two bunches of mountain bison, one of twenty-five head and the other of eleven. These have probably been killed. There are none in Dakota, though eighteen months ago thirty were known to be there. It was estimated in 1887 that there were twenty-seven in Nebraska, and about fifty more scattered in the western part of the Indian Territory and Kansas. Those in Nebraska have since been killed by the Sioux. Of the thousands that once inhabited Texas, only two small bunches remain. Thirty-two head are near the Ratons, in the northwestern part of the Panhandle, and eight in the sand-hills on the Staked Plains north of the Pecos River. These were seen and counted on the 1st of April of last year. This estimate of the remnant of a great race is believed to be essentially correct. It was obtained from reliable and well-informed persons throughout the West, and in part from personal observation during the past years.

It is often asked why an attempt has not been made to save the buffalo by domesticating it, and questioning whether the profits derived from its flesh, horns, and hide would not be much greater than from raising common cattle. The experiment has been tried by Mr. Charles Goodnight on his Paladura Cañon Range, in Armstrong County, Texas. Ten calves were roped by Mr. Goodnight in the spring of 1879, and raised. It was found that they were very troublesome and hard to handle. They bred more slowly than common cattle. Mr. Goodnight has ten domesticated buffaloes now on his ranch. He has endeavored to cross them with Hereford cattle, with but poor results. Out of hundreds of trials he succeeded in procuring but one hybrid. This, a cow-calf, was bred to a buffalo bull, and the result was a bull-calf which in appearance closely resembled a pure buffalo, thus proving the strength of the buffalo blood. Several of the domesticated herd, however, had issue. They were found to defend their young with great ferocity, and at no time has it been safe for strangers or women to go afoot among them. Mr. Goodnight is at present trying a series of experiments in buffalo breeding, but with poor success. Unless the domestic cow is reared with the buffalo they will not cross. The experiment has best succeeded with dun colored cows. I understand that Goodnight has sold his band, and that they finally passed to Mr. W. F. Cody.

While Mr. Goodnight's trials at breeding the buffalo were no doubt original with him, he is by no means the first to experiment in breeding the buffalo in a domesticated state. We are told by Mr. Audubon that as early as 1813 Mr. Robert

Wickliffe, of Kentucky, commenced some interesting experiments. He began breeding from two buffalo cows, from which he raised a small herd. The cows came from the upper Missouri River. At first they were confined in a separate park with some buffalo bulls, but later on they were all allowed to herd and feed with the common cattle; nor did their owner find his buffaloes more furious or wild than common cattle of the same age that grazed with them.

On getting possession of the tame buffalo bulls, Mr. Wickliffe endeavored to cross them as much as he could with common cows, which met with some success, but he found the common bulls always shy of buffalo cows, and unwilling to accede to the same experiment of crossing. From the domestic cow he had several half-breeds, one of which was a heifer. This he put with a domestic bull, and it produced a bull-calf. This when killed as a steer produced very fine beef. He bred from the same heifer several calves, and then, that the experiment might be perfect, he put one of them to a buffalo bull, and she produced a bull-calf, which was raised to be a very fine large animal, a three-quarter, half-quarter, and half-quarter of the common blood. After making these experiments he left them to propagate their breed themselves, so that he only had a few half-breeds, and they always proved the same, even by a buffalo bull. The full-blood was found not to be as large as the improved stock of common cattle, but as large as the ordinary cattle of the country.

The udder, or bag, of the buffalo is smaller than that of the common cow, and while the calves of both were allowed to run with their dams upon the same pasture, those of the buffalo were always the fattest. It was the experience of old hunters of that time that when a young buffalo calf was taken it required the milk of two common cows to raise it.

Unfortunately Mr. Wickliffe had no opportunity of testing the longevity of the buffalo, as all his died, either being killed by accident or because they were aged. He, however, raised some cows that at twenty years old were healthy and vigorous and capable of suckling their calves. It was his experience that a half-bred buffalo bull would not produce again, while a half-bred heifer was productive from either race, beyond the possibility of a doubt.

It is certainly interesting to compare the widely differing experience of Mr. Goodnight with a remnant of a most persecuted race, and that of Mr. Wickliffe's, fifty years ago, when the buffalo had few other enemies in the land than the Indian and the wolf.

In Mexico, it is said that a large band still exists on the big plains some seven hundred miles south of the northern frontier, and west of the Mexican Central Railroad. While hunting in the winter of 1887 in the Sierra Tierra Nate I learned from some Yaqui Indians that the herd was not a myth; that it was a very large one; and, owing to the almost inaccessible country in which it was located, that its numbers had not been depleted. How accurate these reports may be I do not know. In other respects the information given by the Yaquis regarding the country in which I was hunting, and the best game localities there, was found to be accurate. As it is well known that formerly there were large bands of buffaloes in Sonora and Chihuahua, they may have migrated southward. For some years past those who have been best informed have refrained from making known the exact localities where the few remaining bands of buffaloes could be found. They did this trusting that Congress would take steps to check their absolute extermination. This has not been done. The sportsman, therefore, who desires to belong to the party that "kills the last buffalo" should betake himself at once to the east side of the National Park, where, by skirting its edge, he may chance to get a shot. This is the best locality left in the United States to kill a buffalo.

Turning to the now doomed elk, we find that twenty years ago they were almost the most abundant game animal in the Western country, perhaps not even excepting the buffalo. In former times their range existed all over North America. Their horns have been discovered in the Adirondack region and in Lower Canada, while in northern California the elk in small numbers still are found. In 1870 it was very abundant in the valley of the Missouri River, and almost everywhere to the west of that stream. It is an easy animal to kill, and in consequence has been hunted to death. The sportsman in those days could work up to a band of elk, and fire, if he chose, a hundred shots at them. There are occasions when, being shot at, the elk, instead of running away, merely jump about, while the repeaters are mowing their fellows down.

Their decrease in the last eight to ten years has been enormous; yet while the skin-hunters are partly to blame for this, the elk have of late years been killed mainly for their meat. As soon as the cold weather sets in, the settlers go out, each party with several wagons, to get their stock of winter meat. Three years ago one hundred and twenty wagon-loads of elk meat were brought out of Bate's Hole, south of the North Platte River. In the autumn of 1887 there was not one elk left in this district. What, however, has made the elk more scarce than anything else is the spread of the cattle ranches. The cattle go where the elk live, tramp down the grass and brush, and usurp their beds. Formerly it was not an uncommon sight to see five thousand elk in one scattering band. At that time they were very abundant in the Uinta, Wasatch, and Big Horn mountains in Wyoming, all through the mountains of Montana, and along the Missouri and Loup Fork River in Nebraska. Now the sportsman will find no elk to kill in the last-mentioned State, and will have to hunt hard to get a shot in either Montana or Wyoming.

The best and surest find for elk at this time is along the boundary between Idaho and Wyoming, south of the National Park, and in the Salmon River country in Idaho. There is probably no country in the world as rough to hunt in as that last mentioned. The mountains are very steep, rising from five to six thousand feet out of the valleys. The hunter has to be continually climbing up over the jagged rocks, or descending into the broken cañons. Even to the native hunter the travelling at best is very slow. It requires youth, stout legs, and good wind to follow the trails of the elk in this section. Yet when the hunter goes into these mountains in the morning there is a fair chance that he will find plenty of tracks, and come across game within a few hours. The sportsman, however, who travels in the West is continually meeting small parties of hunters who report elk plentiful at different places. Pinning these men down to particulars, he finds they were told so by "some one." The "some one," if discovered, usually simplifies matters by saying that he saw a small band there several months before.

While elk are not nearly as numerous as they used to be, there are thousands of them left in scattered bands throughout the West. One day in the summer of 1887 an old hunter, a friend of mine, riding south of the National Park, came across six bands of elk. To the visiting sportsman this would indicate that the country was full of game; but let him stop and think of the immense tract of country where the wapiti used to be abundant, and where to-day there is not one left.

In western America there are two bears that claim the sportsman's attention—the grizzly and the black. The former, hunters have endowed with many aliases, such as "silver-tip," "brown," "cinnamon," "bald-face," and "range" bear. These names do not mean anything, for the grizzly, like the dog, is of many colors. These two varieties of bears can, among other things, be distinguished by the formation of their claws. Those of the grizzly are longer on the fore than on the hind feet. The claws of the black bear are short, and are of the same length on all four feet. It is difficult to persuade the hunters of different sections that the "silver-tip," "cinnamon," "brown," "bald-face," and "range" bears are all from the same ancestry, and that the same animal is called by different names in different localities. But while hunters may vary in their nomenclature, they one and all agree that the full-grown grizzly is the gamest animal in the world, and the one to be most dreaded.

Never do these bears stand on their hind legs and pursue the hunter with terrible howls and roars, as is the orthodox way of describing their conflicts with human beings in the ghastly literature of the country. When not hit in the brain or spine, they put their head down, and with a swinging gallop rush upon the hunter. They usually receive their death wound without demonstration, sinking down and dying mute. The majority of grizzlies shot by our famous Eastern sportsmen are those that have first been trapped. They are killed when in this crippled condition, after dragging often for miles a large steel-trap with a huge trailing log attached.

The grizzly is found west of the Missouri River, and very rarely, if ever, east of it. They inhabit both the plains and mountains. A dozen years ago they could be seen almost anywhere in the mountain ranges, but since their destruction has been compassed by baiting and traps they have become shy, and difficult to approach near enough for a certain killing shot. Bears are the most wary animals of all the big game in America. They go singly, and usually see the hunter before he catches a glimpse of them. They then cunningly slip away, and are difficult to trail. At this time they are fairly abundant in the mountains of Montana, a sure find being in Crazy Women's Mountain, north of the Northern Pacific Railroad. There is also a goodly number of bears distributed over the mountains of Idaho and Wyoming, some in southern California, scattered in the Sierra Madres and on the junction waters of the Santa Maria River in San Luis Obispo County. They are also numerous in the Rocky Mountains and Sierra Nevadas.

The black bear has a far wider range than the grizzly, but in the West it is confined mostly to the mountains, and rarely comes out on the prairies. It is well distributed, however, and is especially abundant in the timbered country, moving about to where the mast and berries are most plentiful. Black bears are very numerous in northern Montana. On the Pacific coast they outnumber the grizzlies, where both species feed on the salmon. The destruction of the grizzlies has been much greater than that of the black. Bears, though still abundant, are very difficult animals to hunt and kill in a sportsman-like way.

In these days the hardest game to hunt in America is the big-horn, or mountain-sheep. Twelve years ago they used to be wonderfully abundant in the Bad Lands of the Missouri and Yellowstone. When the first white men went there the sheep used to be so tame that they would stand and look at the intruders on their domain, and show no distrust at their approach. It was then a familiar sight, while drifting down the Missouri River in a skiff, to see these gallant-looking animals grouped on all points of the bluffs. Since then their decrease has been very great; not so much from being killed by hunters as from the settlement of the country. In rapid succession they have been forced to migrate from one place to another, and this has caused a majority of the sheep to retire into the high mountains of the remote Northwest, no one knows where. From the regions where they were but a short time ago so abundant they have gone forever. To-day they can be found in small companies on the high rough peaks of the unsettled country bordering the National Park. The Salmon River country of Idaho is an excellent place to find them—and to see them get away. They are scattered throughout western Colorado on the rough peaks and in the almost inaccessible mountain regions. Their range extends into British Columbia and the North. The big-horn is now as vigilant and shy as it was once gentle. Its successful pursuit requires experience, untiring patience, and good marksmanship, and a steady head for heights. The flesh of the mountain-sheep is considered in delicacy of flavor the best that the game of the West affords.

The glory of killing a mountain-goat consists in having courage and endurance sufficient to climb to its home on the loftiest peaks in the almost inaccessible mountains. As for the animal itself, it is the most stupid animal that came out of the ark, while its meat is poor and its skin worthless. They have decreased in Washington and Oregon, where but a few years ago they were abundant. Their range extends to Alaska, while a few have been known to straggle as far south as Colorado. Like the mountain-sheep, their decrease is not from shooting, but from the settlement of the country. There are a few goats left in the Deer Lodge country in southern Montana, and in the Salmon River country in Idaho. Only a very few are killed every year, and the sportsman might "climb the mountains o'er" for a week and then not find this variety of game or get a shot.

Although the slaughter of antelopes for their hides has been enormous, there are places where they can be found in great abundance. In the summer season they are numerous in the North Park, Colorado, and along the Arkansas River, and back on the plains in the Indian Territory. In the winter they also collect along the line of the Union Pacific Railroad, being very abundant on the Laramie Plains in Wyoming. Despite the fact that the antelope is a very wary animal, and, owing to the character of the grounds which it inhabits, is very difficult to approach, they are daily diminishing very rapidly. The sportsman, therefore, who desires to kill this variety of game should as soon as possible anticipate its certain extermination.

The decrease of the three varieties of

deer—the "white-tail," "black-tail," and mule-deer—has been much less than the other varieties of Western big game. As yet the people have not made it a business to hunt them for either skins or meat. The meat-hunters are still devoting their attention to the killing of larger game; but as it decreases, the deers' turn will surely come. There are yet plenty of deer in the mountains of the West. The "white-tails" haunt the willowy stream bottoms, while the mule-deer, almost universally known as the "black-tail," resorts to the high mountain lands in summer, and comes down to the rough foot-hills in the winter. The true black-tail deer is only found on the northern Pacific coast. Mule-deer are abundant enough along the upper Missouri River, but their centre of abundance is on the high dry plateau between the Rocky Mountains and the Sierra Nevada. The sportsman who wishes to shoot "white-tails" cannot go far wrong by hunting in any of the river-bottom countries of the West. Both the "white-tails" and mule-deer were very plentiful several years ago in the Black Hills of Dakota. In this section the first-named variety was more abundant than in any other part of the country. They have been shot off along the Platte River. Good shooting, however, can still be had along the Loup Fork.

Straggling moose are to be met with in Washington, Oregon, Idaho, Montana, and northern California. Their range is limited, however, and they are becoming exterminated. Even in the British Possessions, this, the grandest of our native ruminants, is becoming more scarce as the conditions of its old homes are changed and its old feeding-grounds destroyed by the settlements of the white man.

Thus we see on all sides, and even in the most remote and inaccessible sections of our country, our "big game" diminishing with terrible rapidity. Our only hope therefore in preventing the thorough extermination of the game lies in the maintenance of the National Park and the protection of the animals that now harbor there. Until July, 1885, there was no pretence made to protect the game in the Park, but even with inadequate protection the animals that make their home there have increased in number, and now there are more buffaloes within the reservation than there were two or three years ago. Left undisturbed, the game in the Park will breed and multiply, showing the necessity for its thorough protection, which can only be enforced by vigorous measures regulated by Congress.

It has long been known that the Indians are the only real preservers of big game. On their ranges, where the white man did not dare to go, game of all kinds was most abundant. For this reason the Sierra Madres in Mexico are still virgin of sportsmen and skin-hunters. The ranchmen as yet have not driven their cattle and sheep into the grassy cañons, and at this writing there is a wide section that has been but little shot over. There deer, bears, mountain-lions, antelope, and turkeys are in abundance; and the sportsman in search of novelty may pass several months in a country of which little is known. On one of the spurs of these mountains I found admirable sport in January last.

No idea can be formed of the annual destruction of big game from the skins that are brought into the trading post, for their number is very small compared to that of animals killed. Nor can any estimate be deduced from the statements of the sporting ammunition manufacturers, as it is impossible for them to decide what part of their production is actually employed in killing game. The rough figuring of the Winchester Repeating Arms Company, the largest manufacturers of cartridges in this country, is interesting, however. It is largely made up of guess-work, and must be accepted as such. This firm made last year 250,000,000 of all kinds of cartridges. Of this number it is thought two-thirds were sold in the West. Mr. T. G. Bennett, vice-president of the company, says: "From my own experience in an ordinary summer's shooting, about one-tenth of one per cent. of cartridges fired may be said to be used on game. The rest are expended in target practice." On this very modest basis of figuring, about 167,000 cartridges of only one manufactory are shot annually at game, without taking into account that a great many hunters reload their empty shells once to ten times. Mr. M. Hartley, president of the Union Metallic Cartridge Company, from an experience of twenty years, expresses his opinion that a smaller quantity of large-sized cartridges for shooting large game is sold now than in former years, which he attributes to the decrease of the number of large game in this country. The United States Cartridge

Company, one of the three large cartridge manufacturers in this country, is unable to estimate what part of its production is used in the West.

More interesting, perhaps, to the majority of Eastern sportsmen is the small-game outlook in the Western country. We find that during the past fifteen years the two most popular birds of the gallinaceous order, the prairie-chicken and the quail, have increased their domain very materially. As settlements began to crop up, and Indian-corn and grain fields took the place of wild prairie lands, the sport-providing birds were found to follow in the wake of civilization. Where only the coyote and jack-rabbit had heretofore been found, the grouse and quail began to appear. As long as the sequence of mild winters followed their emigration to their new homes they increased in astonishing numbers. This was especially the case in Kansas. For some years after their appearance in this State all went well. Then came the terrible snows and blizzards of the winter of 1885 and 1886, and at one fell swoop the quail were buried in their winding-sheets. The snow melted, and the frozen birds were found by hundreds of thousands along the Osage-orange hedge-rows where they had sought shelter from the storms. The grouse fared somewhat better, for they appear to have anticipated the approach of the "northers," and to have invaded the Indian Territory, and to have passed across it into Texas. So extended was their southern migration that they infested the southern Rio Grande section, where hitherto they had never been seen, and where they have since remained to populate that portion of Texas. All this indicates that the best shooting of the future will be in the Southwest, especially on those lands which will be irrigated and cultivated for the production of grain. While a succession of mild winters will again occasion the restocking of Kansas, and propitious breeding seasons replenish the crop in Missouri and Iowa, the absolute certainty of good shooting in these States is anything but assured. The sportsman would do well, therefore, to look for his sport in the Indian Territory, Arkansas, and northern and northeastern Texas. The shooting in the Indian country for the next dozen years will be the cream of all the sport in this country.

Within the remembrance of many East-ern sportsmen the prairie-chicken did not inhabit Nebraska, while now, owing to the cultivation of the cereals, the State has been fairly stocked. In those times the sharp-tailed grouse had its eastern limit in Michigan. As this State became settled it returned westward, the prairie-chicken following it into Minnesota and Nebraska. The range of the sharp-tailed grouse at this time is from the western limit of the range of the prairie-chicken on to the Pacific coast. It is very abundant in the Sierra Nevadas and other mountain ranges. It lies well to a dog, is bold on the wing, and is one of the most delicious of all the grouse family. The sage-hen, which is a very large bird, is found on the sage plains of the Rocky Mountain region. It is not often seen east of Sherman, on the line of the Union Pacific Railroad, and follows down the Missouri River as far as Wolf Point. While large bags of sage-hens are made every year, for the sport of shooting them over dogs, they are still very abundant.

Wild turkeys are still very numerous in the Indian Territory and Texas. Their decrease is marked in Arkansas, New Mexico, and Arizona, owing to the practice of killing the birds whenever an opportunity offers. There is no pretence made in the West to observe the breeding season of these magnificent birds; indeed, the native hunters avail themselves of the known habits of the birds at such time to compass their destruction.

In California and Oregon the greatest abundance of game of many varieties still exists. The ruffed grouse shooting in the last-named State is excellent, while the valley quail in southern California are on the increase. They are well distributed in the foot-hills of the Sierra Nevadas and Coast Range, where the sportsmen will see thousands of them in one day. The same may be said of the mountain quail of California, the Arizona quail, and the scaled quail of Texas, Arizona, New Mexico, and Mexico. All these varieties are very abundant, and increasing in their several localities, as is the gentle and talkative Massena quail of Mexico, which is found on the parched deserts and in the rocky cañons of all the mountain ranges.

The shooting in the West is so much controlled by the weather conditions, by early and late seasons, by droughts and floods, that it is impossible to anticipate the season's crop of game in any one section. Wild-fowl and the waders, of all varieties, continue to swarm along the great rivers and their tributaries; yet, while geese and ducks are abundant early in the autumn in Dakota, and migrate in myriads to Texas, where they remain all winter, they are nowhere found as numerous as on the Pacific coast. In California, along the Sacramento River, in the San Joaquin Valley, and at Lake Tulare, the finest wild-fowl shooting is to be had, though it is not what it was some years ago.

STUDIES OF THE GREAT WEST —
CHICAGO
(PART 1)

CHICAGO is becoming modest. Perhaps the inhabitants may still be able to conceal their modesty, but nevertheless they feel it. The explanation is simple. The city has grown not only beyond the most sanguine expectations of those who indulged in the most inflated hope of its future, but it has grown beyond what they said they expected. This gives the citizens pause—as it might an eagle that laid a roc's egg.

The fact is, Chicago has become an independent organism, growing by a combination of forces and opportunities beyond the contrivance of any combination of men to help or hinder, beyond the need of flaming circulars and reports of boards of trade, and process pictures. It has passed the danger or the fear of rivalry, and reached the point where the growth of any other portion of the great Northwest, or of any city in it (whatever rivalry that city may show in industries or in commerce), is in some way a contribution to the power and wealth of Chicago. To them that have shall be given. Cities, under favoring conditions for local expansion, which reach a certain amount of population and wealth, grow by a kind of natural increment, the law of attraction, very well known in human nature, which draws a person to an active city of two hundred thousand rather than to a stagnant city of one hundred thousand. And it is a fortunate thing for civilization that this attraction is almost as strong to men of letters as it is to men of affairs. Chicago has, it seems to me, only recently turned this point of assured expansion, and, as I intimated, the inhabitants have hardly yet become accustomed to this idea; but I believe that the time is near when they will be as indifferent to what strangers think of Chicago as the New-Yorkers are to what strangers think of New York. New York is to-day the only American city free from this anxious note of provincialism—though in Boston it rather takes the form of pity for the unenlightened man who doubts its superiority; but the impartial student of Chicago to-day can see plenty of signs of the sure growth of this metropolitan indifference. And yet there is still here enough of the old Chicago stamp to make the place interesting.

It is everything in getting a point of view. Last summer a lady of New Orleans who had never before been out of her native French city, and who would look upon the whole North with the impartial eyes of a foreigner—and more than that, with Continental eyes—visited Chicago, and afterward New York. "Which city did you like best?" I asked, without taking myself seriously in the question. To my surprise, she hesitated. This hesitation was fatal to all my preconceived notions. It mattered not thereafter which she preferred: she had hesitated. She was actually comparing Chicago to New York in her mind, as one might compare Paris and London. The audacity of the comparison I saw was excused by its innocence. I confess that it had never occurred to me to think of Chicago in that Continental light. "Well," she said, not seeing at all the humor of my remark, "Chicago seems to me to have finer buildings and residences, to be the more beautiful city; but of course there is more in New York; it is a greater city; and I should prefer to live there for what I want." This naïve observation set me thinking, and I wondered if there was a point of view, say that of divine omniscience and fairness, in which Chicago

would appear as one of the great cities of the world, in fact a metropolis, by-and-by to rival in population and wealth any city of the seaboard. It has certainly better commercial advantages, so far as water communication and railways go, than Paris or Pekin or Berlin, and a territory to supply and receive from infinitely vaster, richer, and more promising than either. This territory will have many big cities, but in the nature of things only one of surpassing importance. And taking into account its geographical position —a thousand miles from the Atlantic seaboard on the one side, and from the mountains on the other, with the acknowledged tendency of people and of money to it as a continental centre—it seems to me that Chicago is to be that one.

The growth of Chicago is one of the marvels of the world. I do not wonder that it is incomprehensible even to those who have seen it year by year. As I remember it in 1860, it was one of the shabbiest and most unattractive cities of about a hundred thousand inhabitants anywhere to be found; but even then it had more than trebled its size in ten years; the streets were mud sloughs, the sidewalks were a series of stairs and more or less rotten planks, half the town was in process of elevation above the tadpole level, and a considerable part of it was on wheels—the moving house being about the only wheeled vehicle that could get around with any comfort to the passengers. The west side was a straggling shanty-town, the north side was a country village with two or three "aristocratic" houses occupying a square, the south side had not a handsome business building in it, nor a public edifice of any merit except a couple of churches, but there were a few pleasant residences on Michigan Avenue fronting the encroaching lake, and on Wabash Avenue. Yet I am not sure that even then the exceedingly busy and excited traders and speculators did not feel that the town was more important than New York. For it had a great business. Aside from its real estate operations, its trade that year was set down at $97,000,000, embracing its dealing in produce, its wholesale supply business, and its manufacturing.

No one then, however, would have dared to predict that the value of trade in 1887 would be, as it was, $1,103,000,000. Nor could any one have believed that the population of 100,000 would reach in 1887 nearly 800,000 (estimated 782,644), likely to reach in 1888, with the annexation of contiguous villages that have become physically a part of the city, the amount of 900,000. Growing at its usual rate for several years past, the city is certain in a couple of years to count its million of people. And there is not probably anywhere congregated a more active and aggressive million, with so great a proportion of young, ambitious blood. Other figures keep pace with those of trade and population. I will mention only one or two of them here. The national banks, in 1887, had a capital of $15,800,000, in which the deposits were $80,473,746, the loans and discounts $63,113,821, the surplus and profits $6,320,559. The First National is, I believe, the second or third largest banking house in the country, having a deposit account of over twenty-two millions. The figures given only include the national banks; add to these the private banks, and the deposits of Chicago in 1887 were $105,367,000. The aggregate bank clearings of the city were $2,969,216,210 60, an increase of 14 per cent. over 1886. It should be noted that there were only twenty-one banks in the clearing house (with an aggregate capital and surplus of $28,514,000), and that the fewer the banks the smaller the total clearings will be. The aggregate Board of Trade clearings for 1887 were $78,179,869. In the year 1886 Chicago imported merchandise entered for consumption to the value of $11,574,449, and paid $4,349,237 duties on it. I did not intend to go into statistics, but these and a few other figures will give some idea of the volume of business in this new city. I found on inquiry that—owing to legislation that need not be gone into—there are few savings-banks, and the visible savings of labor cut a small figure in this way. The explanation is that there are several important loan and building associations. Money is received on deposit in small amounts, and loaned at a good rate of interest to those wishing to build or buy houses, the latter paying in small instalments. The result is that these loan institutions have been very profitable to those who have put money in them, and that the laborers who have borrowed to build have also been benefited by putting all their savings into houses. I believe there is no other large city, except Philadelphia perhaps, where so large a proportion of the inhabitants own the houses they live in. There is no better prevention of the spread of anarchical notions and communist foolishness than this.

It is an item of interest that the wholesale dry-goods jobbing establishments increased their business in 1887 12½ per cent. over 1886. Five houses have a capital of $9,000,000, and the sales in 1887 were nearly $74,000,000. And it is worth special mention that one man in Chicago, Marshall Field, is the largest wholesale and retail dry-goods merchant in the world. In his retail shop and wholesale store there are 3000 employés on the payroll. As to being first in his specialty, the same may be said of Philip D. Armour, who not only distances all rivals in the world as a packer, but no doubt also as a merchant of such products as the hog contributes to the support of life. His sales in one year have been over $51,000,000. The city has also the distinction of having among its citizens Henry W. King, the largest dealer, in establishments here and elsewhere, in clothing in the world.

In nothing has the growth of Chicago been more marked in the past five years than in manufactures. I cannot go into the details of all the products, but the totals of manufacture for 1887 were, in 2396 firms, $113,960,000 capital employed, 134,615 workers, $74,567,000 paid in wages, and the value of the product was $403,109,500—an increase of product over 1886 of about 15½ per cent. A surprising item in this is the book and publishing business. The increase of sales of books in 1887 over 1886 was 20 per cent. The wholesale sales for 1887 are estimated at $10,000,000. It is now claimed that as a book-publishing centre Chicago ranks second only to New York, and that in the issue of subscription-books it does more business than New York, Boston, and Philadelphia combined. In regard to musical instruments the statement is not less surprising. In 1887 the sales of pianos amounted to about $2,600,000—a gain of $300,000 over 1886. My authority for this, and for some, but not all, of the other figures given, is the *Tribune*, which says that Chicago is not only the largest reed-organ market in the world, but that more organs are manufactured here than in any other city in Europe or America. The sales for 1887 were $2,000,000—an increase over 1886 of $500,000. There were

$1,000,000 worth of small musical instruments sold, and of sheet music and music-books a total of $450,000. This speaks well for the cultivation of musical taste in the West, especially as there was a marked improvement in the class of the music bought.

The product of the iron manufactures in 1887, including rolling-mills ($23,952,000) and founderies ($10,000,000),was $61,187,000 against $46,790,000 in 1886, and the wages paid in iron and steel work was $14,899,000. In 1887 there were erected 4833 buildings, at a reported cost of $19,778,100—a few more buildings, but yet at nearly two millions less cost, than in 1886. A couple of items interested me: that Chicago made in 1887 $900,000 worth of toys and $500,000 worth of perfumes. The soap-makers waged a gallant but entirely unsuccessful war against the soot and smoke of the town in producing $6,250,000 worth of soap and candles. I do not see it mentioned, but I should think the laundry business in Chicago would be the most profitable one at present.

Without attempting at all to set forth the business of Chicago in detail, a few more figures will help to indicate its volume. At the beginning of 1887 the storage capacity for grain in 29 elevators was 27,025,000 bushels. The total receipts of flour and grain in 1882, '3, '4, '5, and '6, in bushels, were respectively, 126,155,483, 164,924,732, 159,561,474, 156,408,228, and 151,932,995. In 1887 the receipts in bushels were: flour, 6,873,544; wheat, 21,848,251; corn, 51,578,410; oats, 45,750,842; rye, 852,726; barley, 12,476,547;—total, 139,380,320. It is useless to go into details of the meat products, but interesting to know that in 1886 Chicago shipped 310,039,600 pounds of lard and 573,496,012 pounds of dressed beef.

I was surprised at the amount of the lake commerce, the railway traffic (nearly 50,000 miles tributary to the city) making so much more show. In 1882 the tonnage of vessels clearing this port was 4,904,999; in 1886 it was 3,950,762. The report of the Board of Trade for 1886 says the arrivals and clearances, foreign and coastwise, for this port for the year ending June 30th were 22,096, which was 869 more than at the ports of Baltimore, Boston, New Orleans, Philadelphia, Portland and Falmouth, and San Francisco combined; 315 more than at New York, New Orleans, Portland and Falmouth,

and San Francisco; and 100 more than at New York, Baltimore, and Portland and Falmouth. It will not be overlooked that this lake commerce is training a race of hardy sailors, who would come to the front in case of a naval war, though they might have to go out on rafts.

In 1888 Chicago is a magnificent city. Although it has been incorporated fifty years, during which period its accession of population has been rapid and steady—hardly checked by the devastating fires of 1871 and 1874—its metropolitan character and appearance is the work of less than fifteen years. There is in history no parallel to this product of a freely acting democracy: not St. Petersburg rising out of the marshes at an imperial edict, nor Berlin, the magic creation of a consolidated empire and a Cæsar's power. The northside village has become a city of broad streets, running northward to the parks, lined with handsome residences interspersed with stately mansions of most varied and agreeable architecture, marred by very little that is bizarre and pretentious—a region of churches and club-houses and public buildings of importance. The west side, the largest section, and containing more population than the other two divisions combined, stretching out over the prairie to a horizon fringed with villages, expanding in three directions, is more mediocre in buildings, but impressive in its vastness; and the stranger driving out the stately avenue of Washington some four miles to Garfield Park will be astonished by the evidences of wealth and the vigor of the city expansion.

But it is the business portion of the south side that is the miracle of the time, the solid creation of energy and capital since the fire—the square mile containing the Post-office and City Hall, the giant hotels, the opera-houses and theatres, the Board of Trade building, the many-storied offices, the great shops, the club-houses, the vast retail and wholesale warehouses. This area has the advantage of some other great business centres in having broad streets at right angles, but with all this openness for movement, the throng of passengers and traffic, the intersecting street and cable railways, the loads of freight and the crush of carriages, the life and hurry and excitement are sufficient to satisfy the most eager lover of metropolitan pandemonium. Unfortunately for a clear comprehension of it, the manufactories vomit dense clouds of bituminous coal smoke, which settle in a black mass in this part of the town, so that one can scarcely see across the streets in a damp day, and the huge buildings loom up in the black sky in ghostly dimness. The climate of Chicago, though some ten degrees warmer than the average of its immediately tributary territory, is a harsh one, and in the short winter days the centre of the city is not only black, but damp and chilly. In some of the November and December days I could without any stretch of the imagination fancy myself in London. On a Sunday, when business gives place to amusement and religion, the stately city is seen in all its fine proportions. No other city in the Union can show business warehouses and offices of more architectural nobility. The mind inevitably goes to Florence for comparison with the structures of the Medicean merchant princes. One might name the Pullman Building for offices as an example, and the wholesale warehouse of Marshall Field, the work of that truly original American architect, Richardson, which in massiveness, simplicity of lines, and admirable blending of artistic beauty with adaptability to its purpose, seems to me unrivalled in this country. A few of these buildings are exceptions to the general style of architecture, which is only good of its utilitarian American kind, but they give distinction to the town, and I am sure are prophetic of the concrete form the wealth of the city will take. The visitor is likely to be surprised at the number and size of the structures devoted to offices, and to think, as he sees some of them unfilled, that the business is overdone. At any given moment it may be, but the demand for "offices" is always surprising to those who pay most attention to this subject, and I am told that if the erection of office buildings should cease for a year, the demand would pass beyond the means of satisfying it.

Leaving the business portion of the south side, the city runs in apparently limitless broad avenues southward into suburban villages and a region thickly populated to the Indiana line. The continuous slightly curving lake front of the city is about seven miles, pretty solidly occupied with houses. The Michigan Avenue of 1860, with its wooden fronts and cheap boarding-houses, has taken on quite another appearance, and extends its broad way in unbroken lines of fine residences five miles, which will be six miles next summer, when its opening is completed to the entrance of Washington Park. I do not know such another street in the world. In the evening the converging lines of gas lamps offer a prospective of unequalled beauty of its kind. The south parks are reached now by turning either into the Drexel Boulevard or the Grand Boulevard, a magnificent avenue a mile in length, tree-planted, gay with flower beds in the season, and crowded in the sleighing time with fast teams and fancy turnouts.

This leads me to speak of another feature of Chicago, which has no rival in this country: I mean the facility for pleasure driving and riding. Michigan Avenue from the mouth of the river, the centre of town, is macadamized. It and the other avenues immediately connected with the park system are not included in the city street department, but are under the care of the Commissioners of Parks. No traffic is permitted on them, and consequently they are in superb condition for driving, summer and winter. The whole length of Michigan Avenue you will never see a loaded team. These roads, that is, Michigan Avenue and the others of the park system, and the park drives, are superb for driving or riding, perfectly made for drainage and permanency, with a top-dressing of pulverized granite. The cost of the Michigan Avenue drive was two hundred thousand dollars a mile. The cost of the parks and boulevards in each of the three divisions is met by a tax on the property in that division. The tax is considerable, but the wise liberality of the citizens has done for the town what only royalty usually accomplishes—given it magnificent roads. And if good roads are a criterion of civilization, Chicago must stand very high. But it needed a community with a great deal of daring and confidence in the future to create this park system.

One in the heart of the city has not to drive three or four miles over cobble-stones and ruts to get to good driving-ground. When he has entered Michigan Avenue, he need not pull rein for twenty to thirty miles. This is almost literally true as to extent, without counting the miles of fine drives in the parks. For the city proper is circled by great parks, already laid out as pleasure-grounds, tree-planted and beau

tified to a high degree, although they are
nothing to what cultivation will make
them in ten years more. On the lake
shore, at the south, is Jackson Park; next
is Washington Park, twice as large as Central Park, New York; then, further to the
west, and north, Douglas Park and Garfield Park; then Humboldt Park, until we
come round to Lincoln Park, on the lake
shore on the north side. These parks are
all connected by broad boulevards, some
of which are not yet fully developed, thus
forming a continuous park drive, with
enough of nature and enough of varied
architecture for variety, unsurpassed, I
should say, in the world within any city
limits. Washington Park, with a slightly rolling surface and beautiful landscape
gardening, has not only fine driveways,
but a splendid road set apart for horsemen. This is a dirt road, always well
sprinkled, and the equestrian has a chance
besides of a gallop over springy turf. Water is now so abundantly provided that this
park is kept green in the driest season.
From anywhere in the south side one may
mount his horse or enter his carriage for
a turn of fifteen or twenty miles on what
is equivalent to a country road, that is to
say, an English country road. Of the effect of this facility on social life I shall
have occasion to speak. On the lake side
of Washington Park are the grounds
of the Washington Park Racing Club,
with a splendid track, and stables and
other facilities which, I am told, exceed
anything in the country of the kind. The
club-house itself is very handsome and
commodious, is open to the members and
their families summer and winter, and
makes a favorite rendezvous for that part
of society which shares its privileges. Besides its large dining and dancing halls, it
has elegant apartments set apart for ladies.
In winter its hospitable rooms and big
wood fires are very attractive after a zero
drive.

Almost equal facility for driving and
riding is had on the north side by taking
the lake-shore drive to Lincoln Park.
Too much cannot be said of the beauty
of this drive along the curving shore of
an inland sea, ever attractive in the play
of changing lights and colors, and beginning to be fronted by palatial houses—a
foretaste of the coming Venetian variety
and splendor. The park itself, dignified
by the Lincoln statue, is an exquisite
piece of restful landscape, looked over by

a thickening assemblage of stately residences. It is a quarter of spacious elegance.

One hardly knows how to speak justly
of either the physical aspect or the social
life of Chicago, the present performance
suggesting such promise and immediate
change. The excited admiration waits a
little upon expectation. I should like to
see it in five years—in ten years; it is a
formative period, but one of such excellence of execution that the imagination
takes a very high flight in anticipating
the result of another quarter of a century. What other city has begun so nobly or has planned so liberally for metropolitan solidity, elegance, and recreation? What other has such magnificent
avenues and boulevards, and such a system of parks? The boy is born here who
will see the town expanded far beyond
these splendid pleasure-grounds, and what
is now the circumference of the city will
be to Chicago what the vernal gardens
from St. James to Hampton are to London. This anticipation hardly seems
strange when one remembers what Chicago was fifteen years ago.

Architecturally Chicago is more interesting than many older cities. Its wealth
and opportunity for fine building coming
when our national taste is beginning to
be individual, it has escaped the monotony and mediocrity in which New York
for so many years put its money, and out
of the sameness of which it is escaping in
spots. Having also plenty of room, Chicago has been able to avoid the block system in its residences, and to give play to
variety and creative genius. It is impossible to do much with the interior of a
house in a block, however much you may
load the front with ornament. Confined
to a long parallelogram, and limited as to
light and air, neither comfort nor individual taste can be consulted or satisfied.
Chicago is a city of detached houses, in
the humbler quarters as well as in the
magnificent avenues, and the effect is
home-like and beautiful at the same time.
There is great variety, stone, brick, and
wood intermingled, plain and ornamental; but drive where you will in the favorite residence parts of the vast city,
you will be continually surprised with
the sight of noble and artistic houses and
homes displaying taste as well as luxury.
In addition to the business and public
buildings of which I spoke, there are sev-

eral, like the Art Museum, the Studebaker Building, and the new Auditorium, which would be conspicuous and admired in any city in the world. The city is rich in a few specimens of private houses by Mr. Richardson (whose loss to the country is still apparently irreparable), houses worth a long journey to see, so simple, so noble, so full of comfort, sentiment, unique, having what may be called a charming personality. As to interiors, there has been plenty of money spent in Chicago in mere show, but, after all, I know of no other city that has more character and individuality in its interiors, more evidences of personal refinement and taste. There is, of course—Boston knows that—a grace and richness in a dwelling in which generations have accumulated the best fruits of wealth and cultivation; but any tasteful stranger here, I am sure, will be surprised to find in a city so new so many homes pervaded by the atmosphere of books and art and refined sensibility, due, I imagine, mainly to the taste of the women, for while there are plenty of men here who have taste, there are very few who have leisure to indulge it; and I doubt if there was ever anywhere a livable house—a man can build a palace, but he cannot make a home—that was not the creation of a refined woman. I do not mean to say that Chicago is not still very much the victim of the upholsterer, and that the eye is not offended by a good deal that is gaudy and pretentious, but there is so much here that is in exquisite taste that one has a hopeful heart about its future. Everybody is not yet educated up to the "Richardson houses," but nothing is more certain than that they will powerfully influence all the future architecture of the town.

Perhaps there never was before such an opportunity to study the growth of an enormous city, physically and socially, as is offered now in Chicago, where the development of half a century is condensed into a decade. In one respect it differs from all other cities of anything like its size. It is not only surrounded by a complete net-work of railways, but it is permeated by them. The converging lines of twenty-one (I think it is) railways paralleling each other or crisscrossing in the suburbs concentrate upon fewer tracks as they enter the dense part of the city, but they literally surround it, and actually pierce its heart. So complete

is this environment and interlacing that you cannot enter the city from any direction without encountering a net-work of tracks. None of the water-front, except a strip on the north side, is free from them. The finest residence part of the south side, including the boulevards and parks, is surrounded and cut by them. There are a few viaducts, but for the most part the tracks occupy streets, and the crossings are at grade. Along the Michigan Avenue water-front and down the lake shore to Hyde Park, on the Illinois Central and the Michigan Central and their connections, the foreign and local trains pass incessantly (I believe over sixty a day), and the Illinois crosses above Sixteenth Street, cutting all the great southward avenues; and further down, the tracks run between Jackson Park and Washington Park, crossing at grade the 500-feet-wide boulevard which connects these great parks and makes them one.

These tracks and grade crossings, from which so few parts of the city are free, are a serious evil and danger, and the annoyance is increased by the multiplicity of street railways, and by the swiftly running cable-cars, which are a constant source of alarm to the timid. The railways present a difficult problem. The town covers such a vast area (always extending in a ratio that cannot be calculated) that to place all the passenger stations outside would be a great inconvenience, to unite the lines in a single station probably impracticable. In time, however, the roads must come in on elevated viaducts, or concentrate in three or four stations which communicate with the central parts of the town by elevated roads.

This state of things arose from the fact that the railways antedated, and we may say made, the town, which has grown up along their lines. To a town of pure business, transportation was the first requisite, and the newer roads have been encouraged to penetrate as far into the city as they could. Now that it is necessary to make it a city to live in safely and agreeably, the railways are regarded from another point of view. I suppose a sociologist would make some reflections on the effect of such a thorough permeation of tracks, trains, engines, and traffic upon the temperament of a town, the action of these exciting and irritating causes upon its nervous centres. Living in a big railway station must have an effect on the nerves. At present this seems a legitimate part of the excited activity of the city; but if it continues, with the rapid increase of wealth and the growth of a leisure class, the inhabitants who can afford to get away will live here only the few months necessary to do their business and take a short season of social gayety, and then go to quieter places early in the spring and for the summer months.

It is at this point of view that the value of the park system appears, not only as a relief, as easily accessible recreation-grounds for the inhabitants in every part of the city, but as an element in society life. These parks, which I have already named, contain 1742 acres. The two south parks, connected so as to be substantially one, have 957 acres. Their great connecting boulevards are interfered with somewhat by railway tracks, and none of them, except Lincoln, can be reached without crossing tracks on which locomotives run, yet, as has been said, the most important of them are led to by good driving-roads from the heart of the city. They have excellent roads set apart for equestrians as well as for driving. These facilities induce the keeping of horses, the setting up of fine equipages, and a display for which no other city has better opportunity. This cannot but have an appreciable effect upon the growth of luxury and display in this direction. Indeed, it is already true that the city keeps more private carriages—for the pleasure not only of the rich, but of the well-to-do —in proportion to its population, than any other large city I know. These broad thoroughfares, kept free from traffic, furnish excellent sleighing when it does not exist in the city streets generally, and in the summer unequalled avenues for the show of wealth and beauty and style. In a few years the turnouts on the Grand Boulevard and the Lincoln Park drive will be worth going far to see for those who admire—and who does not, for the world over, wealth has no spectacle more attractive to all classes—fine horses and the splendor of moving equipages. And here is no cramped mile or two for parade, like most of the fashionable drives of the world, but space inviting healthful exercise as well as display. These broad avenues and park outlooks, with ample ground-room, stimulate architectural rivalry, and this opportunity for driving and riding and being on view cannot but

affect very strongly the social tone. The foresight of the busy men who planned this park system is already vindicated. The public appreciate their privileges. On fair days the driving avenues are thronged. One Sunday afternoon in January, when the sleighing was good, some one estimated that there were as many as ten thousand teams flying up and down Michigan Avenue and the Grand Boulevard. This was, of course, an overestimate, but the throng made a ten-thousand impression on the mind. Perhaps it was a note of Western independence that a woman was here and there seen "speeding" a fast horse, in a cutter, alone.

I suppose that most of these people had been to church in the morning, for Chicago, which does everything it puts its hand to with tremendous energy, is a church-going city, and I believe presents some contrast to Cincinnati in this respect. Religious, mission, and Sunday-school work is very active, churches are many, whatever the liberality of the creeds of a majority of them, and there are several congregations of over two thousand people. One vast music hall and one theatre are thronged Sunday after Sunday with organized, vigorous, worshipful congregations. Besides these are the Sunday meetings for ethical culture and Christian science. It is true that many of the theatres are open as on weekdays, and there is a vast foreign population that takes its day of rest in idleness or base-ball and garden amusements, but the prevailing aspect of the city is that of Sunday observance. There is a good deal of wholesome New England in its tone. And it welcomes any form of activity— orthodoxy, liberalism, revivals, ethical culture.

A special interest in Chicago at the moment is because it is forming—full of contrasts and of promise, palaces and shanties side by side. Its forces are gathered and accumulating, but not assimilated. What a mass of crude, undigested material it has! In one region on the west side are twenty thousand Bohemians and Poles; the street signs are all foreign and of unpronounceable names—a physically strong, but mentally and morally brutal, people for the most part; the adults generally do not speak English, and clanning as they do, they probably never will. There is no hope that this generation will be intelligent American citizens, or be otherwise than the political prey of demagogues. But their children are in the excellent public schools, and will take in American ideas and take on American ways. Still, the mill has about as much grist as it can grind at present.

Social life is, speaking generally, as unformed, unselected, as the city—that is, more fluid and undetermined than in Eastern large cities. That is merely to say, however, that while it is American, it is young. When you come to individuals, the people in society are largely from the East, or have Eastern connections that determine their conduct. For twenty years the great universities, Harvard, Yale, Amherst, Princeton, and the rest, have been pouring in their young men here. There is no better element in the world, and it is felt in every pulse of the town. Young couples marry and come here from every sort of Eastern circle. But the town has grown so fast, and so many new people have come into the ability suddenly to spend money in fine houses and equipages, that the people do not know each other. You may drive past miles of good houses, with a man who has grown up with the town, who cannot tell you who any of the occupants of the houses are. Men know each other on change, in the courts, in business, and are beginning to know each other in clubs, but society has not got itself sorted out and arranged, or discovered its elements. This is a metropolitan trait, it is true, but the condition is socially very different from what it is in New York or Boston ; the small village associations survive a little yet, struggling against the territorial distances, but the social mass is still unorganized, although "society" is a prominent feature in the newspapers. Of course it is understood that there are people "in society," and dinners, and all that, in no wise different from the same people and events the world over.

A striking feature of the town is "youth," visible in social life as well as in business. An Eastern man is surprised to see so many young men in responsible positions, at the head, or taking the managing oar, in great moneyed institutions, in railway corporations, and in societies of charity and culture. A young man, graduate of the city high-school, is at the same time president of a prominent bank, president of the Board of Trade, and president of the Art Institute.

This youthful spirit must be contagious, for apparently the more elderly men do not permit themselves to become old, either in the business or the pleasures of life. Everything goes on with youthful vim and spirit.

Next to the youth, and perhaps more noticeable, the characteristic feature of Chicago is money-making, and the money power is as obtrusive socially as on change. When we come to speak of educational and intellectual tendencies, it will be seen how this spirit is being at once utilized and mitigated; but for the moment money is the recognized power. How could it be otherwise? Youth and energy did not flock here for pleasure or for society, but simply for fortune. And success in money-getting was about the only one considered. And it is still that by which Chicago is chiefly known abroad, by that and by a certain consciousness of it which is noticed. And as women reflect social conditions most vividly, it cannot be denied that there is a type known in Europe and in the East as the Chicago young woman, capable rather than timid, dashing rather than retiring, quite able to take care of herself. But this is not by any means an exhaustive account of the Chicago woman of to-day.

While it must be said that the men, as a rule, are too much absorbed in business to give heed to anything else, yet even this statement will need more qualification than would appear at first, when we come to consider the educational, industrial, and reformatory projects. And indeed a veritable exception is the Literary Club, of nearly two hundred members, a mingling of business and professional men, who have fine rooms in the Art Building, and meet weekly for papers and discussions. It is not in every city that an equal number of busy men will give the time to this sort of intellectual recreation. The energy here is superabundant; in whatever direction it is exerted it is very effective; and it may be said, in the language of the street, that if the men of Chicago seriously take hold of culture, they will make it hum.

Still it remains true here, as elsewhere in the United States, that women are in advance in the intellectual revival. One cannot yet predict what will be the result of this continental furor for literary, scientific, and study clubs—in some places in the East the literary wave has already risen to the height of the scientific study of whist—but for the time being Chicago women are in the full swing of literary life. Mr. Browning says that more of his books are sold in Chicago than in any other American city. Granting some affectation, some passing fashion, in the Browning, Dante, and Shakespeare clubs, I think it is true that the Chicago woman, who is imbued with the energy of the place, is more serious in her work than are women in many other places; at least she is more enthusiastic. Her spirit is open, more that of frank admiration than of criticism of both literature and of authors. This carries her not only further into the heart of literature itself, but into a genuine enjoyment of it—wanting almost to some circles at the East, who are too cultivated to admire with warmth or to surrender themselves to the delights of learning, but find their avocation rather in what may be called literary detraction, the spirit being that of dissection of authors and books, much as social gossips pick to pieces the characters of those of their own set. And one occupation is as good as the other. Chicago has some reputation for beauty, for having pretty, dashing, and attractive women; it is as much entitled to be considered for its intelligent women who are intellectually agreeable. Comparisons are very unsafe, but it is my impression that there is more love for books in Chicago than in New York society, and less of the critical, *nil admirari* spirit than in Boston.

It might be an indication of no value (only of the taste of individuals) that books should be the principal "favors" at a fashionable german, but there is a bookstore in the city whose evidence cannot be set aside by reference to any freak of fashion. McClurg's book-store is a very extensive establishment in all departments—publishing, manufacturing, retailing, wholesaling, and importing. In some respects it has not its equal in this country. The book-lover, whether he comes from London or New York, will find there a stock, constantly sold and constantly replenished, of books rare, curious, interesting, that will surprise him. The general intelligence that sustains a retail shop of this variety and magnitude must be considerable, and speaks of a taste for books with which the city has not been credited; but the cultivation, the special love of books for themselves, which makes

possible this rich corner of rare and imported books at McClurg's, would be noticeable in any city, and women as well as men in Chicago are buyers and appreciators of first editions, autograph and presentation copies, and books valued because they are scarce and rare.

Chicago has a physical peculiarity that radically affects its social condition, and prevents its becoming homogeneous. It has one business centre and three distinct residence parts, divided by the branching river. Communication between the residence sections has to be made through the business city, and is further hindered by the bridge crossings, which cause irritating delays the greater part of the year. The result is that three villages grew up, now become cities in size, and each with a peculiar character. The north side was originally the more aristocratic, and having fewer railways and a less-occupied-with-business lake front, was the more agreeable as a place of residence, always having the drawback of the bridge crossings to the business part. After the great fire, building lots were cheaper there than on the south side within reasonable distance of the active city. It has grown amazingly, and is beautified by stately houses and fine architecture, and would probably still be called the more desirable place of residence. But the south side has two great advantages—easy access to the business centre and to the great southern parks and pleasure-grounds. This latter would decide many to live there. The vast west side, with its lumber-yards and factories, its foreign settlements, and its population outnumbering the two other sections combined, is practically an unknown region socially to the north side and south side. The causes which produced three villages surrounding a common business centre will continue to operate. The west side will continue to expand with cheap houses, or even elegant residences on the park avenues—it is the glory of Chicago that such a large proportion of its houses are owned by their occupants, and that there are few tenement rookeries, and even few gigantic apartment houses—over a limitless prairie; the north side will grow in increasing beauty about Lincoln Park; and the south side will more and more gravitate with imposing houses about the attractive south parks. Thus the two fashionable parts of the city, separated by five, eight, and ten miles, will develop a social life of their own, about as distinct as New York and Brooklyn. It remains to be seen which will call the other "Brooklyn." At present these divisions account for much of the disorganization of social life, and prevent that concentration which seems essential to the highest social development.

In this situation Chicago is original, as she is in many other ways, and it makes one of the interesting phases in the guesses at her future.

—I must defer to another paper other characteristics of the town which has the greatest merchant in Dry-goods, the greatest dealer in Clothing, the greatest Packer, in the country, and probably in the world.

STUDIES OF THE GREAT WEST —
CHICAGO
(PART 2)

THE country gets its impression of Chicago largely from the Chicago newspapers. In my observation, the impression is wrong. The press is able, vigorous, voluminous, full of enterprise, alert, spirited; its news columns are marvellous in quantity, if not in quality; nowhere are important events, public meetings, and demonstrations more fully, graphically, and satisfactorily reported; it has keen and competent writers in several departments of criticism—theatrical, musical, and occasionally literary; independence, with less of personal bias than in some other cities; the editorial pages of most of the newspapers are bright, sparkling, witty, not seldom spiced with knowing drollery, and strong, vivid, well-informed and well-written, in the discussion of public questions, with an allowance always to be made for the "personal equation" in dealing with particular men and measures—as little provincial in this respect as any press in the country.

But it lacks tone, elevation of purpose; it represents to the world the inferior elements of a great city rather than the better, under a mistaken notion in the press and the public, not confined to Chicago, as to what is "news." It cannot escape the charge of being highly sensational; that is, the elevation into notoriety of mean persons and mean events by every rhetorical and pictorial device. Day after day the leading news, the most displayed and most conspicuous, will be of vulgar men and women, and all the more expanded if it have in it a spice of scandal. This sort of reading creates a diseased appetite, which requires a stronger dose daily to satisfy. And people who read it lose their relish for the higher,

more decent, if less piquant, news of the world. Of course the Chicago newspapers are not by any means alone in this course; it is a disease of the time. Even New York has recently imitated successfully this feature of what is called Western journalism.

But it is largely from the Chicago newspapers that the impression has gone abroad that the city is pre-eminent in divorces, pre-eminent in scandals, that its society is fast, that it is vulgar and pretentious, that its tone is "shoddy," and its culture a sham. The laws of Illinois in regard to divorces are not more lax than in some Eastern States, and divorces are not more numerous there of residents (according to population) than in some Eastern towns; but while the press of the latter give merely an official line to the court separations, the Chicago papers parade all the details, and illustrate them with pictures. Many people go there to get divorces, because they avoid scandal at their homes, and because the Chicago courts offer unusual facilities in being open every month in the year. Chicago has a young, mobile population, an immense foreign brutal element. I watched for some weeks the daily reports of divorces and scandals. Almost without exception they related to the lower, not to say the more vulgar, portions of social life. In several years the city has had, I believe, only two *causes célèbres* in what is called good society—a remarkable record for a city of its size. Of course a city of this magnitude and mobility is not free from vice and immorality and fast living; but I am compelled to record the deliberate opinion, formed on a good deal of observation and inquiry, that the moral tone in Chicago society, in all the well-to-do industrious classes which give the town its distinctive character, is purer and higher than in any other city of its size with which I am acquainted, and purer than in many much smaller. The tone is not so fast, public opinion is more restrictive, and women take, and are disposed to take, less latitude in conduct. This was not my impression from the newspapers. But it is true not only that social life holds itself to great propriety, but that the moral atmosphere is uncommonly pure and wholesome. At the same time, the city does not lack gayety of movement, and it would not be called prudish, nor in some respects conventional.

It is curious also that the newspapers, or some of them, take pleasure in mocking at the culture of the town. Outside papers catch this spirit, and the "culture" of Chicago is the butt of the paragraphers. It is a singular attitude for newspapers to take regarding their own city. Not long ago Mr. McClurg published a very neat volume, in vellum, of the fragments of Sappho, with translations. If the volume had appeared in Boston it would have been welcomed and most respectfully received in Chicago. But instead of regarding it as an evidence of the growing literary taste of the new town, the humorists saw occasion in it for exquisite mockery in the juxtaposition of Sappho with the modern ability to kill seven pigs a minute, and in the cleverest and most humorous manner set all the country in a roar over the incongruity. It goes without saying that the business men of Chicago were not sitting up nights to study the Greek poets in the original; but the fact was that there was enough literary taste in the city to make the volume a profitable venture, and that its appearance was an evidence of intellectual activity and scholarly inclination that would be creditable to any city in the land. It was not at all my intention to intrude my impressions of a newspaper press so very able and with such magnificent opportunities as that of Chicago, but it was unavoidable to mention one of the causes of the misapprehension of the social and moral condition of the city.

The business statistics of Chicago, and the story of its growth, and the social movement, which have been touched on in a previous paper, give only a half-picture of the life of the town. The prophecy for its great and more hopeful future is in other exhibitions of its incessant activity. My limits permit only a reference to its churches, extensive charities (which alone would make a remarkable and most creditable chapter), hospitals, medical schools, and conservatories of music. Club life is attaining metropolitan proportions. There is on the south side the Chicago, the Union League, the University, the Calumet, and on the north side the Union—all vigorous, and most of them housed in superb buildings of their own. The Women's Exchange is a most useful organization, and the Ladies' Fortnightly ranks with the best intellectual associations in the country. The Commercial Club, composed of sixty representative business men in all departments, is a most vital element in the prosperity of the city. I cannot dwell upon these. But at least a word must be said about the charities, and some space must be given to the schools.

The number of solicitors for far West churches and colleges who pass by Chicago and come to New York and New England for money have created the impression that Chicago is not a good place to go for this purpose. Whatever may be the truth of this, the city does give royally for private charities, and liberally for mission work beyond her borders. It is estimated by those familiar with the subject that Chicago contributes for charitable and religious purposes, exclusive of the public charities of the city and county, not less than five millions of dollars annually. I have not room to give even the partial list of the benevolent societies that lies before me, but beginning with the Chicago Relief and Aid, and the Armour Mission, and going down to lesser organizations, the sum annually given by them is considerably over half a million dollars. The amount raised by the churches of various denominations for religious purposes is not less than four millions yearly. These figures prove the liberality, and I am able to add that the charities are most sympathetically and intelligently administered.

Inviting, by its opportunities for labor and its facilities for business, comers from all the world, a large proportion of whom are aliens to the language and institutions of America, Chicago is making a noble fight to assimilate this material into good citizenship. The popular schools are liberally sustained, intelligently directed, practise the most advanced and inspiring methods, and exhibit excellent results. I have not the statistics of 1887; but in 1886, when the population was only 703,000, there were 129,000 between the ages of six and sixteen, of whom 83,000 were enrolled as pupils, and the average daily attendance in schools was over 65,000. Besides these there were about 43,000 in private schools. The census of 1886 reports only 34 children between the ages of six and twenty-one who could neither read nor write. There were 91 school buildings owned by the city, and two rented. Of these three are high-schools, one in each division, the newest, on the west side, having 1000 students. The school attendance increases by a large per cent. each year. The principals of the high-schools were men; of the grammar and primary schools, 35 men and 42 women. The total of teachers was 1440, of whom 56 were men. By the census of 1886 there were 106,929 children in the city under six years of age. No kindergartens are attached to the public schools, but the question of attaching them is agitated. In the lower grades, however, the instruction is by object lessons, drawing, writing, modelling, and exercises that train the eye to observe, the tongue to describe, and that awaken attention without weariness. The alertness of the scholars and the enthusiasm of the teachers were marked. It should be added that German is extensively taught in the grammar-schools, and that the number enrolled in the German classes in 1886 was over 28,000. There is some public sentiment for throwing out German from the public schools, and generally for restricting studies in the higher branches. The argument against this is that very few of the children, and the majority of those girls, enter the high-schools; the boys are taken out early for business, and get no education afterward. In 1885 were organized public elementary evening schools (which had, in 1886, 6709 pupils), and an evening high-school, in which book-keeping, stenography, mechanical drawing, and advanced mathematics were taught. The School Committee also have in charge day schools for the education of deaf and dumb children.

The total expenditure for 1886 was $2,060,803; this includes $1,023,394 paid to superintendents and teachers, and large sums for new buildings, apparatus, and repairs. The total cash receipts for school purposes were $2,091,951. Of this was from the school tax fund $1,758,053 (the total city tax for all purposes was $5,368,409), and the rest from State dividend and school fund bonds and miscellaneous sources. These figures show that education is not neglected.

Of the quality and efficacy of this education there cannot be two opinions, as seen in the schools which I visited. The high-school on the west side is a model of its kind; but perhaps as interesting an example of popular education as any is the Franklin grammar and primary school on the north side, in a district of laboring people. Here were 1700 pupils, all children of working people, mostly Swedes and Germans, from the age of six years upward. Here were found some of the children of the late anarchists, and nowhere else can one see a more interesting attempt to manufacture intelligent American citizens. The instruction rises through the several grades from object lessons, drawing, writing and reading (and writing and reading well), to elementary physiology, political and constitutional history, and physical geography. Here is taught to young children what they cannot learn at home, and might never clearly comprehend otherwise; not only something of the geography and history of the country, but the distinctive principles of our government, its constitutional ideas, the growth, creeds, and relations of political parties, and the personality of the great men who have represented them. That the pupils comprehend these subjects fairly well I had evidence in recitations that were as pleasing as surprising. In this way Chicago is teaching its alien population American ideas, and it is fair to presume that the rising generation will have some notion of the nature and value of our institutions that will save them from the inclination to destroy them.

The public mind is agitated a good deal on the question of the introduction of manual training into the public schools. The idea of some people is that manual training should only be used as an aid to mental training, in order to give definiteness and accuracy to thought; others would like actual trades taught; and others think that it is outside the function of the State to teach anything but elementary mental studies. The subject would require an essay by itself, and I only allude to it to say that Chicago is quite alive to the problems and the most advanced educational ideas. If one would like to study the philosophy and the practical working of what may be called physicomental training, I know no better place in the country to do so than the Cook County Normal School, near Englewood, under the charge of Colonel F. W. Parker, the originator of what is known as the Quincy (Massachusetts) System. This is a training school for about 100 teachers, in a building where they have practice on about 500 children in all stages of education, from the kindergarten up to the eighth grade. This may be called a thorough manual training school, but not to teach trades, work being done in drawing, modelling in clay, making raised maps, and wood-carving. The Quincy System, which is sometimes described as the development of character by developing mind and body, has a literature to itself. This remarkable school, which draws teachers for training from all over the country, is a notable instance of the hospitality of the West to new and advanced ideas. It does not neglect the literary side in education. Here and in some of the grammarschools of Chicago the experiment is successfully tried of interesting young children in the best literature by reading to them from the works of the best authors, ancient and modern, and giving them a taste for what is excellent, instead of the trash that is likely to fall into their hands —the cultivation of sustained and consecutive interest in narratives, essays, and descriptions in good literature, in place of the scrappy selections and reading-books written down to the childish level. The written comments and criticisms of the children on what they acquire in this way are a perfect vindication of the experiment. It is to be said also that this sort of education, coupled with the manual training, and the inculcated love for order and neatness, is beginning to tell on the homes of these children. The parents are actually being educated and civilized through the public schools.

An opportunity for superior technical education is given in the Chicago Manual Training School, founded and sustained by the Commercial Club. It has a handsome and commodious building on the corner of Michigan Avenue and Twelfth Street, which accommodates over two hundred pupils, under the direction

of Dr. Henry H. Belfield, assisted by an able corps of teachers and practical mechanics. It has only been in operation since 1884, but has fully demonstrated its usefulness in the training of young men for places of responsibility and profit. Some of the pupils are from the city schools, but it is open to all boys of good character and promise. The course is three years, in which the tuition is $80, $100, and $120 a year; but the club provides for the payment of the tuition of a limited number of deserving boys whose parents lack the means to give them this sort of education. The course includes the higher mathematics, English, and French or Latin, physics, chemistry—in short, a high-school course—with drawing, and all sorts of technical training in work in wood and iron, the use and making of tools, and the building of machinery, up to the construction of steam-engines, stationary and locomotive. Throughout the course one hour each day is given to drawing, two hours to shop-work, and the remainder of the school day to study and recitation. The shops—the wood-work rooms, the foundery, the forge-room, the machineshop—are exceedingly well equipped and well managed. The visitor cannot but be pleased by the tone of the school and the intelligent enthusiasm of the pupils. It is an institution likely to grow, and perhaps become the nucleus of a great technical school, which the West much needs. It is worthy of notice also as an illustration of the public spirit, sagacity, and liberality of the Chicago business men. They probably see that if the city is greatly to increase its importance as a manufacturing centre, it must train a considerable proportion of its population to the highest skilled labor, and that splendidly equipped and ably taught technical schools would do for Chicago what similar institutions in Zürich have done for Switzerland. Chicago is ready for a really comprehensive technical and industrial college, and probably no other investment would now add more to the solid prosperity and wealth of the town.

Such an institution would not hinder, but rather help, the higher education, without which the best technical education tends to materialize life. Chicago must before long recognize the value of the intellectual side by beginning the foundation of a college of pure learning.

For in nothing is the Western society of to-day more in danger than in the superficial half-education which is called "practical," and in the lack of logic and philosophy. The tendency to the literary side—awakening a love for good books—in the public schools is very hopeful. The existence of some well-chosen private libraries shows the same tendency. In art and archæology there is also much promise. The Art Institute is a very fine building, with a vigorous school in drawing and painting, and its occasional loan exhibitions show that the city contains a good many fine pictures, though scarcely proportioned to its wealth. The Historical Society, which has had the irreparable misfortune twice to lose its entire collections by fire, is beginning anew with vigor, and will shortly erect a building from its own funds. Among the private collections which have a historical value is that relating to the Indian history of the West made by Mr. Edward Ayer, and a large library of rare and scarce books, mostly of the English Shakespeare period, by the Rev. Frank M. Bristoll. These, together with the remarkable collection of Mr. C. F. Gunther (of which further mention will be made), are prophecies of a great literary and archæological museum.

The city has reason to be proud of its Free Public Library, organized under the general library law of Illinois, which permits the support of a free library in every incorporated city, town, and township by taxation. This library is sustained by a tax of one half-mill on the assessed value of all the city property. This brings it in now about $80,000 a year, which makes its income for 1888, together with its fund and fines, about $90,000. It is at present housed in the City Hall, but will soon have a building of its own (on Dearborn Park), toward the erection of which it has a considerable fund. It has about 130,000 volumes, including a fair reference library and many expensive art books. The institution has been well managed hitherto, notwithstanding its connection with politics in the appointment of the trustees by the Mayor, and its dependence upon the city councils. The reading-rooms are thronged daily; the average daily circulation has increased yearly; it was 2263 in 1887—a gain of eleven per cent. over the preceding year. This is stimulated by the establishment of eight delivering sta-

tions in different parts of the city. The cosmopolitan character of the users of the library is indicated by the uncommon number of German, French, Dutch, Bohemian, Polish, and Scandinavian books. Of the books issued at the delivery stations in 1887 twelve per cent. were in the Bohemian language. The encouraging thing about this free library is that it is not only freely used, but that it is as freely sustained by the voting population.

Another institution, which promises to have still more influence on the city, and indeed on the whole Northwest, is the Newberry Library, now organizing under an able board of trustees, who have chosen Mr. W. F. Poole as librarian. The munificent fund of the donor is now reckoned at about $2,500,000, but the value of the property will be very much more than this in a few years. A temporary building for the library, which is slowly forming, will be erected at once, but the library, which is to occupy a square on the north side, will not be erected until the plans are fully matured. It is to be a library of reference and study solely, and it is in contemplation to have the books distributed in separate rooms for each department, with ample facilities for reading and study in each room. If the library is built and the collections are made in accordance with the ample means at command, and in the spirit of its projectors, it will powerfully tend to make Chicago not only the money but the intellectual centre of the Northwest, and attract to it hosts of students from all quarters. One can hardly overestimate the influence that such a library as this may be will have upon the character and the attractiveness of the city.

I hope that it will have ample space for, and that it will receive, certain literary collections, such as are the glory and the attraction, both to students and sight-seers, of the great libraries of the world. And this leads me to speak of the treasures of Mr. Gunther, the most remarkable private collection I have ever seen, and already worthy to rank with some of the most famous on public exhibition. Mr. Gunther is a candy manufacturer, who has an archæological and "curio" taste, and for many years has devoted an amount of money to the purchase of historical relics that if known would probably astonish the public. Only specimens of what he has can be displayed in the large apartment set apart for the purpose over his shop. The collection is miscellaneous, forming a varied and most interesting museum. It contains relics—many of them unique, and most of them having a historical value—from many lands and all periods since the Middle Ages, and is strong in relics and documents relating to our own history, from the colonial period down to the close of our civil war. But the distinction of the collection is in its original letters and manuscripts of famous people, and its missals, illuminated manuscripts, and rare books. It is hardly possible to mention a name famous since America was discovered that is not here represented by an autograph letter or some personal relics. We may pass by such mementos as the Appomattox table, a sampler worked by Queen Elizabeth, a prayerbook of Mary, Queen of Scots, personal belongings of Washington, Lincoln, and hundreds of other historical characters, but we must give a little space to the books and manuscripts, in order that it may be seen that all the wealth of Chicago is not in grain and meat.

It is only possible here to name a few of the original letters, manuscripts, and historical papers in this wonderful collection of over seventeen thousand. Most of the great names in the literature of our era are represented. There is an autograph letter of Molière, the only one known outside of France, except one in the British Museum; there are letters of Voltaire, Victor Hugo, Madame Roland, and other French writers. It is understood that this is not a collection of mere autographs, but of letters or original manuscripts of those named. In Germany, nearly all the great poets and writers—Goethe, Schiller, Uhland, Lessing, etc.: in England, Milton, Pope, Shelley, Keats, Wordsworth, Coleridge, Cowper, Hunt, Gray, etc.; the manuscript of Byron's "Prometheus," the "Auld Lang Syne" of Burns, and his "Journal in the Highlands"; "Sweet Home" in the author's hand; a poem by Thackeray; manuscript stories of Scott and Dickens. Among the Italians, Tasso. In America, the known authors, almost without exception. There are letters from nearly all the prominent reformers—Calvin, Melanchthon, Zwingle, Erasmus, Savonarola; a letter of Luther in regard to the Pope's bull; letters of prominent leaders—William the Silent, John the Steadfast, Gustavus Adolphus.

Wallenstein. There is a curious collection of letters of the saints—St. Francis de Sales, St. Vincent de Paul, St. Borromeo; letters of the Popes for three centuries and a half, and of many of the great cardinals.

I must set down a few more of the noted names, and that without much order. There is a manuscript of Charlotte Corday (probably the only one in this country), John Bunyan, Izaak Walton, John Cotton, Michael Angelo, Galileo, Lorenzo the Magnificent; letters of Queen Elizabeth, Mary, Queen of Scots, Mary of England, Anne, several of Victoria (one at the age of twelve), Catherine de' Medici, Marie Antoinette, Josephine, Marie Louise; letters of all the Napoleons, of Frederick the Great, Marat, Robespierre, St. Just; a letter of Hernando Cortez to Charles the Fifth; a letter of Alverez; letters of kings of all European nations, and statesmen and generals without number.

The collection is rich in colonial and Revolutionary material: original letters from Plymouth Colony, 1621, 1622, 1623— I believe the only ones known; manuscript sermons of the early American ministers; letters of the first bishops, White and Seabury; letters of John André, Nathan Hale, Kosciusko, Pulaski, De Kalb, Steuben, and of great numbers of the general and subordinate officers of the French and Revolutionary wars: William Tudor's manuscript account of the battle of Bunker Hill; a letter of Aide-de-camp Robert Orhm to the Governor of Pennsylvania relating Braddock's defeat: the original of Washington's first Thanksgiving proclamation; the report of the committee of the Continental Congress on its visit to Valley Forge on the distress of the army; the original proceedings of the Commissioners of the Colonies at Cambridge for the organization of the Continental army; original returns of the Hessians captured at Princeton; orderly books of the Continental army; manuscripts and surveys of the early explorers; letters of Lafitte, the pirate, Paul Jones, Captain Lawrence, Bainbridge, and so on. Documents relating to the Washington family are very remarkable: the original will of Lawrence Washington bequeathing Mount Vernon to George; will of John Custis to his family; letters of Martha, of Mary, the mother of George, of Betty Lewis, his sister, of all his step and grand children of the Custis family.

In music there are the original manuscript compositions of all the leading musicians in our modern world, and there is a large collection of the choral books from ancient monasteries and churches. There are exquisite illuminated missals on parchment of all periods from the eighth century. Of the large array of Bibles and other early printed books it is impossible to speak, except in a general way. There is a copy of the first English Bible, Coverdale's, also of the very rare second Matthews, and of most of the other editions of the English Bible; the first Scotch, Irish, French, Welsh, and German Luther Bibles; the first Eliot's Indian Bible, of 1662, and the second, of 1685; the first American Bibles; the first American primers, almanacs, newspapers, and the first patent, issued in 1794; the first book printed in Boston; the first printed accounts of New York, Pennsylvania, New Jersey, Virginia, South Carolina, Georgia; the first picture of New York city, an original plan of the city in 1700, and one of it in 1765; early surveys of Boston, Philadelphia, and New York; the earliest maps of America, including the first, second, and third map of the world in which America appears.

Returning to England, there are the Shakespeare folio editions of 1632 and 1685; the first of his printed *Poems* and the *Rape of Lucrece;* an early quarto of *Othello;* the first edition of Ben Jonson, 1616, in which Shakespeare's name appears in the cast for a play; and letters from the Earl of Southampton, Shakespeare's friend, and Sir Walter Raleigh, Francis Bacon, and Essex. There is also a letter written by Oliver Cromwell while he was engaged in the conquest of Ireland.

The relics, documents, and letters illustrating our civil war are constantly being added to. There are many old engravings, caricatures, and broadsides. Of oil-portraits there are three originals of Washington, one by Stuart, one by Peale, one by Polk, and I think I remember one or two miniatures. There is also a portrait in oil of Shakespeare which may become important. The original canvas has been remounted, and there are indubitable signs of its age, although the picture can be traced back only about one hundred and fifty years. The owner hopes to be able to prove that it is a contemporary work. The interesting fact about it is that while it is not remarkable as a work of art, it is recognizable at once as a likeness of what we suppose from other portraits and the busts to be the face and head of Shakespeare, and yet it is different from all other pictures we know, so that it does not suggest itself as a copy.

The most important of Mr. Gunther's collection is an autograph of Shakespeare; if it prove to be genuine, it will be one of the four in the world, and a great possession for America. This autograph is pasted on the fly-leaf of a folio of 1632, which was the property of one John Ward. In 1839 there was published in London, from manuscripts in possession of the Medical Society, extracts from the diary of John Ward (1648–1679), who was vicar and doctor at Stratford-on-Avon. It is to this diary that we owe certain facts theretofore unknown about Shakespeare. The editor, Mr. Stevens, had this volume in his hands while he was compiling his book, and refers to it in his preface. He supposed it to have belonged to the John Ward, vicar, who kept the diary. It turns out, however, to have been the property of John Ward the actor, who was in Stratford in 1740, was an enthusiast in the revival of Shakespeare, and played *Hamlet* there in order to raise money to repair the bust of the poet in the church. This folio has the appearance of being much used. On the fly-leaf is writing by Ward and his signature; there are marginal notes and directions in his hand, and several of the pages from which parts were torn off have been repaired by manuscript text neatly joined.

The Shakespeare signature is pasted on the leaf above Ward's name. The paper on which it is written is unlike that of the book in texture. The slip was pasted on when the leaf was not as brown as it is now, as can be seen at one end where it is lifted. The signature is written out fairly and in full, *William Shakspeare,* like the one to the will, and differs from the two others, which are hasty scrawls, as if the writer were cramped for room, or finished off the last syllable with a flourish, indifferent to the formation of the letters. I had the opportunity to compare it with a careful tracing of the signature to the will sent over by Mr. Hallowell-Phillips. At first sight the two signatures appear to be identical; but on examination they are not; there is just that difference in the strokes, spaces, and formation of the letters that always appears in two signatures by the same hand. One is not a copy of the other, and the one in the folio had to me the unmistakable stamp of genuineness. The experts in handwriting and the microscopists in this country who have examined ink and paper as to antiquity, I understand, regard it as genuine.

There seems to be all along the line no reason to suspect forgery. What more natural than that John Ward, the owner of the book, and a Shakespeare enthusiast, should have enriched his beloved volume with an autograph which he found somewhere in Stratford? And in 1740 there was no craze or controversy about Shakespeare to make the forgery of his autograph an object. And there is no suspicion that the book has been doctored for a market. It never was sold for a price. It was found in Utah, whither it had drifted from England in the possession of an emigrant, and he readily gave it in exchange for a new and fresh edition of Shakespeare's works.

I have dwelt upon this collection at some length, first because of its intrinsic value, second because of its importance to Chicago as a nucleus for what (I hope in connection with the Newberry Library) will become one of the most interesting museums in the country, and lastly as an illustration of what a Western business man may do with his money.

New York is the first and Chicago the second base of operations on this continent—the second in point of departure, I will not say for another civilization, but for a great civilizing and conquering movement, at once a reservoir and distributing point of energy, power, and money. And precisely here is to be fought out and settled some of the most important problems concerning labor, supply, and transportation. Striking as are the operations of merchants, manufacturers, and traders, nothing in the city makes a greater appeal to the imagination than the railways that centre there, whether we consider their fifty thousand miles of track, the enormous investment in them, or their competition for the carrying trade of the vast regions they pierce, and apparently compel to be tributary to the central city. The story of their building would read like a romance, and

a simple statement of their organization, management, and business rivals the affairs of an empire. The present development of a belt road round the city, to serve as a track of freight exchange for all the lines, like the transfer grounds between St. Paul and Minneapolis, is found to be an affair of great magnitude, as must needs be to accommodate lines of traffic that represent an investment in stock and bonds of $1,305,000,000.

As it is not my purpose to describe the railway systems of the West, but only to speak of some of the problems involved in them, it will suffice to mention two of the leading corporations. Passing by the great eastern lines, and those like the Illinois Central, and the Chicago, Alton, and St. Louis, and the Atchison, Topeka, and Sante Fe, which are operating mainly to the south and southwest, and the Chicago, Milwaukee, and St. Paul, one of the greatest corporations, with a mileage which had reached 4921 December 1, 1885, and has increased since, we may name the Chicago and Northwestern, and the Chicago, Burlington, and Quincy. Each of these great systems, which has grown by accretion and extension and consolidations of small roads, operates over four thousand miles of road, leaving out from the Northwestern's mileage that of the Omaha system, which it controls. Looked at on the map, each of these systems completely occupies a vast territory, the one mainly to the north of the other, but they interlace to some extent and parallel each other in very important competitions.

The Northwestern system, which includes, besides the lines that have its name, the St. Paul, Minneapolis, and Omaha, the Fremont, Elkhorn, and Missouri Valley, and several minor roads, occupies northern Illinois and southern Wisconsin, sends a line along Lake Michigan to Lake Superior, with branches, a line to St. Paul, with branches tapping Lake Superior again at Bayfield and Duluth, sends another trunk line, with branches, into the far fields of Dakota, drops down a tangle of lines through Iowa and into Nebraska, sends another great line through northern Nebraska into Wyoming, with a divergence into the Black Hills, and runs all these feeders into Chicago by another trunk line from Omaha. By the report of 1887 the gross earnings of this system (in round numbers) were over twenty-six millions, expenses over twenty millions, leaving a net income of over six million dollars. In these items the receipts for freight were over nineteen millions, and from passengers less than six millions. Not to enter into confusing details, the magnitude of the system is shown in the general balance-sheet for May, 1887, when the cost of road (4101 miles), the sinking funds, the general assets, and the operating assets foot up $176,048,000. Over 3500 miles of this road are laid with steel rails; the equipment required 735 engines and over 23,000 cars of all sorts. It is worthy of note that a table makes the net earnings of 4000 miles of road, 1887, only a little more than those of 3000 miles of road in 1882—a greater gain evidently to the public than to the railroad.

In speaking of this system territorially, I have included the Chicago, St. Paul, Minneapolis, and Omaha, but not in the above figures. The two systems have the same president, but different general managers and other officials, and the reports are separate. To the over 4000 miles of the other Northwestern lines, therefore, are to be added the 1360 miles of the Omaha system (report of December, 1886, since considerably increased). The balance-sheet of the Omaha system (December, 1886) shows a cost of over fifty-seven millions. Its total net earnings over operating expenses and taxes were about $2,304,000. It then required an equipment of 194 locomotives and about 6000 cars. These figures are not, of course, given for specific railroad information, but merely to give a general idea of the magnitude of operations. This may be illustrated by another item. During the year for which the above figures have been given the entire Northwestern system ran on the average 415 passenger and 732 freight trains each day through the year. It may also be an interesting comparison to say that all the railways in Connecticut, including those that run into other States, have 416 locomotives, 668 passenger cars, and 11,502 other cars, and that their total mileage in the State is 1405 miles.

The Chicago, Burlington, and Quincy (report of December, 1886) was operating 4036 miles of road. Its only eccentric development was the recent Burlington and Northern, up the Mississippi River to St. Paul. Its main stem from Chicago branches out over northern and western Illinois, runs down to St. Louis, from thence to Kansas City by way of Han-nibal, has a trunk line to Omaha, crisscrosses northern Missouri and southern Iowa, skirts and pierces Kansas, and fairly occupies three-quarters of Nebraska with a net-work of tracks, sending out lines north of the Platte, and one to Cheyenne and one to Denver. The whole amount of stock and bonds, December, 1886, was reported at $155,920,000. The gross earnings for 1886 were over twenty-six millions (over nineteen of which was for freight and over five for passengers), operating expenses over fourteen millions, leaving over twelve millions net earnings. The system that year paid eight per cent. dividends (as it had done for a long series of years), leaving over fixed charges and dividends about a million and a half to be carried to surplus or construction outlays. The equipment for the year required 619 engines and over 24,000 cars. These figures do not give the exact present condition of the road, but only indicate the magnitude of its affairs.

Both these great systems have been well managed, and both have been, and continue to be, great agents in developing the West. Both have been profitable to investors. The comparatively small cost of building roads in the West and the profit hitherto have invited capital, and stimulated the construction of roads not absolutely needed. There are too many miles of road for capitalists. Are there too many for the accommodation of the public? What locality would be willing to surrender its road?

It is difficult to understand the attitude of the Western Granger and the Western Legislatures toward the railways, or it would be if we didn't understand pretty well the nature of demagogues the world over. The people are everywhere crazy for roads, for more and more roads. The whole West we are considering is made by railways. Without them the larger part of it would be uninhabitable, the lands of small value, produce useless for want of a market. No railways, no civilization. Year by year settlements have increased in all regions touched by railways, land has risen in price, and freight charges have diminished. And yet no sooner do the people get the railways near them than they become hostile to the companies: hostility to railway corporations seems to be the dominant sentiment in the Western mind, and the one most naturally invoked by any political demagogue who wants to climb up higher in elective office. The roads are denounced as "monopolies"—a word getting to be applied to any private persons who are successful in business—and their consolidation is regarded as a standing menace to society.

Of course it goes without saying that great corporations with exceptional privileges are apt to be arrogant, unjust, and grasping, and especially when, as in the case of railways, they unite private interests and public functions, they need the restraint of law and careful limitations of powers. But the Western situation is nevertheless a very curious one. Naturally when capital takes great risks it is entitled to proportionate profits; but profits always encourage competition, and the great Western lines are already in a war for existence that does not need much unfriendly legislation to make fatal. In fact, the lowering of rates in railway wars has gone on so rapidly of late years that the most active Granger Legislature cannot frame hostile bills fast enough to keep pace with it. Consolidation is objected to. Yet this consideration must not be lost sight of: the West is cut up by local roads that could not be maintained; they would not pay running expenses if they had not been made parts of a great system. Whatever may be the danger of the consolidation system, the country has doubtless benefited by it.

The present tendency of legislation, pushed to its logical conclusion, is toward a practical confiscation of railway property; that is, its tendency is to so interfere with management, so restrict freedom of arrangement, so reduce rates, that the companies will with difficulty continue operations. The first effect of this will be, necessarily, poorer service and deteriorated equipments and tracks. Roads that do not prosper cannot keep up safe lines. Experienced travellers usually shun those that are in the hands of a receiver. The Western roads of which I speak have been noted for their excellent service and the liberality toward the public in accommodations, especially in fine cars and matters pertaining to the comfort of passengers. Some dining cars on the Omaha system were maintained last year at a cost to the company of ten thousand dollars over receipts. The Western Legislatures assume that because a railway which is thickly strung with cities

can carry passengers for two cents a mile, a railway running over an almost unsettled plain can carry for the same price. They assume also that because railway companies in a foolish fight for business cut rates, the lowest rate they touch is a living one for them. The same logic that induces Legislatures to fix rates of transportation, directly or by means of a commission, would lead it to set a price on meat, wheat, and groceries. Legislative restriction is one thing; legislative destruction is another. There is a craze of prohibition and interference. Iowa has an attack of it. In Nebraska, not only the Legislature but the courts have been so hostile to railway enterprise that one hundred and fifty miles of new road graded last year, which was to receive its rails this spring, will not be railed, because it is not safe for the company to make further investments in that State. Between the Grangers on the one side and the labor unions on the other, the railways are in a tight place. Whatever restrictions great corporations may need, the sort of attack now made on them in the West is altogether irrational. Is it always made from public motives? The legislators of one Western State had been accustomed to receive from the various lines that centred at the capital trip passes, in addition to their personal annual passes. Trip passes are passes that the members can send to their relations, friends, and political allies who want to visit the capital. One year the several roads agreed that they would not issue trip passes. When the members asked the agent for them they were told that they were not ready. As days passed and no trip passes were ready, hostile and annoying bills began to be introduced into the Legislature. In six weeks there was a shower of them. The roads yielded, and began to give out the passes. After that, nothing more was heard of the bills.

What the public have a right to complain of is the manipulation of railways in Wall Street gambling. But this does not account for the hostility to the corporations which are developing the West by an extraordinary outlay of money, and cutting their own throats by a war of rates. The vast interests at stake, and the ignorance of the relation of legislation to the laws of business, make the railway problem to a spectator in Chicago one of absorbing interest.

In a thorough discussion of all interests it must be admitted that the railways have brought many of their troubles upon themselves by their greedy wars with each other, and perhaps in some cases by teaching Legislatures that have bettered their instructions, and that tyrannies in management and unjust discriminations (such as the Inter-State Commerce Law was meant to stop) have much to do in provoking hostility that survives many of its causes.

I cannot leave Chicago without a word concerning the town of Pullman, although it has already been fully studied in the pages of this Magazine. It is one of the most interesting experiments in the world. · As it is only a little over seven years old, it would be idle to prophesy about it, and I can only say that thus far many of the predictions as to the effect of "paternalism" have not come true. If it shall turn out that its only valuable result is an "object lesson" in decent and orderly living, the experiment will not have been in vain. It is to be remembered that it is not a philanthropic scheme, but a purely business operation, conducted on the idea that comfort, cleanliness, and agreeable surroundings conduce more to the prosperity of labor and of capital than the opposites.

Pullman is the only city in existence built from the foundation on scientific and sanitary principles, and not more or less the result of accident and variety of purpose and incapacity. Before anything else was done on the flat prairie, perfect drainage, sewerage, and water supply were provided. The shops, the houses, the public buildings, the parks, the streets, the recreation grounds, then followed in intelligent creation. Its public buildings are fine, and the grouping of them about the open flower-planted spaces is very effective. It is a handsome city, with the single drawback of monotony in the well-built houses. Pullman is within the limits of the village of Hyde Park, but it is not included in the annexation of the latter to Chicago.

It is certainly a pleasing industrial city. The workshops are spacious, light, and well ventilated, perfectly systematized; for instance, timber goes into one end of the long car shop and. without turning back, comes out a freight-car at the other, the capacity of the shop being one freight-car every fifteen minutes of

the working hours. There are a variety of industries, which employ about 4500 workmen. Of these about 500 live outside the city, and there are about 1000 workmen who live in the city and work elsewhere. The company keeps in order the streets, parks, lawns, and shade trees, but nothing else except the schools is free. The schools are excellent, and there are over 1360 children enrolled in them. The company has a well-selected library of over 6000 volumes, containing many scientific and art books, which is open to all residents on payment of an annual subscription of three dollars. Its use increases yearly, and study classes are formed in connection with it. The company rents shops to dealers, but it carries on none of its own. Wages are paid to employés without deduction, except as to rent, and the women appreciate a provision that secures them a home beyond peradventure. The competition among dealers brings prices to the Chicago rates, or lower, and then the great city is easily accessible for shopping. House rent is a little higher for ordinary workmen than in Chicago, but not higher in proportion to accommodations, and living is reckoned a little cheaper. The reports show that the earnings of operatives exceed those of other working communities, averaging per capita (exclusive of the higher pay of the general management) $590 a year. I noticed that piece-wages were generally paid, and always when possible. The town is a hive of busy workers; employment is furnished to all classes except the school-children, and the fine moral and physical appearance of the young women in the upholstery and other work rooms would please a philanthropist.

Both the health and the morale of the town are exceptional; and the moral tone of the workmen has constantly improved under the agreeable surroundings. Those who prefer the kind of independence that gives them filthy homes and demoralizing associations seem to like to live elsewhere. Pullman has a population of 10,000. I do not know another city of 10,000 that has not a place where liquor is sold, nor a house nor a professional woman of ill repute. With the restrictions as to decent living, the community is free in its political action, its church and other societies, and in all healthful social activity. It has several ministers; it seems to require the services of only one or two policemen; it supports four doctors and one lawyer.

I know that any control, any interference with individual responsibility, is un-American. Our theory is that every person knows what is best for himself. It is not true, but it may be safer, in working out all the social problems, than any lessening of responsibility either in the home or in civil affairs. When I contrast the dirty tenements, with contiguous seductions to vice and idleness, in some parts of Chicago, with the homes of Pullman, I am glad that this experiment has been made. It may be worth some sacrifice to teach people that it is better for them, morally and pecuniarily, to live cleanly and under educational influences that increase their self-respect. No doubt it is best that people should own their homes, and that they should assume all the responsibilities of citizenship. But let us wait the full evolution of the Pullman idea. The town could not have been built as an object lesson in any other way than it was built. The hope is that laboring people will voluntarily do hereafter what they have here been induced to accept. The model city stands there as a lesson, the wonderful creation of less than eight years. The company is now preparing to sell lots on the west side of the railway tracks, and we shall see what influence this nucleus of order, cleanliness, and system will have upon the larger community rapidly gathering about it. Of course people should be free to go up or go down. Will they be injured by the opportunity of seeing how much pleasanter it is to go up than to go down?